Object Relations
Individual Therapy

THE LIBRARY OF OBJECT RELATIONS

A Series of Books Edited By
David E. Scharff and Jill Savege Scharff

Object relations theories of human interaction and development provide an expanding, increasingly useful body of theory for the understanding of individual development and pathology, for generating theories of human interaction, and for offering new avenues of treatment. They apply across the realms of human experience from the internal world of the individual to the human community, and from the clinical situation to everyday life. They inform clinical technique in every format from individual psychoanalysis and psychotherapy, through group therapy, to couple and family therapy.

The Library of Object Relations aims to introduce works that approach psychodynamic theory and therapy from an object relations point of view. It includes works from established and new writers who employ diverse aspects of British, American, and international object relations theory in helping individuals, families, couples, and groups. It features books that stress integration of psychoanalytic approaches with marital, family, and group therapy, as well as those centered on individual psychotherapy and psychoanalysis.

Object Relations
Individual Therapy

Jill Savege Scharff, M. D.
David E. Scharff, M. D.

JASON ARONSON INC.
Northvale, New Jersey
London

First softcover printing 2000

Production Editor: Judith D. Cohen

This book was set in 11 pt. Granjon by Alpha Graphics of Pittsfield, New Hampshire and printed and bound by Book-mart Press, Inc. of North Bergen, NJ.

Library of Congress Cataloging-in-Publication Data

Scharff, Jill Savege.
   Object relations individual therapy / Jill Savege Scharff,
  David E. Scharff
     p.   cm.
   Includes bibliographical references and index.
   ISBN 0-7657-0117-0 (alk. paper)
   1. Object relations (Psychoanalysis). 2. Psychotherapy.
  I. Scharff, David E., 1941- . II. Title.
  RC489.025S338   1998
  616.89'14—dc21   97-23357
   ISBN 0-7657-0251-7 (softcover)

Printed in the United States of America on acid-free paper. For information and catalog write to Jason Aronson Inc., 230 Livingston Street, Northvale, NJ 07647-1726, or visit our website: www.aronson.com

Dedicated to our colleagues, students, and friends at the

International Institute of Object Relations Therapy

Contents

Contents

Part II   *Object Relations Therapy*

Section 4   TECHNIQUE

Section 5   ASSESSMENT

Section 6   BRIEF THERAPY

Section 7   INTENSIVE THERAPY

Preface and Acknowledgments

We thank all our patients, students and supervisees for contributing to our understanding. In writing about our work with them, we hope to demonstrate the value of in-depth object relations therapy, both in its traditionally intensive, open-ended form and in its abbreviated format when constrained by managed care. We sincerely hope that patients and colleagues are not upset by what they read about themselves or us, and on the other hand that they do not feel hurt if not chosen for the purpose of illustration. We hope that they feel adequately protected by our attention to disguising their identity through using imaginary names. We have selected sessions or treatments where the material helped us to make a point, or where we thought that we knew what was happening. At other times we felt too lost to commit our ideas to paper, which we regret, because these moments are probably the closest to the everyday experience of most therapists, but describing them distorts their essential chaos. As yet, we have not found a way of doing this effectively. So, suffice it to say that, for now, we acknowledge the universal experience of uncertainty and we teach a way of working that values not-knowing and waiting for meaning to emerge from experience.

We try to write about failures, at least the ones we understand, and to present honestly the full range of outcomes. But we also realize that the very act of writing about the process creates an unnaturally clear view of it that is both a help and a hindrance. In particular, we do not want to give the impression that we are always so precise in linking theory and practice as it may appear in this book, where we have an educational aim. One couple in therapy who had read one of our books complained, "You hardly ever talk to us about our projective identifications!" Of course not, because in therapy our way of communicating our ideas is much more natural and human than the concepts of internal object relationships presented in a textbook. After all, the internal objects that we get so excited about, feel so rejected by, or write about endlessly reside in the bodies of human beings and in their relationships to loved ones and to us. We need to use simple, ordinary language, with plenty of the most useful four-letter words—like milk, eyes, arms, pain, pine, part, work, wait, look, long, love, and hate.

Our aim is to present basic theory in a clear, creative way that does justice to the originality of the ideas and yet integrates the concepts into a working model of the human personality *in interaction* that applies to the therapeutic relationship in individual therapy and psychoanalysis. We have given some of the clinical illustrations to make theoretical points clear and others to give an appreciation of theory and technique in process. We have drawn vignettes as well as longer descriptions of assessment, brief therapy, and the early phase of therapy from our psychotherapy practice, while providing examples of longer-term work from our psychoanalytic practices.

The predominance of examples drawn from analysis reflects the situation in our practices in which patients who want intensive work tend to select analysis when they work with us. We are not trying to teach the practice of psychoanalysis. We are simply benefiting from the luxury of the research opportunity provided by analysis to explore in detail the transference–countertransference dynamics and the unconscious communication—between self and object, self and other—in the therapeutic situation, where the therapist can be used as a transformational object. Therapists who practice only psychotherapy know that intensive work can be done in psychotherapy as well as in psychoanalysis.

We note that there are more examples of work with women than men, and feel that this is not a result of women needing therapy more than men, but a reflection of a wider trend in which women more readily admit to problems.

Whether in brief therapy, long-term therapy, or psychoanalysis, the therapeutic relationship is the key. We try to show how to build a good psychological holding environment that supports the emergence of contextual transference both about the holding environment itself, and the more focused transferences when the individual's internal object-relations set engages in specific ways with the internal object-relations set of the therapist. Then work with countertransference elucidates the nature of the transference and is the medium for its resolution in the context of the therapeutic relationship.

We thank Jason Aronson and his staff for their unfailing support, especially Sigrid Asmus and Judy Cohen, who took the editing in hand; Peter Ellman, Rosanna Mazzei, Norma Pomerantz, and Juliann Popp, who devised the promotional materials; and Nancy D'Arrigo, who designed the jacket. Anna Innes, our terrific administrator, and her assistant, Mary Thomas, typed early drafts and generally kept things going in the office while we were absorbed in the writing task, while Maribel Puma took care of the home and the children's needs for daytime driving. We are grateful for consultation received from E. James Anthony, the late Dexter Bullard, Jr., and Harold Searles. We are most appreciative of the generosity of Earl Hopper, who gave feedback on the transference geography chapter, Mary Sue Moore, who checked the research chapter for accuracy and transformed it by guiding us to additional sources, and Drew Westen who helped with citations. Yolanda Varela thoughtfully reviewed the manuscript prior to selecting parts for translation into Spanish. We are grateful to John Birtchnell, who scored data and printed out the octagons used in Chapter 7, and to Michael Stadter for sharing his expertise in brief therapy. We owe thanks to Richard Simon, a young man we have not met, but whose 1991 eighth-grade science fair project on the fractal similarity of shorelines introduced us to the concept of fractals which immediately struck us as relevant to personality development.

Xanthe Scharff did the painstaking job of checking the references cheerfully and carefully. We are grateful to all our children for giving us space to write and for welcoming us back at the end of the day ready to engage with us again.

Lastly we thank the board, faculty, distinguished guest faculty, and course participants of the International Institute of Object Relations Therapy for contributing to this book by their support, friendship, suggestions, encouragement, and engagement in learning and teaching object relations therapy.

I

Object Relations Theory

Section 1

INTRODUCTION

1

The Therapist's Internal Objects

The Therapist's Experience: The Internal Group
of Object Relations

As individual therapists and psychoanalysts, we work alone with one patient at a time. Yet we are embedded in a matrix of other relationships, and so are they. An internal group accompanies us, hindering and helping us, as we work each day. It combines experience, perception, memory, feeling, and thought in our psychic structure, at various levels: first, our internal images of the people in our household, based on our history together and our recent inter-actions; second, the internal characters who travel from the past with us; third, our accumulated clinical experience with previous patients; fourth, our present group of patients; and, lastly, the group of ideas that we use to make sense of our therapeutic experience. Our self-analysis of this internal group's effect on the way that we relate to each patient is fundamental to the object relations therapy approach.

We begin each day in the company of our internal objects. We take them into our office. We bring with us our internal versions of our spouse, children, and parents, our professional colleagues, supervisors, friends, and enemies. We carry with us, in our inner world, our memories of previous patients, some of them gratifying, some puzzling, and some of them abandoning objects. We are filled with our experiences with the patients of that day. We may be taunted, amused, exhausted, uplifted, bored, and intrigued. At every level, these are the objects of our dreams, our hopes and fears, our preoccupations and musings. Then we have the thoughts that help us through to understanding, as new ideas, triggered by working with this man or that woman, build upon old ideas, sometimes transforming them.

Like us, individual patients bring into our office an internal group based on the people in their lives. As patients tell us at length about their conflicts with husbands and wives, mothers and fathers, brothers and sisters, uncles and aunts, children and grandchildren, friends and enemies, we see the contours of this internal group emerging. Patients talk seriously about the bosses and employees they like to work with and those they hate. They tell us about the friends with whom they relax. They may refer to the loss of a previous therapist and expect us to be as wonderful, or fear that we will be equally useless. They roam over their relationships—of the past, the present, and the unknown future. As therapy progresses, the patient's individual internal group presents itself as a living reality that interacts with our own internal group, based on our personal and family experience and current clinical experience with patients.

As we meet the patients one by one, they build up our daily experience of work and form a clinical group. As we listen, we receive a cast of hundreds who jostle for space, find something to identify with inside us, and click with myriad parts of us that accept or reject them. Present patients join the group of family and friends in being the stuff of our internal worlds, the people to whom we relate in intimate ways, with whom or against whom we identify, through whom our own hopes and fears are fulfilled and frustrated. They do not know each other, but they form a group in our minds nevertheless, and each one has a place in that internal group.

> A man reported a fantasy in which he presided over the people that he saw in the waiting room before and after his appointments, and others that he imagined. He pretended that he convened these people to work with the two of us. He had largely imaginary chats with them and he liked to think of himself as overseeing their welfare. In his gregarious, omnipotent way, he partly identified with his image of his therapist and partly expressed his pride of place in his therapist's world. He called himself the "dean of the waiting room."

His idea called our attention to those who occupy the waiting room as a special group in the therapist's or analyst's mind. The waiting room is more than an actual space. It represents a transitional zone between actual and potential interactions. As one patient or family waits to enter the office while another is leaving, old images linger in our minds as we prepare to enter the world of the next patient. Patients who have terminated may still haunt our internal world or come back for a fleeting visit in association to something that a current patient says.

We also filter images arising from the phone calls made when we have a few minutes between sessions. There is a group on the telephone line too, as calls bring in a new referral, a message from a patient not heard from in several years, or news of cancellation from a new patient seen in assessment calling to say that she did not find what she wanted and has decided not to continue. There are other faceless calls. The voice of the man had an arresting accent and a note of wariness. What will he look like? How will he be to work with? The woman cannot afford my fee. Who will I refer her to? The couple has to be seen right away, but only if I have an evening hour. Some calls usher in a new patient who becomes an important part of our daily work. Others bring a former patient back for a follow-up visit.

A former patient, Julie Watson calls to ask for an appointment. I (DES) have known her for twenty years, since before her marriage. I was listening when she struggled through her fear that the marriage might not work for her, brought her husband and children for family sessions, and ultimately found the joy that her family is a loving one—although not perfect. Now she wants to come back to discuss her later life—the evolution of her marriage and her aging now that she has experienced menopause resulting in sexual difficulty. I look forward to seeing her as I would an old friend, even though my pleasure will be tinged with the sadness of disappointment that she needs to come back for more work. We set up an appointment for next week.

Back to the present, Antonio Morales, my first patient of the day, leaves my office. Today he struggled with the distance between us, but he did not manage to bridge it. I am disappointed that I could not reach him either. He crosses the waiting room where a mother reads, waiting for a child my wife is seeing. They do not look at each other. Nothing unusual in that, but it reminds me of how Mr. Morales ignores his own wife and child at this stage of his analysis. The waiting room scene serves as an image of the boy ignoring the mother that he longs for, and it helps me to formulate my next interpretation of Mr. Morales's transference.

As he leaves, a couple arrives for their appointment with me. I know Mr. Morales and the woman in the couple share professional interests although they do not know each other. As I welcome the couple into the office, a fleeting thought crosses my mind about how Mr. Morales might interact with her if they knew each other. Perhaps I am thinking that it is a female element in me that Mr. Morales wants to connect with and cannot. Having thought that, my image of their fantasized interaction fades as I am absorbed into the couple's world.

The couple came at the brink of divorce, but the thought of its consequences to their young children has made them hesitate. They work well in therapy, each building on what they learned in previous intensive individual work that they have valued. I find myself admiring their capacity to work. They enable me to work particularly well with helping them understand their dreams and accept their projections. I am full of hope. I find myself admiring my own capacity to work as well. But our shared excitement also covers up their rejecting objects. I remember that however well they worked in individual therapy, they did not learn to adjust to each other, and however well they work in this therapy, they may not refind each other in a lasting, satisfying marriage. Then I anticipate a feeling of sadness.

I have a brief break when the couple leaves, refill my coffee cup, take the message from voice mail to call the tutor of an adolescent patient who drags her feet at finishing her work and getting to school on time. I glance at the newspaper: "Mass Suicide of 39 Cult Members." Incredulous and overwhelmed with the horror of what happened in that group, I find my spirits sinking.

I'm relieved to be pulled out of the gloom when the bell rings just exactly on time for Alma Schultz. Mrs. Schultz always comes just on time— the most efficient patient I've had in a long time. She gets things done, but her efficiency, which lets her manage an ambitious professional life and a family, hides great sadness and a conviction that no one knows how bad and destructive she is, and how little her life is worth. I think of the suicide I just read about, and hope that she is never drawn toward death. I like her, and admire her, but last week she told me that she has felt from the beginning that she irritated me, that I barely put up with her. How can someone about whom I feel so positively be so convinced I do not like her? I am far from understanding her. Then I realize that I am having evoked in me parts of her that she gets rid of: while I identify her with the exciting object, she identifies the rejecting object with me. Bridging this distance in my sense of her helps me, during the next session, to appreciate and communicate my understanding of Mrs. Schultz's distance from herself.

As Mrs. Schultz leaves, I see Eric Hamburg in the waiting room, sitting restlessly at the edge of his chair, his leather jacket across his lap, its collar held tight in his clenched left hand. He is from a poor family where his uneducated father was physically abusive to him. His anxiety transmits itself to me and joins with the lingering sadness I feel for Mrs. Schultz. I move beyond that past hour to think about Mr. Hamburg. Earlier this week, I told him that his self-defeating symptoms were his way of beating himself up to maintain allegiance to the abusive father that he longed for and loved. I said that he kept the physically abusive relationship to his father alive through verbal outbursts at his wife and children. He looked as if I had hit him. Today Mr. Hamburg reminds me of a British coal worker, cleaned up to ask a favor from the boss.

I'm not sure what this fantasy about him means to me or what it says about him. Maybe he hopes that I will be kinder to him today. I find myself also thinking of the characters in the North-of-England coal town in D. H. Lawrence's *Lady Chatterley's Lover*. In that story, the lonely wife of a damaged and impotent husband is driven by longing to find a secret, physical love. Perhaps in the transference Mr. Hamburg has an unspoken longing for me, as he has for his father, and only when I "hit" him could I become aware of it.

And so it goes through the day. Patients tell us about their lives—some interesting, some mundane—in narratives that hold our attention and may move us deeply, although we do not respond by sharing similar narratives of our own. They leave imperceptible traces or deep footprints through the years. They interact in our minds, sometimes quite openly as they preoccupy us or appear in a dream, stir a fantasy, or create a connection with something we have read.

Patients do more than cross paths in the waiting room. They form a group that assembles only in the mind of the therapist. As they interact with each other and with us, they also, to some degree, comment on our competence. Their success and growth fosters our conviction that our form of therapy offers repair; their difficulty erodes our sense of goodness. Even when the patients do not talk to each other, and we do not talk about them, the group of internal objects based on them comprises an internal teaching seminar, a promotions committee, a reference group for our well-being, and an inner circle of privileged communication. Even when we come to write about them for teaching by using their examples, the process of disguising, condensing, and fictionalizing them means that no one truly knows how they form a part of our own internal cast of characters. And yet when the disguised material is all compiled into a book, we are struck again by the vivid reality of the group that teaches us and furthers our understanding.

We live in, among, and through our patients. We make mistakes with them, set things right with them. Although they are not the only members of our internal worlds, professionally they are the most important ones. They bump shoulders (without seeing or being seen) with our colleagues, supervisors, teachers, and students. They resemble aspects of our children, parents, and spouses, and like them are subject to our affection, discomfort, envy, admiration, or thank-God-it's-not-me reactions. They are with us every day, near or far, around and within.

The Therapist's Ideas: The Internal Group of Related Theories

In object relations therapy, we focus on the individual patient's internal group and its effect on the patient's perceptions of us, as well as their effect on us, their way of using us as objects, and their experience of us. We are not simply monitoring the relationship to maintain a good alliance. We are not avoiding confrontation or empathic failures. We are there to provide a space for thinking and feeling. We are there as objects for use. We use whatever occurs in the laboratory of the therapeutic relationship as a shared experience for examination. In summary, the therapeutic relationship is now at the core of clinical practice.

The ideas that we use and present in this book derive from a loosely allied group of theorists, many of them working in the United Kingdom where object relations theory has become the dominant philosophy in psychoanalysis. In the chapters that follow, we refer primarily to the work of Fairbairn, Winnicott, Klein, and Bion. To the mix we add concepts from sex education and therapy, conjoint therapies, and play therapy. We take information from the child development literature and childhood memory research. We put together research findings from the areas of nonhuman primate attachment and human object relations. We relate object relations theory to the theory of chaos and fractals. Always we remain aware that object relations therapy, even though it challenges classical theoretical constructs, is nevertheless a development that rests on the psychoanalytic foundation that began with Freud.

In this introduction to the basis for our approach, we begin with a brief review of Freud, Fairbairn, Winnicott, Klein, and Bion, and close with a summary of our technique. We expand and integrate their theories in a more comprehensive review in Chapter 2. We then elaborate on these and other ideas from theory and research one by one in the subsequent chapters of Part I.

Following Freud

Object relations therapy takes a clinical and theoretical stance that may seem to be a far cry from the scientific objectivity and surgical detachment of Freud's earliest case reports. We are not looking at patients as if through a microscope, the patient being like a histological preparation fixed on a slide or a butterfly immobilized with pins through its wings, as Freud appeared to do. In his view of development, the individual unfolds along a pre-set route determined by fixed, constitutionally derived instinctual forces and the emergent structures for the disposal of innate energy, rather than by the influence of the environment. He knew that the environment could distort development, as a flower or tree is distorted by having too much water, poor soil, not enough sun or minerals. Therefore, theoretically, parents and the environment that they provided might do harm, but there was little they could do to improve on the theoretical givens of the patient's or child's inborn directions and capacities. What Freud did not have was a holistic view of the relational context of life.

At the same time that he believed in the primacy of biological development, however, Freud originally believed that sexual trauma universally shaped psychopathology. Every child who developed psychological symptoms, he thought then, had actually been seduced and suffered a traumatic neurosis. Then he discovered that these traumata were not universal in his patients (including himself), and he made his landmark discovery of the infantile neurosis. The distortion of experience through the influence of the child's oedipal strivings was now seen to account for symptom-producing fears, rivalries, and conflicts. Once he discovered the infantile neurosis and began to trace the transformations wrought by the child's own fantasy life, the pendulum swung the other way, and then Freud underestimated the clinical evidence for the impingement of actual trauma on the growing personality. What Freud did not have was a theoretically interactive point of view that allowed him to bridge psychic and actual reality.

He was highly interactive himself, however. Despite his ambition to be a man of science, Freud could no more keep himself out of his clinical work than he could keep his own emotional experience out of his lively and immediate writing. Consequently, we can often infer where he stood emotionally as he studied and treated his patients. In modifying his views on ego development to include the superego, formed during the reorganization of psychic structure at the time of the Oedipus complex, he astutely described the family situation of his patients, and showed that he was well aware of the influence of parents on children's development. The first rudimentary elements of an object relational point of view can be found in his theory and will be discussed fully in Chapter 4. But without an interactive theory, Freud was limited in his ability to see the transformational possibilities inherent in early relationships, possibilities that can help the child to become more than the sum of inbuilt tendencies, as each developmental stage presents radically new views of the parents and new possibilities for growth.

Just as an enlarged horizon becomes available to toddlers once they can walk, the wider view of the family made possible once children can conceive of the importance of their parents' relationship to each other marks an immense maturational shift from the previous position of considering the parents important solely as they pertain to the child's own well-being. There is a similar leap in potential as children acquire the capacity for abstract thinking and can enlarge their view of relationships beyond the circle of the family to include their peer group, their community, or the wider society. More than classical theory does, object relational theories offer the therapist a comprehensive view of intrapsychic and social development, and of treatment as a process between partners working toward growth and development.

Freud seems to have felt free to interact with the fullness of his personality during treatment, even though he contended that psychoanalysis was only a research method. However, many of his students chose to follow the letter of his theory rather than identify with the humanity of his discourse. His followers began to constrict the accepted standards of what comprised proper psychoanalytic behavior, and what contributed to therapeutic process. Perhaps this was partly in reaction to early experimentation with active or collaborative techniques such as Ferenczi's ill-fated experiment in which patient and analyst took turns analyzing each other. Whatever the reason, the result was the creation of a myth that the analyst was a *blank screen* on whom the patient's inner world would be projected like a movie. The analyst's personality was felt to have little or nothing to do with the process. Psychoanalysis became reified as a model for the understanding of the patient's life and difficulties from a scientifically objective, theoretical, and cognitive set of principles.

This trend culminated in the narrow understanding of papers by Strachey (1934) on the mutative effect of interpretation and Eissler (1953) on parameters in psychoanalytic technique. Strachey was read as arguing that the transference interpretation alone was the mutative force in psychoanalysis, even though most of his paper deals with the importance of the *context* of the therapeutic relationship and therapeutic action achieved through projection and introjection. In the same way, a slavish devotion to Eissler's view of non-transference interventions as *parameters* that make analysis less than pure gold, ignored or denigrated the totality of the analyst's behavior and experience. From an object relational point of view, we ask: Without creating analysis as a total situation, how can there be much transference to interpret?

Freud did put transference at the center of the therapeutic action of psychoanalysis, but he understood countertransference as a much more limited phenomenon than we do today. He used the term *countertransference* to refer to the unconscious problems of the analyst that interfered with the treatment process and called for more treatment of the therapist, but he did not use countertransference in his formulations. Nevertheless, his clinical writing is replete with indications and descriptions of his own responses to his patients and of the inferences he drew from them, so that we can begin to guess at his use of his inner experience, the same experience that we would now call counter-transference. In a number of places in *The Interpretation of Dreams* (1900), in the Dora case (1905a), and especially in Freud's letters, there is material about his response to patients, including dreams like the dream of Irma's injection (Gay 1988). Because his theory limited his vision, these subjective experiences were not linked theoretically to his clinical descriptions and we are left to speculate about their meaning.

Despite the human aspects of his work, Freud continued to aspire to objectivity and scientific method in his clinical research, and to view the person as an individual biological unit. In contrast, object relations therapy is highly subjective, more of an art than a science. We do not claim to be objective, but we try to be as objective as we can in observing ourselves, our patients, and the relationships that we construct together. In the clinical chapters that follow in Part II, we say what happened as we remember it, we enter our findings, test our hypotheses, and report the results of our interventions so that others may have a basis for disputing their relevance, trying out the technique, or arguing against the theory.

Fairbairn, Klein, Winnicott, and Bion

The evolution of analytic theory into relational form, beginning with the work of Fairbairn, Klein, Winnicott, and Bion, changed our view of the analyst's role.

Fairbairn was the first to write that it was the relationship to the analyst that was the central feature of the therapeutic process. His conclusion came from the theory of personality he developed in the 1940s. In contrast to Freud, who viewed development as instinctually based, Fairbairn held that the infant was primarily object-seeking, and that growth, development, and pathology represented the vicissitudes of the need to be in relationship throughout life. In the late 1940s and 1950s, Klein, Winnicott, Bion, Balint, and other analysts in Great Britain; Jacobson, Sullivan, Fromm, and later Kernberg in the United States; and Racker in Argentina, began to build an interactional model of the therapeutic process based on new theoretical and clinical premises.

There are several starting points for the relational set of theories which to greater or lesser degree emerged independently of each other. We trace the process of this development in Chapters 4, 5, and 6, where we begin with Freud and follow these various threads of development toward a relational point of view. Where Freud's nineteenth-century physics and Platonic philosophical background kept him in a dualistic framework in which matter and energy, content and structure were separate entities, Fairbairn moved from a nineteenth- to a twentieth-century philosophy of science in which matter and energy are interchangeable, and content influences structure and is intimately determined by it.

Fairbairn applied his philosophic training in the Aristotelian tradition to revise psychoanalytic theory from an intellectual base. He drew specifically on nineteenth-century German philosophy as epitomized in Hegel, whose description of the increase in one person's desire for another person under conditions of frustration inspired Fairbairn's description of the child's object-seeking behavior and the relations between the libidinal ego and the exciting object (see Chapter 3). Klein and other contemporary British contributors explored similar territory essentially from an intuitive base, discovering the relational basis of development and its vicissitudes in the clinical situation. Klein described the importance of object relations from the beginning of life. In so doing she flew in the face of Freud's concept of primary narcissism in which the infant originally invests mostly in itself, even though at the same time, and unlike Fairbairn, she remained true to Freud's concept of the instinctual basis of development.

Further development of the concepts of transference and countertransference naturally flowed from the conviction that the therapeutic relationship is at the center of the therapeutic process. Two countervailing trends developed. On the negative side of the ledger, the process of change was viewed as concentrated in the transference; the resulting tunnel vision blinded us to the value of the *whole* of the therapeutic relationship. On the positive side, the study of transference as a total situation (Klein 1952), and on countertransference as the totality of the therapist's response (Heimann 1950, Money-Kyrle 1956, Racker 1957, Winnicott 1947), gave a clinical view of patient and therapist in a *two-person* interaction, which warranted study of both patient and therapist contributions to the therapeutic relationship, and even of the interactional life of the pair. Fairbairnian, Kleinian, and Winnicottian object relations theories are revisited in detail in Chapters 3 and 6.

It adds up to this: the focus on transference as the contribution of the patient, if taken in the context of a transference to a "blank-screen" analyst, tends to narrow our understanding of the fullness of the therapeutic process. However, when transference and countertransference are paired as collateral, mutually interacting subjective experiences, the focus widens to include the entire experience of patient and therapist and of the interactive space between them. The exploration of this point of view occupies the field today. It is an enlarging field of focus, in which we can now train a high-powered microscope on the minute shifts in the therapeutic relationship to give us fresh ways of understanding the complex human situation in psychotherapy and psychoanalysis.

The treatment relationship is different from all other relationships, but it is equally human. It is as different from, let us say, the mother–child, husband–wife, teacher–student, or boss–employee relationship as they are from each other. All have certain similarities and areas of overlap in terms of dependency, authority, gender differences, sexual tension, and fears of abandonment. Each has clearly definable differences from the others. All are important in the patient's internal object relations set. Each internal object relationship, distinguished by role structures and boundaries, is reflected, re-experienced, and reintegrated in the therapeutic relationship.

The Object Relations Therapy Approach

The approach that we describe in this book values the patient–therapist relationship as the center of the psychotherapeutic contract and process. Much of what we will look at concerns transference–countertransference interaction as mediated through the processes of projective and introjective identification, in which diverse conscious and unconscious elements between patient and therapist meet and are blended to form new mixtures of thought, feeling, and perception, combinations of behaviors, and patterns of relating. But we do not believe that this is all there is to the relationship between patient and therapist. Just as the carbon atom takes many shapes and forms bonds with other elements in diverse ways to form the universe of organic compounds, so the therapeutic relationship draws on all the elements common to human relationships to form those structures and processes of the therapeutic relationship essential for healing.

We do believe in the importance of transference interpretation. But we also believe, with Fairbairn, Guntrip, and Sutherland, that its contribution lies in clarifying the problems and possibilities inherent in a therapeutic relationship whose overall purpose is to develop insight into the nature of that relationship and to allow its eventual transformation, with concomitant change in the patient's internal object relations. This cannot happen without attention to securing the treatment situation and creating what Winnicott called a holding environment. Important aspects of the treatment relationship include clarification, linking, and questioning—all of which extend the patient's powers of observation. Empathy is a fundamental part of the therapist's response, and failures of empathy can lead to emotional understanding of what went wrong earlier in life. We try to put into words this understanding of the patient's dilemma. Examined failures of cognitive understanding can also lead to understanding. Other significant factors are the nonverbal components of active listening and absorbing of shared experience, the ability to tolerate being used in difficult ways, the unconscious metabolizing of the patient's experience, and finally, toward termination, the acceptance of the growth that presages loss of the patient.

Equally relevant to our study are the nonanalytic factors—often by-products or unintended communications delivered by tone of voice or a moment's hesitation—such as advice and reassurance, doubt, support, or criticism. Advice and support, or condolence and congratulation usually play an intentionally minor role in a psychoanalytic process, but there are times when withholding them may be such a violation of the human side of the relationship that to do so may badly undermine treatment. Conversely, dwelling on advice and support will certainly obliterate the potential space that must grow between patient and therapist in any dynamic therapy.

The growth of this potential space is supported by attention to boundaries. Therapists need to set limits both on their patients' behavior, as when therapists help anxious patients stop calling them frequently at night so as to promote exploring the pain of separation during sessions, and on their own behavior, as when therapists avoid sexual behavior with patients so as to create space for understanding the intensity of the patient's fantasy rather than becoming a real object to gratify the patient's infantile longings and so closing off avenues for growth of the self.

The model of therapy we present is one of a therapeutic relationship in action and under study. There are specifics to it, items of technique, principles and procedures of process and review. But these serve only to get us in the territory, to land us on the unexplored continent of self and object relations which each therapist has to explore anew together with each patient. In the beginning of each journey with a new patient, therapists come equipped with their own life experience, their therapeutic skills, their analyzed personalities, and clinical experience, all blended into the character of their internal group. Some journeys are brief, some long, some over the rocks of obsessional character, some in the schizoid desert, some in the treacherously lush valleys of overblown sexualization. Each journey is different, and so each touches the therapist differently and draws on various capacities within the same therapist. In the pages that follow, we hope to convey the variety, complexity, and challenge that provide the pleasure and the peril of our work as object relations therapists and analysts.

2

A Clinical Guided Tour

To introduce object relations theory and therapy, we will present some clinical material, and then review the theory and technique of assessment and therapy that it demonstrates. We hope to provide a shared clinical basis from which to approach the next chapters: in Part I we immerse ourselves in the fundamentals of object relations theory, recent advances, and our own new ideas; in Part II we delve intensely into technique and clinical process. For now, a single interview will serve as the clinical example to introduce an overview of theory and practice. Following our presentation of the clinical material, we discuss the theoretical and technical concepts that it demonstrates and key them to the chapters on theory, technique of assessment, and structure and process of therapy, in which they will be discussed more fully.

This summary of clinical process has been constructed from review of a filmed demonstration of a clinical interview by Dr. Jill Scharff in which she provides a single-session individual therapeutic encounter with a young man and assesses his suitability for object relations therapy. The videotape can be found as Dr. Jill Scharff's contribution to a series on different varieties of individual psychotherapy, made in the television studio at the university where the man was studying (Carlson and Kjos 1997). For the purpose of this chapter, we will call him Geoff.

Before the interview began, Geoff, a 26-year-old married student in the final year of his degree course in business network systems, was chatting with studio staff members who were congratulating him on receiving an award at a university ceremony they had attended earlier that month. I (JSS) noted that Geoff, who had previously participated in seven interviews with various individual therapists in this television studio over the past year, knew the crew and seemed comfortable in his role in the studio setting. I had been told that he understood that the main purpose of the interview was to give him a trial experience of object relations therapy, while at the same time giving the series another videotape for teaching. Now it was time for the interview to begin.

The Initial Countertransference

I felt vaguely tense as Geoff sat back in the chair and looked at me, waiting for me to start. He had the appearance of a college student who was still interested in being one of the guys, dating, and having fun. I felt surprised that he was married. I had the idea that he was waiting for action. But what kind? His unshaven face, his shifting glance, and his slightly defiant, mocking smile made me think of him momentarily as a convict. Anxious at the start of the interview, I took a sip of water. Geoff did too. At that moment, we were like two friends in a pub searching for a drink together to ease the flow of our conversation. He was already quite connected to me. This generated some feeling of sexual tension and I was definitely aware of a seductive pull. I suspected that his physical mirroring of my movements stemmed from a capacity for unconscious communication with a woman's anxiety and a wish to make things all right between him and her. I also noted that his deep-set eyes moved from left to right as if dodging my gaze, and his body followed suit, as if dodging me or dribbling past me. It seemed to me that he wanted to connect, but he had something to fear from me.

Establishing the Contextual Holding Relationship

I began by telling Geoff that we had forty-five minutes to talk together and that I was open to hearing whatever was on his mind. He needed no prompting.

The Symptom Focus

Geoff said that he felt totally overwhelmed with two months' work to complete by the end of the trimester, in one month's time. He described at length his exhaustion from the steady pressure of work and studying and the extra strain of losing a precious day to influenza.

The Contextual Countertransference

He evoked in me a sense of concern about him and a wish to relieve his stress, like the response of a mother whose child who is busy with exams. I might have pointed this out, but it felt premature, and I sensed that it might be felt as infantilizing and belittling. He soon got on to the topic of his mother anyway.

Elaborating on the Symptom Focus

In further discussion, Geoff clarified that his difficulty lies not in doing the work, but in having enough time to do it as well as he would like. He told me that it is hard when he has to work a twenty-nine-hour job to pay for school, spend time having fun with his wife whom he loves very much, and meet family obligations such as having to attend the coed baby shower that his mother will give for his pregnant sister in their home town some distance from the university.

Introducing the Dynamic Focus

Geoff said that he was unable to tell his mother that he could not spare six hours to drive home for the baby shower, because he cannot hurt her feelings.

I felt myself wanting to persuade Geoff to explain directly to his mother why he could not attend. But it was not so simple. Geoff preferred to go and suffer, apparently because he could not say "No" to his mother. I thought that he must be feeling that this baby shower had special importance to her, far more than for his sister, and that there was an unconscious reason for his participation that went beyond the usual pleasure in a family reunion and celebration. I began to wonder about his attachment to his mother.

When I asked him to tell me more about his mother, Geoff sighed and said, "I can't deal with talking about my Mom right now." But he did not cut me off completely. He continued, "I tend to feel that I can't say things directly to her, and then I'll suddenly go 'ppff!' and get it out there."

A Focused Countertransference Response

I had the fantasy of him as a baby burping and spitting out milk. His head dodging from side to side was like that of a baby who will not fix on the nipple and who feels smothered by the breast.

Pursuing the Dynamic Focus

I suggested that his mother must be pretty formidable and asked what she did when he hurt her feelings. Again he sighed, shook his head, and said, "I don't know. It's just that I feel guilty." He knew that he was special to his mother as her youngest child and the only boy. It was natural that she would want him at the celebration of the baby who was about to be born.

"You were her baby," I said. "So she would want you there."

"Well, yeah, I was, and I left home." Geoff explained that he had come down here to go to school. He had been a C student in college but now that he was married he was doing well.

Following the Defense Against the Transference

I noted that being away from his family and his single lifestyle had enabled him to do well. Similarly, doing well had become a defense against family enmeshment. I also noted his satisfaction with his improvement and I asked more about the awards that I had heard mentioned earlier, so as to follow his lead from the topic of mother to autonomous self.

Geoff smiled and dissembled. He said, "I got a few awards, a National Scholar, or a merit scholar, or something like that, I dunno. I got a plaque with some cool stuff on it."

The Maternal Countertransference Builds and Gets Addressed in a Trial Transference Interpretation

He must be bright, but he was sounding like an idiot. I knew he was proud of his awards, but he did not want to be pinned down to giving an accurate list. I felt excluded from the fullness of his success, and so I was surprised when he told me that his parents had attended the awards ceremony.

I pointed out that he must have felt proud of his success, but that he wanted to blow it off with me. I asked him, "Do I sound too much like a mother interested in your achievement?"

Geoff laughed that off. "They're just some awards." But he added with conviction, "The ones that mean a lot to me, I know what they are."

I thought that he was dealing with an issue of autonomy again. He wanted to do well for himself, not to satisfy someone else.

Returning to the Symptom Focus and Linking It to Internal Dynamics

Then Geoff put himself down for trying so hard, and said that it is pathetic that school is so stressful. His wife talks to him about the trade-off between an A and a B. I thought that he meant that she thought that he should relax about it, but he then said that she is driven too. She was an A student, and is now a teacher. He will graduate in December in computer networking systems and should be highly marketable in Dallas where he wants to settle. The future looks good for him. I said that I got the impression that he is desperate to be finished with school. He said that that could be, but he is also afraid of graduating and worries about whether he will get job offers. He had a good work history since adolescence, and now has a 4.0 average, so it did not make sense that he was worried.

I said, "Despite being so marketable you're afraid no one wants you. Could you be suffering from a legacy of being a screw-up?"

He laughed with relief and told me what a wiseass he had been as a fraternity brother. He didn't know why he was in college, and spent the whole time drunk. Now, however, he had been sober for six and a half years with the help of Alcoholics Anonymous.

I said to Geoff that he had benefited from dealing with the out-of-control part of himself by stopping drinking, but that the experience of having been out of control had left him rather hard on himself, driving himself to get perfect scores. I asked what he already knew about his insecurity and wondered if it preceded his alcoholism as well.

Working on His Self-Esteem, Both Positive and Negative

He said, "I know it did. I know I have low self-esteem. I never feel like I fit in. I played sports but I didn't fit in with the jocks. I used alcohol to play along. But I didn't know who I was, or why I was in college, or what I was doing. I got kicked out for drinking and that sobered me up. I learned from that, and things are going well now. I'm glad I'm in college. I'm glad I'm married to someone that loves me."

I had heard about his insecurity and low self-esteem, and I made a mental note to return to that later. But he was moving into the present source of satisfaction, his marriage, and so I wanted to follow his lead into the area of his ability to love and his strength in his wife's eyes.

I said, "Why do you think your wife loves you?"

At first he blocked. Then he said that she loves who he is, how he treats her, and what he brings to her life. When I asked what he brings, he replied, "Making her lunch, being sensitive to her feelings, keeping up my end of a conversation, and doing sweet things."

I noted Geoff's capacity to love her in ways that she appreciated. He said that she is supportive of his being back in college. Here in college he is in class with drinkers like the ones he used to hang out with, but he avoids that now. He said he was over that.

Exploring the Catastrophe Inherent in the Symptom
Allows the Emergence of a Part of the Self

I said, "You look like you feel you got over it just in time. What was going to happen to you?"

"I would have ended up in jail," he replied, without a moment's hesitation.

Immediately I thought of my fantasy in the opening moments imagining Geoff as a convict.

"Did you have a few brushes with the law?" I asked.

"I had a third-degree felony charge," he said. "Threatening to cause a catastrophe. I was in a blackout and I banged two propane cylinders together until they leaked. If I'd been a smoker, half the building and me with it wouldn't be here today."

I felt appalled at how close to total destruction he had been. I thought of the cylinders as two breasts that he was desperately trying to get something out of. I thought of two parents engaged in intercourse that was filled with the violence of a child's rage. Whatever his fantasy had been, its enactment had usefully led to a confrontation with his false self. What an explosive way to find himself. No wonder he felt a bit shaky.

I asked whether he was afraid that a prospective employer would see the felony charge on his record. I suggested that perhaps that was why he was afraid no one would want him. He said that it had been erased because he had served two years of probation, and if it came up he would willingly admit it because it was past. He said that his shaky self-worth went back before that, and so, taking his cue, I asked about his childhood development.

Taking a History of an Earlier Developmental Phase

"When I was a kid," he said. "I was less mature than most." He took more pauses and really began to think about his inner world. "I don't know," he began. "I had values, I had jobs. People, grown-ups, thought I was a nice person, but . . ." he trailed off.

I said, "You were a nice kid, but there was also a part of you that was irresponsible and hurtful to yourself."

"Adults liked me. My own age group didn't. I didn't have enough friends. I had three friends I'm still in touch with, but most people would tell me to grow up. They'd say, 'Grow up, Turk'—that's my nickname. I was a late developer." He laughed. "I was slow to hit puberty, and was a year younger than the others besides."

Moving into the Center of the Dynamic Focus: Self and Object Relations

Geoff returned to the subject of his mother and how she told him what to do. "There were just the two of us," he said. "Me and my sister, and for some reason, she seemed to want to hold on to me. To this day she still tells me what to do, how to dress, how to be a person. There is no reason for her to hold on," he concluded.

As he spoke, I noticed that his body and his eyes had stopped shifting from side to side. He no longer needed his false-self behavior, and his true self was connecting with me. He must be feeling trusting of the contextual relationship that I was providing. He was looking intently at me. Our body postures and arm gestures were in mirror image. I felt that we were in a state of deep unconscious communication that reflected the early direct relating of the eye-to-eye relationship. His phrase "just the two of us" came back to my mind.

I asked him, "Was there supposed to be someone else?"

He looked a bit stunned, recovered his balance, metaphorically went "ppff," and got it out there. "My mom's sister told me my mother had an abortion. That's a family secret. My aunt and I have a relationship like that. My family's dysfunctional and full of secrets, like, my dad's sister's husband abused all her younger sisters, and when her sisters told that aunt, she wouldn't believe it. But I haven't discussed the abortion with my mom."

"Do you have any thoughts about your mother's abortion?" I asked.

"Can't think of any," he said. Then he thought of one. "Hypocrite," he said. He seemed anxious, but shrugged it off. "It's not my business what stuff my mom does." He went on to describe some other stuff she does. "For instance, she is pleased with my scores and says things like 'I always knew you had it in you—if you just applied yourself.' She roots for me and digs at the same time. 'Good for you!' Then, jab." He thrust his arm forward as if stabbing the groin of someone nearby.

I had the fantasy of a crude abortion implement being inserted. Perhaps he was wondering why his mother was making such a fuss over the new baby when she had got rid of one. Was love a cover for murderousness? I thought of how he sticks it to himself by playing down his accomplishments. Perhaps as a little boy, he had imagined that he and his mother had created the baby that she had to destroy. But before I could make anything of my thoughts or elicit his thoughts, he whisked me off the subject.

Defending Against Catastrophe by Changing the Subject

Geoff took a detour over the topic of one of his secrets that he will not tell his parents, namely that he and his wife have had to join Debtors Anonymous for overspending their budget on meals, entertainment, and car rentals. He will not divulge this to his parents because their finances are a mess and they have no room to comment on his mismanagement. He told me something that he would not tell them. It occurred to me that what he had told me might cover over what he would not tell me too. I thought that he might be avoiding the subject of abortion, and that he might be avoiding me, but I stayed with his debt topic until I had connected with him and given him a response.

I linked his overuse of his charge card to his overuse of alcohol and his longing to have the things he wants without waiting any longer.

I said, "Part of you feels impatient to have things and feel good now."

He agreed that he'd like to have lots of things and catch up with his friends, but he reminds himself that unlike them he's getting a degree, will eventually get paid well, and has traveled.

Returning to the Dynamic Focus

I had accepted being pulled aside to listen to the secret of his debt, which was where he wanted to go, but now I wanted to get back to the secret of the abortion.

I told Geoff that I wondered whether thoughts occurred to him about the abortion, since so many were occurring to me. He looked blank and then gave an answer. He said that he had the impression that his mother got pregnant too soon after he was born and she felt that she wasn't ready for another child. His father was worried about the financial responsibility.

I said, "So her decision to have an abortion was made to make room for you as a baby. This leads me to guess that she might have had feelings about taking that loss. Having lost one child might have meant that she felt that you were all the more precious and so she became especially attached to you."

He seemed to relax and he stayed connected with me.

I said, "It could mean many things, and I'm only guessing, but you could get a better idea if you talked to her about it." But he did not like the idea of discussing this openly with his mother because he would betray his aunt with whom he had a valued relationship.

Exploring the Rejecting and the Exciting Object Constellations

I said, "But who is more important. Your mother or your aunt?"

"My mother," he said, and went on to qualify his response. "That's the answer I'm supposed to give. But my aunt is more open, easier to talk to, and easier to disagree with. She cared what I did, but she didn't insist that I do what she thought. With her, there was no jab."

"She just wasn't your mother and you liked that," I said. "You felt your mother was too close in on you."

"She didn't back off for a second," he replied.

I asked where his father was in all this. I suggested that perhaps he didn't protect his son from his mother's controlling him. Geoff gave a noncommittal answer that suggested to me that his father had not been emotionally present enough to warrant any criticism.

I felt that his father was only peripheral to the centrality of Geoff's intense relationship with his mother, and its re-creation with me in the transference. Perhaps a male therapist would have elicited a different aspect of the transference. I felt quite in tune with Geoff, and I sensed that I could try again to talk to him about his experience of me as being like a mother to be played with, but kept from going too far. I sensed a focused transference of me as a controlling mother that he was keeping at bay so that it would not interfere with the contextual transference toward me as an easy person like his aunt.

Interpreting the Early Sign of the Focused Transference

I said, "I've had the feeling at times in this interview that you've felt wary of letting me in too close. It's been easier to pretend you don't know what awards you got, or to talk about other things, but I feel that your relationship with your mother is affecting how you are dealing with me."

"Oh, it's always easier to talk about other things," he said.

I said, "Underneath your hard-driving self and its laid-back cover, there might be some unhappiness."

Interpreting His Fear of the Intrusive Maternal Object

Geoff felt criticized. "I do the best I can," he said. "I didn't hide anything."

"I appreciate that," I said. "You told me things I didn't ask, and you've shown me how you are. You're very engaging and you relate well to me up to a point, and then I feel kept at bay. You do it by being charming."

He laughed with pleasure, then joked, "Is that a compliment?" Then he looked thoughtful and seriously asked me what I meant.

I said, "You use your easy manner to make me think we are getting along fine but I sense that you are wary, ready to shift or dodge an imminent intrusiveness that you feel from me. I think of it as a fear of the jab."

Geoff remained quiet and thoughtful and put his hands over his genitals.

We were nearly at the end of the interview. I found myself wishing that I had been able to reach this understanding of the transference sooner. But earlier comments had been fended off. He did not want to talk about his mother. He did not want to talk about me being like a mother wanting to bask in the glory of his awards. He did not want to confront his mother. And he did not want to let me in too deep. His charm had drawn me in, and so his keeping me out felt all the more disappointing. He wanted me to be more like his exciting, nonjudgmental aunt with whom he shared secrets and who was never disappointed in him. I noted that Geoff stayed still to take in my interpretation of the meaning of his way of relating. I felt that he could show and work with his distrust in the contextual and focused transference.

It was time to draw the interview to a close. I commented that he looked rather surprised at where we had got to. Geoff closed by saying, "I'm always a bit surprised at myself."

I found that Geoff could work well in object relations therapy and thought that he would benefit from individual therapy with the same therapist on a once-a-week basis at a reduced fee.

Principles of Assessment and Therapy

Summaries of some of the main points of theory and technique shown in this example will introduce the principles to be discussed more fully in the chapters listed after the headings.

Establishing a Holding Environment within a Frame (Chapters 12 and 13)

The *boundaries* of the single therapeutic encounter were clearly spelled out. Patient and therapist agreed to work within the *frame* established, and to *separate and terminate* within that short time span. Even within the constraints of meeting in a television studio and a single-session format, the patient responded to *the holding environment* and entered a *psychological space* in which to share and think about his issues. Dr. Jill Scharff listened with *free-floating attention* and allowed herself to respond to the roles assigned to her by Geoff. She allowed herself to be *used as an object*—like the intrusive aspect of his mother, the accepting aspect of his aunt—and she maintained a state of *involved impartiality* to the different aspects of Geoff's narrative. Geoff responded to her *nonjudgmental listening*, and to her *interpretation of his resistance* being due to his fear of finding her like an intrusive mother, by telling her things that he was not proud of and by revealing information about the contextual and focused relationships to his mother. By *containing anxiety, using tact and timing, going without an agenda of questions, and tolerating not knowing*, she allowed the unconscious process to flow in a free-form way, so that meaning could emerge from the experience.

Assessing Developmental Level and Capability (Chapters 7 and 13)

In the Freudian language of psychosexual development, Geoff shows symptoms characteristic of problems at the oral stage. He tells of alcoholism and compulsive spending in order to satisfy longings to have things. Having a wife who loves him has bolstered his sense of self so that he can be dedicated to success.

In the Fairbairnian language, he uses various developmental techniques of dealing with the object and his personality style is not dominated by any one of them. For instance, he begins the interview by showing that he projects the bad object into his demanding teachers and mother and experiences them as persecutory (a paranoid technique). Using a hysterical technique, he projects the good object outside (his loving wife, his mother to whom he is special) and introjects the bad object (himself as a screwup, unworthy of praise and job offers).

In the Kleinian language of developmental positions, he is mostly functioning in a depressive position with care and concern for himself and others, but he was well aware of the need to guard against slipping back into paranoid-schizoid mechanisms where he would cause damage to himself and others, lose relationships, and be exposed to societal controls.

In terms of attachment theory, Geoff has a history of anxious/dismissive behavior as a younger college student. At the time when he used alcohol, he created for himself a false sense of relatedness and a dissociated state of blackout in which he did not relate to anyone. At the time of the interview, his attachment seems relatively secure, in the sense that he maintains his family connections while pursuing his own aims, has made a commitment to marriage with a self-supporting woman, and shows trust in the context provided by his interviewer. The anxious/dismissive traits are modified by his charm.

Assessing Internal Conflict and External Impingements *(Chapter 13)*

Geoff describes external impingements in the form of academic pressure, family obligations, and financial hardship. His internal conflict, expressed as a fight against the compulsive addiction to alcohol, entertainment, or work, is due to his guilty vacillation between accepting and rejecting his attachment to his mother.

Capacity to Work in Therapy *(Chapter 12)*

Geoff was shown his *defensive functioning* in dissembling, shutting out Dr. Scharff, and talking about other things than the central point. He gave some relevant *object relations history* concerning his overly attached and intrusive mother, his exciting aunt, and the composition of his sibship. His omission of detail about his father suggests the presence of a male figure experienced as absent. Dr. Scharff expressed an attitude of *empathy*, gave *support*, and made *clarifying* and *linking* comments. She gave *advice* on the usefulness of talking about family secrets. She also gave an *interpretation of the transference* based on her *countertransference*.

Countertransference and Transference Geography in Interpretation of Transference (Chapter 11)

In the countertransference, Dr. Scharff felt charmed yet distanced. She felt well-related to Geoff, but she knew he was holding back. She used this feeling to detect Geoff's wariness underneath his easy manner, and the underlying ambivalence toward his maternal introject.

In the *contextual transference*, Geoff viewed Dr. Scharff positively as someone he could trust in general and who would care about hearing his story. Within this context, he found himself up against the focused transference in which he feared her.

In the *focused transference* he saw her as a woman to be avoided, because, like his mother, her offer of closeness might be followed by a jab, perhaps because of envy of his youth and promise. So he remained on the lookout. When he did share more with her, he changed the subject to talk about his debt, as if to avoid becoming hungry for what she had to offer him. Geoff monitored the contextual holding for signs of impingement from Dr. Scharff's potential nastiness and from his own longing. The focused transference threatened his capacity to trust in her contextual holding of the therapeutic relationship. It is likely that his wariness would intensify when the focused transference was stimulated in an extended therapy.

In the *here-and-now transference*, Geoff recovered from his wary contextual transference and became affectively connected to the therapist as shown by synchrony of body movements. He was then able to experience and work on a focused transference.

In the *here-and-back-then transference*, Geoff re-enacted his guarded relationship to his devoted but intrusive mother as he charmed Dr. Scharff and yet evaded affective connection with her. He re-created his internal object relationship to the accepting aspect of his aunt which stands in for his object relationship with the split-off good maternal object. There was little mention of his father, and he may have been showing object exclusion of his paternal object.

In the *here-and-if-and-when transference*, Geoff might have developed a concept of a future relationship with Dr. Scharff, but both of them knew that this would be their only meeting. This dimension of the transference was not fully explored, partly because of that constraint. It might also have been avoided since it is painful to make a connection, learn so much, and leave so much undone.

In the *there-and-now transference*, Geoff expressed his drive to autonomy in his discussion of his studying habits, ambition, and financial goals. He showed that positive aspects of his internal object relations had enabled him to marry a woman by whom he felt loved. The material may seem devoid of transference when the patient discusses everyday life, but in those details lie the elements of transference as a total situation.

In the *there-and-back-then transference*, Geoff revealed his identification with and against the alcoholism, poverty, and financial mismanagement that dominated the family culture in which he was raised.

In the *there-and-if-and-when transference*, Geoff struggles against his identifying responses to societal influence with the help of his participation in Alcoholics Anonymous and Debtors Anonymous. He looks forward to a better, self-sufficent life further from his roots. Perhaps he wonders if his attempts at self-help will win the therapist's approval. He may or may not develop a vision of future therapy.

Contained in the therapist, Geoff's transference of wanting to depend on and please his mother was experienced as a countertransference feeling of concern. Dr. Scharff also experienced feelings of being shied away from that led her to Geoff's transference of expecting a jab from her.

Contained in the patient, Geoff's transference was one of feeling overwhelmed. He was conscious of feeling burdened by having to study, work, and be with his family. Unconsciously he was experiencing a resigned transference to Dr. Scharff, as if she were just one more obligation that interfered with his studies. He rapidly associated to being unable to disappoint his mother.

Contained in the space between patient and therapist, the transference affected the atmosphere of the session. It changed to a lighter tone when Dr. Scharff recognized that Geoff had been a "screwup." He relaxed and told her about his adolescent awkwardness and delinquency. The atmosphere changed again to one of seriousness as he approached his conflict about separating from his mother. As he and Dr. Scharff mirrored each other's body movements, she experienced a feeling of togetherness with Geoff. In other words, the defensive distance between them lessened and a potential space opened up in which to explore Geoff's experience of being an adored son and the last baby to survive.

Interpretation and Response
(Chapter 12)

Dr. Scharff made a number of clarifying and interpretive comments, such as that Geoff was creating either a charming, laid-back appearance, or a hard-driving self to cover unhappiness. The most complete example of an interpretation illustrates the use of *the because clause*. It occurred when Dr. Scharff said that Geoff used his easy manner to make her think they were getting along fine (*the required relationship*) and to hide his wary relationship to her (*the avoided relationship*) in which he was ready to shift or dodge *because* he feared an imminent intrusiveness from her (the *catastrophic relationship* linked to the annihilation anxiety associated with the abortion).

Geoff responded to Dr. Scharff's comments, sometimes defensively, but then he became able to explore the most difficult issue of the re-creation of his focused relationship to his mother in the transference. He started with a positive expectation of the interview context, and then he showed that he was capable of expressing his focused transference and working with Dr. Scharff's interpretation toward understanding it.

Use of Medication, Adjunctive Therapies, and Modifications
(Chapters 12 and 13)

Geoff's anxiety felt overwhelming to him, but it was not disrupting his functioning or his sleep. Instead it served as a useful stimulus to get him to meet his obligations. No medication was recommended. The group support of Alcoholics Anonymous will be a necessary adjunct to therapy so that Geoff maintains his sobriety while exploring his dynamics. Occasional collateral visits with his wife, or conjoint marital therapy, may also be required. He will require a low fee while he is still a full-time student.

Making a Dynamic Formulation
(Chapters 12 and 13)

Geoff was shown that his symptoms express a longing to feel related, to feel good inside, and to feel worthwhile. They stem from an insecurity in his relationship with his mother. Although he trusts the context of her love, he is afraid of her control and intrusion. This dynamic makes him reject his mother's need for proximity and affects his functioning in other settings—like this assessment interview where he is compelled to protect himself from the interviewer. This dynamic also led him to accept a peculiar therapy situation in which he does not get a sustained therapeutic relationship. What could be born in the session with Dr. Scharff was constrained by the initial conditions of growth set by the videotape project, just as his baby sibling was not born because of family circumstances. On the other hand, he may have found a safe way to have the therapy that he needs, by limiting his involvement to what he can bear. Perhaps he is repeating the abortion trauma, by aborting each individual interview rather than going to term with one therapist.

Within these limits, Geoff showed that he was able to use object relations individual therapy. In this setting, it was not Dr. Scharff's responsibility to arrange the treatment plan, choose the therapist, or set the fee at a manageable level, but in the clinical setting these arrangements would have to be made.

Geoff's Internal Object Relations
(*Chapters 3 and 6*)

Geoff had grown up in a dysfunctional family with crises due to financial mismanagement and alcoholism. He both identified with those traits and staunchly rejected them. In an out-of-control environment, he felt overly focused on and controlled by his mother, and still feels that way. He simultaneously sought the therapist's focus on him seductively (as with his aunt) and fended it off (as with his mother). Geoff has found good enough objects in his environment to build an effective central self capable of work, love, concern, and commitment to ideal objects. He can feel satisfied. But he has also split his objects. He has an exciting internal object relationship that has him full of craving for acceptance, material possessions, and, in the past, alcohol. He has an internal rejecting object relationship that represses his longings which, at their source, are for a secure sense of autonomy, apart from a sought-after, but engulfing mother from whom he wants to separate. He has a lot of strengths in work, relatedness, and love.

Geoff should do well in individual therapy, where he could rework his issues of autonomy. He would need to maintain his participation in Alcoholics Anonymous to support his sobriety while addressing underlying issues. Within the security of an individual therapeutic relationship, he could hope to develop more confidence in allowing his exciting object system to pervade his central self without threat of expressing itself in the compulsive search for substitute gratifications in alcohol, purchases, or overwork, so that he could enjoy his work and his relaxation more. Being free of the pressure from his compulsive exciting object system would permit him to develop a more flexible self-regulatory function than the rigid, rejecting object system needed at present.

The Recommendation and Referral
(*Chapter 12*)

Geoff was able to have a therapeutic experience in the single-session interview, but much was left unsaid. We are left wanting to know more about him. For instance, it would have been good to have a dream from Geoff, and to have heard more about his fantasy of life in Texas. Nevertheless, Dr. Scharff learned enough about his symptoms, his dynamics, his capacity for sobriety, and his ability to talk about himself, to recommend him for object relations therapy. So there is no need for her to extend the assessment. When referral is to be made to another therapist it is better not to prolong the initial assessment so as not to develop a more intense positive transference that could make transfer difficult.

We would like to recommend that Geoff have individual therapy with the same therapist on a once-a-week basis at a reduced fee, but we recognize that his fears of intimacy may preclude that. Before ongoing individual therapy can be considered, Geoff will complete his assignment for the videotape series and hopefully will then continue on the path of self-exploration in individual therapy provided in the counseling center at his university.

Further Assessment During Therapy
(*Chapter 12*)

If Geoff were to continue in therapy, we would expect his therapist to continue to *assess the endopsychic situation* and *refine the dynamic formulation*, while moving into therapeutic action. We would like to know, for instance, how he got his nickname, because that might tell more about his self-image and his peer relations. We might guess that his fear of intrusiveness might affect his capacity for intimacy, and so we would want to know more about his domestic life with his wife, their intimate conversations about feelings, and their sexual relationship. The therapist could usefully ask more about Geoff's fantasy of going to Texas and what it represented for him.

We would be interested to know whether he eventually talked to his mother about the abortion and about her relationship to him when he was a baby, and if so what he learned. This would allow us to *imagine the mother–infant relationship*. But we would not be surprised or disappointed to learn that he had maintained the family's secretive style. In either case, we would want to know what further thoughts he had about his mother's abortion, and his position in her inner world as a determinant of his personality.

We would be most interested in his reactions to the previous session and any *memories or dreams* that came up in association to it. It would be helpful if he had a dream to tell, and if not, the therapist could let him know to bring in dreams as a way of getting access to his inner world.

We would be especially interested in Geoff's *transference reactions*. The new therapist should review the transference reactions to Dr. Scharff, partly to get information about the transference, and partly to release it from its adherence to Dr. Scharff and draw it into the present therapeutic relationship. If circumstances were different and Geoff were to continue in therapy with Dr. Scharff, she would wait for him to bring up those connections to the previous session, or she might detect them in his way of dealing with her. If nothing came up, she might ask directly. Then she would use that information to generate more of a sense of his transference to her. We base our interpretations in our awareness of the patient's transference through using our countertransference response to it as a compass. Transference–countertransference experiences are core-affective moments of psychological arousal that guide us to areas of deep connection in which learning takes place and therapeutic action is most likely to occur.

This unusual circumstance of a single-session therapeutic encounter provided us with a sample of clinical material that doubled as an assessment, a brief therapy, and a trial of therapy. In discussing the case, we have illustrated theoretical concepts drawn from the chapters on fundamentals and advances in object relations theory, and demonstrated techniques described in the chapters on assessment, brief therapy, and the structure and process of intensive therapy.

The book now offers the reader a number of paths. Reading straight through from theory to clinical illustration gives you all the building blocks in orderly progression toward our integration of object relations individual therapy. But that is not the only way. If you know the fundamental theory already, you might proceed to the section on advances. If you don't need to know about research, you can omit that and go straight on with theory. If you don't care for theory, you can turn to Part II. There, you could read the technique chapters on the geography of the transference, assessment, and the structure and process of therapy, and then proceed to the clinical section that applies to your type of practice. That way, you would probably find enough recapping of theory to keep you oriented. After reading the technique section, the brief therapist will then find that the brief therapy section stands alone, while the intensive therapist can omit the brief therapy section if it is not relevant. When a clinical moment interests you, you can then go back and read about the underlying theory in earlier chapters. Once you have read the theory and technique chapters, you might return to this chapter for summary and review or to check how much you have assimilated.

We now turn to the fundamentals of theory in Section 2.

Section 2

FUNDAMENTALS

3

Origins: Fairbairn, Klein, Winnicott, Bion

A psychology of object relations puts the individual's need to relate to others at the center of human development. The infant's efforts to relate to the mother constitute the first and most important tendency in the baby. This experience with the caretaking person is internalized and so provides the building blocks of psychic structure. Object relations theorists coming from different theoretical orientations follow Klein and Fairbairn in agreeing that the fundamental defense against psychic pain is splitting of the object and repression of its anxiety-provoking aspects. This way of dealing with experience forms the basis for psychic structure, the configuration of which gives rise to characteristic ways of dealing with new experience at different developmental levels and with people other than the infant's original caretakers.

These fundamental ideas first achieved prominence through the work of Ronald Fairbairn, Melanie Klein, and slightly later, Donald Winnicott. These three were joined at various stages by analysts Bowlby, Balint, Guntrip, Sutherland, and Bollas of the British Independent group and by Kleinians Bion, Rosenfeld, Segal, Spillius, Joseph, and others, who contributed the elements of what has collectively come to be known as object relations theory. Within this context, the work of Fairbairn, Klein, and Winnicott has continued to constitute the basic framework for our elaboration, based on our integration of their distinctive philosophies.

Where did that unwieldy term *object relations* come from? It was first used by Fairbairn for his new theory of the endopsychic situation. In order to pay respect to Freud's vision even while totally disagreeing with him, Fairbairn derived the term "object relations" from two of Freud's concepts. Freud used *object* to refer to the need-satisfying place that the sexual instinct aimed at for gratification and tension reduction. He used the phrase the *ego's relation to the object* when describing the ego's defensive attitudes toward the aim and target of the instinct. The sexual instinct was thought to derive from the id, an unconscious, physically based source of energy that must seek discharge. As we show in Chapter 4, Freud was aware of the importance of family relationships, but he did not appreciate their significance for psychic structure-building until the child's achievement of the oedipal period, where he saw conflict and identification as forces that secure the development of the managing ego and supervising superego. In various papers, he moved toward recognizing the defining relevance of family and group dynamics for human development, but he always returned to a physiologically based theory in which the human personality was thought of as deriving from the management of drive tension and the resolution of conflict between the ego aided by the superego, and the disruptive forces of the id. Freud did not fully develop a psychological theory of the relations between ego and objects, and so it fell to Fairbairn, Klein, Winnicott, and others of the British Independent or Kleinian traditions to pursue that path of inquiry.

Each of these three major theoreticians—Fairbairn, Klein, and Winnicott—is, in his or her own way, a complex writer whose work may be found difficult to digest for different reasons. Klein, a native German speaker without scientific or philosophic training, wrote descriptively of her wonderful observations and speculations. Her discursive writing is intuitive and persuasive, but to the critical reader it is confusing, because it is presented to be believed rather than argued. However, the power of her observation and thinking accumulates over time, and she has come to be perhaps the greatest single force in psychoanalytic observation since Freud.

Fairbairn's writing is difficult in a different way. It is detailed, thorough, abstruse, and dense. Fairbairn had considerable philosophical training during his first degree at university in Edinburgh, before he was a field officer in the First World War, and then he went on to medical school. He is unique among the major contributors to psychoanalytic theory in the rigor of his thought, which stems from the synthesis of philosophy and scientific method. While his earliest published papers were full of independent, astute clinical observation, his other early papers and lectures on analytic theory that have only recently been published show his keen intellect attempting to make sense of the inconsistencies and potential strengths of Freud's work (D. Scharff and

Birtles 1994). His inquiries reached fruition in the papers written in the 1940s and 1950s, many of them printed in the only book he published himself, *A Psychoanalytic Study of the Personality*. His writing is a model of tight reasoning, condensed language, and rigor, derived from his adherence to scientific and philosophical principles. The theory which emerged in this book was elaborated and explained in later papers that are also now collected for the first time (D. Scharff and Birtles 1994). These papers filled out the theory, linked it to the contemporary concerns of developing psychoanalytic theory, answered objections, and again addressed his early concern with methodological and scientific shortcomings in Freud's theory.

Winnicott's style is different yet again. It is loose and whimsical, yet immediate. Winnicott was a pediatrician who fell in with the vibrant group of analysts thinking and writing in London in the 1920s and 1930s, but who maintained his grounding in pediatrics, and whose definition of his task as therapist, consultant, or theory-builder was always influenced by his early professional training in the observation of the child, the mother, and the family. To his careful clinical and developmental observations, he gives an idiosyncratic, imaginative twist that spins off a theory of development written in metaphorical and evocative language. Not surprisingly, the result is like quicksilver: beautiful, but elusive, suggestive, evanescent. Now you follow it, now you don't! The logical links are not always there, but still there is something powerful, creative, and convincing. Reading Winnicott calls for letting go of logic and understanding to arrive slowly at a comprehension of his ideas from inside our own experience of his words. Powerful, magical—and confounding. There are some good guides to Winnicott's various concepts, which gradually adumbrate a theory of development, but the summaries cannot offer clarity and still retain the magical creative confusion which Winnicott's own words offer.

Winnicott's magic covers the child's coming into being, creating a sense of self within the intimacies of the relationship with the mother, the mother's role in the child's development, and the implications of these observations for assessment and therapy with infants, play-age children, and adults. He shows us how to apply what we learn from analysis of children to our therapeutic technique with adults. Most useful, moving, and evocative of our own clinical experience are his contributions on countertransference. Along with therapeutic care and concern, he permits and values hate.

These three writers came to analysis from different backgrounds that led each to focus the analytic spotlight on a different aspect of human development, and therefore to generate a different set of theoretical perspectives and techniques. They have all been criticized for the partial nature of their views. But each of their individual, intensive investigations contributes a crucial element to our working synthesis of a theoretical model for contemporary object relations therapy.

The Development of Fairbairn's Model of the Mind

Fairbairn began his work with an intensely scholarly interest in developing a thorough understanding of Freud's theory. We can trace the progression in his comprehension by studying the notes he made in preparation for seminars he taught medical and other students at the University of Edinburgh (Birtles and Scharff 1994). His work on these early lectures led him to pose a series of questions about Freud's theoretical structure, questions which he could not fully answer until his own formulation of the 1940s, when he took up some of the objections from the standpoint of his new theory. He did not, however, fully outline his differences with Freud and the reasons for them until the late papers, only recently published (Scharff and Birtles 1994). Meanwhile, in his clinical reports, written as early as 1927, Fairbairn considered the relationship of the patient to her family and others to be of central clinical importance, but without yet having a theoretical framework which differentiated such a perspective from the standard Freudian point of view.

From distant Scotland, Fairbairn closely followed the London scene and the work of Klein and her group. He was profoundly influenced by their papers, since the Kleinian emphasis on the experience of the infant in relating to the mother fit well with his own ideas. He incorporated many of her ideas as his writing progressed, most notably in two papers he wrote on a psychology of art published in 1936, where he applied Klein's ideas on relating to the object, symbolism, and symbolic repair in an uncritical, unmetabolized way. More usually, however, he did not accept her ideas without question.

Splitting and Represssion

In his first original theoretical paper (1940) on "Schizoid Factors in the Personality," written a few years after the papers on a psychology of art, Fairbairn outlined his concept of the process of splitting of the ego in normal development and pathology, and proposed that this constituted an earlier phenomenon than "the depressive position" which Klein had described. In the *depressive position,* the infant becomes capable of recognizing the mother as a whole person and of feeling ambivalence and concern for her as a separate person. In the meantime, Klein had also described an earlier stage that she called *the paranoid position*, to refer to a phase in which the infant defends against anxiety by using early processes of projection of aggression that split the object. Having read Fairbairn's paper on splitting of the ego, Klein agreed with him, and renamed this early paranoid state *the paranoid-schizoid position*, a more complete name for this early position that the infant takes in regard to its object, one which is characterized by the pairing of splitting and projection. Thus, for both theorists, splitting of the object came to represent an early and fundamental psychic defense against pain in relationships. However, while Klein emphasized splitting of the object, Fairbairn was more concerned with splitting of the ego.

We can see the differing emphasis in Fairbairn's and Klein's viewpoints already emerging. Klein emphasized the infant's role in projection and splitting of the *object*. She thought that the infant mainly tried to get unpleasant experience and affect outside the self by locating it in the mother who was then perceived as wholly bad for that moment. Fairbairn emphasized splitting of the *self*. He argued that the infant took these unpleasant experiences and affects inside the self and disposed of them by splitting them off from the main core of the self in the form of objects and subsidiary egos, and then burying them in the unconscious.

Soon, Fairbairn also suggested that Klein's concept of "unconscious phantasy," which she had postulated as the fundamental link between the drives and reality, should be replaced by his more useful concept of the "internal object." He thought that unconscious phantasy was just one aspect of the internal object. Phantasy is an activity of the ego that invests an experience with the quality of its needing to be internalized, at which point an internal object is created inside the self and then exerts its influence over future experience, determining perceptions of and creating unconscious phantasy about subsequent versions of the external object. Fairbairn's point continues to make logical sense, but the term "unconscious phantasy" has remained, alive and well, used alongside its counterpart "internal object." We tend to use the word *fantasy* (spelled in the American way) to refer to conscious fantasy, unconscious phantasy, and to activities of the corresponding internal objects, without distinguishing between them as Klein and Fairbairn would have done.

Fairbairn's fundamental reorientation of analytic theory was published in 1944 in his paper on endopsychic structure. There he stated that the infant is motivated, from the beginning, by a fundamental need for relationships, and that all development takes place and derives meaning in the context of the relationship to the mother. We can see here the origin of Winnicott's later, more evocative idea that there is no such thing as an infant without a mother. In Fairbairn's theory, the first defense against the inevitable disappointments in the relationship to the mother is to incorporate the experience with her as an internal object in an attempt to control disappointment over real or imagined rejection by her, but with the result that the infant is then saddled with an internalized somewhat rejecting object. To deal with that object and the associated painful affects, the infant's second defense is to split off the painfully exciting and rejecting parts of it and to repress them in the unconscious, leaving a relatively unencumbered central ego to relate to the outside world in a relatively reasonable way. As the object is split into acceptable and rejected exciting and rejecting elements, so a part of the ego splits too: because the idea of an object can have no meaning without an ego to relate to it, each part of the object (or part-object) requires a part-ego or part of the self to be in relation with it, along with the relevant affects.

Fairbairn invoked the mechanism of splitting at the later oedipal phase of development, as well, in order to explain the phenomenon of the family romance. He thought that the reorganization of internal structure during the oedipal phase is a creation by the child that is triggered by the experience of ambivalent relationships with both mother and father. The child tries to organize and simplify this complex situation, he said, by using the familiar technique of splitting the object, in this case by making one parent the good object and one the bad, organized along gender lines. Klein, on the other hand, dated the Oedipus complex much earlier, and based the infant's rage and envy of the parental couple in the infant's inborn awareness of their intercourse from which it was excluded.

By 1944, with his paper on endopsychic structure, the central orientation of Fairbairn's point of view had emerged. In summary, Fairbairn holds that the infant is born prepared (or hard-wired as the modern infant researchers put it) to take in experience with its object world, and this biological readiness to form relationships is the central fact of human experience.

Fairbairn's model emphasizes that the internal world is organized by internalizing experience with the outer world. He is specific about the growing psyche's own input in creating a distinctive inner world that is not simply a carbon copy of the outer experience. His model of mind is one that is capable of blending outer influence with inner structuring throughout development. This balance makes his the most flexible of models, able to consider the full influence of both external reality and the inner forces which determine and modify development. For instance, Fairbairn's model can accept and understand the full force of external trauma such as physical or sexual abuse or the loss of a parent, while it also allows for the rich elaboration of the child's inner distortions and modifications of outer experience. It is this flexibility that warrants placing Fairbairn's model at the center of a comprehensive understanding of psychic development.

Fairbairn organized his theoretical statement on a single page, published in the *International Journal of Psycho-Analysis* in 1963, the year he died. It has the tight logical reasoning and spareness of a philosophical formulation. For this reason, it can also be captured in a diagram which allows us to consider graphically some of the major aspects of his theory, and later to relate them to Klein and Winnicott. (See Figure 3–1.)

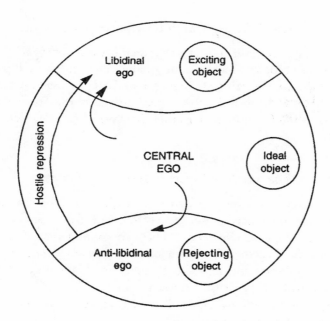

FIGURE 3–1. Fairbairn's model of psychic organization. The central ego in relation to the ideal object is in conscious interaction with the caretaker. The central ego represses the split-off libidinal and anti-libidinal aspects of its experience along with corresponding parts of the ego and relevant affects that remain unconscious. The libidinal system is further repressed by the anti-libidinal system. Copyright © 1982 David Scharff.

Fairbairn's Endopsychic Situation

The Central Ego and Object Relationship System

The central ego and its ideal object comprise the relatively conscious and rational aspect of psychic functioning, free to relate to the outside world and to learn from experience, and characterized by affects of satisfaction and hope. Split off from the central ego, and repressed by it, are the bad internal object relationships (bad because they represent the internalization of painful interactions with the parents). In each case, an aspect of the ego is split off in relation to these split-off and repressed objects and associated affects. The central ego and object relationship system is responsible for learning, thinking, managing feelings, relating to others, and for repressing the less functional object relationship systems.

The Rejecting Object Relationship System

The frustrating or rejecting object is that memory trace of the mother felt to be rejecting of need, and Fairbairn originally called the ego component attached to it the *internal saboteur* (Figure 3–2). Later he used the name *anti-libidinal ego* for this sub-unit of the ego. Ego and object are connected by affects of rage and frustration. Together they form a *rejecting internal object relationship*.

The Exciting Object Relationship System

The other image of the mother associated with pain is the mother who is excessively exciting of need, the *exciting object*. The part-ego associated with this Fairbairn called the *libidinal ego*. These are connected by affects of craving and longing. Together they form an *exciting internal object relationship*. While the central ego acts to repress both these constellations in order to avoid awareness of pain, there is also *secondary repression* carried out by the anti-libidinal ego on the libidinal ego and its exciting object in order to further avoid the pain of unsatisfied longing.

In describing this mechanism of repression in the interaction of internal structures, Fairbairn introduced the first example of *dynamic internal object relations*. We now understand that the dynamic quality works in all directions, so that it is equally the case that the libidinal ego can, and does, act to repress the anti-libidinal ego and object, for example in situations in which a person assumes an excessively sweet disposition to avoid the pain of experiencing rejection. The point is that internal relations between self and object are subject to dynamic flux. In health, the internal object relations are in open exchange with the environment. Only in pathological situations do they become frozen in one or another static situation, forming then a fixed and closed internal system.

Fairbairn's theory has been used as a model for a general psychology and for the development of the self, not just as an explanation of pathology. When it is used this way, it has to take into account the forces that the libidinal and anti-libidinal constellations represent for relating in both health and disease. With this in mind, we have come to see the libidinal ego as the part of the self that pulls toward the object both pleasantly and in a clinging way, and the anti-libidinal ego as the part that distances from the object both to express angry rejection and to seek autonomy within the context of relationships. Object-seeking and autonomy-preserving are the dominant trends in relating, and it is only the excesses of these trends which have to do with pathology. The exciting object and rejecting object also represent trends in the force of internal objects, and only the excesses represent the pathological objects. All aspects of the self—both ego and object, central and repressed internal object relationships—are in dynamic internal relationship with each other, and these dynamics influence and are influenced by external object relations. Accordingly, we have modified the diagram of Fairbairn's theory to show the place of the libidinal and anti-libidinal constellations in development and pathology, as shown in Figure 3–2.

Klein's Model of the Psyche

Klein began to develop her theories from her observations of child development and psychopathology viewed from the standpoint of the mind of a child in relation to the mother, but not from the position of a child who is dependent on the mother's care. Klein was aware of the role of mothers, and commented on them often enough so that it would be unfair for us to say she ignored them, but her theory overlooks their importance for psychic structure. Fathers are overlooked too, but not just by Klein. They do not figure prominently in the work of any of the early theorists on whose work we build. Not until the 1970s are they considered, and even now it is commonly assumed that their role is secondary to whoever does the "mothering," whether it is a woman or a man. We still need a theory that addresses the child's processing of experiencing two parents and their relation to each other from birth.

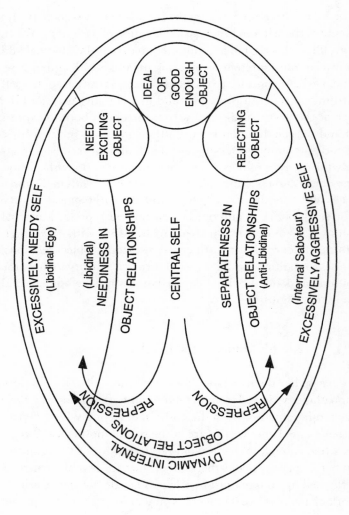

FIGURE 3–2. Amplification of Fairbairn's Model of Psychic Organization. Neediness and separateness are aspects of the Central Self. Exciting and Rejecting Objects partly communicate with the Ideal Object and are partly repressed. All aspects of self and objects are in dynamic relations.

There is, however, a certain power in the singlemindedness of Klein's perspective which enabled her to make new observations, despite her adherence to old ideas about instinctual energies. She saw life from inside the child's mind as it coped with the unfolding of the drives that Freud had described. He had begun by describing the sexual instinct as the fundamental drive, according to the pleasure principle. Later he broadened the sexual instinct to include a more comprehensive life-instinct or *eros*. Against this, he posited a death drive, or *thanatos*, which led to the disintegration and deterioration of life seen in individual self-destruction and the social forces of brutality and war. Klein shared Freud's views on the instinctual basis of development and was particularly struck by the ubiquitous force of the death instinct.

Klein took Freud's formulation of the life and death instincts seriously, and put them at the center of her orientation, but she also differed from Freud, who thought that drives fortuitously happen upon the objects of their gratification. Instead, Klein assumes that drives are immediately directed toward, attracted by, and attached to objects that they color according to the quality of the operative instinct. Klein is both a drive theorist and an object relations theorist. Whereas Freud's drives are physiological, hers are psychological (Spillius 1994). The infant Klein describes is haunted by the death instinct, terrified of the resulting aggression and its effects on the self and the other, and is, at the same time, motivated by the life instinct to feel concern and to undo the damage caused from directing omnipotent phantasies of excessive aggression (biting, excreting, devouring) against the primary objects.

The Paranoid-Schizoid Position

Klein described an infant at the earliest stage of psychological life, struggling to ward off the terror of annihilation and to deal with the persecutory objects that result from the projection of aggression. She called this constellation the *paranoid-schizoid position* to indicate that it was not a single developmental step, but a lifelong struggle. The word *paranoid* refers to the projection of aggression outward. As we noted earlier, Klein first used the term *paranoid position*, but she soon took Fairbairn's suggestion that splitting of the ego was involved in the projection process, and so renamed the process to reflect the *pairing* of splitting and projection. Still, Klein saw projective processes as dominant where Fairbairn saw repression. In our experience, both processes operate at the same time, but some patients emphasize one more than the other. The projection of a part of mental contents is only possible when that part has been split off from the core, so that indeed splitting and repression must operate together as the infant tries to manage anger and destructiveness.

The Depressive Position

At about four months of age, the infant begins the lifelong job of developing concern for the other, of understanding the situation of the mother who has had to put up with the difficult baby, and who, herself, while not perfect, is still the infant's loving mother. Klein called this internal struggle the *depressive position*. She made it clear that this position has nothing to do with clinical depression, but refers to the capacity for bearing responsibility and feeling guilt and concern. It leads to a desire to *make reparation* to the mother. The child in the paranoid-schizoid position *envies* the mother for having what the child needs and wants—embodied in the envy of her breast for having the milk the child needs and giving the pleasure of sucking that the child craves—while the child in the depressive position is capable of *gratitude* for what the mother gives.

Klein contributed many other highly original insights, usually from the standpoint of seeing the child at the center of the relational universe. She conceived of *unconscious phantasy* as the *unconscious* embodiment of the drives, a concept later made popular by Isaacs (1948). Phantasies are primitive organizations of mind which operate entirely unconsciously but which, acting from underneath, determine everything that happens at more conscious and rational levels of organization. Klein described many of the unconscious phantasies of the very young child, who, she felt, understood the essence of relational processes in bodily terms—sucking, biting, excreting, spitting up. She felt that the triangular oedipal situation, which Freud (1905b) had described many years earlier, occurred in a primitive, essentially oral version in the 1-year-old child, and that the child's unconscious phantasy of the mother and father in intercourse, of the mother having orally and sadistically incorporated the father's penis inside her body, was the prototype of a triangular situation to be envied.

Klein chose to use the word *position* in contrast to Freud's *developmental stages*. She did not regard her positions as stages to be gone through according to a preset sequence governed by the drives. Instead she saw them as a lifelong continuum in a state of dynamic flux throughout the life cycle. Her followers (Bion, and later Joseph, and then Steiner), extended the concept of fluctuation between positions in personality development, group process, and in psychotherapy and psychoanalytic sessions.

Projective and Introjective Identification

The best known of Klein's concepts is that of *projective identification* paired with its counterpart, *introjective identification* (J. Scharff 1992) (See Figure 3–3). In projective identification, the infant (or any person) unconsciously takes an aspect of its internal world—object or self—and projects it out and into the other person with whom it is in relationship, identifying the other person with that aspect of the self. This process is carried out by unconscious communication—supported by facial and bodily gestures, intonation, and context. It rides, as it were, piggyback on conscious communication. The other person *introjectively identifies* with these elements and is, without knowing it, partly taken over by the projected elements, and acts in some ways to live them out. In a cycle of projective and introjective identification, this second person (let's assume it is the mother) then re-projects aspects of herself which the infant takes in through introjective identification. This cycle is the bedrock of unconscious communication. In conditions of painful, bad internal object relations, the infant projectively identifies with the painful aspects of itself it locates in the mother in order to get them outside the self (in phantasy) to avoid their spoiling its internal world, but also in the hope that after their sojourn in the mother, they will come back detoxified. Alternatively, the infant projects out good aspects of its self for safekeeping in the mother, or uses aspects of the personality to control her and keep her nearby when separation threatens.

Figure 3–3 depicts one type of projective and introjective identificatory process between infant and mother in which a child unconsciously seeks the exciting object—for instance, by anxiously seeking a feed when no longer hungry—and the mother rejects the child's unconscious initiative. She might do so simply by not feeding the child. If she shakes the child angrily for being spoiled, the child experiences a more severe rejection and introjects an enlarged experience of the persecutory object. A more thorough rejection, or a refusal to take in the child's anxiety at all, leaves the child to introject a feeling of nameless dread, while the mother introjects her child as an anxious, unsatisfiable, persecutory object.

Klein's early work analyzing children as young as 2½ convinced her that infants understand a great deal about the nature of sexuality and destruction. When Klein located these infantile problems of the disposal of the drives of sexuality and death at the center of children's psychological development, she gave analysis a powerful way of understanding the difficulty each of us causes ourselves when excesses of anger, sexual feeling, longing, and rejection torment us. In treatment the child or adult is seen as reliving these earliest

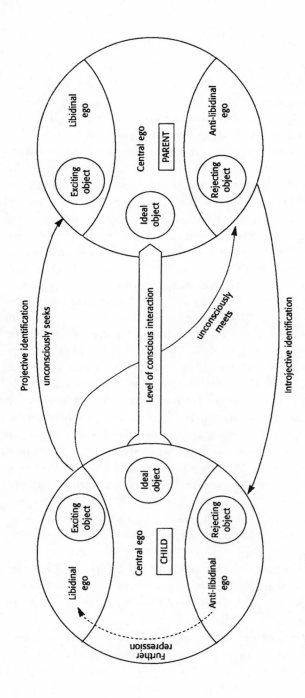

FIGURE 3–3. The action of projective and introjective identification. The mechanism here is the interaction of the child's projective and introjective identifications with the parent as the child meets frustration, unrequited yearning, or trauma. The diagram depicts the child longing to have his needs met and identifying with similar trends in the parent via projective identification. The child meeting with rejection identifies with the frustration of the parent's own anti-libidinal system via introjective identification. In an internal reaction to the frustration, the libidinal system is further repressed by the renewed force of the child's antilibidinal system. Copyright © 1982 David Scharff.

struggles within the analytic setting. Klein's concept of inner phantasy organization has given us access to the richness of the inner world and its continuing influence on external life through projective identification and other interactive processes. Her concept of positions enriched many developmental concepts, which could then be understood in relational terms for the first time.

Although she acknowledged the trauma of birth and the effect of bad experience with bad objects, Klein does not explore them as thoroughly as in her unparalleled offerings on the effects of internal phantasy on the child's inner world. Like Freud before her, she constructed a theory in which human development proceeds according to an inevitable plan shaped only by the forces of opposing instincts. The growing child seems like a flower, unfolding from seed to bud to blossom in a preset pattern so long as it is supported adequately by the sun, water, and nutrients of the ordinary environment. It is almost as though the mother is merely the provider of these elements, a benign but vague and impersonal figure who exerts no personal influence.

Bion's Theory of the Container and the Contained

Bion (1967, 1970) made up for this shortcoming of Klein's orientation in his theory of the *container and the contained*, a model of the mental processes of the mother as she relates to her anxiously projecting baby. In a state of reverie, she attends to her infant's needs and anxieties. In her mind she bears her infant's distress and tries to figure out what could account for it. She is able to think through the problem and in so doing detoxifies the unthinkable anxieties and gives them back to the infant in a thinkable, manageable form. Mommy makes it better, and Bion explains how. She has not simply held her child's mental contents, she has *contained* them in her active processing of experience. The infant is not only relieved of painful mental contents but also identifies with her containing function and becomes more able to use thought to handle anxiety in future. This theory of the container and the contained provides a Kleinian model for mutual unconscious interaction that is helpful in couple and family therapy and in the understanding of transference and countertransference in individual therapy and psychoanalysis.

Even Bion did not address the issue of primary external influence on the child's developing personality. We have to look to other contributors—those in the tradition of Fairbairn and Winnicott—for a study of the influence of external factors. Fairbairn provided a theoretical structure that granted full value to the influence of the parents and significant others in fundamentally shaping the growing child, but it was Winnicott who first described the crucial importance of the actual elements of the mother's (or mothering person's) treatment of the child in shaping development.

Winnicott's Model of Mother and Baby

Winnicott came to analysis as a pediatrician with a lifelong interest in the development of babies and the care their mothers exercised with them. He was influenced by Klein's ideas of unconscious phantasy, and projective and introjective identification, but he rebelled against the constraints of becoming a formal member of her group. It must have seemed to him that the Kleinians valued the child's fantasy to the detriment of understanding the whole world of the psychosomatic partnership of the mother and infant—while to the Kleinians, he might have seemed too involved in physical, child-rearing realities and gratifying activities. He was most interested in the relationship and in the space between the mother and her infant. Like Klein and Fairbairn, Winnicott had almost nothing to say about fathers. The center of his contribution was an evocative exploration of the actualities of the mother–infant relationship, which he applied to the treatment of children and adults, where he saw a reliving of processes of infant and child development.

The Good-Enough Mother

For Winnicott, the adequacy of the maternal caretaking activity had a pervasive influence on the child's psychological development. Where, in response to frustration, Klein had put projection, and Fairbairn the child's splitting and repression, Winnicott saw developmental failure and the growth of the false self as a response to maternal failures. He observed the ordinary mother as preoccupied with and devoted to her infant's growth and well-being. Just as the *good-enough mother*'s functioning facilitated development, so a mother's failures could be expected to handicap her child's maturational processes. The mother begins her task with a state of mind which Winnicott called *primary maternal preoccupation*. This singleminded state of intense absorption with the well-being of her infant includes being open to the infant's anxieties, and being willing to be used by the infant. Winnicott's famous aphorism that there is no such thing as a baby without a mother captures the life-giving quality of the relationship between them.

This has led some to conclude that Winnicott's contribution supplies only a deficit model of psychopathology. It implies that what is wrong with troubled children comes solely from deficiencies in their treatment by others, inadequate supplies, or lack of security. His contribution is usefully applied to understanding the way shortcomings in the enviromental provisions for a child are translated into psychic difficulty, in contrast to Klein, who largely ignored this area, and to Fairbairn who did not supply any details about it. But it is inaccurate to say that Winnicott did not appreciate the child's own contribution to the development of a self. He insisted that the growth of a self and the realization of a true self were a joint matter. His view is, in many ways, closely balanced between self and other. There are several places where he carefully and sensitively describes the state of mind and travails of the parents, and especially the mother. For instance, he describes the need for the parents to survive the aggression of the infant, without retaliation, as a prerequisite for the child to be able to feel confidently assertive and secure in the knowledge the parents survived the child's murderous feelings.

The mother has two kinds of functions to offer. First, as *environment mother*, she sets the context for growth by providing an envelope of safety and comfort to support the existence and growth of the child, an *arms-around* relationship which *holds* the child safely and confidently. Within this envelope, she offers herself as an *object mother*—that is, she offers herself to be used as an object by the infant as the *focused* subject of its love and hate, as the object of its experience, without being devoured or killed off. She offers to survive the experience of answering the infant's needs as a person and as a thing, and at many times does so without demanding anything in return. She survives the infant's love and hate, without dying, retaliating, or exploiting the child. In doing this, she reacts, and the infant learns to see itself as mirrored in her face, her reactions, and her treatment of her child. As she becomes the first external object for the child, the child finds a self in her reaction and in her handling. And at the same time, the child internalizes the experience with her—that is, she becomes the material out of which the internal world is populated. In his concept of *the use of an object*, Winnicott described the way the mother must offer herself as an object to be used and abused *ruthlessly* in the sense that the infant can make use of her with no obligation to have her experience in mind, and in that sense she is the subject of benign abuse. It is her own *ruth* or selfless concern for the infant which allows her to offer herself in this way.

Having described the two functions of the mother, Winnicott describes how the self is formed in the relational matrix. The child's psychological existence begins in the mother's mind while her *primary maternal preoccupa-*

tion holds the baby's needs, moods, and being in her attention, and supports the baby psychologically. In addition to this, the beginning of the self has twin origins at the core of the infant self as it reaches out to the world. It derives from (1) the external world of objects in and out of reach, and (2) the infant's own *spontaneous gestures* at the core of its being. The taking in of outer experience through manipulation of actual physical objects parallels the process of taking in the experience with the mother. Winnicott described this in his paper on his clinical invention of the spatula game, a game in which the child takes into the hand and mouth an inert neutral object while in the presence of an approving mother who holds the environment in which the infant can explore. So the baby begins in itself *and* in its mother, simultaneously and paradoxically.

Winnicott conceived of the beginning relationship between mother and baby as a *psychosomatic partnership*, that is, as a relationship equally grounded in the bodily and physical aspects of relating and in the psychological partnership. After its greatest intensity in the earliest months, this partnership becomes attenuated as a physical, bodily one, but the intense psychological partnership carries on throughout the rest of the child's life. It derives from the initial bodily closeness and communication which gives power, poignancy, and intensity to the way that primary relationships penetrate the bodily being of the child, and will do so later when the child is an adult in a sexually committed relationship. The mother takes care of her tasks through her *holding and handling* of the infant, conveying her environmental care so that the infant can become a going concern and get the capacity for *going on being* through being held in the security of her arms and through her abiding, responsive attention.

Transitional Objects and Phenomena

As the mother–infant pair relate over time, they do so across a widening distance between parent and child, a physical gap between them which is echoed in a widening psychological separateness which holds the essential potential for creativity and communication mediated by what Winnicott called *transitional objects* and *transitional phenomena*. The transitional object is a physical article which the infant treats as though it were the mother, but which is completely under the control of the child. Thus the blanket, teddy bear, or other object is a companion, an object to be used and abused, a source of comfort, and a tireless companion. The child uses other phenomena in a similar way, perhaps at an early stage playing with the mother's face, breast, hair, or clothes, making use of an object of clothing in a habitual way even though the piece of clothing itself is interchangeable, or, as an adolescent, using other objects in such a way as to open a potential space—which we now also call a transitional space—in which internal and social issues can be elaborated and experimented with. This gap area fosters simultaneously an internal experience of the child, and the imaginary meeting of the child with another person. Whether the experience is internal or external is never quite clear, and this ambiguity is one of the sustained paradoxes Winnicott asks us to live with. Mothers may put objects there for their children to find, but children must also have the experience of feeling that they invented them, while the parent agrees never to force the question, "Did the baby find this or invent it?"

Figure 3–4 summarizes some of the elements of Winnicott's formulation superimposed on Fairbairn's formulation of internal organization, which can now be seen to be consistent with Winnicott's contributions.

The arms-around functions of the environmental mother occur in the zone of contextual holding.

This provides the baby with a sense of background security supplied by a mother in whose care and concern he can trust.

The I-to-I, eye-to-eye relating of the object mother occurs in the area of focused relating.

This refers to the way mother and baby become each other's discrete objects of love and hate as they engage in arousal sequences that include looking into each other's eyes (relating eye-to-eye), speaking, and responding directly to each other's gestures and vocal tones.

The True and the False Self

Many of Winnicott's formulations are most evocative in their paradoxical and enigmatic quality, which makes it difficult and even pointless to pin him down to precise formulations. He seems to have intended this, stating that it is from uncertainty that growth and creativity occur. This enigmatic quality also characterizes his concept of *true and false self.* The false self is a quality or state of the personality which is reactive to the mother's (and significant others') needs, which come to take precedence over those of the child itself. The true self, while hard to define, is an internal pole at the core of the child's personality, often covered by the social pole of the false self which, in pathology, is overly responsive to the demands of others. On the other hand, the false self is not a bad or fake attribute, but rather the part of the self that is tuned to the outer reality, that protects the true self in doing so, and that facilitates relatedness to others.

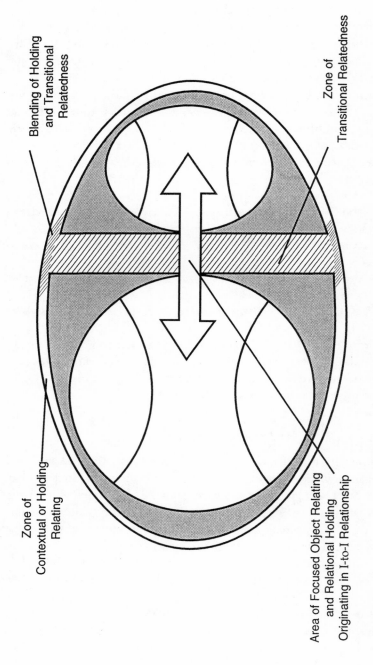

Zone of
Contextual or Holding
Relating

Blending of Holding
and Transitional
Relatedness

Zone of
Transitional Relatedness

Area of Focused Object Relating
and Relational Holding
Originating in I-to-I Relationship

FIGURE 3–4. Contextual holding, the transitional space, and focused relating. Focused (or centered or I-to-I) relating occurs in and across the transitional space. The transitional space is in contact with both contextual relating and focused relating, and is also the zone which blends the two.

Play and Holding

Many of Winnicott's concepts are essentially clinical findings and developmental observations transformed by being given evocative names that create
his unique brand of clinical theory. Not surprisingly, his contributions have
been applicable to the clinical situation with both children and adults. His
clinical concepts, like his developmental ones, center around the concept of
play as a necessary experience. It is through the child's play in the potential space
between itself and the parent—in the transitional space—that growth and
experimentation occur. Psychotherapy and psychoanalysis are conceived of
as an experience of *play in the area of the gap between patient and therapist.* The
child must be able to play to be healthy. The adult must be helped to play with
ideas, with significant others, with concepts of a relationship—and with the
therapist—for healing to occur.

Because of his background as a pediatrician, and his lifelong orientation
as a doctor to children with physical ills, Winnicott did some unconventional
things as an analyst, such as encouraging some patients to get off the couch
and walk around, giving a time-out to a child in a temper tantrum, and
physically holding some patients in states of regression. While some of these
acts, especially the physical contact, would be unacceptable to most modern analytic therapists, it is from the ideas conveyed in these actions that
Winnicott's most important clinical contributions have come. It is with the
clinical concept of *holding*, as a psychological state of mind of the therapist,
or *relating and mirroring*, that the modern therapist works. The analyst's state
of mind may include feelings of care and concern when these are evoked
by the patient, but at other times accurate mirroring may reveal a tremendous amount of hate. An aggressive boy who was unresponsive to kindness
and interpretation benefited when a furious Winnicott put him outside the
door. Winnicott's management of his countertransference to this boy, who
was utterly enraging, shows the therapeutic use of the analyst's hatred in
the treatment of aggression. Empathy does not always assume the mantle
of kindness. Only within a broadly defined context of empathy, can interpretation make its impact.

A Contemporary Understanding of Drives and Their Operation

Today, many analysts understand the drives as operating in more general
ways. Rather than positing the sexual instinct as a universal basis for human

motivation, analysts view physical and genital sexuality as including the tendencies toward closeness in relatedness, mastery of new situations, and growth. Instead of seeing the death instinct as the motivator of destruction, they see it as aggression, which, in excess leads to human violence, war, and destruction, but which, in its positive role also operates toward autonomy in relationships and supports mastery of new situations. For instance, instead of conceptualizing the death instinct as an innate potential or a biological drive, we can think of it as a relational context encased in a closed system that engenders feelings of hopelessness, doom, or massive protest. The relational dead-end leads to an identification with being dead, being killed off, wishing to destroy, and longing for death (D. Scharff 1992). In contemporary times, we are inclined to reframe the sexual and aggressive instinctual poles of behavior which Freud described in the early 1900s as counterbalancing tendencies toward affiliation and aggressive distancing in relationships (see Figure 3–2 for the pictorial representation of a modification of Fairbairn's theory that captures these elements).

Freud would not necessarily have agreed with this analysis, and certainly Klein would not. Klein views the inner world from the orientation of an infant who might expect to have a competent mother *only if the infant's innate aggression does not damage her or drive her away.* Fairbairn and Winnicott expect *a reasonably good mother who will nevertheless inevitably be somewhat frustrating and so cause an aggressive response,* as her infant tries to alert her to what is needed. Where Fairbairn saw an infant frustrated by the inevitability of being let down or rejected by its mother some of the time, Klein saw an infant filled with rage due to its fear of annihilation emanating from the death instinct, a situation that is independent of the mother. For Klein, it is the strength of this constitutionally given aggression that presents the initial psychological challenge. The infant handles this internal threat by projecting this aggression into the mother, and then experiencing her as if she is the source of the rageful feelings. Klein admits that external experience contributes to the situation too, but she emphasizes the role of the infant's innate aggression.

Lastly, whereas Klein holds that the trauma of birth subjects the infant to the impact of the death instinct and so contributes to the *fear of annihilation of the self,* for Fairbairn it raises the issue of *fear of loss of the object.* In Klein's view, infantile anger stems from the projection of the death instinct to protect the self from annihilation by it. In Fairbairn's view, at birth the infant loses the state of uterine bliss in which need has been met automatically and physiologically with no perceived need of an object. After birth, there is total *dependency on the primary object* and this leads to frustration of autonomous strivings and anger at the object.

Klein died in 1960, Fairbairn in 1963, and Winnicott in 1971. Even before their deaths, other contributors had picked up the threads of the rich tapestry they began. Such seminal writers as British Independents Michael Balint, John Bowlby, Harry Guntrip, Christopher Bollas, and Kleinians Wilfred Bion, Harold Rosenfeld, Hanna Segal, Paula Heimann, and Susan Isaacs, all made central contributions to theory and clinical practice. They continued the tradition of using direct clinical observation to advance the theory of infant, child, and adolescent development and its application to the treatment of children and adults.

In the last two decades, the work has continued, increasingly on both sides of the Atlantic, throughout Europe, and in North and South America. Object relations no longer resides solely in the British Isles. It has become a worldwide influence in psychoanalysis and the basis for work in psychotherapy, infant research and treatment, child and adult development, and understanding groups and institutions. The relational paradigm first described by Fairbairn, Klein, and Winnicott has become the organizing set of ideas in modern psychoanalysis, and has influenced literature, philosophy, and organizational development.

The human condition is far too complex for any single theory to suffice, and so we look for a way to integrate findings from all theories that have clinical application. Fairbairn's contribution has emerged for us as the single most consistent conceptualization, even though it is no more complete or flawless than any other, and does not replace the others, but it functions for us as the hub of a wheel to which other concepts and clinical observations can relate. Fairbairn's construction emerges as the most centered, the most logical, and the most helpful to us in organizing our thinking about other psychoanalytic theories, not only those of Klein and Winnicott, but also the contributions of Bowlby on attachment, Kohut on self psychology, and Mitchell on relational–conflict theory, as well as articulating the links between Freudian drive and ego psychology and the relational theories. The result is an integrated theoretical perspective embedded in a Fairbairnian matrix with range and flexibility in application to group, couple, and family therapy, and community psychiatry, as well as to individual psychotherapy and psychoanalysis (D. Scharff and J. Scharff 1987, 1991). Within the clinical sphere, and beyond it, to wider fields of human endeavor, the opportunities offered by object relations theory have yet to be fully explored.

In the chapter that follows, we will begin with the origin of object relations terminology and theory in the work of Freud. From that beginning, we will then look at the writings of Fairbairn, Klein, Bion, and Winnicott in the wider context of American psychoanalysis, including early American object-relations theory. Then we move on to new theoretical developments in object relations theory.

4

Freud's Contributions

The current trend in contemporary psychoanalysis is toward a theory of human development built on a personal, relational basis instead of the instinctual basis on which classical Freudian theory was founded. This general path subtends a number of directions, including self psychology, intersubjectivity, relational psychology, and object relations theories. No longer restricted by the vision of the monolithic era of psychoanalysis, we are now developing many versions of psychoanalysis (Wallerstein 1988). Any one of these may mistakenly regard itself as the only way to understanding, but all of them are needed to expand knowledge of the human condition.

In France, for instance, where philosophy is an important aspect of education, psychoanalysis is regarded as an intellectual discipline as well as a treatment method. There, theoretical developments have emphasized the tensions and paradoxes of instinctual life, primitive signifiers of the hidden meaning of language, and the unconscious. In Great Britain, coexisting contemporary Freudian, Kleinian, and British Independent object relations schools primarily emphasize ego defense psychology, unconscious phantasy relationships determined by the quality of the instincts (especially the death instinct), and preoedipal aspects of the patient–therapist relationship, respectively. In Scotland, relatively isolated from mainstream psychoanalysis in Britain and Europe, Fairbairn challenged the instinctual basis for behavior that was central to Freudian theory, and developed a theory of endopsychic structure based on the infant's need for relationships. In the United States, with its culture of science and technology and where instrumentality is important, the emphasis in psychoanalytic theory has been on the competence of the ego. In the absence of tradition in a new country, Americans, concerned about uniformity and the guarding of standards, preferred classical Freudian theory and technique that adhered to principles of abstinence, neutrality, and the inviolable analytic frame. In reaction to this trend, the self psychology school developed a much less abstinent stance, one that values positive affirmation of needs and an empathic relationship devoted to mirroring and attunement, with analysis focused on lapses in empathy. In the anarchic cultures of South America, Kleinian theory, with its emphasis on the forces of death and destruction, seemed more relevant to an understanding of the human problems experienced there.

None of the theories stand alone, and all of them need modifying as culture progresses. The welcome new developments that reflect the sociocultural diversity, philosophical influences, and scientific advances of the twentieth century derive from and challenge the original psychoanalytic findings and theories discussed by Freud. While in some cases contemporary views are incompatible with Freud's, in other cases they develop aspects that he identified but did not take further because of the inevitable constraints upon his thinking due largely to his gender, his ethnicity, and his historical period.

Overviews of Freudian Theory

The following discussion of Freudian theory draws mainly on Jones's biography (1955a,b,c) and Rapaport's (1960) marvelous overview of various aspects of early instinct theory and their distinction from later Freudian structural theory. Moving from there to object relations, we have also referred to Yankelovich and Barrett's (1970) treatise on ego and instinct, Shapiro's (1978) paper on ego psychology, Sullivanian and object relations theories, and Greenberg and Mitchell's (1983) examination of Freudian theories for evidence of inherent object relational ideas. In the next chapters on post-Freudian theories, the discussion of contemporary object relations–based psychoanalysis is based on historical and theoretical material in Greenberg and Mitchell (1983), Mitchell and Black (1995), D. Scharff and Birtles's (1994) and Birtles and D. Scharff's (1994) co-edited books on Fairbairn, D. Scharff's (1996) edited selection of classics in object relations theory and practice, and J. Scharff's (1994) edited book on the work of John D. Sutherland.

Nineteenth-Century Influences on Freud's Thinking

Freud invented psychoanalysis, a theory for understanding the human condition. He wanted to provide a theory that gave meaning to human experience. He was born with an excellent mind, driving ambition, a strong constitution that supported intensive mental work, and a facilitating family environment. He was encouraged to prepare himself for a life of intellectual accomplishment by his adoring mother, who relieved him of domestic expectations and kept the rest of the household quiet so that he, her eldest son, could study in peace (Jones 1955a). His education gave him access to literature, the arts, cultural anthropology, religion, travel, science, and medicine. During his twelve-year courtship, marriage, and family life with six children, his wife continued the tradition of supporting his devotion to work.

Freud was trained as a physician and neurologist. His studies of hysterical conversion reactions convinced him of the power of primitive ideas and feelings over physical and psychological functioning. He was influenced by the new Darwinian evolutionary theory to emphasize biology as destiny, a point of view that was amplified by his training as a physician. His specialization as a neurologist immersed him in modern neuroanatomy, where he was introduced to the Jacksonian concept of structures whose functions are arranged in a hierarchy, and where the output of lower-level structures is inhibited and organized by higher-level structures of the brain and spinal cord. From this neuroanatomical model, Freud developed his idea of mental structure and function.

Freud saw himself as a man of science. He developed his theories by analogy from scientific models and promoted psychoanalysis as a scientific theory. He found inspiration in the advances of nineteenth-century physics, which featured the transfer and conservation of energy as governed by laws of thermodynamics. These laws of thermodynamics, together with the principle of entropy—which stated that organisms always tend to return to the resting state—fed his hydraulic view of the human personality, whose major task was seen as the disposition of energy. In the area of philosophy, the nineteenth century emphasized dualism: for every force there was a countervailing tendency to achieve harmony, balance, and control. For instance, in religion there was a preoccupation with the balance between the forces of good and evil. So when Freud thought of energy, he drew on biology for his concept of the instincts as sources of energy. Then he looked for opposing forces in the environment to redress the balance and return the energy to its source. In keeping with the principle of dualism, he also looked for sets of instincts to oppose each other's aims, such as those responsible for sexual longing and aggressive attack. In his early theory building, his attention was primarily oriented toward the discharge of energy under the influence of the pleasure principle and the restoration of the resting state under the influence of the constancy principle.

In addition to these scientific influences, Freud was exposed to Talmudic study methods. Discussion, argument, and the formulation of questions were the basis of his approach. He continued to question and develop new ideas, never throwing out the old ones, even if there were theoretical inconsistencies. There was always room for a new angle. In later years he tried to accommodate new ideas and to assimilate them into his own theories. Nevertheless, despite his view of himself as a man of science, he did discourage outright disagreement, and tended to split from those who developed systems of analytic thinking too divergent from his own.

Freud turned his back upon religion, and yet the Jewish mystical tradition informed his imagery and his interest in dreams. He studied the literature on dreams, and he collected, reported, and analyzed his own dreams as examples of the mental life of the unconscious. Add to the mix his lifelong interest in cultural anthropology and great literature, and Freud emerges as a genius who thinks like a scholar, develops and tests hyopotheses like a scientist, observes like an artist, writes like a novelist, argues like a logician, and persuades with the rhetorical power of a politician.

Freudian Theory in 1900: Seduction Theory, Dream Analysis, and the Unconscious

In his work as a neurologist (Breuer and Freud 1895), Freud observed that the fear of a bodily injury that could have been sustained during a traumatic assault on the body might lead to physical symptoms as surely as a physical injury itself, provided that the affected person had a constitutional or cultural predisposition to enter a hypnotic state at the time of the trauma, and especially if verbal outrage was not possible. Freud thought that hysterical symptoms resulted from the mental reaction to the psychological trauma of a physical event of sexual threat in which the immature child's mind had been overwhelmed by excitation arising from premature and sometimes incestuous genital stimulation. The body sought affective discharge in the absence of words, substituted a physical symptom for a verbal protest, simultaneously recreated the wished-for stimulation in disguise and opposed it, and tried to return to the preferred state of non-excitement. The mind dissociated the memory of what had occurred, the wish for sexual pleasure, and the accompanying affect in the traumatic sexual situation. So Freud developed his concept of *dissociation as a defence against trauma.* Dissociation, however, left the mind in a divided state. Hysterical patients could thus experience different states of mind, but be aware of the existence of only one state of mind. Freud referred to the presence of mutually exclusive states of mind as *double consciousness.*

While engaged in neurological work at the clinic, in private Freud was studying the literature on dreams and reporting his own dream specimens (Freud 1900). He recognized that dreams bore some relation to the day's events, to internal somatic signals, and to unfulfilled wishes for repetitions of pleasurable situations that represented the demands of the instincts. Through processes of distortion, displacement, and condensation, dreams transformed the basic human experience into a bizarre narrative, a collage or graphic puzzle that could be understood, however, by using the decoding principles that Freud discovered. He thought of dreams as the royal road to the unconscious part of the mind where the instincts were pooled. His analysis of dreams led him to discover the mode of operation of the unconscious. Freud (1901) also detected the functioning of the unconscious when it emerged in slips of the tongue that betrayed hidden thoughts and feelings.

According to Freud (1915a,b, 1916–1917), the unconscious could be understood only by realizing that it was not governed by logical thought. He found that *the unconscious is organized by primary process*, a primitive way of distributing impulses and ideas in a chaotic matrix in which an idea may get split off from its originating impulse to defuse its impact but may then connect to a feeling that actually originated elsewhere, so that apparently random and illogical connections actually organize a defense against the power that the impulse, the idea, and the associated affect would have had, if they had remained connected.

In contrast to this, Freud described another state of mind, a level of mental functioning of which the person is normally aware. He referred to this conscious layer of the mind as *consciousness*. He found that, unlike the unconscious, *consciousness is governed by secondary process*, a form of thinking in which reason and logical sequencing predominate. Consciousness is bombarded by ideas and affects pressing for discharge from the unconscious. The conscious mind might discharge the energy impulse or might inhibit discharge by sending impulses that are unbearable back along the reflex arc to bury them in the unconscious for more primary-process management, or deposit slightly less intolerable impulses in the preconscious for later assimilation.

Freud's discovery of the unconscious through his research in dream analysis and studies in hysteria, together with his understanding of neuroanatomical heirarchies of structure and function, led him to the conceptualization of the hierarchy of the unconscious, preconscious, and conscious layers of the mind, with their primary and secondary thinking capacities, and years later to the model of ego, ego ideal, superego, and id and the concept of repression. Meantime, he retained his interest in dreams and the unconscious, but he moved beyond the seduction theory as the basis for psychological problems, because he realized that seduction had not always occurred in the histories of patients with psychoneuroses, and in other cases had been imagined because of the perceptually distorting impact of oedipal longing and the maturational impetus of renunciation on perception and memory of which he had now become aware. As he moved on to newer theories, he tended not to discard the older ones, but he publicly turned his back on the seduction theory as the universal cause of mental illness. Perhaps Freud did this in case a sexually repressed and hypocritical Victorian society compelled to disavow his concrete formulations of sexual exploitation and trauma might then also reject his more universally applicable emerging ideas on normal infantile sexuality.

Freudian Theory Prior to 1923: Instinct (Drive) Theory and the Pleasure Principle

Instinct theory derives from biological, scientific, neuroanatomical, and philosophical concepts of energy, hierarchy, and dualism. Instincts are biological givens. Freudian instinct theory (Freud 1910, 1915a) holds that instincts consist of impulses of energy that seek expression and gratification. After years of evolution, they are there to ensure procreation and survival. They are not evoked by experience. They exist independent of the person's circumstances. Individual drive has autonomy from the environment, except that the civilized state opposes unlimited expression of individual drive.

The primary instinct was thought to be the *sex instinct,* which Freud called the *libido.* The sex instinct lies in the deepest reaches of the mind in the area that Freud called the unconscious, a seething cauldron of energy and ungovernable processes. The energy deriving from this instinct wells up and seeks discharge with the aim of finding pleasure and relieving the tension of unpleasure. At first, the infant's energy finds a suitable object of gratification in the self through the activity of thumbsucking and creating hallucinations of pleasure. Freud thought that this state of *narcissism* was primary.

In the next stage, the libido develops *object cathexis*, that is, its energy is aimed at an object outside the self. The object to which the energy attaches is likely to be the mother, because she is there as an alternative to the self, and because she can gratify the instinct. In this theory, the infant is not looking for a mother, for a relationship, or for food. The infant is at the mercy of the instinct by which it is driven to seek sexual satisfaction through stimulation of the oral orifice that happens to occur during feeding. The mother is the *object* that the drive attaches to, but she is not the object of attachment for her infant. In the Freudian theory of adult development, the adult in a sexual relationship seeks a partner with whom to gratify the libido in fully genital sexual intercourse and in foreplay that gratifies the component pregenital instincts by stimulation of the relevant erogenous zones.

To comply with the demands of civilized life, the libido (or sex instinct) somehow had to be dealt with. At this stage in the development of his theory, Freud invoked the dualistic notion of equal and opposite forces. At first he thought that the *sex instinct* was suppressed by the opposing *self-preservative instinct* in order to face reality and secure survival. Later, after he was disturbed by the terrible destructiveness of the First World War, Freud (1920, 1930) invoked the *death instinct* or *thanatos* to counter the force of the libido, a concept which by then had been broadened to include the desire for life as well as sexual pleasure.

Aspects of Early Freudian Drive Theory

Various aspects of the theory concerning the source, expression, and control of the drives reveal their origin in the cultural influences on Freud mentioned earlier. They concern environmental, topographical, economic, dynamic, and genetic factors.

Environmental Aspects

Freud conceived of the impulses as seeking expression in a hostile environment. The drives might be opposed by considerations of social propriety and self-respect, and, when the drives could not be gratified, a traumatic experience might result. For instance, when the libido is driven by the hormonal surge of puberty and seeks a genital sexual outlet, its postponement for fear of pregnancy or respect for chastity and marriage could dam up the libido and lead to problems in spontaneity and ordinary affection, and, later, to sexual dysfunction. The sudden seduction of a young girl could awaken the drives and stimulate associated ideas of sexual intercourse and feelings of anticipated physical pleasure that, being denied to her, could be painful. When the object stimulating these drives was an incestuous one, the situation was traumatic to the young woman. If she defended herself by dissociation, the reason for her actions and feelings of repudiation and revulsion in the face of excitement could be forgotten, and the idea might be converted into a physical equivalent such as vomiting or a later symptom, such as frigidity in a socially sanctioned sexual relationship.

Freud's use of the term "environment" preserves an aura of scientific objectivity about the fate of the drives in the hostile environment, and minimizes the human reality of the people and families who failed to protect and confide in each other.

Topographical Aspects

This aspect underlines the neurophysiological aspects of the model. Setting out from the unconscious, the energy impulse from instinct in the unconscious is registered as a stimulus that proceeds in a reflex arc from the unconscious through the preconscious to the conscious level of the brain, where an action occurs either to discharge the impulse of energy and the associated affect, or to inhibit it by returning it along the arc to the preconscious where it waits for future attempts at becoming conscious. The topographical theory is Freud's first tripartite theory, dividing the mind into unconscious, preconscious, and conscious components.

Economic Aspects

These aspects derive from thermodynamics. The economic theory rests on the principle of entropy and conservation of energy. Instinct is viewed as releasing impulses of energy toward consciousness. The pressure of the instinct leads to a state of instinctual tension for which tension-reduction processes are necessary to avoid discomfort due to inhibition or the embarrassment that would result from inappropriate expression. The person needs a way of controlling these instincts either because the instincts are too strong and therefore overwhelming, or the person is "too imperfectly organized and feeble" to cope with them (Freud 1910, p. 53). The primary automatic mechanism of tension reduction is *repression*, but with greater maturity the more advanced mechanism of sublimation may be used. In *sublimation*, the drive is turned into some other kind of energy that is socially acceptable, such as doing good works, painting or, indeed, studying development and writing about theories. The goal is to return to the state of non-excitation.

Dynamic Aspects

Here the neuroanatomical model predominates. As usual, the drives are the ultimate determinants of experience and psychic geography. Once inhibited according to the topographic and economic principles outlined above, the drives and the relevant affects are distributed in layers of inhibition that correspond to levels of censorship in a dynamic hierarchy. The impulse may be divorced from the associated affect and each may be stored at a different level of inhibition to reduce the tension resulting from both knowing and feeling too much about a particular idea or experience. Furthermore, the thought process may be thought of as dynamically inhibiting the feeling by removing ideational content from the affect.

Genetic Aspects

This aspect of the theory refers to Freud's concept of the psychosexual stages of development, a biology-based idea of human development. The libido seeks expression by being gratified at the site of the pleasure zone that predominates at different ages, in the oral, anal, phallic, and genital stages. In the oral stage, the infant seeks stimulation of the oral mucosa. In the anal stage, the pleasure of the feeling of a stool in the rectum and the satisfaction of releasing it gratify the libido. In the phallic-narcissistic stage, gratification comes from exhibiting the competence of the urinary apparatus and displaying the shape and power of the body in general. In the phallic-oedipal phase, the instinct is expressed in sexual and aggressive behavior aimed at defeating the rival parent and possessing the loved object sexually in order to satisfy the ultimate expression of the libido, namely procreation. All these are component instincts that become subsumed by, but not replaced by, the more mature genital orientation in which the libido seeks gratification in relation to a nonincestuous object. The psychosexual stages then determine the mode of expression of the drives, but not the occasion for their expression.

In summary, instinct theory depends upon the *pleasure principle*. Unconscious sexual and aggressive instincts give rise to impulses for pleasure, survival, and destruction. These impulses are in conflict since they compete for expression along the reflex arc to consciousness and their associated affects compete for discharge. This conflict is experienced as anxiety.

In the early instinct theories, anxiety is a discharge affect.

Here the theory begins to require an object-relational focus to explain why the instincts have to be opposed. The instincts will have to be tamed in order not to lose the object, or the love of the object, or the love of the self. As Freud moved on to develop his ideas on the Oedipus complex and explore mourning reactions to lost objects, he gave the objects of the drives an increasingly personal significance. It is as if they are personified only by the need to solve the Oedipus complex. It fell to Erikson (1959) to relate Freud's theory of instincts and psychosexual stages to family expectations for behavior and modes of childrearing.

Freudian Theory after 1923: Structural Theory and the Reality Principle

Freud had continued to study the characteristics of the unconscious where primary process holds sway, in contrast to consciousness where secondary process governs. Being logical and communicable as language, secondary process is more suitable for dealing with reality. Freud (1911) moved beyond the pleasure principle to describe another principle of mental functioning, namely the *reality principle*. The effectiveness of reality as a principle is made possible by maturing cognitive functions that enable the object to be held in mind long enough to hold off the frustrated instinctual impulse until a moment convenient for the object. This principle governs the capacity for delay and for consideration of the object as having a separate reality to which adjustment must be made. The reality principle might have paved the way to a substantially relational theory, but instead provided the basis for the watershed development of structural theory some twelve years later.

Against this backdrop, Freud (1917) moved on to studies of mourning and melancholia. He noted that a depressed patient had often been bereaved of a love object. The depressed patient who had not grieved successfully could become very like a departed family member as a way of dealing with loss. It was as if the lost object was being held inside the self. But in what part of the self, and how did this happen? To answer these questions Freud was led to a new theory that allowed for the identification of different parts of the mind, whether conscious or unconscious, so that the drives are now to be controlled by mental structure rather than by other drives. The motivational principle can no longer be only pleasure. The new theory would be built upon the *reality principle*.

Freud called this new theory *structural theory*. Now he thought of the mind as comprising *ego, id, and superego*—also a tripartite conception, but a more elaborate and specific theory of the mind than the earlier instinct theories. He still saw the mind as divided into the unconscious and the conscious, but he now distinguished various structures in consciousness and in the unconscious. He conceived of these structures arranged in a hierarchy, which suggests a spatial arrangement inside the self, but the term *structures* can more usefully be taken to imply psychic configurations that lead to repeated patterns of behavior that are relatively stable over time (Schafer 1976).

The outstanding feature of conscious mental functioning called for by this new theory was the adult capacity for delay in order to cope with the reality that instant gratification is not always possible or truly satisfying (Rapaport 1960). Freud recognized that the drives that are always pressing for gratification can nevertheless be persuaded to hold off until a later date when their eventual satisfaction can be expected with confidence and greater personal pleasure. The absence of the object is internalized in the form of structured delay. To account for this management capacity for delay, Freud postulated the existence in consciousness of *the ego*, the conscious executive part of the mind, in which absent objects are represented.

Freud did not give up the old topographic theory but superimposed the new theory on it, much as the new ego sat upon the id. He still held that the infant is motivated to relate to the object because it satisfies instinctual demands. At each stage of development, the child moves on through the psychosexual stages, as if progressing inevitably along a predetermined timeline. At each stage a different zone of pleasure is the focus of the instincts' demands for gratification. The object is experienced progressively through the oral, anal, and phallic routes. By 1923, applying his findings in melancholia to normal development, Freud was more aware that, at each stage, the child has to give up the object of the earlier stage. He proposed that the child does so by incorporating the redundant versions of the object that related to the earlier component instincts. It is out of these introjections of lost objects that *the ego* is formed.

Within the ego lies the *ego ideal*, a view of the self in the form that would be most successful in retaining the services of the object. This part of the ego then gives rise to *the superego*, a guiding structure built out of the ego ideal amplified during the late oedipal phase by taking in identifications with selected traits of the personalities of those arbiters of oedipal reality, the parents. Depending on the force of the instincts and the strength of the opposition to them, the identifications might be either with the parental traits or in reaction formation against them. So the resulting superego might be a self-improving, modifying, controlling, or outright punishing part of the mind. It could operate as a conscience in consciousness, usefully aiding the ego to negotiate the demands of reality and meet ideals of morality and altruism, but it could also be sequestered in the unconscious alongside the teeming impulses whose force led to the need for superego enhancement of ego activity. The impulses were now visualized as being located in an area of the unconscious called *the id*, a seething cauldron of instinctually based drive activity.

As the infant matures and mental functioning comes under the force of the reality principle, the instincts undergo delay, detour, binding, and neutralization of their energy. The resulting delay in instinctual expression leads to structure formation that is then capable of securing further delays. Then conflict is experienced between the id, where the drives are located, and the ego as the representative of reality. In other words the conflict is structural. The conflict is experienced as anxiety, a signal to the ego to secure the mind's defences, reinforced by pressure from the superego. Anxiety trips the system to respond defensively. It is a signal of distress.

In structural theory, anxiety is a signal affect.

In summary, structural theory is distinguished by the reality principle, capacity for delay, satisfaction instead of gratification of drives, and signal affect as a stimulus to structure formation.

Here Freud's theory takes account of childhood perceptions of parent figures and the role of the family as the culture carrier and shaper of human ideals and behaviors. Although in "Three Essays on the Theory of Sexuality" (1905b) and in his case histories Freud demonstrated his understanding of the infant's need for holding and handling, and then the older child's need for family support and validation, he gave less attention to the influence of the actualities of family relationships on the child's developing personality structure than to the impact of the child's inherent constitutionally and phylogenetically predetermined characteristics. Although he outlined the way in which the child selectively identifies with or creates reaction formations against the character traits of the parents in the oedipal phase, and although he said that the ego is filled with the lost objects, he mainly claimed that the ego is formed out of the id.

The translator's use of Latin terminology—id, ego, superego—has had the unfortunate effect of reifying Freud's structural concept of the mind. "Ego" seems to suggest a rather mechanistic, reflexively operant management function, as opposed to what Freud meant—a proactive, personal, executive structure for receiving affect signals and managing affect states, integrating experience with the objects, selecting object qualities to identify with or defend against, and in general dealing with internal and external reality. In the original German, Freud had used the term "I" for ego and "it" for id. His use of the first person pronoun is intensely personal and distinct from the impersonal "it" (Bettelheim 1982). To us, the concept of growth and development from the pre-existing "it" to the developing "I" structure has a parallel in the progression in Freud's concepts from the purely physiological to the more personal view of human reality.

Freud progressed over a period of years to the beginning of an object relations view of the mind, but he disguised the radical nature of his ideas even from himself by continuing to subscribe to his earlier model of the mind as generating its own form and development under pressure from the instincts.

Freud on the Object

The Narcissistic Object

At first Freud thought of the object as simply the *object of the drives* that are aimed at it. In the beginning, he thought, there is no external object in the environment, human or nonhuman. The libido is directed internally and finds its primary object in itself. In Freud's words, the internal object is infused with narcissistic libido. In other words, infants look to themselves for stimulation, gratification, and soothing. Freud called this the stage of *primary narcissism*. Infants reach out only when their mothers seem to promise gratification of the libidinal aims. Freud used the term *object cathexis* for the directing of energy outside the self. When the mother proves disappointing, hurtful, rejecting, or traumatic in response to the baby's needs for pleasure, the baby stops looking to her for gratification. In Freud's words, the infant retreats to using the self as the primary object after the external object fails to gratify the libido. Freud called this the stage of *secondary narcissism*.

The Anaclitic Object

The ego may look to the external object not just for gratification but for support when the ego seems weak and the object is viewed as strong. Freud introduced this concept to explain the depression of bereaved people who have relied so heavily on the presence of their loved ones that they are devastated by their departure. But dependency was a pathological condition in Freudian theory, not a natural condition for development. Freud recognized the importance of the parents as objects of the drives, but he did not focus on the infant ego's relation to its objects until the oedipal stage. Even then, when he took the family dynamics into account, he retained a drive-oriented approach. Although he said that "it is inevitable and perfectly normal that a child should take his parents as the first objects of his love" (Freud 1910, p. 48), he nevertheless revealed his commitment to an instinct-based view of the object, when he continued, "But his libido should not remain fixated to these first objects; later on, it should merely take them as a model" (1910, p. 48). Later, he would expand on this view to say that identification "endeavours to mould a person's own ego after the fashion of the one that has been taken as a model" (1921, p. 106).

Freud got to his concept of identification from studying the effect of the absence of the object on development. He saw *the absent object* as an important stimulus to thinking. In its absence, the person learned to hallucinate the missing object to secure wish fulfillment. In this way *the person has the object*. When the person identifies with the lost object that is being hallucinated, the *person becomes the object*. Then the ego is divided into two pieces, one of which rages against the part that is identified with the lost object. In this way, *the ego is split by its relation to the lost object*.

The term "the lost object" originally referred to the object of the mourner's grief after losing a loved one. This concept acquired developmental significance when applied to the lost object of the oedipal phase. The libido that seeks to express itself in relation to the loved parent of either sex is blocked from receiving gratification because the object is not available: the one parent is already the object of the other parent's libido. The child's libido has to be repressed or sublimated until it finds a new, nonincestuous object. At the point of renunciation, the child's ego usefully identifies with parts of the parents upon which it models itself. The superego forms from the identification with these highly valued aspects and in reaction formation against other parts of the parents associated with their prohibition of the child's libidinal longings.

The Adult Narcissistic Object

In later years, the young adult is more or less ready to choose a love object. Freud noted that people in love do not see each other's characteristics objectively. Instead, they overvalue each other because each of them needs the other as a wonderful object to be gratifying to the libido. The object is used to aggrandize the ego rather than being loved and appreciated for its own unique characteristics, its otherness. In Freud's way of putting it, the new love object is overvalued by being infused with narcissistic libido. The new object has to be glorified so that it can serve as a successful substitute for the unattainable oedipal object. Only this level of achievement can satisfy the narcissistic aims of the libido. In the state of falling in love, the lover may become so preoccupied with the loved one that he or she may lose the sense of being a separate person, or the lover's idealization may obstruct the individuality of the loved one. In that case, to use Freud's language, the loved object may consume the lover's ego, or, when the choice is dominated by the narcissistic aims of the libido, the ego may consume the object.

Intrapsychic versus Relational Perspectives in Freud

From his study of primary and secondary narcissism, identification in loss and mourning, and mental structure achieved by the renunciation of the Oedipus complex, Freud produced the concept of parts of the ego and object in dynamic relationship, and so prepared the way for an object relations theory. He could have moved more solidly in this direction himself, but his concept of identification received too little attention from his colleagues and from himself. In summary, Freud thought that identification was the original form of emotional tie to the object, and that it could operate regressively so that the object was introjected into the ego as a substitute for a libidinal object tie. He thought that it could operate healthily to enrich the personality when it occurred in relation to any person with whom one shared a quality in common and who was not an object of the libido. Identification between strangers in a group occurred for the additional reason that they wished to develop emotional ties among themselves to avoid the conflict felt between the pull to the leader and to the individual group member.

Freud seemed to be moving again toward a relational approach when he wrote "Group Psychology and the Analysis of the Ego" (1921). He noted that, "in the individual's mental life someone else is invariably involved, as a model, as an object, as a helper, as an opponent; and so from the very first individual psychology is at the same time a social psychology as well" (p. 69). He observed that human beings tended to want to live and work in groups. In other words, he saw that humans are social animals. This is quite a move beyond his intensely intrapsychic, drive-motivated view of development and, not surprisingly, Freud had to find an instinct to explain it. He named it *the social instinct*. But instead of giving it a solely biological basis, he looked for its origin in social terms. He thought that "the social instinct may not be a primitive one and insusceptible of dissection, and that it may be possible to discover the beginnings of its development in a narrower circle, such as that of the family" (p. 70). As in the case histories where he showed his awareness of the influence of family relationships on development, Freud here acknowledged the family as the possible source of the human tendency to want to live and work in groups.

This direction was not maintained. Two years later, Freud wrote *The Ego and the Id* (1923), a remarkable theoretical advance, in which he outlined a new theory of *anxiety as a stimulus to structure formation* and as a result of conflict between drive and structure. His concepts of the resolution of the Oedipus complex and identification by the child with selected traits of the parents' characters after the renunciation of oedipal desires led to the tripartite structural theory of the development of the personality. These identifications lead to the formation of an ego with differentiating characteristics that prepare the child to deal with reality and that shape the character—to an ego ideal conceived of by identifying with ideals of behavior for preserving the love of the object and maintaining self esteem, and to a superego crystallized out of the ego ideal through the concentration of internalized parental guidance and prohibitions that give the individual a conscience. This autonomy of moral sensibility could be viewed as a highly social development, but Freud saw it as an intrapsychic achievement after the individual renunciation of the Oedipus complex.

Why might Freud have moved back to the intrapsychic focus? One possible explanation lies in his fear of the social instinct gone wild. The social instinct of the small group was but a step away from the herd instinct which could be massively destructive to whole societies, as Freud had seen in the extent of the death and destruction of the First World War, in which millions were killed and in which he lost a favorite nephew. As a Jew, he also experienced discrimination against his own cultural group. Not surprisingly, he held a negative view of the effect of group life on the individual. Freud not only recognized the group's potential for obscuring differences and imposing constraints, but held the "individual's lack of freedom in a group" to be the principal phenomenon of group life (Freud 1921, p. 95). Thinking of the group member's conflict between his tie to the leader and his attachment to his peers in the group, he went on to say, "If each individual is bound in two directions by such an intense emotional tie, we shall find no difficulty in attributing to that circumstance the alteration and limitation which have been observed in his personality" (1921, p. 95).

We have the impression that Freud did not want to be in conflict between the intrapsychic and social aspects of his theory, or between himself as leader and his own group of colleagues who were not ready to elaborate the concepts of identification that could have provided the bridge between the intrapsychic and interpersonal dimensions. Primarily a biologically oriented physician, Freud was unable to free himself from the influence of his earlier theory of the instinctual basis of human behavior. He encouraged loyalty to his ideas in order to further the movement of psychoanalysis, but as much as he benefited from his colleagues' support, he was also constrained by their dependent intellectual attachment to his ideas and to the status quo. So further development of object relational trends in psychoanalysis would have to wait until the 1940s.

5

From Drive/Structure Theories to American Relational Models

Drive/Structure Models

Analytic theorists did eventually follow new directions, some of them more apparently derivative from Freud than others, but all of them taking his work as the starting place. Freud's daughter Anna, who had immigrated with him to Britain, maintained the Freudian tradition in London. Anna Freud contributed to the advancement of structural theory by extending knowledge of the mechanisms of ego defense (A. Freud 1936). She applied this knowledge to understanding the ego development of children, assessing their strengths and weaknesses along developmental lines, and devising a technique for analyzing children with psychopathology (1965). Her students and professional contacts in the United States taught the Anna Freud approach to child analysis (1964). Derivative programs in child psychotherapy and child guidance were then dominated by ego psychology to the exclusion of relational points of view. Her drive/structure theories of child development informed the work of the adult analysts who remained committed to Freudian structural theory. Unlike Freud, however, some of them argued that structural theory was incompatible with Freud's earlier instinct theory. Following the ego psychology approach to drive theory, analysts in the United States developed an American extension of structural theory that focused on ego adaptation to reality.

Adaptive Theory: Hartmann, Kris, and Loewenstein

Hartmann (1939) and his colleagues (Hartmann, Kris, and Loewenstein 1946) did not agree that the ego arises out of the id. They thought that both ego and id develop from the same undifferentiated matrix. They agreed that the id consists of drives and they left it at that. Their focus was on the ego. They conceived of a coexisting ego endowed with adaptive capabilities for coping with the average expectable environmental influences during maturation from dependency. The object was only one among many possible environmental realities to be dealt with. Like Freud, their focus was intrapsychic; but unlike Freud, they diminished the importance of the drive and its object of gratification, because they were more concerned with the ego's adaptation to a wider, impersonal reality. In Hartmann, Kris, and Loewenstein's view, adaptation does not depend on or result in bonding with significant others. It simply depends on the ego's capacity for neutralization of drive material. As a result, their theory of the mind is rather mechanistic and energy-based. It downplays the object, yet it can be thought of as leading obliquely toward a relational view in that it emphasizes the role of the ego rather than the instincts. It has been argued that adaptation, the central concept of ego psychology, is inherently relational and that ego psychology is therefore a relational theory, albeit one in which the bond between infant and mother is invisible (Grotstein and Rinsley 1994b). We disagree with this idea and maintain that ego psychology is a drive/structure theory.

Hartmann, Kris, and Loewenstein thought that the ego derives energy from its own sources and not from the id. The ego does not develop in response to having to control the impulses. Present at birth, it is preadapted to meet the demands of environmental reality. The ego has to function autonomously from the drives to ensure survival. In this way adaptation to actual life circumstances as well as to the impact of the drives on that reality is secured. The ego's autonomous functions of memory and perception, and its threshold of responsiveness and defensiveness are all preset for building an autonomous ego. This view presages current infant research findings of executive competence in week-old infants, findings that confirm the presence of an ego at birth. At the same time, Hartmann, Kris, and Loewenstein diminish the role of the object even more than Freud did.

The French Schools: Lacan and McDougall

Lacan further diminished the role of both the object and the structures of the self (1977, 1988a,b). For Lacan, as for many others in the French intellectual community, Freud's work on the unconscious was his most useful contribution. Lacan viewed the unconscious as organized like a pre-existing language that determines how life events are perceived and communicated. From the matrix of this culturally transmitted language, individuals must learn to distinguish their own words. A dramatic personality himself, Lacan emphasized the importance of illusion, imagery, and imagination in the construction of psychic reality. He scoffed at ego psychology and object relations theories for misunderstanding the complexity of human existence by trying to nail it down. Lacan's challenge to both ego psychology and object relations theories represented on pages 49 and 238 (Lacan 1977) has been summarized by Mitchell and Black.

> Ego psychology, by focusing on the ego, its defects and development, is the psychology of a social construction, a mirage mistaken for a reality (1977, p. 238); object relations theories, in their focus on the real and the fantastic relationships between the self and others, is a psychology of interpersonal fictions. . . . The ordinary subjectivity of the patient, the character that he takes himself to be and acts like, is precisely what needs to be subverted and dispersed in analysis to a deeper connection with the transpersonal, "transindividual" (1977, p. 49) unconscious and a more creative, revitalized life. [Mitchell and Black 1995, p. 198]

McDougall, a native New Zealander living and working in Paris, forms bridges between Freudian drive theory, Lacan and other French analysts, and object relations. She explores themes of identity, sexual identity, sexuality in growth and development, and hysterical communication patterns (1978, 1985, 1989, 1995). Referring to Freud's theories of hysteria and Lacan's sensitivity to the hidden meanings of language, she describes the ways in which the body takes in and remembers overwhelming early experience and continues to express it in physical terms when adequate verbal symbolizing capacity fails to develop. McDougall's focus is on the drama of human identity and the psychosomatic expression of the fight for psychic survival, as shown in the homosexualities, in "normopathic" behavior which uses apparently normal action to disguise inner terror and compromise, in individual struggles with bisexuality that were sculpted in the biparental environment, and in the molding of sexuality to perverse ends when early relationships are fundamentally threatening. Although grounded in Freudian drive theory, she has questioned the narrowness of Freud's culture-bound view of female development and of normality (1978). She draws liberally from Winnicott, Klein, Bion, Kernberg, Limentani, Ogden, and Bollas to explain her ideas and is drawn by their influence toward the object relations perspective.

Contemporary Freudians in Great Britain: Sandler

Another Freudian who reached toward object relations theory was Sandler (1976, 1987). Embracing the contemporary debate on the concept of projective identification, he noted that there had been three phases in its development, from a time when the real object was thought not to be affected by the projective identification to the modern view in which the real object is not only affected but affects the original projective identification. Nevertheless, he retained an ego psychological focus like his American counterparts. Instead of talking about object relationships, he describes role relatedness between one's self representation and the mental representation of another person, namely one's object representation. Other contemporary Freudians are being influenced by exposure to object relations theory. For instance, Duncan (1981) referred to the analyst's interaction with the transference neurosis as *intersubjective knowing* and regarded it as more important than classical interpretation in securing therapeutic shift.

The Psychosocial Approach: Erikson

The psychosocial approach emphasized the role of the object in the mediation of drive experience. Rapaport (1960) thought that the psychosocial was really a subcategory of the adaptive point of view, but it seems to us that it stands alone in illuminating the impact of actual object behavior on the developing identity of the instinct-driven child. Erikson (1950) showed how the dominant erogenous zone at each developmental stage determines the mode of interaction between infant and caretaker. He thought that development proceeded through the solving of physiological and psychological challenges in the relational context. For instance, he thought that, during the oral phase, the biological pleasure of feeding, sucking, and biting was not the only issue. The question facing the infant is whether to take in or spit out, to take in gently or aggressively, to take in the experience with the parent or push it away. The issue is dependency on and trust in the caretaker. During the anal phase, the infant is concerned not just with rectal mucosa sensation, smell, and smearing. The question to be faced is whether to hold on or let go of body products and of parents. The issue is autonomy from the object. By the genital phase, the young person is capable of renouncing instinctually based object choices and is able to relate to family members in an unconflicted way, to enjoy new objects, and to give as well as receive love. Erikson expanded this relational view to the wider social and cultural context.

So far, the theories emanating from the Freudian matrix retain what Greenberg and Mitchell (1983) have described as a drive/structural model.

American Object Relational Developments

Interpersonal Theories: Sullivan

Like Erikson, Sullivan (1962, 1964) appreciated the influence of parents, siblings, families, social groups, even inpatient cultures, on human growth and the derailment of development seen in psychosis. For this reason, his theory was called interpersonalism (1953). In Sullivan's theory, the infant's primary motivation is to avoid anxiety, the source of which is interpersonal. By picking up affective attunement with the state of mind of significant others, the child picks up their anxiety and expresses it in interaction. Unlike Freud and Erikson, Sullivan did not invoke instinct as a motivational theory. He thought that most of Freud's classical concepts could be better explained as a result of social interaction than libido. To this extent he echoed his British contemporary Fairbairn. Unlike Fairbairn, however, he did not value the systematic delineation of personality structure, and unlike Klein, he avoided speculation about an internal world that, in his opinion, was essentially unknowable.

In keeping with his operational and pragmatic approach, Sullivan stayed close to his clinical observational data and described the resulting ideas in terms of process, pattern, and interaction rather than structure. Sullivan seemed wary of developing a model of the structure of the mind because he thought that a firm idea might obscure what could never really be fully known. Indeed Sullivan seemed equally wary of structuring his thoughts into a systematic theory, perhaps in order to avoid stultification or reification, and to retain the flexibility of his work-in-progress attitude. Nevertheless his writings add up to a coherent vision of human experience that gives full weight to the importance of relationships with significant others in the family and the peer group while at the same time respecting the hidden areas of the self, although it does not fully elaborate the connection between interpersonal interaction and psychic structure.

Self Psychological Theory: Kohut

In classical analytic theory, Freud focused on the instincts and their objects, and on the mental structures of the ego and the superego that cope with the instinctual onrush. He did not talk much about the self as such. While Guntrip

(1969) focused on the self in Great Britain, in America this task fell to Kohut (1971, 1977). Kohut thought that the coherence and resilience of the self determined mental health. The immature child has to rely on others for a sense of security and relatedness in which to develop a healthy self. This cohesive self is formed by reliance on the *selfobject*, a psychic structure derived from experience with the external object. But the external object is seen as having been formed also by the actions of the drives. Therefore, the selfobject is infused with the actual personality characteristics of the parents, including their oral, anal, and oedipal level problems, as well as their well-intentioned parenting attributes. This transmission of parental characteristics to the child's selfobject is evidence of a relational point of view. It also echoes the Kleinian mechanism of introjective identification, but differs from it in that introjective identification is described as being under the influence of the child's life and death instincts. Kohut thought of this internal selfobject in the ideal case as being empathically tuned to the infant's needs for mirroring and narcissistic gratification through devotion and selfless admiration. In relation to the selfobject that is ideally responsive and undemanding, the child's ego identifies closely with the ego ideal. Then a normally omnipotent, grandiose self results and gives way to modifications for a healthy self based on further identification with the parents. When the selfobject is less than ideal, the frustrated child self feels attacked by the selfobject, instead of feeling understood or admired, and the child reacts with disintegration of the self. The self develops along these two poles: the grandiose, secure self and the narcissistically injured, insecure self.

Kohut's radical approach to formulating the development of the self has been appreciated by object relations theorists who, however, fault him for underemphasizing the role of aggression in response to frustration and for overemphasizing the bipolar structuring of the self around the early grandiose needs and attachment to idealized objects, as if bipolarity of the self could explain all forms of psychopathology (Sutherland 1994a). The role of the child's aggression in upsetting the selfobject internalization process is not addressed as it is in the object relations theories. Kohut, like Klein, retained an allegiance to the concept of instincts, except that he focused on them only in the oedipal phase, which, unlike Klein, he placed in the same developmental sequence as Freud. Kohut held that in the preoedipal phase the relational experience feeds the internalization that determines personality development, but he evoked the force of the instincts to explain oedipal-phase development. Self psychology theory implies but does not systematically address either the impact of the self upon the object or the mutuality of the relationship, even in the preoedipal phase.

Kohut's self psychology theory is clearly relational in type, at least during the formation of the self in the preoedipal phase, but once the oedipal phase comes on line, Kohut's theory reverts to a drive/structure model. Kohut retained classical drive theory to explain the Oedipus complex, which he viewed as a difficulty arising after the formation of the self and resulting from the force of the libidinal and aggressive drives (Greenberg and Mitchell 1983).

Contemporary self psychologists have moved beyond the empathic focus on the patient toward recognizing the interactive subjectivities of the child and its caretakers, and of the patient and the analyst, as creating an "evolving psychological field" that forms the context for growth and development, and the focus of analytic exploration (Atwood and Stolorow 1984, p. 69). This new approach, known as intersubjectivity, emphasizes affect and relatedness (Stolorow and Atwood 1992, Stolorow et al. 1987). Lichtenberg (1992) also advises awareness of the intersubjectivities of patient and analyst, but cautions that the intersubjective field can be misused unless the focus remains on the patient (Lichtenberg et al. 1992). Lichtenberg (1989) dispenses with the sexual and aggressive drives, and the id, ego, and superego of Freud's structural hypothesis in favor of describing five motivational systems that define the personality. The quality and relative importance of each system is determined by the caretaker's response to five basic needs for psychic regulation of physiological requirements: attachment and affiliation, exploration and assertion, withdrawal and antagonism, sensual enjoyment, and sexual excitement. The self is the superordinate entity for initiating, organizing, and integrating these systems.

American Object Relations: Mahler, Jacobson, Kernberg, Schafer, Loewald, Grotstein, Ogden, Mitchell, Fromm

In the United States, early object relations theory tended to be grafted on to existing drive/structure models, as shown in the work of Mahler, Jacobson, and Kernberg. Unlike the British object relations theorists, who speak of the object relationships as creating the structure of the mind, the American theorists Mahler, Jacobson, and Kernberg conserve the drive-derived Freudian tripartite structure of the mind, and then go on to show how it contains *object- and self-representations*, in keeping with classical terminology.

Mahler followed Hartmann's concept of the autonomous ego and its role in adaptation, but in her experience, adaptation, the earliest form of which was symbiosis with the object, was more personal and related to the actual mother (Mahler 1968, 1974, Mahler et al. 1974). Mahler continued to accept energy-based libidinal drive theory and the role of the Oedipus complex as central to understanding neurosis, but she emphasized the effects of oedipal-stage relationships with external family objects on personality development and pathology. More than that, she pushed back the challenge of separation and individuation from the oedipal phase and showed how it began much earlier, as toddlers left and returned to their mothers. In her view, the infant's relation to the mother is behaviorally and intrapsychically a symbiotic one, in which the glorified mother is experienced as simply a part of the self with no appreciation for her otherness. Once infants hatch out of their symbiotic states, they could enjoy being apart from their mothers for short periods of time, or they might long for a return to the ideal state of symbiosis. Leaving and returning to the mother, like a shuttle returning to the base station for refueling, the infant in the rapprochement phase learns gradually to take and hold inside a version of the mother being left, and so eventually becomes a separate person with stable self- and object-representations.

In other words, the capacity for delay that Freud and Hartmann had attributed to thinking and drive neutralization was, in Mahler's view, accounted for by a satisfactory balance of experience with the need-satisfying, need-rejecting object. Her description of the symbiotic phase preceded by the autistic phase has been rejected recently in the light of contemporary infant research that demonstrates more ego competence for relating at birth than she allowed for, but her findings about the rapprochement phase have stood the test of time.

Mahler did not throw over drive theory, but she infused it with the reality of her observations of infant–mother relationships, which she saw as providing the necessary conditions for modification of the drives. She did not develop a theory of endopsychic structure, and she followed Hartmann's idea of ego functions working alongside drive activity. Instead of conceptualizing structure, she described processes and relationships in response to the drives active in the zones of the psychosexual stages that Freud had described. Mahler's contribution to the American acceptance of object relations theory was her observation of actual separation behaviors by both mothers and children, her attention to the vicissitudes of the preoedipal phase, her emphasis on ego and superego precursors, and ultimately her theory that put the dilemma of fusion and isolation at the center of development and saw failure to resolve it as the major cause of psychopathology.

Jacobson (1954, 1964, 1967) tried to apply the impact of the infant's range of experience with significant others in the environment to illuminate the economic aspects of energy-based drive theory. She never doubted that drive was biologically predetermined. From an undifferentiated matrix, she thought, the drives take the form of sexual or aggressive energy that could be gratified either by discharge or by remaining in a state of tension, depending on the maturational level. Under the influence of the drives, the baby's felt experience of pleasure or frustration determines his perceptions of the mother, and these internal images in turn promote the aim of "merging" with the object. These images then influence further experience of self and object, independent of the drives which colored the earlier experience.

In Jacobson's version, object relations theory modified the pleasure principle, and challenged the viability of the constancy principle too by offering a non-hydraulic way of managing tension. Jacobson held that development depended on the balance and sequencing of these internal images. She commented on the relation between the self and the object world and its internalization in the form of self and object representations, but, by adhering to biological principles and economic views, she prevented her arrival at a position of clarity and commitment to object relational principles.

Influenced by Jacobson, Kernberg (1979) also remained identified as a drive/structure theorist with a particular interest in the effect of object relations on ego development. His object relations orientation was enhanced by his reading of Fairbairn (Kernberg 1963, 1996). His clinical population included borderline patients who vacillated between ego states in which Kernberg as the analyst was perceived as either all good or all bad (1975). Based on his experience of their pathology in the transference, Kernberg noted that it was the analysis of the splitting of good and bad that brought relief and enabled maturation. He thought that the degree of splitting of the object resulted from the constitutional force of the drives. In Kernberg's theory (1976, 1980), the drives color the infant's perception of the object (meaning the human object) as good or bad, depending on whether the object inspires a good or a bad feeling state. (Now it seems to us that in his theory the affect in the relational situation is evoking the nature of the drive activity.) The child internalizes the nature of the object, the affect, and the representation of the self that corresponds to this view of the object. The most primitive levels of object experience in response to the drives give rise to the introjection of unmetabolized self and object images that are subject to splitting. The drives determine the object relations and so organize the functioning of the ego. At higher levels of development, identification with the object is more modulated by awareness of the impact of the self on the object. In maturity, when the ego is reliably capable of neutralization of drive and repression, all these identifications are integrated by the ego. Greenberg and Mitchell (1983) were impressed by the elegance of Kernberg's theory-building, although they took him to task for retaining drive theory language that obscures the extent to which he is truly a relational theorist. But maintaining some ambiguity was a crucial part of Kernberg's contribution, for he presented object relational concepts in the climate of ego psychology in such a way that they were palatable to the mainstream.

Schafer (1976, 1992) objected to the biologically oriented, instinct-driven approach that described the mind as if it were a bounded space like the body from which impersonal drives bursting to escape are pushed back in to conform to reality, leading to an unhappy truce out of which a self with structure gradually emerges. Rather than thinking of the person at the mercy of an id waiting to be tamed, he preferred to think of the self as the master, in charge of formulating one's experience. Instead of the language of drive and structural theory, he invented a new language that communicated his belief in the self as the agent, but his lexicon did not catch on. His more recent concept of analysis as a reconstruction of the patient's narrative of life, together with his view of the importance of the self at the center of experience, has had an impact on psychoanalytic technique.

Loewald (1980) is usually regarded as a Freudian revisionist, but we place him among the American object relations theorists because he did not believe in the primacy of instincts even though he retained Freud's emphasis on sexuality and aggression as defining variables, and because he was interested in personality interaction. Like Winnicott, he tried to redefine Freud to fit his own views, even when they were radically different. Following Freud's (1917) essays on loss and mourning, Loewald read Freud as having redefined the libido as a drive for affiliation and reconnection to lost objects. Loewald redefined cathexis as an organizing mental act that structures material as an object, instead of viewing it simply as an instinctual charge. Like Fairbairn, Loewald views interaction with the mother as determining the nature of the self and its unconscious drives. The drives are seen as differentiating and organizing processes in the psychic matrix of the mother–infant relationship. As for the ego, he disagrees with the idea of separate, autonomous ego functions. Unlike Fairbairn who sees the original unity as the pristine self, Loewald did not view the infant self as the primary agent at birth. Closer to Mahler's views, he thought that the infant and its caregivers provide the original unity, with no differentiation of self and other. Like Fairbairn, he thought that any drives that come into being are derived from the child's interaction with the mother, including the drive to re-establish the original unity with a new love object.

Loewald's view of individual health bears the mark of his sensitivity to unity. He said that in health the loving sensual experience of infancy will blend seamlessly with the acquisition of language and there will be no gap between primary and secondary process functioning. Instead, the conscious level will enhance the unconscious and vice versa, and internal reality will correspond with external reality.

Grotstein, from a background in ego psychology, became fully convinced of the usefulness of Klein's concept of projective identification (1981b) and Bion's extensions of her views (1981a) through firsthand experience in analysis with Bion. Agreeing with Bion that the analyst should eschew memory and desire as elements that impose preconceptions and structure on patients' communications, Grotstein wrote: "The psychoanalytic object must be discovered and rediscovered from different vertices" (1981a, p. 31). But Grotstein also became equally conversant with Fairbairn's theory of endopsychic structure through reading and contact with Sutherland and the Scottish Institute of Human Relations (Grotstein and Rinsley 1994a). He is committed to a "dual track" psychoanalytic theory of feeling, thinking, and knowing in infancy (Grotstein 1978). Infants believe that their drives and feelings can and do harm their objects, but they are also at the mercy of outside forces or fate. A truly effective theory must take account of both perspectives (Grotstein 1994a,b). In other words, the infant is born with a sense of innocence and of potential guilt that remain a dialectical duality, except when overtaken by psychic conflict (1994b). An independent, relational thinker, Grotstein provides a remarkably eclectic, integrated view of the self. He tries to get away from the limitations of dogma and reified terminology and, instead of talking about objects, describes phantasmally altered, transformed montages for which he proposes the terms phantoms and chimerae, all of them defenses that the self constructs against the meaninglessness and phantasmagoric chaos of the void (1990, 1994b).

Ogden (1982) summarized the concept of projective identification after his understanding had matured in the course of sabbatical study in London. Since then, working in the United States, he has moved steadily in an object relations framework to integrate his own theory of human development and of the therapeutic dialogue (1986), particularly in work with primitive psychopathology and autistic levels of neurotic and psychotic experience (1989). He cautions against throwing out the importance of the instinctual basis of the search for objects and the organization of meaning (1994), because he agrees with Freud that human passion is the force that underlies individual psychopathology and cultural achievement in general. Integrating his understanding of the pre-existing structure of language, within which the individual's lexicon develops, with his knowledge of Lacan, Klein, Bion, Tustin, and Fairbairn, Ogden holds that the individual uses biologically determined templates to organize experience in the form of psychic structure that operates along a continuum consisting of three major positions, the paranoid-schizoid and depressive positions that Klein described, and his own idea, the autistic-contiguous position, that refers to a way of relating with sensory appreciation at the surface of the body to give shape to the self at times of painful separation from the nurturing body (1989). These positions do not follow a developmental sequence but are always present as potential modes of organizing experience throughout the life cycle (Ogden 1994, J. Scharff and D. Scharff 1992). Ogden's focus on therapeutic action led him to describe the creation of a new object, the analytic object, also called the analytic third (1994), present as a potential but not recognized until a moment of new meaning brings it into being. He wrote, "I view these new meanings not merely as a lifting of repression within me; rather, I understand the event as a reflection of the fact that a new subject, the analytic third, was being generated . . . analytic experience occurs at the cusp of the past and the present and involves a 'past' that is being created anew (for both analyst and analysand) by means of an experience generated between analyst and analysand (i.e. within the analytic third)" (1994, p. 76).

Greenberg and Mitchell (1983) redirected attention to object relations theory in the United States when they summarized the essential features of each model of psychoanalysis and called to task those drive and structural theory models that were using object relations as an add-on, instead of recognizing the fundamental difference between drive/structural and object relational approaches. Mitchell and Black (1995) extended the discussion on differences in their chapters on controversies in theory and in technique. Going beyond these challenges to the literature, Mitchell (1988, 1993) has developed a contemporary American relational approach that derives both from American theorists Loewald, Schafer, and Sullivan, and British object relations theorist, Fairbairn, and a Kleinian, Racker. It is not a drive-centered model derived from Freud, nor a deficit-centered model derived from Kohut or, as Mitchell read him, Winnicott. Mitchell calls his model a relational/conflict model that views the individual as centered in, interacting with, influencing, and influenced by, the human environment. Human infants are born into a relational matrix by which they are shaped and which they shape (D. Scharff 1990, Sutherland 1994a). Even though the character of the caretaker is important in its effect on the developing child, so is the child's constitution. Even though sexuality is important, it is not the sole motivator for development. Even though infancy is important in determining ways of organizing future experience, adult functioning should not be interpreted solely in the light of the early relational context, because the individual's impact on the current relational matrix, including the transference–countertransference dimension, is important too. In his scholarly and inventive synthesis, Mitchell uses relational/conflict theory to address the continuity between wishes and fears, hope and dread, in the intrapsychic and interpersonal worlds (1993). Like other contemporary relational theorists, he is devoting his attention to the conceptualization of the self (1993).

This review would not be complete without mention of Erich Fromm (1968, 1973) whose work was overlooked in North American psychoanalytic teaching institutes, perhaps because of his prophetic voice, his radical emphasis on the social as well as the characterological issues in his analytic patients, his deviation from the Freudian anxiety/defense orientation, his active, empathic, nonclassical technique, and his disagreeing about the frequency of treatment and the accepted boundaries between supervision and treatment (Cortina and Maccoby 1996b). He emphasized retrieving the authentic self from the burden of faulty or excessive socialization by analyzing three aspects of the central conflict: mother fixation (a preoedipal, asexual, oceanic attachment to the mother), narcissism (difficulty relating to the other into whom one's own fear is projected), and necrophilia (a proactively sadistic and destructive attitude to reason and vitality as a way of transcending the fear of losing the flow of life). Each of these constellations derives from defensive coping strategies for relating to others within the social fabric in which the individual reaches for independence and relatedness (Burston 1991, Fromm 1968, 1973, Fromm and Maccoby 1970, Millan 1994). In Fromm's theory, these conflicts are determined not by the vagaries of the libido, as in classical theory, but by the need for living life within the social fabric. This way of thinking is reminiscent of Fairbairn's concept of techniques appropriate to each developmental stage for dealing with the vicissitudes of infantile dependence (Burston 1991, Cortina and Maccoby 1996a). Despite these elements of similarity between his ideas and Fairbairn's ideas on clinical psychopathology Fromm's work did not develop fully in the same direction, and yet his psychoanalytic techinque, passed down through an oral tradition, has been described as a forerunner of relational approaches (Gojman 1996, Millan 1994).

6

British Object Relations Theory

In this chapter, we revisit British object relations theories that were introduced in Chapters 1 and 2, with a view to focusing on how they differ from and elaborate upon Freudian instinct theory and ego psychology. Unlike early American object-relations theorists who fit their ideas around ego psychology, British object relations theories have challenged classical psychoanalytic assumptions. The challenge has varied in extent and emphasis; for instance, Klein advanced the Oedipus complex to the first year of life yet retained the Freudian concept of the instinctual basis for development, whereas Fairbairn replaced drive theory altogether with a purely object relations motivational perspective.

British object relations theory is represented here primarily by the work of Klein, Bion, and the Kleinian group (Spillius 1987–1997), and by the British Independent group consisting of Balint, Bowlby, Guntrip, Winnicott, Fairbairn, and Sutherland (Kohon 1986, Rayner 1991, Sutherland 1980). Although both Klein's and Winnicott's theories led to therapies that are far removed from classical Freudian or ego psychology approaches, Klein and Winnicott did not want to be seen as challengers of Freud. Where Freud was intensely logical and deductive in reasoning, Klein was discursive and dramatically expressive of unconscious fantasy. Klein saw her theories as elaborating Freud's views on the instinctual basis for development and developing his interest in identification. Where Freud was logical and narrative in style, Winnicott was whimsical, cryptic, and poetic. Winnicott avoided seeming oppositional by not separating his brilliant intuitions from accepted Freud-

ian theory and not bringing them together until the end of his career. But by
then each of his various ideas had already taken on a life of its own.

Unlike the intuitive and impressionistic styles of Klein and Winnicott,
Fairbairn's intellectual and systematic approach led to a direct challenge of
Freud's intensely biological drive-oriented view of motivation. He constructed
a fully elaborated theory on a new premise based on the drive to be in a relationship. Winnicott's unsystematic accumulation of cryptic theoretical ideas
did not directly confront classical theory with the need for change, while
Fairbairn's radical theory of the endopsychic situation as a system was received
for some time as an affront, rather than as a challenge to develop new assumptions more appropriate to the current intellectual climate.

The Kleinian Group

Klein

While Freud's daughter Anna Freud furthered the contributions of Freud's
theory by focusing on the mechanisms of defense of the ego, Melanie Klein
(1955) extended Freud's late-life emphasis on the concept of the death instinct,
the part of the id that could wreak havoc and destruction on self and others.
In this respect she considered herself Freud's true daughter. Always an instinct theorist, she found herself concerned with the impact of the balance of
the life and death instincts on the infant's perceptions of primary objects. In
keeping with an energic basis for development, she thought that infants were
endowed with various degrees of the life and death instincts. Some had anxiety-
provoking amounts of death instinct to cope with, and others had too little
life instinct to counteract the death instinct.

In the Kleinian object relations revision of instinct theory, instincts did not
simply alight upon an object for gratification, or return rejected by consciousness or defeated by other impulses. Instincts had to enter an interpersonal
space. The infant's perceptions of the mother, colored by the force of the life
and death instincts, determined the child's mental functioning. Klein had little
to say about the actualities of the mother and her effect upon her infant. She
focused on the infant's experience as she imagined it from observation of infants, from her analyses of her own and her colleagues' children, and from
detailed work with very young children in analysis.

According to Klein, the infant's most urgent task is to deflect the death
instinct that otherwise threatens the self with destruction. The infant does this

by projecting the destructive wish and the associated aggressive affects toward the object, namely the mother's breast. Filled now with hostility, the breast is lost as a good object. The infant misidentifies the good breast as absent and the remaining breast as actively hostile to the infant by *projective identification*. To deal with the loss, the infant takes in the breast as it now is, experiences it as an internal, persecutory object, and identifies with it by *introjective identification* (Klein 1946, J. Scharff 1992, Segal 1964). Fortunately the situation is ameliorated by the simultaneous projection of loving feelings, thought to emanate from the life instinct, which color the perception of the breast as good. Thus, in Kleinian theory, it is not so much that the instincts themselves are in opposition as that the resulting perceptions of the object are in conflict.

The few-months-old infant, however, is unable to experience conflict and ambivalence, given the immaturity of the cognitive system. The mother is either good, or bad. The object is split into good and bad categories by primitive mental sorting of the perceptions that result from instinctual expression. Having introjected and identified with the good and bad aspects of the split object, the ego is correspondingly subject to splits. The good breast may be turned bad by the infant's greedy devouring of its supplies or envious attack of its goodness, which only leaves the infant feeling deprived and depleted. The infant feels threatened with depletion, disturbance or, at worst, annihilation due to the force of the death instinct. Klein (1946) called this state of infantile anxiety *the paranoid-schizoid position*.

As the infant matures in the first year of life, cognition improves. The death instinct has not caused total destruction of self or other. The life instinct has had sufficient energy for viability to prevail, and even to give a positive coloration to the infant's perceptions of current and past experience and expectations of future experience. The infant enters *the depressive position*, in which good and bad experiences of the object can be remembered and integrated. The object begins to be perceived as a whole object with good and bad aspects. The infant, less anxious about and threatened by internal instinctual forces, becomes capable of concern for the object, and makes reparation to the object for past destructive attacks (Klein 1935).

Some of the attacks on the mother are occasioned by the infant's envy of the parental couple, imagined to be engaged in prolonged intercourse, with the father's penis constantly inside the mother. Under the force of the instincts and their dominant zone of expression in the oral mode, intercourse is imagined as a total body feeding frenzy that stimulates tremendously disorganizing amounts of envy and hatred in the young child. This perception, later colored with anal aggressive and retentive excretory fantasy as well, leads to a primitive view of the internal couple and its exclusion or inclusion of the child. Klein, the first analyst to focus on the infant's awareness of the parents as a couple, thought that this was the basis of the earliest Oedipus complex.

Klein remained committed to her view that the Oedipus complex began in the first year of life, a critical point of departure from Freudian theory. Although she continued to use the language of orality and anality, Klein also departed from the Freudian concept of psychosexual stages of development. She preferred to talk in terms of intrapsychic positions through which the child and later the adult would continually cycle, depending on the level of maturity and the persistence of psychosocial stressors. In addition, in emphasizing unconscious phantasy images of instinctual processes, she developed an easy familiarity with the instinctual processes of the unconscious. To Freudians, her ready use of interpretation based on these concepts seemed not to respect their deference to the needs for ego defenses and for careful analysis of resistance from the outer layers of the superego and ego before approaching the hidden depths of the id. They accused Klein of ruthlessly bypassing necessary defenses and failing to analyze them. Her view of the superego as a structure deriving from oral, cannibalistic, instinctual impulses was suspect because it did not derive from object identifications of the Freudian psychosexual stage of oedipal renunciation.

Klein's major contribution was the elaboration of unconscious process. In some ways it seems as if she was mapping out the id, athough she did not use that terminology. On the other hand, in describing processes like projection, projective and introjective identification, envy and reparation, she was dealing with ego functions, but she tended not to use that terminology either. From her clinical work in child analysis, she had a different, perhaps more direct, access to unconscious phantasy and its somatic and psychological expressions than Freud had achieved in adult work. She described the functioning of internal object relationships, but, because she remained to some extent buried in her intuitive, impressionistic, clinical descriptive style, she was not successful in applying her ideas on object relationships to the development and differentiation of the ego. Klein did not logically and systematically elucidate psychic structure.

Segal (1964, 1979), Klein's early biographer prior to Grosskurth (1986), and her major expositor, restated Klein's views in a succinct, orderly form and developed her own ideas on unconscious phantasy and symbol formation (Segal 1981, 1991). Isaacs (1948) elaborated on unconscious phantasy. Joseph developed Klein's ideas on transference as a total situation and went on to study psychic equilibrium and psychic change achieved through attention to moment-to-moment shifts in the transference (Joseph 1975, 1985, 1989). Spillius (1987–1997) collected various Kleinian contributions from Klein to the present day in *The New Library of Psychoanalysis.*

Bion

Bion (1959, 1962, 1970), best-known of the followers of Klein, and quite unlike her in style, is hard to comprehend because of his rigorous, philosophical thinking and its frequently abstruse expression in mathematical symbols. Yet his complex writing yields enduring ideas of stunning simplicity and relevance for the clinician. He extended the concepts of Freud and Klein on the nature of the mind as an apparatus for thinking, incorporating experience, and relating to reality, based on the role of projective identification in the development of the capacity to think, allay anxiety, and communicate. Bion showed that projective identification occurs along a continuum from massive use of it as a desperate defense, to judicious use of it as a communication and link between ego and object, parent and child, patient and therapist. His field of observation covered the functioning of normal, neurotic, and psychotic personalities in individual and group therapy and in institutional life (D. Scharff 1996).

Bion (1959) became interested in group process through his work as an army psychiatrist. When a group addresses a task, he found, the individuals cooperate in rational ways to get the job done. But other needs pervade the group even while it tries to work: individual needs to be taken care of, to please the leader, to thwart the leader, or to submit an alternative task. He found that individuals team up to create subgroups that cluster around the themes of dependency, fight/flight, and magical pairing. Individuals unconsciously recruit others with whom to enact their internal object relationships in the interpersonal situation of the group. His findings on these subgroup formations have been critically important in the development of the theory of groups and institutions, and in the application of psychoanalysis to group and family therapy (D. Scharff and J. Scharff 1987).

Bion (1962, 1970) thought that the infant, highly anxious under the influence of the instincts, projects that unthinkable anxiety into the mind of the mother (the container). In a state of reverie, she normally transforms it and returns the primitive, infantile communication (the contained) to her child in a thinkable, manageable form. He called this process *containment*, a process of detoxification by the mother. Her containing function is then taken in by the child, who identifies with it. If her containing is faulty or the infant cannot identify with it, the infant is left with *nameless dread*. The envious or psychotic infant who attacks the containing function, or the link between the self and the container, then identifies with a spoiled container. Attacks on linking lead to a damaged thought process that further attacks links and meanings. The infant's experience of the mother's containment is the forerunner of the child's capacity for thought.

Bion (1956) postulated that, in the infant who subsequently becomes psychotic, there is, because of the infant's tremendous fear of an overwhelmingly powerful death instinct, a hatred of internal and external reality, leading to sadistic attacks on the object and on the self and its thought processes, and a concomitant fear of annihilation. To deal with this, the infant projects elements of internal and external reality into objects outside the self and imbues them with fearful, bizarre characteristics that correspond to the sight, smell, feel, or sound of the experience being projected. These *bizarre bits* multiply by fragmentation or cohere into terrifying arrangements that threaten the self in the form of concrete aspects of the senses, as delusions of sight, sound, smell, and touch. This desperate protective mechanism fragments the capacity for thought and denudes the self and its capacity for relationship, leading to a feeling of being neither alive nor dead that is detected in the transference as a tenaciously held attachment, one that is, however, restricted in its range and depth.

When Bion turned his attention to individual development in infancy, he thought in terms of mother and infant functioning in a small group of two, using projective and introjective identification as their unconscious communication. Nevertheless he retained an intrapsychic focus on the mother's and on the infant's mental processing. He thought that the infant is born with a *preconception* of what might be encountered in everyday life. Then experience with the object matches or challenges the preconception and gives rise to a *conception*. An aggregate of conceptions leads to the formation of a *concept*. In describing these processes, Bion developed a psychoanalytic theory of thinking and mental development that is intrapsychic and yet interpersonal, comprising constitutional, experiential, and relational aspects (1962).

Having developed a theory of the influence of past experience on thinking that could impose a set of preconceptions on him, or any therapist who studied him, Bion (1970) urged therapists to remain free of the influence of knowledge and past experience in order to be open to learning in the present.

He proposed that we enter a state of mind *without memory or desire* so that we rid ourselves of preconceptions of what is or should be known about theory, the patient, the past, or the future, and are not propelled by reaching after fact and reason. He called this state *negative capability*, a phrase borrowed from Keats. Bion wanted therapists to be able to tolerate the unknown, indeed to embody the unknown, and to wait for meaning to evolve from experience created in unconscious interaction with the patient. The therapist who does not yet know the best interpretation enters a state of patience, suffering, and tolerance of frustration (which Bion likened to the paranoid-schizoid position) until enough is known to make a comment that will lead to further exploration of the unknown, at which point the therapist experiences the security of the depressive position. In emphasizing the normal, creative, developmentally useful aspects of the paranoid-schizoid position, Bion reminds us that it is a state of mind that is characterized by qualities in addition to the commonly held psychotic regression.

By bringing a sense of reciprocity to the mother—infant relationship, Bion amplified Kleinian concepts of projective and introjective identification as they secure the development of self and object in the earliest months of life. His thoughts on containment provided a theoretical basis for technical interventions through understanding the therapeutic action of transference—countertransference interaction in the patient—therapist relationship. Rigorously thoughtful in his theory-building about thinking and knowledge, in practice Bion equally rigorously let go of all that was known so as to remain personally open to what is present and therefore new in each moment of the analytic encounter.

The British Independent Group

Balint

Balint continued to favor an instinct-theory model alongside his object relational model, and he believed that the libido was seeking sexual satisfaction as well as relatedness with the object. His writing on the need to work at preoedipal levels by allowing therapeutic regression to reach and heal the basic fault in the personality (1968) informed clinical practice, especially in its application to the doctor—patient relationship (1957). Like his mentor Ferenczi (1933) who deviated from Freudian principles to develop a nonhierarchical, interactional, relational field for mutual examination by patient and analyst, Balint was interested in the therapeutic relationship, especially that between patient and medical doctor. His sensitive description of the differences in personal style between those patients who were *philobatic* (those who gained a sense of security from open space because they were fearful of being trapped in close proximity to an object) and those who were *ocnophilic* (those who avoided the spaces between objects because they felt more secure when clinging to an object) was helpful to clinicians and has found its modern equivalent in the work of nonanalytic marital therapists who talk in terms of pursuer–distancer spousal conflicts. Despite the usefulness of his work and his tremendous influence on the clinical acumen of the medical and mental health professions, his work did not constitute a major challenge to classical psychoanalytic theory.

Bowlby

Bowlby (1969, 1973, 1980) developed a theory based on ethology. Drawing on studies of animal behavior across species, Bowlby found common elements governing the behavior of the young and their mothers: all primate infants seek and need proximity to their mothers in order to survive; all infants show fear and aggression when not protected by their mothers; and all infants in all higher species show specific attachment behaviors that result from and reinforce their mothers' nurturing behaviors. Bowlby saw that the infant–mother relationship is crucial and is secured by inbuilt behaviors that may be regarded as instinctual, but that focus on securing survival, not on gratifying sexual or aggressive drives (1958). Bowlby proposed that the infant is motivated by instincts—as are all animals—but that the primary human instinct is the instinct for attachment to the mother in order to secure survival. Pleasure-seeking is entirely secondary to the main goal, and aggression does not result from the death instinct, but from fear when the child is unprotected.

The attachment theory that he devised supports the object relational point of view, and yet has been read as an alternative, instinctually based theory that focuses on the importance of the actual behavior of the object of the drives (Greenberg and Mitchell 1983). Bowlby was interested in instincts, but he did not regard them as primary in determining development. He observed that the purpose of instinctual behaviors, such as crying, smiling, clinging, seeking proximity, and following with the eyes, was to secure the infant's relationship with the caretaking figure, and he regarded that relationship as primary in influencing development. In promoting this view, Bowlby offered a bridge between instinct and object relations theory. His research-based alternative to classical drive theory boosted confidence in clinically oriented object relations theories, but his absorption in the actual, concrete experience of the object and his relative inattention to the child's modification of the internal world limited his own theories, and kept them from amounting to a thoroughly analytic view of the human experience, which led to his being ignored by many analysts (Slade 1996). His work has given rise to the field of attachment theory research (see Chapter 7) which continues to be influential in developing the object relational view of human development.

Winnicott

Winnicott neither followed nor challenged Freud's description of the structure and function of ego, superego, and object. He did not subscribe to instinct theory either, and so did not deal in terms of energy and its control by the opposing drives, the environment, or the ego and superego. Of all the object relations theorists, he was most aware of the influence of the parents on the growing child. He talked in terms of environmental provision for the infant's needs for growth and development, rather than environmental control of drives. Unlike Bowlby, with whose views on the importance for the infant of secure attachment to the mother he agreed, Winnicott did not remain rooted in the actualities of the child's environment, but he focused equally on the internal life of the child, drawing on the rich analytic tradition and especially the Kleinian concepts of unconscious phantasy. He admired both Freudian and Kleinian theories, but he did not preserve their integrity when he assimilated them. Distorting and playing with them as he was taking them in, he created his own theory out of the creative mix into which he dropped the essence of his clinical wisdom. He inferred what he knew from observing the mother–infant relationship in vivo and studying in adult and child analysis the *potential space* between ego and object—the gap for playing, fantasizing, creating, and relating (1951).

Winnicott started from the relational matrix in the human environment. The unintegrated self of the infant has to be held and handled by a good-enough mother who provides a safe and secure environment before her infant can develop at all. In this *psychosomatic partnership*, the infant naturally experiences physical gratification of oral needs, but the greater need to be met is for a loving relationship that gives meaning to experience (1971a). The partnership is not driven by the infant's libido, but by the infant's dependent needs and by the mother's wish to provide for them. The self of the object becomes the integrating function of the infant self. Winnicott does not assume that the infant is ever separate from the mother. On the contrary, the mother must help the infant to learn to be alone in her presence. Gradually the partnership becomes more psychological than somatic, as the child becomes more independent. To cope with the need to preserve the true self while also relating to the world, made more difficult when there are deficiencies in the mother–infant relationship, the infant develops a false self in compliance with the mother's demands. In identification with the mother, this false self then holds and handles the true self and preserves its integrity by covering for it.

In Winnicott's (1960b) concept of *true and false self*, each self is responsible for transactions with reality that drive/structural theory had earlier attributed to ego, superego, or id. Winnicott, who always preferred to downplay his departures from classical views, claimed a connection between the true self and the sexual instinct and between the false self and the ego's adaptation to social reality. He simply ignored the radical difference between his own and Freud's theories. Where Freud was talking about the need to control the drives, Winnicott was trying to establish the primary importance of forming a self with meaning, value, and integrity. Winnicott did not refute drive theory: he simply crowded it out (Greenberg and Mitchell 1983). In other words, Winnicott soared above classical, energic, and mechanistic considerations of structure and function to express concern for the whole person. He made spurious, deferential links between his own relational concepts and Freud's instinct/structural theory concepts to minimize their differences and so he bypassed the real problem of articulating his concepts with those of Freud. That is why it is hard to see the origins of Winnicott's object relational ideas in Freud.

Fairbairn

Trained as a philosopher prior to becoming a physician, Fairbairn was a rigorously logical thinker who developed a systematic theory of personality development (Birtles 1996, Fairbairn 1943a,b, 1944, 1951, 1952, 1954, 1963, Grotstein and Rinsley 1994a, Scharff and Birtles 1994). He took a dispassionate, intellectually critical approach to all theories. In that spirit, he investigated inconsistencies in Freudian theories and reported his disagreement with fundamental tenets. His conclusions propelled him to consider a complete revision of Freudian theory. To Fairbairn, this level of critical attention was a mark of the highest intellectual respect, but to others, including Winnicott, it seemed anarchic. Colleagues were uncomfortable with Fairbairn's intellectual honesty, because it challenged their beliefs and their professed loyalty to Freud. Although trained in medicine and preserving his awareness of bodily symptomatology, Fairbairn did not subscribe to a highly biological approach. Influenced more thoroughly by his training in mental philosophy, Hellenic studies, and theology—especially Hegel's (1807) writings on self and other, spirit and desire—Fairbairn took a philosophical view of the human infant, its desire for the other, and its needs for growth (Birtles 1996, Birtles and Scharff 1994). Bacal (1987), Grotstein and Rinsley (1994b), and Harrow (1996) mention Suttie's (1935) challenge to Freudian theory as a stimulus for Fairbairn's ideas. Certainly both Suttie and Fairbairn viewed the infant as a person in its own right, both were more concerned with love and hate than with sexuality and aggression, and both thought that anxiety and hate arose from frustration of the need to relate; however, Fairbairn did not associate himself with Suttie's approach, which was infused with an uncomfortable amount of love, tenderness, and shared suffering that Fairbairn regarded as controversial.

Fairbairn argued that the infant is motivated by the need to be in a relationship, not propelled by instincts. For Fairbairn, there is no id. At birth, there is already an ego, a pristine, unstressed, unspoiled, undifferentiated ego. Only in dealing with the inevitable frustrations of actual existence in relationship to another person would this ego be stressed to greater or lesser degree, depending on the constitutionally determined strength of the ego and the responsiveness of the mother. Following Freud, Fairbairn retained the terms *object* to refer to the infant's experience of the mother and *libidinal* to refer to the tendency to seek the satisfaction of being in a relationship. In other words, in Fairbairn's theory, the object is intimately connected to the libido. It is not merely an object that the sexual drive alights upon for gratification, as in Freudian terms. In Fairbairn's view, the libido is primarily object-seeking, not gratification-seeking. And, far from simply happening to be there, the object evokes the libidinal behavior. The object is essential for experience, which then gives the ego the material for building psychic structure. Only excessively frustrating mother–infant relationships that excite painful levels of longing in infants who are seriously rejected incite behaviors that aim at sexual and aggressive discharge. In other words, Fairbairn viewed such evidence of drive activity as a relational breakdown product, not a primary motivational, instinctual energy.

In Fairbairn's view, pleasure is the affect accompanying and signalling the successful infant–mother relationship. Similarly, displeasure is an affective sign of a mismatch in the relationship, not evidence of the dominance of the death instinct. When the level of frustration is intolerable to the young ego, Fairbairn thought, it defends itself by splitting of the object, splitting of the ego, and repression of the unsatisfactory parts of object, ego, and the associated affects. In this way frustration is the motivation for personality formation. Splitting and repression provide the mechanism. Now the ego itself has conscious and unconscious parts.

So Fairbairn came up with a new definition of consciousness and a new map of the unconscious. Consciousness is what remains after the vicissitudes of infantile experience. In consciousness, there are the central ego (inheritor of the original pristine ego), the ideal object (a structure reflecting the internal experience of having had a good-enough object), and feelings of satisfaction, pleasure, and joy in living and loving.

The unconscious is formed from precipitates from the original ego and its objects. When frustration is intolerable, the ego splits off the frustrating part of the original object and rejects it from conscious awareness to avoid pain. The ego represses this rejected object and sorts it into two major types of frustrating object. The rejected object might fall into the category of the *exciting object* that excites too much neediness, longing, and craving without satisfaction in the ego. Or it might be a more obviously *rejecting* object, one that evokes feelings of rage, abandonment, and rejection in the ego. In relation to each of these categories of objects, the ego experiences uncomfortable affects, referred to as *libidinal and anti-libidinal*, respectively. To deal with this, the ego splits itself as well into comfortable, ideal ego states that remain in consciousness as the central ego, and represses the intolerable, split-off ego states. Now in the unconscious, there are *libidinal and anti-libidinal egos*, with excited, needy *libidinal affects* and raging, rejecting *anti-libidinal affects* in relation to *exciting and rejecting objects*. Each ego–affect–object constellation forms an internal object relationship. The anti-libidinal object system further represses the libidinal object relationship, which is then the most deeply repressed structure.

Both systems of repressed object relationships tend to press for re-emergence and inclusion in the central ego. Unlike Kleinian theory, Fairbairn's object relations theory here takes account of the actual nature of the object, as well as the infant's perceptions and misperceptions of object experience. With further good-enough object experience, earlier impressions can be modified and repression need not be so severe. With continued frustrating object experience, further splits in the ego occur. In this way, as the infant matures, social learning in the family context modifies or cements intrapsychic structure. Laing (1960) elaborated the concept of the divided self created in the crucible of conflictual and confusing family dynamics.

Fairbairn's contribution goes beyond structuring the unconscious to give a theory of the functioning of the ego as a system of interconnecting parts that operate in conscious and unconscious areas. He views the parts as being in dynamic relation. The crucial point about Fairbairn's theory is that ego is repressing not just unpleasant content or feeling, but that ego represses ego as well. Now the ego is truly executive, not just as a structure in charge of mediating reality in Freudian terms, but as the active manager of the development of the self (Sutherland 1994b). The ego forms its own psychic structure from its experience with the object, and it grows in relation to the original and subsequent objects. The most radical element in Fairbairn's theory is the idea that the psyche at birth is whole and capable of organizing itself, both in response to external experience and in accord with constitutional givens. This inherent self-organizing capacity of mind is fundamental to growth and to the potential for therapeutic change.

Guntrip

Guntrip followed Fairbairn in thinking of human motivation as interpersonally derived (Hazell 1994). He extended and popularized Fairbairn's object relations theory by describing the endopsychic situation in more personal terms that permitted clearer understanding of and communicating about the human self and soul. Guntrip thought that the core of psychopathology is the schizoid self, a part of the ego that has undergone yet another level of splitting than the levels that Fairbairn postulated. In despair and hopelessness, this regressed ego returns to a state of objectlessness. These views on regression within the ego led Guntrip to a departure from Fairbairn's concepts, because Guntrip was raising the possibility that at birth the pristine ego is objectless, in contrast to Fairbairn, who thought that the ego at birth is primarily object-seeking. But like Winnicott who wanted his ideas to derive from Freud, Guntrip wanted to view his work as an extension or minor revision of Fairbairn's—for which he wanted acknowledgement from Fairbairn. At the end of his life, Fairbairn conceded the point, but it is not clear why he would do so, because it introduced a fundamental misunderstanding of the difference between their ideas as to whether the pristine ego was object-seeking or not.

Personally analyzed by both Fairbairn and then by Winnicott, Guntrip was in a position to observe both analysts at work. Guntrip (1986) said that in practice he found Fairbairn's technique to be quite classical while his theory-building was radical, whereas Winnicott's technique was radically different from classical technique although he refused to challenge classical theory.

Sutherland, Bollas

As Fairbairn's major expositor, biographer (Sutherland 1963, 1989), and chronicler and editor of the British object relations theorists (1980), Sutherland spent the first three-quarters of his life fostering and promoting the ideas of others, building bridges between their different psychoanalytic orientations, and moving easily between various levels of complexity and dimensions (Kohon 1996). After a successful late-life self-analysis, in which he himself analyzed the functioning of his self and healed his tendency to split his parents and to identify with only one of them at a time, Sutherland allowed in himself the creative pairing of ideas and aspects of himself that he had previously avoided (Sutherland 1990b). The result was that he became capable of highly original abstract thinking about the nature of the self, how it develops its structures, maintains them, and is sustained in interaction with others and with society's institutions (1990a, 1994a). He defined the self as a dynamic organization of purposes and commitments whose behavior is governed by conscious and unconscious motives and whose development and functioning are inseparably linked to its social environment.

Like Fairbairn, and unlike Klein, Sutherland insisted that instincts are not external to the structures of the self or of sub-selves but are inherent in them (Padel 1995). Sutherland wrote, "Instinctive endowment only becomes identifiable through its realization in the object relations it seeks and meets" (J. Scharff 1994, p. 365). He thought that the fundamental human drive was to be in a meaningful relationship. Unlike Bowlby, however, he thought that attachment was not an end in itself, but simply a necessary gestalt for the gestation of the self. He criticized Klein, who had vividly and usefully described the ego's fantasied object relationships, for not giving enough theoretical attention to the structuring of the self. He conceived of the self as a dynamic structure from the moment of birth, a holistic ego that will structure itself in the shape of a person by splitting and repression in response to experience with its objects. More than Fairbairn, he emphasized the internalization of the good object in consciousness, perhaps influenced by Kleinian concepts of life-affirming introjective identification. Going beyond Fairbairn, and not unlike Sullivan, he spoke in terms of *processes* to emphasize the dynamic, changing quality of the personality over the life cycle.

Sutherland described the structures of the self as processes and subsystems, terms that were suited to describing the internal and external object relationships that the self engaged in over time (Padel 1995). Influenced by open-systems theory models that were not available to Fairbairn (Bertalanffy 1950, Miller 1965, Prigogine 1976), Sutherland specifically refuted Freud's principle of entropy—the organism's motivation to return to the nonexcited, resting state—on the grounds that organisms do not remain static nor their behavior predictable. In modern times of rapid change and adaptation, organisms as a whole do not appear to return to the resting state. They are not organized by negative feedback aimed at conserving energy. In fact, they do not seem to operate on the principle of homeostasis at all. Rather they aspire to ever higher levels of organization. Sutherland thought that parts of the organism might resist change, but that as a whole the organism tends to seek change. It is governed by positive feedback, not negative feedback. It responds to positive feedback by entering a state of disequilibrium that is not totally unpleasant. This state of chaos is generative and leads to the development of new forms, not a return to the resting state. The organism tends to seek higher levels of organization in psychological, social, and cultural structures.

Always one to speak in terms of self rather than ego, Sutherland was influenced by Kohut's (1971, 1977) work on the self and Lichtenstein's (1977) contributions on identity to think more about the self in his last few years. He took Stern's (1985) infant research as a confirmation of his view that the self at birth is capable of, and driven to, a powerful assertion of autonomy and integrity. If this assertion were blocked, the resulting frustration would lead to a noticeable protest by the infantile self. Sutherland had always agreed with Fairbairn that aggression resulted from frustration, but in late life he thought that the major source of frustration was interference with the child's autonomy. He wrote, "Far from being undifferentiated, the self is being formed steadily, and any interference with this self-determined dynamic elicits intense aggression" (Sutherland 1994, in J. Scharff 1994, p. 330).

Sutherland thought that aggression is not only the reaction to the frustration of the need for attachment (as Bowlby thought), or even the frustration of the need to be in a satisfying relationship (as Fairbairn thought), and certainly not the desperate attempt to protect the self from the death instinct (as Klein thought). Sutherland postulated that aggression results from the self's struggle for its autonomy, which it is competent to pursue, but which is inevitably frustrated by the facts of infantile dependence—even when the infant's needs are met in an entirely satisfactory manner. This is Sutherland's most important idea. It serves as a summary of Sutherland's objection to Freud, reaffirms his stance with respect to Fairbairn, and takes him beyond, into his own theory of the autonomous self.

Interest in the self became progressively important to the leading contemporary object relations theorist, Bollas. He writes about recognizing one's personal idiom through being in touch with the unconscious (Bollas 1989), experiencing the self through projection into its objects, and experiencing itself through those objects until the resulting self is a constantly metamorphosing conglomerate of highly condensed internal object relationship textures (1992). He continues to explore the broad question, "What is this thing called self?" (1995, p. 146). Trained in the British Independent tradition where he was especially influenced by Winnicott, he freely incorporates concepts from Klein and Lacan, and any other psychoanalytic scholar or creative writer who can help him toward an appreciation of the uniqueness of the individual. He has kept himself free of the regrettable tendency of analytic schools to polemicize one aspect of analytic life at the expense of another (1989).

Dicks

Psychoanalysis has also tended to emphasize an understanding of the individual derived from psychoanalytic treatment to the exclusion of learning from other modalities. A brilliant exception to being thus hidebound was Dicks (1967). He contributed to understanding male and female adult development from his study of the simultaneous individual therapies of spouses who, not surprisingly, were found to have issues in common. Dicks took the Fairbairnian concept of endopsychic structure as a system of parts of ego, object, and affect in dynamic relation and put it together with Klein's concept of projective identification to explain how two personalities compatible enough on conscious criteria to make the decision to marry could go on to create a way of being that appears to be a marital joint personality. This indicates a degree of unconscious communication between the spouses that Dicks regarded as the real basis for the match and then the determinant of the nature of their marital relationship. Spouses project parts of their egos and objects into each other and look to find lost parts of their selves in their spouses, where they cherish or berate them depending on how they deal with that part of the self (Dicks 1967, Zinner 1976). They choose each other on the basis of their valencies to accept and identify with these projective identifications and yet with enough personal resilience and autonomy so as not to be captured and distorted by them. Couples who experience marital distress are those whose projective identificatory systems are either disavowing or too cementing of projective identifications. In the healthy marriage, the spouses are in reciprocal states of mutual projective identification in which they nourish or modify each other's projective identifications for the sake of enhanced, shared, mutual development through the life cycle. Dicks's study of marital interaction offers more than an application of psychoanalysis to marital therapy. It is the forerunner of the effort to gather information about adult development from the conjoint therapies and to use it to enrich psychoanalytic theory, test its applicability to daily living in families, and extend its relevance throughout the life cycle. We will return to this development in Chapter 10.

From Classical Freud to Contemporary Object Relations Psychoanalysis

With Sutherland's interest in self-regulation, self-renewal, and self-transformaton as life-determining processes that can account for interpersonal behavioral changes, neural development, and ultimately genetic transmission of changes in the phenotype, we come full circle from Freudian, instinct-based, tripartite structural theory to a contemporary object relations theory that includes an integrated consideration of the biological, and constitutional givens of the ego at birth. This bio-psycho-social view of the origins of the self results from and promotes current efforts in infant research to understand the development of the self more fully. Add to this findings from marital and family therapy action research, and we develop a view of the human personality as one that grows in a relational context with a variety of individual relationships, a nuclear family group, and an extended family group, as well as a host of unconscious internal object relationships interacting through projective and introjective identification in dynamic relation in the system, all influencing each other and the child's development (D. Scharff and J. Scharff 1987, Shapiro et al. 1975). Now we can say that, from birth, the infant is motivated to be in relationships that give security and meaning not only to the self but to the other. In this state which comprises multiple actual relationships in a dynamic system, the infant learns both to value the other and preserve the autonomy of the self.

In this decade, things are changing. Analysts of different schools are listening both to their own theories and to other theories, from which they incorporate whatever makes sense. Self psychologists are now studying intersubjectivity (Stolorow and Atwood 1992), Freudian theorists are applying the principles of projective identification in their discussions of clinical enactments of transference–countertransference phenomena (Chused 1991, 1996, Jacobs 1991), and object relations theorists are focusing more thoroughly on the experience of the self (Bollas 1995, Ogden 1994, D. Scharff 1992). From this broader base, we can look forward to further developments in adapting theory so that psychoanalysis, informed by twenty-first-century philosophy and science, will be a sensitive, flexible, and muscular method for studying and treating the various conditions of human experience.

Section 3

ADVANCES

7

Clinical Relevance of Research: Object Relations Testing, Neural Development, and Attachment Theory

Introduction

In object relations theory, the quality of the therapeutic relationship built by patient and therapist is the main determinant of the effectiveness of therapy. So research that addresses attachment behavior, develops ways of measuring relational tendencies, and visualizes the neural basis of psychic structure is highly relevant to elaborating new theory, applying it to technique in clinical work, and conceptualizing therapeutic action. During assessment, the clinician wants to evaluate strengths and weaknesses in the capacity to relate, so as to get an idea of the likely durability of the therapeutic relationship and an overview of the defensive characteristics of the relational capacities which will become the major focus of therapeutic work in object relations individual therapy. We look to current research studies to develop new ways of looking at personality variables, to narrow our focus on particularly relevant items for observation in assessment and in therapy, and to modify our technique in the light of research findings.

It is crucial for clinically based theorists to collaborate with researchers who will test hypotheses with various diagnostic groups and normal populations. Otherwise, we tend to elicit clinical material that conforms to our own theory and supports our views. We have to get over our idea that clinical work is independent of experimental verification. Psychoanalytic concepts can be stripped down to measurable core concepts to allow testing. Marcia (1994) acknowledged that such simplification is impoverishing to the concept, but he maintained that the results of the process in turn allow new ways of looking at old ideas which is enriching to them, as he showed in his research on ego identity as an evolving construct taking off from Erikson (Erikson 1959, D. Scharff 1994).

It is crucial for the school of object relations to collaborate with other schools of psychoanalysis, sociology, and psychology. Bornstein and Masling (1994) have shown how mutual influence between the fields of developmental, social, and cognitive psychology and object relations theory has led to useful formulations by Blatt and Blass (1992), Bocknek and Perna (1994), and Kihlstrom and Cantor (1984) on self-concept representations, Schacter (1987) on implicit memory, Stern (1985) on the development of the infant in the context of attachment, and Hazan and Shaver (1994) on close relationships.

It is also important for one-body and two-body schools of psychology to collaborate and value each other's approach rather than dismissing either one of them. We agree with Beebe and colleagues (1993) who hold that self-regulation and mutual regulation of affect and interaction by mother and infant go hand in hand from the beginning of life, that these two regulatory mechanisms have to be integrated in infancy, and that it would be better if they were integrated in conceptualizing the functions of the therapeutic relationship.

Empirical Research in Object Relations

In their study of changing self-representations through the life cycle and across gender lines, Bocknek and Perna (1994) developed the Who Am I (WAI), a questionnaire of ninety items in each of the categories of affiliation, social role, trait, activity, bodily appearance, and inner hopes and feelings that is easy to score manually or by machine, and the open-ended Fantasy Day (FD) test that is interesting but, being projective in nature, is hard to score, and therefore is rudimentary as yet.

Jefferson Singer and Jerome Singer (1994) reduced transference phenomena to discrete measurable units. They demonstrated that these units are best seen as elements of an evolving story in which transference manifestations are moments of expression of a larger structure that seeks verification and validation in current external relationships as well as influence over them. Singer and Singer came up with a view that goes beyond transference as a limitation imposed by the persistence of early working models. Based on their research, they conceptualize transference as a scanning mechanism for making sense of the newly encountered current situation by locating it in the emotional and perceptual field and then affecting it.

Tangney (1994), in her studies of guilt and shame in adolescence and adulthood, linked classical theories of superego development with recent findings from object relations theory, social cognition, and developmental psychology. She found that women do indeed score higher on questions of guilt and shame than men do, but she proposed that this is not because of moral inferiority due to the castration complex, as Freud had thought, but because they also demonstrate more highly relational behaviors that leave them vulnerable to feeling guilty for having hurt others and ashamed of being bad. Luborsky and Crits-Cristoph (1998) applied their Core Conflictual Relationship Theme measure to the analysis of transference.

Westen (1990) suggested that the time has come to subject existing theories of object relations in development and pathology to more rigorous scrutiny. He challenged various assumptions of object relations theories by reviewing empirical evidence drawn not from psychoanalysis and psychotherapy, but collected from tests devised to examine object relations and given to different diagnostic populations, to normal subjects, and to the children of both those groups. He refers to research on object relations using the Rorshach (Mayman 1967, Lerner and St. Peter 1984) and his own work on the Thematic Apperception Test (Westen, Lohr, Silk, and Kerber 1985). For the research-oriented reader, we list the various tests and coding systems that Westen referred to. One coding system for Rorschach responses measures the affective nature and cognitive quality of relationships (Blatt et al. 1976) and the other measures mutuality of autonomy (Urist 1977, 1980). There are three other object relations tests: Bell's object relations inventory, a self-report measure of interpersonal feelings and behavior in terms of alienation, insecure attachment, egocentrism, and social incompetence (Bell et al. 1988); the comprehensive object relations profile (Burke et al. 1986); and the Quality of Object Relations test, an interview-based measure of lifelong patterns of relating (Piper et al. 1991b). Another test uses structural analysis of social behavior (SASB) to give a dimensional model of interpersonal interaction when results are plotted on three diamond-shaped surfaces each corresponding to the dimensions of relating to other, others relating to self, and self relating to the self and its internal objects (Benjamin 1979, 1985, 1996). Benjamin's protocol has also been used for coding family interactions on videotape (Benjamin et al. 1986).

Most of Westen's findings come from his use of the Thematic Apperception Test scored on a Q-sort procedure called the SCORS-Q (Leigh et al. 1992,

Westen et al. 1985) applied to fantasy narratives (Westen and Segal 1988), early memories, psychiatric interviews, and, of most relevance for the clinician, data from psychotherapy and psychoanalytic session transcripts (Westen et al. 1988). Interviewers using the refined SCORS-Q make assessments that are similar enough to have reliability above 0.75. The correlation between the Q-sorts provided by the interviewer and by the therapist of any given patient is .50, a strong validity coefficient. This result suggests that clinical judgment about object relations can be made reliably and validly (Westen, personal communication).

Westen and his group focus on the measurement of four dimensions of object relations:

- The understanding of social causality;
- The ability to present a complex, differentiated view of self and other (the central self's ability to perceive accurately and be available for complex social learning, as we might put it);
- The affective quality of the object relations (malevolent or benevolent in his words, closed exciting or rejecting object relationships in our words);
- The capacity for emotional investment and commitment to others (need-gratifying or respectful treatment of the object which Westen relates to superego development, but which we see as another way of measuring the balance between the central self and the exciting object system).

Westen (1990) found that adult pathology does not necessarily correlate with a history of disturbance at a particular stage of development, that severe character pathology does not derive in all cases from a time period restricted to the first three years of life, and that its cause is multifactorial. Coates (1997) was on the same track when she asked directly whether it is time to jettison the concept of developmental lines. Westen found that mechanisms such as splitting, projective identification, and narcissistic ways of perceiving the world are not limited to the preoedipal period, and are not transcended by the end of the oedipal period. But he confirmed that the relationship with the mother is far more critical in the determination of object relational pathology than the relationship with the father. The capacity to tolerate ambivalence, thought to be developed by the first year in Kleinian theory and by the end of the oedipal period in Freudian theory, has been shown to be not firmly established in older children, even including pre-teens (Harter 1977, 1986).

Westen (1990) argued that the development of object relations is not linear, and that its multifaceted progression varies with cultural expectations and opportunities for social learning, is motivated by the pleasure of libidinal gratification (as Freud thought) as well as by affiliation and attachment, and continues at least into adolescence. Even then, the dominance of subcategories of object relations varies from time to time in the same individual and becomes exaggerated under particular conditions, as for instance when the subcategory of malevolent object relations characteristic of borderline personality is activated.

Internal object relationships (what Westen calls representations of self and of object) are encoded in multiple sensory modes and narratives and the quality of this internalization is motivated by the accompanying affect. In our clinical work, we find that the internal object relationship is stimulated to emerge when current relationship paradigms (including the therapeutic relationship) evoke a similar affect that spreads to trigger the original one.

American empirical research in object relations theory tends to follow American clinical practice in referring to *self and object representations* as the hallmark of object relations theory, and so we have used that terminology in this section, although it is not exactly how we describe psychic structure in terms of object relations. We regret that the term *representation* suggests some distance from the experience of having been in a relationship, as if it were the infant's way of thinking about it. For us, it is not a matter of how the self conceptualizes the experience. It *is* the self. The defining idea of object relations theory is that self and object are connected by affects, that they are present in a series of internal relationships, all in dynamic relation to each other inside the self, deriving from the interactive dyad and the family group, and that internal object relationships are not simply represented: they are psychic structure.

Setting that argument aside, we welcome the research findings' confirmation of many but not all of the tenets of object relations theory. They confirm that the affective quality of the object world, the capacity to distinguish between self and other, and the ability to invest in self and other are shaped in the preoedipal years, and that the affective tone of the object world is set in interaction with the mother. They do not confirm the idea of the oedipal complex as the final defining moment of personality development. Research shows that object relations are not finalized by the oedipal stage, but continue to develop from immature dependency to mature respect and love until adolescence—and, we would add, continue to grow and change through adult life experience with work, friendships, relocation, marriage, and raising children. In less than three years' time, Westen hopes that the measures will be able to answer such questions as, "Which aspects of object relations change in which kinds of treatment?" and "What kind of developmental experiences predict what kind of object relations?", but Coates and Moore think that questions linking early development and later personality may not be answerable in a linear sense (Coates and Moore, Westen, personal communications). Even so, the findings are already of interest to the clinician, and when the results of ongoing longitudinal family studies become available, we can expect to learn more about the relationship between psychic reality and historical experience, and about the intergenerational transmission of pathological organizations.

Ethologists' Studies of Attachment

Harlow (Harlow 1958, Harlow and Zimmermann 1959) showed that infant rhesus monkeys' attachment behavior (seeking proximity and contact) was more basic than drive/reduction behavior (such as sucking) for satisfying oral need. He found that monkeys preferred to cling to a furry ventral surface when feeding, and that clinging was as important as nursing was for the establishment of a secure base from which to explore the world. Monkeys bottle-fed from a nipple suspended on a wire frame would not feed, while those who could cling to a terrycloth-covered frame took the nipple on the terrycloth frame or reached over to drink from the nipple on the bare frame. The monkeys raised by terrycloth mothers developed normally but superficially: they lacked the subtleties of monkeys raised by a mother in a context of matrilines.

Suomi (1995) reviewed the literature on the attachment behaviors of apes, rhesus monkeys, gibbons, prosimians, macaque monkeys, and capuchins (Byrne and Suomi 1995, Harlow and Suomi 1970, 1986). They found agreement that in virtually all species of Old World monkeys and apes, infants spend their early sleeping and most of their waking hours clinging to their mothers' ventral surface—for weeks and, in the case of apes, months. They all use their mothers as secure bases from which to explore the environment. At first the mother takes responsibility for maintaining contact and then proximity. The infants contribute automatically by having the cute physical characteristics of the vulnerable baby animal that elicit biologically organized mothering responses. They have a repertoire of facial, vocal, and postural expressions for communicating affect that demands attention (H. Harlow and

M. Harlow 1965). They contribute actively to the shared maintenance of proximity as they grow a little older (Suomi 1984).

Apes and monkeys show the instinctual responses of sucking, clinging, crying, and following, and chimpanzees, like humans, show smiling as well—all secure base phenomena highly congruent with human experience, at least in daytime hours. In Western society, human infants do not generally sleep in contact with their parents' bodies, but this is a fairly new development in our evolution. Some Western researchers recommend that human primate infants need that physical contact and stimulation too. The contact provided in co-sleeping with a parent stimulates breathing and may prevent sudden infant death (McKenna et al. 1993).

In summary, Suomi (1995) states that mother–infant relationships in the higher-order primates, namely Old World monkeys and apes, show common behavior patterns, follow similar sequences of developmental change, and appear to be subject to the same influences. Advanced primate species are highly prepared to elicit, establish, and maintain attachment to caregivers. Suomi concludes that these findings support Bowlby's attachment theory (see the next section of this chapter) with the caveat that nevertheless they do not support Bowlby's idea that the infant's attachment to its mother is the prototype for all subsequent social relationships. According to Suomi, the nature of the infant–mother relationship and *how it is played out over time* is what profoundly affects present and future relationships.

At four weeks of age rhesus monkeys can run, but their mothers at first prohibit exploration. Then they encourage the infant to explore and return to contact with mother, explore and recontact mother. There is lots of one-to-one infant–mother interaction, with visual, auditory, tactile, and vestibular stimulation. The nature of the ventral contact that the mother offers her female baby monkey determines the ventral contact that her daughter will offer her own baby, even when the mother was a foster mother, suggesting that the transgenerational transmission of maternal behavior occurs through behavior, not genes. Longitudinal studies of secure, anxious, and ambivalent attachment patterns reveal that each of them shows continuity from one generation to the next. By analogy, we take the information that a particularly nurturant foster-mother monkey can induce social behaviors that go against genetic type as an endorsement of the value of the symbolically nurturant therapeutic relationship offered to the human primate.

Separation studies have shown consistently that monkeys and apes respond to separation with agitation. When the rhesus monkey mother is removed, all play and exploration stops. At seven months of age, when the monkey has already been weaned, the mother goes off into the woods to copulate with her new consorts. The abandoned monkey is distraught, screams in protest, and tries to follow her. In all cases the monkeys protest, but only 20 percent of them show despair with withdrawal and passivity. This, incidentally, is similar to the percentage of avoidant attachment patterns found in a general population (Moore, personal communication). The young monkeys are safe with the social group, the male monkeys going off with their peers and the female monkeys staying with their families, and gradually both genders get used to the separation.

Those that despair get lethargic and show feeding and sleeping problems. They are shy, inhibited, nervous, withdrawn, reactive, and uptight. They show higher levels of plasma cortisol and adrenocorticotropic hormone, decreased levels of norepinephrine, develop a higher heart rate, and may even curl up in a fetal position when their mother leaves. When she returns, they cling to her and play less for days or weeks. Those that despair are likely to continue to display extreme reactions to separation in later childhood, adolescence, and into adulthood. The physiology of the monkeys' adrenal development may be permanently affected (Suomi 1994). Early stress leads to emotional reactivity in adulthood (Suomi 1991). Changes in hormonal physiology measured in animals provide a physiological basis for Bowlby's idea of the psychological creation of internal working models, and find a parallel in human infant studies.

Bowlby thought that infant attachment experiences became internalized as *internal working models* that determine the nature of future relationships with the family of origin and procreation, and with peers. Monkeys, however, are not capable of symbolic thinking, and yet complex behavioral and physiological consequences occur after interference with attachment needs. For instance, rearing monkeys in isolation severely compromises their ability to relate. Even monkeys reared with foster mothers develop relationships that are somewhat insecure. Monkeys reared with peers and no mothers may look socially normal, but they tend to develop anxious attachments (Hinde and Spencer-Booth 1967). They react badly to social separations, and are particularly timid when challenged by a novel situation, and, although most of them become competent mothers, a proportion of them are not good with their firstborn. Some (mostly male) peer-reared monkeys become impulsive and aggressive, and have higher rates of premature expulsion from the troop, and increased risk of death in adolescence. This is reminiscent of the predominance of the diagnosis of attention deficit in males with anxious attachments (Moore 1997).

Of great interest to the therapist is the finding that infant monkeys reared by foster mothers of differing temperaments have different short- and long-term outcomes. Physiologically over-reactive infants reared by especially nurturing foster mothers develop secure attachments and become dominant in the troop despite their temperamental vulnerability, but those reared by punitive foster mothers develop insecure attachments. Physiologically stable infant monkeys develop normally no matter who raises them. This supports the impression that the interaction of *temperament and environment* is important in the outcome for development of children raised in families, and in the matching of patients to therapists.

In lower-order primates, such as capuchin monkeys, whose genetic makeup is less like that of humans even though their capacity to make and use tools is highly advanced, the diversity and frequency of mother–infant interactions is reduced, and attachment phenomena are less obvious (Byrne and Suomi 1995, Welker et al. 1987, 1990). Capuchin monkeys do grow up clinging to their mothers, but they cling to their dorsal surface, perhaps because their mothers have to be free to work with their tools, and so there is very little visual, vocal, or grooming behavior. They take more months to start exploring, but when they do, they leave their mother for longer periods, and have fewer and briefer re-contacts with her. They explore freely and teach themselves to use tools, and if the mother is not there, they use any other monkey as a secure base. They grow up to be less social, less playful, and more work-oriented than ventral-reared Old World monkeys. If they do play, they play in pairs, not in peer groups as the other monkeys do. Interestingly, they cannot teach each other the use of tools. Each one has to learn it anew. The infant on the back of the mother cannot watch her using a tool, or see beyond her to watch other monkeys using their tools. Perhaps the restricted view from the dorsal clinging position prevents the visual acquisition of an *internal* working model for manipulating an inanimate object that could then be culturally transmitted. Dorsal clinging changes the infants' view of their world and provides a template for their environmental and interactive behavioral patterning (Moore, personal communication). Lacking advanced social development, the capuchins cannot build an advancing, tool-using culture. Prosimian monkeys are even less attached to their mothers.

Suomi (1995) concludes that attachment phenomena are most apparent in humans and higher-order primates who are phylogenetically closest to humans. This may represent an evolutionary process of adaptation toward complex, secure attachment higher in the primate orders.

From their studies of the determinants of diversity in the social organization of apes and monkeys and uniformity in the social organization of humans, Sameroff and Suomi (1996) argue that culture transcends the limits of individual biology and yet biological constraints shape the organization of human culture. For human and nonhuman primates, without an interactive environment there is no survival. Behavior and context are always one process—inseparable. The genotype determines the physical characteristics of the monkey or the child, the resulting behavior and temperament produces the phenotype, and the phenotype influences the environtype (the behaviors of the caregivers in their society). The environtype shapes the phenotype. Genotype, phenotype, and environtype all interact in a system. We agree that the experience of the child is shaped by the beliefs, values, and personality of the parents, the family's interactional patterns and transgenerational history, and by the wider context of the social controls and supports of the culture.

Systematic Naturalistic Research: Infant Observation

Infant observation, a rigorous training in observing without interpreting data prior to its collection, was developed by Esther Bick with the support of John Bowlby at the Tavistock Clinic in 1948 to study early modes of mental functioning and the quality of infantile experiences (Shuttleworth 1989). Infant observation does not claim to be a research method, but we put it in the research category for our purposes here because it collects data, develops hypotheses about personality development, and tests them through further observation. The findings have implications for theory-building, psychotherapy training, and object relations therapy that values the use of containment and countertransference. The infant-and-mother couple are observed over two years, a length of time that permits the gradual accumulation of details into recognizable recurring patterns of behavior and feeling, gives time for them to change, and emphasizes the need for reliance on consecutive observations (Williams 1984). Infant observers find behavioral patterns that are thought to correlate with splitting and projective identification of objects with body parts and processes. In the seminar where observations are discussed, students learn to eschew ideas of right and wrong ways to deal with a baby, and to tolerate the process of each nursing couple finding their own way.

Observing without intervening can be quite a difficult role for the student who is in training for a helping profession, and it produces an experience analogous to that of the therapist facing anxiety in the clinical situation. Not having an active role with the baby robs the observer of a way of discharging anxiety through doing something and it leaves a space for receiving the full impact of the baby's sensations—which sets up a reverberation with the observer's own infantile self (Rustin 1989). For instance, when the mother seems detached from her baby and uses her breasts or hands as part-objects not related to a vital and nurturing self, the observer experiences a counter-transference of identifying with the resentful baby and wishing to augment the vitality of the mother. Observers experience primitive emotional distress. They have to bear it, stay out of it, and trust in the future of the mother–baby relationship, much as therapists have to do with a patient or client in non-directive object relations therapy.

Infant observation has found prominence as a useful preparation for clinical work as a psychotherapist (Bick 1964, Henry 1984, Miller et al. 1989). Infant observation sharpens awareness and acceptance of infantile aspects of older children and adults (Henry 1984). It gives students a chance to see how relationships emerge between the infant and the family members (Bick 1964). It gives them an opportunity to experience primitive emotional states in the mother, in the baby, and in themselves as they respond to turbulence in their relationship (Margaret Rustin 1989). The model of observing without judgment and without intervention heightens the capacity for containment as well as the objectivity of the naturalistic observation. The infant observation method convinces students of the importance of observing the patient's total behavior and strengthens their belief in the validity of analytic reconstruction of early development (Bick 1964). It gives therapists a sensitivity to infant modes of communication, and provides the substrate for developing a language for preverbal experience through which to communicate their understanding of transferences stemming from infancy. Internalizing the seminar group's containing function, the student develops an attitude like that of a mother's reverie through which to bear anxiety and create a psychological space for understanding, where thoughts can begin to take shape out of chaos without a premature need for resolution that would close off full understanding.

Infant observation teaches a scientific method in which naturalistic observation is repeated over time until a pattern emerges from which a hypothesis is drawn and subsequently tested by further observation over time. It collects behaviors that reveal the infant's movement between positively good, integrated states of mind and more fragmented states of mind that feel bad and require the integrating help offered by the caregiver, or so bad that they may temporarily prevent the infant from using the help offered. Brazelton ob-

served that comforting contact with the caregiver can be observed transforming the distressed baby's jerky, aimless, poorly coordinated arm movements
to smooth, circular ones that reach successfully toward the object of desire
(Brazelton et al. 1974). Trevarthen's work (1989, 1990) contributed to current
understanding of the growth and education of the hemispheres of the brain,
and his films confirm observations that 2-month-old infants sustain complex
interactive sequences with their mothers (Murray and Trevarthen 1985,
Trevarthen and Aitken 1986). Infant emotional and cognitive development
is stimulated and shaped by repeated interactions with the caregiver (J. Scharff
and D. Scharff 1992, Shuttleworth 1989).

From his observations, Bråten concluded that the infant is born with the
other in mind (1993). He called this the *virtual other*, a companion space to be
fulfilled by actual others (Bråten 1992). He observed that within a month of
birth the infant can create sequences matched to the mother's. Through
attunement and dialogue-like interplay, the infant engages in a duet with the
mother and she fills the image of the virtual other. In response to perturbation of the rhythm of their connection, the infant self-organizes a return to
the virtual other inside the self (Bråten 1992). Observation of the infant's use
of the mother supports Klein's and Fairbairn's beliefs that the human infant
is object-related from birth.

The advantage of naturalistic infant observation over experimental research is that it deals with infants in all states of mind—joyful, composed, and
distressed—and especially examines the transition from one state to another,
instead of dealing with infants only in states of alert inactivity thought to be
suitable for examining their responses to the research agenda (Shuttleworth
1989). Whereas experimental research in developmental psychology has often
focused on the external social relationship, infant observation focuses on observable processes with a view to noting how they contribute to the infant's
feeling held together or fragmented. Feeling gathered together and held in
the mother's mind through her reverie leads to the infant's internalization of
her containing function, which generates a sense of self capable of managing
affect and conceiving of itself as related to but distinct from the object. Internalization and identification with the containing space provided by the mother
is thought to lead to an internal three-dimensional mental/emotional space
filled with metabolized experience out of which an internal object world and
sense of self are built.

Infant observation is one way of seeing the experience of bodily and emotional states being given meaning by the mother, after which the infant be-

comes progressively more able to use thinking to tolerate distress and delay. Both proximity to the mother and manageable degrees of separation from her are essential for growth of the self. The model of the mind that emerges from this approach is no longer one of causality, in which the past of the external world caused the present ways of experiencing the external world, but one in which experience is encoded in the inner space of the mind, and where the development of an internal object world then affects the present in complex ways (Shuttleworth 1989).

Attachment Research: Bowlby

A major area of research in developmental psychology derives from the observational research of Bowlby, whose attachment theory (also mentioned in Chapter 6) inspired many researchers to replicate and elaborate on his findings. Having reviewed the findings of ethologists, he noted that the young of all species have a repertoire of attachment behavior and show aggression when their attachment needs are frustrated. He thought that loss of a parent is devastating to the young child, and that separation could be deeply distressing, a finding shown graphically in classic films of children experiencing a separation of a few days' duration from their parents (Robertson and Robertson 1972). Bowlby proposed that environmental trauma in the form of loss or parental neglect is the main contributor to pathological growth and development and that infants' behavior is normally geared to maintaining proximity with primary caregivers.

Inititally, Bowlby described three types of behaviors—anxiously attached, compulsively caretaking, and compulsively self-reliant—as attempts to secure relationship to pathogenic parents (1977). He linked the compulsively caretaking type to Winnicott's description of the false self (1960b), and he described the self-reliant behaviors as similar to those identified by Parkes (1973). These three types were precursors of the present attachment classification system developed by Ainsworth (Ainsworth et al. 1978) and elaborated by Main (1990, 1995) (see below and Chapter 13). As clinicians, we found Bowlby's original categories quite useful, because they reflect the self's relation to the internal object as shown in current relationships, including the transference, but we have given them up in favor of current classification terms.

Peterfreund (1978) advised against the misapplication of models based on infancy to understand complex adult pathology. Other mainstream Freudian and Kleinian psychoanalysts did not accept the clinical implications of

Bowlby's work, at first, because his theory was hostile to the importance of unconscious fantasy, which Bowlby thought they overvalued. But developmental psychologists, researchers in human behavior, and analysts of the British Independent object relations tradition eventually welcomed Bowlby's ideas and developed protocols to test his principles, which ultimately led to the burgeoning field of infant research. Now infant research findings, together with trauma theories of childhood sexual abuse, draw attention to the specific effects of parental personalities on children's behavior, memory systems, affect regulation, and self-concept. This research methodology for examining the interpersonal field is prompting a re-evaluation of the relevance of Bowlby's contribution to psychotherapy, psychoanalysis, and child and infant psychiatry (Bretherton 1985, V. Hamilton 1985). Coming full circle, human attachment theory is now also influencing the collecting and interpreting of data in the field of ethology from which attachment theory originated (Suomi 1995).

Attachment Research: Ainsworth and Main

Mary Ainsworth was Bowlby's principal follower (Karen 1994). She put his principles into the research world and her work spawned a wealth of research into attachment behavior. The original research on infant attachment by Ainsworth, and subsequent work on adult attachment patterns by her student, Mary Main, have had a major impact on clinical work and developmental understanding (Belsky and Cassidy 1994). Bowlby and Ainsworth focused on reunion as a time when attachment behavior is highly observable. They found that study of the transitional time when the 12- to 18-month-old infant is reunited with the mother after a brief separation is most instructive.

Ainsworth invented and developed the Strange Situation, a laboratory research instrument for assessing the quality of attachment in young children, by observing their *patterns of behavior in seeking comfort* when stressed by a brief separation in unfamiliar circumstances (Ainsworth et al. 1978). In this test, the mother brings her toddler into the laboratory, leaves for a short time, and returns. The child's behavior during separation and reunion is taken as the measure of the security of attachment to that caregiver. The researchers found that differences in the quality of the mothers' responsiveness to their infants earlier in infancy correlated with the behaviors of their toddlers. Different behaviors are observed when the same child parts from and reunites with the father or other caregivers, showing that the same child may be securely attached to one parent and avoidant of the other. In other words, attachment is not an independent characterological quality but is specific to the particular adult, and to the relational context. The regulation of affect is the vehicle for maintaining the child's tie to the parent (Cassidy 1994). The capacity to discriminate between significant others is a survival mechanism that allows the child to recognize danger and respond with a self-protective change in behavior (Moore, personal communication).

Main later studied the quality of the children's parents' own attachments (Main 1995, Main and Goldwyn in press, Main and Hesse 1990). She and her students developed a research protocol that is an interview that inquires into *patterns of memory, thinking, and narrativization* about separation and loss. These researchers categorized the attachment behaviors of the adults and discovered a category of infant attachment patterning called *disorganized/disoriented* that tended to occur in the children of traumatized adults that they categorized as *disorganized/unresolved*. They found a correlation between the parents' attachment classification and that of their children.

Not all the individuals assigned to the various categories showed all the features typical of that category. It is important to remember that there is intragroup variability and to think in terms of tendencies rather than oversimplifications that do not do justice to individual difference, or that prejudice us to see the individual in a way that neatly fits the label. This note of caution is especially important in applying the findings of research populations to individual assessment by a clinician (Moore, personal communication, Slade 1996).

Recent work has documented that the assessment of each adult's capacity for attachment accurately predicts, in about 75 percent of mothers and 75 percent of fathers, the quality of attachment with their firstborn child (Fonagy 1996). As far as we know, no one has yet made predictions for an adult's attachment behavior with more than one child (Moore, personal communication). The 25 percent that defies categorization is important to clinicians because it allows for the variability that we see in family dynamics and in the transference. Ainsworth's infant attachment types and their comparable adult versions give an outline of the ways of relating to each significant other (and to the therapist) that the clinician can expect to find in adulthood, may predict the adult's likely relationship with a firstborn child, and can signal an alert that individuals whose behaviors fit a particular one of the categories (namely the one called disorganized/unresolved) are highly likely to have a substantial history of unresolved childhood trauma.

While these test instruments are as yet valid only for research, the categories that they have identified can helpfully be used in refining our clinical assessment of the quality of patients' attachment relationships. There we look for a picture of their capacity for relating as an external measure of their internal object relationships and their likely expression in close relationships, work, and social life.

Infant Attachment Categories

When reading the broad categories to which researchers assign the attachment behaviors of the infants that they study, we recall that, even in the research study that narrows the focus of observation to that which is measurable, the behavior of about a quarter of the infants does not fit clearly into a category. We must also remember that attachment is not an invariable quality of the infant's character, but a set of behaviors that occur with one adult. In the clinical situation, then, the infant pattern re-invoked in the transference is specific to the particular internal object relationship dominant in the therapeutic relationship at that time. For a summary of categories, see Table 7–1.

Secure

The infant who is securely attached to the mother uses her as a base from which to explore the world. He expects to find comfort in returning to her when he is upset. He has learned that she will be responsive to his expressions of need for protection, nurturing, and calming.

In Fairbairn's terms, this infant finds most of the experience with the object satisfactory and retains it in consciousness. He does not have an intolerable amount of rejecting and exciting object experience and therefore has less need to split off and repress internal objects.

Insecure/Avoidant

The infant who is insecure/avoidant in his attachment to his mother does not use her as a secure base. He turns away from her when he is upset and tries not to show distress. He has learned that she will be consistent in rejecting his needs for physical or emotional comforting. Here we see traits in the infant of pseudo-independence and restricted affect in relation to a mother who has rebuffed his needs for closeness (Cassidy and Kobak 1988).

In Fairbairn's terms, the infant identifies with the rejecting mother who pushes away attempts at closeness. If his mother is even more thoroughly unresponsive, the profound experience of rejection can lead to a schizoid personality.

Insecure/Resistant

The infant who shows insecure/resistant behaviors when interacting with the mother is anxiously dependent on her as a secure base and is visibly upset on separation. In this category, infants may sometimes be simultaneously angry at or clinging to the mother, or at other times unresponsive to her attempts at closeness (Cassidy and Berlin 1994). These infants cannot use the comfort that is provided to develop a sense of security because often, from soon after birth, they have been offered comfort inconsistently by a mother who is sometimes overly available or intrusive and other times uninvolved.

In Fairbairn's terms, this is the exciting mother who stimulates anxiety, need, and longing for her. The alternately overstimulated and let-down infant feels painfully ambivalent and develops hysterical patterns of relating.

Disorganized/Disoriented

A fourth type of attachment, identified by Main, describes an infant who, when interacting with the mother, may show on reunion a frozen response, confused or bizarre behaviors, or both, when she returns from the separation (Main and Solomon 1986, 1990). These children do not know how to organize their need for interpersonal comfort and closeness, because their mother or father may have been unpredictably frightening or frightened in earlier interaction with the infant, due to their own difficulty in regulating affect and behavior. Often this adult has unresolved childhood traumas, frequently due to physical and sexual abuse.

In Fairbairn's terms, this is the mixed exciting and rejecting external object experienced as an internal exciting and rejecting object of terrifying proportions.

TABLE 7–1. Classification of infant and adult attachment types.

Infant Types	Adult Types
Secure	Autonomous/secure
Insecure/avoidant	Avoidant/dismissive
Insecure/resistant	Resistant/preoccupied
Disorganized	Disorganized/unresolved

Adult Attachment Categories

When reading of the adult attachment categories, we bear in mind that many of the adults that we meet as patients or clients have mixed attachment strategies. But the classification helps us to disentangle the motives for the mixed strategies in terms of their object relationships re-experienced in the transference.

Autonomous/Secure

Adults categorized as autonomous/secure were freely able to recall their memories of separation and loss, had a coherent construction of their past experience, and, while able to articulate the importance of their early experience with their own parents (whether positive or negative) had become independent of them. They were free to experience their emotions currently. They either have no need for therapy, or choose it willingly at times of external or internal developmental crisis, in which case they often benefit from brief therapy. On the other hand, if these well-functioning people choose to seek growth and understanding, they are good candidates for benefiting from psychoanalysis.

Avoidant/Dismissive

Adults categorized as avoidant/dismissive were found to have tightly formed structures for regulating affect, and discontinuous memory systems. They often could not recall details of their childhoods but covered over these gaps with a bland portrayal. They spoke in global, idealized terms as if everything had been fine, but their later answers indicated that they had, in fact, felt distant from their parents. They gave an account that was not congruent with their actual past experience, because they tended to repress negativity, emotionality, and the need for attachment. They were inclined to resist the idea of therapy, but if they ever do get to a therapist they behave in rejecting ways or minimize the therapist's potential helpfulness (Dozier 1990, Dozier et al. 1996). Their rejection of help needs to be understood as a defense against experiencing loss and ultimately the fear of being rejected by the therapist.

Resistant/Preoccupied

Adults categorized as resistant/preoccupied were found to have weak structures for regulating affect and for maintaining order in the memory system. They tended to give an incoherent account of their childhoods, flooded as they often were by affect and memories of intensely negative experiences. Frequently they are, as adults, still enmeshed in family relationships. They may use affect desperately, blurring the distinction between self and other in order to maintain closeness. In therapy, they are often needy and demanding. Many of their frequent phone calls, emergencies, outbursts, and calls for extra time, can be understood as attempts to ensure that they are held in mind by the therapist. The therapist has to tolerate being intensely needed, has to remain fully available in each session, and set clear limits on the deluge. Steady object availability within limits is crucial in promoting definition of the self.

Disorganized/Unresolved

Adults categorized as disorganized/unresolved were likely to show episodes of disorientation or confusion with respect to particular traumatic experiences in their past. They often had weak structures for regulating affect, for remembering painful events, and for keeping the self intact. They might suffer from memory lapses, dissociation, or suicidal feelings, often a consequence of childhood physical or sexual abuse. Some of these survivors of childhood abuse were too terrified of repetition of abuse to trust a therapist. In other cases, they might not have taken to therapy because they did not have access to their memories and dreams, because in their early experience the intrusion of reality closed off the transitional space for fantasy. Those who come to therapy defend themselves against painful memory by the substitution of excessively ordinary everyday experience, not because they are resisting, but because this way of going-on-being was crucial to their survival and is essential for the maintenance of the therapeutic relationship (J. Scharff and D. Scharff 1994).

Cannot Classify

Hesse (1996) has recently introduced another category of insecure attachment called *Cannot Classify*. Into this category he assigns the 25 percent of adults who have mixed patterns. We await further research in this category with interest, because we tend to think that study of areas of transition yields information of great use to the clinician.

Slade: The Continuum

Instead of broadly contrasting the qualities of child–adult attachment as either secure or insecure with variations, Slade (1996) importantly views them along a continuum of affect regulation and structure, and—usefully for the clinician—points out the inevitability of some overlap between categories. At one end of the continuum of qualities of adult–child attachment lie the avoidant/dismissive personalities who have rigid structures for affect regulation, and their insecure/avoidant children. At the opposite end are the resistant/preoccupied personalities, with poorly made structures overwhelmed by affect, and their insecure/resistant children. Beyond that point lie the disorganized/unresolved personalities which show even less coherence of structure, due to areas of dissociation, and their disorganized children. Between the poles in the autonomous/secure category are those adults whose affects and structures exist in balance, and their secure children. These correlations are observed in over 76 percent of mother–infant pairs, a result that held up even when the testing of the adult was done before birth of the couple's first baby (Fonagy et al. 1991).

Fonagy: Mentalizing and Transmission of Attachment Patterns

Infant research is now showing how attachment patterns are transmitted across generations (Zeanah and Zeanah 1989). Fonagy and his colleagues (Fonagy et al. 1995) showed that the best predictors of an infant's attachment patterns are the adult attachment patterns of the parents. Fonagy measured the adults' capacity for self-reflection and found that its presence characterized the type of mother found in the autonomous/secure adult category and whose child fell in the secure child category. The parent's capacity for self-reflection extended to understanding, reflecting upon, and conceptualizing the infant's experience, an adult self-reflective function that he called *mentalizing* (Fonagy 1996, Fonagy et al. 1995). We think that Fonagy's concept of *mentalizing* is similar to Bion's concept of *containment,* that process of bearing and metabolizing anxiety and then giving it back to the infant in a more manageable form. We think that his research has provided a way of measuring containment. We also suggest that his research in infant attachment and adult mentalizing together confirms that the containing function of the mother (Bion 1967, 1970) is as important as her provision of a secure holding environment (Winnicott 1945, 1963a,b). Slade (1996) wrote an opinion that reflects our view that "the mother's capacity to enter the child's mind, and give reality to his internal experience, is as vital an aspect of empathic mothering as maternal sensitivity, and is central to the intergenerational transmission of security" (p. 14).

Empirical Research on Adult Relationships

Adult attachment theory has been considered in the context of adult relationships, including the therapeutic relationship. Dozier and Kobak (1992) elaborated Main's (1990) discovery of the use of secondary strategies for *activation and deactivation* of the attachment system by some adults when primary strategies for re-establishing proximity were thwarted, and Cassidy (1994) described a process of *minimizing* affects that might disrupt a tenuous attachment relationship. Assessment of the adult attachment organization has been used in designing the treatment of adults who have serious psychopathological disorders, especially those using deactivating attachment strategies, and in conceptualizing the role of the clinician as caregiver (Dozier 1990, Dozier et al. 1994, Dozier et al. 1996).

Sroufe and Fleeson (1986) showed that internal working models of attachment influenced the construction of intimate relationships in adulthood and affected perceptions of emotional availability of self and partner. Shaver and Clark (1994) reviewed the use of measures of attachment in understanding adult development, romantic attachment, and relational pathology, including depression, dissociation, personality disorder, and abuse. Hazan and Shaver (1987) invented a questionnaire for a sample of newpaper readers who were asked to rate their romantic attachments according to categories based on Ainsworth's infant-attachment categories of avoidant, anxious/ambivalent, and secure. They found that the percentages of adults in each category was similar to the percentages of infants that Ainsworth had found in each category. But Bartholomew pointed out that Hazan and Shaver's operational definition was different from Main's definition used in the Adult Attachment Interview (AAI), where the AAI–avoidant adults were high in repression, denial, and invulnerability, while in the Hazan and Shaver study they were high on depression, vulnerability, and dissatisfaction. Bartholomew's point was that the AAI–avoidant adults were indeed dismissive/avoidant while the Hazan and Shaver avoidant adults were more accurately described as fearful/avoidant (Bartholomew 1990, Bartholomew and Horowitz 1991). Bartholomew's views, which hinged on this discrimination of the affective quality of the attachment behavior, led her to add to the four-category adult attachment typology a positive and negative aspect of the internal working model of self and other (see Table 7–2). An individual with secure attachment to the other views self and other positively. The person who is preoccupied with relationship to the attachment figure views the other positively and the self negatively. The one who is dismissive views the self positively and the other

TABLE 7–2. Two-dimensional, four-category model of adult attachment
© K. Bartholomew. Used by permission.

Positive
Model of Other

SECURE

Comfortable with
intimacy and autonomy
in close relationships

PREOCCUPIED

Preoccupied with close relationships
Overly dependent on others
for self-esteem and support

Positive
Model of
Self

Negative
Model of
Self

DISMISSING

Down-plays importance
of close relationships
Compulsive self-reliance

FEARFUL

Fearful of intimacy
due to fear of rejection
Socially avoidant

Negative
Model of Other

negatively. The person who is fearful/avoidant of attachment views self and other negatively.

The adult attachment interview has been tested with couples in a dating relationship. Following Main's (1990) development of the adult attachment interview and Dozier and Kobak's (1992) elaboration of activation and deactivation of the attachment system, Morrison and colleagues (1995) studied object relations of partners in intimate attachments. Morrison and colleagues

(1997a) used the categorical approach to attachment security in the Hazan and Shaver questionnaire, along with the dimensional approach to attachment activation based on Collins and Read's (1990) attachment questionnaire, as well as the Structural Analysis of Social Behavior (SASB) (Benjamin 1996, Benjamin and Friedrich 1991). They found that mental representations of intimate relationships in adulthood differed among individuals with different types of attachment organization (Morrison et al. 1997a). Greater attachment security and less activation of the attachment system were associated with perception of more affiliative interaction, and perceptions of relationship satisfaction were colored by the realities of interaction in longer relationships, while in shorter relationships the internal working model of attachment was more crucial in governing the sense of satisfaction (Morrison et al. 1997b). Kirkpatrick and Davis (1994) found that couplings between young men and women who both scored as secure were stable over three years, as one might suppose. Couplings between avoidant men with anxious/ambivalent women were also stable, while those between anxious/ambivalent men and avoidant women were not lasting, a result that echoes sex-role stereotypes.

Unfortunately most of the findings on coupling have been collected in university-based research projects on college age participants who have little experience of long-term intimacy. More research projects are needed to study populations of long-term marriages and should focus on the influence of cognitive and affective factors on interaction patterns, interpretation of behaviors, and relationship adjustment (Noller and Ruzzene 1991, Morrison et al. 1997b).

The Tavistock Marital Studies Institute staff is working in this direction, and results should be available in a couple of years. Clinical researchers are studying how the internal working model of attachment in the adult individual influences the complex attachment of partners in long-term marriages by comparing test results with clinical impressions gained over time in marital psychotherapy (Fisher and Crandell 1997). Adapted from the Adult Attachment Interview (AAI), the test that Fisher and Crandell use is the Couple Attachment Joint Interview (CAJI), a semistructured clinical interview conducted with both partners jointly. Their premise is that in couple relationships, attachment is bidirectional, not unidirectional as in parent–infant relationships; each partner is ideally able to be dependent on the other, or be depended upon, their roles shifting flexibly and seamlessly. The nature of the couple bond is called *complex attachment*. Fisher and Crandell's hypothesis is that secure attachment will predict for reciprocity in the couple relationship, while insecure patterns will lead to fixed positions and rigidly defensive patterns of relating in the couple. They hope to demonstrate specifically how every possible combination in the marital joint personality of secure and insecure individual internal working models drawn from each of the adult attachment categories influences the couple's complex attachment.

We are interested in whether this research based on internal working models of attachment may be extended to quantify the nature of the projective and introjective identificatory system of the marital relationship. We think that Fisher and Crandell's CAJI interview may be applicable to this aim. We think that Luborsky and Crits-Christoph's (1989) Core Conflictual Relationship Theme Method, used to track individual transference patterns, could be applied to study of a couple's projective and introjective identificatory system. This type of research holds promise for supporting the integration of attachment theory, Kleinian theory, and object relations theory.

Birtchnell: The Interpersonal Octagon Test

Birtchnell (1993) has gone beyond attachment theory toward a science of relating that values detachment as much as attachment. He uses an upperness/lowerness dimension in addition to the closeness/distance and positive/negative aspects that Bartholomew used (1990). Birtchnell developed the PROQ, the Persons Relating to Others Questionnaire, and the CREOQ, the Couple's Relating to Each Other Questionnaire, self-administered tests that measure relating and being related to, both positively and negatively, in terms of closeness/distance and upperness/lowerness. With closeness/distance on the horizontal axis, and upperness/lowerness on the vertical axis, the scores are plotted to reveal positions in eight octants of the individual *interpersonal octagon*, which allows each dimension to be viewed in its association to other aspects of relating that lie nearby on the octagon. Assessment of self and other is illustrated on octagons in Figure 7–1, a and b. Birtchnell uses another questionnaire called the US given to husband and wife to measure their views of themselves as a couple. Most healthy marriages score no more than five points with a negative value out of a possible total of twenty on the US.

In the US score of the A. marriage shown on the octagons in Figure 7–1 a and b, the negative score was 11 out of 20 by the husband and 12 out of 20 by the wife, indicating that they have a poor relationship.

Birtchnell's reading of the octagons reveals that the wife's assessment of herself and her husband's assessment of her are remarkably similar. Both of them give her scores in the upper-neutral dimension that are almost the same as those on the lower-neutral dimension. So both agree that she swings between being dominating and wanting to be dominated. On the horizontal axis, she scores as clinging and withdrawing, but he sees her as somewhat more clinging, and more poorly related than he is. Both of them record high scores for him in the lower/distant dimension of the octagon which suggests that he draws away from her, keeps out of her way, and sometimes sulks. Instead of seeing this as an attempt at keeping the peace, the wife sees him as remote, secretive, distancing, and unwilling to spend time with her. But, like her, he also scores high on upper-closeness, suggesting that his only way of getting close to her is to take over, which she partly longs for, but when he does, he risks her swinging over to dominating him, which he avoids by withdrawal.

When the A.s were seen in assessment, they presented as quite miserable for most of the thirty years of their life together, but tied together by their commitment to marriage. They had never been happy and never amorous. They wished for a better marriage, but neither was confident that therapy could help.

Each member of the couple seemed to be a likeable person. In his quiet way, Mr. A. could be quite insightful, kindly, and understanding of Mrs. A.'s losses sustained when her family had to flee their homeland, but he also seemed passive and tentative. He was an easygoing, quiet-spoken man who, however, was quite successful in business consulting. A religious man, he did not see the value of a therapeutic relationship because he judged psychiatry as being atheistic and materialistic. He liked to keep busy, read, work on the computer, and take vacations in a remote part of the country where he could spend time alone. An only son, he was controlled and dominated by his mother. As soon as his father died, he left home and did not live with his mother again, although he continued to make business deals as her partner. When he got married, his mother perceived Mrs. A. as having taken him away from her, and hated her for it.

Mrs. A. was lively and entertaining, but rather impossible to satisfy. She was full of energy, talkative, dramatic, and emotionally volatile. She wanted to spend lots of time with her husband, but he was always busy. She loved to relate to her family and felt that talking in therapy could help, as long as he listened and changed. In the years when the children were young, and her husband was working long hours and traveling, she made a life for herself taking care of the children and enjoying their companionship. Now that he worked as a consultant on his own schedule, she had hoped

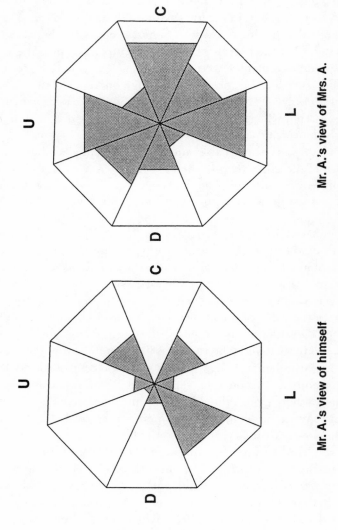

Mr. A.'s view of himself

Mr. A.'s view of Mrs. A.

FIGURE 7–1a. Interpersonal octagons from The CREOQ: Mr. A.
Key: U=upperness, L=lowerness, D=distance, C=closeness

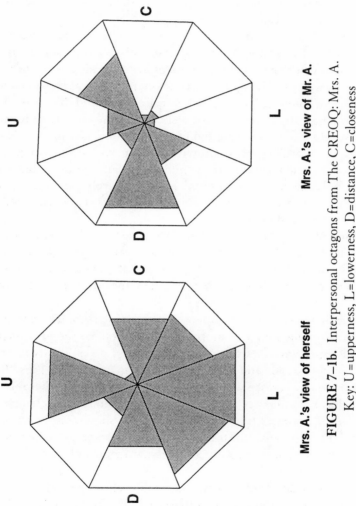

Mrs. A.'s view of herself   **Mrs. A.'s view of Mr. A.**

FIGURE 7–1b. Interpersonal octagons from The CREOQ: Mrs. A.

Key: U=upperness, L=lowerness, D=distance, C=closeness

for time with him, but he still put work first. He put their adult children before her, even though he had not been there for them when they really needed to be attached to him. In her family of origin, Mrs. A. had especially adored her father and the wonderful life he provided for the family in the country that she was from and that she missed. She remained close to her family despite the distance.

Mrs. A. wanted closeness. Mr. A. wanted distance. She wanted to be with him early in the evening, to talk together and be affectionate, but he wanted to read or work on the computer. Later in the evening, when he wanted to have sex with her, she was too tired to bother. She was angry about feeling neglected, but he did not accept her feelings. He said that she had no case, because his extra hours at work were spent protecting their investments. She would love to converse and party. He would like to read. She would love a vacation at a lively resort with dancing, whereas he would be happiest alone in a cabin. He saw their children in planned visits, while she talked to them on the phone at least once a day, yet rarely visited them. The A.'s agreed that he was low-key, never yelled, and never got upset, whereas she was "hotter" and louder.

Mrs. A. was perceived as a demanding woman who dominated by emotional volatility. Mr. A. was perceived as a remote, ungiving person with a stranglehold on his emotions who dominated by withholding himself. Each of them was simultaneously dependent on the other in unsatisfying ways.

While there are problems inherent in reducing complex relational characteristics to a diagram, the interpersonal octagon has the advantage of giving a picture of areas of complementarity and dissimilarity of relational styles for individuals and for couples in intimate relationships. The individual or couple can see where the problems lie, and the therapist can use the results to develop a symptom focus and to demonstrate change. A comparison of the clinical findings and the scores shown on the octagon suggests the conclusion that the test gives a useful corroborating picture of styles of relating, but it does not address the dynamic formulation of the internal object relationships.

Shaver and Clark (1994) predict that studies encompassing long-term day-to-day dynamics of romantic relationships will soon produce results to augment our understanding of how these pairings actually work. Perhaps this research will eventually yield a way of assessing the behaviors of all members of a family and their functioning as an attachment group.

Infant Brain Research

Schore (1994) reviewed the literature on infant brain development and integrated the findings from developmental psychology, psychoanalysis, neuroanatomy, and neurophysiology. He discovered that researchers in all of these areas are interested in adaptive regulatory mechanisms, from the molecular to the societal level. Studying in the transitional zone between these disciplines, he found evidence of demonstrable developments in brain structure and function that underlie the observable developmental shifts previously described at a behavioral level by Bowlby and Mahler. Neurophysiological shifts can now be demonstrated to correlate with the time periods of the practicing phase described by Mahler (1980). Schore emphasized that research shows that the infant brain is sensitive to and dependent upon the socioaffective environment for its development. Interaction with the caregiver mother in the first two years of life is particularly essential for the development of brain tissue, which is then growing at an unprecedented rate. The adult caregiver brain communicates with the immature infant brain through affective signals that release autonomic nervous system activity and neurochemical substances that promote the growth of brain tissue, all of which are the basis for the infant's automatic ability to signal affect and gradually to experience and communicate more complex emotions. Research has now shown that the communication of affect and the expression of emotion is a right-brain function.

The right hemisphere grows much more rapidly than the left and its functioning is dominant in the first year of life. Scientists are now able to document the right brain's role in the expression and regulation of affect and in the formation of high-affect, single-word speech, such as "No," "Mommy," "teddy," and "up," among others (Schore 1994). The right hemisphere is also dominant for the storage of self and object images and for autobiographical memory.

At first, the child's thought emerges as a fused, unpartitioned whole, and that is why the child communicates in the form of single words (Vygotsky 1988). We are fascinated by this finding, which is parallel to Fairbairn's hypothesis that the original ego is pristine, whole, and only later becomes divided by the force of experience. It suggests to us a right-brain form of early thinking that sorts experience into fused categories such as good and bad and accounts for the black-or-white quality of primitive object relations. We think also of a right-brain kind of memory for storing very early experience in an iconic form before the left hemisphere has developed sufficiently for speech to be available to support narrative memory storage, a function of the left brain.

In the first year of life the right hemisphere of the brain develops rapidly, especially in the orbitofrontal cortex (the part underneath and behind the eye) and in the proliferation of its connections to areas of the subcortex, especially to those parts of the brain that comprise the limbic system and the reticular formation. Through these connections, the right hemisphere deals with the expression, communication, and regulation of affect, and with arousal and motivation. But the connections form only if adequately stimulating and comforting interactions with a mothering person are continuously provided by the environment. The mother's regulatory functioning not only modulates the infant's internal state but permanently shapes the emerging self's capacity for self-organization (Schore 1994). The mother's responsiveness is always important, but especially crucial at critical periods. The infant is totally dependent on the mother for affect regulation at first, but later becomes capable of self-regulation. This capacity is exercised through developing brain structures in the orbitofrontal cortex, especially those in the right hemisphere. This part of the cortex forms the apex of the cortico-limbic system that governs all future affective states and the regulation of internal states.

The child is born with the capacity for cue discrimination. Responding to affects and visual cues like the mother's face or the expression in her eyes are survival mechanisms, just as surely as sucking and crying (Moore 1996). Cue discrimination improves with age and experience until, as a toddler, the child can rapidly scan the mother's face and read its expression.

Gaze interaction is a particular focus for the transmission of affect between the infant and the caregiver. The gleam in the mother's eye brings out a sparkle in her child's eye. The gleam in her eye is a result of her physiological arousal at the sight, sound, or smell of her infant. Her dilated pupils reflect the stimulation of her sympathetic nervous system. The dilated pupils then generate a wide-eyed response in her baby. At a neurochemical level, the ventral tegmental dopaminergic area of the brain is stimulated. The infant experiences a rush of endorphins and their opioid effect makes the infant's pupils dilate, which further stimulates its mother's maternal behavior. Neuroanatomists and neurophysiologists have provided us with a neurochemical basis for the eye-to-eye relationship.

By 1 year of age, infants are capable of sustaining high levels of arousal and joyful affect. High arousal, hyperactivity, high levels of exploratory behavior, and positive affect are characteristic of the practicing phase. All are functions of the frontolimbic cortex, whose circuitry has been stimulated by arousal sequences between infant and mother and whose growth is supported by increasing levels of dopamine (Schore 1994). Through affect, mothers mirror their babies' states of elation, build in healthy narcissism, and reinforce their interactions with the wider world.

These socioaffective transactions foster the further development and inter-connectedness of the orbitofrontal cortex with the anterior temporal cortex responsible for vision. A visuo-limbic pathway is created that permits the identification of familiar faces, and the connection between those images and the child's emotional response to them. Further identificatory sequences build more brain structure, until a schema of the face and the response to it can be held in the mind when the mother is absent. This internal affect-associated image is the basis both of attachment and object constancy, and the forma-tion of internal object relationships. In other words, it is the foundation of the self and its relation to the other.

When the infants are toddlers, physically capable of leaving their mothers to explore, they check back or return for emotional refueling. Mahler (1980) noted that toddlers who have gone off to explore on their own return to their mothers in a wilted state and that they perk up rapidly when they get emo-tionally refueled by interaction with the mother. The low-key infant is in a state of energy conservation under the influence of the parasympathetic ner-vous system. The mother, glad to see her child again, experiences arousal of the energy-exciting sympathetic nervous system. Just as these two systems are antagonistic to each other inside the person, in the interpersonal situation, the mother's sympathetic system response moves the infant from the parasym-pathetic mode to the sympathetic mode, in which pleasure is once again ex-perienced and healthy primary narcissism is established. The interaction regu-lates the infant's affect tone in the present moment and leads to structural change in the longer term (Tronick 1989). For instance, at the pathological end of the continuum, autonomic imbalance has been related to hyperactiv-ity, psychopathy, and autism (Porges 1976).

The toddler's refueling commonly occurs across a visual channel for com-munication. Along with mobility comes a new cognitive capacity to read the mother's expression. Toddlers scan for their mothers at high speed and can make affective contact with her eyes in a few seconds, sufficent to continue alone. This is an attenuated version of the earlier intense-gaze interaction, and it is the one now required as the mother moves away from a predominantly caregiving role to a socializing one.

By 4 months, the left hemisphere is at a comparable level of development to the right, and the frontal lobes have developed. Then the capacity for sym-bolic thinking occurs (Moore 1996). These findings seem to us to provide a physiological correlate for Klein's findings of the capacity for thinking of the mother as a whole object beginning at about 4 months of age. By the end of the second year the left hemisphere is sufficently advanced to permit speech that puts words together in sentences. Thinking can now be an effective way of modifying experience, anticipating consequences, and devising behavioral strategies. The left hemisphere supports the autonomy of the self.

Murray: Blank-Face Studies

When a normal mother in normal face-to-face interaction with her infant is asked to stop interacting in a lively way and suddenly sits impassively looking blankly at her baby, the baby begins to do more and more—laughing, cooing, looking away and back to catch her eye, reaching for her with rapid circling movements of the arms to get her to respond. Eventually the baby gives up, looks away from the mother with a depressed expression, and physically slumps. A minute or two of this can be hard for the normal mother to tolerate because she is geared to responding to the cues from her child, but the depressed mother does not look much different doing the test than she usually looks.

From these experiments we can see how much babies use cue discrimination to detect the tenor of a social situation, how hard they try to change the situation to meet their needs for an ongoing infant–mother relationship, and how much they are affected by the mother's mood and maternal attitude as interferences with her capacity to respond (Murray and Trevarthen 1985). These experiments provide evidence for the object relations point of view that the child looks for recognition; if the mother does not reflect the child's experience and interest in the mother, then the child becomes desperate, frightened, and finally depressed.

In a variation on the traditional blank-face studies, Murray (1988) then connected mother and baby to each other through a television hookup. In separate rooms, looking at each other's image on a screen and hearing each other's voice using microphones and speakers, the mother was asked to interact normally with her infant, but at this unusual distance. They had a period to learn how to connect and communicate with each other normally, using the television monitor linkup, and then it was taped. Then they saw a replay of the other from the previously filmed interaction. The mothers were not told that they were now being shown their babies on replayed videotape, and thought that they were engaged in a continued filmed interaction.

When faced with a video replay of their infants, the mothers got upset. Whatever they did, the baby's actions did not respond to the mother's efforts.

The mothers got anxious and showed an increase in expressed negative affect and behavior geared to getting the baby to respond, including telling the baby how to connect. Some blamed the baby for being out of synchrony with them, some blamed themselves, but none guessed what the problem was.

When faced with a video replay of their mothers, on the other hand, the babies looked away, darted glances occasionally at the screen, but did not attempt to interact or pull the mother into engagement as they had in the blank-face experiments. They did not protest toward the filmed version of the moving, lively face of the mother who was not actually present, as they had protested at the blank, still face of the mother who was actually there. It seemed that they knew that their mothers were not really there. Moore (1990) noted that the interactive avoidance behaviors shown by babies in Murray's studies at 6 to 8 weeks of age were identical to the disoriented behaviors of infants categorized by Main as disorganized/disoriented in the Strange Situation test at 12 and 18 months. This finding links the dissociative component from one study to the other, from infancy to toddlerhood, and indicates that there is an inbuilt capacity to respond to dissociated behavior with traumatic disengagement and dissociation.

In summary, we draw from Murray's work the finding that babies who think that they are held in their mother's mind will protest when she is not responding, but babies who get used to depressed mothers do not continue to protest. Babies are so sensitive to interactive cues that they know when the other is emotionally there or not, and whether she is totally inattentive or actively expressing useless concern. The baby's personality is a highly motivated, competent, proactive contributor to the mother–infant dyad, which in turn is memorialized in the baby's internal working model.

We agree with Stern's (1985) point that the relationship pattern created by a mother and her baby is a feature of the dyad, not of the individual. Mother and infant mutually influence the infant's self- and object-representations (Beebe and Lachmann 1988). The system is defined by both self-regulation and interactive-regulation processes (Beebe et al. 1997). We follow Beebe, Jaffe, and Lachmann (1993) in using a process and transformational model: the patterned sequence of interaction between mother and infant is represented by the infant, and changes over time. Object experience is not internalized as a replica of reality unaffected by the child's actions with the object. What is represented at the presymbolic level is *the dynamic interactive process*. Its state of ongoing regulation deals with highly charged affective moments and periods of low-key relating, tolerates disruption, and fosters repair (1997), which ensures that coordinated relating usually proceeds despite strain and even mismatch. What is presented to the child is not simply an object, but an object relation that comprises the actions of the significant other, the actions of the self, the affective regulation by both parties, and the relationship patterns that they engage in (Beebe et al. 1993). These early interactions constitute unconscious organizing structures as well as unconscious memory banks (Zelnick and Bucholz 1990).

Application to the Clinical Situation

Attachment theory has many clinical implications (Belsky and Nezworski 1987, Moore 1992, Slade 1996). In working with patients, we follow Bowlby's idea that the quality of maternal care draws forth specific attachment behaviors and characteristic ways of thinking, feeling, and remembering so as to secure the object and the self in relation to it. This recalls Fairbairn's idea of symptoms as arising from techniques for relating to the object by locating it at a precisely comfortable distance from the ego. We follow Main's (1995) idea that incoherent moments in the structure of the patient's narrative communicate unintegrated experience due to lapses in maternal preoccupation. Slips are not just the sneaking of id material past the censor: they are communications of unthinkable anxiety—what Bollas (1987) called the unthought known —and may signal the effect on psychic structure of early empathic breaks with the mother (Slade 1996).

Attachment theory changes the way we listen to patients' material, and how we interpret the transference. In addition to the content of the narrative, we listen to the structure of thought, we note the choice of iconic or verbal memory, and we process the effect of the communication on us. We listen for memories of attachments and we look for current secure and insecure attachment behaviors. Transference behavior may now be seen not just as a re-edition of past experience, but as a behavior geared to securing the therapist's commitment to providing a secure base. This ties in to Winnicott's concept of the safety-providing environmental mother from which we derived our concept of the contextual transference (see Chapter 3). And we recognize that the patient is an attachment object for us, as we are for the patients who are committed to their therapy with us. If, in terms of attachment theory, we accept that the greatest fear that the therapist faces is abandonment by the patient, then we can correct for those technical errors that arise from failed attempts to secure the therapeutic relationship.

To make full use of attachment theory ideas, however, we have to integrate them with a psychoanalytic perspective on intrapsychic structure—not to say that psychic structure forms from defenses against instinctual drives, but to give weight to the value of the infant's constitution. Unconscious fantasy is stimulated as a response to the attachment situation, further fuels the behavior, and then further affects the object. Although the infant cannot be held accountable for the maintenance of the relationship, the infant does contribute to the quality of the attachment relationship by the behaviors employed. The same mother can do much better with one infant than with another because of differences in constitutional factors such as temperament, cognitive ability, physiological maturity, resilience—and, we add, capacity for unconscious fantasy and unconscious communication. Similarly, the same therapist does better with one patient than another. Like mothers who have family and community support, therapists themselves need a professional relational context as a secure base from which to venture forth into the unknown of therapy. A secure therapist will do better with adults of the dismissive and preoccupied category than a therapist who is insecurely attached (Dozier et al. 1994).

If we apply these findings from attachment theory to the therapeutic relationship, then we see that therapy will have to go on long enough for the patient to build a relationship in which to re-experience old attachment patterns and develop new ones. We must conclude that the therapist who can provide a secure base and contain the unthought known will be the most effective. The literature on attachment is now our firmest research evidence of the importance of the quality of early relationships and the containing function of the mother, not only for early development, but for the passing on of patterns through the medium of the relationship with the next generation, and for the technique of co-creating healthy attachment patterns in a therapeutic relationship. In chapter 13, we show how attachment classification contributes to the way we listen, observe, and process experience during assessment and referral for therapy.

8

Chaos Theory and Fractals in Development, Self and Object Relations, and Transference

In the nineteenth century, scientific theories were aimed at simplifying the natural world to give an illusion of control of nature through knowledge of its laws. Theories tended to view biological phenomena as logical, predictable, linear systems, controlled by negative feedback that preserves the status quo. But nature defeats human attempts at control, because nature does not behave with the simplicity of a linear equation (Prigogine and Stengers 1984). For instance, as Briggs (1992) pointed out, "The equations traditionally used for calculating the gravitational attraction of celestial bodies work wonderfully when the planets are taken two at a time. But when the effect of a third object is added, the equations become unsolvable" (p. 51). Similarly, a problem in maintaining control and order was pointed to by engineers studying the efficiency of their machines. They found that, despite their expert calculations and fine design, their well-functioning machinery was subject to thermodynamic chaos anyway, because, when well-ordered hot molecules cool down, they lose their boundaries and wander about aimlessly.

Since then, scientists have become progressively more aware of the universality of chaos,[1] an unpredictable state of varying degrees of instability, from the utterly random to the relatively stable. Scientists are also aware that any observed state is influenced by the attitudes, cultural experiences, and previous learning of the observers. The field of study is changed by the very state of being observed. As we approach the twenty-first century, we see that nature

---

1. For further discussion of chaos theory, see Gleick (1987).

is too complex and unpredictable to be reduced to formulas, and scientists are never as objective as they wish. No matter how well formulas can document the cause and effect of some behaviors, accurate predictions are impossible, especially in the area of human experience, because of the infinite number of human factors such as constitution, environment, early loss, trauma, schooling, availability of therapy, and cultural influences, all interacting in the complex, holistic, dynamic system out of which personality forms.

Nonlinear Dynamic Systems

The natural world is essentially chaotic. Living and nonliving systems oscillate to and from chaos. Nature consists of nonlinear dynamic systems that are multifaceted, interdependent, and changing from chaos to order and back again. They receive positive feedback from the environment, respond, and adapt. They are sensitive to minor variations in the environment, especially at the moment of starting out. These sensitivities are also especially responsive at transitional moments. The human organism is a nonlinear dynamic system. Psychotherapy and psychoanalysis are nonlinear dynamic systems subject to the forces of chaos. Thinking of our work in this way usefully sets up an oscillation in our thinking that favors the perception of internal states and generates new ways of looking at experience.

In nature, the moments of transition from incomprehensible chaos to recognized order are the most instructive. In the human embryo, for instance, when the organism is starting out, there are critical periods of rapid growth and differentiation of cells when a stage-appropriate stimulus leads to a response that sets the course of development forward. If that moment passes without the necessary feedback, the opportunity for developing in the new direction is irretrievably lost, and the embryo continues its growth around a deficit. Chaos theory holds that dynamic systems are particularly sensitive to the conditions prevailing in the environmental niche in which they find themselves at the time of their origin.

From the random concatenation of phenomena and energies when the system cracks up into chaos or comes out of chaos, stable forms emerge in repeated patterns. The observer notes the emergence of structure and process out of chaos in one part of the system, followed by the return to chaos before a new level of order is achieved in another area. The system of structure and process in a rhythm of chaos, transition, and order may appear to be simple or complex at different times. As Briggs (1992) put it, "chaos and order are different masks the system wears: in some circumstances the system shows one face; in different circumstances it shows another. These systems can appear to be simple or they can be complex; their simplicity and complexity lurk inside each other" (p. 20) and so "paradoxically, the study of chaos is also the study of wholeness" (p. 21).

In studying this area mathematically, Euclidian geometry was found to be inadequate because it dealt in established lines and planes. Linear equations could encompass irregularity only by ignoring the parts of the whole that did not fit neatly into the equation, and resorting to approximations. Equations had to be nonlinear and they were found to be extremely sensitive to the tiniest change in the data. Nonlinear equations were then subjected to multiple reworkings by sophisticated computers. Mathematicians call this process *iterating the equation*, turning it back on itself over and over again, until the endpoint is reached when the equation may produce a stable, periodically returning, or randomly fluctuating number. Dynamic recycling may lead either to stability, periodicity, or chaos, and these outcome states may change depending on the conditions and the time of observation.

Order or Chaos: The Saddle Point

Chaotic dynamics are influenced by their sensitivity to initial conditions to oscillate in one direction, then another. Very slight differences in the starting point lead to major differences in the dynamic as it progresses in time and space. A split may occur in the dynamic so that now there are two dynamics instead of one. The dynamic may stabilize itself as one again or may continue to bifurcate. The outcome is determined by the activity of the saddle point. The *saddle point is the attractor* that attracts the dynamic system toward a value that takes the system into order, but it may equally well repel the system away from that value into chaos. The *homoclinic point is the place of transition* between stable and unstable dynamics. At the homoclinic point, the dynamic could go either way, depending on the activity of the saddle point. If the system self-organizes at the homoclinic point, the disorder is not eradicated, but remains as a latent potential for bifurcating. Even when it remains chaotic, it is a *deterministic chaos*, one that is unstable and unpredictable in which patterns appear and disappear but that has the potential for self-organizing. At the bifurcation there is still the potential for a return to order when two chaotic attractors in the bifurcated system merge to form one attractor of greater symmetry. In this way the dynamic can self-reorganize. If each bifurcation continues to bifurcate in an expanding cascade of bifurcations (or splits), the system goes into endless *entropic chaos* that cannot evolve into order (Briggs and Peat 1989, Field and Golubitsky 1992, Peitgen et al. 1992, Van Eenwyck 1977).

The Limit Cycle Attractor and the Torus

The pattern of repeated motion of a system is called an attractor. When motions repeat in the same, simple way, as in the back and forth movement of a swing or a pendulum, a *single point attractor* brings them to rest while a *limit cycle attractor* keeps them swinging. When the motion creates a recognizable orbit that leaves a predictably circular, or elliptical trace, the attractor takes the form of a *torus* which looks like a regular doughnut with a hole in the middle, often with an additional elliptical trace winding around it (Figure 8–1). It is a three dimensional figure created from plotting the movement of an attractor that revolves around an axis in relation to a number of variables. The torus captures the movement of a classical dynamic system attracted to and functioning in a state of stable, predictable functioning.

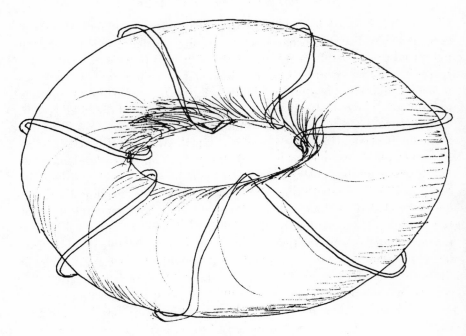

FIGURE 8–1. Classical torus

When the system breaks down or is exposed to variables that cause it to enter a new state, it becomes chaotic. Add the effect of another system for instance, and the original classical system is exposed to turbulence that rocks the boat. The classical system, affected by chaos nearby, moves toward a value that leads to a disturbance in its regularity. Then the newly chaotic system is attracted to a *strange attractor* that creates and follows a disorderly pattern, which, however, has features that are predictably irregular. When the movement of the system is plotted at the time of breakdown or transformation to a new state, it yields a different torus (see Figure 8–2). The torus looks like the long, twisted kind of doughnut showing folds and anomalous shapes where the hole is or was.

FIGURE 8–2. Folding and twisting occurring as the torus of an originally classical dynamic system interacts with another torus. (Generated by the Pyramid3D processor chip, copyright Tritech Microelectronics Inc. Used with permission.)

Cut a cross section through the torus that is exposed to a strange attractor and you find a relatively stable set of patterns in the center with less regular patterns on the outside (see Figure 8–3).

The Strange Attractor

Within a complex system of repetitive motion affected by many variables, such as the weather, the operative attractor is a *strange attractor*—a point that seems to be organizing the system when in fact it is the product of the organization of the system (Lorenz 1963). The behavior of the system governed by the so-called strange attractor cannot be predicted and yet when the equations for studying it are repeated often enough, it seems to tend toward a pattern. Tracked in successive moments, the attractor traces an orbit. Order comes out of chaos through the action of the attractor. "In more complex systems, attractors 'move' (in phase space), split, combine and recombine with others; they can also be graphed and comprehended as images or forms" (Spruiell 1993, p. 19). The pattern is then also the strange attractor that creates and reflects the predictably unpredictable form in which the system eventually settles. Magnify a small portion of the inside of a strange attractor and you find a pattern that is repeated at another place inside it. This self-similarity across time, place, and scale within the strange attractor pattern is typical of the chaotic system. This feature means that strange attractors qualify as *fractal*.

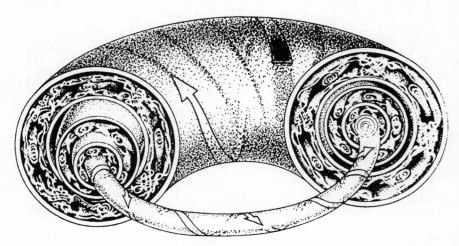

FIGURE 8–3. Cross section through a torus exposed to a strange attractor (Copyright Lucinda Tavernise. Used with permission.)

Fractal Geometry

To cope with measuring the new boundaries of dissolving chaos, Mandelbrot (1977) invented a new theory. He called it *fractal geometry* to reflect its application to the irregular fractured, fractional, fragmentary, fractionated, and refractory areas of experience resulting from dynamic forces. Fractal geometry consists of equations which, when iterated (turned back into themselves over and over), measure convoluted lines, patterns, shapes, and movements, like the Atlantic coastline or the crest of a wave (Simon and Simon 1995). Mandelbrot captured these immensely complicated forms in a two-dimentional image drawn by computer from the iterated equations. The resulting image that records phenomena whose complexity defies the usual categories of measurement is called a *fractal* (Mandelbrot 1982). To put it simply, a fractal is the footprint of a dynamic system. Fractal geometry captures the in-between, the world within a world, and the world between the known worlds.

Computer processing of iterated equations yields a picture of the edge of chaos in a striking fractal image called the *Mandelbrot set* (see Figure 8–4).

FIGURE 8–4. The edge of chaos from an image of the Mandelbrot set. Goddard Space Center.

Fractals are the images of stretching, folding, and unfolding. Briggs (1992) expresses the complexity of fractals when he writes that "fractals are images of the way things fold and unfold, feeding back into each other and themselves" (p. 23). And with this description, Briggs introduces the linked concepts of *fractal scaling* and *self-similarity*. "This means that as viewers peer deeper into the fractal image, they notice that the shapes seen at one scale are similar to the shapes seen in the detail at another scale" (p. 23). For instance, the branching of the limbs of a tree is echoed in the tracing of the veins in its leaf. Fractals are useful in giving us confidence in predicting the whole from looking at a small part. The deeper we look, the closer we attend to detail, the more we find. Greater detail brings greater understanding.

Through fractals, we are given to understand the law of nature in a different way and to respect the limits of our comprehension, control over natural forces, and capacity to predict natural phenomena. Chaos theory offers another way of understanding the development of the human organism in the relational environment and the culture. It helps therapists to appreciate the infinite variety of human behavior. It provides a basis for the clinical position of tolerating ambiguity, respecting the unknowable, and trusting that meaning will emerge. It suggests that we might usefully conceptualize our clinical stance as one of creating a strange attractor in the therapeutical space.

Fractal Scaling, Strange Attractors, the Transference, and Technique

Science discovers and measures what has already been sensed. Even to those who cannot understand the mathematical basis for them, fractals nevertheless make sense. Fine artists create an image that expresses more than its surface content. In the work of the Impressionist painter or the Pointillist, there is a world of color, shape, and texture in any square inch of the canvas. As Mandelbrot himself noted, the detail on the Paris Opera building in relation to its architecture is a fine example of fractal scaling. The part and the whole are in harmony in a dynamic relation. Art expresses worlds within worlds. Art is fractal.

The transference expresses worlds within the world of the therapeutic relationship. The continuity in form between the person, the body, the personality, the internal object relations set, and the transference is an example of fractal scaling. Transference is a fractal of the total personality. In keeping with fractal scaling, small shifts at that level give rise to major changes at the level of the overall personality. To put it another way, "nonlinear dynamic systems are extraordinarily sensitive to some very small alterations of variables" (Spruiell 1993, p. 36). The patient's internal object relationships refind their own form in the external world and in the person of the therapist. The dynamics of the unconscious flow between patient and therapist, sharing in the chaos of unconscious communication, create a new relational formation that is a combined fractal of the transference and countertransference.

Out of the chaos of the artist's creative process, and the patient–therapist experience of unconscious flow, emerges a coherent communication. Out of Shakespeare's *negative capability*, which Keats defined as the capacity for "being in uncertainties, mystery and doubt," emerges a brilliant, universal vision of humanity and the significance of our place within the cosmos (Keats, in Murray 1955, p. 261). Out of the therapist's negative capability emerges meaning drawn from the inner world without any "irritable reaching after fact and reason" (Keats, in Murray 1955, p. 261). The theory of chaos and fractal geometry sets down systematically what is already known. As Freud reportedly said, "the poet-natures have always known everything" (Wilder 1973).

What is the strange attractor that drives the system of the human organism?[2] Moran (1991) located it in the unconscious motivating fantasies which, "though themselves very simple underlying structures, become manifest in complex, multidimensional behavior" (Moran 1991, p. 18). From our perspective, the strange attractor is located in the internal object relations set. It guides the personality system to fill a shape that is then expressed in the form of external ways of relating to others, including the therapist in the transference. As Spruiell (quoted earlier) said, strange attractors move, shift, combine, and recombine, and give rise to images and forms. The internal objects split, combine with parts of the ego, and recombine following modifying experience with the external object. In partnership with ego and affect, the internal object gives rise to an internal image or object relationship that governs the form of the personality and its interactions with others.

Very small shifts in any realm of the internal object relations set produce changes in behavior toward the self and the other, both in development and in therapy. We agree with Moran that interpretations can be likened to frequent, well-timed perturbations that tend to push the system toward chaos and to which the human psyche is highly sensitive. We also see the transference as the strange attractor that is the product of and the organizer of the therapeutic experience. It gives meaning to the pieces of experience.

---

2. See Quinodoz's (1997) update on *strange attractors* and the measurable *tuning variables* that govern state-to-state transitions of psychic structures.

Galatzer-Levy (1995) tested the principle of self-similarity in his study of psychoanalytic process. Having found the process of a few minutes of analysis similar in form to the processes of an hour, of months, and of years, he concluded that a small sample of an analysis of one patient can be regarded as meaningfully representative of the total psychoanalysis. We need not get lost in mounds of analytic data for the sake of representing the truth. We can make a valuable contribution by focusing on one of the folds in the multilayered process of therapy.

The cross-section of the endopsychic situation viewed through the lens of the transference, is a fractal of the personality. The recreation of the internal object relations set as a joint personality or analytic third in the space between the analyst and the patient may be represented by the torus, a shape that captures the depth of the experience.

Lastly, we have looked for applications of chaos theory in psychoanalytic theory and technique prior to the popularity of chaos theory. In writing about the unconscious, Freud described a chaotic mass of seething impulses seeking a path for expression and tension release and connected to thought in only the most primitive primary process (1915b) . Out of the chaos of the id that knows no rules of time or place, order emerges in the form of the ego, governing by the rules of logic and secondary process. Freud tolerated the chaos of unconscious and conscious communication by *evenly suspended attention* and the patient led him to detect the order of the unconscious by *free association* (1912). Freud's (1901) study of parapraxes concerned the typological study of the areas in between.Winnicott's (1951) concept of the potential space, a space between self and other where fantasy, play, and creativity develop, recalls the typological study of the fold between recognized areas. The transitional object eases the chaos of transition. Similar to Bion, Jung (1953–1979) recommended tolerance of paradox to avoid forcibly reducing the unknowable to what is apparently known in order to attain a more complex perception of reality. Jung's concepts of symbols as the mechanisms of psychological growth by which the archetypes (dynamics of the system) influence the organization of the psyche into complexes that reflect more differentiated ego development or instinctually driven ego disorganization has parallels in the functioning of strange attractors in chaotic dynamics (Van Eenwyck 1977). Like Winnicott's transitional object, Jung's transcendent function uses a symbol to ease the transition from one state to another. Bion (1967, 1970), also writing before chaos theory was known, developed a theory of psychotic thinking based on patients' inability to organize experience, resulting in the splintering of experience, registered intrapsychically as bizarre objects and a splintered ego. His theory of normal thinking refers to the process through which the individual organizes experience out of chaos. He advised therapists to eschew memory and desire and to allow meaning to emerge from inside the clinical experience—that is, to allow the pattern to form itself in the interaction of two minds rather than imposing an organization that was already known but unlikely to be relevant to the current situation.

Chaos Theory and Development

Applying chaos theory to neuronal development, we find that the human organism is highly sensitive to its starting conditions. The most important starting condition is the affective attunement that the caregivers offer the infant. Born without sufficient cortical inhibition, the immature brain of the infant depends on the mother to be a regulating, calming, transforming object. It is as if the adult brain programs the immature brain through pathways developed during arousal sequences of high affect. The beginning of life creates the blueprint for the organism's mode of functioning in internal and external dimensions throughout the life cycle. The first months of life are defining. Like the human embryo, the infant brain continues to build order out of chaos at specific moments of transition into increasingly complex areas of development. The infant brain at birth has arrived at its present state after negotiating specific critical phases in the growth of the embryo in the uterus. After birth, the infant brain continues to develop in stages over critical periods of growth and differentiation that are sensitive to and dependent upon environmental influence. Social and emotional encounters with the environment through the agency of the mother stimulate and fine-tune the neuronal circuits that mushroom at some critical periods and require pruning when their function becomes obsolete at the next critical period.

Brain structure in the infant organizes, disorganizes, and reorganizes in the light of environmental influence at critical periods. Postnatal neural development proceeds in leaps, halts, and bounds by a chaotic rapid profusion of neurones in tandem with their destruction. At critical periods, dendrites (the neural tissue that receives messages from the neurones) and synapses (the connections between neurones and dendrites across which messages pass) rapidly multiply. The profusion of these cells is balanced by *parcellation*, a process of elimination in which axons compete for survival, cells are programmed to die when their presence is no longer adaptive, and the overgrowth of synapses is pruned back so as to shape the emergent brain structure. The ultimate prevailing pattern determines the neuronal structure and the competence of the excitatory and inhibitory neuronal pathways. This shaping of ongoing neural structure and function occurs according to a series of timed sequences in interaction with the environment. Neural development, especially in the right hemisphere at first, leads to behavioral communication of affect that calls forth from the caregiver specific responses of a soothing or stimulating quality at specific times (Schore 1994). The key neuronal connections have to be evoked at the proper time by the mother as the appropriately stimulating and modulating object. If either mother or baby misses their appointment, as it were, by chance, neglect, trauma, or faulty genetic programming, a disorder of regulation results (Grotstein 1994c). If they keep their appointment, neural maturation is secured and jump-starts the transition to the next growth spurt.

In summary, the appropriate sequence of interaction with the care and concern of the caregiver is critical for pulling infant neural development out of chaos and into a stable state of order through the selective establishment of further neuronal development (Schore 1994). For more detail on Schore's (1994) findings, see Chapter 7 on research contributions to object relations theory.

Fractal Geometry and Object Relations Theory

Applying chaos theory and Mandelbrot's ideas on fractals to personality development, we note a correspondence between fractal geometry and object relations theory. We see fractal similarity between the societal and the intrapsychic levels of experience. Society consists of families. The person is part of a family. The personality is a part of the whole person and the internal object relationship is a part of the whole personality. The internal object relationships in dynamic relation are fractals of the personality. Each dream is a fractal of the personality, of the transference, and of the course of the analysis. (We illustrate the dream as a fractal in Chapter 26 of Part II on clinical practice.)

Look at the Mandelbrot set (Figure 8–4) superimposed on David Scharff's revised schematic of Fairbairn's endopsychic situation (Figure 3–1) that takes into account the complexity of poles of relating by interpenetrating ego and object (Figure 8–5).

The Mandelbrot set can be viewed as an elaborate amplification of David Scharff's diagram, a more graphic and intricate illustration of the complexity and inextricability of self and object built up in layers by repeated interactions at different developmental levels. But it is still a fanciful application

FIGURE 8–5. Fairbairn's endopsychic situation superimposed on the Mandelbrot set.

of the concept because this image was derived from the study of space, not personality. Yet it leads us to think that, if some research psychologist could devise a questionnaire that measures affect regulation, perceptions of self and other at various levels of experience, and ways of relating to self and other, and then were to process the data by computer in a nonlinear iterating equation, this is the sort of picture of personality that would emerge.

Out of the chaos of early organismic reality (genotype) and experience with the environment (phenotype) emerges psychic structure. The chaos is a mixture of neuronal profusion and destruction, hormonal shifts, sensations of hunger, thirst, deprivation, satisfaction, warmth, cold, pain, comfort, vibration, and position, new affective experiences, and recurring personal interactions with the caretakers. Interactions span the forms of order and chaos. Some of them are planned, predictable, and stable, as in good, reliable at-home parenting, while others are periodically expectable, such as the return of the working parent. Some parenting interactions create a low-intensity background of arms-around, good-enough environmental mothering that promotes going-on-being, while others involve eye-to-eye relating, and sustained gaze interactions that dominate the foreground and challenge the infant to a state of intense arousal for new learning, and still others are randomly fluctuating, such as the mother's mood in the short term, or the size of the sibship, or the effects of divorce in the long-term. Out of all this chaos, order, and the transition between them, emerges a pattern of experience that gives a sense of personal meaning.

Object relations theory holds that experience with the external object in the chaos of early infantile experience is taken into the personality. Random, disorganized experiences can require a strong repressive counterbalance that promotes reorganization, reintegration of parts, and growth, just as confusion can stimulate clarity of thinking. Satisfactory experience remains in the central self, and intolerable experience is split off and repressed in unconsciousness as the rejected object. The repressed rejected object bifurcates into an exciting and a rejecting object. And not only object content is repressed. A part of the ego is repressed with the object. Exciting and rejecting objects are connected by affects to repressed exciting and rejecting parts of the ego. Ego, object, and affect together create a dynamic system of parts in relation, called the *internal object relationship*. The rejecting object relationship further represses the exciting object relationship, and both of them strive to return to consciousness in the central self. Here we have a view of the self as a cybernetic system of parts all in dynamic relation to the whole.

But sometimes the chaos is so great that normal mechanisms of repression are overwhelmed by trauma. The personality resorts to primal repression in order to encapsulate painful experience, and dissociation to avoid feeling the pain and fear of the moment or recalling them in memory. Just as there are gaps inside star clusters and more clusters inside the gaps, the traumatized human personality develops traumatic nuclei because of primal repression, and gaps in the psyche because of dissociation. Inside the nuclei are pointed fragments and gaps. Inside the fragments are gaps. Inside the gaps are sharp pieces of encapsulated experience (Hopper 1991, J. Scharff and D. Scharff 1994).

Order and Chaos in the Development of the Self and Its Object Relations; A Clinical Example from Child Therapy

Lindy Jones was 6½ years old and in first grade. She was suffering from selective mutism, depression, anxiety, and difficulty in relating to anyone outside the family, including other children and teachers at her all-girls school. Her language development was normal, reading ability and school performance were up to grade level, but she was excessively shy, inhibited, and slow to process her work at school, while at home she had violent outbursts at her mother and wrote hate notes to her. It was when Lindy told her parents that she was extremely unhappy with her life and felt utterly sad that they brought her for individual therapy. The course of this therapy is more fully described in *Object Relations Child Therapy* (J. Scharff in press).

In the early phase, Lindy spoke to me (JSS) only twice, both times very softly: once to tell me that she had lost a tooth, and once to tell me how many children had come to her birthday party (far fewer than to her envied brother's). I noted that loss and critical points of transition in development were triggers for her use of speech. Other than on those occasions, the sessions continued in painful silence. Worse than that was Lindy's utter passivity. Although she came in to her sessions willingly, Lindy could sit on the couch for the entire session saying and doing nothing or moving her fingers and feet to make tracings in the air around her. They reminded me of the Brownian movement of molecules that are being heated. I could not detect a pattern in these movements. I was torn between trying to talk to her about my impressions, not so much to give meaning to her experience (at which I could only guess), but to give her the idea of therapy communication. I alternated between engaging with her by mirroring her occasional finger-play and foot kicking, letting her be, and offering her a jump-start to get moving in therapy. I had no idea what was going on and I longed to get the therapy going so that I could get out of the chaos of not-knowing.

I looked for something for Lindy's fingers to do to communicate with me. I took some clay, gave her half of it, and worked the rest myself. This was a breakthrough. From now on she communicated to me in the form of clay sculptures. She eagerly initiated the activity herself, always setting up her worktable in the same place at my feet. This went on for two months, Lindy carefully sculpting shapes of different sizes that looked like a family of meticulously well-formed doughnuts of the twisted kind and I commenting on how they related to each other and what concerns they might reflect. Each doughnut looked to me like a torus, and I was content to think that we were creating this shape of her experience in the play space between us. All my remarks were received in silence and any validation for my comments was completely nonspecific and existed only in the continuance of her thematic play. I drew sketches of her sculptures as a way of letting her know that I had seen what she had shown me and that I was looking for a message and a theme in their developing forms (Figures 8–6 through 8–22).

The only words that Lindy spoke were to ask me if she could use the bathroom, and so I regarded her need to urinate as a focus of intrapsychic conflict that broke out of the play format. I noted that it usually occurred when she was playing with the pointed clay tool and poking it into the clay, or when she was making long, phallic-shaped objects. Later, her parents told me that when she was 4 years old she had been unusually upset at seeing the doctor give her baby brother a shot in his buttocks, and talked about continuing fears of someone hurting their baby. Their information reinforced my way of understanding her play and her bathroom breaks as a repetition of trauma and an attempt at recovery of missing parts.

I was glad of a guiding principle and I used it, perhaps to the point of overemphasis, because I was uncomfortable with the chaos of her silence. I looked too eagerly for verbal explanation and tried to force order out of chaos. While I think that my remarks had validity, I became convinced of a more chaotic interpretation. I think that the pointy things, the holes that she poked in the clay, the marbles that she buried in the clay, and the splitting of masses of clay and their fragmentation, spoke of her ego's overwhelmed but not psychotic response to trauma by resorting to encapsulation of sharp experience, splintering and fragmenting of other experience, and the evacuation of pain leading to gaps in the psyche. The injection given to her brother may have been additionally traumatic because of trauma that Lindy herself sustained from repeated blood tests during her first week of life.

After six months of therapy, Lindy's mother came in to see me for her monthly parent session. She said that she and her husband were pleased that Lindy had stopped writing hate notes to her, seemed less depressed, and was doing much better. Her mother went on to tell me what Lindy had told her about her clay sculpting and the crazy things her dumb doctor said. Her mother said, "Lindy said to me, 'Mom, you know how some people see things in the clouds? Well, Dr. Scharff sees things in clay like others see them in clouds. She thinks that clay can represent feelings, but I think mainly it's all ridiculous. And another thing, every time I go to the bathroom, she's gonna talk about penises. I think she is stupid.' Then she told me that she had begun by making clay mushrooms and made up a game about that and then she made muffins and cupcakes in various colors and then named them according to the colors. She said, 'Dr. Scharff said that I liked cooking with the clay because it made me feel close to Mommy, but it's just that I like making doughnuts.' What really came across to me was Lindy's feeling that her talking was not desired or required, and the way she reacts to speech is it paralyzes her; so don't speak."

I took her mother's advice about saying less to Lindy on the lines of the possible meaning of her play, a useful move on my part, at least for the time being.

Now Lindy's play followed a sustained theme and moved into an abstract level of expression. She took all the separately colorful doughnuts and blended them into a large ball of clay. The colors streaked together and finally became a dull gray mess. They were twisted together in a crude twisted doughnut shape with ribbons of clay lying around them (Figure 8–6). I thought of the torus exposed to a strange attractor.

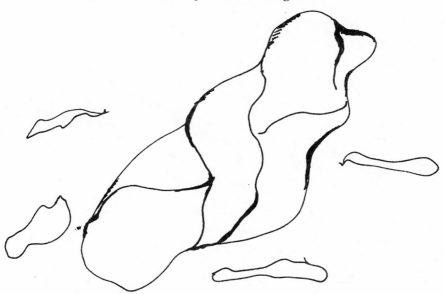

FIGURE 8–6. Original, inchoate mass of clay.

By her bodily responses to my offers, she made it clear that I was not to play with her, but that I was supposed to attend closely to what she was doing. If I felt excluded and turned away, she stopped playing and waited for me to turn back in her direction. My presence was crucial but my words and my participation were unwanted. Accepting this role, I was witness to a remarkable unfolding of order out of chaos.

Lindy moved the clay around, kneaded it, pulled pieces off it, and reattached them to the main mass. She stuck the tools into the mass and tossed it around. She created a huge tunnel in the clay, and subsequently many smaller burrowings into the body of the clay. It always looked a mess of unformed matter, somewhere between fecal and inchoate, with holes in it. I thought of the unconscious with gaps in it. She began to separate the mass into large pieces, squashed them together into a mass again, and stuck it with tools that sported clay ribbons (Figure 8–7).

Then she took a marble and buried it in one of the cavities in the clay, separated the clay into two masses, and connected them by one of the tools. The other tool was balanced on top of it and weighted with clay at its ends so that the tools and clay appeared to be in equilibrium (Figure 8–8). I thought of the buried marble as an encapsulation. I thought of the total structure as a moment of order and balance coming out of chaos.

FIGURE 8–7. Re-formed mass of clay with holes, tools, and ribbons.

FIGURE 8–8. Mass of clay with holes, tools, ribbons, and buried marble.

My comments were simply that it looked to me as though she was working intently with questions of exploring ways of getting inside the body of the clay, sometimes roughly, sometimes gently, and that she was looking for ways of connecting separate parts. If she went to the bathroom after poking with the tool, I tended to comment on the possibility of the sharp, pointy object causing feelings in her bottom that led to the need to go to the bathroom.

A month later, Lindy made a sculpture consisting of figures of eights looped around the clay modeling tool so that it looked like a tree of eights on top of each other (Figure 8–9).

FIGURE 8–9. Tree of eights.

Then she merged the pieces at the bottom of the tree into a mass into which she made a tunnel that she kept looking into. The tunnel reminded me of the birth canal (Figure 8–10).

Suddenly it came to me that Lindy must be 8 on her next birthday. I asked if this was so, and she surprised me by replying that she would be eight on her next birthday, on March 8th. I said that I remembered that her birthdate was 1978, and so I thought that her sculpture must be a way of thinking about her birth. She did not confirm or refute this idea, but she looked pleased, and the play moved on. She took the pencil and broke the circles of the eights (Figure 8–11).

Lindy added the broken circles of clay to the lump around the tunnel, and returned the clay to its original inchoate mass (Figure 8–12).

Now she worked on separating pieces off the mass. Forms appeared and transmogrified into something else. Small balls of clay were lined up in alternation with the tools (Figure 8–13).

The tools were removed and the balls were then gradually amassed to create a floor (Figure 8–14). I thought of isolated capsules of experience being merged to create a floor for her ego development.

Lindy built a wall around the floor and it looked to me like an enclosure for animals. She took some bright blue clay and made a dog. I copied her dog and she included my dog in her game. I felt encouraged that an image of an interpersonal situation was developing, but my attempt to cre-

FIGURE 8–10. Tunnel.

FIGURE 8–11. Broken circles.

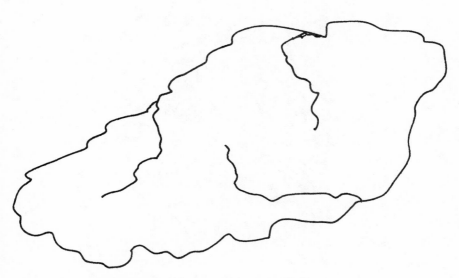

FIGURE 8–12. Return to the inchoate mass.

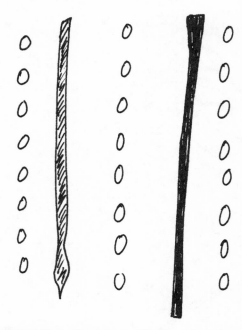

FIGURE 8–13. Lines of balls and tools.

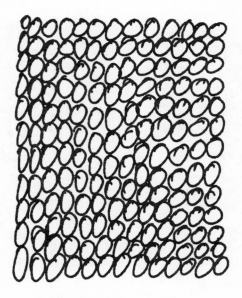

FIGURE 8–14. Floor.

ate a dialogue between the dogs failed. They looked at me, but they did not interact with me (Figure 8–15).

The dogs were put in large collars, perhaps to control them (Figure 8–16).

The walls of the enclosure were cemented over with more clay and smoothed with sensuous stroking movements (Figure 8–17).

FIGURE 8–15. Enclosure with dogs looking out.

FIGURE 8–16. Dogs with collars.

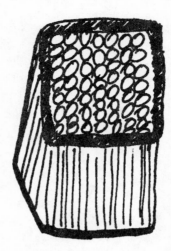

FIGURE 8–17. Enclosure with high, strong, smooth walls.

The repeated stroking made me think of masturbatory excitement, the walls might represent the boundaries around feelings and wishes, and the collars suggested the admonition to control the urge to masturbate.

The walls were then disassembled (Figure 8–18) to create a long ribbon of clay that stretched from the animals to me (Figure 8–19). The solid boundaries between self and other were giving way to a more fluid relatedness.

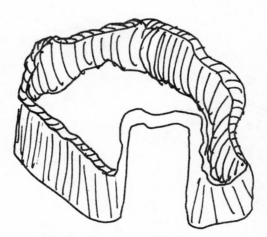

FIGURE 8–18. Walls breaking down.

Window

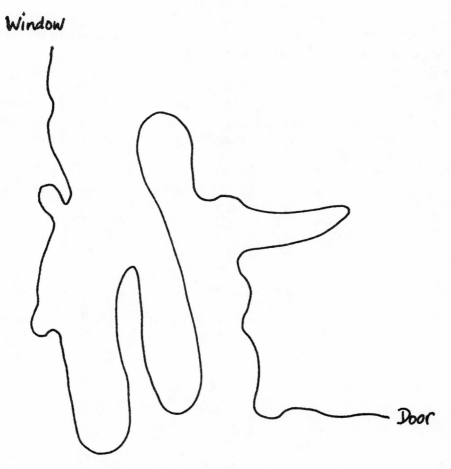

Door

FIGURE 8-19. Ribbon of clay from window to door.

I measured the ribbon by pacing. It was 40 feet in length, and I said that it was the path between Lindy and her animals and me. It was not easy to coil up the ribbon of clay for use again the next day, and I asked if she would like me to help her. I was shocked when she said, "Yes." She was actually relating to me. The animals were dispensed with as the clay from them was merged into the ribbon. I had wanted to think that the animals were symbolic of sexual and aggressive feelings, but I now saw them as a facsimile of symbol formation, easy to dismantle without a loss. The real play was at a much more primitive level.

The clay ribbon now functioned as a path from the window to the door along which she advanced a pair of marbles. At the end of the ribbon, the marbles reached a boundary of two pencils. Next, two pencils and two modeling tools were placed to create three alleys into which the marbles could be rolled on the floor, or dropped from the height of the arm of the couch. Lindy now covered the marbles with the gray clay. Just as it looked as if meaning was about to emerge from chaos again, Lindy dismantled the clay into lots of pieces that lay scattered on the floor in a discarded array of chaos (Figure 8–20).

Then, next to the scene of clay chaos, she fetched some long blocks, pencils, and marbles in a highly purposeful way. It was clear that she had an idea. She used the blocks to create better alleys into which the pencils, tools, and marbles were all aimed. Her focus was now on the alleys, and particularly the center alley. She used one of the remaining rope-like pieces of clay to whip the marbles and pencils into place in the center alley (Figure 8–21).

It looked as though she was trying to get them to align in a certain way to make a desired image. Just before the image became coherent, I could see that this was a rudimentary face, perhaps as a child tries to remember the elements and place them in the memory of the face of the loved one.

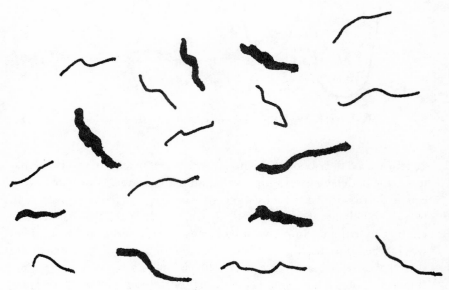

FIGURE 8–20. Fragmented clay.

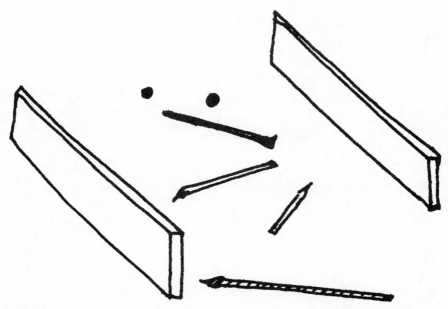

FIGURE 8–21. Marbles and pencils and tools in an alley of wooden blocks.

Finally, Lindy got some more blocks to create a firm outline, and balled up most of the pieces of dismantled clay ribbon and put them to the side, but she kept some to create features for the face and some to twist into a long ponytail (Figure 8–22).

The rest of the month was spent playing with this face. She saved the clay mouth, nose, eyeglasses, and ponytail, and put away the blocks and the clay-covered marbles at the end of each session. Then she quickly re-assembled the face daily. She removed the clay from the marbles and put them inside the clay glasses. With bright marble eyes, the face now looked awake and aware.

I said that out of the chaos of clay and lost animals a person had been born. Lindy went on to play a game of dropping the eyes into the face from the height of the couch, and showing pleasure when they fit properly into their glasses. It seemed to me that this play demonstrated the emergent self (Stern 1985). Lindy was now speaking to me a little bit around the setup and cleanup of the game. I felt as if she had been born into the therapeutic space. I would like to end my report here, where I felt hopeful that she might be able to relate to me now that she had arrived.

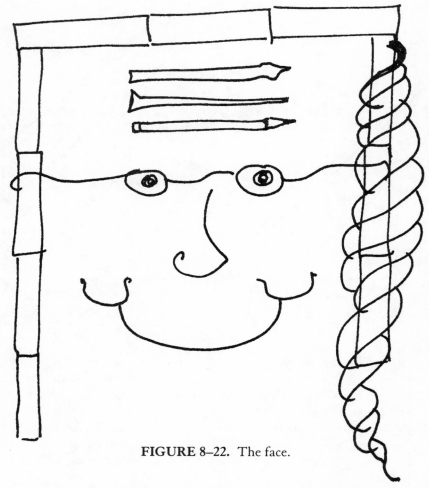

FIGURE 8–22. The face.

But it was not to be. As my vacation approached, we fell into chaos again. I was disappointed when Lindy did not return to the clay face game. She wrote to me in a hieroglyphic code that I could not read, but later figured out to be the letters of her name. So I thought that she might be angry that I was leaving and worried that I would forget her. She responded to these interpretations with further play communications that I could not make sense of. Then she wrote in number code so that I had even less chance of understanding. She scribbled over everything that she had made. All I could say for sure was that her thematic play was completely interrupted. I felt sad for her, and frustrated.

When I resumed with Lindy, she continued scribbling over her drawings, as if there had been no interruption. She pursued the same play day after day as before, but now it was completely incomprehensible. Her capacity for sustaining an activity was intact, but I had trouble detecting the theme. Was she upset that I had been away? She did not validate my comments. I had no idea what she was trying to tell me. I was in the dark. Nonsense words abounded. From squinting at backwards writing, I might be able to disentangle a phrase, but no explanation followed as to what the phrase meant. The main theme seemed to me to be that I should not know what was going on. We had returned to chaos again. I felt anxious and defeated.

Later, out of this chaos emerged a transference relationship in which she played the part of a punishing contemptuous teacher while I was the idiot child trying to please the teacher and getting everything wrong, all of our transactions communicated in the hard currency of paper and pencil. Then each paper would be reused and torn into fragments for further reuse until we were now working in a trail of paper chaos. I often felt like tidying up, putting papers in a folder, throwing out the trash and supplying fresh paper, but I soon learned that I had to bear the chaos for the point to emerge at her point of readiness.

We had been through chaos with clay, now we were in paper chaos. I had an image of living inside her brain at a stage when the dendrites and neurones were in a state of profusion prior to the pruning that would shape the development of the right and left hemispheres. I remembered reading that plenty of socioaffective experience with the caregiver stimulates the growth and the shaping of the neural structure (Schore 1994). I saw my role as simply providing a willing partner for her in the chaotic field, responsive to her affective communications, translating them into narrative form, and waiting for the next development of meaning out of chaos. Occasionally out of that chaos emerged a sentence stunning in its clarity and ordinariness. I am glad to say that the occasions for speech increased as time went on.

This example from a child's therapy is described in brief here to illustrate the fractal nature of play, transference, and internal object relations. The development of self and other were retraced in the play, a fractal of the transference, which is itself a fractal of infantile structure formation, separation, and individuation. As the therapeutic relationship developed greater resilience for bearing chaos, the sadomasochistic transference emerged, a fractal of the negative oedipal relationship. Play, transference, internal object relations, and actual relationships show self-similarity.

There we have to leave this child and her therapist as they toss around together in a sea of chaos with increasingly frequent stops on islands of clarity.

Increasing the Level of Complexity

Most of the research findings of object relations, attachment, and infant development come from study of the dialectic between mother and infant, while the corresponding clinical findings come from infant psychiatry, infant observation, or from clinical experience in the therapeutic dyad of individual therapy or analysis.

Further information comes from couple and family therapy, where we find a similar interaction between dyadic subgroups of spousal partners, or parent and child pairs. Bion's concept of container/contained in the mother–infant relationship is the prototype for interaction between spouses in the emotionally and physically intimate situation of marriage. The internal object relationships of a husband interact with the internal object relationships of a wife through mutual projective and introjective identification so as to form a two-person dynamic system. But the dynamics of individual therapy or marital pairs are insufficient to address the complexity of human interaction. Human behavior cannot be reduced to the study of the dialectic, because most people are raised in the group context of the family. As Briggs (1992) said of the study of two planets, when you add a third object to the field of study, the level of chaos increases. As more members are added to the family, and again after divorce and remarriage when two families are blended, the potential for interaction at the conscious level increases exponentially while at the unconscious level it approaches infinity. The firstborn enters a very different dynamic system, with more interactions in the form of order than the third child, born later into the more chaotic family with parents who have become less anxious about controlling their child's environment. The chaos that the girl child experiences without the penis as a ready focus for identity is of a different order than the anxiety that the boy faces.

In the following chapter we develop the concept of the inextricable nature of self and object. As we expand our views to include the implications of findings from couple and family therapy, we enter another chaotic area, the transition between modalities. In Chapter 9, we hope to present the fruitful aspects of a sojourn at that boundary.

9

The Interpenetration
of Self and Object

In this chapter we examine the central developmental patterns of the relationship between self and object, which we hold to be the strange attractor organizing the chaos of human psychology. The complexity of mutual influence and concern for self and other in the external dimension, and self and object in the internal dimension, develops as a fractal of the total personality, itself a fractal of the family. In this fractal scaling, aspects of personality functioning express larger behavioral, social, and cultural phenomena. In the same way, neurotic symptoms are similar to overall character patterns. When two personalities are interrelated, behavior in one can organize behavior in the other. The internal object relations set of one member of a couple acts as a strange attractor organizing the behaviors and, subsequently, the psychic structure of the other.

We are all born with the potential to relate. Deprived of the opportunity to relate, we wither. But what we require of the people with whom we have the most intimate relationships is not merely that they respond to us, but that they care for us by holding us in mind. When we look at them or talk to them, we want to see ourselves mirrored in them not by an impersonal reflection, but by a responsiveness to us which shows that we matter to them. What we each want is to matter to others who matter to us (D. Scharff 1992).

This principle holds true of all intimate relationships—whether they be ones that span many years, or intimacies of the moment such as those that occur in a brief but intense encounter during a plane trip or a vacation. It also holds true in psychotherapy. We do matter to our patients: they come to discuss the most intimate and important aspects of their lives and their personal difficulties. And, although psychotherapists have hidden the fact from themselves for a hundred years, our patients do matter to us in important ways even though our relationship to them is limited by a professional set of boundaries. It is only through our work with our patients and clients that we can realize our professional desires and ambitions. Through their growth and responsiveness, we realize our worth in our treasured vocation. Professionally, we can do nothing without them. Beyond the enormity of the fact that we rely on them for our income, and despite the sometimes unpleasant fact that we are at their beck and call, we owe everything to our patients. Without them we do not exist.

Clients and patients come to us because of problems in loving and relating that stem from the frustration of their fundamental need for relationships during the vicissitudes of development. The relationship between patient and therapist is at the center of the therapeutic field, just as the relationship between the growing child and parents is at the center of development. In the therapeutic relationship, the interchange of transference and countertransference forms the medium through which intimacies are exchanged, understood, and modified. Transference and countertransference are the clinical vehicles of projective and introjective identification which form the highway for unconscious communication in all intimate relationships (see Chapter 11). We will examine many instances of transference–countertransference exchange in the clinical section of this book. Here we will give one example from David Scharff's work with a transference–countertransference dynamic that will provide a shared clinical base from which to explore the theoretical and developmental basis for the interdependency of self and object which characterizes our object relations approach to therapy.

Albert: Interdependency of Self and Object

Albert is a 35-year-old man. His parents are quite devoted to him, but his mother's relation to him is compromised by her aloofness, while his father is rather tentative and frightened of danger. Both were traumatized by their early years in large families that sustained damage. They have chosen to have a small family for whom they can provide security to avoid a repetition of trauma in this generation. Their love is extensive, but their emotional range is limited.

Albert's link to me goes back to when he was an adolescent, and this made him special to me (DES). He is one of only two patients that I have known for so many years and from such an early age, and the only one I have seen over a period of twenty years. At 15, when I was just out of residency, he was a 1970s counterculture youth. A brilliant student in history, especially of those aspects not on the curriculum, he left the public high school to attend an alternate school, then dropped out of school, and taught nursery school. At this supposedly enlightened preschool, nudity and sexual curiosity were encouraged—fostering conditions that we would now see as abusive and reportable. His dreams repeatedly idealized a young girl with whom he had little actual relationship. Eventually he left therapy, after some improvement, to go to a slightly offbeat but rigorous college and, although socially isolated, he did well academically. He went from there to get a Master's degree in literature and history. He took a job teaching high school while his quirky adolescent interests matured into scholarly pursuits. As a hobby, he investigated overlooked aspects of human experience, including the treatment of themes of homosexuality and perversion in ancient history and literature. After six months of teaching, he experienced panic about being drawn sexually both to a married male faculty colleague and to a male student. He ran from the high school. That was when he asked to see me again for the first time since his junior year in college. He was now 32.

In an early session soon after resuming therapy, he had reported a dream in which he was fleeing some "redcoats" by floating downriver on an oar. He remembered, and subsequently frequently quoted back to me, my interpretation that I was the redcoat because of an association to the bright red chair I always sat in, and that he was riding to safety on a penis. There were frequent instances of his latching on to an interpretation and doing it to death, but this is the most vivid. It was typical of him to take my concern and my comments and turn them into a disembodied phallic object in a way that left me feeling useless. In retrospect, I can see that part of the reason for his doing so was to tease me with the homosexual connection in the dream and in my impulsive interpretation.

I can see the elements of evidence for my comment in his imagery and in my assessment of his developmental level, but as the moment had passed I could no longer remember quite where I got the conviction for making the interpetation. Its main meaning was that he rode my interpretation downriver and floated it back to haunt me. It was one of many interpretations that he held on to and brought back to me to my eventual dismay. Anything pithy I might say would run a particular danger. He would seize on it and it would become "the interpretation." That is to say, he would be so influenced by some of what I said that I could almost see him take it in and become characterized by it. Comments that I thought of as potentially generative were made to seem at once unduly phallic and yet impotent to effect change. Through this process, I became embarrassed by this unwanted power over his views of himself. I became wary of saying anything in case it became memorable.

While inhibiting what I might have to say, I was frequently interested in what Albert had to say. For instance, I was tracking the ambiguous bisexual identification in which he thought of himself at times as a girl. I was impressed by his erudite descriptions of sexual attraction between men and boys in classical Greek vase-painting, philosophy, and drama. This fit with his sexual interest in younger boys, which he had acted on in childhood and adolescence, and for which he had a continuing proclivity that made me so uncomfortable that I once had to warn him that acting on his feelings would require legal reporting to protect both him and the child. Again what I said carried tremendous power. He stopped acting on the feelings, but I worried that despite discharging my ethical duty I had contaminated our work by suppressing his talking freely to me.

Albert had a girlfriend with whom he had lived during graduate school, several close male friends he made in adolescence and college, and one or two couples he felt close to. He rarely saw any of them. He had distant relations with two women he had had friendships with. He had a young niece and nephew whom he loved and felt on a par with, but he felt so stirred sexually by them that he had distanced himself from them rather than act on his impulses.

Albert decided to leave high school teaching for business, a choice designed overtly to support him and allow him to move from therapy to psychoanalysis four times a week. After three years, Albert's analysis with me was completely stalled. He lay silent on the couch, he felt stuck, and he destroyed all of what I said and most of what he thought. He knew that his aim was to destroy my intention of helping him. He said that helping him would be for me, not him. I felt like giving up on him, and I told him that I was considering recommending to him that he stop. When I gave up my own aim for his analysis, Albert was able to find his own therapeutic ambition, to want something from me for himself. Albert came to life slowly but definitely, saying that he did not, in the end, want me to give up, and that he wanted to try again—in his own way. He decided that he preferred to sit up and to resume therapy. I agreed to his proposal that we meet twice a week. He began to respond more to my comments, and he resumed bringing in dreams and material from his vast reading. He gave a more vivid picture of his isolation and his occasional, usually dead-ended, interactions with others. Once again he brought in material from his blocked sexuality, his ambiguous sexual identification, and the longing for love that underlay these issues.

After about eight months in the new therapy arrangement, Albert entered a more animated phase. He seemed to be teasing me about his coming to life again. He dangled pieces of the transference just out of view as he brought in a dream or a story of his relationship to someone else, say, one of his sisters or the 19-year-old girlfriend he met at the community college where he was teaching. At times over the weeks before the session reported below, he had retreated from my interpretations, especially those linking the two of us, and had sunk out of reach, but never so far in the depths as during the analysis of two years before. He then said that he would like to resume analytic frequency, but his income would not bear it since he had to pay for the house that he bought three years before when he moved out of his parents' home.

The Session

As I waited for his session to begin, I thought about my feelings toward him. My countertransference with Albert was complex and painful. Despite a continuing fondness for him, I often felt guilty that I had not helped him more and that analysis and therapy had not given him better capacity for relationships or an improved career. I sensed that my stance about his pedophilic inclinations might be discouraging his self-expression and exploration of sexual fantasies. I sometimes thought that I should stop therapy because of diminishing returns, but I also knew that despite enormous ambivalence about therapy, Albert had regarded me as the most important person in his life for a long time, and perhaps the most real figure in his life even in his adolescence.

I continued to feel guilty about exerting undue influence because of my importance to him. At the same time I felt powerless to prevent his shedding relationships and trashing his teaching career, which he seemed now to have surrendered permanently for a lackluster business job about which he complained. Despite me, he kept ripping things up inadvertently. My best intentions were often turned to shreds. Did I do this, or did he do it to me? I had trouble being sure. One thing I knew—I wasn't going to risk saying anything pithy or clever.

Before the session I am about to describe, Albert left the waiting room to go back to his car for a book and sheaf of paper. At the beginning of the session, he set them on the couch next to his chair and paused.

I looked at them expectantly. He acted as though he were oblivious to evoking my curiosity—a situation I found tantalizing.

He ignored the papers and began to talk. He discussed his difficulties in his career and in relating to others. He told me that he could not get mobilized in his job, and that he was more isolated than ever from others. He was also upset about recent attempts to discuss things with his mother, by whom he felt once again frozen out. He was clearly feeling quite sad.

I was able to experience his sadness directly, in contrast to the usual counter-transference in which I have felt bored and shut out by his empty, non-feeling state.

He continued, "I've been interested in what happened to my grandmother, not the one who is 94 now, but the one I never knew, my mother's mother. Maybe I told you this story. She and my grandfather were immigrants from Italy. My grandfather worked in a factory and had another job. She sewed and did laundry and housecleaning and had five children. They worked hard and saved enough to buy the house they lived in, and then the one next door. I understand she was a gardener, and loved to plant and nurture flowers and trees. Then the Depression came. They were heavily mortgaged, and they lost both houses, and ended up renting one of their own houses from the bank to live in. One day, she couldn't take it. She cracked, and took an ax to their house, the house she had loved and lost.

"They carted her off to the insane asylum, and when she was gone, no one visited her for a long time. My mother was 4 years old, pretty young to lose her mother so suddenly. Finally the family went to visit her. But my grandmother refused to speak to any one of them. Then, after a long time, they left my 4-year-old mother with her, and she began to speak to the little girl. But she never spoke to the rest of the family. And she never spoke to them again, in all the years she stayed in that hospital, which she did for the rest of her life."

"What do you make of such a sad story?" I asked.

"Maybe it says something about my mother's inscrutability," he said. "She destroys nearly everything. She tears up gardens and paves them over. My sister and I seemed to turn to my father for love when we felt so deprived by her. I remember just now that scene of being in the bath with my father watching over me, chanting that ditty about 'Hay foot, straw foot' which seemed to be his nursery rhyme for cheering me up. But that's also a scene in which I wonder if I was abused, but can never be sure. But he was the one who tried even if feebly, to rescue me from my mother's depression."

"And that led you to question whether the rescuing was filled with your desire or fraught with abuse," I said.

"Yes, that's true. But I don't any longer think my father did abuse me. But something was wrong.

"Then there's my grandmother. I think I inherited from her my propensity to cave in, to take an ax to things and relationships I care about. She's the ancestor of my melancholy and my illness. Like me, she was someone who was grossly misunderstood."

I felt quite in touch with him. Perhaps we would get somewhere today, I thought. I also had in mind his father's significant losses, which he had spoken about in previous sessions. His father lost his own grandfather when his paternal grandmother divorced him and moved back to Canada, where he experienced poverty, neglect, and isolation. I remembered a story Albert had relayed to me of how his father had once been so angry he threw his toys out of the window into a construction site next door where they sank into some hardening concrete and disappeared forever. This image of the petrified objects had often been my image of Albert's encasement in a shell himself, a mode I felt he had absorbed from his father. Now the image came back to me as I suddenly I felt him sinking out of my emotional view again.

"Anyway, I want to talk about something else," he said. "Here is a dream:

There is a garden, lush, with a hill rolling to the water, full of trees, flowers, and plants. Then a bulldozer comes to destroy the whole picture. The dreamer runs to tell the father, but he is in the bathroom and stays there for so long it is too late.

It was strange to me that I could not get into this dream even though I heard the reference to his mother who tore up gardens, his grandmother who destroyed her house, and to the father in the bathroom. I had my own associations to his internal father's loss of his toys in rage at neglect. But the distance between him and me seemed great, and now I realized the incongruous grammar of his strange, teasing mention of "the dreamer" rather than himself.

"Who is the dreamer?" I asked.
"It's my sister," he said. "It's her dream."

I felt irritated, tricked, and shut out. It was as if he had taken an ax to the relationship he had allowed me while constructing his family history. Previously he had been connecting with me while telling me about his connection with his grandmother. Now I felt that he was presenting his sister to me instead of himself. But I knew from past experience that he used other people to express his displaced transference. So I pushed myself to listen with renewed attention.

He went on, "I thought it was interesting because it is the same dream I've had about the garden being destroyed. Her dream fits with my fantasy of my parents destroying the garden I planted for them by paving it over. I told my mother I wanted to give my father two small trees for Father's Day to replace a couple of trees that died. She went ballistic! She said, 'It's just more work to do.' I said, 'These are evergreens. They don't take any care.' That didn't change her mind. She "trimmed" some liriope I planted at the edge of the paving stones by ripping it all out. That's my experience of her, too. When I wanted something from her, she'd just rip through me."

"What would you do?" I asked.

"The same thing as in my sister's dream," he said. "We would go to my father. But he would be in the bathroom for long periods of time. We had jokes about how long he would stay there, so the idea of appealing to him to give us what my mother wouldn't, of finding him not available to save us from my mother's destruction, that's my experience too."

I noticed that he relied on his sister's dream to express his experience, as though at this moment he had no experience of his own to draw on, but before I could formulate this, or before I could decide if I wanted to comment on the way he told the story instead of expressing his sadness at being so isolated from both parents, he went on, shifting topics.

"I read a book by a psychiatrist, Wolfgang Taylor, about the Snow Queen and Hans Christian Andersen. I identify with Andersen. He wrote that he thought he never grew beyond childhood. He was like me because he had trouble in relationships. Being childlike was useful to him, and even attractive when he was a young man, but less and less so as time went on. Maybe it was part of his having trouble with relationships as he grew older and found himself alone. You know I used to identify with the situation of the child abandoned to the Snow Queen. It fits with my experience of my mother and her cold aloofness.

"Andersen did a drawing of himself in a bottle, reaching out but trapped in the face of the Snow Queen. I felt something of his plight. He wasn't a great artist, but he was expressive. So I did some drawings!"

He grinned. The cat was out of the bag, as he now reached for the book beside him and took the sheaf of paper from its pages to show me. He knew of my interest in children's drawings from reading some of my books in which drawings are featured, and he had seen drawings by child patients on my office bulletin board for years since he was in therapy as an adolescent. Today's drawings were done before the hour, and were numbered (Figures 9–1 through 9–7). He displayed them to me, commenting on each as he handed it to me.

"This first one is me in a bottle (Figure 9–1).

FIGURE 9–1. Me in a bottle.

"I'm like Hans Christian Andersen, except that he drew himself as an adult. Here I'm a child, hands over my ears, not wanting to hear, almost curled up, with a woman hovering above, seductive but angry. She has a tail like the little mermaid, the girl who had to give up something phallic of her body to try to be near to the man she sought, but without hope of really getting him. The scribble behind her is her anger, which is in the wiggly line of her back as well.

"That's what I wanted to show in this second drawing, just an enlargement of her anger," he continued, showing me the second drawing (Figure 9–2).

"The third picture (Figure 9–3) is a stylized flower, I think," he said.

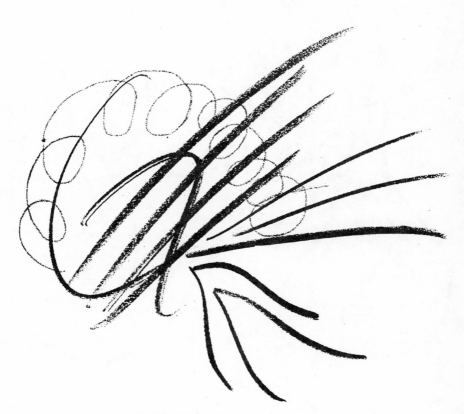

FIGURE 9–2. The woman's anger.

FIGURE 9–3. A stylized flower.

"This flower might represent the garden of the dream, the garden I want to grow, but which my mother is uninterested in and even destroys. But you remember I was talking about Scylla and Charybdis and the whorls of anxiety and depression you thought I am caught between. That's in this flower, too."

"Then I was interested in the fourth drawing (Figure 9–4)," he continued.

"It's a woman, on her back with her hands up and ill-defined hands and no feet, like Hans Christian Andersen's mermaid who lost her tail and never had any feet anyway. Then the red image is a phallus penetrating her. I don't know if those are the testicles around it, or if there are two breasts she reaches for but meets a phallus which penetrates her instead."

This was a disturbing image, but I felt connected to him again despite his use of analytic jargon. The image was more formed and personal to Albert than

FIGURE 9–4. Woman with red phallus.

the ones he usually managed to generate. Usually there was more distance from me, and there was less sense of his reaching out for help.

"This is like an image of you reaching for your mother and meeting something destructive and penetrating instead, like the Snow Queen," I said.

I also thought it was him reaching for me, asking for and fearing penetration. But I felt I should not say so lest the immediacy drive him away.

He nodded. "Yes, I think so too. The breasts have a phallus instead of what I'd be reaching for. And it's a girl who has no feet and whose hands are deformed."

"She wants care and meets invasion," I said. "This picture has an amphibious, metamorphosing quality, with the open mouth, the half smile. There is a lot of sadness which fits with feelings you hide."

"Then here is the fifth picture (Figure 9–5), you'll like because it comes after that one," he said.

"All the faces are associated with wetness, tears in the top one, nose running on the left, slobbering on the right, and emission or urine in the bottom. But the lines hatched across it mean that it is prohibited. I wasn't allowed to feel it."

I saw the sadness illustrated, the emptiness, the symbolic erect sexuality like a pre–Columbian icon relegated to the bottom of the page like his repressed sexuality. I connected the runny nose to a chronic rheumatoid condition which makes Albert's body ache, and wondered if it represented an upward displacement of his longing for phallic expressiveness.

I said, "In the last drawing, I see your sexual turning to others to escape the sadness, the emptiness, and the suffering."

"Yes, but I can't get anything out of it. It's forbidden," he said.

Albert continued, "So the sixth picture (Figure 9–6) is of rage."

"And emptiness," I added.

FIGURE 9–5. Wet faces.

FIGURE 9–6. Rage.

I felt moved more palpably than at any time recently, pulled beyond his intellectual discourse.

"The arrows pointing away have to do with something about not getting what I need and emptying my head," he continued.

When he picked up the theme of emptiness, I began to feel that it would be safe to say something of what I had understood from the nature of our relationship at this time. I would make sure it was a story, not a pithy comment that could get immortalized.

"That goes with the emptiness you feel, and which I so often feel with you," I said. "This series describes what you often feel with me—longing for something, reaching wordlessly as if without hands or feet to reach your mother, then feeling that what I say penetrates you and violates you. But you want that too, just as you reached to your father when you got frozen out by your mother, and felt you could not get it from him either, so you continued your search. You looked to other men longing for and fearing penetration and invasion. Or you would imagine penetrating boys yourself in order to get what you can't get from your father or me. That's the model of our failures here, isn't it?"

"Yes," he said. "Nothing works, and crying is forbidden. So in the seventh picture (Figure 9–7), I've turned back to my computer. That's like being in the bottle, looking at the screen. And now I look like a girl!"

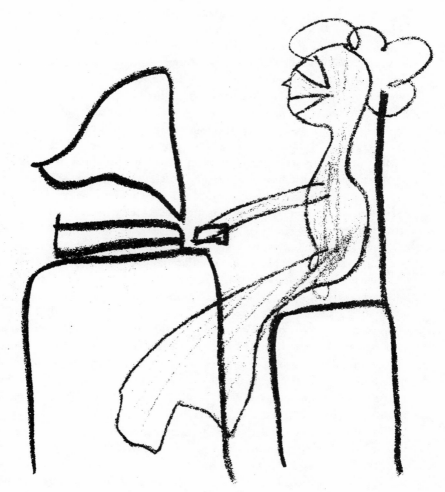

FIGURE 9–7. Like a girl at the screen.

Self and Object in Countertransference

Albert maintained that it was himself in the bottle, with his angry and seductive mother behind. At first I could identify with his object—the angry and seductive mother, trying to seduce him out of his glass bottle, angry too at his stubbornness. But just as self and object are always susceptible to reversal, the picture should also be seen in reverse, as representing his experience of me, or his view of my experience of him. In this perspective, it is I who am bottled up, seduced and abandoned by Albert. He is my tantalizing and unsatisfying object. He left me feeling stripped and exposed, unable to hear or speak safely. I have felt mistreated by Albert, as if he were the sexually ambiguous mermaid toying with me. In this view, it is my garden and horticulture that Albert destroys sadistically, my garden in which he becomes the Snow Queen. Even while he so often idealizes me, Albert sets me up for the failure which he imposes by tearing my words and work to shreds. When his unformed embryonic self reaches toward my breast and phallus, I feel stabbed as he turns my efforts to nothing, when everything I say is forbidden by his stricture on feelings, or when he neatly twists my words to make them sound sadistic. If I didn't feel guilty so often, I might also have felt the rage portrayed in his sixth picture, seeing the arrows slung from my head towards him, as, in the final picture, I turn to my computer (which he has often seen) to write up this impossible situation.

At this stage in the transference–countertransference dynamic, Albert and I are caught in a perverse web of interchangeable self and object. While I am with him, taken over by my concern for him, he is in me, and being in me, he keeps me from having access to parts of myself for which I actively long. And certainly he longs to have me inside him to fill his void. In the central picture of the series (Figure 9–4), neither of us is bottling the other up, nor are we turned away from each other at the computer screen. At the center, he shows his wish for interpenetration, the clinging to a combined male–female image of nurturance and invasion which characterizes his perverse organization and which both expresses and defends against his longing and his fears.

This longed-for connection with its uncomfortably homosexual element was a painful one for me, but one which I had now learned to value. In the course of the frustrating work with Albert, I often longed for ways to get inside his experience, to make a difference. Then I fear that if I get through to him, I will bulldoze his attachment to a man, a woman, or a child, his interest in some of his treasured ideas, or his career. Or I may get hurt myself. Every time I connect, I feel the danger of being sucked into a void as if in intercourse with a yawning vagina, now turned perversely into an organ for excretion that makes feces of whatever comes to it.

There is much to say about Albert's material, but we have focused on the portrayal of self and object in interaction illustrated in the particular trans-ference–countertransference experience that Albert and his therapist shared in the mid-phase of his treatment. It is colored by phallic, developmental stage material, since that is where his oedipal development was stymied because of his underlying schizoid identification with his mother and his weak, although hopeful, connection to his father. In any prolonged therapeutic encounter, self and object of patient and therapist come together in a similarly intense way, at the developmental level determined by the dynamics of that particular patient and by the therapist's ability to allow unconscious resonance there. Patient and therapist internal object relations reverberate, get attached and mixed up. Their objects long for and fear each other, and eventually, we hope, are modified as the transference resolves. In the internal world, internal object relations resettle at a more mature level of functioning and then, in the external world, patient and therapist become subjects and objects of mutual regard.

Theoretical Aspects of the Relationship between Self and Object

Infant research has established Fairbairn's contention that each infant is born with an ego constitutionally structured to relate. It is only through the recip-rocal relationship with devoted parents that the infant's self is born. The self grows optimally within mutually caring relationships through being vali-dated, responded to, and loved by others. From the beginning we need to be recognized and understood. We each need to love and be loved. Albert felt misunderstood. He felt that his mother ripped up his loving gifts to her, just as her mother had destroyed her environment.

For therapists who work from an object relations point of view, it is axi-omatic that the need for relationships motivates development: we are all or-ganized by the way we have taken in the satisfactions and disappointments of our primary relationships. Internal reflections of experience with others structure our experience of ourselves. These *internal objects* of our psychological structure carry our experience of past relationships with the people most important to us, our external objects. Each individual struggles to maintain a self which relates to and is supported by a network of primary relationships.

Psychoanalysis began both as a theory and as a therapy. Freud's early experience with hysterical patients gave him the experience that led to dynamic psychotherapy and psychoanalysis. But those encounters got under his skin, and sometimes left him feeling uncomfortably exposed, altogether too close to his patients. His collaborator, Josef Breuer, fled from his first patient, Anna O. when she attempted to live out her erotic transference with him (Breuer and Freud 1895, Jones 1955a). The patients Freud and Breuer treated at first were suffering from hysterical traumatic neuroses. Their tendencies toward rapidly fluctuating, intense relationships led them to stir others up, tantalize, abandon, and get under their therapists' skins. The theory Freud subsequently elaborated enabled him to keep at a safe distance from such patients, for it stressed the use of analytic theory to know what was happening in the unconscious of the patient.

Freud's theory built a picture of therapists who were trusted scouts for patients' expeditions of discovery in the wilderness of the unconscious. But Freud did not believe that therapists were themselves also on a similar expedition, except in private self-analysis. He maintained that the therapist ought to remain relatively unmoved, even though many of his colleagues had life-changing encounters with their patients, and was so fearful that analysts might succumb fatally to the many perils of psychoanalytic work that he established a clear set of guidelines (Freud 1910, Grosskurth 1991). It was the therapist's job to remain uninfluenced and to understand the patient's transference to the therapist as a re-edition of an object from the patient's past. Countertransference manifestations of patients' effects on therapists were regarded as signs that the therapist's infantile conflicts were interfering and needed further analysis. From this point of view, it could be argued that in his work with Albert, the therapist's unanalyzed conflicts in the negative oedipal area were interfering with the work and causing him to overfunction with clever remarks and then inhibit himself because of castration anxiety. But he was aware of his discomfort and modified his technique in the service of fostering the patient's ability to take in a metabolized experience of him as a whole object, rather than introjecting a part object.

This understanding of the therapeutic relationship for the first half-century of analytic therapy began to change with the contributions of the Kleinians and Independents in the late 1940s and 1950s. These contributors from the

British object relations school paved the way through the exploration of a responsive countertransference in psychotherapy (Balint 1952, Bion 1959, 1967, Fairbairn 1958, Guntrip 1961, 1969, Heimann 1950, Klein 1952, Money-Kyrle 1956, Racker 1957, Winnicott 1958, 1965).

Subsequent contributors from self psychology (Lichtenberg 1989, Stolorow et al. 1987), infant research and attachment theory (Bowlby 1969, Emde 1988a,b, Stern 1985, Beebe and Lachmann 1988, Fonagy et al. 1991), object-relations oriented psychoanalysis (Bollas 1987, 1989, Gill 1984, N. Hamilton 1988, Kernberg 1975, 1976, Khan 1974, 1979, Loewald 1960, 1980, Mitchell 1988, Modell 1984, Money-Kyrle 1978, Ogden 1982, 1986, 1989, Searles 1959, 1965, 1979, 1986, Sutherland 1989, 1994a,b, Wright 1991), and family research (R. Shapiro 1979, Zinner and Shapiro 1972), and many others have enlarged the base of our understanding of relational theory and its application to psychotherapy. We now have a broad and expanding base of understanding of the many ways in which the self forms and is maintained by the presence and action of the other, which in object relations terminology we call the *external object*.

In this vision, each person is not an island, but exists within the context of his or her relationships. Each person's desires and fears, sexuality and aggression, are expressed in relationships of emotional responsiveness that give them meaning. Fairbairn's model of the mind (1952) is a fundamentally anthropomorphic one. As Mitchell (1988) put things more recently, our minds are organized in "relational configurations." We understand each other and ourselves through understanding the internal configurations as they constantly interact with our external relationships. Kohut's *self-selfobject relationship* (1984), Atwood and Stolorow's (1984) *intersubjective context*, and Mitchell's *relational matrix* (1988) are varying expressions of this central point. Interestingly, Albert—in his narrative about his grandmother—and his sister in her dream—both arrive at the same image of the destruction of the relational matrix.

We think, however, that no theory has quite been able to keep an eye on both self and other as both experience each other in constant interplay. Self psychology has focused on the self seeking growth and cohesion through use of the object, but without according that selfobject a reciprocal subjectivity—an equal right to life, conceived in theoretical terms. Object relations theory has focused on the vicissitudes of the object while leaving the growth of the self in relative shadow, a point recognized by Sutherland in his final contributions on the contemporary need to focus on the growth and autonomy of the self (J. Scharff 1994). Mitchell (1988) comes closest, perhaps, but does not elaborate on the reciprocal experience of the parent or the therapist in his work. His theory leaves room for such an extension without distorting it, however. Recent contributions of Bollas (1989), Jacobs (1991), and Ogden (1994), brilliantly develop the clinical implications of an interdependent and mutually responsive way of working, but we still need to elaborate the developmental base for their views.

It is difficult to keep both self and object simultaneously in focus, in development and in therapy. Because they form a figure-and-ground relationship to each other, focusing on one necessarily tends to put the other into the background. For instance, we could look at Albert as the self trapped in the bottle of his defensive identification with the shape of his maternal object, or we can look at the bottle as Albert's self with his object squashed into the bottle as the therapist felt. Figure and ground, object and self, both are crucial to theory and therapy.

There is no self without an object. There is also no object without a self, just as there is no mother without a child. She needs the child to be the kind of self who reflects her being the mother. Inside the individual, both ego and internal object are functions of an overarching self. But the argument we are making here is that the individual ego is not the entire unit that makes up the individual's sense of cohesion and well-being. That sense of cohesion and well-being is a reflection of the functioning of the self which derives from the internalization of a graduated and interlocking series of relationships. The series begins with the earliest caretaking units, the mother–infant pair and the father–infant pair. These original units relate to the larger family, including the couple as a unit, or grandparents, who in turn relate to larger social units. All these external relationships are taken into the internal world of each individual as his or her psychic organization. In Albert's situation, his mother (as he experienced her) was in trouble because she did not want the burden of more gardening, not because she was lazy, but because too much work had seemed to drive her own mother to destruction, a risk to which she did not subject herself and her child. The father–infant pair became a compensatory unit, exciting because any attention was so longed for, and yet not enough to make up for what was missing. The grandparent circle was broken by the madness of the maternal grandmother and the defeat of the paternal grandfather during the Depression. So there was a less than optimal circle of support for their parenting of Albert, and a family system of internal object relationships some of which had to be avoided. It is this full set of self-and-object relationships which form the entirety of the individual psyche and which then guide future ongoing relationships with others and with the wider world.

Because all of us are organized in this way, we are each equipped to be an "other" to whom people can relate and look to have their needs recognized, appreciated, ignored, or met. In being available to others in this way, we are guided by our own lifelong need to be another's object as an integral part of being ourselves. From birth to death, this endless process organizes our internal world and our relationship to others.

The Individual's Relation to External Objects

Although Freud was the first to explore the ego's relations to its object, Fairbairn and Klein moved object relating to the center of personality growth and of psychopathology. Where Freud put the unfolding of the drives as the engine of personal development, Fairbairn put the fundamental need for relationships. It is only within the context of this need for relationships that the unfolding of drives—of desire and aggression—and the gradual structuring of our psyches have meaning. As we have seen, in Fairbairn's (1952) theory of the relationship between self and object, psychic structure is built from the experience individuals have with the people most important to them. The operations of splitting and repression are fundamental to the handling of object relations as well as to the progressive structuring of the ego. And, in Fairbairn's view, self and object are always in intimate contact. The relationship between an internal object and a corresponding part of the ego that is bound to it by relevant affect constitutes the basic building block of psychological structure.

Although Fairbairn used the term *ego* in referring to the part of the self which was in intimate relationship to the internal object, he accepted Guntrip's amendment that*self* was a better term for ego (Sutherland 1989). We may slip into using the term *self* instead of ego at times, but we prefer to reserve the term *self* for the whole of the personality and its parts in dynamic relation, including the central ego-ideal object in consciousness and the repressed internal object relationships consisting of the libidinal ego/exciting object and antilibidinal ego/rejecting object systems.

Fairbairn's clinical and theoretical writing led to the idea that ego and object were inextricably intertwined and interdependent. We are always dependent on our objects, but development leads us from infantile dependency to a mature form of dependency. Fairbairn thought that children were influenced by the actual treatment they received at the hands of their primary objects. This experience was then incorporated as psychic structure.

Klein's ideas are more firmly based on Freud's drive theory. In her view, infants' early relationships to their mothers and other external objects are governed by their constitutionally given drives and the instinctual tensions which come from them as excesses of hate and desire. In her theory, the actual treatment by the parents does not get much attention. She conceived of children as driven by their instincts to impose their aggression and their love on the primary external objects, fear the consequences of aggression destroying love, and react further to those fears. Klein's was a theory with relatively little regard to what the external object actually did in relating to the child. Only when Klein's work was elaborated by Bion (1967) did we get a model of mothers as containers for their infants' unmanageable, primitive anxieties. This model enabled Kleinian theory to consider the role of the actual psychological functioning of the mother and parents as an influence on the infant from the beginning. Now we can imagine the combination of Albert's constitutionally determined psychological vulnerability inherited from both sides of the family and his precocious intellectual development exaggerating his anxiety by leading to thoughts and perceptions in advance of the emotional maturity needed for their integration (see Chapter 8). These vulnerabilities operated in concert with his mother's difficulty in containing anxiety since she had not learned it from her mother—who could not contain her own anxiety much less that of her child. How remote he found her. How he must have pushed her until he learned concerned restraint.

Blending these views of the primacy of experience with the object and the primacy of the child's constitutional makeup lets us consider the reciprocal influence of primary objects on the developing child, and the influence of children on the parents and family as well as on their own psychological growth. Over the years Winnicott (1971a), Kohut (1984), Stern (1985), Mitchell (1988), Lichtenberg (1989), and Fonagy et al. (1991) have moved us toward a growing understanding of the relationship of self and object during early development as it provides the foundation for psychological structure and its continuing differentiation.

Special Aspects of the Self's Relations to Objects

Some people live as though their selves are inside their objects, and some relate to others in terms of internal couples.

Living in the Object

Those people who present themselves as though they lived inside their objects are living out an internal object relationship based on an entrenched projective identification. In this constellation, they have projected their self into one special object, so that it is only through dealing with, satisfying, modifying, healing, or more likely substituting for the object that they feel satisfied with their self. The following case vignette illustrates this object relations set.

Vince always began his sessions by telling me about his wife, Flora. She was the problem to be fixed. She had done one or another outrageous thing to him or the children, or she had failed to live up to a promise. On repeated occasions, she fell sick or took to bed in a depressed way, collapsing and ordering the servants and Vince around. She had screamed yet again at their provocative son, demanded that Vince set limits with him, and then berated him for doing it the wrong way. She had taken their daughter into bed with her despite her having been told by the girl's therapist that it was not good for the girl.

Then he would tell me (DES) what he had done to try to manage the situation. He had put more money in her account to appease her, or he had spoken to her mother about her. Since she did not know how to manage Flora either, they would commiserate, plan how to deal with her, and support each other.

In the sessions, it was no use my trying to get him to talk about himself. Dealing with Flora and her family was his life! He attenuated his relationship with his own family when he married Flora. Her family adopted him with the unspoken agreement that he would take care of her and they would take care of him. He would become head of the family-run business in manufacturing mattresses and would eventually inherit a minority interest in it, but the bulk of the proceeds would continue to go to Flora and her brother, who also needed to be supported and who worked only sporadically in the business because he had become an occasional artist. Vince was the younger son in his own family, and his family's business had been taken over by his older brother, so it was natural that he would find another venue. As a young married man, he had been dominated by his late father-in-law, who had controlled everyone, including Flora, until his death. Now Vince felt dominated by Flora in his place. But what could he do? He did not want to break up his family. He was devoted to the children, and he enjoyed a successful career in Flora's family business. He had built up the company so that it had taken over the major market share in the area, but because it now belonged to Flora's mother, he continued to be dependent on her good will for his job and his lifestyle. When she died, he would be dependent on Flora and her brother for his job, even though in fact they were all dependent on him to run the business.

Therapy had an air of impossibility to it. It was difficult to discuss Vince's setting limits on his wife's provocative and destructive behavior. She tried to assert herself by manipulating other family members to share her point of view and ended up by creating triangles by which she got excluded and belittled. When frustrated, she threw a fit, flew into a rage, or, when Vince did not respond, sulked. He thought well of her, continued to feel hopeful and trusting, and then was frequently disappointed. When she was anxious, she avoided public situations or had to leave in a panic. Most worrisome of all was her overspending, which threatened to bankrupt the family and jeopardize the business despite its success. She had an independent trust from which she had plenty of income, but she overspent whatever bonuses came her way as well. Neither her mother nor Vince could stop her. Vince could not say "No" to her until the business was actually in danger. Only then would he come into the session and tell me that now he could say "No" because the external situation demanded it.

From time to time, Vince thought of leaving to begin a life of his own. But he would lose the family that he loved and that formed the entire context of his life. Still, it was easier to think of limiting his involvement with Flora by leaving her than to set limits while with her. In fact, he could do neither.

I took up with Vince the absence of a life outside his relationship to Flora. I pointed out that he felt entirely hostage to her moods, whims, and commands. In sum, his life was governed by the contour of her personality. He agreed, but was powerless to do otherwise. Since she seemed to him to be essentially unchangeable even when in therapy, he defined his own situation as unchangeable in consequence. He presented me with an impossible job: there could be no change in her, he thought he had nothing to work on but her, so what did he want therapy for? Our job was to enable him to live with constraints in a relationship that left him feeling belittled and humiliated so that he could remain connected to his objects and to his adopted environment.

In the countertransference, I lived with the projective identification of helplessness and uselessness. Since he could do nothing about his situation, he could do nothing with anything I said about it. And so we came to be in it together: both of us helpless to stave off the humiliation and bondage imposed by Flora.

Of course, the constraints were actually self-imposed. He defined his self as bound to, identified with, and shaped in reaction to his primary object and the context she imposed on her life and his. He defined himself as unable to have any other existence, and lived his life as a fantasy which proved to him that it was true. Therapy, constrained by this internal fantasy, therefore could only prove the same: he had no life outside hers.

The end to the story is not a happy one. In response to my interpretations of his insistence on thinking only of her and living within her rules to avoid asserting himself and risking loss, Vince began to set small limits on his own behavior. He would not, for instance, berate their son solely because Flora insisted he do so, but began to evaluate independently what the boy needed. He refused to buy her a gift she had selected because it was too expensive and unnecessary, even when there was money in their bank account. She rightly assumed that his therapy had something to do with his new-found backbone, but wrongly thought that I was telling Vince what to do. In retaliation, she told him that unless he left therapy, she would leave him. He sadly told me that, although he liked working with me, he felt he had no choice. His life was still with her and he was doubtful if he would ever be able to stake out an existence independently of her as long as she would have him. He terminated therapy, and asked her to find him a new therapist who would be acceptable to her.

This man lives a life completely defined by his object. In a metaphorical and fantasy sense, he lives under his wife's domination, and, far more, he lives as though inside her, limited and defined by her rules, perceptions, and feelings of despair and emptiness. He lives to fill her up, to care for and take care of her, and he lives with the repeated expectation of failure to satisfy her. He lives as if he has no life beyond or outside her, and given the choice between this life and any independence, he chooses to continue to live in and through her. He is the opposite of the narcissist whose objects exist to serve him: he exists to serve his objects, the anti-narcissist who tries endlessly to fill his own emptiness by filling an endlessly empty object. His despair, defeat, humiliation, and emptiness are countered only by his determination to keep on trying like Sisyphus to put energy and love into her, and in the transference to put hope into the therapist. In the countertransference, the therapist repeatedly experienced defeated hope, pity for the patient, and anger at his intransigence, not surprisingly displaced onto his commanding object.

While Vince's early history remained vague, it looked to the therapist as though he lived through his wife to compensate for the feeling that he had meant very little to his parents. It is also possible that Vince lived through his wife because his mother had lived through him when he was a child. As an adult, he identified with his mother and lived through his object. A variety of early experiences and internal constellations can produce the picture of living through the object.

Despite this patient's decision to continue living self-destructively in his object, many patients can use their therapists as objects to relate to differently, and so can learn to make other choices and to move beyond their unconscious fantasy of living only in the orbit of their objects.

Defining the Self in Relation to the Internal Couple

Klein (1928, 1945) was the first writer to describe the way children before the age of 1 expressed intense interest in their parents as a couple, in terms of sexualized phantasies of genital interaction. There has since been research confirmation that children become interested in the parental relationship and think about it and its implications beginning at 7 or 8 months (Abelin 1971, 1975). We have written extensively on the role of the internal couple in the development of the child's internal object relations (D. and J. Scharff 1987, 1991, J. Scharff 1992). The internal couple is not exclusively a sexual couple: it is variously a caring couple, an abandoning couple, a secure couple that provides the basis for a firm foundation, or a fighting couple whose relationship persecutes the individual. The internal couple is built up of the same combination of actual experience with the parents (and other important primary couples) mixed with fantasy elaboration that modifies the child's internal understanding of the meaning of their relationship. The chief rival to the child's forming a couple with each parent during the oedipal phase is not the rivalrous parent (who is usually, but not always, the opposite sex parent). The chief rival to oedipal victory is the parental couple's *relationship* and the high value the child places on his parents being married. The security of the foundation provided by their togetherness means more to children than an oedipal victory that would, in fantasy or actuality, destroy the couple and the security that stems from being in relationship with it.

The internal couple is an internal structure like other internal objects, and each individual is defined in part by his or her relation to the internal couple. There is a similar internalization of the family as a whole, but it is more complex and less readily detected in individual therapy. It is more frequently evoked in family therapy, however, but in family therapy the issues concerning the internal family group are often treated unconsciously as only involving one or two family members, just as group issues are narrowed in transference. We discuss this narrowing of group issues in Chapter 10.

The following vignette illustrates the use of the concept of the internal couple in therapy.

Vicki began her session by mentioning that she had seen my wife in the waiting room. Other times when she had passed by, Vicki had found my wife threatening, but on this occasion Vicki had felt that she was cordial although reserved. This was in contrast to her feeling about her own mother, whose support Vicki felt she did not have. She told me (DES) that, when she had been out with her mother and father, her father mentioned that a colleague for whom Vicki had worked for a summer during college had asked after her, and so Vicki's father now suggested that she get a letter from him in support of a contract she was trying to get. As her father was talking about this, Vicki sensed her mother become cold and felt that she withdrew from their conversation, a typical distancing move that happened whenever Vicki and her father moved closer together in discussion.

Vicki then went on to talk about the female associate of a male architect who was in charge of her renovation. The associate had reviewed plans that had already been reviewed, had done so extremely slowly, and had suggested changes that Vicki thought might not pass the zoning laws. She worried that this woman was going to represent her at the zoning hearing, and so she called the chief architect himself and said that she wanted to be sure that he would be there during the hearing. He assured her that this woman was just learning the trade, and that he would be there. Vicki said that she did not want this woman to be learning at her expense.

Then she went on to talk about how there had been a fire in her office building. The owner, who occupies the first two floors of the building, is a man she particularly likes and has even had a crush on. Occasionally she meets his girlfriend, who is co-owner of the building. There is something she cannot quite describe but knows she does not like about the interaction with this woman. But what got to her the most over the weekend concerned an incident with a fire from a booster heater in the hallway. She had previously warned the owner that this heater was a fire hazard. The fire department had to come and she selflessly placed herself at risk by staying in the building far too long, opening windows when she should have left.

What angered her was that the owner of the building and his girlfriend came out of the building together just as she finally left the building. It was as though they were so involved with each other that they had no concern for Vicki or the building.

I now commented that she was having trouble being in relationship to couples. In each of these instances she wanted to be in relationship to the man, only to feel that the woman presented a persecuting element. The man remained exclusively related to the woman, or, if she got the man's attention, then the woman would be resentful and likely to attack. Her getting upset with the women in each case had to do with her wish to form a couple consisting of herself and the man. As soon as she did, she feared she would be attacked by the other woman—the wife/girlfriend/woman-architect, or mother. The fire represents the danger that she often put herself in because the couple she carries inside is too excitedly preoccupied with its own interests to provide safety and concern for her.

She now said that was why she turned to men sexually. Maybe then they would care for her. Her mother had withdrawn from her, and so she had been drawn to her father's teasing emotional seduction, and then resented it. In turn, her mother resented the closeness between them.

I said that this conflict was being reexperienced in the relationship to me: she felt my wife's suspicion and hostility rise because she felt closer to me. Vicki answered that she knew my wife had no relationship to her, but she could not help feeling these things. I said to her that the feelings about my wife arose because she was trying to deal with me not only as a threatening and exciting man, but was trying to understand her relationship to the couple at a time when she was looking for understanding and concern, as a child looks to her parents. Feeling she could not get it from her parents, she had turned to her father in an overexcited relationship as a substitute. Then she hoped a woman would protect her from the invasion she felt from her father after she felt taken in by him. Through it all, she feared she would destroy any safe, well-functioning parental couple, such as the one she imagined I formed with my wife.

Vicki's transference to the couple reveals her oedipal complex, in which she desires possession of the father and is rivalrous with and rejected by the mother. This formulation is consistent with standard psychoanalytic theory. But, in an object relations formulation, we note that her transference also concerns her fear of the disruption of the parental couple itself. Vicki feels excited sexually by the man, then feels attacked, and expects to be displaced from him by the woman. The fundamental reason she turns to the man is to be cared for, not to posess him sexually. What she is really after is to be loved and cared for not only by one of the parents, but by a couple who can offer her the safety and security of a good holding environment in which to grow. The most secure environment is one in which the parental couple support each other so that they can offer more than either of the parents could offer individually in terms of security, resilience to the challenges posed by the child, and physical and emotional love. In all these dimensions, nothing short of a couple can offer as much, which is the reason all children—and all patients— wish for, envy, and relate through and to the internal couple as their inner world representative of the parental couple they either had, or, failing experience with a good-enough couple, continue to search for.

Contextual and Focused Object Relating

The *internal* object relationship originates in the relationship with the *external* object. In an analogous way, in therapy, the internal object relationship is modified through the therapeutic relationship. Patient and therapist, working together, provide the holding for each other's work in support of a potential space which becomes the therapeutic space where dreams, fantasies, and generative transference–countertransference experiences occur. The therapist takes the lead, but the patient's cooperation is crucial, even when that cooperation is given with reluctance.

This model of development and psychotherapy derives from the image of the mother or the father with the baby. They each provide for the growth of the infant. Both offer to secure the environment, to hold the infant in their arms, and to be receptive to the infant's needs and efforts to return their concern with the first innuendos of encouragement—through gestures, sighs, and changes of mood. These signals, quiet and subtle at first, let parents proceed with their caregiving tasks—and with becoming parents in relation to their particular infant.

A series of concentric circles holds each infant. At first unable to hold themselves, infants rely on the parents one at a time and both together, to hold them in their arms, to look into their eyes, touch and comfort them, clean and feed them. But an infant's responses also strengthen and hold the parents in their task—and even more, hold them in their relationship with the infant. What infants cannot do for themselves directly in the beginning, they can do indirectly nevertheless by sending their attachment signals through to their parents where they are responded to, and amplified in the process, and come back to the infant. Now the infant's own capacity for holding the parent in mind is interwoven with the adults' ability to hold the child in mind, and an augmented experience of reciprocal holding is taken in. As this process continues over time, the parents hold the infant who holds their attention by returning their concern.

There is also an important widening circle. As the mother and child hold each other, a father holds the two of them by his concern for the baby, for the mother, and for the two of them as a pair. In a reciprocal way, the mother holds the father and infant as they reach for and hold each other. Then the parents as a pair provide concentric enveloping circles of holding for the infant, for the three of them as a family, and for the larger family of the other children or extended kin. The enlarged circle that the external objects provide through their relationships to each other and, in turn, to the infant provides a universe of object relationships that holds the baby and provides a medium for the fertilization of the infant's mind with meaning achieved through relatedness. In Albert's case, he was held by a mother who had been dropped by her mother when she was 4 years old. Perhaps this left her with the sense of herself as a baby who could not hold her mother, at least not until her mother was mad, at which point, in a reversal of the usual holding relationship centered on the child, she became the only one who could talk with her mother. It must have left her with an internal object relationship that expressed itself in tremendous conflict about nurturing her child, partly enacted and reflected in his object relations, and partly displaced onto rejecting the garden's need for tending. In addition, his father's internalization of loss, neglect, and petrified need made it hard to compensate when Albert turned to him, leaving Albert with a model of an internal couple unable to tend their garden or their children.

We do not mean to imply that this process only occurs with the "ideal" two-parent family. On the contrary, it is the same process with any family constellation: a mother and grandmother, a same-sex couple, or a mother or father alone supported by other adults. If any parent or caretaker has to go it alone, the situation is more difficult, and they will have to fall back on their inner resources of internalized object relations, which to a considerable extent can support the single parent. Ogden (1989) has described the presentation of the father and the oedipal situation through the transmission of the mother's internal object relations to the infant as the original way the child takes in triangular relationships. In a similar way, the single parent conveys the richness of available relationships which support or fail to support her in relating to the infant, and in the absence of additional adult support, she uses her internal object relations to create the network of relatedness.

The parents also become the first objects of the infant's desires and hopes, fears and aggression, love and hate (Winnicott 1960a). Fathers and mothers are similar in being primary objects for the infant, and yet they also have different intrinsic qualities in relationship to children—mothers offering a biological propensity for steadiness, and fathers for enhanced stimulation (Yogman 1982).

In the relationship with parents, the infant finds its objects, explores ways of relating with them, internalizes them, and lives with them, both as real external people and as internalizations. The infant forms a direct relationship with each parent as an object of desire and aggression. We call this the focused or eye-to-eye, I-to-I relationship, emphasizing the importance of gaze interactions in an intimate relationship between self and other. This eye-to-eye or *centered relationship* provides the experience of objects out of which the infant's internal world is built (D. Scharff and J. Scharff 1987).

In the focused eye-to-eye centered relationship, created by the parents' willingness to engage directly, the infant finds its object. In the arms-around envelope, created by the parents' readiness to be relatively in the background as providers and guards, the infant finds its self.

In this safe harbor, or in the ravages of rough or violent holding, the self is born and nurtured, and begins the development which will eventually enable the growing person to take over from the parents the acts of providing, guarding, and navigating the self (D. Scharff and J. Scharff 1987).

The therapeutic relationship has many similarities to the relationship between parent and infant. Like the parent, the therapist takes the lead in the provision of the therapeutic space, but is encouraged by the patient's reciprocation, even if the signs of reciprocity are at first almost as small and subtle in their own way as those of the newborn. This mutuality need not be conscious and rational, but it has to be there if therapy is to thrive. Like the single parent who has to hold in mind the entire potential of human development and represent the possibility of a generative, central male–female couple, the therapist has to provide a therapeutic relationship that carries a larger potential than that of a two-person relationship. Each male therapist must be able to represent the female element in relation to his own maleness, and each woman therapist the male connection. Therapists do so by using their own internal object relations which include themselves in relation to others, analyzed to allow full acceptance of male and female elements, and which provide an internal universe receptive to the patient's experience. Ogden's (1989) model of the way the mother introduces the father and the triangular relationship when she presents her internal object relations to the child helps us to understand the analogous situation in psychotherapy and psychoanalysis.

Therapists are also like parents in offering both arms-around and focused experiences to their patients. They provide a background of holding analogous to the parental arms-around experience which allows patients to deliver aspects of their internal worlds into the therapeutic space and so discover their selves. And on the other hand, in the eye-to-eye, I-to-I relationship therapists offer themselves as objects of the patient's desires, hates, and fears, which convey the dynamics of the patient's internal object relations.

Both the focused and contextual aspects of relationships are relevant to therapy. Patients come to therapy with both sets of experience from their previous primary relationships, and therefore bring transferences both to the therapeutic space provided—the contextual transference—and to the person of the therapist—the focused transference. Context and focus are intertwined in every intimate relationship. We will explore the contextual and focused aspects of transference in the discussion of transference geography in Chapter 11.

The Self and the Object

Fairbairn's (1941) description of *techniques of relating* to objects as methods of compensation for unsatisfying relationships was an early effort to define the particular use of objects by the self during the transition from infantile dependence to mature dependence. Kohut (1977, 1984) coined the term *self-object* to capture the individual's attempt to get another person, including a therapist, to fill a function for the self, and to absorb the fragmenting effects of aggression so as to promote a sense of self-cohesion. This well describes the clinical situation when this use is imposed on us. But it gives a one-sided view of relationships. In contrast, Fairbairn's formulation of object relations (1952) emphasizes the *mutual relation* betwen self and object rather than the *unidirectional use of the object* conveyed by Kohut's term. The sense we have of ourselves is always inextricable from the quality of our relationships to objects.

Referring to Searles (1963), Wright describes the developmental situation by summarizing Searles's "central point that the mother's face is the child's first emotional mirror, and that it is through her responsiveness (her reflections) that the child is able to come to know his own emotions" (Wright 1991, p. 5). Similarly in the therapeutic situation, as Searles himself put it, "[I]n the therapeutically symbiotic, core phase of the work with any one patient, each of the two participants' facial expressions 'belong,' in a sense, as much to the other as to oneself" (Searles 1963, p. 379).

The self is always defined in relationship to its objects, while internal objects have no meaning except in relationship to the self. Fairbairn's early description (1952) of the internal object emphasized that it was organized inevitably in relationship to a part of the self, bound together by the set of affects that characterized the repressed relationship. It has been less recognized, partly because it was less emphasized by Fairbairn himself, that internalization of an object (a memory trace of an experience with a part of a primary person) is a shorthand description for the building in the mind of a model of a relationship of that object with a part of the self (Ogden 1986, Sutherland 1989). In our relationships, we see ourselves in the reflection of the other person's eyes, gaze, expression, mirroring body responses, and echoing sounds, and the structure we build in our psyche reflects that way of knowing ourselves.

In our inner world, we cannot structure an image of ourselves without reference to our objects.

Just as we have a self defined by our bodies—that is, we cannot have a disembodied self—so *we cannot have a dis-othered self.* Our relationships to others in the external world and to the traces of these in our internal worlds continue to define our selves throughout life.

The Normal Need to Be Another's Mutually Held Object

The object is also defined by the self. To Winnicott's aphorism "there is no such thing as an infant, meaning . . . without maternal care there would be no infant" (1960a, p. 39), we have added that *there is no mother without a baby.* No one can be an other without someone to whom they belong, by whom their otherness is defined and validated. Love and development form a reverberating circuit in a relationship of reciprocity. We each need the parent to love, and we need the parent to love us. And then later, as parents, husbands, wives, or lovers ourselves, we need to feel we can care for others with love—that they will grow in our holding. We need this from the beginning: the baby also needs to feel that the parent grows in the light of the baby's love and care.

Now we want to discuss the final dimension. We too need to have taken in an image of the object of our love which is also felt to be loving to us in return. Internal objects—the loving, hating, the beckoning, accepting, and rejecting objects—are embedded within us in a particular way. Deep within us, they must also have us inside them: a fractal of mutual concern (Figure 9–1). Fairbairn summarized this in theoretical terms when he wrote, "[T]he object in which the individual is incorporated is incorporated in the individual" (1941, pp. 42–43).

The image of the object we carry must have room for us within it—that is, it must be an object capable of relating to us, whether kindly or cruelly, lest it be felt to have abandoned us altogether. The image that we find helpful here is of parallel mirrors facing each other, each containing the image of the other with its own image inside. A series of these mutually contained images extends back to the individual's beginning and forward toward the infinity of the imagined future.

We can now offer a simpler description: what is carried inside is an *ongoing object relationship*, one either characterized by aspects of mutual concern and caring, or by antagonism, rejection, and rage. When parents show care and concern for their child, the child learns to have concern for the well-being of the external object as a whole person and to care for, repair, and modify the internal object. Love may be there, but where mutuality and concern are insufficient, the internal object relationships become static, skewed, and distorted, as they were in Albert. When they go badly, the individual operates in what Klein called the paranoid-schizoid position, where part-object relationships predominate in relation to a fragmented experience of the self. When they go well, the person operates largely in the depressive position, where whole object relations predominate and are characterized by concern for the object and a capacity to mourn losses. The vitality of the self and the quality of its relationships with others rest on, and are expressed by, the degree to which relations between self and object are mutually caring and concerned.

The term *object relations* is itself problematic, in that it obscures the problems and centrality of the self. On the other hand, the term *self psychology* obscures the centrality of the object, not only as an object to be of service to the self, but as a structure in intimate and mutually defining interaction with the self. A complete study has to take into consideration the mutual influence and concern of self and object, of what we might call personal relations (Sutherland 1989). This study is informed not only by psychoanalysis, object relations, and self psychology, but by the fields of infant research, and of family and marital studies as well. Clinical work with individuals like Albert whose relationships are impoverished, with children and parents in hostile interaction, or with wives and husbands in marriages of frustration and despair, leads us back again to individuals' inner worlds, to those regions where blocked paths of mutual concern lead to the destructive patterns, to the narcissistic disorders of an arrogant, empty triumph of self over object, to the despairing loss of self at the hands of the inner object, or to the substitution of aggression for caring in attempts to keep alive relationships between self and object.

The internal world of each individual is given meaning through external interaction, while these internal object relations, at the same time, impart meaning to personal interaction. Born originally in the cradle of our primary relationships, our inner worlds seek meaning from and give meaning to our everyday interactions and to the transferences and countertransferences of our treatment relationships.

10

The Formation of New Objects through the Life Cycle: Object Construction, Object Sorting, and Object Exclusion

In this chapter, we explore the formation of new internal objects and their continuing role throughout adult development. We hope to show that the findings of this exploration, informed by clinical experience in couple and family therapy, fundamentally alter basic analytic theory, in ways that Fairbairn partly foresaw, but which we can now articulate more fully. The newly formed internal object of adulthood is a trace, not a replica, of the external object. New internal objects are fractals of the internal object relationship modified by interaction with the external object.

As we have described, Fairbairn put the need for relationships throughout life at the center of development. In summary, he wrote that the infant, in the face of the intrinsic need for relationships and of inevitable disappointment with them, takes in the experience with the object and then splits off and represses the intolerable part and divides it into painfully rejecting and exciting aspects. Here is a bifurcation that establishes a new order. Sorting of experience leads to structuring of mind. Thus introjection is the hallmark of Fairbairn's model, in contrast to Klein's model where there is more emphasis on projective processes for ridding the self of the excesses of drive derivatives. In Fairbairn's model, however, the introjection of good experience comes as a kind of afterthought: good objects are only introjected to compensate for bad (1952). Klein disagreed with Fairbairn's ideas that introjection of good experience was secondary. She thought that under the influence of the life instinct, good experience is also taken in from the beginning (1946). Current infant research demonstrates that she was right that infants, and all of us, take in good and bad experience. But we think that it happens, not because of the life and death instincts (as she thought), but simply because we are built to take in all kinds of experience as we relate in order to grow into a person. The realities of all aspects of external experience and our perceptions of them provide the building blocks for our psychic structure. Fairbairn's student, Sutherland, wrote that the need to love and be loved is primary, and that the human organism grows naturally through the construction of progressively integrated and complex organizations of the self in relation to others (1994a). In the service of this growth, children and adults do more than simply introject or project. They take in experience to use as material to construct an inner world, and they then actively seek to realize that inner world in the outer world, both through interaction with others and through internal modification of their selves. In this process, each individual constructs relations with the outer world in a way that will give realization to the developing self and to the inner relations between internal object and self.

The Application of Fairbairn's Theory to Marital Dynamics

Henry Dicks first applied Fairbairn's work systematically to marriage, much as Bion (1962) had applied Klein and Freud to non-family groups in the 1950s. Dicks described the reciprocity of object relations in marital spouses, using his original amalgam of Fairbairn's system of endopsychic organization and Klein's concept of projective identification as his explanatory vehicle. In his landmark book *Marital Tensions* (1967), Dicks gave detailed descriptions of the way couples found their repressed libidinal and anti-libidinal objects in each other, recovered lost parts of themselves through the return of the repressed in the marital relationship, and shared in the creation of a new *joint marital personality*, a quality belonging to the relationship that the couple shares rather than to either partner individually.

Dicks synthesized the contributions of Fairbairn and Klein to yield a relational psychology focused on explicit interaction governed by the unconscious processes of projective and introjective identification (see Figure 10–1). Dicks's endeavor is still continued at a few places, including the Tavistock Marital Studies Institute, the Tavistock Clinic, and the Scottish Institute of Human Relations in Great Britain, in the relational track of the New York University Post-Doctoral Program in Psychoanalysis in New York, and at the International Institute of Object Relations Therapy in Washington, DC. Fam-

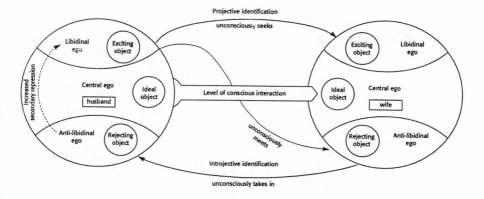

FIGURE 10–1. Object construction through projective and introjective identification in marriage.

Husband and wife interact at the conscious level and also communicate unconsciously through mutual processes of projective and introjective identification to create a marital joint personality. This allows for the return of each spouse's repressed internal objects and parts of ego when these are refound in the spouse's personality. New versions of internal objects and parts of ego are continually re-created for better or worse from experience of the adult self in the culture medium of the marital relationship.

This diagram traces one example: the modification of an internal object when a husband craves affection from an attractive but busy wife. He hopes she will long for him as he longs for her, but she is preoccupied and pushes him away. His exciting object relationship seeks to return from repression by projective identification with the wife's exciting object relationship. Instead, it is further repressed by her rejecting object relationship with which he now introjectively identifies. When his rejecting object relationship is reinforced as a result, it acts to increase the unconscious secondary repression of his exciting object relationship. If such interactions predominate in the marriage, they will form the model for the husband to construct a new enhanced version of his rejecting object and a crushed exciting object. In the healthy marriage, when the rejecting pattern is not regularly reinforced, the husband will instead construct ameliorated versions of his rejecting and exciting objects.

ily studies and family therapy enlarged the laboratory for the study of intimate human interaction and the effect it has on the growth of the individual
throughout life, and for the study of the model for couple dynamics, which
Dicks invented.

Despite his discovery of the importance of relationships throughout life,
Fairbairn focused on the intrapsychic level and remained an individual therapist. He was particularly concerned with the return of the repressed bad object (1943b) which has been split off and repressed early in life, and is reorganized in the oedipal phase (1944). Nevertheless, there are papers in which he
goes much further. The superego, he thought, is a function rather than a specific structure (1956). It consists of suborganizations of ego and object—the
internal saboteur (also known as the anti-libidinal ego), the rejecting object,
and the ideal object—working together as combined internal critic and guide.
He continued to develop this concept until he got it the way he wanted it late
in his life (1963).

In describing this set of combined functions, he was describing more than
the working together of sub-units of the self. The functioning unit also has
new qualities, created by the process that we call *object construction*, a process
intrinsic to continuing self-modification that is central to emotional growth.
The concept of object construction calls for us to take into account more than
the return of repressed bad objects. The concept has to include the self's continual capacity to internalize experiences with new external objects, to blend
those with *old internal* objects to make *new internal* objects, and finally to
reconfigure the self in relationship to these new internal objects. It is a process that goes on throughout life.

Introjection in Object Construction

Fairbairn taught that introjection was central in individual development from
the beginning of life. With the contribution of Dicks and others, we can now
explore its role later in the life cycle, where we can see that introjection is
fundamental in adult development, too. Internal object development continues in mate selection, marital adjustment, and the birth of children and their
development through various stages including leaving home, divorce, illness,
and death.

We can now see from Dicks's work on marriage, from study of the family, from experience in group therapy, from the study of introjective identification (J. Scharff 1992), and from the accumulated experience of psychoanaly-

sis and psychoanalytic therapy, that the internalization of new experience and the building of new internal objects occurs throughout life. It is fundamental to the process through which the self develops cohesion and vitality, maintains its sense of self, and grows in complexity over time.

The Study of Marriage

Let us return to Dicks's starting point, the study of marriage. Whether to get married and whom to marry are usually the defining decisions of adult development. The choice not to have a partner, to have a homosexual partner, or a series of partners, is as defining as the choice of a heterosexual mate, for each road determines the kind of object the self will meet in intimate encounters and in social exchanges with the culture, and the subsequent path of maturation. Having children and the growth of those children is similarly intricately interwoven with a person's continued development. The point is that spouse and children provide the material for new objects whose internal shape and contours change over time in concert with the developmental changes in the external object. The internal objects also change in ways determined by internal forces, by the influence of already existing aspects of self and object.

One implication of this point is that the Oedipus complex need not be viewed as the fulcrum of development, as ego psychology has taught. Oedipal delineation was important historically because it was the stage in which Freud (1923) first studied the internalization of new objects, and where he also saw the implications for the reorganization of the ego or self. In doing so, he contributed the first major study in the object relations literature, building on his earlier work on internalization and mourning (1917). Oedipal development remains a prototype of the birth and reorganization of new objects.

The object relations theorists, on the other hand, have been imperfectly understood to focus on infancy as the center of development and of introjection of new objects. But neither the oedipal era nor infancy are unique in being stages in which new objects are constructed out of a blend of introjection and internal modification, and neither stands alone as the theoretical center of development.

Rather, we can now say that emotional development always centers on the capacity of each individual to keep making internal objects throughout life. The capacity is first exercised in infancy where the first "working models" of self and other (Bowlby 1969) are formed. The fundamental human propensity to keep internalizing experience so as to build psychic structure—in other words, to keep taking in and building new internal objects—is the central organizing principle. This taking in and constructing of new internal objects happens at every major developmental step. Each time the new object comes with a set of affects that convey meaning to the relationship. We are all familiar with falling in love at the birth of a new internal object and grieving at the loss of an important object. Falling in love is an affective marker for the trans-formation of an external object into the most highly valued internal object. Grieving is the affective marker for the loss of the external person who had been taken in as an internal object. These affective events are subjectively experienced by the person, and they can also be observed by outsiders.

But we have to move beyond noting the affective markers that help iden-tify the quality of internal objects if we are going to understand this process. The birth of internal objects follows interactions between a person and his or her external objects, and it is this interaction—this relationship between self and other—that is internalized (Beebe et al. 1993). The internalizing of bad objects is characterized by affects such as fear, disappointment, anxiety, and anger, which accompany interactions of rejection, neglect, and persecution. But a principal condition for the internalization of good objects is that the process should be mutual. To put it colloquially, as Sutherland used to say, everybody wants to be somebody's somebody, or more intellectually as Fairbairn did, "[T]he object in which the individual is incorporated is incor-porated in the individual" (1941, pp. 42–43). This is to say, we look for an object in which to be incorporated, as the infant does in Bion's container/contained model (1967), but we also take that very process back inside us as a mainstay of our own makeup. Throughout life we are looking to introject objects that will contain us through their regard for us. In this way, we feel held, as the baby does in its mother's arms and in her eyes (Winnicott 1960a). Only then can we feel understood, loved, and valued—only then do we feel that our life has meaning. And to the extent that we create objects from experiences of being misunderstood, rejected, or persecuted, we feel hurt and diminished. These are the positive and negative objects that transform the meaning of both outer and inner life experience for better and for worse.

Developmental Stages of Object Formation

Throughout life we take in new objects with their various wrinkles at differ-ing stages of the life cycle. A schematic outline of the birth of new objects and of their internal modification at different life stages will introduce some of the central principles involved.

In infancy, the baby introjects objects based on experience with mother, father, and a handful of other caretakers and siblings. The first introjections are especially powerful because they are nonverbal, because, being first, they have no competition, and because they are there to influence the formation of all later ones. We want to emphasize that the mother is most often *not* the only person taken in. There is usually a father or someone who has a father-like presence. Whenever there are others, they are also extremely important. This leads to our next point about the internal couple.

Soon, and certainly by 7 or 8 months, children are cognizant of the relationship of their external objects to each other (Abelin 1971, 1975). What we call the internal couple is an internalization of the experience with the two parents as they love, fight, cooperate, and form a tantalizing and reassuring combined object for the child. While Klein described a sexualized internal parental couple (1945), other internal couples are formed out of other dyads, for instance that between a parent and one of the child's siblings. A school-age child may create an internal couple based on a mother and a caretaking older brother whose interaction draws attention away from the young child. A 2- or 3-year-old who cannot have ready access to the mother once she has a new baby may create an internal couple based on the nursing couple from which he is excluded. A parent and grandparent who share care and concern for the child may be paired as an internal couple.

Fairbairn was the first to suggest that between 3 and 5 years of age, oedipal resolution allows for the sorting and sifting of images, and the reorganization of ambivalence about each individual object relationship through splitting and reassignment of good and bad between the two members of the parental couple, usually along sexual lines (1944). But he did not take into account the influence of the external objects' relationships to each other, something Freud noticed in passing, Klein focused on as occurring in infancy, and family therapists see all the time. We can now say that the actual treatment of the child by the external couple, and especially the quality of the parents' relationship to each other, is the largest single influence on children's oedipal reorganization of their internal objects and selves (D. Scharff 1992).

The Internal Family and Internal Group

The child's relating to various internal couples leads to an internalization of a family group. This family group is made up of combinations of the internal couples, modified, reduced, and elaborated to yield an internal organization that is more than the sum of the parts represented in it. The larger group—containing all the subgroupings of all the external objects individually and in relationship—cannot be represented by the relatively simple structures we call internal objects or even internal couples. The internal family comprises an exceedingly complex structure that requires us to conceive of internal object organization in a significantly modified way which goes beyond any current psychoanalytic conceptualization. It draws on Nelson and Greundel's (1981) concept of Generalized Event Structures, their term for the psychic structure-building in which the infant represents a group of similar, repeated events so as to build cognitive and emotional expectations, and Stern's Representations of Interactions that have been Generalized (RIGs) (1985), a kind of averaging of experience from a series of experiences with others. For instance, Stern describes the way a baby uses many encounters with its mother's face to construct a generalized image which she may never have actually presented but which is the infant's guide to understanding the many expressions she does present.

Building an internal family relies on an analogous generalizing process applied to object construction and object sorting. Conceiving of experience with a group of people seems to be beyond the mental organizing ability of individuals most of the time, requiring a barely tolerable complexity of thought. To solve this conceptual difficulty, individuals—not only small children but the rest of us too—interpret experience as though it were located in individual internal objects. Instead of feeling loved or unloved by the group as a whole, the child often reads the experience as though it were located in one object, often *constructing* an internal object relationship which represents experience with the group. Then the child searches for an external object who best fits this relationship between self and object, usually distorting its experience with that one external person by generalizing it and attempting to pin the experience with the group on one object, substituting an individual object for a group object. Here the child uses splitting, as Fairbairn described it. For instance, just as bad experience is split and sorted onto one parent and good experience onto another, so experience with a complex group is imposed on individual objects and split among them. But it is also important to recognize that through generalizing and sorting, the child is essentially constructing fundamentally new objects in its internal world.

The child does not merely split actual experience, but actually makes up new versions of experience which it imposes on the outer world and then experiences them as coming from outside.

This also gives us new ideas for projective identification as a mode for the solution of difficulty in constructing internal objects that adequately resonate with external experience. In other words, the need to make new objects fit with the averaging of previous series of experiences drives the need for splitting to distort the new object in the old image.

This process involves active construction in the inner world and employs a series of operations including splitting, object relations sorting of experience, and putting together new constructions. It is more than a cut-and-paste operation, because new bits are also taken in from the outside world, and perhaps new things are added with which the child has little actual experience but which come from precursors such as stories that speak to an inner need. The child cannot keep in mind the complexity of large-scale, complex, group-level experience, and resorts to sorting and coding, understanding, and storing. We emphasize that it is not just children who cannot comprehend group-level experience, and who focus on individuals in groups as the source of meaning. In families, this process accounts for the construction of a family scapegoat, hero, or dependency object. Developmentally, the process begins in the early years at home in the move from individual to family group experience, and it takes a developmental leap when the child goes to school and experiences a widening group there.

Beyond the concept of processing group experience through assignment to individual inner objects, the point to keep in mind is this: as children are moving from family to school and the wider world, they are also making new objects—taking in experience with teachers and other children as friends, competitors, and foes. In the healthy personality, good and bad objects visit the open system of the internal world and are subjected to sorting. Some are installed and others are let go.

There are new individual objects, and new levels of object construction. Now experience with the group in the wider world must be internalized and an internal group model built. While the new objects are built on the model of earlier objects, they are also radically different. The process of understanding the new objects involves new levels of complexity and new organizational principles which do not simply flow from early object experience. The new object relations can modify early experience fundamentally, making it seem better or worse retrospectively, or may maintain and confirm early internal objects while adding to them. The new objects, and the new internal group, are built through principles of organization like the ones involved in internalizing the family group, ones which require new complexity in brain development and social understanding.

At each major developmental stage, new objects are introduced. Going to school brings the acquisition of teachers and peers as new external and internal objects. Children now oscillate between relations with one or two friends and with small and large groups. Adolescence means further developments in the individual's capacity to relate to groups, and new subtlety in the move from dyadic and triadic relationships to larger groups. As adolescents attach to new peers, separate from incestuous internal objects, and experience the gradual sexualization of relationship between self and others, they develop a sense of the future for the self in object relationships. The capacity to internalize new kinds of objects is spurred by sexual and intellectual development and the capacity to conceptualize and choose among alternative paths that may shift in direction and meaning every few days as new futures are tried on and discarded. As all these well-described changes occur, teenagers also develop a new and ever more subtle capacity to move between pair-ing and peer-ing, to be intimate with one or two others and yet remain a functioning part of the wider group and even the wider society. They develop the sense that the intimate relationships remain with them when they are in the group, and that the group provides an outer and inner context for the dyads and triads.

Object Exclusion

Another principle of object construction not previously described is emphasized in adolescence—the process of *object exclusion*. The principle of keeping parents out of the adolescent's life and mind may overlap with installing them as bad objects, but it is not synonymous with it. The process of rejecting parents, of making it clear that there is internal territory parents should not inhabit as internal objects, is a fundamental part of object sorting and construction which cannot be fully subsumed by the notion of bad object construction, for it has more to do with clearing out internal space for the construction of new objects and new aspects of the self when the parental objects are felt to be crowding the teenager's internal world. When adolescents keep their family life entirely separate from their life with peers, they enact with the outer world an internal mechanism of object sorting. In the case of leaving the actual parents behind in order to invest in peers, there is also likely to be object exclusion of the internal parental objects.

The excluded object loses its dynamic importance. Object exclusion of painful objects is not just a form of objectification or neutralization of the object. It is not a form of dissociation, for there the self experiences the object in other states of mind. It is not a form of repression, for there the self retains an active, though hidden, relationship with the repressed. In object exclusion, the object is mourned and eliminated from the internal space. Object exclusion means finished business with the external object and detachment from the internal object.

The internal object no longer matters. Where does it go? The self gives up its attachment to this object and projects its affects of hate, longing, frustration, or sadness that characterized the internal object relationship back into the original external object. We think that the internal object goes back to the source and is reinvested in the actual external object which exists independently of its being in relation to the person and has no special meaning any more.

The same developmental principles apply to acquisition of new objects in adult partnerships, most importantly in marriage, and in the birth of children who become new objects that dramatically reorganize the parents' sense of themselves. The growth and eventual attenuation of these relationships when children leave home and the advent of grandchildren as further new objects, are all events of the life cycle which elaborate on the processes we have been discussing.

The following example illustrates the reorganization of an adult's internal family at the birth of a child.

Mr. C. was in his mid-40s when his second wife unexpectedly became pregnant. Stricken with fear, he became significantly depressed. He had been reluctant to have a child with his second wife and had withdrawn from her sexually out of a sense of loyalty to the children of his first marriage, and out of guilt and loyalty for the damage he had done in sexually betraying his first wife when he left her for his second wife. After significant work had highlighted the way he was hanging on to the old objects as painful ghosts of lost opportunity, he could respond to the birth of the baby as a new opportunity for investing in a new object. This son, his first, became a source of joy, offered him a new focus and a sense of repair, and gave him a reason to let go of the guilty bond to his first wife and finally attach to his second wife in a new way that could now include sexual pleasure.

The acceptance of a new external object and the building of new aspects of the self around it spurred a major transformation of Mr. C.'s self and, in consequence, of several of his internal and external relationships.

The second, more extensive example of building a new object is taken from a consultation interview with David Scharff. It explores the way that the new love object gives meaning to the world of previous internal objects, and at the same time represents totally new possibilities for the self and its object relations. It illustrates some of the processes involved in the birth of new objects: the re-sorting of old object experiences, the repair of trauma and loss, and the continuation of what has been valued while keeping it safe from the damage of everyday life, from the return of repressed bad objects, and from the damage of the external object itself. It demonstrates the gamut of processes: refinding of old objects, object sorting, object construction, object exclusion, and, indirectly, the process of locating painful group experience in a single individual.

William and Janis, a young black couple, sought consultation with me (DES) for sexual difficulties. They had been living together and had planned to be married when they graduated from college, but they postponed their wedding when Janis told William that she was not enjoying sex. When I saw them for a consultation, they had seen a couple therapist six times with some improvement, but they were in a hurry. Their therapist was not confident of her ability to help them with sexual dysfunction and so they sought consultation with me.

Right away I learned that there was no dysfunction. There was a problem with desire. Janis told me, "The act itself is fine, but getting me to want to participate is the problem." William said that not only was he upset that she did not enjoy sex, but he also felt deceived that she had not told him before, since he felt that they should be able to work things out if he knew about them. She said, "I didn't want to hurt him. Something like that can really damage a male's perspective on himself, and I thought I could make things better on my own. But as we got closer to getting married, I got more frightened. After a year passed and we were having sex less, I felt I had to tell him."

Janis said that they didn't communicate well. She felt that no one, not even William, really understood her. For his part, he did not always tell her what he was thinking or feeling, but when he did she could become too upset. For instance, when she pushed him to buy a car they didn't really need, he did not tell her that he felt angry at her for overspending. On another occasion, he willingly paid for necessary groceries after she had overspent on clothes, but he would not buy her a soda treat because he considered that a luxury. She was outraged that he refused such a small request, while he felt that he was being reasonable. "I wasn't being mean," he explained. "I was only saying 'No' because it needed to be said."

Janis told me that she was the middle of three children. In a resigned, flat tone, she qualified that by saying that both her brothers had been murdered. Her older brother was an outstanding young man, full of good qualities, and like a father to her. He was gunned down without cause in a neighborhood shooting. In the wake of his death, her younger brother became depressed, dropped out of school, and started selling drugs, in the course of which he was killed. "My older brother was our only positive male role model," she said. When she talked more about him, she cried and looked at William to ask if he understood what her brother had meant to her. Perhaps she had never told him. He said quietly that he did understand. Janis then said that she had recently had a dream that her brother had come to her and told her not to worry because he was okay. She felt deeply relieved and thought that it meant that he was indeed all right. She had awakened William to tell him the dream. I thought her dream and her telling it to him indicated that because she had found William, she had re-found her brother, her own internal object relations felt satisfactory, and therefore she felt all right in her self for the first time.

Janis's father was alcoholic, and her mother took Janis and left him when Janis was 4. Her grandmother, who was also alcoholic, raised her while her mother worked. Janis never experienced any direct abuse, but had seen arguing and violence among many drunken adults in the household. Janis focused on the disappointment she experienced from her father, who repeatedly promised to help but never showed up. "On one occasion, after my older brother's death, he did come," she said. "But he was so drunk that my younger brother said 'I wish he hadn't even come, he's such a disappointment.'" Janis continued, "If he had been the man, my younger brother might not have been dead. But to say he'll help, and then show up like that! Get outta here! I never want to see him again." While she said this, I could feel the contrast between the father who "was not the man" and William who she knew would stand by her.

William's father was not an alcoholic, but he was a perfectionist, and the son of an alcoholic. When William was young, his father left William and two younger brothers with his alcoholic mother. Later when William and his brothers briefly lived with their father, William took some abuse when he tried to protect his younger brothers from the violence that was mainly directed at them. Mostly, he took care of his mother, and in his teen years, supported her and the children.

By now I had a sense of their relational pattern: William was the older brother Janis had lost, offering to repair her traumatized family, while she was the mother and brothers he longed to care for. Therefore he could hardly stand to say "No" to her. Both of them longed for him to be a better father than either of them had had, to repair old objects and damage to their selves, and to form a couple that would compensate for their devastated internal couples. Although we had not yet discussed sex beyond the initial statement of difficulty, I began to guess at why sex would be so threatening to Janis: penetration might threaten her with the return of the repressed persecuting and abandoning object which, in fantasy, she must have split and repressed into the genitals (D. Scharff 1982).

Now Janis said that she had never really liked sex. It had been easier to go along with it in the beginning. Back then, she and William had made love as often as every day or two. All her previous sexual relationships had felt pressured and abusive. The boyfriend immediately preceding William had forced sex on her and then tried to persuade her he had not, which had left her confused and upset. William was different from the start. He was kind, gentle, and caring. Even so, as in all her previous relationships, she soon became reluctant about sex. When the frequency of sexual interaction decreased to about once a month, William felt that there was too little sex, and she felt that he increased the sexual pressure on her. Once they began a sexual encounter, however, Janis felt it always went well. When they did make love, she enjoyed it. He was a good lover, and he had not understood why sex had become so infrequent, until she finally told him her difficulty.

William had no previous difficulty with sex, but he had never had a girlfriend he actually cared for greatly before, so his pattern was to have sex without intimacy or commitment—a pattern that seemed to have stopped short of exploitation of his various partners, but had nevertheless split off caring from sex.

I now said that the pattern in sex was that she felt she had to say "No" to protect herself from damage, and that most men that she had known previously would not let her be in control like that. In the relationship generally, however, she pressured William not to say "No" so that she did not feel denied. But then she was afraid she had damaged him because she wanted him to stand up to her to rein her in. She agreed: "I need him to say 'No' or I'll go broke. And the funny thing is, I can't say 'No' to my mother. She used my credit card and ran up a lot of debt that I have to pay because I couldn't say, 'You can't do that, Ma.'"

"That's right," said William. "She has the same thing with her mother that I have with Janis. I tell her, 'You just have to say "No" to her,' but she has a lot of trouble doing it."

As we closed the consultation, I asked about their progress in therapy. They felt reassured and understood by their therapist, and planned to continue with her. Janis had already warmed toward William sexually. Their description of the therapy and the sexual improvement led me to think that the therapist's provision of a firm, benign holding was the main factor in allowing the growth of a physical intimacy that was new for both of them. Janis had never before experienced desire that could be satisfied without fear, and William had never experienced sexual intimacy integrated with a caring relationship.

Discussion

In this interview we can see most of the elements of object relating and its effect on the self. We do see what Fairbairn described—splitting and the return of the repressed bad object, as both Janis and William locate the bad object in fathers and try to contain and repair it there. We can see that they share the oedipal reorganization through which they locate badness in the father, although Janis also tries to find in William the image of her good object, the lost older brother who made up for her alcoholic and abandoning father. In locating badness in the fathers and avoiding sexual penetration during genital interaction (through the mechanism of shared projective identification), they spare their mothers who are seen as good even if damaged. Janis kept out the information about her mother's invasion of her finances until close to the end of the interview.

But we also see changes in the inner world beyond those that Fairbairn described. William is not merely a replacement and repair for the lost bad object, enhanced through sorting of old part objects. He is also a new independent object for Janis. Rather than seeing him as a replacement whose image is grafted onto the lost internal object, we can see him as a new object whose importance is enhanced and given meaning from the many connections to her group of inner objects, reviving some, repairing some, extending some, and helping to exclude others. He also fills the space left open by the object exclusion of Janis's father, represented by her saying, "Get outta here! I never want to see him again." William becomes a new internal object that moves to the center of her galaxy of internal objects, providing a new organizational center to her internal relationships. In the process of relating to him as a new external object, she seeks to redefine aspects of her self, for instance by modulating her excessive spending and neediness. She wants to become a better, less impulsive, and less needy person who is more easily satisfied, and more giving than grasping.

Janis has had a painful experience, not only with her father, but with most of the people in her family group, certainly including her mother. To deal with her experience, she has generalized the bad experience and located it in her father, whom she now consciously tries to exclude as an object, while locating the good experience in her dead brother. When she finds a new object in William, she seeks to solve the painful experience with her whole family group through locating good family experience in him individually and through building a new version of her internal couple, one she has never experienced before. Membership in a loving couple who are slowly learning to negotiate boundaries and limits gives her a new internal object modeled on William and a working model of a new internal couple, which each of them are building and installing in their inner worlds. These newly constructed objects support the growth of new aspects of her self, ones which can respond positively to William's efforts to say "No" because it needed to be said. Through all of this we can see the processes of object sorting, object construction, object exclusion, and their accompanying effects on the self.

William, in turn, is seeking an external object to whom he can offer care in order to repair damaged inner objects and build esteem for a shaky self. He treats Janis as a re-edition of his internal object that was damaged by abuse and alcoholism in his family and he fears the return of the repressed bad father and alcoholic, irrepressible mother. But Janis has also become a new object for him. In this interview, William gives less detail than Janis does about the contours of his new object, as he waits in the shadows behind her more dramatic presentation. Dealing with her weakness, he grapples with the defects he sees in his own personality—especially the tendency to cling to her, which compels him to give in to her demands when firm limit-setting would serve them both better. He searches for an object that can be made ideal both through his caretaking and his limit setting. Janis is unlike any previous object he has had. He is searching for a new self and sorting out bits of himself in relation to the new internal object he is attempting to construct through relating to her. He shares an unconscious pattern with Janis in the wish to exclude his father as an object, wanting to build a new self to replace him and create a new external couple with Janis and so generate an internal couple to replace the disastrous one he carries inside from his experience as the child of divorced and persecutory parents.

In relating to and repairing an injured and damaged object, William is repairing his own self through projective identification. In this interview, we see him join with Janis to construct a self in relation to a newly constructed object and a new internal couple while sorting other aspects of internal objects and excluding a bad object father and disappointing aspects of his alcoholic mother. In both Janis and William, we can even get a preliminary idea of the group issues through an understanding of the way they use each other as primary objects to repair their wider family group. Their family group situations are too complex to be held in mind or solved, so they both condense group matters into the relationship with each other, where they hope to solve everything about their lives. In summary, as we examine the situation William and Janis present, we begin to see how self-definition and growth are intrinsically tied to object choice, object exclusion, object construction, and object relating.

Conclusion

The psychoanalytic and developmental literatures have undervalued the possibilities of new object relating throughout the life cycle, focusing instead on the relatively well-explored areas of infancy, young childhood, and even adolescence. As psychoanalysts and individual therapists, we must take far greater account of the evolving processes of object relating, object sorting, object construction, and object exclusion in the continual remodeling of the self, a process which persists into adulthood and throughout life, and which goes on in any therapy, whether during adulthood or childhood. An essential point remains to be made.

Infants building their internal object worlds are fundamentally dependent on their parents' taking them in as new objects for themselves. That parents build a new object is a requirement for the infant's feeling loved and filled with good objects.

The process of object and self construction also occurs in the therapist–patient relationship. Therapists provide the material out of which patients make their new objects. We are the new material of their internal worlds—as they are new material of ours. Dicks's (1967) *joint marital personality*, Ogden's (1994) concept of *the analytic third*, or Bollas's (1992) concept of *genera*—the new constructions jointly made by analyst and patient—all refer to versions of a shared venture which has the power to offer new internal objects to both partners in the two intimate venues of marriage and the therapeutic relationship. As therapists, we offer ourselves as partners in a life-sustaining and life-changing process, one in which we cannot help being modified too.

We cannot avoid taking our patients into ourselves—sometimes more, sometimes less—and in the process they take up residence as denizens of our own internal worlds.

The process of therapy begins, as Fairbairn said, with an object relationship. He wrote (1958):

> In my own opinion, the really decisive factor is the relationship of the patient to the analyst, and it is upon this relationship that the other factors . . . depend not only for their effectiveness, but for their very existence, since in the absence of a therapeutic relationship with the analyst, they simply do not occur. [pp. 82–83]

We can combine Fairbairn's statement with his ideas on introjection: The therapeutic relationship is the central factor in treatment *because it is internalized as a new internal object organization.* As is always the case, the internalizing of one intimate relationship reorganizes the entire internal world. This fundamental process occurs at any age. We take advantage of it to offer something new to the patient. When the new external relationship becomes a new internal object relationship, the patient is fundamentally changed. In any such encounter, we ourselves cannot remain as we were before. In that relationship of mutual influence lies the hope for our patients and our selves.

II

Object Relations Therapy

Section 4

TECHNIQUE

11

Geography of Transference and Countertransference

Transference has been the cornerstone of psychoanalysis and analytic psychotherapy since Freud discovered it. In contemporary psychotherapy, its scope and application have continued to evolve in concert with increasing understanding of its counterpart, countertransference. In this chapter, we explore current analytic ideas of transference and countertransference, and some concepts from marital and group therapy, to arrive at a flexible, adaptable, relational concept of transference. From our integration of these ideas, we isolate elements that can be used to locate the transference in terms of time and space, context and focus, and its containment within the patient, within the individual therapist, or in the potential space between them. These elements yield a *geography of the transference and countertransference*, a map for understanding the transference as a total situation.

Countertransference is usually the compass that guides us toward understanding of the transference, but sometimes it can actively obscure our sense of position in the therapeutic relationship, and then it blocks our thinking and our intuition. Nevertheless, transference is always there even when we think that we cannot see it. At those times, clinicians can pull out this map as an orienting guide.

History of Transference

Understanding of transference changed over the years. Transference that was viewed at first as an impediment later became valued as a source of information and eventually as the main work of the analysis. In the Freudian era alone, its role in treatment progressed from being an inconvenience, a re-edition of old impulses transferred to the analyst, a resistance to the emergence of the unconscious, to a re-creation of the infantile neurosis. Since then, transference has gone from being viewed as a display of internal conflict projected onto the "blank screen" of the analyst, to being seen now as the patient's contribution to the co-creation of the therapeutic relationship through which internal object relations are experienced and modified.

At first, Freud thought of transference as an inconvenience resulting from the reviving of unconscious impulses and fantasies from the past and their being attached by misperception to the person. He quickly recognized that these perceptions and feelings were also about perceptions of the therapist now. He realized that each patient built a new version of reality within the treatment. In 1901 when he wrote the Dora case (1905a), he understood the power of transference to disrupt treatment. With further study, he moved beyond his idea of transference as resistance to seeing transference as the vehicle for understanding the patient's infantile neurosis as re-created in the analysis.

Strachey (1934) applied Klein's ideas on introjection and projection to show that in transference it is the internal objects that are transferred onto the person of the analyst. His paper is most remembered, however, for singling out transference interpretation as the engine driving analytic work. Following that impression, all other forms of intervention took a distant second place, either to be avoided or held in some degree of contempt. A later practical paper on psychoanalytic and psychotherapeutic technique by Bibring (1954) went some distance to rehabilitate activities such as clarification and establishing links as activities also useful in their own right when used in preparation for transference interpretation, while pointing out a more limited role for such forms of the analyst's activity as suggestion, advice, and support.

Klein (1952) reformulated transference as the urge to transfer early object relations, infantile experience, and emotion from the unconscious onto the person of the analyst. In analysis, anxieties and conflicts are reactivated, emerge from the unconscious, and are subjected to the same mental mechanisms and defenses as were in use in early life. She vividly described the emergence of early annihilation anxiety, experienced as persecutory anxiety. The feeling of being attacked from hostile sources is focused on the analyst as the presumed source of the destructive energy. Splitting of the object, idealization of the good object, and introjective and projective identification, are the mechanisms of defense expressed by the transference. Deriving from slightly later when the infant is capable of not splitting the object, feeling ambivalence, and experiencing concern for the object, the transference will be colored by depressive anxiety. Later oedipal guilt and anxiety, which were dealt with by projecting goodness on to one object who is loved and badness on to the other object who is hated, account for further passionate transference attitudes toward the analyst.

In summary, Klein held that transference originates in the same processes that determine early object relations. The analyst may be viewed as a multitude of swiftly changing and sometimes simultaneously present objects because the infant experiences the actual people in the environment in their various aspects, not as whole people. To understand positive and negative transferences, she advised returning over and over to the fluctuation between loved and hated, external and internal objects.

The transference situation is often expressed less directly than when early anxieties are projected clearly onto the analyst. Transference is displaced into the currents of everyday life and relationships. The investigation of transference covers all that lies between the current experience and the earliest experiences, and it links them over and over again until the whole of mental life has been encompassed. Joseph (1985) views transference as a framework in which there is movement and activity. She sees transference and interpretation as living, experiencing, and shifting. Transference includes everything— words, stories, silence, emotion, behavior, ways of getting us to respond, ways of constraining us—everything that the patient brings into the relationship. Most of all, transference lives and changes by evoking a countertransference, which the analyst experiences in resonance with the patient, monitors, and uses to make the transference conscious—a much more effective technique than reconstruction.

The successful analysis of the transference yields changes that are evident in altered attitudes toward the analyst and improvements in the patient's life.

History of Countertransference

Freud did not study or write about countertransference as much as transference. He understood countertransference as the manifestation of the analyst's pathology and evidence of the need for further analysis. His ideas on countertransference did not evolve in tandem with his ideas on transference. Following Kleinian and Independent developments in British object relations theory, countertransference took its place alongside transference as a guiding system, beginning about 1950. Winnicott's paper on hate in the countertransference (1947) was followed by other papers on countertransference from Heimann (1950, 1954), Money-Kyrle (1956), and Racker (1957). The trend of making countertransference the single most important guide to the therapeutic experience continued with the writing of Joseph (1985), followed by Bollas (1987), Casement (1991), Jacobs (1991) and, in the application of object relations to conjoint therapy, J. Scharff and D. Scharff (1987, 1992). In these papers, countertransference was described as a useful emotional response in which affects, reactions, fantasies, and identifications were added to the field of study, offering a depth not previously available when the model had been one of "blank screen" neutrality.

The theoretical basis for understanding the import and effect of countertransference was provided by Klein's (1946) concepts of projective and introjective identification, powerfully communicative mental mechanisms of defense driven by the life and death instincts. Through projective identification, the patient's state of mind is communicated unconsciously to the analyst who introjectively identifies with it until the patient's state of mind is actually evoked in the analyst. The analyst may identify with any part of the patient's ego or object system, often rapidly shifting among them. From this countertransference experience, the analyst can interpret the transference, which can then shift into a new form and so proceed toward psychic change.

Racker (1968) found that he could be more specific about the nature of the transference to the analyst by careful attention to the countertransference. Through projective identification, the patient communicates a part of the ego or the object and evokes a corresponding state of mind in the analyst. This state of mind might be complementary to the patient's or concordant with it. When complementary, the analyst has identified with a projected part of the patient's object and feels pulled to experience the patient in a way similar to the way the original external object was presumed to have felt. When concordant, the analyst has identified with a projected part of the patient's ego and is given to feel the way the patient did in dealing with the external object.

In a series of papers in the late 1950s and 1960s, republished together as *Second Thoughts* (1967), and elaborated in *Attention and Interpretation* (1970), Bion developed Kleinian concepts into an immensely useful theory of thinking and of unconscious communication in growth and development culminating in his idea of the *container/contained* which addresses the mental processing of the mother–infant relationship.

Transference and countertransference go hand in hand. They are always present even when not apparent. They are buried in the intricacies of everyday life and in the therapeutic relationship. We think of introjective and projective identificatory processes as the basis for transference and countertransference. We agree with Heimann (1954) that there is mutual introjective identification between analyst and analysand. We note that introjective and projective identificatory processes are reciprocal between therapist and patient (J. Scharff 1992). We think that countertransference is both the mode of discovery of the transference and the vehicle for its resolution.

In the clinical setting, the countertransference is our trusted compass for following the transference, but we find it useful to have an orienting map as well for those times when the transference is not being picked up in the countertransference. In this chapter, we build a geography of the transference and countertransference, we arrive at the map derived from it, and we conclude with two clinical illustrations.

Concepts Contributing to the Geography of the Transference

We will now introduce the concepts that we use to build our geography of the transference and countertransference.

Container/Contained

We use Bion's concept of container/contained to illuminate the mechanism of transference and countertransference and provide one of the elements in the geography that we are working toward.

In his model of container/contained, Bion developed an interactive theory of the growth of the mind. The infant has unformed anxieties and sense impressions that are not yet thoughts. Through projective identification, the infant puts them into the mother in order to evacuate unstructured and untenable anxiety and to communicate with her. These mental contents have a sojourn inside the mother's mind, and are processed in the realm of thought by her *reverie*, which Bion calls the organ of her mental process. Thus detoxified, metabolized, understood unconsciously, and given an increment of added mental structure through the meaning provided by being understood, they become understandable and are reprojected back into the infant, who takes in the detoxified, modified anxiety, the added increment of cognitive struc-

ture, and also, importantly, a sense of being understood by the mother. Fonagy
has recently described an adult capacity for *mentalizing infant experience* that
we regard as correlating with the process of containment (Fonagy 1996).

We can see that while both mother and child are involved in projecting
mental states into each other, each must sequentially introject what has been
put there by the other. This process requires the partnership of the parent as
a condition for the provision of building blocks of sense experience (sights,
sounds, smells, touch) and their use by the infant for creating an inner mental experience. Both projective and introjective identification inside the infant self, inside the maternal self, and between self and other are simultaneously involved in a mutual process which is, in effect, an unending cycle
out of which the infant and growing child's mind is structured. The whole
process is repeated in therapy, a cycle of relatedness out of which the patient's
mind is restructured.

Countertransference is seen as the mental container for the transference,
while transference is the contained, that unmodified, relatively less-structured
content of the patient's material. The analyst's containment of what is unknown and unstructured of the patient's mind is the foundation for the growth
of understanding.

Now we acknowledge that the patient's mind is, at the same time, a place
for the growth of understanding of the analyst's mind (D. Scharff 1992). There
is a kind of fearful symmetry here that analysts have been slow to acknowledge. Their reluctance came from the twin fears of being influenced by patients, and of being all too influential with their patients in a way too personal
to control. If they followed Freud and the classical approach, they could take
refuge in an impersonal, disinterested, scientific mode of influence. Lately,
however, analytic therapists of many stripes have been embracing the idea of
the mutuality or intersubjectivity of work in therapy and analysis.

The model of containment is one in which the parent's mind is the processor for the raw anxieties and unstructured potentialities of the infant. Although one-sided, this model does approximate the situation of the parent–
infant dyad, but is clearly not applicable to the relationship between the older
child and adult, nor between adult and adult, where the experience is one of
mutual projective identification and mutual processing between two developed egos fully capable of cognition and affect management.

In the clinical setting, we notice that we and our patients act as though a
one-way model applies, and some of our patients act to freeze the system so
that we are given access to them only in certain ways, consigned to being a

frozen container or a dumpster on the one hand, or protected from raw anxieties that must not reach us on the other. When this happens, we may become aware of missing the ordinary mutuality of the parent and baby, and we become painfully aware of functioning as a partial object container, or of not being allowed to offer containment at all to those patients who fear that putting anxiety into us will damage us, kill us off, or destroy their own internal objects. Such patients act as their own unsatisfactory pseudo-containers, leaving us outside the protective shell with which they isolate their inner world for fear that letting out their feelings and entering a state of unconscious communication will project harm into their objects.

Bion's concept of container/contained gives us a theory of how the countertransference receives and transmutes the transference. The therapist's unconscious is the container. The patient's unconscious transference is the contained. The containing function is the therapist's countertransference. We think that the countertransference forms an image of the contained. Sometimes the countertransference may be so invaded by the defensiveness inherent in the transference that it obscures understanding. In this case, countertransference operates as a resistance. Other times it functions like a clear mirror that gives an unmistakable reflection of the interior of the patient's mind.

The transference may be contained, however unsatisfactorily, in the fearful or desperately self-sufficient patient, leaving the therapist feeling nothing. When the patient attributes to the therapist feelings that are not actually felt, the patient is projecting the transference into the therapist, but the therapist is not identifying with it. At some point, the therapist may register a feeling of being excluded. Then the transference has moved into the therapist as a countertransference identification with a part of the patient's ego or internal object. On the other hand, the transference may not be felt by the patient, but instead is only projected into the therapist who contains it in the countertransference. Patient and therapist may both be aware or unaware of transference and countertransference simultaneously or separately, and either of them may evacuate their feelings into the space between them.

So the location of containment of the transference may remain in the patient, be projected into the therapist, be projectively identified with by the therapist, or be projected into the space between them.

The location of countertransference is in the therapist. When it is not recognized, however, it may be projected into the patient, who is forced to contain it to protect the therapist from the triggering of personal reverberations with the patient's material. It may also be felt as a perturbation in the atmosphere of the session when it is projected into the space between patient and therapist.

Concordant and Complementary Identification

The countertransference may be complementary to or concordant with the transference (Racker 1957, 1968). In other words, the analyst may identify with a projected part of the patient's object (the complementary countertransference) or a projected part of the patient's ego (concordant countertransference). We usually find that these identifications shift from session to session. Patient and analyst recreate the patient's internal object relationships from either pole of ego or object.

The location of the transference may be split between the patient and the therapist due to the projection of a part of either ego or object.

Potential Space: The Analytic Third

What else do we know about the space between patient and therapist? Moving on from Winnicott's idea of the potential space between mother and infant, that space for creativity and imagination, various authors from different schools of thought have been writing about the shared experience between patient and therapist that leads to growth. There are several overlapping ideas: the "x factor" (Symington 1983), genera (Bollas 1989), intersubjectivity (Stolorow and Atwood 1992), the co-construction of meaning between patient and analyst (Gill 1994), and the analytic third (Ogden 1994). These concepts all refer to ways of understanding that what is created between patient and therapist could not have the form it takes without the particular combination of personalities and the process unique to these two people. It is a third structure related to the subjective experience of each of them, but finding its shape in the particular, idiosyncratic union of their two personalities. This structure is built from events that happen in the space between the two individuals, not simply within either of them, although it is intimately related to what happens within each of them as they experience each other.

This structure formed by patient and therapist recalls the *marital joint personality* (Dicks 1967; see Chapter 10). Each couple relationship can be described as somehow apart from the personalities of the two partners while still allowing for similarities and differences in personalities (Dicks 1967). The creation of the marital joint personality (Dicks 1967) through the projective and introjective identification of aspects of the self and the object refound in the spouse, provides a prototype for the construction of the analytic third in the therapeutic relationship (see Figure 10–1). Mutual projective identificatory processes go on between spouses as they do between a baby and each of its parents. They go on between siblings, students and teachers, employers and employees. All intimate relationships acquire a joint personality, or third entity with qualities unique to that relationship, which is both larger and smaller than the sum of the two personalities that it comprises.

Another influence on the creation of the joint personality is the patient's and the therapist's internal couples, an internal object relationship based on the child's versions of the parental couple experienced at different developmental stages. Klein (1945) noted the child's interest in the parental couple, not only as an actual and literal couple, but as a pair who form the stuff of fantasy. She described the child's sexualized fantasy of the mother as containing the father's penis and the child then carries forward this early version of the internal couple. The couple formed by therapist and patient is influenced by such *internal couples* in both patient and therapist, and in turn changes them as the joint creation by therapist and patient is itself introjected in each of them where, like a strange attractor, it is organized by and appears to organize experience.

In summary, the transference may be located in a joint object-relational construction in the potential space between patient and therapist co-created by mutual projective and introjective identificatory processes.

Hopper's Four-Cell Square

Working both as an analyst and group analyst, Hopper (1996) was in a unique position to observe and describe four areas of experience which describe the therapeutic relationship in terms of time and space:

1. Here-and-now (what is happening in the affective unconscious communication right now between patient and analyst).
2. Here-and-then (what happened in primary relationships in the past when it is experienced again in a shared therapy experience between patient and therapist).
3. There-and-now (what happens out there with others, the family, at work, in society—but in present time).
4. There-and-then (what was happening in the culture, and in the family as the culture carrier, when this person was growing up).

The first three categories refer to the intrapsychic and interpersonal dimensions. Hopper likens them to the three nodal points of Malan's triangle: person, other, and therapist (Malan 1976), which we discuss in Chapter 17. Hopper suggests adding a fourth dimension, as did Stadter (1996), which we will also discuss in Chapter 17. But where Stadter's additional fourth component concerning the way the person relates to himself is placed internal to the triangle, Hopper prefers to "square the therapeutic triangle" by adding a fourth angle that represents the social unconscious (Hopper 1996) (see Table 11–1).

As we interpret Hopper's categories, the here-and-now refers to the therapeutic relationship; the here-and-then to the internal object relations derived from infancy and early childhood and their expression in the interpersonal arena including the transference; and the there-and-now refers to the interpersonal expression of internal object relations in the present—at work, at play, and in the family. The there-and-then is infrequently attended to in psychoanalytic therapy and has almost no standing in psychoanalytic theory, where concern with external reality is often interpreted only as a displacement of intrapsychic anxiety. Hopper's interest in the there-and-then realm of experience derives from his interest in the social unconscious—those events and attitudes of the wider society experienced in common but the importance of which is almost always overlooked.

The resulting pattern forms a square divided in four cells or quadrants that represent the four areas of experience of the intrapsychic and social unconscious in place and time—here, there, now, and then. These four quadrants constitute a simple framework for constructing the geography of transference.

Here-and-Now

Events that happen to patient and therapist in the shared participation of an encounter in the here-and-now have an immediacy of time and place that lends power and a sense of conviction to the therapeutic process (Rickman 1951). When the therapist can identify something as "happening to you or me or us right here and right now," the exploration of affect, behavioral patterns in interactional events, and inner world contributions to those shared moments has a poignancy beyond intellectual conjecture or speculation about

TABLE 11–1. Hopper's four-cell therapeutic square.

	SPACE	
TIME	**Here**	**There**
Now	Here-and-now	There-and-now
Then	Here-and-then	There-and-then

more distant events. This aspect of life together in therapy requires the full presence and participation of the therapist for its authenticity.

There-and-Now

The there-and-now constitutes the events of the patient's present life, brought into the therapeutic space as the narrative the patient weaves for the analyst: the tales about his current life, the characterizations of his wife, boss, children, parents. This is material apparently devoid of current transference, but we shall see that to separate this material from its transference meaning and context is an important misreading and underestimation of transference as a total situation.

Here-and-Then

There are two aspects of the here-and-then dimension. First, it constitutes the heart of analytic transference. A situation from "then" in the past—often the patient's infancy or early childhood—is imposed "here" on the treatment. The therapist is taken to be like an internal object understood as an object from the past but carried in a living form inside the patient. It is as though the therapist is a new and immediately present version of aspects of the patient's mother, father, or other internalized figure brought once more to life in the therapy through an enactment and a current affective identification. This here-and-then relationship is not truly about the past, for it happens between the patient's current internal objects and self-components and the therapist. It is actually a form of here-and-now relating between internal parts of patient and therapist which are currently operational, but which are *experienced* as being about past object relationships. Like other here-and-now interactions, this kind of shared experience also carries the feeling of conviction. The patient, and frequently the therapist, feel as though the past is coming to life in the consulting room. To deny that sense would be to deny the mode of experience for both patient and therapist; for internal objects, while not faithful and accurate representations of the past, are our only living record of it nevertheless.

In our view, the here-and-then situation also refers to the narrative of the therapeutic situation, all that has happened between patient and therapist over time as their own relationship gathers a history, the memories of a few moments ago, the last session, all that has happened over the last year in therapy, or in a previous therapeutic contact. It carries the richness of shared accumulated interactions which make up the shared therapeutic experience.

Object Relations Individual Therapy*

There-and-Then

In Hopper's view, this category refers to social reality as it exists in the social unconscious. It affects growth and development through the influence of social, cultural, and communicational arrangements of which most people remain unaware. Only the mature can remain indentified with their culture and actively involved in it, and yet regard it objectively and seek to change its influence over self and others for the better. Hopper uses the there-and-then category for mention of phenomena that impinge on life and safety such as a bomb threat or shifts in managed care benefits, and emphasizes that they have universal relevance and meaning beyond whatever symbolic function they may also serve in intrapsychic life. He makes the point that analyzing the influence of the wider culture on mental life is essential to understanding self and transcending the limits of a particular background.

Modifying Hopper's Four-Cell Square to Include the Future

The word "then" may be used to refer to the future as well as to the past. We think that there is also a transference to the future as patient and therapist imagine what will transpire in their lives and in the therapeutic relationship. We want to extend the here-and-then and the there-and-then category to apply to the future dimension.

The If-and-When of the Here-and-Then

We regard fantasies about the future as complementary to concerns about the past. The here-and-back-then determines the transference, but the transference also includes a future dimension which is structured similarly to the way the past is carried psychically: the future of the transference consists of the hopes and fears of how the therapeutic relationship will turn out. This focus on the future of the patient's actual relationship with the therapist led us to a dimension that we call the *if-and-when* of the transference. The relationship between patient and therapist has a history (a past, a back-then) on which to base this vision of the future. The perception of the past relates to the hope for the future of the therapeutic relationship (including its being no longer necessary). Both past and future are areas subject to transference. These thoughts and feelings about the future of the therapeutic relationship require reinterpretation and reworking in the same way that a growing girl uses and revises her vision of her past relationship with her parents, and uses and revises her vision of future relationships to them. That is, just as adult children make transference use of the past and future of their internal parents even when in the room with their actual parents, so individual patients make transference use of past and and future relationships with their therapists even while experiencing current relationships with them.

Modifying Hopper's There-and-Then

To Hopper's concept of the realm of the there-and-then, we also add an element of importance to us as individual therapists who also work with families. We think that the there-and-then includes the impact of cultural experiences on the family which is then conveyed to the individual in the family setting, as well as by the wider world. Social issues such as the Holocaust or nuclear threat may only be remembered as aspects of parental treatment of the child, may be specifically recalled as events, may be named and struggled with in family debate, or may simply be experienced as a nameless dread or fond hope regarding society, depending on how the family has metabolized its experiences at the unconscious level. For us, the there-and-then realm of the social unconscious includes its mediation by the family unconscious, which forms the vehicle for conveying and modifying the influence of the wider culture.

In our view, the mediator of this reality for the growing child is the family. The family is the major carrier of the culture. The patient's past is shaped as much by social forces on his family as by the specific personalities of his parents and siblings, and by the family's style of denying, narrativizing, and adjusting to social reality. The family may have been part of a privileged or underprivileged majority or a minority characterized by class, race, religion, and nationality, to mention a few. The there-and-then world occupies our attention, for instance, when a woman recounts her experience as a child with warring parents in whose culture divorce was prohibited, a man describes his school days among the cultural elite, or another woman describes her childhood search for safety in an urban ghetto. In practice, we use the there-and-then to refer to experience from the past, including the recent past outside the consulting room.

The If-and-When of the There-and-Then

The future is also a neglected aspect of the there-and-then. To Hopper's there-and-then category, which refers to the past, we suggest adding ideas about the future of society. We propose calling this dimension the *if-and-when of the there-and-then*. Here we are concerned about the patient's hopes and fears about the outside world: fears of social defeat, persecution, and exposure to war; questions about the future implications of the current economic status; longings for work satisfaction; and hopes for future well-being of self as a self-sustaining person, usually within some form of family or social structure. All of these issues motivate the patient to seek analysis and are always in the background of intra-psychic work, even if they come to the center of attention only occasionally.

Hopper argues that the if-and-when mode of experience is not a separate aspect of mental and transference organization because a patient's imagination occurs in the present time, even though it is about the future (Hopper, personal communication). To his objection, we respond that expectations, thoughts, and memories deriving from the "there-and-back-then" also occur as a mental organization in the present, even though they are about the past. The common experience that people (and societies) rewrite history in the light of contemporary experience makes the point that personal and social history is a matter of current understanding and current importance. The same applies to the future: individuals and societies are constantly revising their visions of their futures, which are carried personally and collectively as a current mental and social organization. Bearing in mind that the past and the future both contribute to the formation of mental organizations, we suggest that both are active in the organization of transference and countertransference.

In summary, transference emanates from four areas of experience—here-and-now, there-and-now, here-and-then, and there-and-then. The here-and-then and the there-and-then include both the back-then and the if-and-when aspects of then. The here-and-then includes the history of the transference.

Context and Focus

Two other dimensions of transference derive from Winnicott's division of the relationship between mother and infant into two fundamental categories, the *object mother* and the *environment mother* (D. Scharff and J. Scharff 1987, J. Scharff and D. Scharff 1994, Winnicott 1945, 1963a,b).

As the environment mother, the mother offers a context for the infant's going-on-being, *a contextual holding relationship* to support the infant by providing safety and security.

As the object mother, she offers a *centered relationship* in which she is the object of her child's desire for love and meaning, the person who fulfills or frustrates longings, and is the object of intense curiosity, love, fear, and rage.

Context: The Environmental Parent and the Holding Relationship

The *contextual holding relationship* recalls the arms-around holding that the mother provides physically to the baby, and functions as a metaphor for the general provision of psychological holding. Within this arms-around emotional posture, she positions the baby, provides food, keeps the child clean, protects from harm, and provides for the child's well-being and general sense of safety. In this mode of relating over time, she prepares the ground so that the child can grow and relate. While the mother may be the principle provider of holding, there are many variants on that situation, all of which can meet the baby's needs. The father, a live-in grandparent or housekeeper, a reliable day care person, or an older caretaking sibling provide holding just as well. Modern attachment research has demonstrated that a child forms specific and differentiated patterns of attachment to each parent or primary caretaker, so that a child may have a secure attachment to one parent and an anxious attachment to the other. The quality of holding is specific to each situation and primary holding object (Fonagy 1996, Slade 1996).

In addition, we recognize the importance of the spousal partnership itself to the provision of a context. When holding is provided, for instance, by a mother and father who have a primary partnership with each other, their couple relationship is itself a source of the holding whose importance goes far beyond the support a father can give a mother. We are emphasizing here that the parents' relationship itself has an independent quality due to the joint personality that we have discussed, and that this parental pair itself provides a quality of valuable holding to infants and children. Children know this, and in times of loss or separation from one parent, they miss the relationship with the paired parents just as they miss the individual who is gone. This same quality of an independent joint personality applies to other situations, a mother and grandmother who form the parental pair, a father and housekeeper, or a mother and older sibling who share the care of the child.

The family group itself, in whatever constellation it exists, contributes to the overall holding of the child. For instance, a child with two working parents who is cared for by a housekeeper during the day develops a sense of how the parents returning home in the evening relate to the daytime housekeeper and to the child's overall situation. The child learns to relate to the group, to differentiate among the individuals, and to assess which individual is likely to respond to which need. All in all, contextual holding provides an environmental extension of the mother's presence.

We have pursued this line of reasoning in order to make the case that holding is a quality not only of the mother–child situation, but of the group parent–child situation, including mother, father, and other caretaking individuals. We hasten to add, however, that such a group should be a small one in which all the individuals know the baby or young child intimately and in which they know and interact with each other. We cannot substitute a large group of interchangeable adults who are unable to focus on the child reliably, and with whom the child has a repeated experience of discontinuity.

The provision of holding does not fall solely to the parenting group. The infant must provide part of the holding, too, which contributes to a shared, strong holding environment. When an infant cannot offer aspects of holding in return and at the same time as the parents, it is the parents who are apt to feel dropped.

So too in therapy. When patients cannot hold us in mind, we feel on fragile, dangerous ground. When they cannot remember to attend their sessions or pay their bills, or when they cannot trust our competence or our method of working, they cannot support the treatment. Holding is a mutual project co-constructed by patient and therapist. Both contribute to the transferential here-and-now experience based on the qualities of their separate cultures and there-and-back-then experiences that color the contextual holding transference (Hopper 1985, 1995, personal communication).

Focus: Centered Holding

The *centered relationship* occurs when the mothering person opens the transitional space between her (or him) and the baby and offers herself as an object for direct relating. She becomes the focus of the baby's love, hate, interest, hopes, and fears. Within the protected arms-around envelope provided by the environmental parent, the object parent and child have the space and safety for centered relating to form a centered relationship which has an external reality and groundedness based on the parent's preoccupation with and handling of the baby, and which is the stuff out of which the child forms internal object relationships. They speak to each other, look into each other's eyes and form an eye-to eye, I-to-I relationship. Here the mother, father, and few other primary others are each experienced as discrete objects and part-objects who are each in a dyadic relationship to the child, who develops strong affective responses to them. These various responses characterize each part of the relationship. In the area of central focus, the parents' relationship to each other becomes itself a single object, the experience from which the *internal couple* is fashioned as a form of discrete internal object for the child.

Nothing holds a relationship as firmly as properly functioning, centered relating in which two people become each other's objects, whether in the context of a mutually loving or a hateful relationship. So in the end, the centered relationship has a holding function of its own, a kind of grab-hook into the core of the other person which complements and fortifies the arms-around of the contextual relationship. In practice, when both contextual and focused relationships go well, they operate seamlessly to provide arms-around and centered holding. But in individual pathology, damaged relationships, and difficult therapeutic relationships, we see the two components of relating, the contextual and the centered, leading to contextual and focused transferences respectively, and generating corresponding elements of countertransference.

In the centered relationship, the child finds its *objects* and peoples its inner world with them.

In the contextual holding relationship, the child is supported to find its *self*.

Focused and Contextual Transference and Countertransference

Winnicott's model of environmental and object mothers forms the basis of two types of transference, the contextual transference to the therapist's analogue of the parents' holding capacity, and the focused transference as the analogue to the relationship with the object parent (D. Scharff and J. Scharff 1987, 1992, D. Scharff 1992) (Figure 11–1).

The *contextual transference* derives from the early experiences of environmental provision and, by analogy, consists of those experiences of holding and its vicissitudes in the therapeutic situation that pertain to the provision of therapeutic space and the facilitation of understanding, growth, and development. When the contextual transference is positive, the patient experiences the therapist as understanding and caring, like the kind of parent or teacher who can be taken for granted in a benign way—used as an object in Winnicott's sense. In the positive *contextual countertransference*, the therapist feels much as a good parent or teacher might, satisfied with the work and reaffirmed as a helpful person. When the contextual transference is negative, the patient feels the therapist is not to be trusted and may not have the patient's best interests in mind. Therapy is experienced as not entirely safe. In the negative

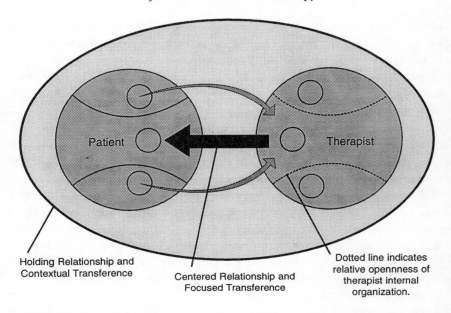

FIGURE 11–1. Focused and contextual transference in individual therapy.
Within the envelope of the holding relationship, patient and therapist examine the patient's inner object relations and their effect on relationships. In the
focused transference, these are projected into the therapist, where they are
modified in interaction with the therapist's less rigid splitting and repression
of internal object relations, and then fed back to the patient in modified form.
The relationship itself is the agent of change.

contextual countertransference, therapists feel treated with suspicion. They
feel attacked, misused and misunderstood, or useless—signs of projective
identification of the patient's threatened self's experience of lack of safety and
of previous aggressive attacks on weak holding.

The *focused transference* is that aspect of the relationship in which the therapist becomes the recipient of discrete projections of internal objects and self.
Aspects of the critical parent, the seductive or overanxious parent, the negligent, tantalizing uncle, the smothering nanny or grandparent, the inspiring
or punitive teacher, the rivalrous sibling are all internalized as loved, feared,
and longed-for objects. In addition, parts of the self in relation to these discrete objects are located in the therapist through projective identification. In
the process, the therapist also becomes a new internal object for the patient
through introjection, object sorting, and object construction (see Chapter 10).

In the *focused countertransference* we feel treated as though we actually were the critical or adoring parent who seduces and loves, neglects, persecutes, and hates. And at times we fall into an enactment of the corresponding state of mind that is invoked in us.

In summary:

In the transference emanating from the centered relationship, the patient's self finds the objects within the therapist and peoples its inner world with them.

In the transference emanating from the contextual holding relationship, the patient feels supported to find the self within the therapeutic relationship.

The Geography of Transference

We are now ready to describe the geography of the transference and construct a map for therapists to use. This map will be a help in determining the location and action of transference and its impact on the countertransference in the clinical situation. To build the geography, we have consulted the old maps of theory and have surveyed the new findings. In working toward making the map, we have isolated elements analogous to longitude, latitude, depth, and altitude. The compass we employ is always our countertransference, but for those moments when intuition fails to give us a reading, we can use our cognitive apparatus and refer to the elements in the map.

The First Element of Transference: Locating the Containment

First we ask ourselves *where in the therapeutic setting does the impact of the transference occur?* Is it felt to be located between the patient and therapist in the transitional space where the therapeutic third holds sway, in the internal world of the patient, and/or in the internal world of the therapist? Describing this element is difficult, because an effect in one of these areas must affect the other two, but in the shared experience of patient and therapist, there is often agreement about where the experience is felt to occur, with the effect that the other two spaces are relatively less available to direct experience. At times, the patient will seem to be intensely moved while the therapist is curiously untouched; other times, the therapist may be full of feeling while the patient is unmoved; and at some times of mutual involvement, an event seems to touch both, or more precisely, to be a matter of the whole atmosphere of the session or space that they share (Duncan 1990). As we shall see when we come to the question of interpretation (Chapter 12), understanding the location of the processing space within the transference–countertransference interchange is a vital clue in arriving at the most helpful way of speaking to the patient, for at times patients will experience things as residing in themselves and then we direct comments to them about their immediate experience of self, but at other times the experience is *as if* it is in the therapist, and the most useful comments describe the patient's experience of the therapist. At still other times, the most accurate or helpful comments will focus on shared experience stemming from the analytic third, in which the experience of therapist and patient has condensed.

The Second and Third Elements of Transference: Locating the Transference in Space and Time

Containment can be located within the session, but it also occurs outside therapy where it cannot be observed. To understand containment in all its locations in therapy and in life, we require the next two elements of transference, those of space and time. Together they supply coordinates with which to locate events that occur in different time zones and emotional spaces of the patient's intra-psychic and social unconscious, and yet affect the therapeutic relationship.

To introduce the element of time we ask ourselves *when is the impact of an event understood to be felt*. Is it felt now, was it felt in early life, or will it be felt in future relationships?

To introduce the element of space we ask ourselves *where the event is understood to occur*. Is it here in the therapeutic space or out there in the patient's life outside therapy?

We consider the elements of time and space together and plot the results according to our version of Hopper's four-cell square extended by two categories to include the future dimension. We change his use of "then" when referring to the past to "back then" in order to distinguish it from "then" which can also refer to time in the future. Now we have six cells to consider. Lastly we differentiate two aspects of "there." To the "there" of society which fits Hopper's usage, we add a closer-in aspect of "there" that is the "there" of family life. Now we have eight cells to consider (see Table 11–2). Using these loci on the map, we should be able to demonstrate where the transference is at any given moment, whether or not the therapist can (or needs to) locate the role of transference consciously during the session. Important transference work goes on all the time in those spheres of transference that are largely out of sight but nevertheless active.

TABLE 11–2. Transference in terms of time and space.

TIME:	SPACE:		
	Here In therapy	**There** In family	In society
Past	Here-and-back-then	There-and-back-then	
Present	Here-and-now	There-and-now	
Future	Here-and-if-and-when	There-and-if-and-when	

So far, we can locate our discussion of transference in dimensions of time (past, present, and future), space (here in therapy or there in life outside therapy), and containment (in the therapist, in the patient, or in the space between).

Locating Containment in the Here-and-Now

Now we return to the dimension we discussed previously: the location of containment within the therapeutic experience. Within the here-and-now experience of the therapeutic relationship, we attend to the location of experience between and within patient and therapist. Therefore, we put a magnifying glass on the here-and-now, to see *where the transference is being experienced.* We look to see whether the transference during therapy is being experienced within the patient, in the therapist as countertransference, or in the space between them (Figure 11–2).

In the patient / The space between / In the therapist

FIGURE 11–2. Expanded view of the here-and-now.

By locating the action of containment within the here-and-now experience of the therapy, we can connect its action to other modes of experience of the patient. We can begin, for instance, to deduce the way the patient uses the community for containment in the there-and-now and the way he did so there-and-back then. When we come to speak with the patient about the link to the here-and-then we can ask "Is it possible that the way you are experiencing me now is like the experience you had with your mother or father then?"

The Fourth Element of Transference Geography:
Contextual and Focused Transference

We then ask ourselves *whether the transference applies to the contextual holding relationship provided by the therapist, or the focused centered relationship.*

The contextual transference can be observed from the moment therapy begins. It represents the patient's concerns about trust in the provision of safety, on the one hand, and on the other, fears of invasion, persecution, and deprivation. It is the contextual transference that needs to be grasped early in treatment. When it is under attack, it needs understanding and interpretation in order to support the entire treatment project. Hopper (1995) links up the second (there-and-now) and the fourth (there-and-then) cells of his paradigm with the contextual transference and countertransference.

The focused transference takes longer to develop because it depends on the growth of a relationship adequate to find and confirm resonance with the patient's inner world. Ordinarily, it takes several months or even years of intensive treatment before it emerges and eventually crystallizes as a transference neurosis which has a pattern that expresses in a condensed way the patient's object relational difficulties. The transference that is prominent early in treatment is the contextual one, except when the patient prematurely rushes to a focused object transference in order to obliterate fears about inadequate emotional holding. For instance, patients with borderline functioning or those with a history of trauma may rush to identify the therapist as being like a mistrusted parental figure in order to narrow the area of anxiety by personifying the early, acute lack of trust they bring to treatment. Other patients may identify the therapist as the best in the country, someone who is unbelievably skillful and devoted to them—a picture built on the basis of no evidence at all. Such prematurely focused transferences can best be understood in terms of expressed or denied fear and mistrust in the contexual transference. Hopper (personal communication) agrees that the contextual transference may also operate as a defense against the focused transference, but we find that less usual, especially in the opening phase of treatment.

Mapping Countertransference

Like transference, countertransference may be felt at different locations. Countertransference usually occurs in the here-and-now and is located in the therapist. It may be felt as a physical sensation, a thought, a fantasy, a smell, or an emotional response. In other words the transference may be projected into the therapist's psyche or soma.

Countertransference is not always contained in the therapist, but may be projected out into the patient or into the space between them. For instance, countertransference may be projected out of the here-and-now into the there-and-now of the therapist's personal space outside the session when the therapist may dream or fantasize about the patient. The therapist may analyze the dream to free the countertransference of personal infantile elements so that treatment can proceed without impediment, or may use the dream images that involve the patient to arrive at understanding of the transference. The therapeutic space that has temporarily expanded then moves back inside the here-and-now boundary.

Countertransference in the here-and-now also occurs in the here-and-then because it has a history. The present countertransference may be like that felt in an earlier time in the therapy. The most usual interference with the countertransference comes from the therapist's here-and-then, when the therapist's internal object relationship is refound in relation to the patient. Countertransference has a future dimension. We might long for it to be different. We might have in mind an image of the way we would rather feel in relation to the patient.

There is also a there-and-then of the countertransference, in that therapists are subject to the influence of current ideas on the countertransference that hold sway in the analytic literature or the societies where they train. Another there-and-then influence on the countertransference is the activity of the countertransference in response to other patients, past and present, in the therapist's internal group. The future dimension of the there-and-then is active when the therapist thinks of using an example from the patient to contribute to the pool of ideas that changes the analytic culture. Countertransference is also affected by the there-and-now of cultural attitudinal shifts regarding analytic ways of thinking about unconscious process and internal object relations in society.

Countertransference forms in reaction to the focused and contextual transferences. We can ask ourselves whether we are experiencing a countertransference to transference directed to our contextual holding or to our centered relating.

Countertransference also forms in relation to the projected part of ego or object. We can ask ourselves if our countertransferece is concordant (aligned with part of the patient's ego) or complementary (aligned with part of the patient's object).

A Multidimensional Model
of Transference and Countertransference

We find that this way of allocating elements of transference and countertransference helps us detect the areas, ways, and means of transference action. Putting this together with the basic framework, we now propose an integrated model for locating the aspect of transference active in the therapeutic encounter and studying the impact and efficacy of various interventions. The map is also useful for elaborating corresponding aspects of countertransference that have hitherto been difficult to see or use.

Transference and countertransference can be understood to occur along the vertices of all the dimensions we have been discussing:

1. Location of the contained anxieties in the therapeutic space: inside the patient, inside the therapist, or a shared independent creation in the space between them;
2. Locations of projected parts of self or object;
3. Inside or outside of the therapeutic space: here or there; in the relationship between patient and therapist, or in other relationships outside their immediate experience, including the family or the wider society;
4. In time: now, back then in memory, or in the future of anticipated experience;
5. In the contextual holding or the focused, centered relationship.

These five elements relate to each other in intimate ways. In analytic literature, usually only one element has been the subject of study at a time. For instance, Freud emphasized the recall of past experience imposed on the person of the therapist. He was describing a focused, here-and-then transference as the creation of the patient which the therapist understood but did not experience in a significant personal way. More recent analytic literature has described focused transference—understanding and interpretation in the here-and-now, sometimes as a creation of the patient, often recently with reference to the subjective experience of the analyst, and more occasionally as part of a joint creation of patient and analyst (Jacobs 1991, Joseph 1989, McDougall 1985, Ogden 1994, Symington 1983). Group therapy and family therapy have been concerned with the problem of context (Hopper 1985, D. Scharff and J. Scharff 1987). What is needed is a comprehensive view that accommodates input from all these modalities.

Table 11–3 summarizes the elements that comprise the multidimensional view of the geography of transference.

TABLE 11–3. The elements of transference geography.

Space	Here	There	
	In Therapy	In Society	In Family
Time	Now	Then	
		Back then	If-and-when
Contained experience	In patient	In space between	In therapist
Transference type	Focused	Contextual	
	Ego	Object	

The Geography of Two Transference Enactments

We believe that a richer and fuller understanding of the transference–countertransference situation is possible using this model. It provides a map against which to compare findings gathered from intellectual appraisal and from process and review of countertransference feelings and fantasies. It ensures that we do not shortchange the power of transference work and interpretation by overlooking any of its dimensions. This model helps us to see transference where it is occurring and how its influence pervades the therapeutic project. When we come to the discussion of interpreting transference (Chapter 12) we will be able to use transference geography as a practical guide when we wish to speak about elements of the transference relationship—focusing our understanding on experience as seeming to be contained in the patient, in the therapist, or in the space between them; about the relationship as experienced with reference to the present, past or future; inside or outside the therapy in family life or in the wider society; and in the contextual or centered relationship. We illustrate the elements more graphically in Figure 11–3.

We will now give two examples of mapping transference geography. In the first, a negative focused transference suddenly emerges to replace an apparently good contextual transference. In the second, we demonstrate the actual transference situation when there appears to be an absence of focused transference.

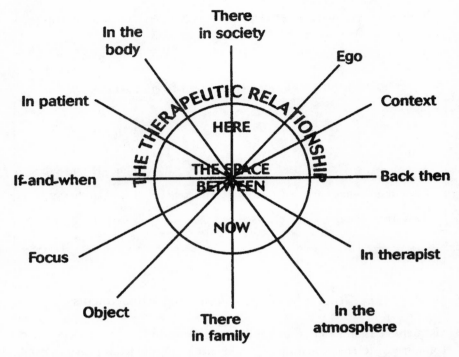

FIGURE 11–3. The multidimensional compass of the total transference and countertransference.

A Focused Negative Transference Breaks through a Positive Contextual Transference

Catherine had recently sought therapy with me (DES) for a renewed on-set of depression related to feeling underused and unappreciated by her boss whom she may have alienated by her demands for more interesting work. Catherine had been a tireless worker all her life, really an over-worker. Since she was twice divorced and without children, she spent her weekends and time off at the same frantic pace in hobbies and volunteer activities that gave her considerable pleasure while not fully compensat-ing for the lack of a satisfying intimate relationship. She had transferred to the Washington area after a successful career with her company, and had been given what was considered to be a plum in the national headquarters. But when she arrived at her new post, there was little to do. The inactivity made her incredibly anxious, and she began to agitate for more work, explaining to her current boss in the words of her previous boss that "a bored Catherine is a dangerous Catherine." Taking this as a threat rather than an offer of service, the new boss warned her to calm down, shape up, and adjust to the pace of the work, or risk being shipped back to her previous job.

In this crisis, she began therapy. She told me that perhaps she might choose to go back to her previous job, but she did not want to be sent in humiliation and defeat. And in her depression at this work confrontation, she saw some echoes of the failures in her two marriages and her current lack of relationships with men. She trusted my judgment that therapy should be twice a week for an indefinite length of time because she recognized that her issues would persist beyond the period of adjustment at the new job, and she chose to use the couch. We agreed that her need to overwork served to cover an emptiness in close relationships and a depression that descended whenever work stopped. She committed herself fully to the treatment and arrived for her sessions with a cheerful, eager attitude despite her depression. She also had a characteristic slightly sheepish demeanor, as if she had been caught doing something playful.

In the session that I am about to describe, Catherine began by talking about her mother in a forthcoming way, as if comfortably assuming my interest in the there-and-then of her experience with a mother who, like many women of her social class in the '50s, was a full-time homemaker. Catherine's contextual transference appeared quite positive. She told me that unlike her present boss who would be happier with less effort on her part, her mother said that Catherine never did enough. A 98 percent in school should have been 100 percent. Catherine's mother frequently gave the children chores to do when they got home from school, at which point she herself went to bed and left them to it, even though she had been home all day and could have rested earlier while the children were in school. Catherine's father worked too hard and was not there in the early evening either. Catherine then thought that her mother was lazy. Now as an adult she could see that her mother was mainly drained by her own private angst, probably depressed in a way with which Catherine could now identify. As a child, Catherine had felt driven, unappreciated, and exploited, and she was still angry about it.

I said to her, "When you don't have enough to do at work, you panic at the thought of becoming like your 'lazy' mother who retreated to bed."

"Absolutely," she said. "Basically, I am lazy, too, and I would like to give in to it. But then I would be like some of my co-workers who loaf along and whom no one respects. I wouldn't respect myself."

"So your panic at having too little work is the fear that you would find in yourself the part of your mother that fills you with resentment and scorn," I suggested.

"Yes, I've known that for a long time," she replied, confirming my comment in a tone of appreciation.

I realized that she was not learning anything new, but was responding to the validating aspects of my comments. She did not seem to need much from me, but carried forward her thoughts without impediment. I listened, making occasional comments.

At length, Catherine described the there-and-now of her upset over being criticized for not doing the job in the slow and gracious way the boss wanted, when Catherine felt capable of doing so much more. It left her feeling distressed and anxious, sometimes even panicky.

"Do you think that your boss seemed like your mother in saying you were doing things the wrong way no matter how hard you wanted to work?" I asked.

"I suppose so," she allowed. "Although he is a man," she added, as if that point of difference might disqualify the comparison. "But he certainly was telling me I was screwing up, which was my mother's role," she agreed.

"And you'd already been telling yourself you were screwing up by not working more," I said. "So your mother is both in the boss and in you. The situation makes you fear that you'll become nothing else than the lazy mother you resented."

"I can see that," she said. Then she fell silent. After a few moments she asked, "What's next? I'm waiting for you to tell me where to go from here."

I felt challenged. Had I been telling her my ideas too forcefully? I had said only this in the space of more than half the session, so I did not think so. So why had she suddenly become dependent on me to do the work for her? I felt pushed, and I felt stingy about saying any more. In retrospect, I can see that in working in a relaxed way with her, saying fairly little in the hour, I had also been identified with the lazy mother and the lazy Catherine, and now I was feeling guilty that I had done something wrong and as though she were her mother telling me so.

I did not answer her challenge, but simply said, "We'll have to see what comes next." She remained silent. Minutes of silence.

As we neared the end of the hour, I began to feel withholding. Responding to the unorganized sense that I had not been working hard enough to help her, I reluctantly took the lead in a way that was peculiar for this late in the hour.

I asked, "Maybe you've had a dream?"
She quickly responded, "Oh, sure. I had one last night. I was going some-where and someone told me I wasn't allowed to wear shorts. Later another woman came along who had a wound on her thigh. A ball the size of a tennis ball was attached to a tank the size of a scuba diving tank and they were put on her wound to treat it. Then the wound was on my own leg, with the ball and tank attached."

I felt quite interested in hearing this dream and would have liked to hear her associations, but there was no time to work on it, and I wished I had asked ear-lier or had not asked at all. I felt guilty that I had not done this piece of work properly and I compounded the error by going on to respond without having heard any associations.

I said, "The critical voice telling you not to wear shorts sounds like your mother's. But we're at the end of our time for today, so more work on the dream will have to wait."
The hour was up. Standing, Catherine turned and said, "Do you think it would be possible to cancel tomorrow's appointment? You scheduled it a day early because you have to be out of town the next day, but I would like to cancel it, mostly because I'm tired and would like not to do any-thing that involves traveling, like coming here."

I was caught. The hour was over, yet the question demanded an answer. I was in an awkward situation partly of her making, partly of mine. I could not yet fully understand it and had no time to work on it. I would have to be brief.

I said, "I think we need the time and that you should come. But you think it over and let me know."
She said she would call me, and left.

Mapping Transference Geography to Understand the Session

At the end of the session, the there-and-then and the there-and-now came together with the here-and-now in a powerful affective exchange, but it was outside the potential space of the hour, which had in a way run dry, and had certainly run out of time. From the moment Catherine stood up ready to cancel the next hour, I felt that we were replaying in the here-and-now a core-affective exchange that drew on sources outside the hour. In recent literature (Chused 1991, 1996, Jacobs 1991) these events have been termed *enactments*, inevitable replays in the here-and-now of the transference of situations from the past. Catherine's enactment with me came to the surface at the boundary ending the hour, when she became like her mother, going off to take a nap, leaving the work of making sense of this to me, having not "worked" in the hour, while I felt pressed to overwork like her father or her childhood self.

This enactment is a complex, unanalyzed early transference manifestation. To the here-and-now of therapy the patient brings material from the there-and-then of interaction with her mother, all in order to make sense of there-and-now situations comprising the work situation which brought her to treatment and her difficulty in forming relationships with men. While I had thought that such events might show up in our relationship in due course, they did not appear to do so during the formally bounded part of this session. During the hour, there had seemed to be relative quiet in the potential space between us. She was simply reporting to me on things that had already gone on inside herself. My comments seemed only to confirm what she already knew, although the information was new to me. For a long time, there was an absence of projection of intense affect into me during this part of the hour, during which the contextual transference seemed benignly positive. I was being used as an understanding background figure who could contain her anxiety. The problem areas seemed to be seated firmly in her and I was spared any intense, unmanageable affect. Affect is commonly low-key and mildly positive when the patient is reporting there-and-now and there-and-then events in this way, using the therapist as an understanding sounding board much as a child may report to the parent on the day at school.

The calm ended when Catherine began to pressure me to tell her what to do next. Perhaps she had a sense that I was not contributing much to the process, although we did not have time to find out if she was aware of this. I had supplied an interpretation which linked the there-and-then with the there-and-now, noticing the role of her internal mother in her current work pattern. We do not ordinarily consider that a transference comment, but Catherine's subsequent action makes it clear that it had hidden transference implications which gave her to feel that I was saying she was not working hard enough, as her mother might have done, while not napping or relaxing herself. Her request that I should tell her what to do next speaks of an empty space that she had left in her mind for me to fill. She conveys the emptiness to me, and it now does not reside solely in her, but in the space between us.

Now, I also sensed the empty space and felt increasing anxiety about it, an anxiety to which I could not attach words. In retrospect, I think I may have asked her about dreams in order to get her back to work, to get her to fill the emptiness in the potential space between us. That is, I acted out a countertransference which only later could I see corresponded to her transference wish for me to fill in a space. She complied with mental content which could not be fully linked up—because the real link between us was being saved for the end of the hour and because we had filled the hour with a sort of nap like her mother's nap. She was quiet while I tried to work and felt her absence. That replay left no time in the hour for giving shape to unconscious mental content of this sort—no link had been prepared for it by her or by me. That is, she wanted me to put something into her mind, which would have been a substitute for a joint creation that would have occurred if we had been talking together.

I then signalled the end of the hour, and suddenly, from around the corner of that ending, direct transference material rushed out: as she stood up, she made a request that seemed clearly related to the content of the hour concerning her mother who was too tired to work and took naps when there was work to be done. The request to cancel the next hour refers both to my having rescheduled it to fit my needs and to the mother who made Catherine work while not working herself. In that moment, I could finally feel the anxiety she had kept centered in the story about her mother, which now she acted on directly. When she asked to cancel the hour, she named me as the mother who made unreasonable demands (to reschedule the hour for my convenience), but at the same time she took the role of the exhausted and anxious mother who is too tired to work, the mother toward whom she still feels such resentment, showing the current standing of the there-and-then story she had been telling. The transference has suddenly become a here-and-now event, giving affective immediacy to the stories about her mother which she told me she knew all about. Until that moment, she had been informing me about this relationship with her mother, but without transmitting anxiety. At the moment of the enactment, I felt the full force of the anxiety. In feeling my own sense of inadequacy, Catherine's internal experience had taken shape inside me and given me a fuller, more truly informed understanding of the way she felt.

At first blush, it might seem that Catherine has presented a focused transference, as content located inside herself for most of the session suddenly floods the potential space between patient and therapist. However, these prematurely focused transferences typical of early treatment come in the service of testing the holding, and thereby primarily express worries about the contextual transference. Catherine is worried that her therapist will be the kind of mother who will put her to work and retire himself, signified when she asked him to take over in the middle of the hour. Although she put him on the spot when she demanded a decision to let her cancel or not, the fundamental decision is about the boundary that he will hold around treatment—the contextual situation. Both sides of the non-holding situation are presented simultaneously in the enactment: he will be like or unlike her mother in requiring her to work when he does not, in providing safety and comfort when her mother did not require it of herself. Catherine also challenges him to be like her disapproving self in asking if he will allow her to be like her mother who demands time to rest.

Although this enactment has elements of a focused transference, fundamentally it is not the thoroughly focused transference of later treatment. When fully developed, the patient's conviction that, like other figures, the analyst is heartless, lazy, and demanding would be delivered into the mature contextual holding of the analytic relationship. Catherine's is a hasty transference which shifts there-and-now and there-and-back-then material into the here-and-now which is then linked to the here-and-then. It is aimed at weighing the overall holding capacity of the therapist whose likeness in the here-and-now to her internal objects is principally of interest for putting him to the test. The here-and-now transference becomes one of testing the ability of the therapist to tolerate anxiety internally and in the transitional space between patient and therapist. The here-and-now test is principally about holding and containment. Material which had seemed to be contained in her is suddenly off-loaded into the therapist, for the moment destroying the sense of a shared work space. The therapist can feel the anxiety as it is dumped into him, and reflexively does the best he can to preserve the possibility of a future work space by indicating his reluctance to cancel without placing a demand on the patient which would further the sense of an unconscious enactment. He will expect to resume shared analytic work on the enactment in their next session.

A Contextual Transference as a Defense against the Focused Positive Transference

Ivan maintained a capsule around himself in therapy with David Scharff. A determinedly self-containing person, Ivan produced a blockade on the here-and-now of the therapeutic relationship. He left a vacuum in the space between him and his therapist. His frozen containment was arrived at as a response to the there-and-back-then trauma of divorce and abandonment by his father and multiple losses in his mother's family due to the Holocaust. He lived in the there-and-now of his tenuous current relationships and the impact of the social factor of HIV infection on his life as a gay man.

A 35-year-old naval officer, Ivan was successful in a demanding, interesting post, but his home life was in turmoil. Joe, his lover of ten years, had become extremely difficult to deal with because his behavior and thinking processes were affected by organic brain damage due to AIDS. This committed relationship had been a source of joy, but now it was ruined by Joe's illness and his impulsive infidelity. Ivan was HIV negative and had not exposed himself to risk as Joe had, an area in which his defensive encapsulating style had served him well. Although he longed to stand by Joe during his illness, he could neither stand living with Joe, nor could he let him go.

In twice-weekly therapy, Ivan lay on the couch and implacably recounted his experiences to me (DES). He never mentioned my name, but simply called me "the analyst." He reported that he now thought of his life as getting on a train for the death camps of the Holocaust where others would die, but he knew he would come back. Although these are dramatic words, from the way that Ivan delivered them, I could not tell how he felt.

I found it hard to know where to intervene. I felt restless, kept at bay, and had the recurrent sense that my words would bounce off the transparent shield that I imagined surrounded him. I was far more silent than usual. Surprisingly, if I spoke, even after being silent for a considerable time, he felt it as an intrusion. Not that he was hostile, just surprised. He thought that "the analyst" was supposed to be mainly silent, as if only to provide space for the patient. There was far less of a sense of shared ex-

perience than with any other patient I can remember. With Ivan, I felt
walled out by a well-functioning person who existed inside the capsule
around his experience.

The first part of the treatment comprised reports on daily difficulties
with Joe who, as his AIDS progressed, became increasingly tempestuous
and unreasonable. In spite of mounting levels of abuse from Joe, Ivan stuck
by him. It was Joe who eventually wrenched himself away from Ivan and
went home to complain to his parents about how mean and controlling Ivan
was. They took Joe's side, and cut off relations with Ivan, to whom they
had been like a second family. After all that distress, Ivan got over his grief
surprisingly quickly—too quickly, it seemed to me.

Nevertheless, Ivan stayed in therapy, explaining, "I'm here to deal with
the loss of my mother." I seized on this richly ambiguous sentence. His
mother had not died, as the sentence seemed to imply. He meant to say that
eventually she would die, and, having lost his lover, he wanted to prepare
for the fearful eventuality of losing her. But I heard it differently: that he
was in therapy to deal with her losses, as though she could not do it herself, or, more to the point, that her losses were unresolved inside him. Ivan's
mother had lost numerous close family members in the Holocaust, and her
marriage failed when Ivan was a young teen. But as far as he knew, she
had dealt with these losses reasonably well.

And Ivan had early losses of his own to deal with. His father was an
admiral who had little to do with him during his childhood, and even less
since the parents' divorce. Preoccupied with numerous lovers and with his
military career, he ignored Ivan. Periodically, he promised emotional and
financial help that never materialized. Finally, Joe, Ivan's lover had AIDS.

The loss of Joe was even more complete than Ivan knew. After leaving
Ivan, Joe had developed end-stage pneumonia and had died. The rupture
with Joe's family meant that Ivan did not find out about his death until six
months later. When he heard it from a mutual friend, he hardly seemed to
respond to the news. I commented that Ivan was not connected to his feelings about losing Joe. His theory was that he had mourned the Joe he loved
before his death. I agreed that he had done some anticipatory mourning, but
I thought that, given the tenacity of his attachment, it was remarkably little.
It was a sign, I thought, of a traumatic pattern of attachment: keeping a tight
grip on the relationship, then suddenly letting go without a trace.

The strength of my wish for Ivan to experience the loss more directly
was fueled by his reluctance to do so. Pressuring him to experience pain
would be unfair and inappropriate, despite my recurrent conviction that

he ought to be feeling the loss more acutely. But I had no good inner im-age of what he was feeling, because he was not letting me in on it, what-ever it was. I believe that my wish to press him to experience his grief rep-resented my wish to penetrate his shell—a way of rebounding from feeling shut out by him as he felt excluded by his father.

Ivan began speaking about a group of new friends and potential lovers he had met in a bar. When he made an exclusive relationship with a new partner, he found him attractive, friendly, kind, and loyal, but denigrated him and compared him unfavorably to Joe because he was not as intelli-gent and did not share the same values and interests. He talked a lot about the new partner, but he did not let him in either. He was there, he sounded like a decent man, he clearly cared about Ivan, but Ivan constantly let me know—and reminded himself—that the new man could not occupy the same inner space as Joe. Why, I wondered, did Ivan keep saying this? He seemed to long for someone who could fill the space, and yet he kept this new partner out emotionally.

Finally I began to realize that I felt as I imagined the new partner must feel—excluded from a space I wanted to be in. I felt Ivan valued me; he talked freely to me and he came to his appointments more or less faith-fully, although he did take vacations easily and without any sign of miss-ing me. But I felt that he continued to come into my presence with his shield firmly around him.

Then came a time when Ivan decided he would try to visit Joe's grave as a way of saying goodbye. Seeking to find the grave, he intended to call telephone information for the numbers of cemeteries in Joe's hometown, but dialed Joe's parents' number instead. On the spur of the moment, he decided to talk to Joe's mother, who told him that her son had been cre-mated, and the ashes scattered on their land in Colorado. Ivan was full of distrust and scorn about the family's treatment of their son and his ashes. He held them responsible for killing their son by failing to safeguard him during his depression and physical decline from AIDS, which resulted in the pneumonia from which he died. But Ivan had a lot of contempt for those who did not live up to his standards—which meant almost everyone except his mother, Joe, a number of shadowy idealized figures in the Navy who seemed to escape his scorn for the time being—and me. His father certainly did not. I often had the feeling that Ivan's emotional shield pro-tected me from becoming the object of his contempt.

As he talked, I was following his story, imagining the scene, taking in his outrage, feeling his coldness, and wondering why he was turning his grief to scorn. Suddenly interrupting his expression of the scorn with which he regarded Joe's family's treatment of the ashes, Ivan said, "I realize I've been thinking something crazy: I want Joe's ashes so I can eat them."

I was shocked out of my reverie. The image that burst through the shield that Ivan usually kept between us suggested an appalling way of filling emptiness and spoke of enormous hunger, not of his usual self-sufficiency. I thought of the ashes of the Holocaust. His longing for Joe in the there-and-now could be a longing for his mother in the here-and-then, and if he let himself relate to me, his worry must be that he would hunger for me too, and then feel frustrated.

Ivan went on to say that he realized how empty he felt without Joe, that he had been longing for him desperately, and that he was obviously wanting some way to get him back inside and keep him there.

In the next session, Ivan did not refer to Joe, ashes, or hunger. Instead he talked, once again, about keeping the new partner out. He didn't want to tell him about the feelings about Joe and began to speak of Joe mainly as "my lover." When he reported things to the new partner, he gave him a briefing, but no sense of what was actually going on. Ivan was back to reporting on experience, but, based on the previous session, I could understand what was happening between us. For the moment, something had gotten past the shield—not that I as a person had gotten past the shield, but something had gotten through.

I said, "You often give me a briefing that's like telling your superior officers what has happened in a sea battle. But you're not letting me in on the action, any more than you'd take them to the actual scene of the battle. That's just for you. And in your mind, it was reserved. Only Joe could be there with you. The way you feel now, you'll never let me in any more than you'll let your new partner in."

"You're right," Ivan said. "I keep my new partner out. When my mother dies, it will give me the same feeling of a void because she's part of me. I feel a void now. I have to confront my lover's loss and my disappointment about what happened between him and me. The void is there because a lot of space is empty. Somehow I'm making sure my new partner won't enter that space. I don't know how, but six months after meeting my lover, I already had to hang on to him because of a fear of losing him. He did it to me somehow. As I think about my new partner and I building something, I can't make the commitment to him. I'm scared to go through a separation which will be traumatic again. When my lover was on the way out, I felt unprotected, no defenses. It was like a war I entered totally defenseless. I hope it won't be like that forever."

He continued, "But I am lowering my shield now with my new partner, slowly, in a natural way. The damage my lover created almost kept me from starting again. One of my new partner's friends turned out to be HIV positive, and I thought 'God, here we have to deal with that again!' With Joe, I was in the inner circle. Intimate! With my new partner's friend, I was a member of the outer circle. I've needed to get outside the inner circle, but meeting my new partner has given me energy to move on, even to invest in my job again."

The image of the inner circle brought us full circle—an image of being inside intimate experience or outside it. I realized sadly that I was back to feeling the void as Ivan moved imperceptibly into another monologue, protected by the circle of his shield that excluded me. Perhaps he would let the new partner in eventually, but there would still be no room for me.

"It's the same with my mother," Ivan continued. "She sees herself as a victim. And she is! She carries it with her. I told her once: she did survive the war. Okay, she had a failed marriage, but she did what she wanted to do and came out well, good-looking and healthy. She's overcome a nearly fatal car accident ten years ago, too. It's the same with me: I've had trauma, but in the end I'm lucky, so I'm not down. But I'm reassuring myself, like trying to convince you."

Now I felt as if I were an opponent in a logical argument about the need to let me in. I hadn't known we were in an argument, but I realized that indeed I didn't agree with him about how smoothly all this was going and would go in the future.

I said, "Why would you be trying to convince me you're well and happy?"

"I shouldn't have to sell you on that, should I? There must be a lot you see and I don't. But you have to get to know me, so the advantage has to be with me: I'm in daily interaction with me. So the process is that you steer me through things, but I'm in the driver's seat. It's like I have to debrief you so you know where things are at, in my work, with my lovers, as if I am keeping you up to date."

Ivan was talking about how he could include me, but I still felt excluded. I identified a jealous feeling about his relationship with himself in which he appeared to me as a self-contained couple.

I said, "You have to keep me briefed so I can help navigate your voyage, but I'm not actually on the voyage with you. It's like mission control at Houston. The people there may have a hand in steering things, but they're not actually on the trip."

"Yes, in the end, it's still the patient's world, not the analyst's. Someone else would say, 'I'm fine!' In the end it boils down to that. I'm not fine certainly—there's the void of the lover from when Joe left."

I thought of the similarity between "the void of the lover," the earlier phrase "the loss of my mother" that I remarked on, and his referring to me as "the analyst." Ivan was living in the void of the space between objects, and he experienced the space where he lived as objectless.

He went on, "The issue with my new partner is, 'How far can I take him in?' If I do, he pushes my lover out. Happiness kills my lover. How can I find the balance?"

I felt bleak. Again Joe had lost his name and was simply referred to as "my lover."

Ivan concluded, "How do I displace my lover without killing him?"

Mapping Transference and Countertransference with Ivan

If I had talked about myself and my relationship directly with Ivan—about transference and countertransference—he would have experienced an intrusion. If I were to do so, I would have felt that I was inappropriately assuming or forcing a focused transference relationship. Our argument was over the question of whether I could ever become a focused object for him, an external object with my own subjectivity, ready for centered relating in which he could re-experience and modify his internal objects. He insisted that I remain only a fixed context, which is what I came to feel he meant by "the analyst." He kept me as the holding and understanding mother who cannot become an object in her own right lest she take over the controls and have the journey instead of him. The role of object mother is reserved for his actual mother and for Joe. So I felt frozen out by his shield, kept at the cold, lifeless periphery of his personal envelope. I was required to be the envelope without the freedom to move back and forth between context and focus, between offering him a holding environment and being an object in my own right with my own experience and needs.

I became aware at times of avoiding saying things because I feared becoming an object of contempt and abandonment as his father was. While I felt that Ivan's contempt disguised the longing for his father, I did not feel able as yet to convey this to him. But Ivan also shut me out to avoid allowing a potentially dead mother and lover to be displaced, "killed off" by allowing me to be alive in the center of his object world. To avoid me he lived largely in a sealed capsule with petrified objects inside, instead of in a live interaction with his new partner and with me.

Understanding the geography of Ivan's transference centers on his insistence on immobilizing his therapist, keeping him as an environmental parent only, and cutting him off from being a subjective object, that is, a person of importance in his own right. This means that containment is skewed: everything important goes on inside Ivan and inside the capsule in which he lives, but as though it happens without being processed through the mind of the therapist. Anything else is a scorned and worthless space. The potential space between patient and therapist is also cut off by Ivan's protective shield, and the therapist's inner space feels as though it is atrophied, deprived as he is of reciprocal holding. Perhaps Ivan's internal space is filled with his mother's Holocaust objects and therefore he has to keep the space clear between him and others, so that at least there is room for him somewhere.

In his here-and-now countertransference experience with Ivan, the therapist experiences him as an absence or a rejecting figure of restricted access because Ivan's life goes on within his capsule. He keeps the therapist safe from his aggression and he defends against the intrusiveness, abandonment, or retaliatory contempt that he may fear from him. Dr. Scharff is left with a lifeless experience, at the mercy of Ivan's reporting. Perhaps Ivan is giving him to feel what it was like for him as an abandoned child waiting for a postcard from his father who had sailed to the other end of the earth—a concordant countertransference. Dr. Scharff experienced the countertransference as an emotional response to Ivan. Another therapist might have experienced a painful, hungry feeling in the stomach long before Ivan mentioned his fantasy of eating the ashes, a bodily way of appreciating the here-and-now transference.

Yet another might have been more aware of a lack of liveliness in the atmosphere of the session.

Ivan tells Dr. Scharff of the immediate there-and-now of his family life, but is reluctant to link it either to there-and-back-then experiences which might allow them to explore the origin of his difficulties and so experience meaning. The there-and-now of his conflict as an officer in the military who must isolate his homosexual life is not addressed as such, but melds with his intrapsychic defense of living in a capsule. And he is armed solidly against linking to here-and-now or here-and-then experiences which would enliven the therapeutic relationship and move the therapist toward the center, where he could become the focus of scorn and longing. There was more life to their work when they discussed the there-and-now situation of life in his home, than if the therapist had focused directly on the implications for the transference with him in the here-and-now. Because of his fear of losing Joe as an internal object, Ivan constrained his longings for a new lover. He did not want to feel sad and empty with the new lover in the there-and-now, with Dr. Scharff in the here-and-now, and in the if-and-when of the therapeutic relationship.

Using Transference Geography—And Letting It Go

We think of the map that we have devised as a fractal of the transference–countertransference. It gives us a visuo-spatial, multidimensional view of the transference as a system, so that we need not be imprisoned in thinking of transference–countertransference as a solvable linear equation. Transference and countertransference can better be represented by a non-linear equation whose solution can only be approximated through multiple iterations. Remembering all the contributing concepts as part of a whole, we can use any one of them as they occur to us without narrowing our vision or being imprisoned in any of them.

We have presented transference geography as a conceptual aid for doing therapy—a map to consult when we lose ourselves in unknown realms of the transference. When the transference seems absent or obscure, we can use the map to locate it in one of the protean forms where it rests in time and space. Using our countertransference as a compass orients us to the transference. The map gives us a way of marking out unfamiliar terrain. It is never our only tool, however. We want to use it in concert with every instrumentality we can bring to the process of therapy.

We do not propose slavish use of this or any other device. Once we understand the principles of mapping transference, we want to put the map away, and travel using our intuitive sense of direction. We go with the patient on a shared voyage, noting the sights, learning new and old things, letting ourselves get lost, finding our way out of blind alleys, trudging through dense forests, or following the path along a river. We let go of our map, and "by indirections find directions out." Usually that will get us where we need to go. And every once in a while, when we feel puzzled for too long, or get lost yet again in a familiar place, we remember to pull out our map and compass as guides to finding our way once again. The use of the map is systematically illustrated in Chapter 2, and various of its elements are referred to as they occur to us during therapies illustrated in the clinical section of this book. As you will see, periodically, to differing degrees on different voyages and with differing emphasis in different phases of each voyage, mapping and analysis of transference will be a valuable guide.

12

Structure and Process of Therapy

This chapter presents the principles of object relations individual therapy and analysis. Although we give descriptions of various techniques, we always keep in mind that they are embedded in an overall therapeutic relationship. It is the relationship with the therapist that organizes the therapeutic process, not any one of the elements that we are about to describe, for in the absence of the general therapeutic relationship, none of the other factors matter (Fairbairn 1958). (See Table 12–1.)

Arranging the Frame

Setting Boundaries

From the first contact with the person who presents for therapy, it is the therapist's responsibility to set the conditions within which they will meet and work. Conditions of work include the time and place of meeting, the frequency of sessions, cancellation policy, the amount and method of payment, use of the couch, and the use of the telephone or other means of contacting the therapist in emergencies. These conditions constitute in part a business arrangement and in part a psychological contract. They form the literal boundaries around the therapy. The patient's compliance with and testing of them as features of the therapeutic relationship reveal the patient's ways of relating in general. Of course it is up to the patient to agree or disagree with

TABLE 12–1. Summary of principles of object relations therapy.

Arranging the frame
    Setting boundaries
    Management of the therapy
    Psychoanalysis or psychotherapy?
Creating psychological space
    Free-floating attention and role responsiveness
    Neutrality and involved impartiality
    Treating resistance
    Tact and timing
    Negative capability
    Listening without memory or desire
Listening for conflict, defense, and anxiety
Working with dreams and fantasy
Eliciting patterns of internal object relations
Working with transference and countertransference
    Transference as total situation
    Use of the therapist's self
    Evolution of the transference/countertransference relationship
Tolerating and understanding silence
Giving surface feedback: clarification, linking, support, advice
Giving in-depth feedback: interpretation
    Interpreting transference–countertransference and enactments
    The behavioral interpretation
    The because clause
On being wrong, being threatened with quitting, having doubts
Adding ancillary and adjunctive methods (drawing, play)
Using medication
Modifying technique
    With survivors of trauma
    Reduced-fee arrangements
Working through
Continuing assessment as therapy evolves
Separating and terminating

the therapist's conditions. Most of the therapist's policies should have come up for discussion during the assessment period, but may not become fully apparent until therapy is beginning. It does not go well for a therapist to assume that any conditions which happen to suit the therapist should automatically be acceptable to the patient, but neither will things go well if the patient is free to disregard elements of the frame without challenge and discussion. When a patient does disregard elements of the frame, or accepts them too readily, it is likely that an aspect of the patient's object relations is being enacted, which should be addressed without delay (see the vignette of Mr. Morales in Chapter 20).

Management of the Therapy

In object relations therapy and psychoanalysis, we do not prescribe homework or ways of dealing with situations, nor do we instruct our patients in changing the way they think about life and its challenges as in cognitive–behavioral therapies. The management we do is of our selves and our role in the treatment. We manage the boundaries of the therapy (for example set the fee, keep to time, regular sessions) and the processing of the countertransference as we direct our attention to an ever-increasing understanding of the patient's situation. It is incumbent on us to be available at the times we say we will be there, to be reliable, to remain nonjudgmental when hearing difficult material or when subject to the swings of our own feelings, to remain neutral when we would like to be nasty or nice to our patients, and to remain true to the task of understanding. Above all, we manage ourselves in order to provide the psychological space for the patient.

Remaining neutral also requires avoiding social relations with patients and accepting a complete embargo on sexual relations with patients even after therapy is over, no matter how long after therapy the possibility presents itself. Only such firm boundaries can allow the analyst or therapist free rein to experience and resonate with the patient's fantasy without the threat of the possibility of acting on such fantasies.

The following example demonstrates an aspect of therapeutic management involved in setting limits.

Lottie, a 37-year-old woman, called her therapist frequently, drove by his house, and pressed for more attention. When the therapist limited the phone calls and indicated that he would be available only at the times of their appointments, she began to bring her anger into the therapy. Only when the therapist could stand to deprive her so as to protect his own privacy were the conditions set which made it possible to explore her rage at years of feeling deprived and the way it drove others away.

When we work with patients who act out, it is not possible to begin to work in depth with them until we manage the boundaries around the therapy. Setting appropriate limits amounts to a behavioral interpretation which conveys a message that may not be understood in verbal form (see page 303 later in this chapter).

Psychoanalysis or Psychotherapy?

The Couch or the Chair

The most obvious criteria that give a rough and ready differentiation between psychotherapy and psychoanalysis are the frequency of meetings and the use of the couch. These surface attributes often correspond to the intensity of engagement in the therapeutic process, but not invariably. Selecting the couch or the chair and the frequency of sessions is often equally a matter of patient and therapist choice, rather than of deciding whether the patient meets some arbitrary criteria for psychoanalysis.

Frequency of Therapeutic Sessions

Originally, Freud saw his patients six hours a week, or five when his practice was overcrowded with Americans (Gay 1988, Kardiner 1977). Now the standard for psychoanalytically oriented therapy is forty-five or fifty minutes, with analysis taking place three, four, or five times a week, depending on the analytic school. We agree with the assumption that greater frequency tends to facilitate in-depth treatment, and we prefer four or five times a week to two or three when intensive work is the intention. Some patients' problems will not yield significantly without an analytic frequency, because of how embedded the patients' defenses are in their character structure. Paradoxically, patients who have considerable strength of personality may need an analytic frequency precisely because things tend to work pretty well for them just as they are, and it takes an extremely well-held therapy to crack the existing structures and allow fundamental change.

We think of once-weekly or less frequent meetings such as every two or three weeks as offering a limited chance to plumb the depths, but adequate time for the review of matters of daily concern. Working infrequently, and at the surface of difficulty, we must use more guesswork in arriving at an interpretation. Nevertheless, it must be said that some patients can work in considerable depth on a weekly basis, and that some can move toward analytic depth in twice-weekly therapy, using dreams and free association more readily than many analysts have thought possible in the past. The problem with once- or twice-weekly therapy, when patients are attempting analytic work without frequent sessions that best facilitate analytic work, is that the patient has to have a greater tolerance for pain and upset in order to expose the underlying anxieties and then go two to four days before the next session. In a less-intensive therapy, with sessions once or twice a week, the low frequency tends not to precipitate the kind of rapid uncovering that is associated with anxiety, and the therapist is more active in helping the patient to stand the feelings that stem from the therapy itself. There is, however, variation in the correlation of frequency and depth in the practice of any analyst/therapist because patients in the same modality work differently.

The debate about the distinguishing characteristics that separate psychotherapy from analysis has been going on for years. Some writers such as Bollas and McDougall tend to blur the distinction between psychotherapy and psychoanalysis. They disregard artificial distinctions between one, three, or five times weekly. They define analysis by the activity of the analytic mind in sessions of any frequency rather than on the logistical arrangements. We follow their lead in proposing that logistics do not in themselves distinguish between the two forms. Intensity and frequency are not for everyone, nor is every analytic therapist interested in practicing formal psychoanalysis or in the exhaustive training that it requires. Patients who come only once a week may work in depth, while others who come five times a week may stay on the surface despite their analyst's best efforts. There is no easy definition of what is psychotherapy and what is psychoanalysis.

We tend to think of psychotherapy as a treatment method in which therapists provide their patients with a good holding environment in which they can safely discuss their symptoms and explore their underlying dynamic issues. The therapeutic relationship becomes an object of study for revealing the nature of the internal object relations. The treatment may be brief or long-term, once a week or more often.

We tend to think of psychoanalysis as an intensive form of psychotherapy, with the patient usually lying on the couch but sometimes sitting on the chair, with enough sessions to allow the patient to work in depth with an analyst who is capable of creating a psychological space, engaging in a therapeutic relationship, and then experiencing, reflecting on, and interpreting unconscious aspects of the patient's internal world through work in the transference.

Whether object relations therapy or analysis is being practiced is not determined by frequency alone, but by the motivation and psychological-mindedness of the patient, and by the therapist's capacity for unconscious communication, reflection, and interpretation.

The Couch

Nevertheless, we tend to associate psychoanalysis with frequent sessions and the use of the couch. The use of the couch with the analyst seated behind or to the side and just out of easy sight of the patient offers many patients and analysts a relaxed atmosphere for working, although we recognize that some patients' anxiety is increased by the removal of the reassuring aspects of face-to-face contact and readier access to an external object relationship. Depriving of such social contact, the couch arrangement induces a degree of object hunger which we find helps to expose the inner world in the space between us and the patient. With some twice-a-week therapy patients, the couch can facilitate the same relaxation that promotes free association as it does in analysis, and can catalyze the therapy. We both tend to like the freedom of not having the patient read our faces and monitor our responsiveness. It leaves us freer to relax into a reverie that facilitates unconscious communication in depth with patients.

Some patients, however, are too anxious to use the couch, too worried about the sexual threat it arouses in them, or too worried and lonely without the contact of seeing us. Adolescents are usually too anxious for the couch, and this applies to many young adults as well. Late in his career, Fairbairn (1958) abandoned the use of the couch because he felt it produced too much deprivation for many of his poorly related patients. There is no need to insist on using the couch for the sake of orthodoxy: thoroughgoing analyses have been conducted with the patient sitting, but they are more of a strain on us as analysts because we work best with a transitional space. For other analysts, engagement is more important than space, and they choose to do analysis face-to-face. Psychotherapy twice, or even once a week with the patient seated can produce an in-depth therapy.

In practice, we generally suggest using the couch in therapies that are three or four times a week, and sometimes in twice-weekly therapy, depending on its intent and the motivation of the patient, and hardly ever in once-weekly therapy.

Creating Psychological Space

The principle function of any therapeutic relationship is the offering and maintaining of a psychological space in which the patients can review their lives, examine their internal object relations, and explore the nature of their effect in personal relations and work. Therapists create this space by offering active (but not inquisitive) listening, which invites patients to tell their stories, to tell the therapist about themselves through every modality, verbal and nonverbal, while therapists take in the experience, and allow it to resonate with their inner worlds. The external dimension of the space is bounded by an agreed, weekly time frame and by the double doors of the office, but the primary setting for the space is the internal dimension of the well-analyzed, trained mind of the therapist. Good work can go on in physical spaces that are significantly compromised, for instance in a video studio (see Chapter 2) or in the presence of students or colleagues. Therapy and analysis can be conducted on the telephone, if the patient's level of trust and the therapist's capacity to focus on the patient are sufficient to maintain the psychological space (Zalusky 1996).

Psychological space is created by the therapist's capacity for contextual holding and containment. Into this space, the shared psychological life of the patient–therapist pair comes into being, and is nurtured by them, or attacked. This co-construction has been called *the analytic third* (Ogden 1994). Here there is an overlap of capacities and concerns of patient and therapist where they are free to play with ideas, states of mind, anxieties, hopes, and fears. Over time, they become able to play with fantasies, enactments, and ways of relating in relation to the therapist. In this way both patient and therapist can become aware of the way the patient's strengths and difficulties are expressed and new ways of managing conflict and relating can be tried out. The psychological space corresponds to the potential or transitional space described by Winnicott (1971a).

Free-Floating Attention and Role Responsiveness

In the early psychoanalytic literature, the maintenance of psychological space was often described as a matter of *abstinence* and *neutrality*. Freud wrote that the proper state of mind was that of "*evenly suspended attention*" (1912, p. 111). And more recently, a number of writers have thought that this useful recommendation could be broadened to include a state of attuned *free-floating responsiveness*, which includes not only thinking about the meaning of the patient's words, but a willingness to receive the whole range of unconscious meaning signaled by thoughts, affective states, and role responsiveness to enactments that subsequently gives new understanding to patients' inner worlds (Sandler 1976). With this broadened definition, the concepts of therapeutic abstinence and neutrality have different operational definitions than they had in classical drive-oriented or ego psychological analytic teaching.

Neutrality and Involved Impartiality

By neutrality, we mean that we are neutral about the patient's right to choose for himself what course he will follow, although we acknowledge that we are on the side of life, growth, and development. That is, we do not accept self-destructiveness or a refusal to grow as equally valid outcomes of our work, but we do not want to impose our ideas of development and health on our patients. We are not parents raising a child to our standards.

In place of neutrality, we tend to use the term *involved impartiality*. We care for the patient, and we accept it when the patient cares for us, hates us, or is anxious about us, but we understand that the patient's inner world is characterized by many part-object relationships that pull him in different directions. At one moment he is driven by one set, and the next by another set. We do not make a prejudgment that one is him and one is the enemy. Rather we accept and explore the functioning of all parts so that they become familiar to the patient, who can then choose how to integrate into the personality these splits that otherwise deprive him of the full enjoyment in his capacity to relate and to live.

Treating Resistance

During therapy, patients often express excuses as to why it is impossible to attend sessions, or why they are occasionally or habitually late for sessions, why they should not talk about certain things, or why they may simply remain silent, withold information, inhibit free association, and forget dreams. These are manifestations of *resistance*, a term that Freud (1917) introduced to describe the patients' efforts to repress painful feelings and fantasies, and to keep them hidden from themselves and their therapists. Classical psychoanalysis centered its theory of technique first and foremost on the analysis of the patient's resistance against giving up defenses for controlling drive energies and the resulting structural conflict (A. Freud 1936). Then work on fantasies of shame, embarrassment, and guilt would help patients de-repress the previously hidden unconscious drive material.

Object relations theory views resistance somewhat differently (Fairbairn 1958, Guntrip 1969). Fairbairn thought that resistance arose from a defensive need to cling to old forms of object relating because giving them up would mean losing part of the self. Guntrip thought that resistance occurred when the adult self tried to defend itself against feeling ashamed at experiencing the child part of the self. Fairbairn wrote that the most important source of resistance was to the person of the therapist, because shame was experienced at revealing parts of the self in front of the therapist. At first, patients long for the therapist to rescue them from their painful relationship to inner parental objects (the contextual transference), but they then become afraid that they will meet those very parents again in the person of the therapist (the focused transference). When change finally seems possible, they fear that therapists will rob them of these objects and expose them to the underlying void. Thus object relations theory has redefined resistance and defense and no longer sees them as stemming primarily from a need to keep id material unconscious. Now we see resistance and defense as arising from the need to maintain split-off and repressed internal object relations as a closed internal system, safe from the threat of therapy, analysis, and the person of the analyst who attempts to breach the patient's closed inner system (Fairbairn 1958).

Tact and Timing: What Not to Say and When Not to Say It

Winnicott (1971a) wrote about the importance of letting patients take the lead in speaking, and warned against therapists interpreting simply in order to prove that they have something to say. Often if therapists wait, patients discover something for themselves, a creative activity of the true self in the transitional space which we obliterate if we speak too quickly. Abstinence means that we do not speak or act to please ourselves and relieve anxiety, but only to further the patient's progress.

The hardest part of clinical learning is when not to say things that present themselves and may seem compelling. The clue lies in recognizing a slight feeling of doubt or hesitation. This may consist simply of a whiff of misgiving, or, on examination, it may be a developed sense that something we are about to say is too much for the patient to hear, or an appreciation that it would be showing off to anticipate the work the patient is doing. Casement's (1991) concept of the *internal supervisor* outlines a way of putting ourselves in the patient's shoes. Invoking the internal supervisor helps us to reflect on whether it would be helpful or intrusive to say something. The way out of the internal debate may be to discuss the conflict with the patient, but more often, if we wait, the situation will clarify itself, and we will often find that the patient comes across the material without our having to speak. Another way of being tactful is to take the heat off the patient by speaking about the analyst's behavior or characteristics rather than the patient's.

Steiner (1994) differentiated analyst-centered and patient-centered interpretations. He recommended an analyst-centered interpretive position for facilitating containment with certain patients who are deep in the paranoid-schizoid position and cannot stand to look at their own fears. Even for those who are only temporarily in this position, it is gentler and more acceptable to the patient if the therapist couches any interpretations in terms of the patient's understanding and fears concerning the therapist's incapacities and limited understanding. Working with this interpretive stance in mind, we might say that a patient is afraid that the therapist will be unable to tolerate certain states of mind of the patient, or that the patient fears the therapist will misunderstand the patient, rather than focusing on the patient's state of mind directly.

This approach displaces patients' anxieties from the self to the object, represented by the therapist, and focuses attention on the object's capacity for holding and containment. Ideas about the patients' view of the object rather than the self may be easier to absorb when the patient is unable to introject the therapist as a containing figure, and therefore is excessively reliant on the actual presence of the therapist and experiences heightened worry about separation or misunderstanding by the therapist because of the missing capacity within the self. We find Steiner's (1994) contribution helpful to our intention to use tact and timing in adjusting our interpretation to fit the current state of the relationship between self and object during treatment. We will add to his contribution later in this chapter.

Negative Capability

In describing the analyst's ideal state of mind, Bion (1970) used the term *negative capability*, borrowed from John Keats's description of Shakespeare's poetic capacity for "being in uncertainties, mysteries and doubts without irritable reaching after fact and reason" (Keats, in Murray 1955, p. 261). In advocating this state of mind, Bion (1970) taught that the analyst should be *without memory or desire* in order to be as open as possible to what the patient brings to the therapy in the here-and-now of each moment. Clinging to theory prejudices the therapist to hear what the theory teaches should be heard. Feeling too tied to exactly what the patient said in the previous session prejudices the therapist to hear what has already been said and to learn what is already known. Only by abandoning what is already known as fully as possible can therapist and patient be open to what is not yet known. The *unthought known* is lived out without being able to be thought about (Bollas 1987).

In practice, it is not possible, nor is it advisable, to forget everything about the patient's history or the previous course of therapy. Nor is it possible to have *no* desires for patients—such as desires for their growth or a lessening of their self-destructiveness. Making links and holding potential shapes for patients to grow into are also crucial parts of our function. We do not advocate a literal surrender to Bion's dictum of being entirely without memory or desire. But we do advocate a relaxed capacity to let go of what is known, remembered, and understood in order to escape its tyranny and become free to learn anew in each moment and able to understand things not previously experienced and understood. We are also free to remember what we learned before and to apply it anew, to associate previous experiences with the patient to those in the present moment, and to create links that facilitate growth and change.

Finding Our Own Way of Listening without Memory or Desire

We are not entirely without memories of previous experiences with the patient or memories of our own life either. Rather it is that we are open to the flux of our own fantasies, thoughts, swings of feeling, and memories of what patient or therapist has said before. We have a free-floating attention and an open capacity for responding with our own free association to the patient's material and tolerating the wandering of our attention until it is triggered to respond keenly and in depth. We want to be able to get lost in the patient's material, in our selves, and in the space between which is our shared area for work. Yet there is anxiety about this suspension of purposeful attention; for the chance of simply getting and staying lost or of missing something the patient feels to be important is always there. We should not expect to listen perfectly, to roam freely and still catch everything. Giving up the intention of hearing everything on the surface that is presented to us is the only way to be ready for the depth. This kind of listening can be described and illustrated—as it is, in these chapters and elsewhere (Bollas 1987, 1989, Jacobs 1991, D. Scharff 1992, J. Scharff 1992, J. Scharff and D. Scharff 1994). But it cannot

be copied. David Scharff gives the following vignette about the realization of
the need to find your own way of listening and thinking without memory or
desire of an ideal:

> During a year at the Tavistock Clinic, I (DES) used to listen to the free and en-
> tirely amusing associations of my supervisor, then chair of the adolescent depart-
> ment, Arthur Hyatt Williams. His associations were invariably surprising, shock-
> ingly vivid, and often full of literary references to Keats or Shakespeare, evocative
> of new and vital ways of understanding the patient under discussion. "Now that,"
> I thought, "is the way an analyst ought to think." And I set out to find out how to
> spout Keats and Shakespeare. Alas! It did not work that way, and I felt pedes-
> trian and deflated in comparison to my idealization.
>
> It took me some years to realize that Hyatt Williams had his style, and I had
> mine. When I have gradually, and with some sense of loss to be sure, given in
> to being myself, I have found that the inner world, like the outer one, is usually
> pretty ordinary in the material it chooses, but extraordinary in the way it uses
> it and makes illuminating links that go beyond the ones I could consciously
> construct. With the descent to ordinariness, I am freer to admire Hyatt
> Williams's capacity to find his ways, which are not mine, but also to find my
> own new ways which are not his.

We have to be ourselves. We do not have to come up with extraordinary ways
of looking at things—our patients will do that if we encourage them to be themselves. So, finally, we have to let our minds be what they will. On a good day,
we pick up the patients' language and our inner accent moves toward the
patient's and connects with those aspects of cultural reference we may share.
We do not impose our own references. If we insist on showering Shakespeare
or James Joyce on a patient who is raising children and may not have literature
on her mind, we will not connect. Use your own self and all its aspects in your
own idiom and you will encounter all aspects of the patient in a way that will
produce an authentic shared experience for understanding.

Listening for Conflict, Defense, and Anxiety

We are not asking specifically, or expecting to hear, about any one thing. But
in general we are interested in listening for areas of inner conflict, repeating
patterns of external impingement, inconsistencies in the stories patients tell
and the pictures they paint, vulnerabilities that defeat them over and over,
and for strengths that appear without warning to help them and others in

defiance of their own expectations and self-destructiveness. We are interested in patients' associations to aspects of what they have said, whether to pieces of a dream, a sudden impulse to action, a fantasy, or a recurrent and habitual way of doing things only now recognized. We may have to help them widen their way of thinking, by asking about the history of something, or asking directly for associations to a dream or an action. Even the question conveys our interest in the matters they have introduced, avoided, and now linked. We are interested both in the internal conflicts themselves and the defenses against anxiety, and in the way patients keep the pain of their lives at bay both through habit and at times of acute threat.

Working with Dreams and Fantasies

We are interested in dreams and fantasies—the unconscious nighttime dreams that Freud taught us to follow to their roots in the unconscious, and the subconscious dreams for the future which hover behind the surface of patients' narratives. We are interested in fantasies as manifestations of unconscious organization—for instance those that accompany masturbation or daydreaming—and motivating fantasies that pull the person toward an ideal.

Analytic therapists have always had a special fondness for working with dreams, which as Freud first pointed out, are a *royal road to the unconscious*. On the other hand, we no longer follow his view of dreams as being solely organized by wishes, governed by the pleasure principle, and expressed in primary process thinking. Fairbairn taught us to see dreams as being representative of the entire endopsychic structure of the patient. We see the dream as a fractal of the person's internal object relations that communicates an image of the patient to the therapist (see Chapters 8 and 26). Kleinian analysts have seen dreams as crucial aids to the understanding of the *transference as a total situation* (Joseph 1985). David Scharff has written extensively about the role of dreams in individual therapy communicating the totality of the patient's situation in individual therapy, and fostering communication between family members in conjoint therapy (1992).

The same applies to working with fantasy; it represents the patient's internal world as it scans, reacts to, and modifies the patient's external interactions. We value all forms of fantasy, and try to understand them in the gestalt of our relationship with the patient.

Because we believe that dreams and fantasies are best understood within the total situation—the patient's endopsychic structure, the patient's relationships outside therapy, and the transference–countertransference relationship—our work with dreams reappears under many headings throughout the clinical chapters, and is illustrated later in this chapter where we discuss tolerating silence.

Eliciting Patterns of Internal Object Relations

We are interested also in the object relations history of many events. We look for the relationship patterns that accompany fantasies and dream sequences. We convey to the patient that we welcome thinking about connections to past relationships, and at times ask about them specifically, because this gives us a shared sense of how things developed. But the patient's report of the past gives us not only history, but provides the prototype for persisting patterns of relating. Past relationships and events are described as though they are only about the patient's past history, which they may or may not represent accurately. What they also tell us about is the current organization of the patient's internal object relations inside the self.

In short, we are interested in virtually everything about our patients, in the ebb and flow of their interests, in the way their attention is at first in one place and then in another, in the rhythm of their thought, and its effect on us. We cannot keep all these interests in the front of our mind at the same time, so we surrender focused listening in favor of listening as a totality. Having worked at our training through personal therapy or psychoanalysis, supervision and reading, we listen with the accumulation of our experience and interests and are guided by both conscious and unconscious navigation at the same time.

Working with Transference and Countertransference

Transference as the Total Situation

We discussed transference extensively from a theoretical point of view in Chapter 11 and provided examples of using transference geography to map the meaning of the therapeutic relationship to the patient. Using transference geography too explicitly has the same pitfalls, however, as conducting a minute-to-minute defense analysis: it generally interferes with our capacity to listen. We do take the transference as central, but we understand it as the *total situation* that characterizes the patient's overall relationship to us, to treatment, and to life in general (Joseph 1985, Klein 1952). So we want to listen *through* our countertransference, noting the totality of our response to the patient by letting go and absorbing the experience, by including our own associations, and by listening inside ourselves as well as to patients. Conscious and unconscious listening and processing are at the heart of object relations psychotherapy and psychoanalysis. No one example can adequately convey the complexity, the spontaneity, and the variability of this process, but from the accumulation of varied examples throughout this book, we hope a compelling picture will emerge.

The Use of the Therapist's Self

Exactly how we process our countertransference is perhaps the hardest thing to describe. We teach the use of countertransference in supervision when we investigate the supervisee's affective responses to the patient or client. We cannot show our countertransference on videotape because it is an internal event, although it may have some external behavioral and relational signs. We cannot show countertransference in a traditional case writeup. So we include our responses in the clinical examples given in this chapter and throughout the book. We try to become aware of our responses to the patient, or more accurately, to as many of our responses as possible without prejudging which of them are actually responses to the patient and which come from us as though they have nothing to do with the patient. What we are aiming for is the resonance between the patient's and our inner object relations, so we do not try to separate one from the other before we have a chance to understand.

We do not simply want to respond to our feelings or thoughts as though they automatically represent truths about the patient or our relationship. For instance, if we are feeling angry or annoyed with a patient, or if we feel erotically aroused, we rarely say so directly. We take it as a starting point for thought and for inner analysis, letting the feeling percolate while wondering silently what it represents. Then, when we have made something of it, we speak about it in one way or another—perhaps commenting on the patient's anger that has been put into us through projective identification, perhaps commenting on the sadness beyond the anger. Very occasionally, and usually only after the contextual transference has solidified, we might comment directly on the anger or arousal we felt as a commentary on our shared relationship with the patient. We do so only when we know that the patient is likely to understand that we do so to convey what we understand of the patient from inside her dilemma, not from a hostile or self-justifying stance. We speak about the transference and countertransference directly only when patients have come to value this resource for working on their life situation.

Some analytic papers on the role of spontaneity in therapy and analysis describe how thoughts that suddenly burst through the therapist's reserve can break through a stalemate and bring new understanding (Symington 1983). We have no doubt that this happens, and that there are times, perhaps more than traditional training suggests, when spontaneity revitalizes a bureaucratized treatment. Some of those spontaneous utterances, however, catch the patient in a sore spot, create an empathic failure, and leave us wondering why we thought it was such a great idea to sound off. And then every so often, we blurt out something that helps. What we want to promote is a way of exchange where spontaneity and tactful plain speaking are valued, but not overvalued, where the impact of a rash remark can be reviewed, and where therapies that are stuck can be talked about as being stuck, so that therapists do not have to rely on a magical outburst.

The Evolution of the Transference/ Countertransference Relationship

In addition to working with the transference and countertransference in each session, we want to monitor the *evolution of the transference and countertransference* over time. As patients change during therapy, the matrix of their attitudes toward us evolves as they experience our perceived feelings and attitudes toward them. The changing countertransference consists of the whole pattern of feeling and understanding we develop about the patient. If we keep an eye and an ear on this process, it gives us a gauge for growth and change in patients' relational capacities and growth and change in their selves.

Tolerating and Understanding Silence

Object relations therapy and analysis often calls for the therapist's tolerance of silence for shorter or longer periods. Some patients are rarely silent for more than a few seconds; others are silent periodically for a few moments; and still others go through long stretches of silence, even for whole sessions over a period of weeks or months. There is no single formula for how to deal with silence. Indeed, there may be no need to *do* anything about it at all except to treat it as any other communication or blocking of communication. Our minds wander over the experience of the patient and the therapy. We can break the silence to ask what it might contain or conjecture about its meaning, but we are not responsible for making the patient talk. Indeed, some patients, after a long period of silence, may be grateful that they have been allowed to be silent without having to speak, and find that being able to be silent in the presence of someone else is an important change from having felt compelled to fill up interpersonal space for most of their lives in a way that was false to their true selves.

When silence does go on for a long time, we can occupy ourselves, and free the patient of having to speak to satisfy our longing to engage, by thinking our own thoughts. On occasion, patients may need us to empty out our thoughts about therapy, and not be preoccupied about them, and not be looking to them for anything. It is really hard for a conscientious therapist to remove all investment in the process in this way. At these times, we have found it helpful to draw or read while sitting with a silence of this kind. When a patient continues to come but has been silent for quite a while, for instance over a period of several sessions, or for the most part of sessions over time, we might say to the patient that, although we are not speaking, we are there and willing to respond or not. Then we would spend part of each session inwardly reviewing the evolving relationship with the patient, commenting from time to time, but probably not in every session, on the meaning of the silence or whatever else occurs to us (see the vignette of Mr. Morales in Chapter 20).

Giving Surface Feedback: Clarification, Linking, Support, and Advice

Our words have more impact than their purely verbal message. How we say things, what sorts of things we comment on, whether we speak in statements or questions, our silences, gestures, tone of voice, and facial expression on arrival all provide the patient with an experience of our internal object relations. Language and the process of speaking are the transmission of our thinking process about events and forces in the patient's life and in the therapeutic relationship. We speak to patients at many levels, from the commonly caricatured utterance "Hmm" to the idealized genetic reconstruction of the patients' unconscious situation based on their transference and object relations history as understood over time. We do not disparage any level of verbal interaction, but want to be thoughtful about each level of comment and how it is received.

The simplest level of comment conveys simply that the therapist is here and paying attention. Sometimes there is nothing else worth saying. The "Hmm" conveys this, or perhaps registers surprise or ambiguity. Other simple comments such as "I see!" and simple questions or comments that repeat what the patient has said mark our presence and confirm that we are listening. Some contributions simply summarize what patients have been saying. Others clarify what is meant, or work toward the implications of a train of thought without yet offering insight. The analyst may contribute more by linking things that the patient has not put together, as in saying, "Being angry at your wife might be connected with your feeling harrassed at work," or by pointing out the absence of linking between two sets of feelings or between ideas and feelings. Linking comments are especially important, since they convey the value of connectedness in arriving at understanding.

Support and advice are relegated to an inferior position as being part of counseling, teaching, or supervision, and are not acknowledged as being part of a psychoanalytic approach. True, support and advice do not power our analytic work, but they do not kill it either. Most current therapists, and many analysts, offer both support and advice at times in their work. They just do not talk about it. For instance, one patient being seen for sex therapy reported how helped he had been when his classical analyst suggested he wear a jock strap instead of boxer shorts to treat minor but persistent testicular discomfort. That suggestion seemed not to have undermined his analytic work, and he remembered it as evidence of concern. At times, acknowledging that a patient is having a rough time, lending an umbrella to one who is caught in a rainstorm, or sharing your telephone with one whose car dies, need not undermine the process of analytic investigation. To refuse help breaks the ideal of neutrality, too. Many patients will use minor advice about childrearing, or referral for adjunctive treatment, or even insistence on consulting a physician instead of ignoring a health problem, as evidence of concern and added safety in the therapeutic process and will continue to work analytically. Some, however, will take one episode of advice as a reason to ask for more. Then is the time to interpret the patient's attempt to use the opportunity to turn the treatment into something else so as to gratify the longing for a particular type of object relationship that serves to defend the self. We are free to respond naturally to emergencies and special requests if we investigate what we have said or done and what it has meant to the patient. In Chapter 17 we give an example of a brief therapy where much of the work centered on the validation provided by supportive listening.

Giving In-Depth Feedback: Interpretation

Working in depth involves the use of interpretation of defense, anxiety, unconscious fantasy, the dynamics of internal object relations, and transference.

Interpreting Transference–Countertransference and Enactments

Enactments of transference–countertransference happen when patient and therapist fall into living out patterns of entrenched object relations. Memories are repeated instead of being consciously remembered (Freud 1917). We think that this repetition compulsion occurs not because of the death instinct, as Freud thought, but because the memories are organized not just as memories but as psychic structure that is both a current way of being and a model for future experience. Such a constellation causes an enactment when the patient projects into the analyst an internal object relationship with which the analyst's internal object organization resonates so thoroughly that he or she is at first unaware of the resulting pattern of interaction. The therapist falls into the patient's illness, in the therapist's own style. A transference–countertransference enactment is unconsciously designed to evoke responses in the therapist that are like those of parts of the patient's own ego or object. Such an enactment is not in itself curative. It does not work by providing a corrective emotional experience when the therapist is not exactly like the patient's expectations. Only when the therapist returns to the neutral position and reflects clearly on what has happened is there any benefit to having experienced a transference–countertransference enactment (Chused 1996). Then as awareness dawns, it becomes possible to speak interpretively and meaningfully about these events from inside the shared experience and to substitute thinking and understanding for enactment.

The best interpretations are given in short and easily understandable form. When something more complicated needs saying, it will be more readily absorbed if it is presented in small pieces over a period of discussion. Long speeches tend not to be well understood. But there is no hard and fast rule about what single mode of speaking best informs a particular patient. The discussion of what has been enacted becomes part of the interpretive conversation of the evolving transference, and of where the patient has been and seems to be going in the therapeutic process.

Part of the effect of interpretation rests with the tact with which it is given. As we noted earlier in this chapter, Steiner (1994) has discussed the role of focusing interpretations on the patient's experience or on the patient's experience of the therapist as a way of modulating the impact a message may have. To this we now add that using the aspect of transference geography which locates the experience of containment in the patient, in the therapist, or in the space between them is a useful guide in this activity. Other aspects of transference geography can also help therapists decide where the patient is most open to intervention—when direct interpretation of the here-and-now transference would be out of place and when it would clarify shared experience, when interpretation of the here-and-then would help, or when it is best to focus more on the there-and-then or there-and-now.

The following vignette illustrates a transference interpretation which combines the there-and-back-then with the here-and-now, and uses the analyst's momentary countertransference to understand the here-and-then.

Interpreting a Transference Incident about Spoiling

Marianne was telling me (DES) about her mother's extended family in a particularly interesting way. She had told me about her mother's suffering from cancer, and now she was giving a long list of damaged people. She suddenly looked around from the couch and angrily demanded, "Are you listening?"

I was surprised at the way she fractured a moment of intensity. I asked why she thought I was not listening, and she said it was because I wasn't looking at her. I was staring off at the floor.

I said it was strange that she would think I wasn't listening when I happened to have been listening with particular absorption. I wondered if, when she was getting something she wanted very much, she often spoiled it.

She said that she did. She said that she felt guilty that while her mother is suffering with cancer, she was getting so much from me. She remembered feeling guilty about getting things when she was little, too, when her mother seemed so unhappy. Her mother used to spoil things by her nastiness.

I said that now she does it for herself, keeping her spoiling mother alive inside her through the spoiling of her good opportunities now.

The Behavioral Interpretation

Some of our most important interpretations are not spoken but acted. In the same way that we live and act our reliability and respect for the therapeutic frame, we must at times convey a message by our behavior which cannot be adequately conveyed by words alone. Often it is not possible to put such a message into words until the patient has first experienced it. For instance, if a particularly needy patient is pressuring the therapist to extend the hour, it is not enough to talk about why it is not a good idea to change the frame (which we have probably already explained during the assessment anyway). It may take an insistence on ending the session on time to evoke a response. Then the affects and the underlying object relationship can be analyzed. Generally, behavioral interpretations happen when words have already failed and a more dramatic impact is required (see the clinical example of setting the frame with Mr. Morales in Chapter 20).

The Because Clause

Henry Ezriel, a consultant at the Tavistock Clinic from the 1950s through the 1970s, described the ideal interpretation as a complete one which spoke to the patient's internal object relationships (1950, 1952). In teaching about individual and group treatment, he taught that therapists should not interpret until they understand the relationship the patient requires, the one that is avoided, and the calamity that is feared. For instance, a patient might fear that unless an exciting object relationship could be used to further repress a rejecting object, the calamity of loss of the self to the persecutor would ensue. Furthermore, Ezriel wanted the complete interpretation to center on the transference wishes toward the analyst. Then he would interpret that the patient wanted such-and-such from him in order to protect himself from recognizing another way of being with him that he was afraid of, *because* it would cause a calamity, as was felt to have occurred earlier in the patient's experience. Hence, Ezriel's form of interpretation earned the name *the because clause*. Looked at in terms of Fairbairn's theory, Ezriel was describing a threat to the central ego which the patient felt would occur if one repressed relationship could not further repress another.

We have been impressed by the explanatory power in Ezriel's formulation of *the because clause*. But we teach it as an attitude to guide our working together, not as a counsel of perfection. We do not wait to speak until we have an entire and wholly formed interpretive message for our patients, for, as we have been saying, we believe understanding arises through our joint efforts. We want to be able to say to a patient, "You do these things that shortchange yourself and cause you distress *because it protects you from something else more painful*." Once we discover what that greater pain is, then we work together to unravel the calamity that is unconsciously expected at the next level of anxiety. Often patients do self-destructive things over and over because they feel that no one will love them if they carry on differently; they feel unloved anyway so they'd better take care of themselves, which indeed causes others to avoid them; or they are afraid they will be exploited, plundered, or go crazy. Acknowledging the way that behavior makes sense in the context of required and avoided relationships comes as a considerable relief to patients, and lets them take in interpretations about fears which otherwise might be too painful to accept. If we can understand how and why patients are compelled to do things with us as they do, they may not be bound to relate that way in the future.

On Being Wrong, on Being Threatened with Quitting, and on Having Doubts

On Being Wrong

One of our teachers once said that one of the main reasons for making interpretations was to prove that the analyst could be wrong. We do not need to offer proof that we can be wrong. It happens often and without any need to try. But we do need not to be afraid of being wrong and making mistakes of understanding and timing. We need to be open to knowing less than our patients. It is, after all, their inner world and their lives that we are exploring, and all the evidence we use begins with them. There is no shame in having them correct us: being open to their doing so is a model for them. It demonstrates that we are together with them in working away at getting things right and in growing a sense of understanding together. Imposing a theory whether it fits or not and stubbornly insisting on being in the right will not bring about understanding. Being wrong and being willing to reconsider how we understand things are building blocks to collaboration and shared understanding, both central to the method we value.

On Being Threatened with Quitting

Some patients stop therapy when we feel it would be to their benefit to continue. Other patients have a feeling of wanting to stop that indicates other needs that can be analyzed rather than decided upon. There are some patients who eventually manage to stay in a long therapy or psychoanalysis whose work is nevertheless marked by the repeated feeling of wanting to quit. The therapist may feel too alarmed to carry on analyzing disruptive elements, but steady analysis is what is called for. We cannot require our patients to stay, but we can ask them to delay their departure so as to consider the meaning of their call to action, and we can continue to analyze and interpret as long as they are with us.

Angela first announced that she wanted to stop treatment early in her second year of analysis. She knew that the analyst cared, but she felt that it was all for nothing. She had married the wrong man who was abusing her in the process of their divorce, and she was unable to take care of her children adequately. Analysis was a waste of her money and time. In this first run-through of her wish to quit, I (DES) reacted more than I wished, saying I thought that she was upset that I had not been able to help her solve her difficult marriage, that she felt more lost and alone than ever, and that she was punishing me for several things—failing to understand her situation, having things she did not have, and for taking a recent vacation. We both knew, I said, that she felt she still needed the treatment.

Although she tearfully agreed to stay, I felt guilty, as if I had had a childish tantrum to bludgeon her into remaining. The next time she threatened to quit some months later, I was able to recall that childish feeling that unless I "threatened" her by recalling her need for treatment and for me, she would not stay.

This led me to say to her that she might be invoking in me a childhood wish to get her parents to stay with her when she feared they would not. In response, she told me about her parents' divorce, for which she felt responsible. When her father took her on a business trip to Europe, he openly had an affair, and took her out on delightful evenings with his new companion. On her return from the trip, her mother had quizzed her about her father's behavior, and when Angela confirmed her suspicions, her mother threw him out of the house. For some years afterwards, Angela saw little of her father. Now she felt that her talking with me and revealing her guilty secrets meant that I would throw myself out of her life and leave her as her father had. And on the other hand, her threat to leave me carried the identification with her father who had left her, and it effectively burdened me with the fear of abandonment.

Later in the analysis, she made further threats to quit, each of which had different meanings. By then I learned to take them as indicating a feeling state or a memory that could be understood. As I conveyed this confidence to her by my non-anxious silence, she struggled to find the meaning behind them. At first, she was grudging in sharing her discoveries, because she still feared that I would leave if she told. Over time, she was more able to talk with me in solving the mystery behind the new rendition of the wish to quit. The next level of inquiry revealed that she must quit because I was, she said, "a good analyst," and she, she said, was "a hopeless patient." In a self-destructive way, she longed for her father as a fun-loving, exciting object, and felt stuck with her angry mother whose abrasive style she emphasized and experienced as bad and rejecting because she overlooked her mother's faithfulness and support through the divorce. The cost of maintaining the split in which her father was the exciting object and her mother the rejecting one was the lack of a good, ideal object to nourish her central ego. So her main identification was with her mother as a rejecting object and this left her feeling bad, rejectable, and depressed about herself. Quitting signified a hopelessness about mourning, making reparation to her objects and her self for these splits, and moving on to a gentler identification with her steady mother as a good-enough object.

In the last phase of what turned out to be a long analysis, Angela was ambivalent about stopping treatment. She was in a much improved second marriage, but one with compromises nevertheless. She mourned her losses and talked sadly of how ties to bad objects had impinged on a fuller development of her potential. Nevertheless, she had insight into how she could improve her life or handicap herself, and had grown generally happier and at the same time easier to live with. Now the appropriateness of the parting changed the defensive wish to stop into a time of mutual mourning for the limitation of her potential by commitments already made, the loss of the therapeutic relationship, and mutual acknowledgment of her gains.

The wish to stop therapy has as many potential meanings as any other transference event in therapy. It requires the same steady and thoughtful approach to understanding as the others. For the patient who is basically motivated for treatment and held in an adequate contextual tranference, the interpretive work yields understanding and a re-secured treatment. A longer example of work with a patient around the issue of stopping treatment is given in the case of Marianne in Chapter 21.

On Having Doubts

Psychotherapy is not a field for someone who wants to be sure and confident of what they are doing at every moment. Since we are advocating a process of being willing to dwell in mysteries without unreasonable reaching for the facts, we have to acknowledge that we find ourselves mired in ignorance or swimming in doubt more of the time than is comfortable. This book offers principles of technique to help us tolerate and emerge from chaos. It gives examples of therapeutic process, some of which seemed to yield gratifying progress while others show mistakes and less-good outcomes. But we have found it more difficult to write about the sessions that do not stand out. How do you make the unremarkable interesting to someone else? Nevertheless, we acknowledge that much of the work is mundane, plodding, and devoid of inspiration or reassurance. When the patient is stuck, we feel stuck, and all too often we fear that we lack skill, which surely someone wiser must posess. At these times, we feel awful, not just in a theoretical way, but just plain lousy. Not in each case or at every moment, but the power of the transference in one case can obliterate the value of the rest of the week's work. Our sense of well-being depends on our patients' experience of us. There seems to be no way around it: we depend on patients as they do on us.

Loneliness and vulnerability in private practice have to be attended to by sharing the ups and downs of our work with supportive, yet critical, colleagues, and by having pleasure from nonprofessional relationships. We recognize the importance of a well-distributed emotional investment in a rich tapestry of personal relationships so that no one area of life, including the professional one, has too much power to inflate the sense of self or strip it from us. In that context we find support to continue to live with recurring doubt, to work to understand the dark areas, and to reach the light, until further work takes us into the shadow of the next venture with another patient's unknown.

Adding Ancillary and Adjunctive Methods

Individual object relations therapy may be conducted in a hospital or day-care setting as part of a milieu that includes bodily, artistic, and cognitive approaches to self-expression, such as movement therapies, dance therapy, psychodrama, therapeutic sports, art therapy, and patient education. In outpatient settings it is more often integrated with group, couple, sex, and family therapies. But even on its own, individual therapy includes more than verbal communication. In individual therapy with children and in family therapy, we employ play and drawing along with talking because young children express themselves better through play than verbally (D. Scharff 1982, D. Scharff and J. Scharff 1987). In object relations individual therapy we have both had adult patients who drew occasionally or brought in drawings made outside the sessions and used them for further elaboration of themes in their work (see the example of Albert in Chapter 9). A number of patients have brought photographs of families to facilitate discussion of the relationships of an earlier period in their lives. Occasionally a patient will bring a home movie or video from their early life. A number of patients will read from a journal or from finished pieces. Here the therapist does not give a critical review of a piece of art, but tries to appreciate the meaning of the work to the patient and, with the patient's collaboration, looks for the dynamic meaning of the writing or painting and its relevance to the therapeutic process.

Using Medication

We discuss the use of medication in the following chapter on assessment. Here we only want to say that our continuing assessment during therapy includes a readiness to re-evaluate the need for medication, adding it for patients who may become overwhelmingly anxious or depressed or in whom a psychotic potential is revealed in the course of therapy, or helping patients stop medication as their increased maturity and firmer capacity to stand anxiety and move past crippling depression takes hold. For the majority of therapists who are not physicians, it is crucial to work closely with a psychiatrist who is fully supportive of the psychodynamic work, does not take the stand that only medication is important, does not institute dramatic changes in medication without collaboration with the therapist or analyst, and does not engage with the patient in ways likely to cultivate a split in the transference. Patients benefit from their experience of therapist and physician as a couple working to facilitate growth. For the psychiatrist-psychotherapist, the challenge is to be able to medicate without losing sight of the psychodynamic meanings of the medication and its impact on the transference.

Modifying Technique
With Survivors of Trauma

Treating the survivors of physical and sexual trauma requires an understanding of the way they fear for their safety even within what would otherwise be an adequate holding environment, because earlier in their lives trauma has often followed safety, breaking through unpredictably. Because they have learned to be always on their guard, they present a guarded exterior in therapy.

Because they had to go on being to survive horror, they may keep the therapy at a similarly welcome mundane level. Because their transitional space for fantasy and creativity was invaded by a painful reality that collapsed it, they do not dream freely. The therapist must learn to value the mundane and to understand it as representing the patient's method of unconscious communication about the struggle to keep alive, rather than seeing this as merely a defense against seemingly more analytic material that might be more gratifying to the analyst (Bollas 1989, J. Scharff and D. Scharff 1994).

Traumatized patients may have problems with dissociative processes at all levels, from a tendency to numbness or absentmindedness and mildly altered states of consciousness to frank multiple personality disorder. Even the less severely dissociative patients may see their experience as more thoroughly split between good and bad, their objects more threatening and idealized, than other patients. Direct recall of trauma and its details may elude us until well into a long-term therapy, even several years after therapy has begun. Therapists seeing these patients should value the everyday realities, pace their work more slowly in order to focus on the quality of safety, maintain good holding in the contextual aspects of the work, and tolerate heightened fears.

The children of trauma survivors who have not been directly traumatized themselves have nevertheless inevitably absorbed the object relations of trauma from fearful parents through projective identification. In Chapter 9, we presented the therapist's dilemma in working with Albert, whose parents had been traumatized and were therefore hypervigilant, and who was left with a lifelong question about how to deal with the absence of a direct trauma in his own life. In that chapter, we revisited the issue of working with aspects of uncertainty. In Chapter 26, we relate dreams from the analysis of a survivor of trauma that occurred in his childhood, his adolescence, and his early adulthood, and had also occurred to family members in the previous generation.

In Reduced-Fee Arrangements

When patients are seen for a low fee or with an unusual fee arrangement, transference and countertransference complexities are inevitably introduced into the therapy, which must be taken into account. Both of us have seen many patients for reduced fees, and even for no fee, when seeing patients in training, working in Britain's National Health Service where no fee is charged, when a patient we are already seeing suffers a financial reversal, or at times when the patient's internal object relations are of interest for our clinical research. It is frequently the case, when analysts wish to practice psychoanalysis nowadays, that analytic patients have to be given special fee considerations because of the enormous expense involved in paying for treatments of three to five times weekly without reimbursement. Knowing that these situations involve transference–countertransference complications should not deter therapists from making appropriate fee arrangements, but the meaning of these arrangements must be investigated throughout the therapy.

The following case represents an extremely unusual fee arrangement undertaken by one of us (DES), with large-scale implications for the countertransference and the therapy.

A Boom-or-Bust Therapy

Max came in despair about the meaninglessness of his life. He had no worthwhile relationships, no job, and was 150 pounds overweight. His health was severely jeopardized by his obesity, resulting in a dangerous degree of edema in his legs and coronary occlusion which had already been treated with angioplasty. As a young adult, Max had been a cocaine and heroin addict, but with addiction treatment he had stopped abusing and had remained drug-free for twenty years. He had, however, lived with a boom-or-bust mentality ever since. At times he scored big in business, and at other times he was completely broke. He was able to support himself by beginning and selling venture businesses, some of which succeeded, while others failed, but he had always been able to scramble. He had been married once, but, much to his regret, the marriage had come apart when he went through one of his bust cycles.

What appealed to him in our initial consultation was my focus on his inner emptiness, which I tied to his object relations history of parental neglect and his father's alcoholism. His father was a successful ship's captain. During Max's childhood and adolescence, his father came home between voyages, drank heavily, raged at Max and the family, and then lapsed into a neglectful presence the rest of the time he was home. His mother stood by at a distance, so that Max felt he had no one to turn to. His father's alcoholism grew worse, and resulted in his being fired from one command after another. Finally, when he could no longer find work, he became more tyrannical at home, and soon thereafter, Max left.

Max had two therapies before seeing me, neither of them satisfactorily steady, including one by telephone with a man whose orientation stemmed from a theory of power and control. Nevertheless, Max felt that therapy had been helpful, but not sustaining. He came to see me after seeking help from another therapist who seemed strangely inappropriate and who taunted Max with an offer of marijuana during the initial consultation.

So Max felt reassured first by my ordinary professional approach, and then by my focusing on his lifelong habit of betting the store in each venture in order to cover his inner emptiness. He asked to come for weekly therapy, which was all he could afford from savings, with the hope that if his current venture panned out, he would intensify the treatment.

For my part, I found this an interesting venture. I had just left an administrative position, and had the intention to expand my practice. Meanwhile I had extra time. I liked Max, and my immediate liking of him corresponded to what he said of his world: people were enormously committed to him, although he did not understand why. So I found myself considering an unusual arrangement to accommodate him. I understood that if his current venture did not pan out, I was unlikely to be paid my regular fee for long. I knew from the beginning I would be gambling on whether I would be paid if he continued in therapy, but I was interested in him and had time to offer without otherwise jeopardizing my livelihood. I like to offer some reduced-fee time as a community service, but only when it is agreed upon as an expectable reduced fee. I found Max's circumstances equally deserving of consideration. So I took a chance with an arrangement I have never made before or since. He would pay me a somewhat reduced fee for the time being, with the understanding that the fee would go up when he could afford it. In the meanwhile, if his current project did not materialize, I would wait to be paid the bulk of the fee until his next major venture. He assured me that he had never failed to repay his debts, even large ones, and that he would pay me, even if it took a long time.

The first venture failed promptly, and Max soon suffered a number of other reversals which meant that he could barely pay me any fee. He had another venture idea, which seemed strong and worthwhile, and he began to work through his contacts in the network of ex-addicts who supported each other quite well. At this point his income fell to nothing, and it was clear that he would soon be unable to pay me at all until and unless another new venture took off, one he had already initiated, or until he abandoned that one too, and took an ordinary job. Once more, I gulped and again decided I would see it through with him.

So far I have said nothing about the therapy, which went quite well. Max took stock of the boom-or-bust pattern of his life and the enormously self-destructive elements that powered it, linked it to his wishes to have me rescue him, and explored the emptiness underneath. He came faithfully, made occasional payments when there were small windfalls, and discussed the pattern that had put him in this position with me. He could not understand why I had agreed to take him on, and felt grateful, which made it hard for him to express the anger that he felt periodically at me for withholding advice and answers. But he also began to feel that he was finding his own voice, and that he could face the emptiness inside him without taking actions that made things worse. He developed restraint and a capacity for delay. He had been periodically depressed, and after about a year of therapy, at a time when he became suicidal, he agreed to take antidepressant medication that he had previously refused because of his history of addiction. The medication resulted in greater resilience and less severe depressive episodes. Max was also finally able to begin a regimen of diet and exercise, which resulted in a notable improvement in his health, significant weight loss, and a much improved social and sexual life.

What I have not so far conveyed is the way I felt about this project with Max. I continued to believe that his venture would eventually come to pass and he would be able to repay the accumulating fees. Yet I was also fully aware that there was no assurance that it would happen. I could well be out of pocket for all he owed me. On the one hand I knew I could survive without the income for this one hour a week, but on the other hand I did not want to be an altruistic fool. I felt an odd dissociation from my concern, which I knew matched a dissociation inside Max. I came to realize that I had taken him on at a time when I felt in a "bust" mentality myself after leaving my administrative job, and that my vicarious investment in him represented an identification with his state of impending failure and with his unsubstantiated hopes for his future ventures.

As therapy progressed without substantial payment, we talked frequently about his way of running his life, even as he redesigned many aspects of it, gave up counting on a number of relationships which had perverse and destructive elements at their core, and learned to tolerate his emptiness. His continued hope in his business venture, which received increasingly wide support in the business world, put off the day of reckoning for him and for us. The intention we both had, which survived as a fantasy, was that when the venture was finally funded, he would intensify treatment and would be able to face his lifelong inner emptiness more adequately. But the day kept receding before us.

Within this context of suspended animation, I continued to feel that Max worked in the treatment, confronted his self-destructiveness, and dealt honestly with me. I had to absorb a deepening sense of risk and possible defeat over time. Although I still felt bound by actions I had taken during a time of unconscious identification with him, I was able to move beyond my own sense of defeat and so was no longer identified with his defeat. I now had to cope with new feelings about him. I developed a hollow feeling inside about my naïve assumption of his risk, and a fantasy of being lashed to the mast together with him as our ship must surely sink, a metaphor that indicated to me that he and I were bound to the object relations of the abusive relationship to his seagoing father. Although my father was not abusive, as his had been, my memory of him leaving to go to work as a naval officer in wartime opened me to sharing Max's experience. These feelings continued over many months, during which I shared his experience in a way that gave me a new understanding of living with risk and despair. My situation was like the one he described for himself: I felt bound by having given my word, more or less knowing what I was getting into, and there was no getting out of the situation with integrity. I felt that the validation of my judgment rested with the outcome of his venture, for I had failed to protect myself in the usual way of only working with patients who could pay a fee that was agreed on from the outset.

And then his ship came in! The business venture he had been brokering for two years was sealed. He was assured a salary over a substantial period of time which would allow him to pay therapy fees at a twice-weekly frequency and at the same time to retire his past debts with scheduled payments. I felt as if I had weathered a trans-Pacific crossing in a two-man ship, and that now we would have to reconstruct the ship's log, come to understand the dangers that had been weathered without being fully understood, and face the emptiness which had characterized the voyage from the beginning. The hollow feeling inside that was related to the narrow escape from disaster and to the risk I had taken with him, which only now could I fully see, began to abate. The voyage seemed more grounded now and I felt that we were ready to begin it together.

Max's point of view was not very different. He had built a relationship with me because I had stood by him as his parents had not. More than gratitude— which he did feel—he felt that now he had a chance to begin living in a different way, a way that was not yet charted, but that could at last begin.

Working Through

Long-term therapy offers the opportunity to work over problems from more than one perspective. The shape of personality structure and the form of psychopathology are overdetermined, built by repetitive experience and patterns

of conflict in relationships which resolve into a psychic structure that determines the individual's characteristic way of doing and being. These have staying power because they have many origins that converge in the final common
pathway of the organized structure of the psyche.

Troublesome symptoms and personality traits are not resolved or changed
because of a single new way of understanding them found in a single session
or as a result of a single thread of understanding developed by therapist and
patient. The only time this does happen is in the case of an externally imposed
crisis or relatively simple developmental impasse of the kind that responds to
brief, crisis-oriented psychotherapy (see Section 6). These developmental crises
are relatively common in patients seen in primary care medical practices, student health clinics, and in employee assistance programs.

But the large number of patients who require long-term object relations
therapy and analysis need time to work through their issues by approaching
them again and again from slightly differing angles—by starting with problems that seem unrelated to any other, then picking up a different problem
only to have the experience of arriving at the same point and thinking, finally,
"There it is again"; by experiencing something as a there-and-then problem,
and later having the same pattern emerge in the here-and-now of the transference; and by finding a dream that reveals the conflict in yesterday's encounter with a partner. Finding confirmation in these several overlapping ways,
patient and therapist gradually develop conviction in their understanding of
the patterns of the patient's ways of relating, defenses, anxieties, conflicts,
growth and development, life outside therapy, and the nature of the therapeutic relationship. It takes experience in all these modes, exploring overlapping areas, modifying understanding, and confirming interpretations, to lead
to growth and change.

After trying self-defeating ways of running their lives and fighting to prevent change in therapy, patients finally become aware of just how futile the
pattern is, and exhaust their habit of doing themselves in. These are the times
we wait for, when change is not so much a surprise as it is inevitable, no longer
a defeat for the old ways, but a welcome relief. The denouement to the process of working through is often not so much a bang as a whimper!

Continuing Assessment as Therapy Evolves

The need for assessment continues during the conduct of therapy, as we
monitor emerging needs, progress, and changing goals. We have already

addressed an aspect of the continuing assessment when we described monitoring the evolution of transference and countertransference during therapy. Our impressions change as we learn more about the patient and as the patient changes, for instance when a patient gives up rigid obsessional defenses and becomes more overtly depressed, or another remembers a history of trauma for the first time.

Therapeutic progress changes the profile of a patient's vulnerabilities and defensive structures. For example, in the opening and mid-phases of this treatment described in Chapters 20 and 21, Mr. Morales's use of splitting and isolation of affect, and his blaming of his wife for imposing on him, decreased. As this happened, his capacity to focus on internal issues as the cause of his limitations, and his concern for the impact of his actions and attitudes on others signalled an ever-growing capacity to live in the depressive position. His perception that this was so, and his therapist's understanding and confirmation of this, formed an important part of the therapeutic dialogue.

A man with a significant degree of dissociative vulnerability who became more integrated as a consequence of therapy was then able to join his partner in sex therapy and face his sexual anxieties, which he could not tolerate before. A depressed woman who moved beyond her tendency to severe mood collapse was able to stop medication. Another woman with borderline oscillations in mood and quality of relationships who allowed herself to experience her internal persecution through a therapeutic regression to a psychotic transference which fully expressed the internal problem, then needed help to return to reality by sitting up for a while and receiving more direct and concrete interpretations.

There is wisdom in pulling back from an ongoing therapy periodically to assess changes in patients' developmental capacities and their treatment of external impingements and inner conflicts. The value of doing this is now further emphasized in the current climate of managed care and the societal pressure to produce results quickly.

Separating and Terminating

There are many separations during therapy: the separation between one session and the next, weekends, cancelled sessions, vacations, and illnesses. Each provides a challenge to patients' anxiety by evoking the loss of contextual support and by recalling previous losses and separations. We illustrate work with these separations in many of the examples given throughout this volume. These small experiences provide a basis for working on separation and loss which anticipates and prepares for the eventual loss of the therapy itself at termination.

The facilitation of mourning underlies all the work we do. People in need of therapy need help to mourn the losses and deprivations that have beset their lives, whether we see them through a long analysis or work with them briefly. In Angela's case, earlier in this chapter, the loss of therapy was the equivalent to the loss of her father and the loss of the kind of relationship to her mother that she longed for. Only in the termination of analysis could she finally mourn the loss of a good relationship with the analyst, and use that experience to mourn her other losses. The process of termination itself is such an important opportunity for revisiting earlier ways of relating, mourning, and consolidating gains that we illustrate it in detail in Chapter 24.

13

Theory and Technique
of Assessment

Offering an assessment is a useful way to approach the possibility of therapy. Patients or clients need make only a limited commitment to reviewing their needs and exploring possible therapy or referral. Assessment may be completed in a single session, but more commonly requires an extended series of about four interviews. This gives the therapist time to evaluate the patient's needs and likeliness to benefit from therapy or psychoanalysis, and to recommend the appropriate treatment or combination of therapies. It gives patients a window for reflection without feeling pressured into a commitment. They can review their present circumstances, learn how they are connected to past experience, and decide what if anything they want to do about it. They get to experience what therapy could be like and how it could help. Most of all, they get to assess whether they can get along with the consultant, and if so then they may choose to enter therapy on an informed basis.

Assessment functions as a trial of therapy. The goal of assessment is to enable patients with psychological problems to make the investment in themselves and proceed to therapy or psychoanalysis. Most of the same principles that we discussed at length in the last chapter on the structure and process of ongoing therapy apply to the assessment process, even if they are used in an abbreviated form. But assessment also has a form of its own, designed to help therapist and patient make practical decisions about whether to undertake therapy, to assess the degree of commitment to treatment, to understand what the patient is asking for and what the therapist is willing to offer, and to decide on the most effective modality and intensity of treatment. The task of arriving at a conclusion adds pressure to assessment interviews which is not usually present in ongoing psychotherapy or analysis.

In Table 13–1, we provide a framework for thinking about the assessment process.

Establishing a Holding Environment

Setting the Frame

The creation of psychological space begins with the initial contact with the patient, usually made by telephone to the therapist directly or to the clinic receptionist or intake worker. It is important to listen for any questions the potential patient has and answer any of them directly when they involve practical matters of general orientation, fee, appointment hours, office location, directions, and the qualifications of the therapist. Place, time, and initial consultation fee are agreed on.

The appointed hour for the initial visit arrives. We can set the patient at ease by establishing an introductory phase in which we get or confirm identifying information—correct spelling of names, addresses, phone numbers, and billing information. We give a general overview of the assessment as a process that may require between one and six sessions of whatever length is agreed. Usually we use an hour or an hour and a half for the first consultation session, and therafter move to forty-five minutes. We describe the function of the assessment process as simply a chance to explore the problem and its meaning and to see whether there is a good fit between patient and therapist. We describe the form of the process as a flexible one that accommodates the patient's individual needs, but once it is agreed on, we stick to our boundaries of beginning and stopping on time, and expecting payment on the schedule that is mutually acceptable. Usually we bill at the end of the month, but some patients prefer to pay by the session. The boundaries are needed to create a safe space in which the patient can feel protected yet free to communicate, explore, and experience.

We answer initial practical questions. Some patients ply us with other questions early on, and we then let them know that we do not usually answer questions directly, because an exploration of the meaning behind the question will generally tell us more than any answer we might offer, but there is no fast and firm rule against answering questions.

TABLE 13–1. Principles of assessment

The holding environment
    Setting a frame for the assessment
    Creating psychological space
    Nonjudgmental listening
    Containment
Developmental level and capacities
    Developmental techniques of relating
    The balance of developmental positions
Attachment behaviors and memories
Standardized diagnosis
Areas of inner conflict and external impingement
Capacity to work in therapy
    Naming patterns of defense
    Object relations history, especially of loss and injury
    Following the affect
    Working with dreams and fantasies
Feedback
    Surface feedback: Clarification, linking, support, advice
    Depth feedback: Interpretation
    Transference/countertransference interpretation
Response to interpretation and assessment format
Medication, adjunctive therapies
Formulation and recommendation
Agreeing on a treatment plan

One question we always answer is the one about our qualifications for conducting therapy or analysis. Even though the beginning therapist may feel exposed by this question, the patient has a right to know our professional credentials, and this is not a place to hide behind a policy of refusal to answer questions. In any case, it is not up to the patient to know that we generally do not answer questions, or that personal questions are out of bounds. It is our job to tactfully but directly let the patient know our policy and our reasons for it, and then to begin work when the patient tests us in this area, perhaps setting limits and reaffirming the boundaries, perhaps parrying a persistent inquiry with humor or responding with interpretation.

Creating the Psychological Space

With agreement about the form and function of the assessment in process, we proceed to discuss the problem. Even if the patient has given enough information on the phone to establish the reason for a consultation, we prefer to begin at the beginning in the first interview, asking for the reasons for seeking consultation, and going from there. At times, patients will press for treatment plans before therapists have much experience with the patient, but practical matters about possible ongoing therapy should be deferred until nearer the end of the assessment when there is more understanding about what makes most sense. Here we are encouraging a capacity for delay. This leaves time for the creation of the psychological space.

The creation of space and time are the fundamental aspects of the holding environment that we create. Within the boundaries of the frame, we use our reflective, process-and-review orientation to generate a psychological space in which the patient can be herself, share her pain, work, and play with ideas.

Nonjudgmental Listening

As we listen, we have an open, nonjudgmental attitude, asking questions or offering clarifications, occasionally putting back to the patient our understanding of what is being said. Our focus is on understanding the core of the problem and what led the patient to seek consultation at this point.

We want to understand the patient's story and the difficulties as he or she understands them himself, but we are listening more particularly for the underbelly of the story, for the unconscious picture that begins to emerge from silence, gestures, the flow of associations, dream, and fantasy. To best absorb this, we are partly gathering facts and taking in a conscious narrative, and partly we have an attitude of relaxed, nondirective unconscious attunement which allows for resonance with our own unconscious organization.

Containment

We use the capacity for tolerating anxiety that we have built from clinical experience and personal therapy or psychoanalysis to hold the patient's worries and distress. We want to create space where anything can be said and anything can be felt, even if it does not make sense. We will look for the sense in it by seeking connections to earlier experience, but we will not force sense on material the essence of which is to communicate fragmentation and broken links. We use our *negative capability*, our capacity for being without irritable reaching after fact and reason, to let the story emerge, partly in the telling and partly in the effect it has on our relationship to the patient as we listen. We use our training in process-and-review to monitor our interactions as we go along, all the time assessing the impact the patient has on us. In the brief time of assessment, we will develop a working hypothesis about the internal object relationships that are guiding the patient's experience of us.

We contain anxiety. By this we do not mean simply that we bear it. We mean that we take in the patient's experience, feel affected by it, reflect upon it, and find words for it to communicate to the patient. We developed the concept of *containment* in the last chapter on therapy. Our containment is a processing function, like the mother's who in her reverie can temper her infant's distress and give form to his unthinkable anxiety (Bion 1967). The infant not only gets his anxiety back in a metabolized, thinkable form, but he gets the idea of his mother as a containing person who can help him, an idea of his self as understandable, and he identifies with her containing function and learns to do it for himself.

Assessing Developmental Level and Capacities

Here we want to consider where in the patient's growth and development difficulty has ensued, from which developmental phases the person has emerged with an unsatisfactory balance of conflict. In Freud's psychoanalytic theory, development was assessed according to the stages of psychosexual development, beginning with the oral stage, and proceeding to the anal, phallic, and oedipal. He thought that fixations at various stages led to relatively specific syndromes, and that the diagnosis of a syndrome led more or less reliably to a point of fixation at a specific developmental stage.

Nowadays, some of the syndromes which were thought to have psychodynamic causes are understood to be largely organic in origin, such as schizophrenia or autism. Even some of the main psychodynamic diagnostic entities such as depression, obsessive-compulsive disorders, or anxiety may be intensified by changes in the central nervous system which trigger them easily or cause such sensitivity to small environmental triggers that the patient has major reactions to relatively minor impingements from outside.

Nevertheless, Freud's way of assessing levels of growth and development remains of some use because it allows us to understand the person's overall levels of achievement, the relative strengths and weaknesses which mark his growth, and the vulnerabilities which provide pitfalls to future functioning under certain circumstances. It also provides a well-known language through which therapists can communicate in shorthand their shared understanding of the meaning of stage-specific oral dependence or sadism, of the anal, controlling attributes of the obsessive-complusive personality, and the phallic qualities of showing off, taking over, and thrusting oneself forward.

Developmental Techniques of Relating

The object relations therapist who does not accept the drive-oriented basis for development no longer ties these qualities to their source in the energies and erogenous zones of a single developmental period. For us, the concept of psychosexual stages remains useful only as a metaphor for the quality of object relating that emerges from the child's developmental mastery of the conflict with the external object at each developmental phase. Instead, we use Fairbairn's revision of developmental phases as a progression of *transitional techniques* for relating to the object in the transition from the infantile dependency of childhood to the mature dependency of adulthood. The persistence of these techniques leads to characteristic symptoms and character types, depending on the location of accepted (good) and rejected (bad) objects that have been unconsciously distributed as the individual struggles between the urge to cling and surrender to the infantile object and the effort to separate from it.

Phobic and obsessional techniques are, therefore, two methods of dealing with the same issue, by splitting and managing the alignment of the self with regard to good and bad objects. By externalizing both good and bad objects and fleeing from them, the person in a phobic state of mind passively avoids surrender to the bad object and clings anxiously to the good, safe object. In contrast, the person in an obsessional state aggressively relates to both good and bad by taking them inside and managing them actively. In the hysterical state of mind, the person internalizes the bad object and externalizes the good object, which is overvalued and needed desperately, while the self is depreciated, and then vacillates between accepting and rejecting the overvalued good object. The person in a paranoid state of mind projects the bad object into external objects who are then regarded as persecutors, and attempts to locate the good object in the inner world, and so the self is overvalued.

Because these states of mind are not based in developmental fixations but rather correspond to strategies for relating, a person can exchange one pattern for another at different points or under changing conditions without major diagnostic implications. Table 13–2 summarizes the characteristics of Fairbairn's techniques:

TABLE 13–2. Transitional techniques of relating

Technique	Accepted (Good) Object	Rejected (Bad) Object
Obsessional	Internalized	Internalized
Phobic	Externalized	Externalized
Paranoid	Internalized	Externalized
Hysterical	Externalized	Internalized

Modified from Fairbairn (1952). Used with permission of Routledge.

What we assess is the internalization or externalization of objects, and we determine the predominant way of relating to external objects. We consider whether the person appreciates good objects, craves unsatisfying exciting objects, expresses rage at or fear of rejecting objects, and vacillates or withdraws from objects.

The Balance of Developmental Positions

Newer gauges of developmental achievement based on Kleinian theory are also useful. Klein (1946) described two fundamental positions characteristic of infancy. The infant begins with the capacity to understand relationships only in partial ways because of an intolerance of aggression and anxiety inside its self. The earliest *paranoid-schizoid position* gives the infant a way of dealing with this intolerance by using projective identification to rid the self of unmanageable anxiety, splitting the object into good and bad, identifying with the object of its projection, and repressing it inside the self. By the end of the first year, the infant is usually more often in the *depressive position*. Finding its aggression more tolerable and having become able to hold in mind the whole object that used to be split, the infant begins to show concern for its objects and a capacity for guilt and mourning. In this position, there is also a vulnerability to use manic defenses to avoid mourning in favor of impulsive, magical solutions that leap over the need for taking responsibility. These capacities are developed more fully over time. Klein's idea of development is that once a position is attained, it stays with the individual as a potential mental state. To Klein's schema, Ogden (1989) added an earlier position, the autistic-

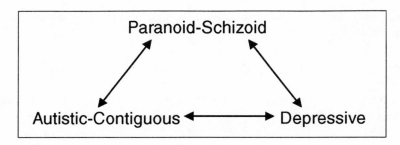

FIGURE 13–3. Positions in normal development.

contiguous position, which refers to the individual's degree of preoccupation with cohesion of the self. This position predominates when the person relies on proximity to an object to maintain the physical and emotional intactness of the self. Ogden posits that the autistic-contiguous position predates the paranoid-schizoid position, but, like Klein's two positions, remains potentially active in the individual throughout life.

In assessing the developmental schema, we ask where on this continuum the individual's leading anxieties tend to fall. All of us have the potential to operate at any point along the continuum, but one of the positions better describes our way of thinking about ourselves and our way of relating to our objects during certain phases of our lives. However, the fact that one of these is present at a given time does not mean that the other positions are absent or will not take over at a later time. What we assess is the balance between the positions and the repeating pattern of tending to operate mostly in any one of them under stressful circumstances. In normal personality, these positions alternate and the concerns of one position are adequately subsumed during the dominance of the others.

Assessing Attachment Behaviors and Memories

We need not be bound by the traditional developmental schemata that are fifty or a hundred years old, now that we have the advantage of the new perspectives offered by current research in infant attachment spawned by the work of John Bowlby. These findings are easily assimilated into our clinical object-relations perspective because the field of attachment research stemmed from object relations theory refracted through the ethological lens of Bowlby and the elaboration of his work by Mary Ainsworth, Mary Main,

Peter Fonagy and Mary Target, Arietta Slade, Mary Sue Moore, and others (see Chapter 7).

Here are some simple descriptions of personality functioning organized by categories that are abstracted from the literature on attachment classification that is presented in Chapter 7. This gives us another angle on assessing development along the continuum of affect regulation, structure, and object relations through observing or asking about attachment behaviors and memories.

Autonomous/Secure

Adults with secure attachments value their relationships highly but do not despair at separation or loss. Relationships, which are usually high on their list of priorities, provide a background of holding or a foreground of pleasure or concern in a relaxed way.

Resistant/Preoccupied

People with anxious attachment of the resistant/preoccupied kind have overly dependent relationships as adults and are fearful in many circumstances. They often cling to their objects, and may seek promiscuous closeness. They fear losses and separations, and try desperately to avoid them by a show of affect that induces attachment behavior in the therapist. If they cannot avoid a separation, then they try to blunt the pain they feel and punish the significant other by their withdrawal. They are nevertheless often loyal to their attachment figures and value the closeness that they achieve.

We think that women have often been culturally induced to behave in resistant/preoccupied ways so as to keep them at home and devoted to their families, and the pathology of this pattern is only now being fully addressed.

Avoidant/Dismissive

People with avoidant/dismissive patterns handle their anxiety by truncating relationships, often devaluing them and maintaining a distant, often walled-off existence. They may seem schizoid, living in their inner world as a way of controlling access by their loved ones for fear of giving others control over their sense of well-being, or they may maintain many superficial relationships so that no one other person has power over them. Some seem isolated, others seem promiscuous and uncommitted in relationships. The pseudo-independent behavior characteristic of this group and seen among toddlers in day care has been highly valued by some in our society, and in the past has tended to be culturally imposed on men more than on women.

Disorganized/Unresolved

People with disorganized attachment patterns oscillate rapidly between patterns of attachment. The vascillating quality of their relating will be re-created in psychotherapy, but may require a few sessions to become apparent. They often give off a feeling of lurking chaos and wariness, or flexibility and pseudo-adaptability that caves in easily under minor stress. This group of adults with disorganized attachment includes a high proportion of trauma survivors, and a significant number of others who were not victims of overt trauma themselves but whose parents had disorganized patterns of attachment, a residue of direct trauma to the parents. In either case, the patient has learned to expect the unexpected, to be wary of large fluctuations of anxiety in relationships, and to protect against having the rug pulled out from under without warning.

Within these broad categories there are many subtle variations in the person's ability to relate. Our clinical appreciation of the person's individual attachment patterns comes partly from the early life history, partly from the present way of remembering and thinking about attachment, and partly from the feel of the assessment session, in which the patient relates to us in characteristic ways. We process our countertransference to amplify our understanding of the transference and so arrive at a picture of the patient's internal object relations. We described transference and countertransference more fully in Chapter 11 and will return to the topic later in this chapter.

Giving a Standardized Diagnosis

The therapist is usually obligated to make an official diagnostic assessment of overall functioning along various axes according to the categories of the current edition of the *Diagnostic and Statistical Manual*, and to make a prognosis and estimate the length of treatment. Therapists who think in terms of dynamic formulations and who keep an open mind on the possibility of progress and changing goals in treatment feel compromised by this requirement. They have to take on a different professional identity to fill out the forms that will document a diagnosis consistent with securing reimbursement for the patient or client. While we understand that insurance and managed care companies need standardized diagnoses, complying with their requirements distorts our thinking to fit a culture driven more by the economics of corporate profitability than by concerns for the quality of patient care. Attempting to offer the least possible care is not consistent with the best care, but assessing what can be done within the limits of what is available is a present-day necessity. DSM diagnosis is most useful for establishing basic or accompanying organic conditions and for distinguishing between the main groups of major mental illness, because it then determines the choice of medication. Some advances have been made in including consideration of dynamics, but DSM is still mainly symptom-focused. We are more interested in such issues as motivation, psychological-mindedness, the capacity for sustaining a therapeutic relationship, the dynamics of conflict and object relationships, problems of self and other, and in exploring what is possible for the individual person, regardless of DSM category.

Exploring Areas of Inner Conflict and External Impingement

One of the crucial distinctions to be made is in the area of the source of conflict. Does it arise primarily from external or internal sources? Patients often come to us complaining of trouble caused by a boss, spouse, or child. Indeed, it may not be possible at first to determine how much of a patient's difficulty is externally imposed. At times the patient will know that the external object's behavior is independently troublesome to many others, and simply requests help in tolerating, managing, or leaving a bad situation. Others may be aware that they cause their external objects to mistreat them. They demonstrate a pattern of repeated difficulties in relating which represents the persistent effect of repressed internal object relationships. Other patients have a propensity to accept blame for relational difficulties that are imposed principally from external objects. Such patients contribute to their situation by their readiness to accept blame, but it does not always follow that they will provoke blame in future if they can extricate themselves from the current relationship. We try to assess the balance between external and internal forces and recognize that our perception of this balance will change over time as the patient works on the conflict, and explores relating to alternative objects.

Capacity to Work in Therapy

Assessment functions as a trial of therapy, and so uses most of the basic ways of working in brief. For this reason, several of the basic tasks were discussed more fully in the previous chapter on therapeutic process. So here, in brief, is a review of the ways of working used in the assessment process. Through the patient's response to these techniques, we can form an idea of the patient's capacity to sustain a therapeutic relationship and work psychodynamically. For further discussion of the ways of working, see Chapter 12.

Naming Patterns of Defense

First we want to see how patients demonstrate defensive functioning. As they let us know about themselves, do they fend off certain areas through unlinking affect from content, by ignoring links that should be obvious, or by externalizing blame onto others in their life for problems that seem to rest with them? Do they split good and bad objects without seeing that they are doing so, or do they take blame for events which seem not to be their responsibility? In short, how do they handle the various sorts of anxieties and losses that they come to tell us about? We comment on the repeating patterns of defense, name them, and ask the patient to join us in thinking about the need to engage in these ways.

Object Relations History

On the way to understanding these matters, we like to get some object relations history, that is, the narrative of the life with significant objects throughout development. We are especially interested in the child's experience of loss and injury. We get this information not by taking a formal history, but by asking about parents or former important relationships at moments when this question seems relevant to something the patient is talking about in the session already. We cannot, in the space of any assessment period, learn all the things about a patient's past that we will eventually see as important, but we can get an idea of how the past influences the current relationships and the way the patient organizes life.

Following the Affect

We ask for associations to the previous family experience when there is a show of affect about current experience. Thus at a moment when the patient is talking about being mistreated by her spouse and cries like a child, or shows that this hurts her because it is like the relationship between her parents before their divorce, we might ask her to elaborate about her parents at that point. The object relations we want to know about are those that are affectively alive in the session, those that convey pain, separation, and loss, and that we have become aware of in the session because of affective shifts, defensive functioning, and inconsistencies in memory and behavior.

Sometimes there seems to be no affect. In those disorganized/unresolved patients who have been severely traumatized, there will be gaps in their memories of old relationships, and corresponding areas of distance between them and others—including the therapist—now. When we see a patient who tells us blandly that childhood was fine and whose spouse complains of a sense of distance or absence at times, and with whom we have times of disconnection, we can suspect that there was an important area of unbearable pain which we cannot know about directly in such a short encounter. The internal object that is the live remnant of the trauma may be too painful to be linked consciously to current experience, and can only become linked through therapy.

Working with Dreams and Fantasies

We want access to dreams and fantasies even in the assessment phase, and we tell patients this in the first session when we describe our ways of working. If they are not forthcoming, we will ask directly about them. As with getting the object relations history, we prefer the story of a dream or fantasy to emerge naturally in context, but when dreams and fantasies have been omitted or referred to indirectly we will ask directly about the lack of focus on them. Fantasies, not restricted to masturbation fantasies, may lead to or emerge from a discussion of sexual pleasure or difficulty. Other fantasies relate to the more mundane matters of imagining an alternative situation to the one in which the patient finds himself, the "dream" person they wish to be or be related to, or the fantasy of another career or life course. Unconscious fantasies reveal themselves in dreams and in the way the self relates to the other and to the therapist.

We are interested in these unverbalized guiding fantasies that operate as unconscious assumptions that structure anxiety. A man may believe without knowing it that the troubles he experiences repeatedly are an inevitable part of his life. Even in assessment he may come to see that he continues to impose this on himself because of unconscious guilt stemming from a childhood situation. His unconscious fantasy is that he has caused trouble before and deserves to be punished for it by being pursued by trouble, according to the law of talion. A woman survivor of abuse who keeps her relationships as splintered as her ego may realize that she is doing so to ensure that she is never again at the mercy of someone of importance to her. As therapy proceeds, the level of understanding of such motivating fantasies deepens, but even in assessment a superficial formulation can give patients an orienting principle that persuades them of the value of further therapeutic exploration.

Feedback

The kind of feedback we give in assessment is designed to show the patient how we work. We are demonstrating our ways of working for the patient to try out, and we want to see in return how the patient works with our input at the surface and in depth.

Surface Feedback: Clarification, Support, Advice

At the surface, we make comments that show the patient we have understood what he has said, ask him to clarify a murky point, or link one set of concerns with something else that he has told us about. At times, a patient may come with a question about a child or the management of an aging parent, and we may express our empathy with her in a difficult situation or give useful advice. At the same time we are aware that the offering of this kind of support and advice may become a model of a way of working together which has the potential to undermine thematic psychodynamic work. There is no rule against offering support or advice, but since these tend to build an expectation of more supportive therapy, we monitor the use the patient makes of asking for answers, and then we ask the patient to think about the meaning of the request and their experience of our not giving the answer they expected. Many patients gratefully accept such help in assessment without then trying to move into a nonanalytic mode of relating. Support and advice are not against the rules, but they are not the workhorses of object relations therapy and assessment.

Depth Feedback: Interpretation

In every assessment, we would like to have the opportunity to offer trial interpretations, those aspects of feedback that operate in more depth. Here we can interpret how and why a patient shields himself from pain and anxiety, the function his fantasies serve, the interpersonal conflicts revealed in a dream, or the structure of his internal object relations and the struggle between opposing aspects of the self.

Transference–Countertransference

Interpretation is most effective when it derives from our experience of the transference in the countertransference. In Chapter 11 on the geography of transference and countertransference, and in Chapter 12 on therapeutic process, we give a map for tracking where the transference is. Transference and countertransference already operate in the first interview, as people enter our space with expectations about our capacity to be therapeutic and as we react to them as potential patients. We name the problems in the patient's experience with us in the here-and-now and link them to similar experiences (the here-and-then) with important figures in the past (the there-and-then of family life) and in current relationships (the there-and-now of family life). We notice where on the map the transference is operating—here in therapy, there in life, here in therapy or there in relation to significant others, located in the patient, in the therapist, or in the space between. We look for whether we are being used as one of the patient's objects or as a part of the patient's self.

We may or may not become aware of specific contextual or focused transference elements that we wish to comment on. When we find that the beginning contextual transference is generally a positive and accepting one and we understand its origins in secure early attachment, there is little to interpret beyond acknowledging that there seems to be a good possibility of working together. Even here, the transference–countertransference dynamic has been registered and used, though not interpreted. Sometimes the positive contextual transference is too good and we have to be sensitive to tiny cracks in the idealization through which we can help the patient look at the problem so that the unrecognized negativity does not derail the move into therapy. In other cases, we may find a negative contextual transference. Through our dawning awareness of discomfort, we become aware of the patient's reservations. These must be addressed promptly and forthrightly in the first session, and revisited during the assessment phase. Sometimes a specific focused negative transference develops prematurely as a defense against facing the more amorphous anxieties about the context, or it may arise as a result of an extraordinary level of valency in the therapist to receive such a projection. If we can interpret the fear of the therapeutic relationship so that patients feel understood, they will have a basis for considering the value of the therapeutic relationship as a laboratory for exploring their difficulties.

Testing Response to Interpretation and Format

We cannot tell patients everything we think about our experience with them, but we want to try an interpretation or two to see how they respond. Do they become defensive and deny what we say? Do they react thoughtfully even if they disagree? Do they produce more material which expands, clarifies, or improves our understanding? Addressing these directly, preferably in the first session, as we become aware of them and come to understand them, is the best way to reinforce the holding capacity for the therapy which may follow.

Medication and Adjunctive Therapies

It is now commonplace to see patients for psychotherapy who are already on medication, or for whom the possibility of medication arises during evaluation or subsequent therapy. Although psychoanalysts were wary for many years about the use of medication in case it blunted the motivation for therapy by prompt removal of current symptoms or obscured issues emerging in the course of therapy, there is no longer any reason for conflict between these two modes of treatment. Patients who use medication properly for overwhelming anxiety or depression, for psychotic vulnerability, or dissociative tendencies, can work better in psychotherapy and in psychoanalysis. In a similar way, children and adults who are properly diagnosed with attention deficit disorder settle down on stimulants, and are more available for treatment. Patients with frank psychosis, violently acting-out behaviors, unrelenting suicidal depression, refractory mania, or acute alcoholism and severe chronic drug use can all be treated effectively with object relations therapy, especially if their therapists have hospital affiliations that secure the holding environment.

While suitable medication properly prescribed by a specialist or a family doctor can by itself give relief for conditions such as panic disorder, intractable depression, or obsessive-compulsive disorder, it is more effective when combined with talking through problems and relational difficulties. We recommend a full assessment before any drugs are prescribed, and, in most cases, we prefer to have a trial of therapy before deciding on a combined pharmacological approach. One of us (DES) worked for several years with the family practitioners who offered primary care to the well-functioning population of medical students and their families at the Uniformed Services University of the Health Sciences. Over several years there when almost a quarter of the students asked for some form of psychotherapy, he prescribed psychotropic medication in only a handful of cases. Object relations therapy or analysis offers a more lasting amelioration of suffering and may lower or end the need for medication.

Our point is not to compete with medication in its areas of legitimate use, but to argue against its overuse as a panacea. Object relations therapy and analysis are effective treatments in their own right, either in conjunction with medication, or in preference to it.

Offering a Formulation and Recommendation

After we have given enough feedback so that the patient understands how we work, we offer a brief formulation, distilled perhaps from the more extensive and tentative one that we have arrived at ourselves. We want to say enough so that patients can see how we are understanding their situation, but not so much that we seem to have reached a conclusion. We follow our hypothesis with suggestions for treatment, offering more than one possible plan when we feel there is more than one reasonable way of working. For instance, we might offer a choice between once- or twice-a-week psychotherapy, or between psychotherapy and psychoanalysis, or discuss the merits of therapy with or without medication. We may suggest couple or family therapy as an alternative, adjunctive, or preliminary approach to individual therapy. In some situations, we may tell a patient why treatment does not seem essential, why they would do better with a different specialist, or why this is not the best time to consider treatment. Our recommendation is a combination of what we think the patient needs, and where the patient is in terms of facing conflicts and investing in treatment.

Agreeing on a Treatment Plan

Then, through discussion with the patient, we agree on a frame for the therapy. The frame committed to by both therapist and patient should be sturdy enough to withstand attempts to bend it for the purpose of avoiding anxiety. On the other hand, it does not have to be set in stone. For instance, we may agree to begin therapy at a frequency of once weekly, but reserve the right to recommend a collateral visit or to increase the frequency of sessions if the need arises.

At the end of the assessment and before any therapy is agreed to, we discuss the practical conditions that apply in therapy but were not required in assessment. For instance, we do not routinely charge for cancellations during an assessment since there is no ongoing commitment, but we do charge for missed sessions once a regular time and frequency of therapy or analysis is agreed on. We discuss fee, payment procedure, and anticipated vacations of both therapist and patient, and any other practical questions which arise. We discuss the option of the use of the couch for those patients who are most able to follow the free associational method of psychoanalysis. Then we negotiate any difficulties in arriving at agreement, modify or confirm our usual policies, set the agreed conditions for beginning treatment, and look forward to the next phase of working together.

In Chapter 2, we showed these principles in action. We gave a simple example of an individual assessment closely tied to the theoretical concepts that we have presented here, rather like a teaching exercise. In clinical practice, we do not always think so systematically as that. We do not try to make the clinical material fit the theory. We let go of theory and follow the material. Theory then becomes an unconscious guiding system. The three chapters in the next section present a more typically complex clinical situation, an extended assessment of a man and a woman separately, and then an assessment of their couple relationship.

Section 5

ASSESSMENT

14

Extended Assessment of a Woman

After writing the last chapter on the theory of assessment, we agreed that we wanted to provide a lengthy clinical example of assessment. Rather than go back over old notes and pick the most satisfactory individual assessment, we decided to take the next individual referral and write it up, no matter what the outcome, to give a fair idea of how an assessment may go. Months before, a therapist had called us from the West Coast. His client, Mrs. Secombe, had had a major depression that had been successfully treated with psychotherapy and medication, but he was worried that she might become depressed again with the stress of a move to Washington, DC. He said that he would refer Mrs. Secombe to Dr. Jill Scharff, but months had gone by without a call from her. As we waited for the next referral for assessment, Mrs. Secombe happened to call to discuss whether she should have individual or marital therapy, and so it fell to Jill Scharff to provide the clinical illustration of assessment presented here and in the next two chapters.

Mrs. Secombe's First Individual Interview

Liseanne Secombe was early for her appointment. A small, 30-year-old woman with graying hair, she wore jeans and a sweater and carried a large bag of the sort that mothers need for carrying all their infant supplies. I wrote down Mrs. Secombe's name and address, and explained that the assessment process might take a few sessions, including a meeting with her husband, before I would be ready to give her my recommendation. She reminded me that she had been in therapy before and that she had been referred by her former therapist. I told her what he had told me, and said that I would like to hear from her how she viewed her situation.

Mrs. Secombe explained that she had moved here from the West Coast and had taken some time to settle into her new neighborhood and arrange for child care. Now she was all set to reinvest in therapy again, she said, and she began to tell me the history of her previous treatments. She had been in a series of therapies for a total of ten years, including individual therapy, marital therapy, and group therapy for chronic, recurrent depression. Five years ago she had suffered a major depressive episode and had required treatment with Prozac for one and one-half years. This major depressive episode had been triggered by the death of her mother and the stress of being newly married at 25. She had stopped taking Prozac when she decided to become pregnant and now had a 1½-year-old toddler with whom she was staying home. She had been mildly depressed for a long time, she said, but she had not had a relapse into a major depression despite being off Prozac and being under strain from moving.

I asked what was the main trigger for her depression, and she told me that it was isolation. She explained that she has always been dependent on her work environment to find a community of friends, but her work as a health science magazine production editor was not compatible with caring for a baby. She needs to get back to work, but only part-time, and so she needs to make a shift. She has a plan to work on her own time at home by writing for a health-care newsletter and eventually to self-publish a full health-care newsletter for the disadvantaged. She now has reliable child care once a week and she will use those days to research such opportunities and to learn how to write grants and locate foundation monies. She told me that she had found it hard to step out until now because she had been deeply immersed in the early months with her child, and it had been a joy to her to have that luxury.

I noted that Mrs. Secombe talked freely and thoughtfully about herself. She listened to my responses and connected with me. She smiled in recognition when I understood what she had said, but every so often she looked fleetingly far away and sad.

I was puzzled. She seemed to be doing so well, I wondered why she had asked to see me. What did that occasional sad look mean?

I said, "Your life-long depression seems not to be interfering at this point. You have been able to come off Prozac, go through a pregnancy, a delivery, the postpartum period, the isolation of being home with a baby, and the stress of a move without relapsing into depression. So, why are you here?"

Mrs. Secombe said that she was here mainly for help in dealing with her relationship with her husband. Previous couple therapy had helped a lot when she was pregnant. She said, "My relationship with my father affects how I feel about Hugh, men, and marriage. My father died when I was 18. I had a total lack of relationship with him. Now I find I'm very angry with Hugh a lot of the time and I'm not happy about that. I worry about whether I want to stay married to him, but I don't want to be divorced. I want to be a family with him, but I have black thoughts and fall into despair over our relationship. I feel like giving up on it. He sometimes feels like that, too. We've been married five years now, and we really had a tough beginning because he's so passive. For the first years I did all the fixing of problems, all the emoting, and all of the carrying of the chores. It was not good. I told him that he needed therapy and couple therapy because I couldn't carry the relationship all by myself. He went into therapy and it helped him a lot, so we were able to stay married. So, that's why I'm here. My marriage is not making me happy."

I felt that Mrs. Secombe looked very sad and lonely, as if she were needing a hug. My next thought was "Who would dare to hug her?" She wasn't an aggressive person, she wasn't prickly, so why did I feel that way? She connected well with me, but part of her seemed remote. I saw her as staying inside a boundary that ought to be respected. Perhaps her husband had a similar impression, and if so, perhaps it inhibited him from taking initiatives toward her in their intimate life as well.

I asked whether her husband was passive sexually as well. She said they had stopped having sex, or perhaps they had it every three or four months. Early in the relationship he had suffered from premature ejaculation, which was still sometimes a problem, but not a major interference, since he had learned mental control of premature ejaculation from advice given by the couple therapist.

I asked why she was most angry at Hugh. She said mainly it was about his passivity. He doesn't take care of anything. For instance, he doesn't do chores. He doesn't plan for the baby. He doesn't seem to realize that the baby needs care. If they are going on a trip, he will just go out the door without realizing that you have to transport equipment, take food and diapers, and plan the trip to accommodate naps. The same is true with the cat. If she takes the baby away for a week to visit his family, he simply doesn't remember to feed the cat or change her litter.

I asked, "Does he take care of himself?"

"Not always," she replied. "He wants me to take care of him. He doesn't do his laundry. He doesn't even go to the doctor when I ask him to find out what's wrong with his stomach. He's just selfish. He'll go to the store and get what he needs and doesn't remember to get what I need. This triggers memories of my parents, who were pretty neglectful. They made me crazy. I think I am hypersensitive to being neglected and I'm always on the lookout for it."

Earlier I had felt a physical distancing. Now I felt an emotional remove. I felt held at bay, a countertransference feeling that fit with my observation that Mrs. Secombe had held at bay any mention of her mother while she emphasized her relationship to her father. I noted that she then turned from her father to focus on Hugh. This transition confirmed her earlier suggestion that the way she feels about her father affects how she thinks of Hugh. I felt that if I said too much about her projecting perceptions of her parents onto her husband, she might have felt accused, and so I simply asked for memories of her parents' neglect.

"They didn't have time for me," she replied. "I simply didn't exist for my dad. He barely knew I was there. I have two older sisters, and my parents were in their forties when they had me. They were so wrapped up in their own problems that they couldn't tune in to my needs as a child. I was left alone a whole lot. I had to be very competent for their sake. I had nobody to turn to. My mom had depression, too. I think it was because my dad left us for three or four months every year. We lived in Pittsburgh and he went to Southern California. My dad was a tennis pro and so from November to April we saw no dad. Mom was depressed by that. She would get completely incapacitated and not leave the house. Every now and then I lose it, just like she did. Since moving here, I've had one or two bad days and Hugh had to come home." Mrs. Secombe wiped away a tear.

I said, "I see that you're looking upset."

She nodded.

I said, "What is it that you're feeling at this moment?"

She could not tell me.

I said, "It looks to me as if you were very upset to have to admit that you were not super-self-sufficient and that you needed fatherly support like your mother did."

She said, "That's it. It is really scary for me."

I decided to survey her network of support. She told me that it is hard for her to reach out to people. She depends on others reaching out to her. Nevertheless, she had landed in a neighborhood with plenty of young families. She had been invited to join a play group already, and a baby-sitting co-op, and she lives near a playground with a lot of children. She told me that she would soon be ready to start building on her professional contacts as well.

I said, "Well, I hear a lot of strengths here, in that you've been able to survive the move, you've chosen a neighborhood that's supportive, and you've already arranged some activities for you and your child. So, as I understand it, the main problem is dealing with the internal life in your marriage."

Mrs. Secombe replied to my comment with more information about her father. This tended to confirm my hypothesis that the rejecting internal object relationship dominates the center of her marriage. But again her mother is a minor figure. The rejecting object has been located in her father.

"Yes," she said. "My father ruled through fear. He was angry, always on the verge of blowing up. He would be angry about things and never talk about them until months later, and suddenly blow up. When I look back on it, I think he was a big baby. Really, life was much more comfortable when he was gone. When he was there, everybody tiptoed around him. Everybody upset him. I could never say the right thing. He was extremely critical and very controlling. My mother would come to me and say 'You shouldn't have said that to your father—look how you've upset him.' But it didn't seem like what I'd said should have upset him that much. I'm so angry with him—what was he in the family for? Why could he not control himself?"

I asked if he had been drinking.

She said, "They were not heavy drinkers, but they did both drink. They certainly had two drinks every night. Seems unusual for an athlete, now that I think about it. Every now and then he'd have a big blowout. Not related to alcohol as far as I know, but related to something that someone did. Like when my sister dropped out of school. He yelled and yelled at her, and actually he hit her, too. With me, he just ignored me. I'm not as messed up as my older brother and sister, probably because he ignored me. My older brother is a recluse, my sister is on probation. They are both unhappy, pathetic people, married and divorced several times."

I said, "Well, you didn't get in trouble like that. You chose marriage with a controlled man who won't yell at you as your father did. But then he can't get through to you either. Does his passivity provoke you to outbursts?"

"Yes," she said, "I get angry, but I'm not quite as bad as my dad. I don't get nasty, and I don't storm out. But I do yell. And really, I'm not a yeller. I was not like that at work. In fact, I was known as 'the calmest in the business.' I hated people who yelled at work. Of course, that's probably how my father was regarded, too. He was very well-liked on the tennis circuit. He really was the good guy. He loved the children in his classes. He never mistreated or yelled at them. He never ran the top-level players into the ground like some coaches do. And he helped out the other pros. My sister went on the tournament circuit with him every vacation, and that seemed to work out for her. I tried to go and my mother often encouraged me to go, but when I did, I always got shunted aside. I was always in the way, and people were always telling me I was in the way. He didn't teach me to play tennis anyway. He did that for my brother and sister, but not me. So I stopped going. By the time they had me, they were just too tired to be bothered. I think I was born unexpectedly, after a couple of miscarriages, in my mother's mid-forties.

"There were a lot of secrets in my mother's life," she went on. "I found out that she had had two abortions after I was born. I didn't find this out until late in her life. I was helping her fill out forms in hospital and she told me to add that in. She said that she'd had six years of infertility after her first child, gave up hoping, then the second pregnancy came out of the blue. Then another four years of infertility, and miscarriage, and suddenly I came along. After that she kept getting pregnant in her mid-forties and she couldn't believe it. Yes, there's a lot of mystery in her life. I never knew any of her family members. We knew that she left home at 17 and never went back. She wouldn't tell us anything about her life at home, except her mother died when she was 2 years old, so that was probably very painful for her, but she didn't talk about it. All that I knew was that she hated her stepmother. She wouldn't tell me my cousins' names, although I know that I have cousins in the Pittsburgh area. When she died, I got her parents' names off her death certificate, and so I could trace my cousins through them. I also found out from the death certificate that her maiden name was Rudnitsky, not Brown, as we had always been told. What did that mean? Had she had a previous marriage, or a name change? If so, why?"

I said to her, "Do you have a hypothesis?"

She said, "A few. One: she could have been adopted, but why wouldn't she just tell us that? Two: she simply wanted to erase her immigrant past and picked an anglo name. At first I thought the name might have been Brunowski, and that it had been changed to Brown. But what kind of name could Rudnitsky be? Is that Russian? Polish? I don't know. Three: I think it's most likely that she wanted to erase her past, whatever that was. I know she hated her stepmother, and maybe her father was mean and cruel to her. We would ask her lots of times, and she would always blow us off, or lie about it. Once she told us he was a carpenter. Another time she told us he was something else. Every time I tried to ask her, she would get really angry and upset. She would say, 'I don't know anything to tell you.' I really wish I could have told her how much it would mean to me to know about the family background."

I would have thought that, being in therapy for years and looking into the influence of the past on her current state of mind, Mrs. Secombe might have been particularly motivated to find these things out. I kept wondering why it was left so vague.

I said, "I guess that when your mother was alive, you might not have wanted to invade her privacy, but with both parents gone, I would imagine you would want to know." I said, "Here you are a science writer, used to using all the research tools on the Internet. Of all people, you would know how to find things out. I'm surprised that after sixteen years of therapy you didn't insist on knowing more."

She said, "We always treated Mom with kid gloves. We just couldn't ask. But after she died, I did make some inquiries by phone. I've discovered that if you want to know things you have to show up at the various offices. I may do that some day. I really want these questions answered."

Her need to know had been freed by her mother's death and by becoming a mother herself. But her curiosity was still underdeveloped. While she spoke clearly and freely and looked at me in her low-key way, I was monitoring her effect on me. She had handsome features and yet they added up to a nondescript whole. Her dark hair was quite gray around her face. While her speech was clear, focused, and direct, her feeling tone was flat. In general, she seemed faded and shrouded. I thought that she had a competent false self that was effective at work and with her baby, but her true self was repressed by the internal rejecting object relationship which she refinds with her husband. She did not appear to find it or provoke it in me, nor had I felt her to be rejecting of me. Then again, I felt that I had handled her with kid gloves, as when I chose not to make the link between her father and her husband. But later, when I felt more confident, I dared to confront her about not knowing. She took the confrontation quite well and this encouraged me to give her feedback on how she had affected me.

We were almost at the end of the interview and it was time to wrap it up. I said, "I have an impression of you as being very damped down. It's as though you are under a blanket or a veil. You don't act in a mysterious way, however, and unlike your mother, you've told me quite fully the things that you are aware of about your life, your development, and your marriage. But as you do so, everything is kept very calm. I have the feeling that you have learned to live your life in such a way as to not be intrusive into anyone's space, not just your mother's. I think you are motivated by not wanting to impinge upon or bother the other person, including me. This may be why it's taken you a few months to get in to here to see me, and why you spare me your feelings now."

She nodded.

I continued, "I'd like to see you for a second meeting, so that you have a chance to talk to me about anything you haven't felt comfortable with today. I'm interested in your reactions to this meeting, any memories that have occurred to you after you have been here, any feelings that you have had about me. I am interested in your dreams. Then next time when we meet, we'll pick up the themes that we have touched on today and begin to think about what we do from here; individual or couple therapy, and if it's individual therapy, how intensively you would want to work."

She asked about how I worked with her insurance company, and I explained that I expected payment within ten days of her receiving the bill that I sent at the end of the month, even though she might have to wait a while for reimbursement to come directly from her insurance company to her. I told her my consultation fee, and said that my therapy fee would be determined by the frequency of the therapy chosen and by her resources. I told her that if she needed a fee much lower than mine, or for any other reason preferred not to work with me, I would arrange referral to someone else who could offer what she needed. We arranged to meet in a week's time.

Principles of Assessment Illustrated in This Example

In this first interview, Dr. Jill Scharff established a holding environment by setting the frame for the assessment, by acknowledging the connection to the previous therapist, but preferring to have Mrs. Secombe's own perspective. Mrs. Secombe was able to tell Dr. Scharff a great deal about her situation, and to give her a sense of her internal world as well. Dr. Scharff set the frame for the assessment by explaining that they might need a few sessions to complete the assessment before giving a recommendation. She listened with free-floating attention and let Mrs. Secombe determine the flow of the conversation. She registered and contained an element of low-key distress that did not match the content of Mrs. Secombe's words. She followed the affects of remoteness, loneliness, and sadness.

Mrs. Secombe shows that she uses the developmental technique of meeting her own and others' dependency needs because she cannot rely on anyone else to do this for her. It leaves her longing for someone to recognize what she needs and to help her meet the baby's needs and her own needs for physical affection and holding. She projects the good object into her husband, but then feels rejected by the good object.

Assessment of her developmental position shows that she functions in the depressive position most of the time. She is able to love and care for her child. She has made a commitment to her husband and she takes responsibility for her share of the marital distress. She feels bad for causing him unhappiness. But when she has been functioning autonomously for too long, she becomes anxious and obsessional. She slips into paranoid-schizoid functioning and thinks that her husband is ignoring her. She loses her sexual desire.

In terms of her attachment pattern, Mrs. Secombe was anxiously attached to both her parents while they were dismissive of her attachment needs. She has developed an ambivalent attachment to her husband. She is working on making sure that her son's attachment is secure. Concern about this is making it hard to leave him for appropriate lengths of time.

External impingement in the form of a move has interrupted her network of support. Her husband's desire for sex is experienced as an external pressure because she has lost her sexual desire because of being angry about his passivity. The drive to resume her creative work is creating an internal conflict because of her wish to stay home with her child. Her financial circumstances make it hard for her to afford therapy and introduce an additional external pressure.

Mrs. Secombe already shows an excellent capacity to work in therapy. She freely gave her object relations history. She listened to Dr. Scharff's naming of the defense in which she damps down her affect and minimizes her impact on the other person in relationship to her. Dr. Scharff made some clarifying comments, gave support for her good adjustment to the move, and gave the advice to investigate her family history.

Dr. Scharff's countertransference feeling of caution about making links and conveying her impressions in the form of interpretation back to Mrs. Secombe leads to a tentative dynamic formulation that there is an element of inhibition and caution in Mrs. Secombe's inner world, probably based on an identification with her mother's secretiveness, which has kept her from knowing how much she longed for her chronically absent father, and from moving beyond her inner resentment because it cannot be fully felt or expressed. So far, this forms the beginning of a hypothesis about Mrs. Secombe's recurring depression and her frequent return to bad or negligent inner objects, now experienced in her self as the unhappiness of her marriage.

But Dr. Scharff also feels that full interpretation at this early juncture would overwhelm Mrs. Secombe. While this feeling may be viewed as clinical intuition acquired with experience, it is also a countertransference clue to Mrs. Secombe's own inner inhibitions. Dr. Scharff sets up a second interview to test whether a stronger therapeutic relationship develops or whether referral is indicated. In the next session Dr. Scharff will be interested to see if her tentative hypotheses are confirmed. She will be assessing Mrs. Secombe's reactions to the first session and will be hoping for a dream to work on. She will be trying to get a deeper understanding of the transference.

Second Assessment Interview with Mrs. Secombe

At 1:30 P.M. I was waiting for Mrs. Secombe, who had been early last time. At 1:40 P.M. she arrived.

She said, "It starts at 1:40, right?"

I said, "We had agreed to start at 1:30, but we'll have plenty of time. Did we have a misunderstanding?"

She said, "Well, I knew you said 1:30, but I assumed that that meant 1:40, because the last session was at 10:10, so I assumed you always started at ten minutes past the hour, like my last therapist did."

I thought that this did not quite make sense, but it said to me that she was looking for something that would be familiar.

I said, "You were expecting it to be like therapy was before."
She said, "Yes."
I said, "Well, where would you like to pick up from last time?"
She said, "I've been thinking it over and I called the insurance company, and the bottom line is, I can't afford you. They only pay 50 percent of the usual and customary fee. I talked to my husband and we agreed that we could only afford $30 per week, out of pocket. That is, whether therapy should be twice a week, whether it's for him or me, or both of us as a couple. It seems to me that the relationship really needs it most, but I'm the only one with the time to put into therapy."

I felt disappointed. I could see her every other week for a fee that they could afford, and that might be enough to meet her need for therapy and keep her going at her current level of growth, but not enough to produce more lasting development. I could not afford to see her twice a week for that amount, and she could not afford to see me even once a week and also pay for couple therapy and individual therapy for him, if he should want that. I took what she said about her financial limitations at face value, but I also wondered whether her statement represented some resistance to therapy in general or to me in particular. Nevertheless, I thought that this interesting consultation was likely to lead to therapy. I realized that I had been hoping to work with her without quite realizing the extent of my interest in her. As I adjusted to the likelihood that she would go elsewhere for therapy, I felt the loss. I could feel my energy staying with doing a thorough assessment for referral rather than moving on to an assessment for entry into therapy with me.

"After talking with you last time, I thought a lot more about myself and whether therapy was the right thing for me," Mrs. Secombe went on. "I realized that I've come a long way, and perhaps I don't need it that much right now. I need to stand on my own some. The area of greatest difficulty, and where I don't have a handle on it, is our relationship. I realized after talking to you that, yes, I am handling the depression, I do have a game plan. The fact of the matter is, my husband needs a lot of therapy. Now, maybe it's wrong for me to think that, as if I'm saying that he just needs to change and things will be fine, like there's nothing wrong with me."

I said, "Well, I can see that if the problem in the relationship is that you find that he's passive, then you wouldn't want to fix that by doing all the work in therapy as well."

"You are so right," she replied. "I want him to have the space to do for himself. Really I think he should come here, but his department is not near here. If he did agree to it, it would have to be with a therapist near the campus so he could go on a lunch break. Maybe we should both come here."

How could it be possible for him to come with her if he really needed a thera-pist in a better location? I realized that she was expressing her own resistance, perhaps brought on by the previous session. Perhaps financial constraint was not simply a practical issue, but a vehicle for expressing her reluctance. She was putting obstacles in the way of affording to work with me herself, and telling me her husband would not choose to work with me before knowing what hours I had to offer him. On the other hand she was willing to come here with him, so I thought that she was perhaps scared of seeing me alone, and yet wanting to keep me for herself.

I approached the problem on a reality basis at first by responding to her review of their various needs. I said, "In view of what you're saying, I think we should extend the consultation to include a couple meeting, and indi-vidual meetings for him. Then, at the end of it, we'll get together and think about how to proceed with what will be most useful to you both."

Then I moved to address the resistance by inquiring about her experi-ence of me in the last session.

"Whatever you may decide in future, this session today is just for you," I continued. "We might as well use the time to proceed with thinking about your situation. I'd like to hear more about your reactions after talking with me last week."

"Well I found it quite jarring," she replied. "I felt that you were critical of me, and most of all, I missed my therapist from Los Angeles." Mrs. Secombe began to cry quietly. "She became motherly towards me. I don't know you. I felt the strangeness of it." She dried her tears, and seemed to return to the present. She said, "Your observations were extremely help-ful. And I do find that feedback stirs a lot in me, and is helpful to me. It's the only way that I can see myself and can know how to change. So, I appreciated it, but I felt unhappy.

"I was particularly sensitive about your saying I had not found out about my mother's background. It really stings to think about that. The truth of what you said made me think about how different being in therapy is now than it was in the beginning. Then, I spent many sessions in total silence. It took me a long time to get going. I believe that my family's influence was so much over me then, and that I hadn't come to grips with my relationships with them, that I didn't dare to say anything. I look back on that time. I can hardly believe I was so unasking. I didn't bring it up much at all. In Los Angeles, yes, I thought about my mother in that therapy, but as you said, I really haven't looked into the whole mystery."

I felt slightly anxious to think that I could have blown it by going too fast, and I felt relieved that she had weathered the impact of my interpretation. Her reason for saying that she could not see me was partly in reaction to what I had said, despite my caution. So my concerns about her vulnerability were confirmed. On the other hand she had come back to talk about her concerns quite openly and this made me feel hopeful that she could benefit from confrontation as well as support, and work well in therapy.

I said, "When I pointed that out, you felt that I was really criticizing you for that being the case."

"Yes," she said, "because I'm critical of myself. It reminds me of something that often happens to me. I often feel suddenly naïve, and when someone says something that makes me see things differently, it feels like a kick in the chest. It has terrified me at times, and I'll think to myself, 'My God, how could I not have noticed that?' I think that this stems from the secretiveness in my family. Everyone kept information from me in the name of protecting me, because I was the youngest.

"Even when my dad died, they kept it from me. He was in the hospital for a week and no one told me. I was in college at the time, and no one called to tell me that he had gone to the hospital. But one day I had a premonition of things not being right and I actually got on a train and went home. I even got a friend out of the shower to drive me to the train, I felt so urgent. I got home. I rang the bell and my mother opened the door. She was in tears and she said, 'Your father just died.' We got into the car and went over to the hospital. That kind of thing went on so much. Like when Dad went to Southern California each winter. They never explained that to me, either. I never knew when he was leaving, and I had no way of planning on when he would be back. Everything was kept completely vague."

I said, "So then, when I say something to you quite directly, and without any mystery, it seems unfamiliar and is felt to be critical and hurtful to you. I think you didn't feel safe with me, as you did with your therapist in Los Angeles, whom you got to know well."

"Yeah, it's like, how could I have not realized how little I knew? I read the story about Madeline Albright and how it came out that her family was Jewish and from Czechoslovakia and she never knew it. Now, my mother was from somewhere over there, too. She was raised Episcopalian, but she always hinted that it wasn't really her religion. As soon as I read the story, I realized that there are parallels here. This is something I'm going to think more about."

I said, "Well, yes, as I talked with you last time, I realized that you'd come a long way. I know you said that what you needed to work on was your relationship with Hugh, your relationship with your father, and its impact on your marriage, but the underlying mystery in the relationship with your mother seemed to me to need work too—as you are doing now."

Dr. Scharff realized that she had moved too fast to confront the maternal internal object the week before even though she had been quite attuned to Mrs. Secombe's vulnerability. A counterphobic move perhaps. Dr. Scharff's acceptance of Mrs. Secombe's disquiet and her acknowledgment of her recovery from Dr. Scharff's empathic failure re-established a safe holding environment in which Mrs. Secombe could return to the consciously difficult subject of her father. It did not, however, secure the space for exploring her feelings for her mother, at least not yet.

"Well, I thought I'd work on my relationship with my father and how it affects my relationship with Hugh," she said. "He died such a long time ago. He kept me at arm's length. I felt neglected by him. Really, he was just as elusive as my mother. I knew so little of him, too. He was a taciturn person. I just don't have much memory of him at all. My relationship with him is a void. Both of my parents lost a parent when they were very little, so that may explain some of their difficulties. He left his home in South Carolina. He had a strong family, and mostly they're still there. He became the only Northerner. I do know those relatives, unlike my mother's side. But I never really saw them much. I don't know why my father became a Northerner. I've heard it had something to do with the war, but I can't remember how we ended up in Pittsburgh. He didn't retain a southern accent. He was a bit of an outcast. There's a big blank there."

I said, "So there's a void there, too. When your relationship with both parents seems hard to get a hold of, I'm not surprised that you'd want to work on the relationship with your husband, because at least the problems there are current and can be spoken to. As you say, they've been influenced by your relationship with your father. And, I have to add, by your mother, an influence which I think you underestimate, because the problem with your father is so compelling and so obvious."

Once she heard my interpretation of the reason for her avoidance of her maternal object, Mrs. Secombe was able to stay with the topic of her mother. She went on, "My brother didn't bother with her, but my sister and I had to take care of her. As an adult, I'd try to see her every week, and I never felt I could do enough. It was impossible to give her a gift, or take her to a meal, because something was always off. I laugh about it now, but really it was plaguing. When she died, taking care of her was gone out of my life and, much as I hated it, I found that I missed it. I have those feelings now with the baby. I feel I can never do enough. But I tell myself, 'That is enough. You can't be responsible for his every emotion.' I hadn't understood that before.

"I had a couple of confrontations with Mom too. They were disturbing. I said to her, 'I feel that you're never happy. What will make you happy?' She got very upset. That was one of the biggest confrontations we ever had. There's some of that in my relationship with Hugh, too. He doesn't express what he's feeling and I get very angry. I have too much responsibility for his emotions and his feelings."

I said, "Well, I can see that if he's a quiet and passive person, he could bring that out in you, but we have to see that you have the potential from your family experiences to want to know what's hidden."

"Oh yes," she agreed. "And I thought more about what you said about me being under a blanket last time. I agree with that. I predigest things for people so that it doesn't upset them, or put me in a bad light with them. That's the negative side of it. On the other hand, I'm a good storyteller."

I said, "Well, today you told me quite directly what it had been like for you to be here last week, and I appreciate that."

She said, "That's learned behavior. It was a breakthrough in my first therapy, and it didn't occur until the end. I felt that my therapist was really angry with me, and I walked out of treatment. But I made myself go back. She was telling me that I was stuck, and that I was more competent than I gave myself credit for. And I kept saying, 'But you don't understand, I feel incompetent.'

"So she may have felt that I did not understand how she felt when I talked about her strengths, but I did not bring this into the transference yet. Then it happened when I was in group therapy. There I was, the new patient, an Easterner in this hip L.A. group, and all the Californians were so cool about accepting whatever, they carried on as if nothing new had happened. But I experienced it as if basically they just ignored me, and I got very upset. Well, I confronted my fear of speaking up and engaging with people. I told them that they were very rude to ignore me so much. I said I couldn't believe they didn't want to know who I am and what I'm about. But normally, it is pretty difficult for me to engage with people."

I had already sensed that in her relationship to me. She was telling me what I needed to know, but I kept feeling that she wasn't quite there. I thought that she was projecting that silent, remote part of herself into her husband. I decided to make that interpretation, and see how she took it.

I said, "Yes, I've seen how that has been a problem in engaging with me. Nevertheless you have given me the information I need and you've talked to me quite openly, I think. At the same time, the silent part of you inside that used to block you in therapy can still cause trouble. I think that you learned to get over that part of you, and now you are refinding it in the way that your husband behaves. It troubles you to see the same kind of behavior in him."

"My husband doesn't take in what I say as well as he should, and it makes me crazy. Your idea about a silent part of me is really very interesting. I was so quiet as a child, and all through my twenties. People would still say that I'm fairly quiet, but I'm not paralyzed by silence. My husband just blocks me out. He doesn't hear what I say, and so he doesn't respond. And yet, he's an easygoing and gregarious person. Friends like him so much. In fact, that's why I was interested in him. But at home he blocks things out and he's very quiet and he simply doesn't say what's going on in his head. It's funny, I don't see that that is like me."

Mrs. Secombe used the interpretation as a stimulus to think more about her husband, and she refused the interpretation of her projective identification. Dr. Scharff acknowledges the patient's point of view, and then changes her tack for reaching the unconscious.

I said, "You're more willing to say what you're thinking than he is. Then you get very anxious to hear what he is thinking.

"I'm wondering if there are some thoughts that you are not aware of which might have made an appearance in your dreams. Do you remember, I asked you if you would tell me of a dream this time."

"Oh, usually I have a ton of them," she said. "But I haven't been dreaming at all. Usually I dream about my male friends being supportive and giving me a hug. Like last night, I think I dreamed about a friend from Pittsburgh. A short, warm, fuzzy dream. I can't remember anything about it."

I felt her resistance to exploring the unconscious. Her reluctance to tell me her dreams reminded me of her avoidance of the silent areas in herself, especially in relation to her mother. I noted that she did not think of any women in her dreams, and I knew that she did not think of me as a supportive woman. But before I could comment on her view of me as a woman who could not be trusted with her unconscious, she surprised me by gaining access to a helpful dream.

She said with sudden animation, "But I did have something a few nights ago—Oh yes! Now I know what it was. Hugh and I were on a table. One table was put on top of another, like jugglers might do. It was precarious, and I was really scared. I had a feeling of extreme fear of heights, as I had when I was pregnant. Hugh was holding on to me to keep me from falling off of this thing. I said, 'I have to get down off this. I'm so frightened.' He helped me down quite kindly. Another part of that dream is a recurring dream for me. I dream about skating a lot, and it's something I do on a regular basis. In my dream I was doing that figure, what you do call it? It's a figure I can't do, like this . . ."

"A spiral?" I guessed.

She continued, "I was doing a perfect spiral, perfect. Effortless and amazing. So that was fun. I've never thought of myself as a good skater, because my oldest brother has that title in our family. Actually, he had all the titles in the family. Skater, computer wizard, etc. Cutup, too. But, actually, most people would say I am really a good skater.

"As I was saying the thing about the table, I was thinking of it as our marriage. But then, it's odd that Hugh was really helping me, and I trusted him."

I said, "I've been wondering if the precarious table relates to your appointment here. I brought up something that was frightening to you, and then you've been thinking about having your next sessions with Hugh, or that Hugh should help you by doing therapy alone."

"Well, it was frightening, and I don't understand it, because really you were pointing out how strong I was. You were only asking me to look at the more mysterious aspects from a position of strength. So, I'll have to think about that some more. Meantime, I'd like to go ahead with a couple's meeting and individual meetings for my husband. I think it would be best for you to see him alone next, and then we'll both come in."

Principles of Assessment Continued

This session begins with two signs of Mrs. Secombe's resistance—her lateness and her discussion of financial constraints against working with Dr. Scharff. Dr. Scharff explores the transference resistance and learns that Mrs. Secombe has felt criticized. Dr. Scharff's comments about the void concerning her mother has triggered a focused transference toward Dr. Scharff as not being there for her. By acknowledging her empathic failure and Mrs. Secombe's response and recovery, Dr. Scharff secures the contextual transference. Mrs. Secombe mourns the therapist that she has lost. This makes way for an exploration of the sources of her fright about the emergence of painful material with Dr. Scharff who was more confrontational than her former therapist. Mrs. Secombe proceeds to work with her reluctance, deepen her individual exploration, and generally demonstrate her capacity to benefit from individual therapy.

Mrs. Secombe goes further in showing how her internal object-relations history of always feeling inadequate to provide for her mother's pleasure is being re-enacted with her baby.

Another defense is pointed out: the silent part of her seeks expression through projective identification with her husband's passivity. She shows that she can work with the idea well, even though she ultimately rejects it.

She is enabled to recall two dreams. One dream shows that she performs well and the other captures her feelings of shakiness about her marriage. Dr. Scharff works with the second dream as a transference communication about her fear of therapy and her transference to Dr. Scharff as an unsafe woman. Together the dreams convey two aspects of Mrs. Secombe's personality. In short, Mrs Secombe shows that she can work well in individual therapy.

Mrs. Secombe confirms with Dr. Scharff that she would like to continue with the plan for evaluation of the need for marital therapy. She may reveal how much she projects into her marriage. But this is not just a plan. It is a statement of the state of the transference. In choosing to have a couple session, she has projected her here-and-now transference to Dr. Scharff, based on her here-and-then relationship to her mother, into the space between her and Dr. Scharff where the couple assessment will take place. It seems that she has projected her paternal transference onto her husband at whom she rages for being as neglectful as her father, while she identifies with her own vague and unresponsive mother in terms of her intimate and sexual functioning in the couple relationship.

Dr. Scharff tests the response to interpretation. In the first interview, Mrs. Secombe acknowledges her defense of damping down her affect. In the second interview, Dr. Scharff tells her that she is driven to focus on her rejecting father because active rejection is easier to deal with than the amorphous feeling of her mother as a void. Mrs. Secombe takes this interpretation and responds by talking at greater length about her mother.

Medication is not suggested. Ancillary therapies are not suggested, but a collateral visit with the husband and a couple assessment session will be part of the assessment process.

Dr. Scharff and Mrs. Secombe are considering treatment options. They design an extended consultation format that will allow these choices to be explored. Formulation, recommendation, and treatment plan will be postponed until the end of the assessment. Whether Mrs. Secombe eventually works with Dr. Scharff or chooses to accept a referral from her, whether she works in individual or in marital therapy, she has the psychological-mindedness and resilience that predict a good outcome.

15

Assessment of Her Husband

Hugh Secombe, husband of Liseanne, the woman described in the last chapter, arrived in good time for his appointment and smiled agreeably in the waiting room, but he looked uncomfortable once he was in my office.

I asked, "How do you feel about being here today since it was your wife who suggested that you come here to see me?"

He said, "I have mixed feelings. On the one hand it seemed that this is a good time to get back into it because I no longer have a lot of problems at work which dominated discussion in my previous therapy. On the other hand, I wouldn't choose to come back into therapy right now because I'm very busy in my new job at the University—which is just great by the way, I love it. Things are going well for me. Basically, I am here because of Liseanne." He paused.

So far he seemed to be as his wife had described him, pleasant, likable, well-related, but unacknowledging of problems. I thought that this was not going to be easy. I approached the problem by stating what he had communicated to me, to let him see that I knew that he did not feel in need of help.

I said, "So you, yourself, have not experienced strain."

He corrected me, "No, I have been feeling strained, but I have not been feeling ready to plunge into therapy."

*I noted his careful way of taking responsibility while straightening my per-
ceptions. I could sense his reluctance to deal with me on an emotional level, and
so I was surprised when I did not have to work more on his resistance. Once it
was established and understood by me that he did have feelings but that he did
not want or need to work on them, he talked freely and spontaneously. It was
not difficult after all. He did not seem passive in the circumstance of talking
about himself with me. In fact he managed quite well without me, which I
registered both as a strength and as a subtle way of making sure that I did not
have too much effect.*

Without a pause, he continued, "Liseanne feels better when I am in
therapy because she feels it is better for the relationship and better for me.
But I can't help thinking that maybe she wants me in therapy because she
can't get through what she is trying to deal with—and she does have a
lot to deal with from her childhood. Her parents were really neglectful,
whereas mine were really quite loving and devoted to me, even though they
had their problems—which I found out about only as an adult when I was
in therapy before. I have made progress in identifying what I have to work
on. I felt that I had gone as far I could with the person I was seeing in Los
Angeles before we moved here. At that time I was stuck at the assistant
professor level and I spent a lot of time talking about my frustration on
the job. Then I got a tenured position in the music department here, moved,
and that solved all that. I love the job. All the work anxieties are removed.
I have this wonderful feeling that there is so much in front of me. So what
remains are family-related issues."

*I thought that he was trying to tell me that the previous therapy had done its
job, and that what remained were largely his wife's issues. I thought that perhaps he was right that she was trying to get him to bear the brunt of the therapy
work for a change. My main feeling was that there was not much room for me,
and I wondered if his wife might be feeling similarly peripheral and experiencing it as his being neglectful of her.*

He continued, "I was my parents' only child and they were loving and
devoted to me, but recently I've become aware that something is missing.
It must be so, because I have insecurities and I feel real pain and anguish
whenever I try to think back to my childhood. I only learned in the last
year that my parents were not living together for the first two years of my
life. They kept it secret. I was born before they were married. My mother

had had four miscarriages before me with her previous husband. She was still living with him when she met my father and fell in love with him. Then he went back to his posting in Korea, and she thought she'd never see him again. She was surprised to become pregnant with me. She had thought that she couldn't have children, and no child came after me. I was the only child that she bore. She wanted to keep the pregnancy, but my dad wasn't there. So she told her then-husband that I was his child, although she knew that I wasn't. He was alcoholic and very abusive with her, and finally he threw my mom and me out of the house, and we lived for six months in an apartment near my aunt in New Hampshire. Somehow my dad found us on his next leave and he said he'd come back once she got her divorce. See, my mother was living in New Hampshire and my father was living in Korea the first two years of my life. Apparently we saw him occasionally when he was on leave but not that much. Then when they could be married, we moved again. It must have been hard on me and my mother, and hard on him. Now that I have a child of my own, I see the importance of daily contact."

Mr. Secombe was getting a lot into this visit with me. I began to think that he was relating to me in the paternal transference, cramming a lot into a short time and trying not to need me at the same time. I did not feel excluded because my listening seemed to matter to him, but I felt a bit redundant.

"My mother loves me, but she's a troubled individual," he said compassionately. "She lost her own mother at the age of 18, and her father was a womanizing gambler who wasn't home a lot. She had her own issues and she's often depressed. I see that now. She's volatile emotionally and physically nondemonstrative." Pointing to his chest, he said, "There is something locked up in there and it's trying to get out, and when I try to deal with it, I feel as if I am entering this miasma that I can't understand. The consequences of all this in daily life are that I chafe under a block or an inability to seize the moment, and then I can't claim what I want to do. For instance, I'm a successful composer, but I'm stuck doing short pieces. I'll have an idea for a symphony, but I can't get myself to write it because I approach the task with a measure of defeat."

As he spoke of his music, I felt that he was relating to me quite intensely even though I was not required to give any verbal feedback. I thought of Freud's interpretive work with Mahler whose composing was inhibited by his avoid-

ance of passionate passages that might reawaken the anxious feelings he had when his parents were in a rage. Perhaps that was the problem here too, but I didn't interrupt, because he was talking freely.

"To keep her sanity, my mother keeps control of everything with lists and attention to detail. I know it is an expression of love, but it is very controlling and it typifies her relationship with me. Liseanne took Hugh Junior to visit my mother, and when she came back, she told me that when my mother plays with him, she takes away what he is playing with and suggests something else."

Perhaps he kept turning his talent to the next small piece of music because he was used to a mother who kept introducing something new. Is that why I was required to say not much? Perhaps he didn't want me to get him off onto another subject and interrupt a precious stream of thought. I did not want to fall into this maternal transference. I stayed quiet.

"Mom has to be on top of everything. That's why I'm not good at doing for myself. Because of the way she is, I developed a way of tuning her out. Now that's created problems with Liseanne because I do that with her. I don't listen and I don't pay attention. It's not because I don't love her, or want to piss her off. It's just because that's what I've learned to do. In couple therapy, I could work on that with her."

I found myself liking this man, because he was undefensive in confirming his wife's concerns, he recognized his problem areas, connected them to his history, and related easily to me. When I found myself thinking that it was too bad that he was reluctant to engage in individual therapy, I realized that he was projecting his longing into me, as he must do with his wife, as he did with his mother who doted on him, and as he could not do with the absent father of his infancy for whom, like his mother, he must have had to keep his longing at bay.

I thought to myself, here was a man who, as an infant, made a devoted pair with his mother, and had very little time with his father. He must long for a centered relationship, but be afraid that it would be suffocating and skewed in the sense that it would exclude the father. I could feel the alternation between maternal and paternal poles in the transference. He was creating a couple as an individual with me at one level and yet alluding to the marital couple as the couple I should be concerned with.

I began to think that couple therapy would be the acceptable recommenda-
tion. I saw this thought not only as a clinical decision in the making, but also as
a reflection of the wish to repair both their internal couples, which could be done
either in couple therapy or in parallel individual therapies.

I asked, "Do you find Liseanne overstimulating like your mother?"

He replied, "Well, they're both perfectionists and they both want things
their way. I get a whole lot of instructions and it creates a lot of resentment."

"Do you say so?" I asked, knowing that he did not.

"No," he replied. "I withdraw. I should say so but if I do she always says,
'I can't tell you anything.'"

"What do you think of your wife's instructions? Do you think that hers
is a good methodology, or are her ways unnecessary?"

"Oh," he said, "I have a tremendous respect for how she manages. She
is very in tune, and I'm often not. She won't let things ride and I admire
that. The problem is that when she's feeling badly about herself, she gets
critical toward me. I think that comes from growing up with neglectful
parents and an absolutely horrible sister and brother. Liseanne bears a tremendous amount of anguish and she lashes out when she feels it most
acutely. That's when I withdraw. I don't want to lash out.

"My mother called the shots and my father went along with everything.
I never once saw him express one of his own needs. He never stood up to
her, never ever. He avoids conflict. I've learned from Liseanne to stick up
for myself a bit more, but I'm very sensitive to criticism. When it comes
my way, my tendency is to stew. But I'm getting better. I'm not as dependent on positive feedback as before. I used to live for my parents' praise,
and my father was very ready to give it. My mother, on the other hand,
hardly ever did. So now I'm really trying to do things for myself."

I noticed that I did not feel the wariness I had felt with his wife—which
was odd in view of the couple's agreement that it was he who could not take
confrontation. I decided to comment on the negative cycle of interaction, partly
to summarize what I had understood so far and partly to see how he took an
intervention.

I said, "So when Liseanne gets angry with you for not listening and not
paying attention, you withdraw even more and this makes her all the more
angry."

"Right," he said, "I wish she would decide what is important."

His response puzzled me because it contradicted what he had said before about admiring her ways of doing things. So I asked, "Could it be that you don't like taking advice because it sounds like criticism?"

"Absolutely right," he said, and then was quite silent.

I said, "Are you suppressing other feelings perhaps?"

He said, "A lot of the things she singles out just don't make a difference. For example, the other night she was upset because I left the bread out while I cleaned the kitchen. I am thinking thirty minutes isn't going to make a difference to whether the bread gets hard or not, whereas she wanted it done right then. So I'm suppressing a lot of anger about having to do things on her schedule when I don't really agree with the necessity of what she is suggesting."

I said, "What do you imagine would happen if you were to express this anger?"

He paused. "I'm really not sure. From a very early age, my father taught me not to be angry. You count to ten before you say anything. I mean literally—one, two, three—you know. The times I've lost it—and I have lost it once or twice—I've been shouting and screaming at Lise-anne. I expected the sky to fall in! And she was, like, 'Oh, good, you're saying what you feel' and I'm like, 'Wow, that's pretty cool.' It's hard to let it out, though."

I said, "Well, when you are angry she welcomes it, but you haven't learned to trust that because when she is angry you don't welcome it."

"No, I don't," he replied. "She has to release those feelings and I respect that, but I'm glad that she's gotten better at moderating them. She used to throw things and scream. That really frightened me into retreat mode. She doesn't do that anymore. My mother used to have these episodes. She would go into a tantrum about how nobody loved her. She would get the car keys and disappear for hours and not even be home before I got to bed. Once she locked herself in a bathroom. When my father opened the door, she had crawled out the window. I was 5 or 6."

I felt myself in the place of the little boy. What a frightening image for a child to see that open window and not know whether he would see his mother again. He could well be afraid of refinding this internal couple in his marriage.

Mr. Secombe looked small and frightened on the couch. "It scared the shit out of me," he said. "My father would just say, 'Oh, she just needs to go. It will be okay.' Somehow he put up with it, but anger triggers fear of abandonment in me, I think."

I remembered his wife saying that she feels emotionally abandoned by him. He may be projecting his own unbearable feeling of abandonment into her and she certainly has a valency for feeling it. Then her resulting anger returns the projective identification to him and he feels paralyzed by the fear of abandonment.

"Well, I don't know really," he said.

I said, "You do know. You've just been telling me. You know a lot about it, I think."

"Well, yes," he realized. "I know that my problem with expressing anger has consequences in my family and in my career. I would like to really take a sabbatical and devote all my energy to composing a major work, but I'm worried about taking that initiative. Maybe it's the same problem. I might be afraid of really putting all my talent and all my ideas together in something that lasts and doesn't get thrown away like a discarded music exercise. Most of all I am afraid of taking that year and wasting it away through inaction and indecision. I'm a musician steeped in teaching music and writing practice pieces for students and what I would really like to do is compose symphonies. But I'm not sure they would be any good. My composition is good enough for teaching, and it is probably good enough for a longer concert piece, but getting myself to feel that I can do it, and then do it, that's the problem."

I said to him, "A symphony would have to come from the center of yourself."

"Yes," he said, "It would, and that's a frightening idea."

When we talked about his music, I felt that he was in deep communication with me. He was appreciative of my understanding of his need for centering to be fully creative. He must long for a centered relationship, but must feel equally afraid of it becoming controlling or suffocating over the long term. I felt that we had worked on this topic just enough to notice that he was interested in the problem, even though it was not currently causing any strain for him. I took note that he was responsive to the potential for helping him analyze this self-defeating behavior. I wanted to give him a taste of interpretive work on which to base his decision regarding treatment, even though he was presenting himself primarily as part of a wider assessment. His wife had told me that, even if he decided on individual therapy, because of his schedule, he would have to find a

therapist with an office near the campus, which mine was not—partly a real-
ity, and partly her setting conditions to keep me for herself, and partly a state-
ment of his wish to avoid a geographical separation that might remind him of
his early separation from his father.

So I moved on to complete the assessment task promptly and without creat-
ing a transference and countertransference that would make referral difficult.

I said, "Well, whether you write a symphony or not, doesn't compromise your career. It only concerns your personal satisfaction and growth
as an artist, and it's something you could choose to work on in individual
therapy at some point or not. But let's return to the current situation of
interferences with your life now. We're nearly at the end of our interview,
and I'm thinking about how to proceed. I understand you have a limited
amount of money to put toward therapy. What I've talked with your wife
about is whether to invest that money in individual therapy for her, individual therapy for you, or couple therapy for both of you. What do you
think?"

He said, "I think couple therapy is best. We have both done some individual work, and I think couple therapy would allow us to work on our
individual issues while mainly dealing with their impact on our relationship. She hasn't explored her relationship with her father and his absence
in her life. She sees me through the eyes of her father."

I noted this turn of phrase. He meant to say that his wife looks at him and
sees her father. But I also thought that the phrase 'she sees me through the eyes
of her father' unconsciously meant that he must experience her as if she becomes
an angry father while dealing with him at times when he, like her father, does
not give her his attention. He did not have to learn to deal with an angry father
when he was a child, and it is unfamiliar and frightening to him. Like Liseanne,
he does not recognize the impact of Liseanne's rage and remoteness because of
her mother's secrecy and whatever trauma it covers.

He continued, "In couple therapy, she really saw how her problems with
her father come out, and it was hard for her. If we are not to do couple
therapy, then it should be individual therapy for her because she would
benefit the most from it. I'd benefit too, but I get a lot from my job and she
doesn't have that. It's been hard for her to be home with no intellectual
stimulation of the sort that I get on my job, and she really needs that, too.
On the other hand, it would be good to work on these individual areas right

now because my career is going so well and the remaining areas are so much clearer now."

I said, "It seems to me you prefer to put her first."

"Oh, yes," he replied without a moment's hesitation. "That's what I do. That's what my father always did."

"So how shall we proceed?" I asked. "Do you want to see me for a second session as Liseanne did? That would give you a chance to pick up any themes or memories that come to you after the session, dreams, and reactions to me, or do you prefer the couple session to be the next part of the assessment process?"

He answered, "Let's go ahead with the couple session. Liseanne told me you have a time open next Monday when she has a sitter. I can do that. Do you still have that time?"

I made the appointment for a couple session in a week's time.

I was impressed at how much understanding of himself Hugh had gained from a short and nonintensive exposure to individual and couple therapy. He was clearly psychologically minded and could benefit from more intensive therapy, including psychoanalysis, but I had the impression that he was not motivated for individual therapy because he was not suffering enough, because he was identified with his father's attitude of putting others first, and because it was his priority to repair the internal couple. In choosing not to have individual therapy, he could undo his longing for an independent relationship with the absent father of his infancy and his guilt at having sole possession of his sad and lonely mother at that time.

Principles of Assessment

This session covers areas that could not be reached in individual meetings with Mrs. Secombe. First, Dr. Scharff gets the chance to see that Mrs. Secombe's experience of her husband—and her complaints about the limitations in their relationship—are congruent with his views of his limitations. Secondly, she can see that both members of the couple support and welcome change and growth. This situation augurs well for any treatment choice—couple therapy, individual therapy for Mrs. Secombe, or combined individual and couple work. Thirdly, Dr. Scharff can assess Mr. Secombe's own interest and capacity for therapy and change.

Dr. Scharff finds Mr. Secombe insightful and open-minded. He talks freely about himself and he shows his feelings. He gives no dreams, but that does not seem unusual in a first interview. He does share his fantasy that the sky would fall in if he were to express his anger. He responds to surface and depth feedback, but he is not motivated for individual therapy for himself, although he is supportive of his wife's need for help.

Dr. Scharff secures the holding environment as a safe space by acknowledging his mixed feelings about therapy and the distinction that he makes between feeling strain and feeling in need of treatment. Mr. Secombe works well with his ambivalence about therapy and shows that he has learned a lot in previous therapy. He has been able to grow and change, and he has the capacity to work in therapy. He talks easily and has a positive contextual transference to Dr. Scharff in the assessment interview, but not so positive that he expects to enter therapy with her. He recognizes the possibility that Liseanne is projecting her difficulties into him, and he does not want to have individual therapy for her sake. He shares his object relations history and is aware of its re-enactment in the marriage: he knows that his mother's controlling nature has left him unwilling to accept direction and unable to sustain his own momentum; that her rage has left him fearful of Liseanne's ordinary anger and inadequately self-assertive at work; and that his father's advice to contain anger has left him speechless and passive. The preliminary dynamic formulation is that his responses to all of these factors have combined to inhibit his expressions of thought and feeling in his intimate life and in his work. Even though he recognizes his own difficulties and their impact on Liseanne and connects them to his object relations history, which suggests that he is capable of working in therapy, he disconnects these thoughts from the need for therapy. He projects the need for help with intimate relating into his wife, who has a valency to accept that projective identification because of her problems. Perhaps he hopes that she will grow on his behalf while he is too frightened to attempt it, just as he is too inhibited to write a symphony. He may hope that couple therapy will offer him an opportunity to "bootstrap" a personal growth project without having to openly go for it and face change alone.

Dr. Scharff does not have the occasion to say much in this interview, beyond linking and clarifying comments, because the patient speaks so freely. She makes the interpretation that his defense of passivity in the face of his wife's rage stems from his anxiety about abandonment and creates a cycle of interaction that is frighteningly reminiscent of what he is trying to defend against. His attachment style is hard to classify. He seems eager to relate, yet ambivalent, secure in the knowledge of his parents' attachment to him, and yet worried about abandonment.

Dr. Scharff does not interpret the transference, but she is receiving it in the countertransference as a quieting of her speaking. We can tell from her countertransference that the here-and-now focused transference to her as an interested but unobtrusive listener recalls the here-and-then of his devoted mother centered on her nonverbal infant, and the here-and-then of the silence between him and his father because of separation in the first two years. He did a lot of the work for Dr. Scharff and created an assessing couple with her, much as he may have met his mother's needs and created a couple with her to compensate both him and her for the father that both must have been missing. The if-and-when of the here-and-now is in Dr. Scharff's mind as she wishes that this man would get the individual therapy that he needs. The there-and-now of his marriage when his wife lashes out at him in anger recalls the there-and-then of his family life when his mother raged and his father modeled restraint. The there-and-then of military and marital obligation prevented his parents from being together and is re-created now in the difficulty of finding time for sessions.

No medication is suggested. The dynamic formulation concerning his object relations history will be tested in the couple session to follow. The self and object identifications in the marital personality should throw more light on their individual object relations sets. No recommendation or treatment plan is made. On the basis of their individual sessions, Dr. Scharff expects to recommend intensive individual therapy for both of them, but she is waiting to see what the couple session brings.

16

Self and Object Relations
in the Couple

Mr. and Mrs. Secombe's Couple Session

Liseanne and Hugh sat easily together on the couch. The alignment of their bodies gave an impression of closeness and comfort with each other that was belied by Liseanne's looking at the floor and Hugh's looking anxiously at her.

I said, "You've had some individual sessions, and here we are together in a couple session for you to talk about your relationship and what kind of therapy to invest in."

I felt surprised and anxious when an awkward silence followed my opening remark. It reminded me of the missing ten minutes at the opening of Liseanne's second session, and it struck me as being utterly unlike the beginning of Hugh's.

Liseanne began by reporting progress on an issue that had come up in her individual session, saying, "I went to the Archives today, and I found my mother and her sister. All I had was my father's name on his birth certificate. I went to the 1937 census and I actually found him. From there, I found my mother, and then my mother's sister. Her name was Zjeja. I learned that my mother's mother, and her sister, were still alive in 1930, whereas I had always been told that they died when my mother was born. That's obviously not true. She had to have been at least four before she lost her mother. In the metro on my way down to the Archives, I felt quite panicky—something I haven't felt since my early twenties when I used to get panic attacks on the metro. I felt scared, thinking that my mother was looking down at me and not wanting me to do this."

I asked, "This task made you feel alone, frightened, and guilty. Did you feel that you had Hugh's support?"

She said, "Oh, yes."

And he said, "Yes, I am very supportive of this. I think it is extremely important to know what your background is, and to get over the sense of mystery."

She said, "I feel okay about it now. It's left me anxious to know more. I now have a whole cast of characters inside me that I didn't know before. While I was there, I felt lost in another world at the turn of the century. In a way, it was quite pleasurable to me, to be recovering this piece of history."

I felt amazed. Liseanne had felt jarred by my confrontation, and yet she had taken it as a challenge. I did not feel that she was being aggressively compliant, because she took pleasure in what she had done for herself. I admired her taking the initiative and I welcomed this response to her individual session as a good sign. On the other hand, I felt that her return to the past of her previous session by recreating an opening silence and by reintroducing the topic of her need to know about her family of origin was a defense against the present topic of their relationship. Here was a movement that drew me toward thinking of recommending individual therapy for her, but I resumed my focus on the couple's issues.

"You certainly took that ball and ran with it," I said. "I'd like to hear more about it, but now you have a session together so you can talk about couple issues. Where would you like to begin?"

There was a silence while I looked expectantly from one to the other.

Hugh said eventually, "I don't know. I've really been thinking that individual therapy might be better." There was a pause.

I noticed that Liseanne looked down. She seemed depressed, and Hugh seemed anxious. I felt stymied. Each of them had been so responsive in individual sessions, I found myself wishing that I was seeing them individually. Perhaps they felt the same way. Perhaps each of them experienced their relationship as infringing on their individual needs.

I said to Hugh, "Why are you thinking individual work might be better now, when at the end of the individual session you thought couple therapy might be better?"

After another pause, Hugh said, "I thought Liseanne was reluctant to do this consultation. She seemed angry about changing the appointment to suit my work."

Another silence. I asked Liseanne what she thought about what Hugh had said.

She replied, "I'm not sure about that. I know I got angry about couple therapy before."

There was another pause.

I asked Liseanne, "Are you angry about being here today?"

She said, "No, but I'm finding it difficult."

I said, "I notice that it's very difficult for you as a couple to get going here, whereas each of you, in your individual sessions, spoke quite freely. You weren't waiting for me to ask the questions then. You took initiative. But here, it's as if you are inhibiting each other."

Liseanne became more animated and said, "Absolutely! I'm inhibiting myself because I'm afraid that I'll take over, I'm so used to Hugh not sharing his feelings."

Liseanne and Hugh as individuals are afraid of damaging each other and the couple. As a couple they are afraid of neglecting their selves.

I said, "Okay, let's establish some conditions here to make it safer for you to speak. I suggest one: that it will be up to me to make sure that each of you will have more or less equal time to speak." I was waiting for each of them to suggest any other modifications, but Hugh responded immediately by getting over his resistance and taking initiative, as he had done to my surprise in the individual session.

Hugh said, "Okay, I'll volunteer. I thought more about the meaning of my father's absence. I feel pain and anger every time I think about it, and about not being told. I was able to talk to Liseanne about that, at more length than usual. Especially about being pissed off that information was withheld from me for thirty-five years. My mother was angry, I think, about being left to fend for herself when she was pregnant with me and raising me as an infant. She always presented my father as such a saint. Her rescuer, her facilitator, this wonderful man who encouraged her creative side! But she must have had other feelings, too. It was such a messy situation, and he took two years to retire from the army. He was living in Korea while she was raising me with an abusive husband or by herself. It must have been awful."

Liseanne added gently, "Her husband disowned you, didn't he?"

And he said, "Yes, he threw us out of the house. Talking about it makes me feel frightened. It takes a long time to digest this. When I first heard about it . . ."

Liseanne interrupted to say, "You know, it really didn't come out as a statement all at one time. It just sort of percolated through a little bit at a time. It seemed to come out after Hughie was born. Hugh and I would talk about this bit of information and that. Gradually we put two and two together."

"Yes," said Hugh. "Then I go, like, 'Oh, so that's the mystery!' It felt like a relief, a solution. Really it gave me quite a thrill to discover it. Then the implications came up. It really hit us both. I'm sure it's why I feel depressed and very difficult to be around sometimes. I get quite withdrawn. I'm spoiling to be provoked by Liseanne, so I can let it all out."

We note that as individuals, they led Dr. Scharff to be concerned for the couple. As a couple they lead with individual issues.

Liseanne said, "Well this weekend you sure got angry."

Hugh said, "Yes, it was really ugly. But you know what? I felt a lot better afterwards."

I was struck by this interchange. My first thought was still at the individual level. This anger must be partly a response to Hugh's individual session in which we worked on his suppression of anger. It had the quality of immediate response to the analysis of his fear of aggression. I thought that it showed both a positive freeing of aggression as a result of interpretive work, and that it also had an element of acting out, perhaps because he had not given himself a second session in which to experience further individual feelings about me, having withdrawn from me as he does from his wife.

Then, I moved to the couple level. I saw that Liseanne had taken the initiative to enter the psychological space of the couple.

Hugh and Liseanne went on to discuss this incident in an abstruse way. I cannot recreate now exactly what they said because it made no sense to me.

The vague way that they discussed this angry episode reminded me of the obscure quality of their family histories. I noted that I was having to struggle to comprehend what they were saying and not saying, just as they had to struggle with the reality that lay behind their parents' words.

I said, "I realize you're discussing a time when Hugh got angry, but I have no idea what it was like for you, what it was about, how the anger was expressed, or how it was resolved."

Hugh said, "Oh, sorry, sorry. It was Sunday morning and I was looking for physical intimacy, and that triggered it."

Liseanne started talking about how the baby was taking a nap, ostensibly to set the place for the incident, but she got lost in an argument about whether or not that is when the baby usually takes his nap.

I said, "I feel that I am being distracted by the baby too. Let's get back to what you were saying about your anger. Hugh, what did you mean by physical intimacy? What was going on between you?"

Hugh answered, "Well, we had lain down on the bed. I was looking both for affection and for a sexual response."

"That's right," said Liseanne. "He got amorous, and I turned my back."

There was another pause.

I said, "So what happened then?"

Liseanne said, "Hugh got nasty."

Hugh said, "No, I didn't get nasty then. I held it in then. But after that you were on the phone too long. I was supposed to be looking after Hughie, and you kept being on the phone. We were trying to decide whether to go to brunch or not, and I got irritable about the lack of decision. Finally we decided to go to lunch—you're still on the phone—and I was annoyed about having to wait. So, when Hughie started crying, I just ignored him. I'm not proud of this. I've apologized for doing this, because then, of course, Liseanne had to attend to the baby while she was on the phone. Then she was mad at me, and we're yelling at each other over Hughie, and he got upset. We both felt really awful about it. We don't want to upset him."

I said, "Well, I can see that you both prefer to solve this fight by yourselves. Hughie isn't here now, so perhaps we could discuss the incident, and what it represents about your sexual relationship."

Hugh said to Liseanne, "You are always saying that I'm selfish sexually, and you've been mad that I've accused you of not making an effort on sex for a couple of years. But you must admit, you really didn't make an effort the entire time you were pregnant, nor have you done so since Hughie

was born. You're always saying that it's me resisting having a sexual relationship. I admit I was reluctant in the last month of pregnancy because I
was worried about hurting the baby, but since then, I've been making consistent efforts, and you've been brushing me aside."

Liseanne said to me, "Well, for years, I'd been trying to do something,
and he ignored me." Then to Hugh, she said, "Long before I was pregnant. Soon after we got married, you lost interest."

"No I didn't lose interest," said Hugh to me. "I lost all my confidence.
The sexual problems got bad after the marriage. Oh, I had premature ejaculation maybe once when we were dating. But once we were married, I
started having premature ejaculation more and it made her angry. It got
worse and worse. After it began to happen more often, I got afraid of her
anger, and sex became associated with anger. I really don't know why that
was so hard for me."

I said, "Yes you do."

He said, "I do?"

I said, "Yes, you told me in your individual session why a woman's anger
was so hard for you. And you also said 'I don't know' in that session, right
after you made the connection."

He said, "Well, what are you thinking of?"

I said, "You explained to me that anger is very closely tied in your mind
to abandonment."

"Oh," he said, "You mean about my mother?"

"Yes," I said. "Does Liseanne know what we are talking about?"

He said, "Yes, she knows that my mother used to get mad, and lock
herself in the bathroom."

*I felt stunned at the matter-of-fact tone that Hugh used. Unlike his mode of
expression in his individual session, he said this so blandly in the couple session
that he didn't convey the picture of what it was like for him at all. With his loved
one there to hear him, he was stripping emotional meaning from his experiences
of rejection and fear.*

It is now clear that the reason Hugh and Liseanne avoid their couple issues
is to avoid anger and rejection in the present infused with hurt from the past.

I said, "The way you have said this to Liseanne is utterly different than
the way you said it to me. She couldn't possibly sense the childhood feel-

ing you conveyed to me, a feeling of terror when your mother got angry, locked herself in the bathroom, climbed out of the window, drove off in the car for hours, and didn't come back until after you were in bed."

Liseanne looked upset for Hugh. She said, "I never heard it that way. That's awful. I'm so sorry that when I'm angry you have to worry that's what is going to happen. I feel so bad about this, but I have to admit that I really did feel like walking out."

He said, "And so did I. And I said to myself, 'I must not do this. This would be really awful.' Thank you for staying, that was really helpful."

"Okay," said Liseanne to me. "There you have it. He's worried that I'll get angry and abandon him and I'm worried that he won't be there for me, and that if I make an initiative, he'll reject me."

Here we were exploring the way their sexual relationship expressed their combined feared object relations. I wanted to see if they could continue that train of thought despite the way it frightened them both.

I said, "It's really difficult to feel secure enough to enjoy each other."

"Still," said Hugh. "I make initiatives."

Liseanne said, "And I just don't want to risk it. It requires such effort."

I said, "Both of you have become phobic of the sexual situation. Now Liseanne, from your point of view, do you think that in addition to feeling frightened of rejection, there is also an element of paying Hugh back for previous rejection?"

"I hope not," Liseanne replied. "But I was awfully rejected. The way I see it, I just sort of shut down. I felt that I just wasn't going to put out any more. Three years of a problem about 'never having sex' really upset me. The worst of it was Hugh simply didn't want to deal with it." Liseanne became tearful, and Hugh kindly held her hand.

Hugh reminded Liseanne that he loved her and wanted their sexual relationship to be good. He said, "True, for a while I couldn't face it, but once we went to therapy, and once we got pregnant, we talked a lot about it."

"Yes, things did get better then," said Liseanne. "But at a certain point in pregnancy, you didn't want to have sex with me because you were scared of hurting the baby. Do you remember that? And I told you that it couldn't hurt the baby, because they had told us that in the childbirth classes. Do you have any idea how rejected I felt then? You didn't think anything about my needs. I did take care of yours."

Hugh said, "No you didn't."

She said, "Yes I did. But you never took care of mine. Even if you were too scared to have sex with me, you could have given me pleasure, but you never did. You are so selfish."

They argued a little bit about this, and it was established that she had once or twice pleasured Hugh to orgasm. She claimed that he did not want to do this for her, but he protested that he had learned to enjoy pleasuring her. He said that he had often tried. He was hurt that it did not add up in her mind.

Hugh said, "I'm not surprised that you feel I'm selfish, because you always ask for something that's more than I can give. It scares me to have sex with you because of that. I do want to touch you and give you pleasure, but it always seems that sex has become something that is just for you."

I felt impressed at their ability to make sense of their shared projective identifications. I was satisfied with their capacity to work together in couple therapy. It was time to arrive at a plan for them.

I said, "We're just getting into the discussion of your sexual relationship, which I feel is important, but we will need to interrupt there in order to leave time for considering your individual needs, as well as your shared needs, and for thinking how best to proceed with therapy."

I would have liked to work with them and it was a loss for me that they could not afford my fee. In my countertransference to them as a couple, I experienced feelings of interest in their problem, and gratification in working with them, because both of them accepted responsibility for their shared distress, both were already psychologically minded, and because they worked separately and together toward understanding. I knew that they loved each other, enjoyed their child together, and wanted to be good for each other as partners and parents. Their individual needs were obviously interfering massively with their couple relationship.

I recommended a combination of individual therapy and couple therapy with therapists that they could afford at the low-fee clinic. They preferred to invest in one modality of therapy with a therapist in private practice rather than accept referral for low-fee concurrent couple and individual therapies. They agreed that Mrs. Secombe had a need for individual therapy, that Mr. Secombe could use it even though he did not feel an urgent need for it, but they could not afford this at the present time. Mrs. Secombe did not want to do therapy for both of them, and Mr. Secombe would only do therapy with her at this time.

They argued that each of them could usefully work on their individual issues as they addressed their marital strain, and so they preferred to go forward with couple therapy once a week, an amount that they could manage for now. They said that they had found me more confrontational than their previous therapist, which was somewhat uncomfortable for them, but they had also found this beneficial, and so they asked for referral to a therapist who would challenge them as I had, but at a lower fee.

I thought that they might be shortchanging themselves, but I accepted their choice and consoled myself with thinking that perhaps the couple work now would enable Mr. Secombe to confront his work inhibition later in individual therapy, at which point Mrs. Secombe might be earning and be able to resume her individual therapy. They said that they would review their needs for individual therapy after a period of couple therapy, and after they were more established in Washington.

Principles of Assessment Illustrated in This Example

We have reviewed this session to find in it elements of the principles of assessment that have been covered in this example. While it is possible to make this catalogue, we would not have covered all these points if we had been trying to do so methodically. We do not advise following a checklist, and we offer it here only as an instance of how to think about what we are doing in an unstructured interview. We suggest subjecting interviews retrospectively to process-recording and review according to the categories. We advise letting go of intention and simply following the unconscious process.

Establishing a Holding Environment

Dr. Scharff listens to the silence as well as to the words. She contains the anxiety of the opening silence and then interprets the resistance to working in the couple setting. Each of the couple then admit to their anxiety about losing their individual space. They demonstrate a shared contextual transference to her as unable to help them if they show themselves as a frustrated couple, just as they could not as children resolve their parents' marital tensions. Dr. Scharff offers to monitor their participation so that they have equal time in order to hold open the psychological space. When these ground rules are set to establish the holding environment, they are able to get to work.

Assessing Developmental Level

In dealing with each other, Mr. and Mrs. Secombe use the developmental technique of splitting the object and locating it in the ego and in the internal object as replayed in the self and in the partner in various combinations. No single technique predominates. Locating the rejecting object inside Mr. Secombe leaves him seeming inept, thoughtless, and selfish in comparison to Mrs. Secombe. Locating the exciting object in him because he is a less depressed, less compulsive, better balanced, more social person than she is leaves her feeling that she should leave before she ruins his life. Locating the rejecting object in her makes her ordinary anger seem like the prelude to her leaving. Locating the exciting object in her leaves him feeling sexually desirous and frustrated by her rejection.

In the modulated space of therapy with its use of verbal communication, the Secombes are able to operate mainly at the level of the depressive position. They have concern for each other, they each take responsibility for the destructive effect of their resentment on each other and on their child, and they want to work for the repair of their relationship.

Their attachment styles are readily apparent in the couple session. His attachment style is ambivalent. He maintains that his reality is of secure attachment, but his memories are of insecure attachment alternating with his feeling smothered. Her attachment style is fundamentally insecure. She felt thoroughly neglected and actively rejected as a child, and is vulnerable to feeling that way in the marriage, even though her husband is devoted to her.

Demonstrating Capacity to Work in Therapy

They respond to interpretation of resistance. The main defense worked on is the denial of anger and resentment and its emergence in a strained relationship that leaves them afraid of abandonment by the spouse, the very thing that they fear most. It is the possibility of neglect or abandonment that they are both basically angry about and re-enact with each other in order to re-experience, metabolize, and recover from childhood anxieties. Dr. Scharff points out how Hugh minimizes his vulnerability to abandonment to avoid his terror and that this has the effect of preventing Liseanne from being fully empathic.

Dr. Scharff tracks the affect and picks up the shared opening anxiety, the sense of loss of individual space, and their sadness about the spoiling of their sexual relationship by resentment. Dreams and fantasies are not a feature of this session. But the unconscious is expressed mainly in the flow of information about their internal object relations given in their history, enacted in their relationship, and expressed in the unconscious communication of the transference.

Clarifying and linking comments are accepted and worked with. Support is expressed through empathy with their situation. Advice about their way of relating is not given. Interpretation of defenses against anxiety is taken and worked with. The dynamic formulation of the internal object relations is the main work done in this session.

Using Countertransference

Focused transferences are well developed toward each other: Liseanne sees Hugh as a neglectful parent and Hugh sees Liseanne as an angry and rejecting one. These focused transferences tend to threaten the contextual transference. They are not enacted directly toward Dr. Scharff, but are defended against so as not to destroy the contextual transference. As individuals, each of them had been spontaneous and interesting while projecting most of their difficulties into the couple relationship, but as a couple they are tongue-tied. They defend against the individual situation by invoking the couple and use the couple to fend off the painful emergence of individual issues and focused negative transference perceptions of Dr. Scharff.

Dr. Scharff experiences the loss of each individual at the start of the couple session. This is a concordant countertransference with the self of each spouse feeling compromised and changed by having to accommodate to the object as refound in the partner. When they discuss their angry episode, she experiences another concordant identification with their puzzled selves when faced with a vague account of what had happened. These countertransferences reflect their here-and-now transferences to Dr. Scharff as an object, with here-and-then aspects reminiscent of their experience in their tenuous family holding environments. When interpretation secures the holding environment, they develop a positive contextual transference.

Assessing the Secombes' Shared Object Relations History of Loss and Injury

Both Mr. and Mrs. Secombe have mothers who kept a secret that functioned as a void. Both of them carry a sense of mystery about their families. Both of them were conceived unexpectedly after miscarriages. They had shared painful experience, but they grew up in radically different environments. Whereas

Hugh's parents were thrilled to have him, Liseanne's parents were too tired to bother with her. Hugh's father had the patience of a saint, and was endlessly supportive of his mother and tolerant of her moods, while Liseanne's father was alternately absent, neglectful, and irascible. The man that Hugh lived with until he was two had an impulsively aggressive personality like Liseanne's father's.

Hugh's passivity and avoidance of anger evokes in Liseanne angry behavior that he dreads because it speaks to him of abandonment. Hugh finds in Liseanne the embodiment of the repressed rejecting object based on his experience of the "father" of his first two years, combined with the abandoning aspects of his mother when she was angry. Liseanne finds in Hugh a man who can be trusted not to get angry unlike her father, but who, in controlling his anger, becomes withdrawn and seems neglectful and uninterested in her, quite like her father, and unknowable, like her mother. In Liseanne, Hugh finds a woman who is steady, open, and honest, but who, when angered by him, has rages like his mother's that terrified him. He does anything to avoid them so as to avoid the threat of abandonment, which only makes her anger worse. Their shared interacting fears of anger, neglect, abandonment, and cruel domination interfere with establishing the trust required for enjoying their sexual and emotional relationship.

Testing Response to the Assessment Format

The assessment format is designed to meet their needs for deciding how to invest their resources. The assessment includes individual and couple settings which offer trials of therapy on which they can base their decision. They are pulled in all directions, but eventually decide on the most economical approach, not the least expensive, but the one that allows both of them to get something out of the therapy directly.

When we assess an individual and then include the other partner and the marriage itself in our assessment process, as we routinely do, we become aware of the loss of the option that is not taken, a loss that we can avoid when we limit our assessment to the presenting patient only. In other cases, individual assessment does indeed lead to individual psychotherapy or psychoanalysis, and we never know the cost to the life partner whose needs have not come to attention. On the other hand, good therapy for an individual is likely to be helpful to other members of a family system, just as good couple therapy has a positive effect on the partners individually and on their family members. When we conduct each assessment, we like to keep an open mind about its outcome so that we can tailor our recommendations to the needs and situation of the patients to find the best overall treatment plan.

Assessing Suitability for Therapy

Because Hugh and Liseanne were able to recognize the individual feeling states that were interfering with their relationship and were willing to work on them, because they could make intellectual and emotional links, and because previous short-term therapy had been helpful, either individual or marital therapy could be expected to have a satisfactory outcome for each of them and for their marriage.

Recommendation

A combination of individual and couple therapy was recommended, and the couple agreed that this would be optimal. They preferred not to switch to a low-fee clinic, and they could not afford to do couple therapy and individual therapy for each of them concurrently. They decided on a serial approach to therapy and began in couple therapy with a senior trainee who offered them a private practice setting at the fee they required. She reported recently that Mr. and Mrs. Secombe have made substantial progress in the past year, that Mrs. Secombe is now working half-time, and that she is almost ready to return for individual therapy with Dr. Jill Scharff.

Section 6

BRIEF THERAPY

17

An Object Relations Theory of Brief Therapy

Object Relations Applications to Brief Therapy Formats

The tradition of brief therapy goes back to the beginning of psychoanalysis. Many of Freud's earliest cases were brief psychotherapies (Breuer and Freud 1895), and he continued to see patients for brief or even single sessions in his prime (Jones 1955a). Freud interrupted one of his precious holidays to conduct a single four-hour consultation with Gustav Mahler, whose marriage was in trouble. In the course of the extremely brief psychoanalytic process of sorts that occurred during a long walk, Freud found Mahler adept at catching on to psychoanalytic ideas and two moments of insight were thought worthy of reporting (Jones 1955a). Freud made an interpretation linking Mahler's fondness for his mother with his pet name for his wife, and the great composer arrived at the insight that his finest passages of expressive music were marred at their climax by the intrusion of mundane melodies because of his childhood memory of a hurdy-gurdy tune occurring at a time of great emotion following a brutal scene between his parents. Freud linked the there-and-then with the there-and-now, and Mahler made the link to the symbolic area of his creativity. There is no mention of a mutative transference interpretation linking these to the here-and-now, but there is mention of Freud's countertransference to such an important figure as Mahler, for whom he made an exception, interrupted his vacation, and then found to be a gifted analysand. This admiring countertransference enactment may have exerted an unspoken effect on the here-and-now of Mahler's ability to learn from Freud, to communicate his feelings, and to feel capable. We have not seen the original case notes, but venture to suggest that the relief of Mahler's symptoms of lack of potency with his wife that Jones reports as the outcome of the consultation resulted from the selected focus on these two areas and the connection between them, perhaps mediated by their reverberation in the here-and-now of the unspoken transference–countertransference. We would not expect such a brief consultation to be sufficient to address the extent of Mahler's obsessional neurosis or to free him to express his possible homosexual themes.

Early object relations analysts applied their ideas to other modalities of psychotherapy in brief format to various areas of interest—Wilfred Bion to groups, Enid Balint and Henry Dicks to marriage, Ronald Fairbairn to dental practice, John Bowlby and Donald Winnicott to pediatrics, and Michael Balint to primary care medicine. Balint developed an approach for family doctors in which they learned to monitor the doctor–patient relationship to arrive at insight about the patient's way of being, and then to capitalize on the cultivated power of that relationship to improve the reception of the insight to produce change and healing. This method of intervention was thought to maximize the effectiveness of ten-minute brief appointments offered in the National Health Service consulting room. In describing his work with mothers and infants within the pressures of the National Health Service, Winnicott said that the challenge often was not to see how much could be done, but how little need be done. Many of his consultations consisted of a single session, most effective if provided as an emergency when the patient was ready to open up (Winnicott 1971b).

Among the object relations analysts, it was Michael Balint who first became interested in focal brief therapy, and his work was further developed by Malan at the Tavistock Clinic (Balint et al. 1972, Malan 1976). Alexander and French (1946), the forbears of brief therapy in the United States, described the importance of the therapist providing a corrective emotional experience so as to refute the patient's expectations based on internal object relationships and so modify them, and limiting regression in order to shorten the length of treatment. Sifneos (1972), Mann (1973) and more recently, Davanloo (1980), Strupp and Binder (1984), Budman and Gurman (1988), and Stadter (1996) have continued the trend of establishing brief therapy as a legitimate form of psychotherapy with an integrity and range of application of its own, and have expanded our understanding of the role of the therapeutic relationship and the interpretation of dynamic conflict and repressed object relationships in short-term therapy. Malan, Davanloo, and Sifneos emphasize highly discriminating selection, to a greater or lesser degree, and a clear, analytic, interpretive focus, preferably on oedipal conflict. Others such as Budman and Gurman take patients with preoedipal dynamics as well because their flexible definition of brief therapy allows for a custom-tailored approach to any individual patient and can run to a year of sessions.

Each of these contemporary brief therapists emphasizes different technical elements of efficacy. Mann, who focuses on the destructiveness of negative self-image, recommends adhering to a strict twelve-session contract with no extensions in order to zero in on defining issues of separation, loss, and denial of death. Horowitz (1991), like Mann, recommends twelve sessions, but unlike Mann, he does not prohibit extensions and does not use the finality of the length of the contract to focus on separation and loss. Sifneos, on the other hand, usually uses about twenty sessions, and does not focus on separation and loss. Like Davanloo, Sifneos has an anxiety-provoking technique, but only for some patients. For others he uses an anxiety-reducing technique that has drawn less attention. Davanloo (1991) and Bloom (1981) both aim to unlock the unconscious, Davanloo in up to forty sessions for complete eradication of the neurosis, and Bloom in a single session in which he emphasizes the patient's capacity for ongoing growth. Malan and Davanloo interpret the intrusion of object relations into current relationships through their concept of the *triangle of the person* (see p. 391). Like Balint, Strupp and Binder (1984) emphasize the curative factor of the therapeutic relationship, which must be fostered by the early interpretation of negative transference and attention to the countertransference.

In contrast, Piper and his colleagues, who studied the variables of transference interpretation and quality of the therapeutic alliance, found that when therapists responded to resistance and weakening of the therapeutic alliance with transference interpretation, this high proportion of transference interpretation had a negative effect on outcome (Piper et al. 1991a). They found that good outcome was correlated with a high score on their Quality of Object Relations interview, and that this test was a better predictor of outcome than tests of recent interpersonal functioning (Piper et al. 1991b). Their studies support the clinical point of view that holds that it is better to build an alliance based on trust before engaging the patient in transference work, and to select patients on the basis of good fit with the approach being offered.

Object Relations Approach to Brief Therapy

Drawing on this heritage of analytic brief therapy, we will describe and illustrate our way of working in short-term therapy, which derives from object relations theory and technique by centering on the therapeutic relationship and the use of the countertransference in arriving at interpretation in the brief setting. Our own approach has most in common with that of our colleague Michael Stadter, who has brought object relational approaches and brief-therapy formats from other sources together in his book *Object Relations Brief Therapy* (1996). He emphasizes the value of brief therapy in selected cases without undermining the importance of long-term therapy in other cases, and notes that brief therapy is often only one phase in a therapy process of serial brief contacts.

Object relations theory and the techniques derived from it apply to brief therapy just as well as they do to long-term therapy and psychoanalysis. The same principles of attention to the frame, active listening, obtaining an object relations history, and working with the transference from the countertransference, form the core of brief object relations work. The principle shift in technique for the brief therapy format comes from an increased need to identify areas for work, to accept limited goals, to compress the focus of attention, and to feature the issues of separation and loss that are highlighted in the brief format.

The Trend toward Short-Term Care

In the current climate, there is pressure from managed care, insurance third-party payors, and institutions or reduced-fee clinics that offer psychotherapy to keep treatment to a minimum in cases that clearly require long-term care. Much publicity from these sources claims that brief therapy is better therapy, that long-term therapy is most often an indulgence whose primary purpose is to produce income for therapists. The same sources exploit the prevailing sentiment in medicine that medication can do what is required in most mental illness, and that psychotherapy is largely unnecessary. Fortunately, consumers are now aware of research studies that show that psychotherapy is the crucial variable that determines the effectiveness of other therapies, and that longer-term approaches of whatever orientation tend to produce better results over time (*Consumer Reports* 1995). Brief therapy does not allow time for the building of the therapeutic relationship through which faulty lifelong attachment models can be restructured (Slade 1996). We think that it is far better for the integrity of the therapist and the patient to use the few sessions available to do a limited piece of work that is realistic in scope and to give a brief experience of what therapy and psychoanalysis can offer than to pretend that symptom removal or a limited focus for exploration of complex charac-terological issues or mental illness is the extent of the benefit that therapy and psychoanalysis can offer. We do not want to collude with unreal expectations of the effectiveness of cost-saving alternatives to the excellent in-depth medi-cal and psychological care that we are trained to provide. We work by the principle of freeing patients from conflict so as to be able to make choices about their relationships, their behaviors, their lives—and their investment in therapy or psychoanalysis.

While this sort of pressure is never an adequate reason for preferring short-term therapy, it does argue powerfully for us to offer it even when we would prefer to suggest long-term therapy or psychoanalysis. But this is not the only situation where we must offer less than we would like. Some mental health institutions limit what is offered; for instance, some clinics and employee as-sistance programs limit the number of sessions allowed. In other settings, some patients are in our locale only briefly, or are about to move to another city, and other patients' motivation may be limited so that they prefer a brief en-counter to a more thorough one. They impose limitations on their own com-mitment. Other patients limit their goals because they do not require more than a brief intervention to make the minor adjustments necessary for their continued well-being.

All these situations press us to develop a model that does justice to the com-plexity of the patient's situation and the sophistication of our level of under-standing, while honoring the constraints. The challenge of the brief format can bring out the best in our therapeutic functioning, and for selected cases brief therapy will be all that is required.

Selection

Sifneos (1972, 1987) selects for brief therapy only those few patients with oe-dipal level development who agree to focus on oedipal conflict and unresolved grief reactions. Horowitz (1991) chooses those who have an acute reaction to a stressful life event. Davanloo (1991) requires proof of good ego strength and willingness to respond to confrontation as demonstrated in a lengthy assess-ment process. Like Sifneos he intends to focus on a circumscribed area of oedi-pal conflict. Stadter (1996) selects according to the criteria of well-developed focus, psychological-mindedness, and motivation.

We use brief therapy as the treatment of choice for highly motivated pa-tients in those situations that derive from developmental and externally im-posed crises where there is relatively little severe underlying disturbance, or in which the resonance with deeper issues does not principally involve en-trenched characterologic patterns. Patients referred from primary-care medi-cal settings, those seen in student mental health clinics, and many of those seen in employee assistance programs are more likely to qualify for short-term treatment as the method of choice than those seeking psychotherapy through other mental health routes.

Technique in Object Relations Brief Psychotherapy

We want to do the most that we can within the context. We shape our ap-proach to maximize benefit to the patient under the time-limited circum-stances. The principles of conducting a period of assessment, arriving at a treatment plan, listening for conflict through conscious and unconscious lis-tening, and making interpretations still apply. If we believe that more treat-ment would be helpful, we may be able to set the stage by conducting a help-ful therapy now, and by outlining to the patient the areas we believe would offer fruitful opportunities for later work. Or a helpful brief therapy can pave the way for subsequent long-term therapy, or for serial brief therapies with us or with other therapists, and so may offer a good deal over time.

In brief therapy, we must develop a therapeutic focus quickly. Stadter's (1996) paradigm sets a dual focus on (1) symptom and (2) underlying dynam-ics. The approach that focuses only on symptom will be supportive rather than psychoanalytic and change will be less far-reaching. Shift in one symptom can, however, eventually lead to changes in other areas of self-functioning, and this accounts for the long-term success of some short-term therapies.

Focus on Symptom

The focus may be on a cardinal symptom, a developmental crisis, a central self-defeating conviction about the self, or a recurrent self-destructive pattern (Schacht et al. 1984). The symptom focus expresses the therapist's understand-ing of the situation that brought the patient to therapy, put in language that patient and therapist agree expresses the painful situation.

Focus on Dynamics

During the assessment, which in practice may function as the first session in the very brief format, we also attempt to construct a dynamic formulation that best expresses the underlying conflict or internal object situation. It is not always possible to construct such a formulation immediately, but in the cases most suitable for brief therapy, the therapist will be able to have at least a roughly sketched tentative formulation. Then the rest of the therapy works to elaborate the dynamic formulation and to link symptomatic and dynamic foci.

There-and-Now, Here-and-Then

This means that we are working to understand and interpret the external conflict or situation (the there-and-now) with the internal situation (the here-and-then and its effect on the here-and-now). In addition, as in all object relations work, we are interested in the role of transference and countertransference to make sense of the patient's situation, so we call on the here-and-now of the transference–countertransference for our understanding and interpretation too.

The Triangle of the Person

Malan (1963, 1976) in Great Britain and later Davanloo (1980) in the United States devised a way of thinking about the short-term patient termed the *triangle of conflict* and the *triangle of the person*, two images that they keep in mind to organize their thinking about the patient's issues and to guide their interpretive focus. In the triangle of conflict, a concept drawn from drive theory, they trace the connection between impulse, anxiety, and defence. In the triangle of the person, they trace the patient's feelings and actions toward the therapist, the feelings toward important figures from the past such as parents, and those toward others in the present or recent past. Then the therapist uses these three angles in formulating interpretations, Davanloo from a more forceful, confrontational, and relentlessly interpretive stance than Malan. In line with current thinking in object relations and self psychology, Stadter (1996) added the evaluation of how patients treat themselves in order to add the interpretation of attitudes toward self and others now and in the past. The interpretation of these phenomena adds "self" as a fourth nodal point to the interpretive thrust of the triangle of the person, and brings a new dimension of immediacy to the process (Figure 17–1).

In a sample interpretation linking the past and a current external relationship with the patient's self, the therapist might say, "You keep away from your wife sexually now (there-and-now relationship) because you are afraid she will take you over (a self experience) like your mother used to do (there-and-

then relationship)." However, to link such an interpretation to the transference, the therapist might draw on a sense of the patient's reluctance to speak
about the transference by adding, "You are also afraid of being here with me
(here-and-now transference) in case what I say will somehow put you in danger of being taken over by me (self's fear about the future in here) as you feel
dominated by your husband (there-and-now relationship)." In this way, the
two interpretations would link all three angles of the triangle with the position of the self in its center. For a detailed description of a similar use of the
triangle of the person in brief therapy in which marital sexual expression is
linked to the object relations history, the transference, and the attitude toward
the self, see the case of Susan in Chapter 19.

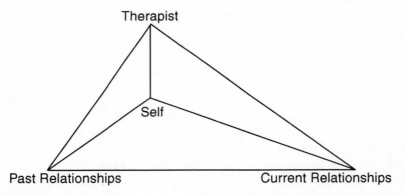

FIGURE 17–1. Interpretive triangle of the self in relationship. Reprinted
from *Object Relations Brief Psychotherapy*, © Michael Stadter (1996). Used with
permission.

The Use of Nondynamic Elements

Budman and Gurman (1988) advocated the judicious use of nonpsychodynamic
elements in the conduct of object relations brief therapy. Such elements as support and advice may play a greater role than they do in long-term therapy, as
they did in the next case example. The patient attended once a week for twenty
sessions, most of which served a supportive rather than an evidently analytic
function. Nevertheless, the support given addressed the development of the
mother–infant–husband triangle and the resolution of the mother's identity as
a woman.

Tracy consulted me (JSS) because she was depressed about her life as the wife of an ambitious executive and mother of three children, aged 4, 2, and 1. She said that she did not know what to do and she had lost sight of who she was. She and her husband Ron were fighting a lot and their sex life had dwindled. They were on the verge of divorce, a step that neither of them wanted to take, because they loved each other and enjoyed their family. The problem was that Tracy was always in a bad mood. She held it together all day to be fun with her children and then she took it out on her husband.

Ron was a terrific husband, made good money, helped with the housework, and adored the children. If he had to be out of town for a few days on business, he came home in the middle of the trip to see the children. At the end of the business day, he immediately tuned in to the children. On the weekend, he could manage both children so that Tracy could get time to herself. The problem was that Ron found his work fascinating and enjoyed his family more than she did. He still had lots of energy in the evening and by then she was wiped out. He had plenty to talk about, while she felt that her day was less interesting in comparison. She had been successful at an interesting career, but it had not been important to her, and she did not regret her choice of staying home with her children. But she found it hard, and her daily life did not provide her with interesting things to say to her husband. Her baby had frequent colds and so Tracy was often sick, which further depleted her reserves. She cooked and ate dinner with her husband on the nights that he was home, but then she retired to bed at 9:00 with little energy left for sexual intimacy. Normally even-tempered, Ron was getting frustrated and tending to flare up at her.

Tracy had money to pay for help with babysitting and housecleaning, and she had lots of friends to spend time with together with their children, so her life was not as burdensome as it seemed. I said that one reason life was hard for Tracy was because the care of the children was not shared. Either she did it all, or he did it all. He could replace her after a day's work, and this reduced her sense of value. Instead of feeling glad of the break, she felt expendable. She also felt jealous that the children had priority for getting time with Ron. I worked with Tracy on how furious she was that Ron was so unavailable to her. It was hard to be angry with such a great guy, especially when their income depended on his job, which required travel, and when he tried so hard to meet her needs as he saw them. She was also jealous that he was so invested in what he was doing and derived a good feeling about himself from the way that he filled his roles, while she felt so lost and uncertain.

Her resentment at her husband reminded her of how she disparaged her practically perfect brother who worked hard to achieve academic honors, but who was a "nerd" in her eyes. She was as bright as he was, but she wanted to be the opposite of him. She aimed at being cool and doing well without working. As a young mother, she was still cool and active with her social group, but she had to work hard night and day caring for a preschooler, a toddler, and a baby. It was a challenge, and it left her feeling depleted and on unfamliar territory.

It took only a few sessions to connect Tracy's envy of her husband to childhood feelings about her brother and to work on her anger at him for his success and satisfaction. She expressed all this to him and he was able to listen. He could not change the facts of his work life, but he could tune in to her now that she was not angry or asleep all the time. She was able to arrange more babysitting for evenings when he was traveling so that she could do things with friends that generated interesting adult conversation. Her marriage improved, her sex life returned, and she was no longer depressed. She stopped worrying about who she was or what she should be doing for herself. She considered terminating in a few more weeks.

Tracy thought that I must be bored with seeing her now that she had nothing to talk about except what adorable thing the baby did that day. True, a managed care company might judge her illness cured in six sessions, and I said that she could certainly choose to finish at this point, but not because I was bored. The main problem was only now coming to the fore: Tracy thought who she is was of no concern, and that the mother–infant relationship was of no interest to anyone outside it. She did not know how to take in and value her experience and present it to her husband so that he could share her pleasure. When I said that she could continue to see me to work on this, she started to cry. She said that her own mother lived abroad, and even though she talked to her often, she really missed being able to sit down with her and tell her about the children. She thought that she had been using me to fill in for her, and it had really helped, but she felt guilty to be using a therapist that way. I said that she was making legitimate use of her therapy to find meaning in her life through having it reflected back to her by me. After a few months of weekly individual therapy, she gained confidence in the worth of her life as a mother, she became able to talk to her husband and allow him to be the mirror for her mothering, and she was then ready to terminate.

This patient was experiencing stress as a young mother with a busy husband, three very young children, and not enough family support. Her depression was due to a developmental crisis. Work on the symptom focus of her depression and irritability led to the dynamic focus on her feelings for her mother and brother. Her anger at her husband's ambition had its source in her envy of her brother. Her resentment at his absence was fueled by missing her mother. Therapy served to relieve the tension arising from the dynamic focus on the triangle of the person, but Tracy did not go on to confront her self—her inhibition of ambition and her lack of a complex view of herself and her future. She did not experience a focused transference as a re-edition of the absent mother, and instead maintained a positive contextual transference, with the therapist seen as a good mother/grandmother. The main work of this brief therapy remained at the level of offering the patient a context of support in which she refound herself as a wife and mother. Incidentally, we think that the extension of this therapy to twenty sessions probably saved more than it cost by buffering the children from the effects of their mother's depression about doing without her own mother, sustaining her self-esteem, and protecting against a relapse by giving time for consolidation of gains and rebuilding of a supportive marital relationship.

Stadter (1996) thinks that elements from cognitive and behavior therapy or hypnosis are consistent with a dynamic brief approach, and notes that Strupp and Binder (1984) and Horowitz et al. (1984) employed some of the techniques of cognitive therapy as part of their work. In our consultative work, we give advice about children in sessions with parents who may consult us briefly about their children. One of us (DES) has used the techniques of sex therapy in brief approaches with individuals and couples (D. Scharff 1982, J. Scharff and D. Scharff 1992). These techniques include prescriptions for the graded exercises involved in sex therapy, instruction about sexual behavior and response, readings, educational information, support, and other kinds of advice. When conducted as dynamic therapies, these ancillary methods are embedded in an exploratory and interpretive matrix, and any reactions and associations by the patients are available for dynamic work. Even when we use these ancillary techniques, we have had little difficulty centering the work in our usual dynamic mode (D. Scharff 1982, D. Scharff and J. Scharff 1987, 1991).

An Example of Brief Therapy

Tom, an older medical student, came to see me (DES) when I was the psychiatrist in the student health clinic at his medical school, because he felt that his marriage had gone dry and because he had begun to drink excessively in the evenings. In an individual session, he and I quickly established a dual focus on the wetness of the symptom and its connection to relieving the dryness in his emotional life. He felt guilty that he was no longer interested in his wife, and he was feeling even more distant now that she was angry and depressed about the change in their relationship. He readily agreed to a couple session.

In the couple session, he began by berating his wife for being so preoccupied with the children and for losing interest in her appearance. She in turn said she felt he had let her down. She was upset that he had lost interest in her sexually, and she felt overburdened with caring for their two sons. She had accepted her role as primary parent with the children because he had to go to school all day and study in the evenings, but she was furious now that he was spending his evenings drinking, which had only started recently. His argument evaporated in a cloud of guilt.

Tom asked to see me alone again, and in this individual session, he revealed that he was having an affair with a classmate. Perhaps because he had not told me of it from the beginning, perhaps because of his guilty tone of voice, I suddenly felt unexpectedly condemning of his behavior. I recognized this as a countertransference evoked in me that must relate to his guilt about an event in the there-and-then. I used this to guide me to a dynamic focus which clarified his symptoms of distress. I asked about earlier experiences of guilt. Now Tom was able to link the drinking that he had previously connected with his avoidance of his wife and family to calamitous circumstances he had experienced as a teenager. He vividly described a scene on a fishing trip with his alcoholic father who got drunk when they were out in the boat. When Tom angrily complained about his father's drunkenness, he threw Tom in the water. Furious, Tom swam ashore, and went straight home to bed without explaining his upset to his mother. Later that night, while Tom slept, his father went out into the woods and shot himself. Tom admitted that he must be angry at his father, but he had cut himself off from feeling anything about the incident. What he did feel was guilt about the effect that the loss of his father had on his mother, who became depressed, thin, and "dried-up." It was as if he had caused his father's death by his silence.

He and I now linked these early events to his current difficulty. The compassion I felt on hearing his story helped me connect to Tom as we established the links between his adolescent story and his current dilemma. He recognized that the drinking, his avoidance of his wife, and the decline of their sexual life had resulted from a resurgence of his guilt as he saw her shrivel up from neglect as his studies had taken more of his time and energy. He recognized that he was killing himself by joining with his father and making his wife suffer as his mother had, and that he was doing this to punish himself for not being able to fix his father and keep him alive for his mother. I advised him that, in view of his family history, it would be wise for him to stop drinking if he could. I said that, sober, he would have a better chance of making good choices about his marriage and family. He stopped drinking altogether, ended the affair, and decided to return to his wife and try to work things out. After a total of five sessions he stopped therapy.

Serial Brief Therapy

We often find that the brief-therapy contract is followed by another request for help, sometimes for another short intervention and sometimes for longer-term work. In a student mental health clinic with medical students and their families at the Uniformed Services University in the 1980s, David Scharff worked with brief-therapy contacts that students often deemed sufficient to allow their development to proceed, although long-term therapy was available without charge. Sometimes a student came for three or four sessions around a crisis, then would come back a few years later, now married, looking for help with his marital adjustment. Sometimes a spouse came for help with adjusting to her husband's heavy work schedule, or for help with her baby's sleep disorder, and found that a few sessions were all that she needed to get back on track. Sometimes one brief-therapy contract involved the couple or family therapy, while a subsequent one called for individual sessions. Or the sessions in any one set might call for a combination of individual and conjoint therapy. Stadter (1996) documented that some of the best results have come with a series of brief therapies with patients who return several times over a period of years.

Tom sought me out four years later, when I was in private practice. He had remained abstinent, as I had advised. Once his wife stopped being angry at him for drinking, he had been able to relate to her again. He stopped feeling guilty about mistreating her, but he had found that he was not able to love her fully, and learned that she did not enjoy her life as the lonely wife of a highly ambitious junior surgeon who worked night and day. None of this could change, and so they separated. He had left his wife within a year of finishing his brief therapy, and was now happily remarried to a self-sufficient woman (not to his classmate with whom he had the affair).

Now Tom wanted to improve his relationship to his children. He had two teenage sons from his first marriage, and a young daughter in his second marriage. He got along well with his daughter, but he felt challenged by the two older boys. Again we were able to work with the there-and-now effects of the there-and-then situation with his parents. The trauma experienced with his father had resurfaced as his sons approached the age at which he had confronted his father and experienced his death. He found he had been worried that the boys would feel angry at him for being unavailable, as he had felt about his father because of the father's alcoholism. He thought he had neglected his sons in favor of his second family so that this marriage would not fail as the first one had, and so that he would not experience a return of the kind of guilt he had felt toward his first wife and the mother whose depression he felt he had caused.

In the countertransference this time I felt more sorrow and loss in response to Tom's fuller range of feeling. I asked him to talk about the losses he had felt in leaving his first marriage. He again linked the loss of his first wife, who had been great as a young woman but who shriveled (only partly due to his neglect, he now realized), to the loss of his mother's vitality (more a feature of her attachment to an abandoning husband, he now realized, than a result of anger at him). He had a frank talk with his sons and told them how his father's death had left him feeling shaky about how to be a good father, asked for their help in building a good relationship with them, and negotiated a more attentive visitation schedule. He felt that he had done what he wanted in three sessions, and he left saying he would call me again if the need arose.

Tom was able to move beyond guilt about damage done to his objects to a stage where he could experience the loss of his objects and accept their limitations. He could allow himself to be concerned for his self and to make choices that were good for him, and to accept the responsibility for making reparation to the children who had suffered the loss of their intact family. But to an intensive therapist, the work is far from complete. He did not look at his oedipal rivalry and murderous feelings toward his father. He did not work through the depths of his guilt at seeming to cause his father's death.

He did not address the disappointment he felt when he had his mother all to himself and found that she was too depressed to respond to him. He did not work on his internal objects in the transference to achieve fundamental change. But he used his therapist as a fatherly person who did not tip the boat, who gave him some advice that enabled him to face his dilemma, and who helped him to make a link between his symptom and his current and past relationships. He did not resolve the trauma in his adolescent development, but by linking there-and-then with here-and-now, brief therapy detoxified its effects sufficiently that he could move on and become a loving husband and father.

In both brief therapy contacts Tom linked past and present, self and object together for an increased understanding of his situation, which enabled him to move forward. He unconsciously communicated his self and object dynamics to his therapist who received them in his countertransference and used his feelings to guide the therapeutic process. In the second series of three sessions, Tom was able to recall and make use of what he had learned in the first brief therapy, and especially to take advantage of the trust that developed. Both series beg the question of whether more could have been done, but each series left Tom feeling considerably helped. In a Christmas card that he sent a few years later, he reported that he was able to enjoy his adolescent sons and could look forward to the teenage years of his young daughter without dread.

In the next two chapters we provide two more examples from the brief therapy of two women. One of the women had previous analytic therapy on which her brief therapy could capitalize, while the other's attitude to therapy was compromised by the disappointing outcome of prior supportive counseling. These examples illustrate the session-by-session development of the therapeutic relationship, the interpretation of the transference, the use of countertransference, the interpretation of dreams and fantasies, and confrontation of the limitations of the brief therapy format.

Follow-Up

We usually end each brief therapy with patients as we did with Tracy and Tom (in this chapter), Adele (whom we present in Chapter 18), and Susan (in Chapter 19) by inviting them to call if they feel we can be of help in the future. Tom and Adele used the opportunity; Tracy and Susan did not. At times, a follow-up session is an opportunity for patients to ask for more treatment, but equally often they use it to amplify aspects of the work and confirm their decision to stop. Some then remain in touch periodically for the next months, or drop a note a year or more later, as Tom did. In that case, the attenuated relationship with the therapist may offer an extended hand which enables the patient to confirm and solidify gains. Equally valid is the brief therapy that is used and then let go.

18

Serial Brief Therapy after Long-Term Therapy

Patients or clients who have had previous psychoanalytically oriented therapy are more experienced in the psychoanalytic approach. They are more able to join in an examination of the transference than those who are in therapy for the first time. The level of work that they can do by taking advantage of knowing how to work analytically shows that the brief format is not necessarily superficial, as some of its opponents have claimed.

Adele had had previous therapy for two years in her twenties, at a time when she was unable to marry because she kept finding fault with all of the men she might have considered as suitable husbands. Always a devoted daughter and family member, Adele was particularly attached to her father, who could do no wrong. On the other hand her mother was perceived as a rather critical and demanding person who wanted things her way—not unlike Adele herself when she was evaluating her marriage prospects. Work with her male therapist enabled Adele to resolve her idealization and denigration of her parents before her mother died. Then she was able to find a man whom she could love. The man that she chose, Ed, a divorced older man with teenage children, offered her a ready-made family to whom she transferred her affections. Ed also supported Adele's feminist interests and her assertive commitment to her career, and yet he encouraged her to relax and find more time for pleasure and her new family.

In her thirties, Adele had an additional year of therapy with me (JSS). She agreed with Ed's assessment that she had a conflict over work and pleasure. Despite enjoying her intimate and sexual life with Ed, despite her love of furnishing their house and cooking gourmet meals, Adele had trouble leaving work at the end of the day until every last item of business was dispatched. A top-rated manager, she always found a little extra time to listen to an employee with a problem. A willing subordinate, she always accepted one more assignment and did it well. Work had been her life and now that it was only part of her existence, Adele was in conflict. A devoted aunt, Adele had loved shopping for her nephews. A loving stepmother, she had welcomed her stepchildren to live in their home. In therapy it became apparent to Adele that her conflict concerned her maternal longings. When she unexpectedly decided that she wanted to have a child with Ed, he supported her through infertility investigations and helped her to give up work so that she could concentrate on her wish to conceive. With her conflict resolved, Adele terminated therapy. The couple were rewarded a couple of years later with the birth of a gorgeous, bright boy.

Now in her mid-forties, the mother of a 4-year-old boy, Adele came to see me again. She was happy with the choices that she had made. She was glad to be out of the stressful work environment, and she was enjoying her domestic life as a mother and homemaker. The last few years had been stressful because her father had died after a miserable illness, her mother-in-law had died suddenly soon after that, her youngest stepchild had left the home, and Ed's company had transferred him to Wyoming where he and Adele had bought a house and settled down, only to find two years later that Ed was out of work because the business failed. With some disappointment at leaving their new home and considerable relief to be rejoining their remaining families on the East Coast, they returned home when Ed found an excellent business opportunity that, however, involved more traveling than they had expected.

This time Adele was in conflict about her mothering behavior. She wanted to be reasonable and loving, but she found herself driven to impulsive anger, like her mother. She said that for the last year and a half, she easily lost control with her child, Noah, an aggressive, high-energy boy. Despite her careful monitoring of his television viewing, Noah was "too weapons-oriented." He told her his dreams of owning a magical weapon to destroy skeletons and ghosts of which he had been afraid since seeing the film *Ghostbusters*. Instead of recognizing his developmental masculine need for defense against his fears, Adele thought that Noah was criminally obsessed with aggression. A family consultation soon established that Noah's fears were age-appropriate, magnified by Adele's responses and stimulated by her frighteningly raging behavior toward him.

Adele had not fully experienced her own aggression, even in the competitive world of business, perhaps because there were so many channels for its sublimated expression. She had transformed her aggression into assertiveness, reversed it to become concern for employees, and turned it against herself by overworking, staying late at the office, and pursuing perfection. Now this naturally aggressive boy had posed a new level of challenge. Former defenses against aggression that were so successful in business were blown away by a 4-year-old boy.

"What happens is, I'm real patient," Adele explained. "Then suddenly I lose it. I yell a lot and then I spank. Time out doesn't work with Noah. He hates it and he's afraid upstairs alone. So I yell and hit. I sound like my mother, and I hate that. My mother worked all her life and didn't like being home. She yelled a lot, especially in menopause. But I like being home, and I'm not in menopause. She was spanking us all the time. She even threw things. Thank God I don't do that, but I don't want to do the other stuff either. I'm not so bad when Ed is home. When he's there I don't get out of control. But he has to travel, so I've got to learn to manage this, but I don't want another two years of therapy. This problem can't wait that long. There's a deadline here. I've got to get this stopped now before Noah is any older."

Adele already knew the child-rearing techniques that were preferable, but she was not taking the time to master the anxiety of using them. Instead she was taken over by her mother's familiar methods, which she hated. I asked Adele to consider analysis so that she could explore thoroughly her maternal identifications, but Adele did not want to invest in changing herself to that extent. Since she had had previous therapy and did not want more, I decided to offer her a brief therapy contract. She thought about it and made a commitment to six sessions.

I liked working with Adele. I enjoyed her spontaneity, her energy, and her dedication to her role, whether as businesswoman, wife, patient, or, now, mother. As a mother of little ones and stepmother of more mature children myself, I could empathize with her frustration in dealing with her challenging younger child. I missed working with her in depth at this new developmental stage concerning her maternality, but I felt optimistic that we could achieve her limited goals by capitalizing on the deadline of the brief therapy format and her previous experience in therapy.

I asked her to think about her goals more specifically and said that we would develop an outline of them when we met for the first session.

In beginning brief therapy, Dr. Jill Scharff has to accept Adele's independent assessment of her needs. She has to absorb and mourn the loss of doing longer-term therapy without demanding to have her own way or becoming critical of Adele, like Adele's maternal internal object. Brief therapy often confronts the therapist with containing a sense of lost opportunity that reflects the patient's internal object relations.

Session 1

Adele did not seem to have any focused goals in mind. She began by exclaiming about the beauty of my ring, an inexpensive, but large, smooth, opaque, deep blue chalcedony set in silver.
"Your ring!" she began. "Look at that! It's gorgeous. Just what I like. I'll select that kind of thing for my birthday." She fell silent.

I felt quite conspicuous and a bit embarrassed by the effusiveness of her praise. I imagined that Adele was waiting for me to tell her where to get one like it. I had bought it to match a bracelet I got as a graduation present from my late grandmother who had been a second mother to me. I asked her to tell me what occurred to her about my ring.

"I love silver," she said. "It reminds me of the two years in Wyoming. There were so many beautiful Indian pieces I would have liked to buy. I look better in silver with my complexion. My older sister who works buys whatever she wants. I used to be able to do that. I'd like to be more generous to myself, but only if I get a bargain. I feel better if I get it at a reasonable price, and the good pieces don't go on sale. Now I did buy myself one thing, a silver and turquoise bracelet, because my big sister said to, because it wasn't my money, it was Ed's money and he said I could spend it, and because he said it was a farewell gift from Wyoming.
"But your ring is really something. It's old-fashioned. It's the color of your eyes and your blouse. It pulls it all together."
As she reveled in this appreciation of beauty, Adele gestured with her right hand toward me, as if she was outlining the curve of the stone, and the circle connecting stone, eye, and blouse. I felt that she was caressing the breast unconsciously, but I did not now feel embarrassed by her love. I

simply thought that the roundness and voluptuousness of the stone and the skin-flattering silver of the ring had led her to the shape and surface of the breast. Since the ring actually did not look like a breast, concern about the breast must be pressing to consciousness. I told her that these thoughts had occurred to me as she made her rapturous gesture.

"Oh!" she exclaimed, taken aback. "Do I want to be a baby? Do I want to nurture or be nurtured?"

"We know that you want to nurture Noah especially, the employees when you worked, me perhaps. But maybe this means that it is time to speak of your own needs," I suggested.

"Oh, I seek approval like a child," she replied. "In business we always say 'it's not personal' but I want it to be. You had to like me. I personalize everything. I expected family feelings in the business environment. I learned in therapy with you before that I was transferring feelings about my family to work. Here I am transferring wishes to be nurtured onto a ring. This is amazing."

Now it was my turn to make it personal. After all it was my ring that she had found so entrancing.

"Your first comment as we began this therapy was a compliment to me about my choice of ring," I said. "This is your way of making therapy more personal. It is your characteristic way of approaching a relationship and beginning a task."

"I tried to have a more personal relationship with my first doctor, too," she confirmed. "Right out he said he wouldn't have that. He was just there, not empathizing, not with me. I got really angry, but it was important for him to be that way. I got much more out of it. My other sister had a more personal relationship with her therapist. She had a crush on him. But I needed someone who wouldn't fall for my traps. I was trying really hard to get him to be more friendly."

"Are you trying to make a more friendly relationship with me?" I asked.

"Yes and no," she replied. "I'm too friendly with service people. We need to have a doctor–patient relationship because it's better for me. I expect that and I want that, but I don't like it."

"How does a friendly feeling help you approach the task?" I asked.

"You feel you're okay," she answered. "When you're not friendly, the jury's out. Like I don't know how you feel about me. It makes me worry about being with you."

"Does that have anything to do with choosing a six-session contract to take care of these anxieties about your feelings and your frustrations with your son, when what you long for is nurturing for yourself?" I asked.

"No," she reminded us. "You'll be businesslike as usual, and I can be any way I want to. You'll just respond to what's germane. You are over there and I am over here."

"Okay," I said. "So the six-session contract can be viewed as if it were the bracelet you longed for—not all the pieces that one might long for, but something special by itself. You can be generous with yourself in taking this special time, in using it to explore your own needs and find nurturance any way you want to." Returning to our focus, I said "First we need to set your goals."

Adele knew exactly what they were and she quickly outlined them:

"To provide time for myself.

"To have a more even temperament.

"To not get pressed and hurried.

"To not spank Noah.

"To not yell at Noah.

"To be less driven about getting jobs done and to be able to postpone work.

"To stop taking time from me and Noah to get jobs done.

"To be better at prioritizing.

"Good," she concluded. "We have a direction and an outline. I'm glad we started."

Here in the first session of the brief contract, the therapist moved quickly to convert an apparently inconsequential remark about her ring to the contextual transference attitude it actually represented. This allowed patient and therapist to convert the longing lodged in the patient and the sense of loss lodged in the therapist's countertransference into a thinkable and talkable matter in the transitional space between them. As they did so, a there-and-then matter (the past wish the patient had for a bracelet) was connected to the here-and-now of the transference–countertransference exchange (the love of the therapist's ring), and led to work on the actual and hoped-for quality of the therapeutic relationship and the symptom focus on her role as a mother, which was important to Adele. The symptomatic focus on managing self and object in her maternal role was linked with the dynamic focus on accepting limited access to the nurturing breast despite envy of the idealized breast belonging both to her sister and to her husband. We note that only some aspects of this formulation are spoken about directly in the session. Others are noted silently. Still others are present but could not be consciously formulated until later review.

Session 2

Adele had called to cancel two sessions because she and Noah were sick, and to request two more sessions at the end of the previously arranged six, so that she would still have a total of six sessions. My contract with her was for six sessions only, and so I agreed to her request and did not charge her for the missed sessions.

She began, "I'm doing and undoing all my decisions. I was out buying a light, I settled on one fixture and then I wondered if I should look somewhere else. I found another, but I didn't buy it either. I can make a case for any kind of decor and then I don't know which is best. A lamp is only a $125 purchase, so it isn't much to worry about. I could have bought both of them. I'm going to call today and settle it—maybe because we have our appointment."

$125 was my fee at that time. "How's that connected?" I asked.

"Maybe I was thinking subconsciously of coming to see you and it reminded me of how I have to change," she replied.

"I think there may be a link between not buying the lamps and not buying the sessions you had to miss," I said.

"Oh, interesting," she said. Her mind was on the money, not on the sessions. "I've always worried about what things cost. The breast surgeon wanted to do biopsies on the lump in my breast even though there was only a 5 percent chance of it being anything other than fibrocystic disease. I insisted on waiting to get an approved doctor so it would be covered by insurance. I have confidence that these sessions with you are of value and they are 80 percent covered. In fact I look forward to them."

I appreciated that she felt fine about her sessions because they were good value and a bargain besides. I felt fine about that too, but I did not feel fine about the missed sessions or her unwillingness to pay for examining problems within the nurturing breast. It was also hard for me to give up the income. More than that, I felt interrupted at the beginning of what was already a short contract, and I felt insecure about its viability. Then how did she feel about not having sessions the last two weeks?

I asked directly, "Did you have feelings about having to miss two sessions?"

"Oh maybe," Adele answered. "I enjoyed the last session with the symbolism of the ring. We made the list of the goals. I felt very positive and I told Ed I'd rather have kept coming each of those weeks."

Since the price of a lamp and the fee for a session was the same, I thought that the two lamps that she did not buy but could have bought referred to the two sessions that she had not had. I thought that she could now purchase a lamp today because she was having her session today, in an act of symbolic equivalence. I said, "I think that you were obsessing over the lamps to avoid thinking about feelings having to do with missing the sessions."

Adele turned to the there-and-now, and the there-and-then. "I've been missing my sister a lot, even though I'm so close to both my sisters," she said. "In Wyoming I missed them terribly, but I put together a social life there from mothers I met at the mommy-and-me classes. I met these two women I really liked and we helped each other with the kids."

Adele continued to tell me in detail about these wonderful friends. I began to say something about them as her substitute sisters, but before I could say more about loss and replacement, Adele rattled on about how frequently she saw her sisters even while she was in Wyoming and how much more often she sees them now, as if to say there had been little loss of friends or sisters.

I felt bleak. I remembered how much support I needed when my children were young, and I would have loved to have had sisters close by. But like Adele, I had left my family home, and so I appreciated my friends all the more. I really needed them to help out, play together, and enjoy the children's growth. One of them had moved out West, as Adele had done, and I missed her and her children terribly.

I said, "It's still a loss. You can't replace friends that you make during the early years as mothers."

Adele started to cry. "Oh it's so true," she sobbed. "It was such a special time. It was so ideal. I was just three doors away from either of them. I feel as if I'll never have friends like that again. They were like me: all of us Jewish, all compulsive, but they were not obsessive. Confident, high-energy, bright, respected and serious women, direct and straightforward. I don't like tiptoeing around and guessing about a friendship. I have one other friend like that, but she's in New Orleans. I love and miss her too."

"Does your grief leave you reluctant to rebuild friendships here at home?" I said, thinking about the strain of getting to know me again as well.

"I do want to do it," she said. "I've got to. I'm just slow. But I'll drive for every school trip. I'll get to know the other mothers. I like some of the women and one of the teachers. I don't know how far any of them will go as a close friend."

Adele wiped her tears and went off.

This session marked the patient's move away from the therapist, enacting the there-and-then move to the West and back, away from the therapist and back in the here-and-now. Adele acknowledged the link to missing the therapist, but gave it passing attention in favor of discussing a connected issue in the there-and-then and there-and-now of missing her friends and sisters. Much less important than them, Dr. Jill Scharff had to bear feeling somewhat devalued, then try to understand this countertransference. She used her identification with the loneliness of being the mother of young children without family nearby to help her understand Adele's emptiness, loss, and longing for support—an extension of the envied nurturing breast theme.

Session 3

Adele described how she had developed a pain in her neck so severe that she had required traction and would have to continue physical therapy twice a week for three weeks. I noted to myself that this added up to six sessions, the same number as in our psychotherapy contract, and so I assumed that her physical situation was a symbolic equivalent to her psychological pain and its treatment. After listening to a long description of her physical discomfort, I told her that I thought that her sore neck was her body's way of giving her to feel pain instead of feeling grief and longing for her sisters and her friends, fear of relying on me alone to help her with her losses, and dread of missing me too when our sessions came to an end.

Adele told me that Ed had suggested that the neck spasm happened because she was too controlling. Now she could see that what she was trying to control were her losses. That fit with something else that Ed had said. He thought that she was angry at him for their having to move to Wyoming and back again and being the cause of her missing her friends. When I said that I thought that Ed was right about this, Adele denied her anger. She said that she had never been angry at him because he had not wanted to move either, and had lost his job only because the company folded, not through any lack of competence on his part.

Adele was relating my comments to her family relationships and not to me. I followed her lead. Instead of seeing her neck pain as a plea for comforting from me, or as anger at me for causing her grief, I thought of how Adele's loss of control occurred when her boy was aggressive. Clearly anger was an emotion that she wished to suppress in herself and in her child.

"Anger is scary to you, and you would like to get rid of it in both you and Noah," I said.

Adele listened thoughtfully and said, "This is the key. I have to get in touch with it to help Noah."

In this session, Dr. Jill Scharff notes Adele's tendency to deny anger by displacing it into bodily expression through trying to rigidly control it lest it take over. Adele's denial of anger obliterates the symptomatic focus altogether: she has not mentioned her son in the second and third sessions at all. Following Dr. Scharff's comment about her fear and suppression of anger, she relocates the symptomatic focus on her inability to control her anger at him. We begin to get the idea that the anger the patient cannot allow herself to direct at her husband may be an important source of the eruptions with her son.

Session 4

"I've been feeling so angry!" Adele began to tell me, even before she was seated. "I had a big fight with Ed over how he didn't care what lamps I bought. He wouldn't come to the store to help me choose. He told me just to buy two lamps and get it over with."

Here, I might have detected a hint of anger at me for agreeing to six sessions in which to get the therapy over with, but I did not gather her feelings to myself. I took a back seat. She had a story to tell, and I let her get on with it.

"Ed shouted at me," she said. "He shouted that he was exhausted from traveling and he just wanted to relax with me and Noah. He wanted to go to the park, not the mall. I could see that, but he lives in the house too. I'm trying to get it right so that he likes it too. I really blew up. I just lost it. I told him he couldn't leave all the making of the home to me. He looked really surprised at my outburst. Then he said quietly that I was right. He would look at the lamps with me on Sunday if we could have Saturday for play.

"I felt so much better. I used to think that if I was angry at the situation and at Ed it was unjustified. I saw it as equivalent to blaming him. We talked and talked. We talked about how I could not feel things if they were unjustified and he told me that he had already guessed that I was mad anyway. He said that he could see I was angry and why wouldn't I be, with two moves in two years and a child to manage while he was traveling.

"I've calmed down a good deal. I'm yelling at Noah a lot less. In a week I'll spank him no more than once, and that's usually a spontaneous reaction, not a big punishment."

I felt relieved that Adele's husband was able to respond to her direct anger, and she was able to stop displacing so much onto her son. But she was still spanking him, and by now he was probably accustomed to presenting himself as a blameworthy object to her. There was still a way to go in showing her that she saw in Noah the angry part of herself.

In this session, the work of the previous sessions bears fruit and is confirmed. Adele has made the links herself and so there is less interpretive work for Dr. Scharff to do. Centering on the symptomatic focus has produced considerable symptomatic relief for the moment. As the patient anticipates the imminent loss of the therapy, however, we expect that she may experience an increase in anxiety (which often brings back the symptomatic behavior), and the therapist should have this in mind when facing the last two sessions.

Session 5

Adele came in looking much brighter, wearing strikingly beautiful silver earrings that did indeed complement her skin tone. She began by referring to them, saying "I remembered the conversation about your silver ring the first therapy session and then I felt like wearing these earrings. It's the second last session today."

"Next week is the final session," I agreed, maintaining the brief therapy focus on ending.

"Don't say that," she chided me.

I felt that perhaps she was right in correcting me. I knew to keep the end in focus, but was I overstating the boundaries of the therapy contract because of anxiety about its brevity? Was I escaping the stress of the second last session and the mountain of work remaining by invoking the terminal session? Was I rushing forward to the termination to avoid the slow process of separating? It had been a loss for me to agree to a brief therapy format in the first place, but having made the contract, I was enjoying the work, including the ease of not getting embroiled in long-term dynamics. I would miss her.

She went on: "Don't say 'the final session' like that. I like coming here. It makes me feel better. I get to talk as much as I like and it's just for me. It's better to understand how I feel and then I talk to my husband about it. It's not just what I've lost that made me lose control of myself. I've been reflecting on what we came back to. We came back to where it all happened—where my father and his mother died and Ed lost his old job in the transfer. No wonder it got me down."

I too was reflecting on what she had come back to, beyond her life in the local area. She had also returned to the world of therapy where personal exploration hurts before it heals. I was glad to hear that she had been able to stay with these thoughts.

"I've thought a lot about our moves and losses, and I've talked them over with Ed," she went on. "Now I feel much perkier, more on the ground. I'm going to a show for the children and then I'm hosting a dinner for the grown-ups at the school. I selected the menu from old family recipes and I'm not changing my mind once. It won't be gourmet, it won't take a lot of time, but they're going to love it."

I noted with some ambivalence that she did not stay with her mourning for long. On the plus side, I was pleased that her improvement was confirming that six sessions was plenty. On the negative side, I was missing the opportunity for more thorough work on how to tolerate and express her sad and angry feelings. I looked for a way to acknowledge the positive aspects of moving on without agreeing to a manic closure.

"It's not perfect, any more than life is, but you know it's good enough and feel confident that they'll like it," I said. "And it still leaves you time to enjoy the show and be with the children. That's a sign of progress for you, so why would you be warning me not to remind you that we are close to the last session?" I asked.

"I'm reporting progress and I'm happy, but in a way I'm sad," she said. "I like coming here and I'll miss talking to you. I've really accomplished something here. I learned so much thinking back about that period in Wyoming and why I missed those friends so much. I know now it was because I leaned on them to lift my spirits. I had so much depression there from feeling dragged about and from losing my father and Ed's mother, and the job, and the hometown, and the house. I couldn't get going. I couldn't decorate the house either. The depression was pervasive and kept me from making a decision. My normally compulsive self wanted to hurry up and get it behind me, but my other side couldn't get to first base. The only jobs I got done were the ones that Ed did with me. I'm not worried now about making him help me choose. Matter of fact I'm not worried about getting the house completely decorated at all. I just take it bit by bit and get it done by myself. That's progress."

"You're feeling more confident, independent, relaxed and still efficient," I commented. "Saving your time for what?"

"To read the newspaper, put my feet up, play with Noah. I fixed the hose. I've always thought that was the man's job and Ed was home. But he prioritizes, and if he's putting his feet up he's not going to fix anything. He works and I'm at home, so I fixed it. Then I put my feet up and didn't try to do more. But I must admit it's on my nerves the way he sits there waiting to be fed. I complain about it and usually he dismisses it, but last night I pursued it and gave him examples he couldn't refute. I said, 'You're living the husband of twenty-five years ago today, like your mother waited on your father hand and foot.' He said, 'I've raised three kids, I've done that, and remember I told you with Noah you'd have to do it by yourself.' I said, 'Look at the other husbands. Just because they work they are not exempt.' He'll be waiting for me to get in the car. I'm still packing Noah's backpack and trying to find his shoes. What's to stop Ed helping instead of complaining that I'm not ready?"

I said, "You and Ed are at different life phases, and so your priorities are different. But now you are dealing openly with your resentment which was fueling your difficulty in dealing with Noah."

"That's terrible, but yes that's it. Still today, Ed admitted it. What a great breakthrough. He says he wants to help in the house. I'm happy, so now our relationship can be really great."

The therapist has the ending in mind throughout the therapy. In this session, therapist and patient are not far apart on the need to mourn the therapy and to put it in context. Adele solidifies the progress on her symptomatic focus, and documents the behavioral changes that were propelled by the dynamic work. She has been able to apply with her family what she has learned in the relationship with Dr. Scharff. Progress on tolerating being alone and enjoying being self-sufficient is promoted by mourning the loss of the therapeutic relationship. As Dr. Scharff silently lets go of her wish that Adele could be available for more intensive therapy, Adele voices her regrets and her satisfactions about the therapy in a forthright way that echoes her new ability to discuss her feelings with her husband.

Session 6

The final session did not seem unbearable after all. Adele no longer seemed sad about leaving me, and I found that I was ready for her to be on her way.

"I'm ready to do this on my own now," Adele began confidently. "I don't know why I'm acting and feeling different. I know we've talked about the reasons, but still it's a surprise. The times I feel dragged down are fewer and farther between. I feel optimistic, energetic, and enthusiastic. I didn't feel that way. I was just doing things on my lists. Now I'm excited about the holidays and I feel very good about that.

"I had another chat with Ed about his noninvolvement and my resentment. He resisted at first, but he came back to it and asked for examples. He thought that I'd painted a realistic picture and did not realize that his behaviors made him seem uninvolved to me. He says that he is involved, wants to be involved and, now that he sees it really matters to me, he will do the helpful things I long for. He says not wanting to help in the house was not because he's finished with raising children. It's because he's 59, he's worried about losing another job and not getting hired again. The economy is terrible and the Iraqi problem is affecting his business. Sales are down, his division quotas are down, and he's overworking and traveling to all the stores around the country in the hope he can fix it. He's acting about work like I used to and in those days he had to call me and tell me to come home. Since that talk, he's really been participating and I've been appreciating it. I had felt that it was such a gift that I was at home while he was working that I felt I could not complain. Since that chat, he's cut down on his traveling, we're together more, and Noah feels so loved. The photographer for the family holiday photo said that he just exudes personality and happiness.

"Overworking and putting up with things just doesn't get you what you want. You get it by speaking up and sharing," she concluded.

As she prepared to take her leave, Adele added in a tone of acceptance and determination, "What it was all about is this: Ed and I got married late in life and we only have half a life to be together in."

Although Adele was confident and committed to making it work, I felt suddenly scared. The death of her parents had been a reminder to Adele of the reality of mortality. Her older husband was closer to it than she was. She must be terrified of losing him too. Adele's six sessions were not even half of what she was used to in therapy, but she made the most of it. I now understood that the time pressure that dictated the brief therapy format was not only the stated one of Noah's urgent need for a reasonable mother. Adele's awareness of the death of parents and the limits to life with her husband led her to choose a treatment format that emphasized learning to make the most of a time-limited opportunity.

In the area of the symptomatic focus, learning to confront Ed directly had helped him with his anxiety and relieved her symptom of yelling at Noah. Now in the area of the dynamic focus, we understood that Adele's impatience and unexpressed anger with her husband, which was landing on her son, was a distorted form of sadness about the loss she had to take in having only "half a life" with Ed and their child. Mourning what might have been in the here-and-now of the therapy and in the there-and-then of her life as a child, as a dislocated married woman, and as an unsupported harried mother, was connected in the final session with the there-and-now, and the there-and-yet-to-be of her current life situation as a woman who had married late, had a child with an older man, and had experienced the death of parents.

Subsequent Brief Therapy

Six years later, Adele returned to see me at Ed's request, because he found her to be too controlling, too entitled to his support, too preoccupied with their child, and too little concerned for him. He had had to take a lower-paying job than others he had been offered so as to keep the family in the area and avoid travel. He had begun to worry about retirement and he was furious that Adele had not yet returned to work, as most of their women friends in business had done.

Adele said she loved her mothering role. She cooked, decorated, volunteered at her son's school, and helped him to overcome his learning disability. Ed had also been attentive to their son, but now he was easily irritated by his noisy protests and stubborn refusals, and Adele had been giving the boy more attention than before. Ed felt that Adele was not attending to him as a wife should, because she was busy with their son and because she also liked to have time alone to read the paper rather than watch television with him. Always the one with the stronger sex drive, Ed had suddenly gone on a sex strike. It seemed incomprehensible at the time, but by now Adele had come to see it as a way of his insisting that she should become independent of him, his love, his sexuality, and his dwindling income. While in a state of worry, unhappiness, and self-imposed sexual deprivation, Ed had had a heart attack that required bypass surgery—for all of which he held Adele responsible. He asked her to see me to learn to stop being so controlling of him and to get her back to work to relieve the family stress. Clearly Ed had faced a major blow to his vitality, but he refused treatment for himself.

Again Adele wanted brief therapy, but this time she could not say how long it would take, because she could not say how long it would be before her husband would be fit enough to work on things with her. Perhaps he never would. To reduce the stress on him, she arranged therapy for her son to help him avoid upsetting his father, and to help him tolerate her gradually separating herself from him. She thoughtfully reorganized Ed's family environment and nursed him to recovery in a loving and supportive way. I was impressed at how well she managed to put up with Ed's continuing withdrawal, to remain committed despite his rejection of her efforts to make up with him, and eventually to encourage him to enjoy lovemaking again. She began to interview for part-time jobs, and told me that she felt hopeful about continued improvement. It took seven sessions to arrive at this point, and she decided that the next session would be her last.

She brought Ed with her to the final session. He looked fit, wearing new clothes she had helped him buy, and he was pleased with the effects on Adele of her talking to me. He reported that she was much less controlling and less stubborn about refusing to work. He was delighted that she was so much better. I felt that Adele's optimism was justified. I thought that her limited goals had been met, and I felt fine about her decision to terminate.

Then Ed threw me by reasserting his position in terms that were unexpected and painful to hear, after what he had been saying. He calmly stated that he had not softened his resolve to stay remote from Adele. He had stared mortality in the face and he now saw his marriage as a stressor and even a mortal threat. It was time for Adele to take over the financial burden of the family. I tried to work with his worries, to understand his need for self-protection, and to remind him of the healing effect of love. Even though they might have sex, he said, it would just be to satisfy her needs, he insisted, not to rebuild their relationship. He did not want to be married any more, and he would stay in the house with her purely to share expenses and keep the family together. Ed was intransigent. His fear of death had led to a rigid defense of avoiding the integration of sex, love, and commitment.

Six years ago when Adele had been so enraged by Ed's entitlement to sit back at home, she expressed her views and he changed. But his previous entitlement was nothing compared to his present demand to be left alone to rest in peace. Instead of anger, Adele now felt compassion and a deep sense of sadness and hopelessness about changing his fixed ideas, and yet her loving commitment to Ed kept her in place, working and hoping that she could save her marriage. "I know what to do, I know how to do it, and I will have to do it without Ed," she said. "He won't let therapy help him, I can't do therapy for him, and therapy has already got me to where I want to be. You can't help me any more."

What a painful position Adele was in, and what a lot of work she faced in persuading Ed of the value of re-creating their relationship. She acknowledged that she could not control Ed's fears or his decision, that she was the only one willing to work on the marriage, and that she might have to raise their child alone. But, since she knew what to do and had the skills to do it, Adele felt that she was back on track, ready to manage her life without further therapy. Therapist and patient both felt that the eight-session therapy had given the patient the fortitude and ability to do the best she could in managing an extremely difficult time in her life.

This example of serial brief therapy lets us see how the therapeutic relationship persists over time as a resource to return to. It reminds us that success at one stage may be challenged at another. Therapy, brief or long-term, cannot protect against future life events or control for psychological change in the external object. So the long-term perspective of serial brief therapy brings humility. It offers the therapist a rich, but bittersweet, opportunity of watching the progression of development as the person moves through the life cycle, and of intervening with more advanced skills and greater experience in each successive treatment.

19

Brief Therapy instead of Long-Term Therapy

In this example, brief therapy functions as a bounded piece of therapy with limited goals and as a trial of therapy on which to base a decision regarding further long-term therapy. Susan consulted Dr. Jill Scharff for assessment and referral for analytic therapy but chose brief therapy instead.

Susan, the 34-year-old American wife of an international development official, was back in the United States for a two-year tour. At previous postings abroad she had tried individual counseling, marital therapy, and medication with various antidepressants and sedatives to relieve her symptoms of anxiety and depression. The supportive therapies, focused on the realities of her life and her marriage, had felt gratifying with her warm and friendly counselor, and various medication combinations had been tried, but no real change had occurred. She looked forward to returning to the United States, to being back in a close relationship with her mother again, and to being in a culture where she could get analytically oriented therapy.

After years of living abroad, she returned to her homeland with relief and good intentions, and was devastated when her longed-for mother unexpectedly died before she got home to see her. Her depression intensified and she lost the momentum to organize a therapeutic consultation until she came to see me almost a year after her return to the United States.

Susan told me that since her mother's death, she was more aware than ever of the lack of emotional engagement in her marriage. As a mother herself, Susan was devoted to her 4- and 6-year-old daughters, as her mother had been to her and her sister, but she felt that she was too dependent on them for love and admiration. As a wife, she felt that she was a good, practical partner, except when she forgot things. She appreciated the security of her husband's commitment to her, but she longed for a less utilitarian arrangement. Her sex life was nonexistent, and she felt unable to speak to her husband or her friends about it. She was increasingly tearful, and she was waking early in the morning. She had no confidence in herself, her appearance as a young woman, or her work as a writer of short stories and songs. She was fretting over her creative productions and judging them so harshly that she could not submit them for publication. Her self-esteem was rock bottom. But the worst problem was with her memory and her thinking: she was forgetting appointments and information, and she experienced herself as wordless, even though she had a degree in literature.

Susan consulted me for assessment and recommendation for analytic therapy, but her husband's agency would provide reimbursement for only six sessions of therapy, and she imagined that she would not feel entitled to pay for more out of her husband's paycheck.

The Assessment

Susan, a tiny, mouselike woman with gorgeous, black curly hair told me she had married her husband while both were foreign students at a French university, she from the United States and he from Mauritius. As a student of French, she understood it perfectly but had great difficulty speaking the language. Speaking to me in her mother tongue, she had a soft, hesitant voice, but her words had the power to evoke images clearly, sensitively, and evocatively. Still she felt dumb, weak, and self-conscious with me, as she had as a student, despite getting top grades. Everyone else seemed so self-assured, including her future husband with whom she spent a lot of time. He rescued her from her insecurity, because he seemed so sure of everything, including assuming that they would be married. He gave her self-confidence: she gave him sensitivity. Sex was always disappointing, but she put it down to her inexperience and pretended that it was fine, hoping that it would become so eventually. When she became pregnant on the IUD soon after marriage, her husband had known immediately that she needed an abortion and arranged it for her. She regretted it, but she knew that he was right. She preferred to think of her husband as "right" and herself as "wrong," so that she remained dependent on him for direction and validation. She had never had a job and had not earned any money from her writing.

Susan described the cultural and gender differences in her marriage first. "My husband always seems so sure about what's right. He convinces me and I go along with it," Susan explained. "Now I see that he's full of hot air, but I never say so. If I left him, I would have no place to be, and he would keep the children. He doesn't want divorce, because it would be embarrassing to him and his family. They are a prominent Catholic family in Mauritius. So we go along in a secure marriage, working partners, raising two children, but he's not emotionally engaged. I'm dramatic, sentimental, and demonstrative, and he just can't provide the affection I want. I pretend it's fine, but I really wish we had an affectionate and physical relationship. I'm close to my daughters, too close, just like my mother who didn't divorce my father, but stayed in a separate room in the same house and lived through me and my sister."

Susan then went on to talk about her learning difficulties. "I'm a totally disorganized person," she said. "I have a terrible memory and I forget everything. I forgot about this appointment with you and so I agreed to keep a child for a friend. I remembered just in time, so then I had to let her down. When I'm being given information, I get nervous and I can't take anything in. Then if I'm asked, I can't say anything. I used to be chatty until I was 6 and we had to move to Kansas, supposedly for a year. We stayed for twenty-five years—always thinking it was just temporary. So in school, I never settled in and I didn't do wonderfully. I'm bad at generalizing and following big concepts. They stop at my eyes and don't go into my mind. It's a processing problem and it shows up when I'm putting out information too. Like in my writing, I could never sustain a lengthy novel. I couldn't hold a narrative together. So, I'm a short story writer. I'm best at libretto. Songs can be distracted. You just put odd things together. I'm not in them."

Then Susan talked about her family.

"My father is a nice man. He was a traveling salesman and an unpublished writer. He was often away and he said very little when he was there. He was an alcoholic, but never mean. He was a quiet drunk, with a good sense of humor. Our mother was a crier, often upset. She was our best friend. She was always there, thought my songs and stories were wonderful. Loved to listen to me sing them. My father was just not around, except on vacation. He was great then. He's a nice man, has a great relationship with my children. My sister is an angry person, confrontational. But not me. I was always trying to go along, make things all right."

After this assessment session, it was clear to me that Susan needed psychometric testing to measure and explore the constitutional or affective sources of her processing problem and memory impairment. One of her children had a documented learning disability, and this made it likely that Susan's difficulty in learning was also constitutional and that tutoring might prove helpful for her. I did not recommend psychoanalysis because Susan could only count on being in Washington for one year. In view of the failure of previous therapies, she really needed intensive therapy and maybe marital therapy as well, but I realized that she might refuse either recommendation for financial reasons, as a cover for her ambivalence about therapy and her perception of herself as unworthy to have what she needed.

Susan welcomed the idea of psychometric testing, which was separately covered by her insurance, and she promptly arranged to meet with the psychologist that I recommended. She could not work with her husband in marital therapy, because he was not willing to do that again. As expected, Susan did not want to invest money in intensive therapy. But her reluctance went deeper than that. She did not want low-fee psychotherapy which I offered to arrange for her with a well-trained therapist in training at the clinic so that she could afford almost a year of sessions out of pocket. Susan chose to have brief therapy at my fee, even though it would not be covered in full, but she limited the contract to the six sessions for which she could expect some reimbursement. The goals we agreed on were:

1. To explore her memory and thinking problems with me while she also underwent psychological testing with a colleague;
2. To experience her feelings about her marriage and her work;
3. To mourn the loss of her mother and think about her relationship with her father;
4. To see how much of this could be accomplished in six sessions of brief psychoanalytically oriented therapy with me;
5. To explore her motivation for, and reluctance to afford, more intensive treatment if that should indeed be necessary.

Just as Susan's husband had rescued her from feeling insecure by his certainty about what was good for her, Dr. Scharff thought that Susan should have intensive therapy. But she did not push her point of view. As with Adele in Chapter 18, Dr. Scharff accepted the limitations of the patient's willingness to invest in long-term therapy. Susan used the insurance company's six-session limit as a vehicle for expressing the limitations that she puts on her self and her objects. In brief therapy the symptomatic focus will be on her memory and learning difficulties, on her unhappiness in her marriage, and on her way of being mean to herself. Susan's inability to plan for and spend the money for a longer therapy, even at a low fee, was part of the problem of not investing in herself and not feeling that she deserved more. She was intent on limiting the usefulness of her therapist as an object, and maybe even of defeating her rather than get something worthwhile from her. The dynamic focus should explore Susan's unconscious determination to define her self and its potential by the limitations and constraints of the external object (her father, her husband, her therapist) and the damaged self (the learning and memory disability).

Session 1

Susan had been feeling preoccupied and embarrassed since our last meeting in which she talked about sex. She was wondering what I was thinking about her and feeling vulnerable because she had admitted her interest in a better sex life. Accustomed and resigned to her husband's way of praising her faintly, as in his saying "You're not that fat," she had been overcome at the grocery store when the store manager said "Hi, nice to see you again. You've got such great hair!" She went into the vegetable section and cried.

I thought that Susan was telling me of her appreciation for my interest and her hope that I might see some worth in her, as the vegetable man had. I felt hopeful that taking in experiences like this could modify her self-esteem and free her from depending only on negative feedback from her husband.

Having told me of being validated, she took charge of the session and went on to describe her learning problems more fully. "Getting back to why I came here," she said. "My memory is shot. I forget which side of the road to drive on. Last night suddenly I was thinking I had already turned off the road. Things drop out of my head. To remember to come here I have to have an elaborate system of signs. I forgot to go to a luncheon last week. The hostess called me and I had no idea what she was talking about. I once forgot to pick up my daughter. It's not new, but it's worse and worse. Since

I started a reading seminar, I find that I don't just forget parts of the book I've read. I forget I've read it. I can't keep my attention on the work. My hand is writing and my brain is not on it."

This sounded like a dissociative phenomenon to me and I asked, "Does it seem so unfamiliar that someone else might have been writing?"

"Yes, someone else could have written it, but I still believe it's me. It's embarrassing to forget things I've talked about before."

"You don't forget what we've talked about here," I noted.

"No, I think about this a lot," she agreed. "I remember metaphor better than actual ideas." She fingered a small ring on her right hand.

Immediately I wondered what the ring meant.

"I found this ring in a Mauritian bazaar," she said. "I had wanted one like it when I was a teenager but I hadn't bought it. A few years ago when we were visiting my in-laws, I bought this for myself. My counselor said that it was nice that I had bought something for myself and I started to cry. I have a thing about having objects as metaphors for my troubles. I collect boxes to keep things contained and held together."

But a deeper metaphor was now to emerge.

"My mother collected jewelry," she went on to say. "She was really good at going to flea markets and finding good stuff. I'd go with her and I start-ed collecting commemorative medals. Like I was trying to be self-congratulatory. A lot of the clothes I wear are her cast-offs, but lately I've been buying myself some new clothes, but always cheap things. And I'm buying this therapy which is not cheap, but I'm buying only a small amount of it, because I feel guilty using my husband's agency's money for some-thing that may lead to a way of leaving him. Right now I don't have any image of the future. I don't have any image of me on my own, or me with the girls, me with a job, me as capable, or me as the wife giving dinner parties."

Susan used the last ten minutes of the session to describe her marital unhappiness. I had to interrupt to say, "Time to finish."

"Sorry," she said. "I'm so sorry." Head down, she scuttled toward the door, looking upset, and muttering apologies. She looked pathetic, like a child who has been scolded.

"Wait," I said. "Sorry for what?"

"Taking too much time," she replied. "My demands are limitless."

We had run over by fifty seconds, hardly a big dent in the frame, and certainly not one of her making. "You took the time I set aside for you," I said. "I decide the exact moment of finishing here."

Susan cried like a miserable child.

I thought that she was guilty about being greedy, and I wondered if there might be unconscious reasons for guilt, having to do with the way she had treated her objects in earlier life, or now, or in her imagination. But we were past our time boundary, so I simply said, "One extra minute won't make a difference. Look, we're considering whether six sessions can do it. If they can't, we'll have to see whether that's because your demands are limitless, or because the limit of six sessions makes them seem so."

In this first session after assessment, Susan expresses her incompetence, neediness, and attachment to her mother. She has an immediate, strongly positive contextual transference to Dr. Scharff. With her assumption that the therapist will provide contextual holding, she pours out the hidden contents of her unhappiness into the space between herself and her therapist, filling the potential space between them. As a result, Dr. Scharff appreciates the need for love that has led Susan to cry when strangers compliment her, feels the neglect and rejection she experiences from her husband, and senses a hint of unconscious guilt. Now the question becomes, "How much of this rejecting object experience is externally imposed by an actually rejecting external object who has no interest in changing himself, and how much does Susan induce the limitations in him through projective identification?"

Session 2

"I'm sorry about the way I left," Susan began, obviously remembering the main point of the last session. "I'm very grateful for this time and I'm so aware of it ticking past. I'm glad my husband won't come, because I like having this for myself, and I am not giving this up. I'm feeling braver because of being here."

"Braver, but sorry about being sorry," I added.

"Yes, I'm sorry about being sorry, because saying I'm in the wrong is my way of avoiding being envied for being powerful and getting what I want."

I remembered how in the last session I had been struck by the pathetic quality of her apology, and I was struck now by how empowered she was to claim her right to therapy. I felt relieved that she had found her voice and was proving to be adept at saying what she was thinking. Her level of trust in me was increasing.

Susan continued to describe herself at length without any prompting or comment from me. She concluded by saying, "Being conceited is the worst thing. I sing my songs too fast or too slow or too deadpan, so as to demean them. If someone says 'I like that,' I say, 'It's better than the first draft.' It's real, real hard for me to say 'I like it,' but I do think it's good, I do. I just don't think anyone else will think so. That's why I can't send anything out to a publisher. They'll think my songs are mundane. Like my dreams. They are very realistic, boring, and too real. It's like I do at night in my dreams all the stuff I can't get done during the day."

I said that I'd be interested to hear any of her dreams because we could learn more from them than was apparent on the surface.

Susan demonstrates that within the limits she has set, she can make therapy a space she can use, but she fills the space with her self observed in the there-and-now, rather than producing material for joint consideration. We note that Dr. Jill Scharff fails to connect ruining the songs with spoiling therapy and has little to say about her own experience of the patient, and so we might guess that she is not yet aware enough of the limitation on her containing function to draw Susan toward examining the transference.

Here we can differentiate between the *holding* and *containing* functions of the transference. The contextual holding is fine: Susan trusts Dr. Scharff enough to bring out new and painful material which is full of affect. But the containment is going less well; there is not enough evidence of therapeutic processing to transform unmanageable anxiety, which sits between patient and therapist like floodwater. Whether the therapist can use her capacity to contain and transform the unmetabolized material will have to be seen in future sessions. The dynamic focus will have to include asking a question: Will there be enough recovery in the therapist's capacity to process and review the experience so that she can share it with the patient and give her an experience of containing function with which she can identify within the time the patient has allowed?

Session 3

Susan began by describing the first session of the psychometric test experience with the psychologist whom she had liked. She gave more examples of her loss of memory, emphasizing one she had forgotten telling me already: having taken notes from a book she was reading for the reading seminar, she found that she had already taken the same notes before and

had no memory of having done it the first time. I wondered what this symptom might mean. The dissociative quality of this remarkable memory lapse
raised the possibility that a traumatic event was being relived, though
memory of it was erased. I wondered silently if there had been sexual abuse.
I asked if there had been an earlier abortion, but there had not. I wondered
if she was working in fantasy on a second marriage, as if the first had not
happened. Susan did not think so. She thought it was simply a consequence
of her preoccupation with other issues.

My attempts to link this peculiar experience to unconscious determinants
happened to be wrong, but Susan was not helping me out. She was blocking the making of links in the session, as she did in her mind.

Susan moved on to tell me what she called a typically utilitarian dream
that she had had the previous week.

> I was in the Smithsonian gift shop with other shoppers comparing prices. I
> don't know what I was shopping for. There was nothing else to it. Just me
> and the other shoppers.

*I associated silently to the Smithsonian sticker on my car and to her buying
my services without shopping around for the best price.*

"But after I had that totally boring dream, then I had another that was unusual for me," she said.

> I dreamed I was in an airport inside the covered tunnel for entering the plane.
> The plane was a space shuttle and I'd be there for fifteen years. It was really
> short and that was it. Just me, standing there in these aluminum walls.

"How could I stand to be there fifteen years?" Susan asked. "I guess it
stands for my marriage and I don't want to go on like that. I was reminded
of *The Andromeda Strain* that I saw with my husband and *Star Wars* that I
watch with my kids. The door to the shuttle was a sliding door to close
everything off. The space shuttle's been on the news a lot."

I thought of the sliding door to the outside of my office, and thought
that her dream was referring to being trapped not just in a marriage, but
in a therapy capsule. "This dream suggests that you are thinking about a
repair mission," I said. "And . . ."

*I had been about go on and be more specific about my evidence from her
associations when Susan suddenly associated to another dream, so I kept quiet.*

I felt that it was a good sign that she was able to allow her mind to make links today.

"One time I had a dream about my mother. It connects to the first dream about the Smithsonian.

We met in a museum, went to the gift shop and then had lunch. It was Heaven, literally, and the food was really good, but the prices were really high.

"It's funny, if there were a gift shop in Heaven that's where she'd be!" said Susan. She began to cry, thinking fondly of her mother and missing her.

"But the Smithsonian dream was very utilitarian. Just me and the other shoppers," she repeated.

When she linked the dreams by association, I felt connected to their unconscious meaning.

"So your apparently utilitarian dream now reveals to us your search for your mother," I said. "More than that, it recalls the consultation in which you shop for therapy. It leads you to the short tunnel in the short dream that stands for this brief therapy that may however lead to a dreaded fifteen years in intensive therapy if you are closed in by the sliding door— and as you can see there is a sliding glass door here in the office."

"And I thought I wasn't thinking about it because I have a paper due for the reading seminar!" Susan said thoughtfully. Now aware that it was the end of the hour, she reached into her purse for her driving glasses and said as an aside, "I've tried to use contact lenses, one for distance and one for close-up, but I can't suppress one eye image, or else I can't integrate both images, I'm not sure which it is." As if her next comment was unrelated, Susan remarked, apparently returning to the theme before leaving her session, "You think there is nothing there, and then you see all these connections!"

At first, Susan rejects Dr. Scharff's attempts to make links between her surface content and underlying dynamics, and then presents a dream that she insists is banal, as if to denude it of relevance. Nevertheless, Susan is able to put her dreams together. She gives additional dream material that links the next dream to the earlier isolated dreams and conveys to Dr. Scharff their latent content. Dr. Scharff makes an interpretation of their dynamic meaning in the transference, which Susan accepts thoughtfully. Then Susan makes a dynamic comment of her own about her difficulty in maintaining the dual focus that she wants, both up-close and distant. This recalls the duality of focus that we aim for in therapy, and we have seen that it is indeed difficult for her to look beyond the there-and-now. The therapist has been unconsciously identified with this unseeing part of the patient's self, but the dream material and the patient's newfound willingness to make links allows the therapist to understand her reluctance about therapy here and now, and in the future where it could go on and on like her longing.

Session 4

"I've completed the psychometric testing," Susan began. "The doctor says that I do not have a constitutional defect. Believe it or not, the tests show that my intelligence is in the very superior range, so I'm not as dumb as I thought. My memory and processing problems are all due to depression."

With new confidence, Susan set about using her intelligence to address her problem about not thinking or remembering anything worthwhile to say. "I realized that I didn't always use to be this way. So I've been thinking about when I lost my voice, or if I've really lost it. I wrote a series of songs about the translations of certain words. A friend arranged the songs together in an album under the title "Finding a Woman's Voice" and I liked her idea. The interesting thing was she had arranged them in the reverse chronological order of their writing. Like I have to go backwards to find my voice.

"Then I thought of times I lost it because of things my husband said. Like the time I told him I was upset with my previous therapist who was so warm and fuzzy and really messed me up. My husband said, 'No, you were always messed up.' What else could I say?

"Then he knows I've lost a check from my mother's estate. I keep thinking I'll find it in a drawer somewhere, but it never shows up. He waits until we're in the middle of a dinner party and asks me about it in front of all these people. I just ran from the room. Then there was the time right after we were married, I got pregnant on the IUD. The doctor advised abortion and I agreed it was best but I was so upset. I tried to talk to him about it and he said, 'Oh that's a shame that the IUD didn't work. You're not ready to be a mother yet.'"

Susan was sobbing. "I can't tell you the whole story of the pregnancy and the abortion, because now I've forgotten it," she said. "Now, if ever I speak to my husband, I babble and he'll only half listen."

"This gives us a clue to your losing your voice," I said.

I was thinking of the devastating impact of the husband's response to the woman's telling him that she is pregnant with their child. Susan had repressed her hurt too thoroughly to get it back, at least for now. But it was another pregnancy that was the real trauma, as she now revealed through her associations, the one that preceded the birth of her sister.

"It goes back before that," she said. " I often wish I could take things back, so as not to feel embarrassed. Like with my sister, I used to tell her things and she'd not listen or she'd get angry. I had to remind myself, 'I mustn't think I'm her friend. Having a nice time with her will never happen.' My sister and I get along okay now because my husband has substituted now as the selfish person I have to live with." After a moment's reflection, Susan noted, "I'm jumping around a lot. Is this the way I'm supposed to do this? Is this what you want me to do?" she asked again.

I had been feeling pleased that Susan was making links for herself, and was following along. Suddenly my concentration was broken, as she interrupted herself. In the here-and-now I was experiencing the dynamic process in which she blocked her own thinking, and I had an idea why it had happened.

I said, "I note that you are trying to be unselfish and to keep me and my needs in mind here so that neither one of us becomes like your sister."

"Yes, I'm always trying to make the other person comfortable, but my husband says that I'm just trying to make a good impression. With my sister I couldn't bear any kind of conflict, even though she doesn't mind it at all. In fact she's quite confrontational."

I was sure that her husband had a point, but his was not the only correct assessment of her motivation. I wanted to hear more of her view of the prototype sibling relationship and to experience it in the transference.

I said, "Sure, there is an upside and a downside to your ability to avoid conflict. There seem to be a lot of difficult feelings about your sister."

"My mother was so in love with her children, she thought we were in love with each other too. She says I was delighted with Sara arriving. The family story is that my first sentence was 'What about Sara?' She says I was crazy about her when she was 2 and 3 years old, and that we only had problems when we were old enough to have opinions. With my own children and friends' children, I've seen the eldest be overly enthusiastic about the baby they really want to throw out the window. I know now that I had that level of anger about her, and now I'm trying to admit it. I'm trying to admit that I have anger. I certainly sound angry after I leave here.

"All the way home in the car, I swore at myself for monopolizing the conversation. It felt a terrible thing to have done. You hardly had a chance to say anything. 'Fucking stupid bitch,' the voice in my head was saying. 'Why can't you shut up?' I actually pointed a finger as a gun at my head. I was beside myself."

"What did the voice sound like?" I asked, wondering if this was the voice of an internal object that we could recognize.

"The opposite of my voice," she said. "I never swear like that. It wasn't anybody's voice."

"What occurs to you about the voice?" I persisted.

"My father might have sworn when he was drunk. At himself," she added. "I imagine he was in a state of quiet desperation."

"About what?" I asked.

"I don't know, I don't know," she cried. A long silence followed.

"Your first response to my question about your dad's pain is to lose your voice. There is something here that you can't bear to hear or tell."

"I don't understand it," she said. "I always thought of him as a nice, quiet man, even a quiet drunk. He never yelled at me, but now I remember he was really abusive to himself. I remember one time he was cursing and swearing at himself because his life was so complicated and he was no good at it. I was in the doorway heading for another room, and I heard it all the way from there and in the next room. I never thought of this at all before now. I love words. They are very powerful for me and I'm afraid of them as well.

"I've been very nervous this week about my presentation for the reading seminar. Two other women had to share the assignment with me, and we worked out who was responsible for what. I told them I was afraid I would dry up—and I did. I couldn't say more. The other two filled in for me, and then I could chime in again. I've been wary of losing my voice all week. I feel like I'm running in an alley full of snipers and my objective is to get out as fast as I can."

"Your associations have taken you to the scene of three women being close and helping each other. It is reminding me of the threesome of your mother, your sister, and you, where you could not be as angry or as assertive as you might have been, but hung close together, perhaps to exclude your father."

"We certainly did," Susan nodded. "We excluded him. We blocked him out. The anger I heard from him, I blocked out until today. His was the only anger I saw and it was hidden and directed only at himself."

I said, "You directed his kind of anger at yourself in the form of a self-demeaning voice to stay close to him in a way that your mother does not know is happening and that I did not know was happening outside the sessions, until you felt able to tell me today."

"I was the one closest to him, more patient with him and more hopeful about him than my mother or sister."

"Your mother was in love with you, you told me," I said. "He must have had some feelings of rage against you and her about that."

"My mother used to say that once you have children there is no point in having a husband. He was 2 percent of her emotional investment. I want it to be different with my husband, but it isn't. He is as angry as my father, but he doesn't drink and so he doesn't ever show it. But I feel it as his coldness, which he denies, and which makes me feel terrible."

"So you go through life silently angry at and guilty about your husband's withdrawal that is somewhat like your father's, and you sense your husband's unspoken anger at your preoccupation with your children, which ties in to your father's anger at you and your mother. And you feel worse and worse."

"I do," she said. "Unless I sweep it all under the rug and say that not having much of a relationship is what being married is about. When I feel better is when I have a triumph of expression outside the family."

As we saw in the previous session, Susan's dense repression of the angry demeaning of her capacities had gotten into Dr. Scharff where it inhibited her thinking too. Dream work in the previous session fostered the emerging capacity for linking, and now in this session, patient and therapist recover their voices and their capacities to think together about her internalization of her father's self as an internal object and her projection of this object into her husband. For the first time, Susan can see how relating to her husband as if he were her envied sister has drawn his contempt toward her. With connections flowing and a state of unconscious communication established and reflected upon, the therapeutic relationship breaches the closed internal system that Susan had managed to maintain until now, and gives her access to old memories and connections that have been buried for her entire life.

This session is the turning point of the therapy. The therapist will be on the lookout for spoiling manic defences or a regression to old ways of splitting and repression.

Session 5

With something resembling a sense of triumph, Susan began by declaring proudly, "I didn't swear all the way home. I feel quite comfortable here today." A moment later, she had to undo her success. "Now I can't think of anything to say!"

This undoing of success was an old habit. I could have interpreted it as her way of preventing my envy, but I felt that she already knew that. She had explored the loss of voice in relation to husband, mother, sister, and ultimately father, and I thought that she would be able to find it again by herself. So I waited.

Susan resumed talking about her father. She concluded, "I have underestimated how much my father has influenced my life. It seems every woman I know had a childhood ruined by her father being critical, abusive, absent, or dead. I didn't have any of that. I had a present absence and it has mattered more than I thought. I never crossed the bridge from my mother to him.

"He quit drinking after my mom died. He's still very quiet and private. He is still hard to talk to, always has a project he's involved in, but he's a nice man, so funny and interesting. He's just not social. You can't chat with him.

"My husband is not very interested in talking. I'll tell him something and he replies but he doesn't really address me. Like the time I said I thought maybe we should split up, all he said was that I'd have to find someone to stay with him in the house to take care of the children. I try to talk and he slams the door.

"As a child, I was in a family that was very physical—lots of hugging and kissing and patting, more than most. I do it with the girls a lot. My husband doesn't like that. We could have sex but not hugging. My husband says kissing is a waste of time. I say without that, without the verbal communication, why bother with sex? It's been three years since we had sex—I won't call it making love—and I feel it is a shameful secret. It hardly seems to bother us. He jokes about it once in a while, but he never approaches me any more. I used to cry all the time, every time we had sex, and it gradually became unbearable."

"Was it pleasurable at one time?" I asked.

"The anticipation was, but I never felt fulfilled. It was so disappointing that gradually the expectation of it was unwelcome too. It was a conjugal duty until it got to be unbearable. I'd rather be in a dentist's chair.

"My previous boyfriend and I kissed a lot and I loved that, but I wasn't serious about him. So when I met my husband, I was excited at the prospect of having sex with someone I was in love with. I thought that the sex didn't go well for me because I was too nervous, too thin, too young, too guilty, or doing it wrong. It was no different when we got married. I always hid my disappointment at the lack of romance and passion. I tried to accept that hugging, touching, and kissing just didn't suit him. I'm slow to come around to things, and he is fast. He walks too fast for me, and he thinks and decides faster than I can. He picks out the important points and he deals with them. It's the same in sex. Get to the point. The act is it. For me, maybe I need a two-hour warmup!"

"You need a daily warmup," I countered. "A daily context of affection."

"That's it, that's it!" she exclaimed. "There is so little affection in him. I try to say this doesn't matter. My parents stopped having sex, so it's part of my expectation. It does matter, but now I don't have enough trust in my husband to break down the barriers I've built up so painfully. I have a loving personality and it's rotten to be so stuck and unable to do anything with it.

"Maybe he and I ended up together because he was so unable to deal with emotion and so he needed someone like me, but I was so sentimental that I needed someone like him to put a check on it."

I was impressed that Susan had described the projective identificatory system of the marriage, but she had not yet understood why her so-called sentimentality might be a feared aspect of herself. I asked about her sexual feelings and masturbatory fantasy.

"I don't masturbate. I wouldn't know how. I do have sexual fantasies, but they're vestigial, like thinking of the thrill of being in the same room with an attractive man, wondering what a professor thinks of me, admiring or being admired. Standing next to someone could be sexual. Subtlety is very sexual to me."

I could see that Susan's sexuality was even more split off and repressed than her anger, and I began to wonder if she had unconsciously used the angry veneer with both her father and her husband to avoid sexuality as a lifelong pattern, perhaps in identification with an avoidance of sexuality in her mother. I felt sad that the limitation in the therapy made it unlikely we would plumb those depths.

I said, "We've got one session left to complete this work and consider whether you want intensive treatment. Do you want to work on recovering your sexual self?"

She replied, "Right now I can't imagine having that level of trust in anybody."

I was relieved to discover the unconscious meaning of choosing a brief therapy contract: it became clear to me that it was a deep fear of unsatisfactory intercourse that led Susan to limit our work to that of a brief attachment. I felt sad for her, and cheated of the chance to make a difference, and at the same time, I felt that the brief format had propelled us through a lot of work to get this far in such a short time.

Manic defenses appeared briefly at the beginning of this session, but then dissolved in favor of further work. The session then picks up where the last one stopped, at the repression of Susan's sexuality and her capacity to make links between ideas. The brief contract ensured that the contextual transference remained positive, by ensuring that it did not last long enough to allow the development of a focused transference in which the therapist would be linked to painful object experience. In the final session, we might expect to see patient and therapist mourn the loss of their brief therapy relationship and the loss of what might have been in life and in therapy, if it were not for the limitations of the patient's trust in her objects to be concerned for her.

Session 6

But the final session did not happen as planned. January snow caused a school closing and Susan was unable to arrange for someone to take her young children for her at the early hour of her appointment. Her husband was traveling. She rescheduled her final session to occur the following week. Later the same week she had taken the children on the train as planned to visit her father at his cabin in Canada for the Martin Luther King Jr. holiday weekend and was snowed in through the next week. The trains were not running and she had not taken a car. She called me to request another rescheduling and offered to pay for the missed two appointments out of pocket. At the same time, she requested an additional session so as to have time for a good ending to the brief therapy which the snow delays had interrupted. I too felt that the flow of the process had been interrupted and I agreed to her request.

Susan arrived for the first of her final two sessions and said that she had two dreams to tell me. She began, "The first occurred while my husband was on his way, when the roads were finally clear enough to drive the car up to join me and the children at my father's for a couple of days and take us home.

It was a fragment of a dream of tearing paper to shreds and banging doors (which I never do).

"Then I had an explicit dream, the day my husband arrived," she went on.

I was in a room with a big picture window. I was with a man. He was naked and I was naked and I was sucking on his penis. He was not anybody I know. It was not thrilling but it was not awful either. I realized people could see us and so we went to another room, but it had picture windows too. We closed the curtains and a lady came in who was like a 1940s movie character, the "millionaire-dressed-up-socialite." (The train we took to my father's place in the mountains had a sleeping car in 1940s style.) She was this man's mother, a brash, Ethel Merman type, really loud. (My high school boyfriend's mother was like that.) Even though we were both nude, we weren't embarrassed. Nothing else happened.

Susan went on to give the daily context for the dreams. She said, "The next day, we had to leave. I stayed at home to clean up and pack the suitcases and my husband took our car and went off at 10:00 A.M. with the children for a couple of hours' skiing. My father stayed to help me and drive me over to the foot of the slopes to join my family about 1:00 P.M. for the drive home. Dad and I were late to meet them, we got there at 2:00 P.M. and they weren't waiting at the foot of the slopes. But we weren't worried. We figured that they had just gone back up in the chairlift for more skiing. After an hour and a half we did get worried.

"At 3:30 P.M. my father decided to drive me home to Washington, even though the trains were running again, because I had ten cases and I couldn't manage them alone on the train. Really, he was taking care of me because

I was so frantic. Twelve hours we were driving with me not knowing what had happened to them, and no one at home was answering the phone.

"It turned out they had left at 1:30 P.M. because they hadn't found me. But I had been there at 2:00 P.M. which wasn't bad since I said I'd be there about 1:00 P.M., by which I meant 1:00 or 2:00 P.M., and he's not an on-the-dot punctual person himself. So why leave without me? He didn't answer the phone, he just went to sleep as soon as he got home and left me a note, assuming that I would get home somehow, sometime. He hadn't even left a message on my father's machine or on our machine after he got home. So I had no idea what was happening until I got home and found the note. It made me so angry. But if I discuss it with him, I'll only lose the argument, so I've not talked to him at all, and I've not slept in the same room either. And I've told the children it's because I'm mad at Daddy.

"This is a big example of what he does in little ways all the time. And it really inconvenienced my father. He was so angry he couldn't say anything, except 'the jerk' and I said 'I need a good divorce lawyer.' He said 'Don't say that' and he shut me up. He didn't want to hear that. We got in at 4:00 A.M. And he wouldn't stay the night. He helped me in with the bags and insisted on driving home immediately. My husband didn't even get out of bed.

"The next day I told my husband that what he had done frightened me. I said I'd been shaking and nauseated and worried that they were dead. He said that he'd been worried about us and thought that we'd had a breakdown. So why did he leave? How could he sleep?

"So the first dream came true. I ripped his note up and threw the shreds on the floor. I slept in the other room."

"I hear how rejected and abandoned you felt, and punished for being only a little late, but I was wondering why you were late," I began.

"Right, I was only a little late, so why didn't he wait?" she interjected. "I had been doing my reading and I left half an hour to pack the car, but it took an hour. We left half an hour late and the drive was longer than my husband had said. At 2:00 P.M. we were at the most an hour late. Since my father would normally be two hours late, we got there an hour early for him. For me, I was the usual amount late."

I felt that Susan was showing me the consequences of her disorganization. I was now more inclined to view her missing of the previous hours as a transference enactment of loss and ambivalence about me in which she hoped that I would be there for her anyway so as to reinforce her feeling justified in condemning him and to deny the role her disorganization played in the family events.

Her husband's indirect expression of anger was so extreme and outrageous, it aroused my sympathy for her and her father, and it could have deflected me from challenging her to look at her role. But the main point was to help her look at her responsibility for her part in the situation.

Before telling me about that incident, she had delivered a dream of frank sexuality, a topic that had previously been completely repressed. Then she had covered that material with such an outrageous story, that it would have been easy to forget the sexual material. So I returned to thinking about her erotic dream concerning the man associated with her high school boyfriend with whom she had enjoyed passionate kissing.

"Did the physical longings you had in your dream leave you feeling uncomfortable when you saw your husband?" I asked. "What had been going on before you were late and he left without you?"

Susan talked about the visit to the mountains without her husband and how it was different with him there. Eventually she reached an insight. "I was angry at him because he'd been away for a while. Also I'd been with my Dad for a while and when I'm there with him I don't feel like a piece of shit any more. I feel entitled to better treatment. I feel I have a right to be angry. When I'm at home with my husband, it's like there is a rock on top of me. Alone at Dad's it's gone, but when my husband's back, it's there."

I said, "You enjoyed being with your father, your self-esteem recovered, your angry feelings returned directly, and your sexual feelings were stirring in your dream, but you don't have a way of discussing them with your husband and so they come out in side ways, like being late."

"Or nasty," she added. "He had driven all that way to get us and I wasn't nice to him. He might have got the idea I'd rather be with my father, so maybe he thought, 'So let him take care of me.'"

Susan defended herself against the emergence of oedipal sexual fantasy shown in the dream she had while with her father by nastiness and rejection of her husband. She splits the there-and-now experience so that her father is the good object and her husband the bad object. She brings her conflict and defensive pattern into the therapy with a here-and-now therapeutic enactment of cancellation which Dr. Scharff deals with differently than the husband dealt with her lateness. The therapist does not precipitously act out but contains the rejection experience and uses it to further exploration and hold out the possibility of an enlarged opportunity for understanding. We can recognize and even feel the transference–countertransference elaboration of her conflict and yet know that we will probably not get to see it through to resolution, at least not for now. More insistent interpretation of the limits that Susan kept imposing might have led her to reconsider the possibility for long-term therapy which we can now clearly see she needs, but she is likely to withdraw in her characteristically defensive way in case the exciting therapy opportunity fails and leaves her guilty and more deeply disappointed.

Session 7

Susan began by acknowledging that this would be our last session. She thought that this brief therapy wasn't enough, but she couldn't see starting intensive therapy or analysis when she couldn't be in Washington longer than another year. She had decided to wait and see where their next posting (most likely a four-year tour) would be and get therapy there. She did not want to accept money for therapy from her husband's agency in case she might decide to leave him. The check from her mother's estate could have paid for therapy independently, but she did not find it nor did she have the executor rewrite the check.

I felt disappointed as I thought over Susan's situation and came to terms with her final decision. I felt that she had shown that she could work in therapy, that she had achieved some insights, but that she was not ready to change. She was not ready to leave her husband, and she was not willing to insist on his participation in marital therapy, or his support for individual therapy. She had not used the brief therapy as an end in itself nor as an entry to further treatment.

On the other hand, therapy had given her a sample experience of an object relations analytic way of working on which to base future choices. She might arrive at therapy in the future later on in her life and some other therapist might take her to the next stage in her growth, just as her father had driven her home, not her husband. I felt some of the abandonment that she had felt from the husband who went off without her. I felt like her and her father, unable to get the job done in the time available, and needing to provide a time extension that was perhaps a mistake. I felt like her adoring mother, thinking of her therapy as having poetic potential. I had the feeling of things unraveling.

Susan told a final dream.

I was in my dining room with all my mother's jewelry spread out on the dining room table. There was lots of it. My husband came in and said it was a terrible mess and I should put it away. But I was sorting it into piles and I wanted to put it into boxes before I put it away. I also wanted more time to look at it. But I had to sweep it all into a box and put it away in the attic.

"There was lots of it, a mixture of good stuff and junk, pretty much like what I got when my mother died. My sister didn't want any of 'that junk,' as she calls it, but I love it. My mother had made a business out of going to flea markets and auctions and picking up stuff. I'd go with her sometimes and I enjoyed it. She had a good eye and I have too. I thought of starting a business from her inventory, but I like to keep the stuff and look at it. Especially the best pieces I wouldn't want to wear, because I don't like to draw attention to myself. But I take them out and hold them and look at them. I have a bag of Czechoslovakian glass for repairing broken pieces and I like to do that when I get around to it."

As she spoke, I was thinking back to the dreams of comparison shopping and finding her mother in the gift shop. I thought of her story of buying herself commemorative, self-congratulatory medals while out shopping with her mother, and later of buying herself a simple ring. I had an image of her lovingly touching her mother spread in pieces on the dining room table. That image dissolved into an image of her own psyche being sorted and identified for repair, but having to be put back into the bag for a time when she might get around to it. But I felt these fragile pieces could not be forced into place before she was ready.

I said, "This is a dream of wanting to refind your mother, and then separate from her to repair yourself, which would mean beginning a longer therapy. This short-term therapy has given you a surface on which to spread out the bits and pieces, the treasured and broken memories and curios. But it has left you with the mixed feeling that has been there from the first time we met: on the one hand, you want more time to look at and repair the parts of yourself that you have learned about here, shown in your asking for today's extra session. And on the other, you want to store these parts of yourself safely and not risk losing or breaking them in therapy. Today, a large part of you wants to keep them in the attic of your mind, out of sight for now. If you change your mind about that, I will work with you in therapy for the rest of your time in the United States, or I can help you later by finding referrals at your husband's next posting. Let me know at any time if I can help."

"Thank you," she said. "I will think about it, and maybe I'll call you."

I thought that I might hear from Susan again when she got ready to get herself down from the attic, but I have not heard from her again. It might have been helpful to schedule a follow-up interview some months after this brief therapy was concluded as we sometimes do to reassess the patient's situation or to see whether such an extenuated period of holding solidi-fied her gains. This might have made a difference to the outcome in Susan's case, but the limit on the number of sessions and her discomfort about the reimbursement being tied to her husband's income or the payments com-ing out of her late mother's estate would probably have continued to work against there being another session, or against a different outcome even if she had committed to therapy. And yet, the doubt remains: Was there more I could have done?

In the end, Susan rejected the option of intensive therapy despite seeming like an excellent candidate for it in terms of her psychological mindedness, the improvement in her capacity for linking, her access to early memories and dreams, and her superior intelligence. Viewed in that light she became an exciting and rejecting object for the therapist, at which moment she may have been revealing in the transference the way she had behaved toward her hus-band and her family of origin. Perhaps she realized that she was scared of falling apart and that a year would not be long enough to put herself together again. Perhaps the loss of her mother was so painful that she could not face another separation from an older woman that she would have to leave be-hind. Certainly she was not ready to experience the full power of her intellect and her feminine appeal. Her choice of accepting the gains of brief therapy rather than the uncertainty of truncated longer-term therapy resolved the struggle in the therapeutic relationship over the limits of growth. Susan's therapy was kept brief by her dread of the there-and-then of the future, which she eliminated by foreshortening the here-and-now possibility. The loss of the opportunity for growth was felt mostly in the countertransference by the therapist whose hope for a more generative future was not fulfilled. The thera-pist who is abandoned in this way develops a feeling of completion and satis-faction within the limits of the work done only if she can understand and withstand the pain of loss and rejection of highly valued long-term therapy and can appreciate the unique attributes of short-term therapy and its value in providing a trial of therapy that informs the patient's choice—whatever it may turn out to be.

In brief therapy, Susan had many gains. She benefited from learning that therapy could be a meaningful experience that, unlike her earlier counselling, was neither warm and fuzzy, nor did it mess her up. She reworked her feel-ings toward her father and mourned the loss of her mother. Her self-esteem improved so that she could feel that she deserved better and could respond positively to loving treatment from her father, and perhaps some day she would feel that she could spend her husband's income or her own inherited or earned income on her self. We hope that she got a glimpse of her potential and sensed the value of analytic therapy for the growth of her self in the future. In this case, brief therapy served as an end in itself for achieving considerable gains, and as a limited experience of what longer-term object relations therapy could offer.

Section 7

INTENSIVE THERAPY

20

Opening Phase

In the opening phase of therapy, securing a good treatment environment is the top priority. The principal transference is the contexual one—that is, the transference to the therapist as a provider of holding and safety. Work on the contextual transference facilitates the patient's growing confidence in the therapist's capacity for containment. The transference–countertransference exchange is relatively uncomplicated compared to later therapy, when complexities accumulate with shared experience over time. In the sessions presented in this chapter, Dr. David Scharff is working with Mr. Morales to re-establish the frame of the treatment at the end of the first year of analysis. With Mrs. Meyer, his work with the contextual transference prepares the ground for her widening exploration in subsequent sessions of psychotherapy.

Setting the Frame

At the beginning of this session, Antonio Morales immediately told me (DES) that he could not come for his session the next day, because he had to have a routine medical procedure in the morning. He explained that his wife would pick him up after the procedure, because it didn't make sense for him to tie up their only working car in the parking lot, and therefore, he could not get to his session. He had already scheduled a lunchtime business meeting, for which he would be late unless he cancelled his early session. He thought that it was fair that I should charge him for the session because he could have called to let me know before the weekend. He then went on to report on his life as usual with no further mention of the upcoming procedure.

I felt puzzled and vaguely anxious. If it was so routine, why had he not told me of his appointment conflict sooner? If it was an emergency, how serious a threat to his bodily health was he facing? Was the doctor available to do the test only at the time of our session? Even so, what did the business meeting have to do with it? And what difference did it make that his wife was doing the driving? I could not quite follow his reasoning for canceling, and I was waiting to hear more.

I thought back over our contract. This patient's work regularly requires frequent travel that irregularly interferes with his therapy schedule. At the time of setting the frame for treatment, I agreed to an unusual contract in which he would try to attend four times a week and in which I would accept cancellation if given with reasonable warning for me to fill the time. With this understanding, he agreed to pay for at least twelve sessions a month. Below that minimum or without adequate warning, he pays for cancelled sessions. There is always a potential for some ambiguity in the interpretation of this unusual frame, and on this day I felt confused by his cancellation for this additional reason, with little warning and even less feeling of conflict about it. He was so used to juggling his schedule and using transportation for travel that he could easily have worked out how to get to my office without a car. I got the idea he did not want to bother with a session and a test in the same day, perhaps because both made him anxious. But there was no sign of anxiety, except in me. Why was I worried, if he was not? The only thing that was clear was that he had not given warning.

I interrupted the flow of his associations to remind him that he had said that he would miss tomorrow's session for which he would be charged, and that he hadn't shared any reaction to this.

He said little other than to agree that it seemed fair enough.

I persisted, "It seems to me that you canceled not because you truly cannot come here, but because it is not convenient to work it out."

He agreed again. "That's right. I made a decision not to squeeze in too many people and things, like we've been working on."

"Fair enough," I said. "But still you canceled your session in a month when business travel will claim more sessions. You have to have a medical procedure done for reasons that are not clear to me and about which you seem to have as little feeling as about missing your session."

"It's just a thalium stress test," he said matter-of-factly. "I'm not worried about it because the doctor isn't and I have confidence in him. He is pretty sure the chest pain I had on my last trip is a passing thing, probably indigestion from hotel food, but he just wants to check it out because of my family history. The only problem is it takes three hours."

Now I remembered. "Didn't your father die of heart disease?" I asked.

"Yes, he did," he confirmed. "But the doctor's not worried." End of discussion!

I felt shut out. Mr. Morales had evacuated an emotional problem of worrying about a lengthy medical procedure and about dying like his father by getting rid of me and the space in which we do that kind of work.

I said, "You've cancelled your session apparently for convenience, and you'd like to simply have me charge you for it and forget about it. But from the sense of worry that you've passed on to me, I guess that you are trying to avoid thinking about your experience because of what you might feel. For my own part, I would rather see you tomorrow and work on this than get paid for the missed session."

"I don't think I'm worried," he insisted. Then he conceded, "But I haven't given it a thought. I probably could come tomorrow. Okay, I'll make it work."

This vignette shows how the patient's attempt to bend the frame of therapy conveys a wish to obliterate the therapeutic space so as to avoid anxiety about the vulnerability of the self, the feared intrusiveness of the doctor-therapist, and the potential worry of identification with the father. The therapist's interventions include clarifying and linking comments, a behavioral interpretation conveyed by limit-setting concerning the frame, and a verbal interpretation of defense against anxiety.

The Holding Environment

The following three sessions are from the opening phase with a different patient.

Menucha Meyer, whose depression and lack of sexual interest had severely undermined her marriage, has seen Dr. David Scharff for individual therapy twice a week for two months. Prior to beginning individual therapy, Mrs.

Meyer and her husband had been seen in twice-weekly couple therapy for a
few months. They were enabled to take back enough of their shared projective identifications that each partner became upset rather than being accusa-
tory toward the other. Husband and wife both thought that they would now
be best served separately by individual therapy. Mr. Meyer already had an
individual therapist, but Mrs. Meyer had felt uneasy with her former therapist and had quit. Since Mr. Meyer was already in therapy with a colleague,
and Mrs. Meyer felt that she could trust Dr. Scharff, the couple had agreed
that Mrs. Meyer would begin therapy with him.

Now Mrs. Meyer is in the second month of individual therapy with Dr.
Scharff. The sessions show work typical of the opening phase in that they focus
on the holding environment of the therapy and the nature of the therapeutic
relationship. Work on these issues builds trust and confidence for approaching the main issues. We can observe the therapist at work to provide psychological holding, both for the patient and for himself, as he begins to relax into
the patient's material with confidence in the containing function of his reverie.

Session 1

Menucha Meyer, a petite, 35-year-old red-haired Israeli-American, worked
as a reporter for the Washington Bureau of an Israeli magazine. Born in
Jerusalem, she had lost her father when she was 10, and had lived in the
United States since the age of 12, when her widowed mother remarried an
American. As a college student, she spent six months in Israel and met her
husband Oded, whose mother's family of Egyptian Jews had emigrated to
Israel before he was born. He joined her in the United States and got a job
with a major international bank in Washington, D.C.

Today, with an engaging but serious look, she came in to the waiting
room breathlessly as I (DES) opened my office door. She threw off her coat
and hurried in, sitting, as she usually did, on the end of the couch as far
from me as possible. She had just gotten off a plane from covering a story
in Chicago. She already knew she had to change the schedule for next week,
but she did not yet know when her source would be available. It would
likely mean we would only have one of the two regular sessions next week.

She said, "This is terrible. I'm just off the plane, and I have to go back
out there next week, so I have to ask you to change one of our sessions, but
I don't know if it's Monday or Thursday yet that I have to change. I'm so
sorry. This is beyond my control."

I said quite agreeably, "I know it is. I may not be able to change the sessions next week, but I'll try."

I liked Mrs. Meyer for being so committed to therapy despite her fright about what she was discovering. Working in Washington, I am used to last-minute changes and do not automatically regard them as evidence of resistance. I have developed a flexible attitude that enables me to accommodate the frequent switches needed by government administration people, trial lawyers, and press. So I felt cooperative about moving sessions, and did not feel pushed around by her requests.

"Well, thank you for trying," she said. "I really don't want it to be like this, but I have to talk to this source whenever he'll talk to me. The magazine is planning to run my story as the lead next month, and my editor is counting on me even though I've never covered anything quite this big."

I must have been feeling something more than I knew, because I now went overboard to repeat that I trust her. I must have been reassuring her about some accusation I had not yet understood.

"I have the sense there's nothing you can do about it," I said. "So I'm not making anything of the need to change, and I will make a switch whenever I can. But we do want to leave room for the possibility that there will be times when there is meaning hidden in changes like this."

Consciously, I was trying to prepare her for the exploration of underground meaning conveyed by changes in the frame.

Consciously, she seemed to accept my caveat and went on. "Okay," she said. "But what's really on my mind is what happened over the weekend. It's movie review time again! Last week I was talking about *The English Patient* with all the land mines exploding people's trust. This weekend in Chicago I went to see the movie *Shine*. It was truly moving. I managed to stay put-together all through it, right until at the very end when I broke down."

In addition to whatever themes may have been brought out by the movie, I realized that when she was telling me about movies seen in another city, she was telling me how she had taken care of herself when she had to be alone away from her family. I knew that this movie included scenes of a young adult alone in a foreign city. Perhaps the unconscious theme was about her arrival in the United States at the age of 10. I remembered her discussion of the precariousness of trust in relationships, and in the relationship with me. So I readied myself for an extension of this theme.

"It was compelling. It's a story of a father who traumatizes his son. He always said to him, 'You are a lucky boy, David, you always have music.' Then over and over he tells David the story of saving money to buy a violin, only to have it smashed by his own father. Then he keeps David far too close to him and won't let him take opportunities that would let him realize his talent. He holds out to him the wonders of the extremely difficult Rachmaninoff Third Piano Concerto, but refuses to let him study abroad.

"Finally David takes off on his own for London, where a mentor brings him along and reluctantly agrees to let him perform the Rachmaninoff in a competition. Following his mentor's advice, he plays 'like there is no tomorrow.' Then he cracks up from the stress of it all, and spends many years in the hospital, until he's finally rescued by a woman whom he eventually marries, and who helps him perform again. It's a true story."

I was aware that Mrs. Meyer frequently felt on the edge of collapse, and that there was considerable resonance between this script and her own history of moving to another country and being in training for a career in the arts. She had been a promising dancer, pushed and praised by her mother, until a series of stress fractures left her feeling that dance was no longer worth the sacrifice, and that in any event, she probably was not good enough to make a career of it. I had seen the movie, as it happened, so without telling her, I was in a position to hear her report of it and to supply my own associations, which included associating the name of the main character with me.

Mrs. Meyer continued, "What broke me up at the end was the visit to the father's grave, where David says to his wife, 'It's no use blaming Daddy any longer, because Daddy is gone.' Then I just lost it and was sobbing and sobbing. I don't know why, it reminded me of all those years as a child trying to please my mother and father. I got so upset. There were my mother and father, thinking Israel was doing so well, and not pleased with how I was doing. I'm so mad at them.

"I just wanted you to be there. I wanted to call you, but I knew you wouldn't like it. This system stinks: I needed a session right then, and I was upset that you weren't there, and I couldn't call you. I have an editor. He knows that I only call him if it's crucial. The magazine has a lot riding on this story. It could be sued if we're wrong. So when I call, he knows it's not trivial and he takes the call, even if he's with the publisher or a member of the Knesset.

"That's what I should be able to get here, but the system is that I have to wait. I have to behave and I have to wait. I called Oded at the bank, and he walked out of a meeting with some important guy from one of the countries he oversees to talk to me on the phone. He said, 'But I'm here for you, you can use me.' But I didn't feel like that mattered."

I said, "You felt like this business was with me, not with your husband."

"Yes, it had to be with you. There is something going on that doesn't involve him," she said. "But it's the system's fault. The system is that you can only be here when the system says so."

I was pleased that Mrs. Meyer understood that therapy business had to be with me. The problem was already beginning to focus within the treatment in a way that can facilitate the work of therapy. On the other hand, she was sidestepping the anger which should have come directly at me. She was right in thinking that I would not like her calling me whenever she felt like it. The specter arose in my mind of the demanding client who calls one of my supervisees several times a day. In retrospect, I can see that the ready reassurance I gave her at the beginning of the hour that she was not impinging on me relates to this image of her as an out-of-control patient, but the image did not really fit with the reality of this overly controlled, highly functional woman. Over a few minutes I realized that she was not making an actual request to call me frequently. She was wanting to convey the feeling that her urgent longing to be understood would be rebuffed in the name of "the system." As I thought this, I felt more sympathetic to her again.

I said, "You're mad at me. It's not just at the system. You talk about the system today like you talked about the magazine a few weeks ago not giving you enough money to live in Washington because of its system, rather than about your stingy, unappreciative boss. In here, it's not the system, it's me you're mad at."

She said, "Yes, but it's the system that sets it up that way."

I said to her, "When your mother and father let you down, would you say that was the system, too?"

"Actually," she said, "It's more my father who let me down. He noticed how I was doing in my schoolwork, but he wasn't there when I needed him. He cared more about Israel than about me. I didn't really look to my mother to be there for me. She was always complaining about the petty inconveniences in our life there. I just gave up on her."

So in her childhood, she felt there was no system—that is, no effective parental couple. But here I found myself insisting that the anger was at me, perhaps as the father who let her down. It was only later that I realized that I was more worried that if she felt I misunderstood her, she would turn away from me altogether, as she had from her mother after her father's death. It was easier to be the controlling and ultimately dead father on whom she focused her anger than to become the mother she blamed more deeply and gave up on. Acting out this anxiety and avoiding the underlying sadness of her father's death, I pulled the transference toward me more directly than necessary.

I said, "It's not the system that's letting you down. At certain moments, like after the movie that upset you, you felt you just had to be with me right away. It's a feeling far beyond logistics or systems. And you could not call me then or any time, because you think I'll turn you away like your father did and say, 'I'm busy. Behave yourself and don't ask for help.'"

"Yes, that's right. And I'm not a troublemaker. Anything but! I always behaved, but I felt they thought I was the bad one anyway."

I said, "You feel that I'm not going to put up with you, especially if you feel needy here. It's not a matter of what you're allowed to do, but what you're allowed to feel and be. Can these needs and feelings of yours find a place here, or do you have to shove them underground and appear to 'shine' here as you did growing up?"

"Okay," she said. "But it's hard. And meanwhile, I have to travel, and then I have to pay you whether I'm here or not, and it bothers me especially when I do want to be here."

I meant to keep a focus on the developing transference, but since this was early therapy, I wanted to use this experience of heightened need to make a point. I had recommended more intensive therapy which she had been unwilling to accept. So I had been waiting for a moment like this to remind her of this option.

I said, "In terms of the way therapy works, you'd find it easier to do this if you could come more frequently. If you came three times a week, it would help you move into the work without having to hold such terrible feelings for so long alone or with your husband."

She said, "That's right, it really doesn't have to do with him, it has to do with being here and working on this with you. And yes, I can see that coming here more often would make it easier. I'll have to think about that."

I continued, "If your travel precludes your being here for some sessions, I'd be willing to talk to you on the telephone."

She asked, "Does that work?"

I said, "It's not as good as you being here, but it's better than missing sessions. I'd be willing to do it when you have to be away."

She said, "I'll give you a call tomorrow, letting you know what my schedule's going to be." Then she caught herself and said, "No, I'll see you tomorrow anyway, because we had to change so I could come two days in a row. I'll tell you then, of course."

In this session, Mrs. Meyer demonstrates that she has learned a good deal about how to work in therapy. She comments on the problem her work schedule poses for the therapeutic frame. She proceeds to use a film story to continue the discussion of her problems with need, trust, relocation, parental expectations and artistic promise, and loss of a parent. As the session goes on, we can see that these problems are present in the here-and-now transference, as she makes it clear that she dare not express her need to Dr. Scharff and expects him to rebuff her. The there-and-then origins of the transference leave her fearful about the future of the growing therapeutic relationship. After all, she lost her father when she was 10.

The hallmark of this early-phase transference is that it usually focuses on the safety and holding that the therapist can provide. Dr. Scharff draws Mrs. Meyer's attention toward a focused transference concerning him as an uncaring *person*, but Mrs. Meyer is clear that her concern is with his provision of a caring *system*, an environment of holding and availability. She wonders whether he will see her as blameworthy for misbehaving. She expects that he will be less available than she would like.

We see Dr. Scharff offer increased availability in a way that can be understood at least partly as an unconscious intention to give her something rather than to interpret her unconscious fear that he will not be there for her, having been unavailable while helping her to develop, as her father had been because he was busy and ultimately because he died. On the other hand, he is also speaking to the way her fear has kept her from agreeing to an arrangement which would better meet her need. A more rounded intervention would have been possible if he could have spoken to the way distrust and fear of another loss had kept her from agreeing to more frequent therapy so far, rather than offering it at a moment when she might well feel pressured by it and distrustful, as the hero of the movie felt pressured by his father's clinging to him.

In the early phase, the therapist experiences resistance too, because he does not yet feel fully trusting of the patient. In addition, transference blocks his thinking, for the patient wants more from him at the same time that she fears he will profit by her neediness. This ambivalence is enacted in their evolving relationship. It is never possible to be free from the influence of the patient's inner object relations. All the therapist can do is offer to absorb them, and then to understand them as soon as possible. This is even more true in this early stage when both patient and therapist are inexperienced with their relationship.

Session 2

Mrs. Meyer called a few minutes before her 8:00 A.M. appointment and left a message in my voice mail to say that she would be late. She arrived about ten minutes later, without saying why she was late, and so I asked.

"I slept through the alarm, which hardly ever happens to me," she replied. "I don't know why it happened. I know I was really upset yesterday that you said I was at fault for having to reschedule."

I was taken aback that she thought I had said that, and I felt unfairly blamed, all the more for being faulted on the very point about which I had been trying to reassure her. I knew instantly that this was like previous episodes with Mrs. Meyer in which she told me she was upset by something I'd said which it had never occurred to me would give offense. I felt guilty, but I had nothing to be guilty about. I had to try to understand what was happening between us in the transference, so I held on to my discomfort without reassuring her or defending myself.

I said, "Tell me what you felt and what you thought I was trying to say to you."

"You said it must be my fault for having to reschedule so much. It's like the reason I don't call you when I wish I could talk to you right then. Once after a couple's session, when we had been coming just a few weeks, I called and asked if I could come in before the next appointment. And you said, 'I don't have anything available this week.' Coldly, just like that! You didn't say, 'I'll call if I have a cancellation,' or 'I'm sorry.' I got the message: 'Don't call!' So I don't, but I hate it."

I said, "You learned lessons like that from your parents who said everything else was more important than you. So now you're interested in finding out what the rules and boundaries are. You're very careful to scan voice tones and attitudes for cues about how to act. You're doing that with me and it doesn't take much to convince you that I don't care about you or that I think of you as a bad patient."

She said, "That's right, I don't want to be 'the patient from Hell.' I feel very worried about that."

I noted that we had established the basis for her reaction to yesterday's session; so now I could work with her fear from its reflection in my countertransference. This time I felt less endangered as the therapist and more confident in working with the here-and-now of the transference.

Dr. Scharff and Mrs. Meyer are dealing with her understanding of his role as the provider of holding and safety, which she experiences as unsafe and attacking. This is the contextual transference, a common feature of early therapeutic work, when the therapist has not yet become an object of the patient's inner world. The contextual holding is secured by prompt transference interpretation of the patient's mistrust of the therapist as the conveyor of a safe holding context. Dr. Scharff decides that this is a time to use his countertransference as evidence of the patient's transferential distortion.

I said, "What I said yesterday was that I was *not* blaming you. In fact, I pretty much went out of my way to reassure you I understood that your schedule was beyond your control and that I did not mind shifting appointments so long as I was able to. But I did also say that we had to leave room for the possibility that at other times such requests might have meaning. Does this episode echo anything you felt with your parents growing up?"

I had a clear memory of what I had said, particularly since I had been somewhat uncomfortable with how much I had reassured her. By saying that "we had to leave room for the possibility that at other times such requests might have meaning," I knew I had consciously intended to be "educating" her for the process of therapy, having in mind that she was fairly new to analytic psychotherapy. I realized now that my warning her had a role in triggering her response. I felt

I needed a few more minutes to understand both why I had reassured her and why I had issued this warning.

"It's my father really," she explained. "He would say that I just wasn't good enough and would have to try harder. He was a national hero, but I saw him as a tyrant. He cared how I did, but he never let me feel I was good enough. My mother didn't get involved. It was like she wasn't there."

"Just when you were trying to walk the straight and narrow and not cause any waves?" I asked.

She nodded, reaching for a tissue and wiping her tears.

Now I realized I had been reacting to her "good girl" false-self behavior, to her having to be good lest I should think she misbehaved. I had been a father wanting to reassure her that she was indeed good, and then, fearing a criticism from my own rejecting object telling me that I had been too gratifying, I had guiltily tried to temper my action by telling her not to let my reassurance go to her head. I felt that I could make an interpretation based both on having identified with her longing for her father's praise and her guilt about it.

I said, "Yesterday, I was actually at pains to tell you I didn't think it was your fault. In fact I've been wondering why I went out of my way to reassure you that I didn't think you were doing anything wrong. You've let me know in several ways that you're worried I'm going to blame you and think you're bad. You want people to reassure you, but any crack in the reassurance is devastating. The question is why you feel I would blame you."

She said, "I'll tell you why. It's because I've come in here every week and had to change the schedule. Yesterday I came in and said I had to change it again, but I wasn't sure whether it would be Monday or Thursday that I couldn't make. Why wouldn't you be mad at me?"

Although at this moment I did seem to be getting annoyed toward her, I knew I had not been upset with her need to change the schedule the day before, or even as I anticipated this session. In the middle of this exchange, however, I was beginning to feel an irritation, not about the change of schedule, but about being misunderstood just when I was trying to be so nice to her. At the moment I said this to myself, I felt I finally got the point. I had identified with her effort to be "so good," and, like her, I got blamed anyway. I now had the complete experience inside and felt calmed by the insight.

I said, "You're terribly worried about being accused. I do know that about you. I was trying to protect you from feeling accused when I said it *wasn't* your fault. But I had doubts about giving you that reassurance, so I tried to leave room for those other times when there would be various hidden meanings to requests like that. You heard blame because you are afraid that people are going to blame you."

"Okay," she acknowledged. "I see what you're saying. I felt so blamed growing up that I look for it everywhere, and you think I read it into what you said."

I felt back on an even keel. While she had not quite grasped what had happened, I had gotten a sense of it myself and felt I could work with it better now. I also realized that her being late this morning was the kind of episode for which I had been wanting to allow room for the discussion of its meaning.

The countertransference enactment was not over, however. When she felt falsely accused, she expressed her anger and upset indirectly in ways that, in the home, probably pushed her parents to be more critical than they might have been otherwise. Although I did allude briefly to this in my last comment of the session, I could not take it up completely. There would be time to cover that ground later.

"We're lucky though," I joked. "This morning you were late because you overslept the alarm. You haven't said that was determined by outside forces, so we could look into that now."

She said, "Well, maybe I was just so exhausted by the worry about this story and rushing back here to see you."

I shook my head. "No, I think you were upset with me."

She took this with a grin. "Well, that could be. I certainly was upset. But why would I oversleep, then?"

"That's a good question," I said.

"I don't know. No thoughts," she replied, shaking her head.

"Actually, you did two things," I said. "You overslept, and then you called me. I wonder how you felt yesterday about my suggesting that we might talk on the phone while you were away."

"I thought it was weird," she answered. "It wouldn't be the same. And it wouldn't work. When I'm on these trips, I'm going like mad. I couldn't count on being able to be at the phone at some time we agreed on."

"Hmm," I said, making it clear I was not too sure of the reasoning here.

She then listed all the things she had done on the recent trip, all the reasons telephoning wouldn't work, and then ended by contradicting her argument. She continued, "But maybe it's the same as my saying to you before we began that there was no way I could come to see you regularly because my schedule was always like that in town, too. And here I am with the time to see you and it's just not a problem. Okay, maybe you're right."

I said, "It's interesting. At the end of yesterday's session I talked to you about using the telephone. And the next thing that happens is you over-sleep in such a way as to make you call me on the phone."

She said, "Yes, but I didn't expect to talk to you directly. I talked to the machine as I intended."

I said, "You did a little experiment in reaching me by telephone that was set in motion by the oversleeping. Oversleeping let you test out what I would do when you did not keep so perfectly to the boundaries you have always set so that you wouldn't make waves. You're making small waves here and seeing how it feels."

"Yes, I can see that," she said.

"What I'm learning," I said, "is that you are always worried about danger in relationships. You feel you never know when you'll be hit by a land mine like the ones that destroy people in *The English Patient*, or in Israel when there is fighting. So we have to be aware that you may feel I set them off when I don't even know I've done it. I thought I was reassuring you, but you felt I had hit you with blame. You're at least partly right: I wanted you to know that I wouldn't always reassure you, wouldn't always accept your reasons, or give you what you want. I was reacting to your fear without being fully aware of it. It's probably not the last time we'll have this kind of experience."

"No," she said. "It's probably not. I think I get lots of them in my life."

Contextual Holding and Transference Evolution

These two sessions covered the contextual transference. We can see that the patient brings material to the first session about trust and fear in caring relationships. Therapist and patient collaborate in relating this fear to their therapeutic relationship. In the second session, the unconscious action of the first session comes to the fore, and this enables the therapist to work with countertransference feelings based on his introjective identification. This introjection takes two forms. Dr. Scharff has a complementary identification with her father feeling misunderstood when he was trying to help her and a concordant identification with her own longing for her father's praise and guilt about it.

What characterizes these sessions as typical of the early treatment process is the concentration on contextual holding in contrast to the nonelaboration of focused object relations and discrete transferences. The patient's relationship to her parents is given without much elaboration, although the feeling of distrust is palpable. The contextual transference to Dr. Scharff as a parent who will not be there to meet her needs is shot through with the transference to him as one who will not be there at all because he has died. But it does not focus yet. For instance, she does not take up possible feelings about contributing to her father's death by demanding more from him, and yet we can see her protecting Dr. Scharff from being burdened by her. It would be premature to say this. Dr. Scharff will wait until Mrs. Meyer feels safe enough to bring it together in the focused transference. The here-and-now transference evolution of the first session does not connect with the here-and-then. It does not yet shed much light on the meaning of her old relationships. This is fairly typical of early sessions.

In the next session, the work done on contextual holding in the previous two sessions opens the transitional space and facilitates an exploration of internal object relations and their origins in past relationships. As Mrs. Meyer elaborates these matters, the transference also begins to develop in parallel with the added detail about internal object relations. Not all of these matters require verbal interpretation. The therapist helps the patient concentrate on the elaboration of the material within the strengthened contextual transference, watching as the more focused transference material crystallizes, but he still does not try to gather the focused transference to himself prematurely. As the therapist facilitates the patient's exploration, he is developing his own capacity for containment. He begins to relax within the session, to feel less guarded against attacks on his holding, and to exercise his capacity for reverie, for holding the patient's material and projective identifications inside. There they communicate with his own internal object relations and can be understood intuitively as they resonate with them. This moves Mrs. Meyer toward exploring and understanding the unconscious.

Session 3

Mrs. Meyer began the next session with vignettes about her parents in her childhood in Israel, some new to me, some previously reported. She referred to a story she had told me bitterly some sessions earlier. On the occasion of her sixth birthday party, her father was at a meeting of the Knesset. She enjoyed the party, although she missed him. But when he came home, he chastised her for not calling him to come home for the party. Then she referred to another painful memory, also recounted last week, of the times when her father had told her to lower the tone of her voice because he disliked high, feminine voices. Mrs. Meyer, whose voice is quite low, said that as a girl she practiced lowering her voice and felt ashamed of how its tone rose when she got excited. Then she recovered a positive memory of her father teaching her to read before she was of school age, and rewarding her for learning and remembering things.

Mrs. Meyer's father was much older than her mother, and had died when she was 10 years old. Two years later her mother remarried and moved to the United States. Once, as a teenager, when recognizing her limitations as a dancer, she worried out loud whether she needed to have a career beyond dance. Her stepfather told her that women in America should be supported by their husbands to do the domestic things. She remembered saying to herself over and over again, "No, no, no! I'm not going to do it like that."

"On the other hand, if it weren't for my stepfather," she continued, "I never would have left home to go to college and become a writer. Even though all four of my grandparents were sent to university in Europe before the war, my *father* would have made me stay home and marry early. He was far more orthodox and culturally conservative than his parents had been. I feel I'm a throwback to what he apparently used to dismiss as their more liberal ways."

It was not clear why she felt this way about her father who had, after all, taught her to read early, but I felt that Mrs. Meyer was elaborating nicely on the emerging memories about her parents as these memories related to aspects of her current life, and so I did not interrupt to challenge her. She was talking easily, even when obviously feeling a good deal about the memories, so I thought it best to encourage the elaborations without intruding.

She now went back to talking about the movie *Shine*, which had occupied the previous session. "That father set up a box for his son, David. On the one hand he fired his ambition. He drove David on by telling him constantly how lucky he was to have music. On the other hand, he kept him from being able to achieve it by not allowing him to leave when opportunities were offered. I think that the father was hurt—maybe by being persecuted, as my father was before he emigrated to Israel. In the movie, David's father wanted to be the one to teach David himself, even though he didn't have the skill. He was reluctant to let him go to the teacher in town, although he did finally do that. In the end, David just had to leave despite his father. And then his father cut him off. I feel like that sort of thing could have happened to me if my father had lived."

I had been wondering about the use of the name "David" in her recounting of the movie, and my own identification with it. Now I began to feel that it heightened my identification with her as the victim of parental pressure and misunderstanding. Her identification with the hero of the movie, David, was having the effect of promoting my identification with her, and so I did not see myself as the teacher or mentor that she might long to work with but also feel reluctant about in case her choice could be felt as disloyal to her parents.

A few minutes later, Mrs. Meyer spoke about ways that her parents had discouraged her development. Then she turned to the parents of her adolescence, her mother and stepfather. She remembered the time her mother took her to buy her first bra.

"I didn't think I was ready, and I didn't want one, but my mother insisted. Then, instead of buying the little elastic training bras that all the girls had, she bought a stiff thing in a huge size that felt like it was made out of cardboard. It had sharp points to it. I couldn't come close to filling it. I was so embarrassed I took a pencil and poked out the pointy bits. I felt my mother had exposed me to ridicule.

"Over and over, in every way, I said to myself 'I don't want to be a girl.' Even though my mother and stepfather pushed me like they did with that bra, mainly they would turn and denigrate feminine things. They would be very sarcastic about girls who were cheerleaders or had feminine frills. My stepfather was like my father in hating those high, shrieking, girlish voices. I learned from them that it was no good being a girl."

I said, "This is still an area of a lot of conflict for you."

"It certainly is," Mrs. Meyer said. "I had a dream last Thursday before I was home from Chicago. It goes perfectly with what I'm feeling."

In the dream we were at a party for Congress and the press. I recognized the people there. I saw Rachel, a columnist at the magazine. At dinner I was eating with Itzak who is one of the senior editors and has kind of been my mentor. After dinner, Rachel said, "Okay, get ready for the dance." So we went off to get ready together. When we got there, there were these two women from high school years, who were my competition back then. One was Nancy Clark, my closest competitor in dancing, the other was Agnes Black, a beautiful girl for whom I was no competition. All the fathers thought Agnes was the model teenager. She was the popular one, the homecoming queen, good academically—the one we all hated and wished we could be.

In the dream, we were all ready for the dance and I said to Rachel, "You have to help me decide what color belt to wear for the dance, because I am going to have the prettiest dress." So I went off to the dance, but it wasn't really a dance. It was a men's bar and at the same time a competitive athletic event. As I got there, some girl was doing running like at a baseball game. All the men were cheering her. I had thought this was going to be a dance, but now it looked like an athletic event. I stood there totally confused about what I was supposed to be doing. When I woke, I thought, "That dream doesn't need interpretation."

"It's less clear now," Mrs. Meyer concluded, "but it was completely clear then."

"What was so clear?" I asked.

"What I learned growing up about how to behave on a competitive basis has taken the place of behaving on a sexual basis," she said. "When I do one, I think it's the other. It's completely messed up. These two girls from high school in Brooklyn represented both areas: one was sexually competitive with me and the other was professionally competitive. They were at an event that had to do with my immediate, current life, where there's just as much mix-up as I had in high school. In the dream it was like, 'What are we doing here, competing or dancing?' Beyond that, I don't know."

I was pleased to have her bring the dream into the session, a sign of her capacity to elaborate on the memories in new ways and to link them to her current life. But I did not want to leave matters at the level of connections that she could make herself, useful as they were. It was still the early phase and she needed some help to associate further to specific elements of the dream which seemed to stand out as emotionally significant. She did this easily, with an expanding range of feeling as she spoke.

I said, "Tell me more about the dream. What about Rachel?"

"She's a classic bitch. She advocates that there's no difference between men and women, and that we women should compete on a gender-blind basis. She started as a reporter late, which is really unusual. Now she's in her fifties. She writes stories about anti-Semitism. She's very powerful with Itzak and the editors, so I keep away from the things that interest her. When I spoke out at an editorial meeting recently, she was beaming and was nice to me. That made me nervous. She's a person you try to stay away from."

I felt that enough material had accumulated from her memories of her mother and the dream that it would now be useful to make some links between them without closing down the transitional space in the session.

I said, "She's a deadly mother figure—the successful woman you don't want to be measured by or be like."

She said, "That's right. If that's what I have to be like to be a successful reporter, I say no thank you!"

I said, "So you feel you have to get rid of being feminine to be a successful woman. That's what your parents taught you, and it's a way of not being like your sexual mother either, the part of her that bought you that large bra. Does Rachel's approval frighten you?"

She said, "No, I don't think so. She's taken no steps to help me. It's just clear that she was pleased with what she saw and heard. On a concrete level, she's into things about prejudice and I keep a safe boundary between us by steering clear of that area. Plus, Itzak has staked me out as his protégée, so she knows not to interfere even though I think she's jealous."

Now I am able to see that this is a transference equivalency. With me, she is the favored woman, as she then splits off the mother who alternates between being critical and sexually exciting. She feels this internal mother would do her in by denigrating feminine things and, at the same time, pushing her to be excessively sexual. She has a good, protective, and exciting father and a persecuting, critical mother who also taunts her with a secret sexual identification. As a defense, she has formed the unconscious fantasy that she can please her father best by working hard without looking feminine or sexual. This oedipal split inhibits her sexuality and her feminine identification. It also indicates a troubled relationship to the internal couple who, as a pair, present her with this dilemma. As I begin to formulate this constellation, I notice that I am pleased with the way she is working. I realize that my countertransference represents my receptiveness to her transference to me as the approving and protective father, leaving out the disapproving father for the moment.

I said, "You're Daddy's girl."

She said, "I guess I did try to be what he wanted. To have a low voice and read well, to be polite to everyone no matter how I felt. All of which I do still."

Here, as I've interpreted her identification with her father and her seeking her father's approval, she seems to be tracking with me. I have a sense of our working together, of her following my lead and my following hers. There is an invisible sense of support from her relationship to her father which is stitching our work together here without need for comment about the working alliance. It's as if it's the two of us against the malignant woman represented in Rachel.

She continued, "So it was Rachel who said, 'Get ready for the dance,' in the dream. But when we get there, it is clear from the men that it didn't have to do with dancing. It had to do with competing like they do."

I said, "So while she seems to invite you to feminine activities, it was really to male athletic activity."

"Right, that's not feminine."

I asked, "How does that fit with your high school rivalries?"

"Nancy Clark was my closest competition," she said. "We were sort of friends, even though she wasn't Jewish, but she was a snippy kind of person. We put in a lot of time together in dance lessons, so she was sort of a friend by being in that group. She was close enough to me in skill in that group that other people thought of her as a competitor of mine. It grated on me because I thought I was so much better—which wasn't really true. So it includes the idea that I *thought* I should have been doing better competitively.

"But sexually, with the girl thing, there was Agnes Black. I wasn't even close to being able to match her, but I longed to be as attractive as she was. I had a total yearning to be and have those things that weren't mine, and were never going to be. My mother's speech about Agnes Black was, 'Don't worry about her. Some day, things will all even out. These girls don't have everything.'"

I'm thinking about Mrs. Meyer's shame and her dislike of her body. Like many dancers, she remains dissatisfied with her body. She is still trim, but envies other women who have what she regards as ideally feminine bodies, an odd contradiction in view of her internal attack on femininity. This contradiction conveys her envy of her mother's sexuality and the denial of her own feminine

*sexuality which has set in as a way of controlling that envy. But I did not want
to interpret this area yet because she is adding to our exploration richly herself,
and I decided, as we went along, simply to support her widening exploration.*

I asked, "What did your mother's saying 'things would even out' mean
to you?"

"It meant, if it were true, that eventually everyone would see that the
things I was good at were more important and long-lasting. The things
Agnes Black was valued for wouldn't last. In the end everyone would
realize I was 'worth it' for what really mattered—whatever those things
were. I wasn't the only one who got that speech from her mother. But Agnes
Black was the sort of girl that all the fathers thought was wonderful right
then. And the girls and their mothers thought, 'Oh yeah! Right!'"

I said, "Meaning?"

"Meaning: men were all attracted to her blond hair and gorgeous figure, and her ability to suck up. She wasn't interested in kissing up to women
of any age, but she was definitely interested in doing well with men, and
she did. That seemed two-faced and shallow to the girls. We weren't impressed. We felt that the men were being stupid and blind."

I said, "No jealousy in that?"

She agreed, "Total jealousy, of course! Was there one of us who wouldn't
have traded places? I doubt it. Total jealousy!"

I said, "The best you could do was a distant second. The push from your
parents against femininity kept you from being the way she was and getting the pleasure that she could have from appealing to men. Your scorn
was a way of trying to protect yourself, too."

She said, "True, but there was also cultural pressure. In the culture
that I was in, the things that Agnes Black stood for were really valued—
cheerleading, pretty dresses, being social. That was part of my parents being
totally against them. They didn't fit well with our values. None of the Jewish girls were comfortable with those things, even though we might have
longed to be in that world at times. Then there was my mother's theory:
you only had one phase of your life in which you could be popular and
successful. If you were on top in high school and college, by marriage you
would have spent your chance, and that was it for your future success.
You'd just have to settle. Isn't that strange?"

I said, "But you still feel that way. You're still waiting for your time,
aren't you?"

She said, "Yes, I sound like that, but I don't know. A lot of times I would say, 'My mother was right. Yep.' I have my own career, a devoted husband—a lot of women would kill to have what I have—and a gorgeous child."

I asked, "So what keeps you from enjoying it all?"

A long sigh. "The fact that I so damage others," she said regretfully. "And now I think maybe my parents were wrong about saying some things weren't important. I go through life and there are some parts of experience I can never have. But a lot of people have to live with disappointment, and they don't have half of what I do. You can't do everything, you can't have everything!"

In this session, the third in a series drawn from the early phase of therapy, Mrs. Meyer explores the links between her current external situation, the cultural contexts in which she grew up and her parents' reaction to them, her fantasy life, her dreams, and her internal object relations. She does so within the context of a widened transitional space which has been prepared by the work in the two previous sessions. She uses Dr. Scharff to supply necessary contextual holding, but that process is almost invisible when they work together without conflict in the transference. We can see the containment the therapist offers. We note his recovery from his resistance to arrive at a state of receptiveness to conflictual elements of the transference–countertransference exchange, which he uses to further his and their shared understanding, but which he processes internally without premature direct comment. The patient continues to elaborate conflicts, and to give an ever-widening picture of her there-and-then object relationships. In the third session of the series, we can see the fruit borne of work done in the two previous sessions, as the patient retrieves material from her unconscious in the form of a dream and learns to associate to it. Lastly, we see the potential for future work that can occur once the transference and countertransference dynamic gets charged with the elements that until then remain at the reflective distance typical of the early phase of therapy.

21

Mid-Phase

In an ideal therapy, the mid-phase of therapeutic work is marked by a sense that patient and therapist are working smoothly together with relatively small fluctuations in their alliance. The patient knows how to work, so that difficulties in the way of working relate primarily to themes that interfere rather than to the difficulties of learning to work together. As there is relative security about the holding context, focused transference issues often take center stage, where patient and therapist can work away at the issues of understanding the patient's characteristic difficulties that are increasingly delivered into the arms of the therapy, prompt therapeutic regressions that lead to understanding through the cycle of projective identification and containment, and lead, through ups and downs and the slow path of growth, to the maturation of the therapy and the patient.

In practice, the mid-phase varies enormously. A relatively smooth course is rare. Patients' lives continue to evolve, new crises erupt, some stages of growth provoke more strain than others. Each therapy is different. Therapy with some patients feels relatively consistent from one session to the next, while others have sessions that show marked contrast.

Nevertheless, there are some characteristics of mid-phase work that we come to expect: work with transference has a sequence and direction that the therapist keeps loosely in mind; patient and therapist do grow a way of working together that both come more or less to expect. If there is work with dreams, they become part of the fabric of the work, as does a working knowledge of the patient's cast of internal and external objects. As the history of their work is established, so too is a sense of the future of the therapeutic relationship, perhaps as an extended one stretching indefinitely into the future, or perhaps as one time-limited to a few months or a year.

Each session has particulars that frame its meaning—the content of the sessions that lead up to it, the data about impending vacations or times the patient or therapist is to be away, the status of the total transference at the time, events in the analysand's life at the moment, and the situation of the analyst's life as well. In the sessions we will look at in this chapter, the patient has kept the future of the analysis up in the air, never making a decision about where she will live and work in the future, with the result that the uncertain future of the analysis looms as a constant theme.

In this first mid-phase analytic session with Marianne (earlier presented briefly in Chapter 12), we will follow the course of transference and countertransference. We will apply to the session the concepts of transference geography and the relation of self and object that we introduced in earlier chapters.

The Early Mid-Phase

Marianne is in the twenty-second month of four-times-weekly analysis with Dr. David Scharff. She has been married for five years and considers her marriage to be extremely unsatisfactory. She is French, but she has lived much of her life in the United States and her English is excellent. Her husband is American. The couple has been in Washington, DC, together since getting married. She is going to Paris tomorrow to visit her parents for three weeks. Her mother is in decline from cancer, but not yet in the terminal stages.

Marianne has just presented a professional paper that she has been writing for several months, and is planning a job change in the next few months that will take her out of the city, may end her marriage, and will terminate her four-times-weekly analysis. Although she has tended to ignore the consequences for analysis of her job search, we have talked about this occasionally, almost always at my instigation. She insists that there are no good academic jobs in this area, although at times she simply acknowledges that she has not tried to develop a job in or near Washington the way she has in several other areas. Her usual method of job searching is to wait for someone to approach her or to give her a hint through the academic grapevine, rather than to conduct a systematic search.

Yesterday she had a dream that she was flying in a plane piloted by her husband. In the dream, the plane crashed in the water and sank, although they were not clearly in danger. Her husband does fly planes, but she will not fly with him because his flying frightens her.

This is the last session before her visit home. Since our schedule often has some irregularity to accommodate both her academic duties and my travels, we begin the hour by checking the schedule for her return and times I will be away after that. She tells me that she will investigate a contract the University of Paris may offer her. The job would give her an entry there, but it is beneath her current academic rank.

I understand these practicalities and her wish to be with her dying mother and family, but I am once again left with the feeling that I value the analysis more than she does. It's curious, because in an immediate, daily way she is devoted to the analysis and gives me the feeling of being valued.

Then she says, "I had a dream last night."

I was going parachuting with a man. I don't know if it was you or my husband. Probably you. We were flying, and perhaps you jumped out or were already in the air to parachute. You or my husband was going to show me how to do the parachute. You opened yours, and then were going to show me how to use it, or maybe you were going to let me go, and then open your own. Then we were floating down with open parachutes. You were going to show me, but then we landed totally gently, a soft landing. I was surprised because I would have thought there would be some speed in hitting the ground.

Then we were in a place like a hotel, and we were with a couple. We were going to have a drink, but I didn't know if I should. I had a glass of orange juice. The couple suggested a whiskey-orange would be good. I thought that would be okay, so I went to the area where there were different whiskeys, one old Chivas Regal, one Black Label, and so on. I wondered what kind would be good in orange juice. Actually, I don't like whiskey, which is why I would have to put it in orange juice. The woman in the couple had short black hair.

She began to give associations without prompting. "The glass of orange juice and ice relates to you because you always have a huge glass of something to drink."

"What about me, then?" I asked.

"The parachute: my old boyfriend David's mother has a vacation house near a mountain with a valley. You see lots of parachute fliers from the terrace. That reminds me that a friend of mine died exactly seven years ago when he was hang gliding. Just about this date!"

I said, "In this dream, I was supposed to show you how."

"Actually, by the time you were going to, we had landed. I was disappointed because I wanted to do it myself."

I felt she was talking about the dangers she was facing by taking off without me, but also the impingement she expected if she stayed with me. Jumping with me (in the analysis) offered something, but she also wanted to jump without me (by leaving). I remembered the dream from the day before which had such a similar theme.

I said, "This dream follows the one yesterday of the danger of flying with your husband."

"This morning I thought, 'God, I'm not going to see Dr. Scharff for three weeks. How will I stand it? How will I survive? Why didn't he tell me I shouldn't do this?' I could have gone for one week. Why did I have to go for three weeks?"

"So why are you flying off this way?" I asked.

She didn't answer my question, but went on her own course, her own flight. "I'm really worried about my husband's weight. He puts on weight like crazy. I told him to check it out, but he blew me off. He said he had no time."

I note that she is worried about her husband's behavior and judgment rather than about her own.

Then her husband had pressed her to go with him to a lecture on health. She said she couldn't because of coming to analysis, but then told him she would go just to get him off her back. "Yesterday we were in a store and there was a barrel of treats for children. I said, 'How cute.' He said, 'We can buy some for our children.' I said, 'That'll be the day!'"

I remember that their sexual activity is almost nil. He has refused to have children, except when she threatens to leave him, at which point he often says, "No, stay and we'll make a baby." At such times, she refuses him. As I think about this way that he withholds and then tantalizes her, I realize that she is doing the same to me: presenting material that holds so much potential the day before she is literally flying away. I think she is introducing the sexual element of seduction and avoidance in regard to me and our work.

I said, "What about the image of parachuting with me?"

"It's very sexual. Flying is orgasm. This is like landing. When my husband offered to take me flying I was frightened because he flies like a reckless child and in the dream the plane landed in the water. As you said, it's my sexuality drowned."

"Is this a rescue?" I asked.

"I don't know. The plane's drowning is my sexuality and my husband's. I wanted to tell someone we were in the water, but he said, 'Be quiet.' I was ambivalent, disappointed yet relieved that no one had to know.

"Remember the dream I had last week? We talked about my mother not letting me do my own thing and ruining things for me. I don't know how these things link up. There's probably a lot that's not coming to the surface. I'm relieved it's coming to the surface but when it does, I'm worried I won't be able to deal with it."

I am thinking of the downing of the plane under water with her and her husband in it, not just as a threat to their lives, but as the sinking of issues below the surface. Marianne herself buried things because they seemed unacceptable, something she often blamed her mother for. I wonder what is in danger of being drowned now.

"Like the sexuality and the parachute jumping together?" I said.

"It has something to do with my identification with you. Take the glass with ice—I'm like you having that."

"What about the whiskey?" I asked.

"I don't like whiskey at all, so I never drink whiskey. My father drinks it though. I took vacations with him. I've said only negative things about him in here, but actually I had some good times, like in kindergarten, and later taking hiking trips with my father. But then my mother would spoil it."

Her father is coming up to the surface in a new way that sounds more positive and oedipal, closer to the exhilaration of a parachute jump with me. I link the mention of whiskey to the Scottish calendar on my office wall which stands

for my connection to Scotland through my wife's family. But I am not sure that
this constitutes a connection for her, so I stay quiet.

"I feel I have all these pieces, like a puzzle, but I can't put them together.
You should help me, because I can't."

"Like I should help you with the parachute," I said.

"Oh, something else," she said, apparently ignoring my comment. "The
couple! And the woman with the very short hair. I think of people I know
who are psychoanalysts. I know them through David. One has very short
hair. Sasha. She's in her early forties. She is alone and would have loved to
have children. Her father's a rabbi. There are a couple of other women
in Paris, too. All single, happy professional women. I always thought I
wouldn't want to be a single professional in my forties."

I said, "In the first part of the dream, you weren't alone. Even though
you had a soft landing, you were disappointed that you couldn't do something for yourself."

"Yes," she said impatiently. "So what?"

"You're not on your own. You think about leaving me so you can be on
your own, but at the same time, although you say you should leave your
husband, you don't because you're afraid of being alone like the single
professional women. Then the feelings you can't afford to let surface with
him come up in here. You solve your fear of being alone, but in a way that
doesn't give you what you want either." She was quiet. I went on. "This
dream is a sequel to the crash in yesterday's dream. In this dream, you
formed a couple, with me instead of with your husband, and instead of
learning from me."

I felt I was saying too much and too abruptly with her. I was feeling pres-
sured by the theme of her wanting to do it by herself at the same time as she was
acting like she couldn't do things without me and yet was fleeing.

"So what about the couple telling me to put whiskey in my orange
juice?" she challenged me.

"Tell me," I said.

"I don't like it. My father drinks it too much."

"So you'd be like him?"

"Yes."

"So the couple tells you to put whiskey in a tall glass of orange juice."

"We call it 'OJ' which is like O. J. Simpson. I was watching the news report on him. They said, 'There's no word on why he forgot his daughter's birthday.' My father forgot my birthday last year. He called me three days late!"

"You're being like your forgetful father who drinks too much. Are you afraid you'll become like him if you're not part of a couple?"

I see in retrospect that as her irritation with me entered the picture, I became defensive about her identifying me with her rejecting and denigrated father. As this happened, I also overlooked the aspect of the dream in which the couple was advising her to become like her father, jumping to pin the wish on her, rather than feel accused of acting like an excluding couple and advising her to become like hated aspects of her father.

"I always wanted to be like my mother, but she would say to me, 'You're just like your father!' when she was mad at me. I was never able to identify with her. That's something I missed badly. She would say I was like my father, that my figure and brain were like him. It's true, I have my father's hands. They're identical. My personality is exactly like his mother, a terrible person who left her kids when they were 2 and 4. After she calls my father a bad person, my mother goes on to say how she hated her mother-in-law. So I'm always like someone who is bad.

"I wanted to be like my mother, but I couldn't identify with her. I have mixed feelings about it. Sometimes, I think I *wish* that I *wished* to be like my mother."

"In this dream, you were considering being like your father."

"Apparently. But also like you!"

I realized with relief that she was avoiding me because of the erotic pull toward me which also included wanting to identify with me and her father. Then she interrupted herself and spoiled the situation just as her mother spoiled things throughout her life, often by attacking her father. I felt we were back on track together in the hour.

"But being like me threatened to make you like him in a way your mother wouldn't let you."

"Maybe. He called me a couple of days ago and said, 'Can't you take your vacation later, because I'll be gone on business the first week you're at home.' I don't know why he said that, because I'll be there another two weeks. My father said, 'I have to talk to you.' I said to my brother, 'I bet he wants to tell me that he's going to marry his girlfriend.' By the way, she's a psychoanalyst, too."

"Oh!" I said, quite surprised. "You never said that before."

"You didn't know that?"

"No. You've never mentioned it. What about her?"

"I don't know why she'd be interested in my father. She's younger, in her fifties."

"Well, it's pretty interesting to tell me that in the last minute before you leave for three weeks."

I am left abruptly, without time to process this new information, about which I would have liked to have said something like, "It's the couple you want to be in, one with me who is married to an analyst, and with your father who would then be like me. You feel excluded from them and from me at the point of leaving here. I think that has to do with why you're leaving." But she has given me this new evidence of how she feels transferentially excluded from the internal couple by throwing me the links as she metaphorically jumps out the side of our plane and opens her parachute without me. I am left holding the surprise, wanting to jump after her to teach her something.

Discussion

This is a mid-phase hour with a patient who works well in the analysis, despite the possibility of its interruption. The transference has developed and she can work with it. She refers throughout to her internal object relations linking the here-and-now of the hour to her there-and-now situation with her husband about whom she is chronically ambivalent, and to the there-and-then of her feelings for the mother she wanted to want to be like and by whom she often felt persecuted, and the father with whom her identification oscillates between anti-libidinal and libidinal forms.

The dream also introduces the internal couple consisting of Dr. David Scharff paired with Dr. Jill Scharff whom the patient occasionally sees in the waiting room. The image of the analyst's wife is echoed by that of her father's girlfriend, offering her an intense identification which is itself fraught with peril. When she dreams of putting "OJ" in her drink, she links that to O. J. Simpson, whose trial was then prominent in the news and whom she identifies as a murderous husband and negligent parent. The drink itself is a drink she hates, because it substitutes whiskey for milk and because it is identified with the father who left her and onto whom she has split an intensely rejecting object. For the analyst, the whiskey provides an association to his wife before the patient specifically invokes the internal couple in the session.

At the same time, Marianne yearns for her analyst excitedly as a potentially helpful parent, only to find him turning into a sexualized oedipal partner. This refers to the way that he brings to the surface material that she finds threatening. Then she fears she will die from soaring (the friend who died hang gliding), or crashing and drowning (with her husband who flies in a frightening way). On the other hand, the analyst could help her parachute to safety, but without teaching her how to protect herself—a sexual image that is exciting and frightening in turn: it threatens her wish to jump from the analysis and land on her own. Then, at the end of the session, she produces an enactment of her ambivalence by giving new information that seems important, but by giving it in the last minute of the session before she leaves for a visit to her parents, she leaves the analyst hanging, opening her own parachute and leaving him wishing to teach her something she is not there to learn.

Transference Geography in the Session

As in most sessions, the locale of the transference changes during the session. The quality of the analyst as an object alternates between exciting and rejecting, maternal and paternal. The discrete focused transference material derived from her internal objects has both an erotic attraction and a persecuting intensity for her. This fits the hysterical object relations set in which the ideal object of the central self is carefully stripped of excitement and aggression, and has little power left for centered holding (Fairbairn 1954).

This is why Marianne's generally positive contextual transference is also shaky. She does trust that Dr. Scharff supports her and has her interests at heart, but she expects that he will become like her rejecting and self-interested parents and husband. She handles this, in part, by withholding helpful information until the last minute as though it would be used against her central interests. The contextual transference is undermined by the focused transference.

The containment possible in the hour changes from one moment to the next, as Dr. Scharff follows the minute fluctuations of the transference as one state of mind succeeds another (Joseph 1989). But Marianne holds so much of the material inside that she does not allow him a full opportunity for reverie precisely because she is afraid that he will be like her self-interested parental objects and will use space to think for himself and against her. Nevertheless, there is an atmosphere of work going on and of exchange between them, so that the potential space opens and closes in a flow during the session. Only in the last minute does she throw him the bone of the information about the father's girlfriend, which forms a solid link between her parental couple and Dr. Scharff's couple, and which should, in time, allow them a fuller range of interpretive work about the envied transferential internal couple.

Holding and containment are alternately compromised and repaired within the session. A full range of use of the transference in time and space gives the sense that in spite of the enactment that is going on, Marianne is working quite fully within the analytic space. The work is centered on the here-and-now, beginning with the opening exchange about logistics of scheduling, and continuing with active discussion of the here-and-now centered on the there-and-back then and here-and-back then (how the patterns with mother and father determined the present moment). Marianne links the there-and-now of relations with her husband and parents to the current situation with Dr. Scharff and to her past experience with them. The area of greatest avoidance is in the future of the analysis, the if-and-when of the here-and-now, overshadowed by her focus on her future life, the if-and-when of the there-and-now. She acts as though planning for her life future will solve issues that are essentially matters of a possible analytic future, which she has often avoided discussing with Dr. Scharff. The difficulty holding in mind a future for the analysis stems from the problems in the focused transference in which Marianne experiences Dr. Scharff as one who will spoil, seduce, or exclude. She avoids linking and thinking, and she foreshortens the analytic future to eliminate her fear.

Responses to the focused transference flood the countertransference and saddle Dr. Scharff with a sense of responsibility for Marianne's future when she cannot bear to consider it fully. Locating this area of the patient's oversight can be used to focus the therapist's future thinking and intervention.

Object Construction and Self Modification

This hour is filled with object sorting, exclusion, and construction (see Chapter 10). Marianne considers which aspects of her mother and father she can accept as objects of her central self, which parts to reject, and which parts to identify with. As they are now less subject to the repression that hides them from her view, she now tries excluding aspects of them, lets aspects back in, and excludes them again. She wishes for parts of her mother and father to accept and laments the spoiling and splitting that she engages in. We see her experiment with new aspects of relating with Dr. Scharff. As shown in the dream's parachute metaphor, she tries to learn from him despite her wish to go it alone. She tries to find an object with which to identify and work, then fearfully moves away. As she thinks about the limitations and destructive patterns that she has invoked repeatedly in her past and current life, she considers the kind of self-organization that she can tolerate and grow toward. We see an exquisite back-and-forth movement in which new construction of elements of her self is intricately involved with the remodeling of her old objects and with attempts to install new and improved objects in her inner world.

In this way, we see her self, striving both for autonomy and relatedness, struggling with external objects and the inner object relations that define her. Marianne worked with her transferential ambivalence, centering on the avoided question of whether to form her life plans in such a way as to truncate the possibility of analysis.

Middle of the Mid-Phase: Working Through in the Transference and Countertransference

Two consecutive sessions in the twenty-eighth month of analysis six months later pick up themes from the previous spring and show an increased capacity to work with them. Incidentally, these sessions also show Marianne's struggle with whether to use medication for her sometimes crippling depression.

It's the first day after Thanksgiving weekend. Marianne does not say that our meeting only three times the previous week had anything to do with it, but she had a lousy weekend. Today she sits on the couch facing me, something she does occasionally. It seems to be a feature of her despair. She says that everything personally and professionally comes to nothing. She feels in despair, and so, as we had been discussing for some time, she finally called a psychiatric colleague this morning to make an appointment for evaluation for antidepressant medication.

She reports a dream:

There was a puzzle in a vitrine, which is a glass antique showcase. The word is the same in French. I don't know the English word. I feel I am under glass. It's one of those puzzles that you move the numbers or pieces of a picture around, except the pieces all were stuck except for two in the lower right-hand corner, which would only go up and down. In part of one corner it looked like a recognizable picture, but otherwise it was a mess.

I remember some feeling like this when I was a teenager in therapy, feeling I was only going forward and back between the past and the present.

In the dream, I wanted to say to my mother that this was all stuck and wouldn't work. I wanted to take all the pieces out and rearrange them before putting them back, because I felt I couldn't do it the way it was, but my mother said, "No, you have to do it the right way."

Then, explaining the problem with the puzzle to me, she said, "You have to screw it from the back." She meant that one has to unscrew the back and remove it to rearrange the puzzle.

I noticed the perverse sexual image in the phrase "screw it from the back," but I only used the image now to talk about how she felt stuck like such an unworkable puzzle.

I said, "Your only hope is to take pieces out of yourself and start over. You don't think you can work things out otherwise because you feel so stuck."

"My mother is the one that says I can only do things a certain backwards way. It's the blind alley. The puzzle is a maze."

"There's no way out," I said. "That way of feeling is what you've brought here. It's the feeling of impossibility and stuckness we have to work on. It leads to the feeling of hopelessness, which takes on a life of its own and gets you really depressed."

"I know that's why you think I need medication now," she said. "Why don't you do the prescribing yourself then? And why did you pick Dr. X?"

I told her I would prefer to leave our work free for the analysis, and that Dr. X was himself an analyst and would be supportive of our work. She said that her uncle who is an analyst and neurologist said to her that she should take the medication, that it would help her analysis. He spoke with her about the depression he had seen in both her parents. We agree she has absorbed the depression that her mother has shoved underground, and has pushed into her. Depression runs right through her upbringing. Her uncle thought her father was actually much more depressed than her mother.

The next day Marianne sat up again for the second day in a row. She had called Dr. X, who did not have an appointment for some time. She wondered if I had called him, because he then called her back with a better time. We discussed leaving room for the meaning of the medication, but meanwhile she was afraid to take it for fear it might decrease her capacity to bear pain, which she feels she should do, perhaps out of guilt.

Then, leaning back against the bolster, she said that she had further thoughts about the dream. "The phrase I used about the puzzle, 'You have to screw it from the back,' is sexual, isn't it? Maybe it's a feeling I don't have a penis. Maybe that's what's wrong down there."

She then went on to talk about times in bed with her father. "On Sunday mornings I would go into my parents' bedroom and my mother would leave me alone with my father. We played the tickle game, which I liked but I also felt it was wrong. He would hold me from behind, my back to his chest and press my chest with his arms. It was almost like lying on the couch here, he was behind me like you're behind me here." She made a face about it. "I keep thinking that I'm so identified with my mother, but I'm beginning to think that there was more trouble with my father.

"Now I remember yesterday's dream. Part of the puzzle was pretty and in order, and then there was the other part of it that was a mess. Maybe the ordered part was the way I thought about my mother, and the disorderly, upsetting part I couldn't solve was about my father—about the way I liked what he did but it was also really uncomfortable."

We now talked about the way in which she could bring things into the analysis, and then, precisely because things would start to move—like the puzzle pieces being able to shift—she would feel guilty.

I said, "We agree the puzzle dream is about how you feel here in analysis. But now I see why you're sitting up. You're worried about yourself as the 'it' that will be 'screwed from the back.' You're worried that I would hold you like your father did in the tickle game and do something to you from behind that also has to do with something being wrong down there."

She jolted, then nodded. "Oh, maybe that's right. I want you to do something to fix me, but I'm frightened too—it doesn't feel right."

A little later, she said, "I really should stay in Washington. What's been frightening me is that analysis is starting to mean a lot to me. I told my husband that this is my home now. My job's not important and our marriage doesn't work. I really don't want to go to New York or Paris, but I'm frightened of staying for analysis. I said something to my cousin about looking for a job here, and she had some interesting ideas about working for an academic society."

I said, "I notice you saved the news that you might consider a job here for the last couple of minutes of the hour. That pattern is still in place."

After this session, Marianne resumed lying on the couch. In the consultation about medication with Dr. X, she decided that her depression had abated enough so that she could agree to his suggestion that she delay a trial of medication for the time being.

In this session, the work we saw Marianne doing six months earlier is still going on, but with an added directness and intensity in the here-and-now of the transference. Analysis is filled with her erotic wish and fear. We see that her sitting up, a minor enactment in the analysis, is used as a defense against her transference fear of being "screwed from the back." She ties this to her bodily fantasies of something being wrong because of not having a penis and longing for something from her father, which took a sexualized form. She thinks that analytic repair will take the form of giving her a penis by "screwing from the back," in keeping with her infantile fantasy.

As she retraces similar territory, Marianne moves in a spiral way into deeper work. The focused transference is now more solidly in place, held by a strengthened contextual holding. Despite periods of intense depression, the process of containment works better, and the material of the session distributes meaning and emotion evenly between her mind, the mind of the analyst, and the space between them. She is more able to consider the excited sexual material and to modulate the feelings of rejection by her objects, less prone to shutting Dr. Scharff out, as she develops a wider associative range. All of these, together with the ebb and flow of the regression, constitute the pattern of preliminary working through typical of the mid-phase.

Mid-Phase: Working with Silence through the Evolving Transference and Countertransference in the Mid-Phase

Antonio Morales (described in Chapter 20) had grown strangely silent during his hours. In almost every hour over a period of weeks, he greeted me (DES) in the waiting room, checked our schedule if a change was indicated, lay down comfortably on the couch—and said nothing. I was used to his giving me full reports of the preceding days, the job situation, or the progress of his friend's analysis. This reporting had been the hallmark of his work. He reported on his life in the there-and-now world beyond the analysis to such an extent that I felt he was not really present in analysis. On the other hand, he was quite engaged with me: he liked being here, he was curious, and he would often answer one of my questions by saying, 'That's interesting because . . .' In keeping with his reporting style, he often used the phrase 'The truth is . . .' to introduce a comment or an opinion about what he had examined, as if to emphasize the accuracy of the report.

I listened, I made obvious links, and asked questions about earlier life experiences that might reveal his early object relations model for the situation he was reporting. I tried to build *model scenes* (Lichtenberg et al. 1992) of early life as a template for later experience. I had given advice about his treatment of his children, and I had encouraged him to stop drinking, which he did—to the great benefit of his family. His marriage improved, he stopped raging at his wife, he reintroduced sex into their relationship, and his commitment to marriage and family increased. He spent more time with his children and put his work into better perspective. Things had gotten vastly better in his life.

During this reporting period, I sometimes felt silenced by a lengthy report because I did not know exactly what I could say to be helpful. And since he did not bring a palpable affect to the exchange with me, I mostly felt that, in a continuing way, he was absent. I did not have access to his feelings, and now that he was silent, I did not have access to his thoughts either.

One day he broke his silence with an observation about the analysis and a question for me. He had begun to wonder if it were time to finish his analysis. He wanted time back for other priorities. What did I think?

It was now that I spoke from my countertransference. I saw him as being in the mid-phase, not the late phase of analysis. Tactfully, I agreed that the changes brought termination to mind as an option, but I said I felt that something intangible but important was missing in our relationship, for he had never been angry at me and never experienced heightened feeling in my presence. He had reported on it to be sure, but never demonstrated it—and apparently hardly ever felt it—with me. While the goal of our work was not explicitly to have him do that, I felt that the experience of himself as an absent father and an uninvolved husband was now being felt in our relationship as the absence of feelings and thoughts about me, and a wish not to see things through with me.

He was surprised. It had never occurred to him that he should feel anything particular about me. He respected me, but he had no feelings of liking or not liking me, and no reason to be angry at me. Sure, he wished that I would give him more advice, or tell him how he was doing in various areas, for instance with his children, but he knew he had to find out for himself at this stage. Nevertheless, he took my intervention seriously, and decided to see what possible meaning lay in the absence of feeling. Over the next weeks, his capacity to be in a state of unconscious communication with me improved.

Mr. Morales now told two dreams which developed the transference in an altogether new way:

> In the first one, I dreamt I was in an old car with you driving, getting to my old home across some hills and valleys. But my house wasn't in sight yet, so I wasn't quite sure we were actually almost there.

He related this dream to the frequent trips his father took away from home and to his feeling that he had no connection to his father in childhood. *He* thought that we were getting somewhere, and *I* thought that he was coming closer to home in the transference.

I felt a sense of hopefulness.

Then he told the second dream.

> I dreamt that I viewed a gated city from a great height, from a place called Washington Heights above New York. I came closer and entered the gates with a couple of teenage thugs. There was a swimming pool inside. I met a crusty old woman who seemed unapproachable but she had something to offer. Wild dogs roamed the city threatening people, and I realized I was in league with the threatening teenagers.

The gated city with a pool referred to my office, which is situated next to a high wooden fence with gates that open to the pool behind my house. I remembered that he had commented on seeing the pool when the gates were blown out by high winds. I felt his aggression had entered the room. He was coming down from the great heights and distance above our Washington analysis to dream of me both as the absent father of his childhood now returning through me, and as his crusty, complaining mother who now seemed to have something to offer. And the thugs and dogs represented the aggression he had kept out of the office, behind and beyond the gates.

I felt we might be getting closer, and I experienced a mild rush at our approach to the gates. Following discussion of his associations, I interpreted the elements of these dreams and the gathering transference to him, and inwardly I expected some form of transference attack. But he pulled back from the approach to the gates, and began to be silent in the hours. A new "nothing" began to happen. I felt his absence all over again, all the more acutely after the hopeful dreams of getting somewhere.

I let the silence grow. In the first few days of silence, I would wait a few minutes, and then ask what was going across his mind. He said that he had just been reporting, and he was no longer happy simply to fill me in with the reports. So I let the silences get longer. Now he would go perhaps for ten or fifteen minutes before speaking. Curiously, I actually felt that he was more with me now than when he had spoken so easily and automatically over the previous couple of years. I did feel connected to him and his experience, but I struggled—as I now felt he was doing—to put meaning to the situation. As in the first dream, we were actually together in the car, perhaps even coming closer to an internal home or to the gated city. Although I had lost my bearings, I now felt that we were lost together.

A new question occurred to me: I asked Mr. Morales to tell me *how* he was thinking in the silences. He said that he was "scrolling through files" in his mind, scanning topics he might talk about, things to be done at work, and things about his family. He knew he could talk about any of them, but it no longer seemed worthwhile to do so, so he continued to scroll.

Finally I understood. For all these years he had been "scrolling," as one does with computer files, scanning things quickly while moving on, never quite pausing or alighting. His description let me into his thinking process: he used his way of thinking both to his enormous advantage at work, and defensively in his analysis. When I described this back to him, he first countered that he valued his way of thinking. He could make connections between patterns at work and recall masses of facts accurately, which gave him his major intellectual advantage. No doubt this was so. No doubt it was the store of evidence that lent authority to his frequent opening phrase "the truth is . . ."

I repeated that his scrolling also operated to his disadvantage, as any strength may do: it represented his fear of opening and sinking into certain "files" that held threatening contents. I said that his scanning, scrolling, and reporting with me had the effect over the years of keeping us from sinking into the material of the threatening files, and therefore from becoming engaged together in understanding the really tough aspects of his self that kept him remote from me and from his family.

Mr. Morales was silent again for a few minutes before saying that he had never seen that in his pattern of thought. He had just felt instinctively that if he stopped scrolling and "running through his thoughts," he would lose his edge.

"I can see how I've tried to keep a step ahead of you, to keep you out because I'm afraid I'll come to a stop. I'll crash the hard drive," he said. "Maybe there is something in those files I'd better look into!"

The view of his mental process built from Mr. Morales's words and my countertransference widened my understanding of his two dreams. His mental process was an identification with his absent father who drove away from him so often, the view of the countryside scrolling past the car windows. Mr. Morales had to keep driving faster than his father by scrolling in his mind in order not to feel left by him, crash into him with longing, or see the faults in his own car. If he stopped scrolling, he would face the grief for the absent father, and that would bring him face-to-face with the complaining, depressed mother. The second dream represented not only the arrival home and the meeting of depression and anger, but a new way of thinking which he had been avoiding just as much as he had avoided the angry and depressed content of the files.

In their mid-phase work, Mr. Morales and Marianne both show consolidation of the contextual transference, which allows the focused transference to emerge. Both show a capacity to analyze their dreams, and work with focused transference. Mr. Morales, who earlier had held Dr. Scharff at bay (Chapter 20), is now able to let him in. Marianne moves her experience into the transference. She links her thought of getting "screwed from the back" to the there-and-then (getting in bed with her father), connects it to the here-and-then (her fear that Dr. Scharff would be like him) and works on it in the here-and-now (working together in the transference). Typical of mid-phase work, the containing function moves into the shared potential space inhabited by the therapeutic relationship. But there is no resolution. We get the sense of work in progress.

22

Late Mid-Phase

This chapter illustrates work from the middle and late stages of the mid-phase of an analysis. We begin with work selected from the middle of the mid-phase in the fourth year, and pick up the same case again in the late mid-phase during the fifth year of analysis.

The Middle of the Mid-Phase

The first sequence of three mid-phase sessions of analysis illustrates work with the impact of the analyst's vacation on the therapeutic relationship, the transference, and the sense of self. It shows the use of dreams to reveal the transference and the patient's endopsychic situation, and it follows the evolution of the transference and countertransference as patient and analyst recover from the effects of the separation. Patient and analyst use the heightening of the transference to rework issues that the patient has already explored but has not completely resolved.

Mrs. Nichols, a woman in her late thirties, married to Lee, and with two children, was in the fourth year of analysis with me (JSS). She had begun analysis to get help with her depression, her lack of self-assertion, not knowing what to do with herself, frustration with her difficult daughter, lack of sexual desire, and resulting tension in her marriage. She had progressed in all areas, but still found it hard to be assertive, to take initiative sexually, and to confront negative feelings.

For the first time, in an assertive but unconsidered move, she had planned her summer vacation of two weeks without regard to when my vacation would be. It happened that her two weeks followed mine without any overlap. So the summer vacation from analysis for her was then four weeks instead of two. After the long vacation break, she had a complicated reaction.

Session 1

When Mrs. Nichols returned for her first session after her two weeks hiking in Norway, I felt pleased to see that she was looking pretty and rosy-complexioned. It was only two weeks since my own vacation, but my vacation glow had faded under a mountain of work at the start of the academic year.

"Sorry I'm late," she began pleasantly. "I had to wait for the painters and then my daughter missed the bus so I had to take her to school and then other parents were seeing their kids into the classroom and I felt that she needed me to stay for a bit." She paused, and her tone of voice took on a peevish quality, as she went on, "I almost felt like cancelling anyway, because I don't feel like getting into things. The vacation was a mixed blessing. There are things I have to talk about, but why tell you? That's what I feel."

"Sounds like you're mad that I didn't give you my self the last four weeks, so why should you give me your self?" I suggested.

"That's it," she agreed. "This is wasting my money. The way I speak to you here doesn't work at home. No one really listens. They certainly don't want to hear how depressed I am. And even if I get better, my daughter is still difficult. Lee thinks so too and yet the psychologist we took her to says she doesn't need treatment. So this is a waste of time and money. I don't want to go on." She fell silent.

Mrs. Nichols is feeling an angry contextual transference at the break in therapy, but she handles it through a focused attack on Dr. Scharff, as though it were her direct fault that she feels let down. The explanation that the anger and her reaction are due to the separation is not a complete one: neither patient nor analyst understands why this separation so many years into their work has hit her so hard, but it is too soon in the sequence to press that question. Dr. Scharff chooses first to speak to Mrs. Nichols's feeling of anger in the contextual transference about the failure of holding and containment.

I had already been through two weeks of returning patients being angry at me for being away for just two weeks, and I was getting used to it. The break of four weeks had been even harder for Mrs. Nichols, and it brought to mind the four years of work we had done together. I did not want to lose her at this stage, but I did not feel threatened that she would abandon her analysis. I felt more punished by her unaccustomed silence.

"You're depriving me to pay me back because you felt deprived," I said. "In so doing you're depriving yourself because it seems easier to do that than tell me you're upset with me for depriving you."

"Yes," she said. "It's always easier. Okay, let me try to do this more directly. You weren't here when I wanted you and you got your vacation, and then when I went away you got the money from me for nothing." She paused before saying, "I feel disrespectful to you for treating you this way and saying these things." She hesitated, and then went on. "What's so special about you that you get to have everything? You're the doctor and I'm the patient and I pay all this money for you to heal me. But to get anywhere here, I have to forget about that and somehow believe that there'll be some give and take, that you are interested in me for who I am and not for how much I can pay you."

Anxiety and rage about the break have taken Mrs. Nichols into the paranoid-schizoid position in which she lambastes Dr. Scharff as a disappointing and neglectful parent. But Mrs. Nichols also signals clearly that she understands the wider context of this material: it is within a respectful, holding relationship with an otherwise caring and trusted analyst that she is delivering this painful material. The descent to the paranoid-schizoid position is followed by a return to depressive-position functioning, as she brings together split parts of the analyst-object, and is able to assume that the analyst understands. In response to the interpretive work, she gives more material.

Mrs. Nichols seemed to interrupt herself to tell me a dream:

I had this dream last night. I came back for my session. Your office was under renovation, you were very caught up with all these trainees and there didn't seem to be anywhere for me to be. You said, "Wait a minute" and I don't know what happened after that. I wandered around and woke up.

"I know you do all these things," she continued, making it clear that the dream was no interruption, but part of her communication of rage at my neglect of her. "Increasingly more. You've expanded your travel, training your students, and writing books, and it feels like this is sort of . . ." She could not complete the sentence, but got to the point with her next try. "Where do your patients fit in? Where do we fall on your priority list?"

"Since the vacation, you're worried that there's no room for you here, that I regard you as unimportant," I said. "You've been late because you've been busy with your other projects—renovating your home and 'training' your children. You want me to know you take better care of your children than I do of you, and your lateness gives me to feel how you feel shut out by me."

Dr. Scharff is now able to contain the material. Instead of threatening to quit, Mrs. Nichols is more directly expressive of her anger, despite feeling disrespectful, while Dr. Scharff resumes her work in tolerating, listening, and understanding. These are signs that the contextual transference is intact and positive, and so the focused transference is freed to become negative without endangering their working partnership. The patient's validation of the contextual holding contributes to the therapist's capacity to make the interpretation that now leads to the return of repressed unconscious material in the form of remembered dreams:

"Oh, I had awful dreams last week," she said, and told me the first of them.

I was on a train. My college boyfriend was there and I dismissed him though I wanted to relate to him. He went off to the end of the train. My best friend, Milly, was on the train. Someone had been murdered, either by Lee or Milly, I didn't want to think who had done it or why. I really had the feeling it was Milly. I didn't want to be left alone with the two of them. Then there was this baby struggling, and while I was looking at it, it stopped breathing and was slumped over on the corner of the seat. I kept saying, "We've got to do something with the baby." But people just left it until we got to the destination. Then someone started moving it and there was hope that the baby was maybe alive. Then I went over and found that, yes, the baby was alive, a boy, but he looked not as rosy as before. He was sallow and unattractive, but he was alive anyway. I took him off and played with him.

"I just woke up feeling really sick and distressed. This dream was too much for me to deal with. I woke up in the middle of the night, because our old cat was panting and uncomfortable. The kids are all upset about whether she's going to die. But the dream really has to do with me. Am I going to slump over? Will anyone notice?"

Mrs. Nichols is threatened in the dream by abandoning objects, by Lee and Milly, and by the murder, as the train moves on, perhaps a symbol of her life's journey with her sexual and aggressive feelings and her fears for her self, or of the course of the analysis. But underlying these losses is the threat of the death of her infantile, needy self, represented by the baby. The anger and denigration aimed at Dr. Scharff for leaving her covers her terror that central aspects of her needy self will die. Now we can see that the therapeutic separation brought her back to worries about self-cohesion and self-survival. She expresses anger to draw attention to her abandonment and ensure she is not left again, and also to jump-start the cohesion of the self around anger. Now we can see that the paranoid-schizoid position behavior was covering up the more fundamental problem of the autistic/contiguous position. Treating Dr. Scharff as a rejecting object at one level obscures Mrs. Nichols's longing for her as an exciting object, and even more fundamentally covers the need for her as an object to secure cohesion of the self. Mrs. Nichols's taking care of her children instead of being on time for her session is a way of expressing the longing that Dr. Scharff care for her own infantile needs.

I said, "You wonder if I'll have the same care for you as you have for your cat and your children. You wonder if I care as much for the baby part of you that comes alive here even if it seems more dead, even if that part of you is angry and envious of me for all I have, made to feel worthless because of it, and feels like retaliating."

"These feelings are such a burden," she replied. "I don't want to have to deal with them. I just want to get rid of them in an aggressive kind of way. I don't like them and I don't want to have them. Like in this dream, this train has a lot of power, but it's very negative; I want to take hold of it but I'm afraid."

Mrs. Nichols closes the session by acknowledging the power of her problems and reassuring Dr. Scharff and herself by making it clear that she is "back on board" in the analysis because she wants to be rid of her difficulties.

Session 2

"I had this dream," Mrs. Nichols began right away.

> I was visiting my grandparents' house, which in reality was razed to the ground when the county built the new highway. But in the dream I was there. It had a wonderful feeling about it. I was strolling with Lee under spreading cherry trees.

The dream describes a holding environment that Mrs. Nichols treasured and misses very much. She is struggling to return to the depressive position, in contrast to yesterday's regression to paranoid-schizoid and autistic-contiguous issues, when she felt abandoned. The recovery in the dream of the wonderful place of the past is magical. She notes that the county has actually razed the old magical place: real progress to the present will require real mourning for what has been lost. For the moment, she looks not to her self but to her husband in the romantic setting under the spreading cherry trees.

"I'm really missing Lee now that he's back at work. It was so nice having all that time together in the mountains," she remarked. She went on to describe the land and the features of the grand country house on rolling acres, and how much Lee would have loved it there.

I thought of the cherry trees that abound in the neighborhood of my office. Each year in springtime a magical canopy of paper-white blossom spreads above our paths.

I said that I thought that her refinding Lee there was referring to her pleasure in recovering a new relationship to him through analysis and now in returning to recover me. That led her to remember another part of the dream:

> In the second part of the dream, I'm in your office. Our positions are reversed. I'm over here on the couch and you are there on the other side. I don't remember too much, but I felt you were attentive. This time there were no distractions. This place was protected from outside interference. I got up to leave. You asked me if I hadn't forgotten something. I'd been playing with a piece of clay nearby and you pointed out that I'd left it on the shelf behind you. I said, "No, that was here when I got here." I got up and realized that I had on the same dress as the day before and it had cookie-dough crumbs all down the back of it as if I'd lain in it at home. I apologized for that and left.

Then Lee was in the dream. I had told Lee it was hard to be back in analysis and that I was upset about the money it costs. So in the dream, he asked me how it went, and I said it was much better but there was a big deal about forgetting something. He rolled his eyes. I said, "No, No. I hadn't forgotten anything. The big deal was *she* stepped out of her role to make sure I hadn't forgotten something."

In this dream Mrs. Nichols shows that the contextual transference is working positively again. She brings in an older child self who has been lying in unformed dough. Within the positive context, she views Dr. Scharff as going out of her way to remind her not to leave things behind. The final condensation of the image of her husband with the analyst and perhaps another female figure in the sentence "*she* stepped out of her role to make sure I hadn't forgotten something" cannot yet be understood, but it heralds work on the transference that Mrs. Nichols is trying to accomplish.

Mrs. Nichols continued, "So I woke up feeling much better I guess. Both of those parts of the dream had been about making good contact and being in a relationship where I felt that you and Lee were both interested in me. But I'm suspicious of losing all the regular feelings. The dirty dress makes me think everything wasn't perfect, that it was still messy from the day before and maybe I wanted to hide it. I'm guilty about what happened yesterday."

The patient is now firmly back in the depressive position with a functioning capacity for concern, and so she can take up issues of guilt and damage to herself and others, and experience their goodness.

"Yesterday you were talking about angry, envious feelings, ruining things, and worries about not caring for the baby part of you," I confirmed. "Today you dreamed of recovering the pleasant connection to your grandmother, the woman for whom you are named, and it feels good to you."

The patient's capacity for concern fosters the goodness of the analyst's ability to think and make connections. Now we see the transference connection between the analyst and the other "she" of the dream condensation.

"Yes," she said. "It was pleasant to be there. It had aged, though. When I think of my grandparents and their international stature, it's weird. I've spent most of my adult life trying to erase it and hide it and remove my-self. I haven't in any way carried on their tradition of service to the coun-try, living abroad, and gracious entertaining all the time with two or three servants. Important government people. I'm not sure how I feel about it. But things are different now, so it makes sense. You couldn't find a more diverse group of grandchildren, all of them wanting to reject that.

"Then there's also my mother's sister who died of malaria, and it devas-tated my grandparents. And yet they never talked about her. And they both had affairs, I learned after they died. So the house held a lot of secrets and tragedy. Yet also a lot of happy memories. I don't know if my grandmother was a depressed person like me, but she sure knew how to throw a good party."

Mrs. Nichols has spent this session securing her sense of Dr. Scharff's ca-pacity for contextual holding and containment. So she can assess her grand-mother, like her analyst, as a woman with faults and assets, someone whose children rebelled but who offered treasures.

Session 3

"What is going on?" Mrs. Nichols confronted me. "You haven't given me my bill and you've not dealt with the dream about you. Maybe I said these things about you charging me, and now you're not going to! But the dream . . ."

Right away, Mrs. Nichols signals that she is back in the paranoid-schizoid position, suspecting Dr. Scharff of not treating her properly.

"Which one?" I wanted to know, momentarily caught off guard.
"About you and me in the office," she said. "The one where you were paying attention after all. In the dream you were, but maybe you weren't paying attention at all yesterday. You just focused on Lee."

For the life of me, I could not remember the dream. I remembered her talk-ing about missing her husband, and my interpretation linking him to me, but I thought that I said very little in that session because she was working away on the dream herself. But why could I not remember the dream? I might be iden-tified with some aspect of the patient's projection that killed off my attentive-ness, or the dream may have been dealing with forgetting. I knew from experi-ence that when this happens, the dream usually comes back later in association to elements brought out by the patient, so I hoped it would now. But I felt anxious and defensive.

Usually if the therapist does not have material in conscious memory, the patient shares her state of mind and it comes back. Today, Mrs. Nichols does the opposite: she attacks the context and destroys Dr. Scharff's capacity for linking. But in this early part of the hour, Dr. Scharff does not realize what is happening, and a transference–countertransference enactment begins. Through projective identification, Mrs. Nichols put her destructive state of mind into Dr. Scharff who now experiences it first-hand. This is just the kind of encounter that we learn the most from.

"The day before, you were angry and envious and feeling neglected by me," I said, half to acknowledge this to her and half to remind myself of what was going on and kick-start my own thinking process. "Then yesterday you had the dream." But the dream would not come to me.

I could have waited and struggled through until she rescued me, but the projection was so gripping and my capacity to hold the patient's material in mind was so destroyed by it, that I did not have the usual confidence in the analytic process of recall. I said to myself, "I am feeling guilty for forgetting" and looked in that phrase for a clue. I remembered that she had mentioned guilt the day before, but I did not remember the issue of forgetting. At that moment what I did remember was the advice of a late supervisor when he wanted detailed process reporting from me. "So look at the notes," he said. "That's why you take them." Fortunately, I happened to have taken notes in yesterday's session. Encouraged by his grandfatherly support, I looked at my notes.

The enactment continues: Mrs. Nichols has put her own need for grandparental support into Dr. Scharff who remembers the support of an older supervisor, and reaches for tangible evidence of that support. What is important here is not the use of the notes—which in any event fails to satisfy the patient and the therapist—but the memory of the helpful figure at a time when the patient has, through projective identification, destroyed her own helpful object.

I said, "Let's go over the details again. Your dream was one of recovering connection through the memory of your grandparents' house. The image of recovery was linked to my office and to me by the image of the spreading trees . . ."

"I didn't link it," she interrupted.

"I know, *I* did," I agreed. "I'm wondering if you felt that I dwelt too much on the recovery, and not enough on the hidden message of mess, damage, and inattention that you thought the cookie-dough crumbs pointed to."

"No, you didn't deal with the recovery either," she complained in a disgruntled tone. "Especially, you didn't seem to appreciate that I'd made things better here."

Mrs. Nichols lets Dr. Scharff know what she is after: recognition both of her difficulties and her capacity to recover and make reparation. Having contributed to the destruction of Dr. Scharff's capacity to think, Mrs. Nichols is now, grudgingly, helping her to understand her through projective identification, which conveys more about her state of mind than she had done through her anger in the first session. Feeling abandoned by Dr. Scharff during the long vacation had destroyed Mrs. Nichols's capacity to function, to think, and to carry on as usual, and she wanted credit for working hard to rebuild good feeling about Dr. Scharff and her self. Dr. Scharff, still in the grip of the projective identification, does not yet feel that things are better, and she works on the projective identification by reviewing what she thinks the patient is feeling about her.

I felt that my notes were making things worse. I could not get it right.

I tried again, this time ignoring the notes and staying with the here-and-now. I said, "You felt I ignored the whole dream and you. I forgot your bill, your dream, and what I remember I'm not getting right."

"Yes," she said. "You don't want to deal with it."

Now that her anger was out in the open, my mind was freed to think and recover the links I had been making in association to her dream the day before. I said, "I am thinking of other elements we could be exploring—the meaning of the solid piece of clay versus the fragments of cookie dough, the reason for the reversal of our positions, what it was you thought I forgot. But I'm not sure if you really want to work on the dream, or if the main point is that you want to challenge me about what I've forgotten and haven't done, about how I haven't taken as good care of you as you have of me by paying for your hours during your vacation."

Mrs. Nichols has helped Dr. Scharff to recover, to think and connect again to the patient's sense of loss so that she can speak to the challenging attitude she has used both to cover it and to convey it. The patient has given the analyst to feel what the patient herself experienced during the analyst's absence: in feeling forgotten by her parents and her analyst, she felt that she lost her own capacity to think and her sense of self. But it does not matter that the analyst does not get everything said, because by bearing and identifying with the sense of difficulty, experiencing it, and reflecting on it, she conveys her capacity to care for and understand the patient, and it is this experience that lets her resume the mourning process which now follows:

"It's always been like that," Mrs. Nichols replied, and fell into a tense silence.

Suddenly she took in a gasp of air and sobbed uncontrollably.

"I don't want to get upset," she said, eventually. "I have to work today. Oh, why is this so hard to say?"

"If you could just say it, you'd feel better," I said. "So what's making it hard?"

"It's just that when you said all that about the dream, I knew you had been listening, you remember things to work on, you really are interested in me." She sobbed anew. "It just feels like you've gathered me up in your arms. And I'm crying with relief and I'm crying for all the times that didn't happen."

I had always felt sympathetic to her as a child feeling excluded by her family's importance to the country, and maybe they were too preoccupied with service and with burying their grief to attend to her, as she said. Now I got the sense that she had contributed to her experience of them as unempathic by the force of her link-destroying anger. Envy of their success led her to feel insignificant, and then silently she could attack their effectiveness as parents by not letting them know what she needed from them.

Both Mrs. Nichols and Dr. Scharff have recovered from the imposition of rejecting and exciting object relations designed to avoid mourning. They together experienced attacks on thinking and linking, and successfully threaded their way through the pathological organization that repeatedly destroys aspects of the patient's self and object relations. This is the essence of working through, a process that must be carried out over and over.

"This time you made it happen by confronting me with your anger, and you got a feeling of goodness," I said.

Now quite composed, she asked, wanting to move on, "So, what are you thinking about the clay?"

I replied, "In the dream, I told you that you had forgotten the clay, and you told me that it belonged here, and so I think of the clay as material being formed here as well as in the dream," I told her. "I think of the clay as your self that you are shaping here, and you couldn't maintain that work on the vacation by yourself. You couldn't use our way of working and talking within your family, and came back with no sense of yourself and just a messy stain of cookie crumbs."

"The clay is myself I'm shaping here," she said. "And I left it here with you. I never did get a sense of myself and what I could do in my family. But here there is hope I can get myself together."

Dr. Scharff is able to interpret the autistic-contiguous position difficulty of maintaining a cohesive sense of self during separation because she has experienced it herself through the patient's projective identification. Her intervention is effective because she speaks from inside the shared experience of the transference–countertransference encounter. Then Mrs. Nichols is able to take on the process for herself, to take up the metaphor of the clay and the cookie-dough crumbs to express, now in dialogue, her crumbling as she grew up with her family, and her effort to form a stable sense of self here in therapy. She takes on the process of thinking analytically for herself, a crucial sign of her internalization of the analyst and of the analytic process. But she is not yet ready for termination, because this ability is still dependent on the analytic context.

Mrs. Nichols went on over the next year to get in touch with her sexuality. She now experienced sexual desire and her husband was pleased, surprised, and responsive. As her desire mushroomed, he felt slightly threatened by her frequent initiatives and by her visions of fantastic, prolonged intercourse, but they were working on building a realistic, mutually agreeable sexual relationship. Any time her husband did not respond with enough excitement and follow-through, Mrs. Nichols felt rejected and became hurt, irritable, and finally hypersensitive to his being thin, a quality that had been appealing before.

The Late Stage of the Mid-Phase

The next sequence shows four later mid-phase sessions in the fifth year of Mrs. Nichols's analysis. These occurred ten months after the three mid-phase sessions described above. She looks again at her vulnerability to loss of the object, this time in a way of working characteristic of the late mid-phase. Mrs. Nichols has missed three sessions the week before the sequence to be presented, because she was away for a mid-week Fourth of July. This short vacation reminded her of the last short vacation that she and her husband took over Memorial Day weekend to celebrate the birthday of one of their children. Their trip had been a catastrophe because her husband had tripped on one of their children's toys and broken his ankle.

Since the Memorial Day weekend, Mrs. Nichols had been in a chronically resentful frame of mind, which she abhors but cannot escape. After the July Fourth break, she became more acutely angry. She fell thoroughly into a paranoid-schizoid position in which she was nasty, attacking, and blaming of her injured husband. Once he was spoiled, she then felt bereft, and was ready to turn the attack onto me and her analysis. She slid back into this earlier way of relating, that was seen most consistently in the second year of the analysis, and that she tended to slip back into at times of separation.

We have already described how Mrs. Nichols re-experienced and recovered from this way of relating after the summer vacation in the fourth year. Here it is again, up for reworking.

In the following sessions, Mrs. Nichols visits the theme of her baby self, experiences and recovers from an attack on her new-found sexuality, analyzes her regression as a defense against progress and termination, and examines her fantasies about Dr. Scharff's attachment to her and ability to tolerate termination. In the activated transference–countertransference, she falls into a pit of nastiness and spoiling, she takes Dr. Scharff with her and leaves her feeling literally like shit, and then she works her way out of it by herself.

The sequence shows work characteristic of the late mid-phase. We can see transference–countertransference that is not just a manifestation but a fully developed, repetitive neurotic pattern in which Mrs. Nichols denigrates the object and her self, and then we see her emerge from it by her self-analytic function. She still complains about Dr. Scharff, but she has concern for her as well, and she does not need her as much as in the previous example. The sequence shows the depth of her regression and her way of working out of it. She works on how she and Dr. Scharff might feel if she were to be ready to terminate. At this late stage, she works more in the transference, does more of the analytic work herself, and faces the loss of her neurosis and her analyst.

Session 1

"I don't want to go back to work," Mrs. Nichols complained. "But being on vacation at the beach was awful too. Lee was worried about getting sand in his cast and he couldn't run after the children anyway, so we couldn't relax at the ocean. We couldn't play golf. Usually I love the beach. Now I'm back at work, and it's no better. People at the office are bothering me. I hate Mondays. Nothing gives me any pleasure anymore. After five years of analysis I'm worse off than ever. I feel so stuck."

I said to myself, "Here we go again." I felt testy. I had been hearing this sort of complaining for a month. But this was the first time she had noted that she was stuck. Maybe she was ready to get on with analyzing her situation and get over it.

"Perhaps analysis is the work you don't want to do, but have to get back into," I said, somewhat nastily.

"I've had a miserable weekend," she said. "No sexual desire at all. What's happened to it? It's affecting everything. I'm miserable with my husband and my view of myself. It's discouraging after all this analysis, and even more so that I have no effort to get out of it. It's just easier to be here."

I was struck by her turn of phrase. Did she mean no wish to get out of it, or no effort or energy for getting out of it, or it would take effort to get out of it, or that it would be no effort to get out of it, and no effort is what she has? When she said "it's easier to be here" I did not know whether she meant here in this nonsexual depressed state, or here in analysis. I guessed that she meant both of these things, and that it would be hard to make an effort, because they were linked. Maintaining the progress in her marriage could mean leaving analysis. For the moment, she was more comfortable returning to her old depressed ways and staying with me. I felt discouraged too.

"Everything was going fine until Memorial Day weekend when Lee broke his ankle. That just killed everything. How can I let something like that happening to him kill everything in me? It seems so punitive. I feel so punitive towards myself and everyone else. I can't move out of it. Lee's legs are like sticks. His ankle broke with the slightest twist. He's too skinny, out of shape, and depressed, and not excited about anything, and not having anywhere to go, no dreams for our future."

Her husband who had always sounded like a tolerant, sensitive, attractive man, now sounded quite unappealing. It was as if, because she was getting better and more desirous of pleasure, she was noticing that he was no longer a match for her. I felt momentarily sorry for her being stuck with him. Then I remembered how she got disgusted with me, most markedly when I had been away. I thought that she felt abandoned by her husband both because he was in some retreat from her ardor and because he was injured and could not help as much as usual. She was defending herself by projective identification, and being unduly critical of her husband for physical attributes that had always sounded quite attractive before. Then I heard her description of him as if it were about her old self. She feels herself to be greedy for love, imagines her object shrinking, and then her self shrivels. At first my view of her mature potential shriveled too, but then I felt encouraged, because her description that I took to be about her old self said to me that she was angry about her depressed functioning and wanting to be rid of it.

"When I got to feeling sexual in myself, I just wanted him to be there for me, and his response was just so . . . I don't know . . . He just wasn't as interested as he used to be before, when I had no interest at all. In that one moment when he tripped, broke his ankle, and couldn't stand up, I just lost it all, all the positive stuff got diffused and this ugly wave of all the things I just said rolled over me. He's too thin, he's got no muscles, he fell over because he's weak. I can't forget it."

I started to feel sorry for her husband now. Poor guy, he was injured, and in need of support. She sounded irretrievably nasty. "Where's your compassion," I thought. I started to feel hopeless, dragged down into a slough of despond.

"I blame myself for this," she said. "How fragile was this great thing I was experiencing if it's so easily wiped out now? Where's my compassion?"

I was interested to hear her ask herself the same question that I had been thinking. It said to me that I was in a good state of unconscious communication with her, and it encouraged me to think that she could do this work by herself.

"It seems it's not him that I was feeling sexual about at all," she continued. "This whole sexual thing was just a fantasy, and he was just there. It seems to me that if I only care about the good things and not the weak things, what kind of relationship is that? It's not good."

I was glad that she could take responsibility for her situation and stop blaming her husband. But now the blame was to shift to me.

"I feel punitive towards you too for not being able to do anything about it and not helping me do anything about it. This is the fourth weekend we've been working on this and it's not going anywhere. You know?"

"Are you wondering whether I only want to hear positive things, or if I'll care about your weaknesses and vulnerability?" I asked.

"I don't know," she replied. "You have in the past. I don't know why I'd feel that. I seem to be backsliding so fast."

I remembered her saying "It's easier to be here" and it gave me the idea she was slipping back for my sake too, regressing to have an excuse for staying in analysis.

"Well then, maybe you're wondering whether I'll be able to keep up with you if you improve," I said. "You know me better as you are now."

"If I go on like this, I'll be here forever," she said. "Every time I get thrown, I'll plunge into this old stuff. It's like it used to be: I'm crying every day. My whole life is focused here. I've given up all of my independence that I'd gained. I don't understand why I'm doing this. Maybe it did get too scary to get out there and feel independent. I was thinking when I was out there and feeling good that there really wasn't much more to resolve. Now I don't know."

I could see that she was having worries about terminating. Then I started to overfunction intellectually. I said to myself that she is not ready to finish, because she has not reliably internalized the analytic function. She has found pleasure and hope in her sexual functioning with her husband, but her sexual self is vulnerable to destruction by his unavailability due to injury. Feeling rejected, she is not capable of tolerating delay and feeling compassion for him. Perhaps envy plays a role in the destruction of her good feeling, but I can't yet see how. All these thoughts may have been accurate, but their main function was to give me things to think while I put up with feeling increasingly rotten, because she had not got enough of what she needed from me to leave with a good feeling.

"If you really connect with Lee and with yourself, you lose me because you don't yet feel yourself as having me with you inside," I said.

"Well, I guess there have been times when I've felt that I didn't have you with me when I wasn't here. When I feel I have myself and feel independent, then it's okay. But if I get connected to Lee then it means I lose you. I have to . . . I don't know. I mean I certainly feel that in the last three weeks I have connected with you, at his expense. As we've talked about all the things in here, I've pulled away from him. It all started with him needing me to help him because of his injury and I couldn't stand to have him demand physical closeness. I hoped I could get those good feelings back from talking to you. Instead, I feel worse and worse about it. I don't think talking to him is going to get them back, but maybe it will. A lot of what's missing for Lee and me is talking about it together. I'm afraid to tell him, but it must be obvious to him that I've lost that fire. I can't handle his rejection. He'd write me off and discount my improvement rather than have any faith that it'll come back. But that's how I feel. *I* don't have any faith that it will come back.

"I guess I'm not sure if he'll ever really be capable of satisfying me sexually in the way I was looking for. Not that we worked on it for very long. I just feel like I may have to settle for what is."

She was feeling unhelped by talking with me, and had momentarily lost faith in analysis. Through my introjective identification with her projective identification of loss of hope and desire for improvement into me, I was wondering if she would ever get her good feeling back and wishing that I could do something, anything, to move her out of this hole. But I did not take an action, and simply tolerated the feeling of despair.

As the session ended, I said, "I think that you're disappointed in me for not giving you a shove out of this. You're wondering if I have faith in the recovery of the good."

Progress in analysis brings Mrs. Nichols to new worries. Obstacles in the form of her husband's inability to fulfill her somewhat manic sexual fantasies or to stay available because of injury threw her back into a paranoid–schizoid position and made her despair of further progress. On the other hand, progress will mean the end of analysis, and so the paranoid–schizoid position serves to prove that Mrs. Nichols still needs it. She is not yet ready to feel compassion for her husband or her self, or to mourn the loss of the relationship with Dr. Scharff.

Session 2

"I had this dream that doesn't seem related at all," Mrs. Nichols began, and went on to give me a bit of background before telling her dream. "Our friend Liz was in it. Her husband seems a very affected guy, but, really he's an optimistic, up person. She called me to get together Friday and we haven't been together in a while since they had another child. She's done well, got her PhD, and her children are fine. Things work out for her. Her child care is absolutely excellent. I don't know what it is about her. Lee doesn't like her at all, finds her very narcissistic. She's short with her husband. She just rubs Lee the wrong way. Here's the dream:

> Somehow I was to take care of Liz's baby while she was taking her two children to the circus at 10:30 A.M. on a Saturday. We hung around. They weren't ready to leave, stopped for food, and just before they did leave, the baby woke up. They left no instructions or supplies and were vague about when they'd be back. I felt foolish for offering to do the job when they weren't thinking about what they were imposing on me. I was not at all sure that their child would know me and I thought I would be a stranger to him and be uncomfortable. It was completely lacking in communication. Lee either called or came by, and he was annoyed that I hadn't put my foot down. It was a really frustrating situation. Then I have some fleeting image of Lee or someone like Lee with those plastic gloves on like dentists or OBGYNs use. He was putting his finger in my vagina and saying "this is your vagina" and his finger in my anus and saying "this is your anus" like he was teaching me. It was strange but not unpleasant. It's more my reaction to it that's negative than the actual experience.

"Liz must be representing you," she said. "My reaction was 'I'm done with this baby thing. I don't want to be stuck all day taking care of this baby.' I don't want to be pressured into looking again into the past. I did feel somewhat better yesterday. It seemed that something got loosened up yesterday. I am really tripped up and arrested by the bursting up of the fantasy that Lee and I would have wonderful sex and that our relationship would lead to all sorts of other great things. I haven't completely finished talking about how disappointed I am about that. Until he slipped, things were getting resolved and I was getting closer to being finished. I don't know whether that was too difficult to hang on to, and so I plunged back down, or whether it has to do with my upset at the business of the sexual secrets I learned at the reunion about Ann, remember my college roommate who had the affair when we were in college with the professor that I admired so much? I was stunned by her confession. It seems like a distraction, a side trip, and yet it was so upsetting. I got so upset and angry about it, and it seemed so significant. I haven't quite connected that with everything else that's going on. Maybe it's related to fears of me getting out of control if I become truly sexual."

I remembered how hard her roommate's revelation about the affair had hit her, and how we had understood it as an oedipal betrayal by her professor that triggered discomfort with family secrecy and reactivated conflict over sibling rivalry. I might have asked more about her fears of becoming an oedipal victor, but I followed her in regarding it as a side issue. Remembering my sense of her envy that I could not quite document in the previous session, I returned to the transference point of the dream in the here-and-now, thinking that she might be envying my position.

"In what way do you experience me as Liz?" I asked.

"Going after what she wanted professionally," she guessed. "Everything so organized. I know there are struggles, but on balance she's done well. You're much more accomplished than she is, but she has child care she can rely on like you do. The part about being so entitled and making assumptions, that's something I feel about you, not during, but at the beginning and ending of sessions. You call the shots on that. There's no accommodation to extend the time. But you do reschedule flexibly, and so that doesn't resonate so much."

So I was right about the envy, and now it was conscious. But I now learn that she is not so much envious of my position, as angry that I have not helped her maintain her more mature position.

"But I think I really have felt regressed this last week or so, being upset about sessions ending and your not paying attention to a couple things. That all feels like baby stuff, punitive stuff. We've been through that and it's very discouraging to have to deal with again. I don't feel you initiated it or pressured me. I do feel that you didn't hold up some good mirror that reminded me of my strengths. You allowed me to get back into that. You weren't helping me hold on to my gains. When Liz called me, it was the day I worked at home and I talked with her longer than I wanted to. I was bummed out that day with work and Lee. It all spilled out to her, not actual confidences, but my general attitude about life and marriage. It was a complaining, poor-me conversation we could have had ten years ago. I really hated that conversation.

"Liz gets me to talk about myself when I don't want to and she doesn't respond in kind. She caught me that day after I was here. She intruded into my personal life, and I let her do it. No, not intruded, she just stepped into a private, infantile place where I don't let anybody come."

Good, I thought, here comes the transference.

"Whereas Ann shares her own stuff, Liz is drawing things out from me, and I don't know what she does with it. There's not the connection between us. There's a voyeurism about it. I suppose that's pretty parallel to what's going on here in analysis. I don't think I end up here talking about things I don't want to, but there have been times I've felt exposed when I lay out all my horrible thoughts and feelings—and you always get to stay put together."

"The dream seems to say you're done with taking care of babies and you don't want to take care of your own baby that you feel is of my making, while I get to be annoyingly adult, like Liz who draws things out of you, or Ann who raises history that leaves you feeling preoccupied and upset," I said.

"No, it's not of your making," she corrected me. "I discovered this baby aspect. I just don't feel very tolerant of it. Liz's baby reminded me of our Andy as a baby. He screamed a lot every evening when I was fixing dinner and when we were eating it. Three hours every evening. She looked, as I probably did, quite unperturbed about it. I was drawn to the baby and would have liked to have held him. So that's not quite accurate," she concluded, reminding herself of her good feelings as a mother.

"I meant the baby part of you," I clarified.

"The relief I felt yesterday was not great," she said. "But it was something—a way to step back for a moment and not feel so wretched. But today I'm just not dealing with it. I'm determined to stay stuck in this shit and feel wretched and beat myself here. If I look at it objectively, that's avoiding it. I'm not going to get through it until I deal with it."

"I think you're wondering if there needs to be more screaming instead of so much shit," I said. "You are not sure if I'll deal with your baby responsibly, and if so will the baby be a boy or a girl, and if a girl, will she know the difference between her anus which is for gathering and expelling shit and her vagina which is for giving as well as receiving pleasure, and for giving birth to babies."

She replied, "Liz wasn't too concerned with the baby who was having to eat sausage and tortillas. She was more interested in a huge plate for herself and paying no attention to me or the child."

Now I see that Mrs. Nichols is experiencing me as selfish. The envy of my being adult is less on her mind than the misery of being stuck with babyish feelings that I don't help enough with. I wonder if she is defending against recognizing her envy, or if I am forcing a theory on her, which indeed would be selfish. Whichever may be the case, I am pleased that she is telling me about her experience and associating to her dream so freely. She is doing most of the work herself, even while complaining about me for not helping her. I'll be interested to see where she is tomorrow.

Dr. Scharff is right about Mrs. Nichols's envy, but she cannot quite nail it down, because she is being affected by it. Dr. Scharff feels too captured by shitty feelings, so that she cannot see that Mrs. Nichols envies her for not being subject to the regression.

Session 3

"I have a vision of clearing this," she began more optimistically. "It's taking shape like a pile of wet leaves; decaying but holding together enough to get rid of it. It's just not so intangible and oppressive."

I noticed that she has been working through by herself, not just in the session, but afterwards, too, and I felt that it was a good sign. I was struck by her metaphor of wet leaves and hopeful that she was about to clean them up.

Mrs. Nichols's metaphor of the decaying leaves represented the pile of shit that she and Dr. Scharff were immersed in yesterday, and the word "leaves" calls to mind the leaving process.

"But yesterday I was just nowhere," she said. "At work, I just felt it was very difficult to make any progress. The folks at the office work hard and yet our project is not going anywhere, although there were a couple of bright spots. This guy spoke eloquently for advocacy for African Americans. The boss and his assistant are African Americans but they are light-skinned and they don't do much advocacy for blacks. At home I was alone because the kids were with their friends, and I felt lonely and depressed."

When Mrs. Nichols goes on to tell about her frustration at the office, she is also alluding to her struggle to represent her minority rights to herself and to Dr. Scharff. Her loneliness at home without her children speaks of the loss of her babyish self that she is working in analysis to be free of.

"I had planned to be with my daughter when Andy was at soccer, but I had nothing incredible to offer her, and so I let her go, but I really wanted her company. Ordinarily, I'd be delighted to have an hour or two to myself in my house. I thought, 'This is what it'll be like when the kids are gone.' It was not a good feeling. Lee called to find out why I had bought a new vacuum cleaner for $500 and I said I feel bad enough without talking about this. I started spilling out about how flat and stuck I was feeling. He wanted to know if it was about my work or my life. So I told him it was everything. He thought I was angry with him and he hung up on me.

"When he got home, fortunately he was able to joke about it, and didn't pressure me or shut me out. He doesn't want to get involved in my depression. He doesn't have his tail between his legs."

Mrs. Nichols is reassured by her husband's resilience. Her expression that he does not have his tail between his legs suggests that she has been afraid that his capacity to have an erect penis has been damaged. Now it appears that the meaning to her of his ankle injury was that of castration following her intense sexual interest. Partly the work that she is now doing in analysis and partly his functioning as a helpfully containing object has enabled a transformation to get under way.

"Maybe I was testing him," she admitted. "So when he didn't dump all over me, fine, I thought, now it's time to get on with it and not sink into this hole of self-pity and depression and discouragement. It's hard moving forward. Every day a new struggle. But I will say today, for the first time in a couple of weeks, I could look at Lee and not be repulsed.

"I've been sexually so turned off. All those feelings about him being bony, and overstressed, and out of shape. I have not been able to get rid of that these last few weeks. But it lifted momentarily. Our mail just piles up and gets so out of control. It's like my life. There's so much to be done and it doesn't get done. Our house is too big and the old paint is awful. How did

I get off on that? Oh, I know, the mail, so much to be done. The piles get bigger. We stayed up till midnight going through it, so I felt better."

I was pleased to hear that there were moments of relief in the depression at home. I thought that she had been able to use Lee, previously the object of her disgust at herself, as a transforming object momentarily. Perhaps she was dealing with a reluctance to express her longings to him instead of to me, because they were not yet metabolized. Now it was time to gather the remaining depression into the transference.

"You are describing the work to do and the messes out there to clean up," I pointed out. "What about the mess in here?"

"It feels as if I've put it all out before us these last two days," she said. "Now I'm waiting for you to help me. I've dug it all up and put it all out. Now help me to organize it so I can get rid of it, or save the parts that are useful."

I pressed on and challenged her again, "So what kind of mess is there between you and me?"

"You see it all and have it organized, but you're not telling me," she accused me. "You're waiting for me, so that it's not you doing it. You don't want to do it for me, or you don't have it organized so it's not clear that you can or can't do it. Either way, I'm stuck with it. You could make suggestions or give me feedback. There's still that shove that I'm looking for. It doesn't seem to be forthcoming."

"The shove you want is for me to tell you to try again," I said. "And you want me to assure you that if you succeed and leave me, that would be okay with me."

"No, I wasn't looking that far ahead," she said, at first denying her wish for me to get her to move on. "But wait, I've been talking about it. When you say that, it makes sense. Then I'd have nothing to stop me but myself. It makes me think of my mother and how I felt from her that it was never okay to leave. Well, why don't I try again? I can't because I'm so turned off. I've been thinking, 'I can't do this by myself.' I have had to pick it all apart and get so far into this mess, and then I can't do it until I get out of the mess. I do feel a little more hopeful that I could step out of it.

"The message I've been getting from you is—you haven't said this, but the message I get is—there is more stuff we haven't gotten to. We have to get down and get dirty again and get angry and get through it. It was good that I could come to the realization of being terrified of the option of being strong and connected with Lee and be off. Because, I guess in a lot of ways, that is the time when I feel most intensely connected with you, that is, when I'm experiencing strong, punitive feelings."

Mrs. Nichols had been a rejecting object to her husband, and then, after she recovered her feelings of excitement, she felt that he was rejecting her. Her transference to Dr. Scharff, which was an idealizing one in the first year of analysis until it gave way to an exciting and then rejecting object relationship, is remembered in its intensity. That is what is familiar to her. Being regressed and punitive connects her to Dr. Scharff and she has still to work on finding a different kind of connection, and then letting go. As the following material shows, she goes back and forth between wanting to be led and wanting to be independent, thankful to Dr. Scharff and frustrated by her, wanting to be allowed to regress and wanting to be pulled out of it. It is not exactly clear what she really thinks, or what period of the analysis she is referring to, or where her thoughts will end up, but this is typical of in-depth work in the late stage of the mid-phase as the patient struggles with ambivalence about letting go of the neurosis and finishing up.

"When I went down in there, you stood by me," she said. "That was the respectful thing to do, but I wanted you to tell me to get out of it and tell me why it was happening. But if you had, it would not have been a good thing. I'm remembering that time months ago that I said you were too directive and that I had to see things for myself. You said then that I was right, and I went on and got beyond it. I had wanted and needed you to lead but I got past it. We gave me the reins and I was frustrated by that, though it's what I was asking for. Not only was I regressing, I felt you were also going back to relating to me in a way I thought had been left behind."

"What was that?" I asked.

"In the last six months, you've not been beginning and ending and wrapping things up," she explained.

I felt defensive. Surely I didn't do that. Even if I had wanted to, this patient had a way of talking in which she paused for breath in the middle of sentences, and then ran over the periods. So there was no warning of the end of a thought, and no good place to end without interrupting. I couldn't imagine how I would have had time to wrap up. But then I figured out that she meant that I had been shaping her material more actively than now, giving it form through interpretations that by this stage in the analysis were less frequent. Or perhaps she meant that it was now timely to wrap up the analysis and I had not been making it happen.

She continued, "But if you were more active sometimes, we could cover ground faster. I could take advantage of things you said, or reject them or whatever. But in the last few weeks you've stopped saying things. Now I feel you came back into it with me, instead of letting me muddle through it and without offering me ways out. As I'm thinking about it, maybe that was the only way for it to happen. I was plunging down, and you with me, rather than holding on to my gains."

Now I got it. She is talking about the experience of regression, which she both hates and appreciates.

Mrs. Nichols is reminding Dr. Scharff of an earlier enactment in which she succeeded in getting Dr. Scharff to take care of her by giving structure to the sessions and limiting the regression and confusion. Now she tells her that there has been another enactment in which she has dragged Dr. Scharff down into the paranoid-schizoid muddle so that both of them failed to hold on to her gains. The implication is that neither of them wants to finish the analysis. Even while complaining, Mrs. Nichols, however, demonstrates her progress. She describes the phenomena of the transference–countertransference enactment of the last few sessions, and she interprets for herself.

Session 4

Mrs. Nichols said cheerfully, "I was busy cooking dinner and I stopped and said, 'Lee, come over and give me a hug.' He smiled and said, 'Good day in analysis, huh? I can always tell.' It was. I got your blessing to go back and try again.

"I can't remember what you said, but it was like, it'd be okay with you, not that you're ready for me to leave, but . . . Funny I can't remember it exactly, I don't want to. And you didn't really say it. You said, 'This is what you want me to say.' It was helpful to me in gathering the energy and motivation to hoist myself out of wherever I had been. I feel sexually alive again, the deep freeze lifted. It was the first time since Memorial Day weekend.

"But I'm uneasy about some things I said yesterday. I'm interested in your reaction. At first I was saying, it was good of you let me get down there and come to my own realization of what was happening with a minimum of directiveness. Then I said you communicated that I had really slid backwards and you needed to treat me that way and had not held on to new developments and had not made suggestions to get me back there. I thought you would not like what I said. I got all caught up in 'Is that a bad thing to say' and 'Do you disagree' and 'Is it presumptuous to talk about you'. It felt good to be struggling toward some understanding of what had been happening. It was like sticking my neck out and feeling unprotected. It was good for me and made me feel better, but then how did you feel? Then I started to feel guilty. The bottom line of what I was suggesting yesterday is (oh, this is incredibly presumptuous) the work we did yesterday assures me that you are emotionally involved in this relationship—which could be completely wrong, and it just feels, like, awkward to say it—and yet it makes sense. Wait, I'd better finish.

"The bottom line is that you were also returning to an earlier way of relating to me and not wanting to encourage me to be independent and take steps to be leaving. Maybe I just wanted to see that in you, to see if it was easy for you to remain professionally cool and controlled or whatever. It's almost like when I feel better, it's like slipping out of this protective womb, stretching, waking up, feeling the sun, and feeling energized, and feeling good, or not needing whatever it was that made me safe before. As soon as that rush settles, I worry and feel that I have to scurry back and make sure you are all right.

"If I can connect with myself and Lee, then I lose you, you lose me too, and where does that leave you? I'm not sure if it's really that or the other. Is worry about your loss a substitute for dealing with my loss?"

"Yes," I affirmed her idea. "I think you're wondering if I'll have hurt feelings like your mother when you tried to connect with your father. I think you are also wondering if I'll have hurt feelings when you and Lee connect, like you did when you discovered that your mother and father were the stronger pair, and so try to keep you here by letting you flounder in a regression."

"Well, I gave up as a girl," she admitted. "I said my dad wasn't available anyway, and then I got to be a teenager and said he wasn't desirable anyway. But if I'm the one in the strong position in the strong relationship, I really identify with the one who's left out instead, and it takes away from my ability to sustain that strong relationship. It happens in friendships with women, too. Whenever a relationship becomes strong, there's someone else who's losing out."

Mrs. Nichols understands that her oedipal feelings persist as a tendency to diminish the importance of her marriage, or any other significant pairing, to appease the hurt and envious feelings of the one who is excluded, like she felt as a little girl. To understand the oedipal complex, we have to trace it back to its roots in the previous adjustment of the infantile relationship to the mother. Similarly in the flow of the session, Mrs. Nichols is about to work backwards to review her relationship with Dr. Scharff. She cannot understand what has helped her to feel better, and she now moves back into confronting the transference.

"I realize now that my family relationships get acted out here," she said. "Dealing with loss and triangles and independence, and all that. But you're not responding to the level of the relationship between you and me. You're just looking at it in terms of my family. Maybe that's your job. I guess I feel like you were the one who brought this up and threw it out and maybe that's why I'm . . . I don't know . . . I'm not sure. There are a lot of questions. It's only two days since I felt, like, completely bogged down, depressed, and cut off from my feelings and my sexuality. Here I am two days later and it's like night and day. When it happens again, will I get out of it? Maybe it has to do with worries about leaving here. Are you always going to translate it into family stuff?"

"Instead of?" I prompted.

"Dealing with the relationship between you and me."

I welcomed her challenge and asked, "Tell me more about you and me."

"Well, I'm sort of trying to fend off these thoughts," she said. "It's not likeable. I hate it that I operate this way. But here goes—I want to hear that you are emotionally invested in this relationship, that it's not just professional. All of which I sort of don't know. You have allowed yourself in here just enough to show me that you are involved, but not enough to interfere with the process and the treatment. I have a lot of respect for how you've done that.

"I'm starting to ask myself 'Why do I need to know this from you?' It's because I can see that I'll be leaving here someday, and it's sad to think of not seeing you any more. I want you to tell me you care about me and that it's hard to let me go."

I feel pleased and proud that she got to the point and was ready for the next stage.

This session is typical of late mid-phase work in that the patient does most of the work, draws attention to the transference, and works it through. She has a positive contextual transference that gives her the confidence to confront Dr. Scharff, call her selfish, use her as a rejecting object without feeling actually rejected by her, and in general creates a vivid transference–countertransference dynamic. Within that context, she experiences therapeutic regression that is terrifying to her and disappointing to Dr. Scharff at this stage in her treatment, but she does not stick there. Her capacity for tolerating depression is much improved and gives her the space in which to analyze the conflict that she is dealing with in the there-and-now of her life with Lee and in the here-and-now of the transference. She attacks her objects and fears for their destruction, then becomes concerned for their well-being and worries if they will stand her faults. She confronts Dr. Scharff with the need to focus on the here-and-now rather than the here-and-then. Finally, she moves beyond the transference in this session to confront the reality of Dr. Scharff's feelings for her as she contemplates being well.

Mrs. Nichols is solving the problem of her attachment to Dr. Scharff, and approaching the mourning to be done as the therapeutic relationship faces eventual termination. Typical of work in the late stages of the mid-phase, she is in the process of resolving her oedipal complex by reworking its underpinnings in the dyadic relationship in analysis and seeking to build a more satisfying sexual relationship with her husband. She is on the point of claiming the fullness of her life with her husband and family, and when that gain is consolidated, she will be ready to terminate.

23

Pretermination

In the late mid-phase, the therapist recognizes that considerable gains have been made and held on to, but remaining issues are still requiring work, especially in the transference. At some point, material emerges that makes it clear that therapy is about to enter the home stretch. In the late phase of analysis with Dr. Jill Scharff, a lengthy dream signalled the patient's readiness for termination of the analytic process and reintroduced the transference for further analysis and resolution.

Esther, aged 31, had been in analysis for eight years, an uncommonly long time for a young adult, and she was beginning to think that she had had enough of it. A crushing depression based in family trauma and loss when she was 11 years old had left her with little zest for living. Two teenage sons from her father's first marriage were killed in a car crash as they were driving home from a visit to their late mother's family, and Esther's parents, who had raised them since they were 4 and 6 years old, were devastated and remained depressed during her adolescence. Her father dealt with it by intense investment in financial success and membership in the right clubs, while her mother devoted herself to Esther's 2-years-older sister Rachel, who was now 33 and married, and to her 4-year-old grandson Saul and his baby sister Ruth. For each parent's adjustment patterns, Esther had enormous contempt, which she expressed openly in rejecting and belittling her father, but hid from her mother to whom she clung for sustenance, except in occasional nasty outbursts.

Despite a good education, Esther remained totally dependent on her family for the first five years of analysis, had little appetite for food or work, and had no social life. She was frequently in severe abdominal pain which accompanied emotional strain and led her to avoid the tension of sexual gratification. She had scanty, irregular periods. She felt that life was not worth living and often felt actively suicidal. Her family took good care of her and supported her analysis, but they were still depressed themselves following their loss and could not help her complete her mourning.

At this point in the analysis, Esther had analyzed her fear of separation, her somatization of conflict, her negative oedipal attachment to her mother, and her envious and contemptuous relation to her father, and she had succeeded in weaning herself from her parents. She was living independently in a group house, working and going to school, but visiting her parents for meals and often staying overnight when she got sucked in to old ways of relating to them. Almost finished with business school, she met Art, a boyishly handsome 41-year-old man with whom she fell in love. She was aware that he reminded her of one of her late half-brothers in his hyperactive style, his looks, his humor and sensitivity, and his sense of devotion to family. But his artistic profession, his lifestyle, and his social class were all welcome points of difference. His adherence to unfamiliar religious beliefs was more of a problem. She thought that her feelings for Art were very positive and likely to endure. They got along well, he appreciated her intellect, loved her looks, encouraged her sexual expressiveness, and wanted to marry and have children with her. Soon she would finish her masters degree in marketing and get an apartment of her own where she could entertain him more freely or ultimately live with him. And if in the course of time the relationship deteriorated, she felt confident that she would find someone else that she could love.

Obviously she would soon be ready to finish analysis but the idea of full-time work at the management level in retail, her chosen field, still scared her and she was not yet ready to accept her professional identity. In addition she had made her gains fairly recently, and there had not been enough time to see whether her health was based on a manic flight to a new object, or whether she was demonstrating a new capacity for object relating that could apply to this or any other relationship. She said that she might be ready to finish soon, but she would like to diminish the number of sessions per week gradually over a year. I asked her to consider the more usual plan of estimating how much time she still needed and then continuing at the four-session level for a planned period of termination until the day she had set for finishing. She regarded my plan as too abrupt and she preferred her idea. She thought that I would be inflexible and unwilling to consider her plan because I was slavish to what all analysts are taught, instead of deciding what is best for each patient. On the day when this was discussed, we both agreed that analysis might come to an end in less than a year, but no date was set, and no decision was taken as to whether there would be a hard-edged ending or a graduated one.

She did not return to the subject, but continued to deal with her conflicts over being fully sexually expressive with Art. Orgasm was associated in her mind with masturbation and did not pertain to the shared situation. She enjoyed intercourse with him and petting and cuddling so much that she seemed not to need the orgasm that he wanted for her. The only problem was that she was spending so much time with him that she was ignoring her parents and therefore felt guilty. Then she told two dreams.

> This dream took place somewhere like a college or a school grounds. School buildings were in the background. A college club was conducting an initiation. To get into the club you had to climb a totally sheer, slate wall that seemed to have no fingerholds. A severe-looking man and woman were standing at the top of the wall looking down on the rest. So they had done it successfully and they were in the club. But I wondered how did they do it? Then I saw that there were tiny fingerholds at five or six foot intervals. A woman did it really well and I watched to see where she put her fingers and how she did it. I don't know why I wanted to try it, but I did. Why did I want to be like those severe people in that club? Then the woman ahead of me fell a hundred feet to her death. I paused, and thought of going back, but I couldn't get down. There was nothing for it but to go on. I just kept climbing up, pausing, and then going on. A man below me was waiting for me to decide about going on. I indicated that he should pass me. Then he fell too. I made it to the top before the dream ended.
>
> I don't know why I did it. I saved my life, but I didn't want to be in the club with the people watching the people below try and fail and die. And they didn't speak to each other. Nobody talked in the dream at all. I just can't remember why I started out to climb. I can picture that wall so clearly. I wish I could draw so as to draw the image away from me. It was dark grey, so slate popped into my mind. Slate is what my Mom used for paving our garden paths. It's rock and it lasts and lasts. The surface of the wall reminded me of the path up to my Mom's front door step and the steps themselves. The walk around back is made of the same slate tablets.

As if walking from step to step, Esther continued on her dream path, and told her next dream:

> The other dream is of me working in a store like the one where I work. A middle-aged woman was carrying a toilet seat. An old woman had asked for one because she had heard that we were giving them out. I was a staff person. So I had to get it for her and show her the bathroom, but I would not wait for her to be done. It was not much of a dream. Just a lot of looking around and talking and being with lots of people and objects. No one talked in the "wall" dream. I can't remember any other dreams.

Esther went on to give her associations. She said, "The first dream sounds like getting my degree. I struggle to achieve it and I don't really want it. I'd rather be making gingerbread men—that sounds so good! I don't remember as many dreams as I used to. Do you think I am letting go of this process?" she asked me.

I had been scanning the imagery of the dream for clues to the latent content. I thought of the wall as the sexual response cycle, the fingerholds as the way towards orgasm, the slate as a pathway to the secrets of the female body. I thought of the wall as her journey through life, punctuated as it had been by major loss of life in her family. Now I focused in on the wall as the story of the analysis, subsuming as it did all the themes I was thinking about, and more. Climbing the sheer wall might also represent the hard-edge termination plan I had asked her to consider, but I was not able to see myself in the cold superior people of the dream at the time of the session.

"Do you think that analysis has been like climbing this wall?" I responded. "You were scared and skeptical of its value, and you didn't want to join the analytic club."

"I wouldn't embrace these cold, superior people," she said. "That's how I view my parents and my socioeconomic class. Though I was raised to join it, I don't want it."

"Do you think that you are uncomfortable to think that these privileged achievers and survivors, they and you, are watching others fail and die?" I asked.

"Yes," she said. "They feel it's weak to help each other. And I was dressed up in fancy clothes and I wanted to take them off. It made no sense. There were men in three-piece suits climbing a wall. If I could just get to the top and save my life, I'd choose something else."

Her businessman father always wore a suit, even when he went to watch
her Saturday soccer games in elementary school, I remembered. Getting
over the wall of grief had been hard for both her parents. She still felt somewhat responsible for staying around to help them feel better, but she was
no longer held back by their level of adjustment to their family trauma and
bereavement. She no longer had to identify with their lifestyle and accommodation to loss.

I pointed out, "In the next dream, there you are in the environment of
your choice, quite engaged in activity and relationship, talking, doing, and
getting on with it, and you didn't want to wait for some old woman to get
off the pot."

"I had so much to do," she went on. "I didn't want to be stuck in some
bathroom."

"Did the old woman remind you of anyone?" I asked, wondering if she
might be me.

"You could say that I was waiting for her to die. So she could be my great-
aunt who is in an old people's home. But she didn't look like her because
she was small, fat, and filled a wheelchair. No, it doesn't remind me of
anyone in particular," she concluded. Then reflecting on the progress of
her session, she added, "I don't know where to go with these dreams. I'm
tired. We went hiking yesterday. You know, it was fun. I have all these
things to do. I don't want to get bogged down in some old dream."

"So the old woman could be you that you want to get away from," I
suggested.

"An old woman with bowel trouble!" she acknowledged laughingly.
"Yes. That was me! I don't have stomachaches any more, and I feel af-
fronted if ever I do. I guess it could also be my mother I'm leaving behind."

I thought that it was time to put the two dreams together. I said, "These
dreams speak of your feeling that it is time to terminate. You've been climbing the wall, often with difficulty. You're there. You've joined the land of
the living, no matter how others are progressing. You are looking at choices
now different than the lack of life that you felt condemned to."

"I'm never going to hear you say that we are going to finish in a week,"
she said, teasingly.

"No, you won't hear that from me," I said. "We will take time to discuss what makes sense."

She associated to a difficult discussion she had had with her boyfriend
on the topic of abortion. A religious man, he did not share her views. He
did not dispute her right as a woman to decide on what should happen to

her body should she become pregnant, but he was uncomfortable with the idea of her playing God, taking such a decision, and letting other people know this about her and him.

"If I did not want to have a child, let's say because it had Down's syndrome, I would have an abortion," she insisted. "It would be saving my life."

In considering her readiness for termination, I noticed that her unconscious was keeping pace with her conscious appreciation of the remaining time left for analysis. On the other hand, she still needed help with analyzing the dream. And her last association about abortion worried me in that she might think that analysis would have to be aborted rather than come to term, as if a sudden way of ending our therapeutic relationship might be the only way to assure her continuing life. She might also be equating my thoughtfulness about termination with procrastination and an unwillingness to let her go.

A few weeks later she told me that she wanted to take a week of summer vacation different than the week when I would be away and to have me not charge her for the missed sessions. Otherwise she would quit on July 1. This would leave two months for us to terminate, or as she preferred to say sarcastically, for her to "jump through my termination phase hoops." One could argue that a two-month termination phase was reasonable for a young adult, and I might have agreed, if there had been a shorter analysis and less difficulty with separation. One could argue that there are examples in the literature of young adults who do not finish in the classical way, but simply move on and maybe return in a later life phase. But I did not think that it would serve Esther well to finish in this way. I wanted her to have time to consolidate her gains, but I did not want to be hostage to her demands, any more than I liked the idea of her feeling that way about me and my policies or practices.

"I've been a good patient," she argued. "I've bent my schedule to yours for years, taking vacation only when you were away. I've been a steady paycheck. You can afford the $500 to let me go. You should be supporting my independence, not blocking me from moving on. 'Consolidate your gains, blah, blah.' You can't keep me in analysis until I get a job, get married, have children. And it's your fault. You've always taken vacation in July or August before, and so does everyone else. You took five weeks off last winter whether it suited me or not, and I was good about it. I was loyal.

So you should let me take my vacation in July or August. But you'll never agree. You are so rigid. No one else's therapist is like that."

Now I was aware of a countertransference interference. My week out of the office in October would not be a vacation, but a teaching engagement. I wouldn't be having a vacation in July, or August, or September. I wanted to say spontaneously "Yes, that's a sore point" when she mentioned my not taking a vacation, but I inhibited the inappropriate response, tried to say something appropriate, and could not remember what it was. The thought left my mind, as I had left my practice. I had missed five weeks of work in winter as she had said, but not by choice. It had happened while I was recovering from emergency surgery. I was already upset at recognizing how dependent I am on income from my practice. That is why there would be no summer vacation for me. And it upset me to be reminded of how this hurt me and others. Having done this work on my countertransference based on my own conflict imported into the situation, I was now free to think about the aspect of countertransference evoked by her attitude and corresponding to her unconscious projective identifications of me.

I asked about the meaning of her request. I wanted to know more about her resentment regarding my absence, and Esther responded by getting angrier and more disparaging. She portrayed me as mean-spirited, ungrateful, domineering, controlling, rigid, exploitative of her, and unfairly dependent on her money. She was outraged.

I felt outraged too. I had to admit that she was right that I felt worried about money, but even though it would be hard for me, her request for the usual two-week vacation seemed reasonable. What was not reasonable was the imperious and coercive way of making her demand. That was familiar, and it triggered the memory of how awful I felt when she had given me similar ultimatums before, except that in earlier years they had taken the form of giving me dates for killing herself. This time the ultimatum concerned killing the analysis in such a way that it looked like I had done it. I hated that feeling, and I defended myself by conceptualizing her position as a termination regression, and hoped that I would have time to rework her way of claiming autonomy, and be able to analyze her need to end this way.

The word "abruption" came to mind. At first I thought this was simply the technical term for an unanticipated ending. Then I realized that this is the medical term for the sudden shearing of the placenta from the uterine wall that may occur due to maternal hypertension. It causes hemorrhage, spontaneous abortion, and premature delivery. This association led me to see that I felt like a mother whose gestation is not complete and who because of a physical strain cannot support the bodily context of safety for her fetus. She finds that the automatically life-giving placenta is torn away from her and the baby has to survive by seeking its own nourishment and care. I must be feeling that my illness had ruined the therapeutic relationship through which Esther's adult self was growing and soon would have been ready for timely delivery.

I admired the way that Esther's parents had been endlessly flexible, helpful, and supportive, and yet I regretted that this had prevented her from expressing anger, because they had no limits. Instead, she turned the anger on her body and devalued her intellectual achievements. So I was wary of acceding to a request for removing my limits. I might rob her of an opportunity to experience her rage. On the other hand, I wanted to make an independent decision about what was reasonable to promote the completion of the analysis by allowing for a termination phase sufficient to work through Esther's major conflict around separation and autonomy. I wanted her to have a strong finish, and I wanted it for me. If, in order to give us both the time necessary for completion, I would have to alter my policy of charging for missed sessions, then I would simply have to take the loss.

As I arrived at this conclusion, Esther offered a compromise. "If you don't agree to that, then we could use this next year to cut down on the sessions, and Monday is the day I would like to drop first," she announced.

The session was almost over. I said that we needed time to think over her ideas and her feelings and keep talking about it. She said that I could have one week, and then she needed my decision. I said that the decision would be a better one if we could reach it together, and we could aim at doing it within the next week.

The following Monday Esther did not show up for her session. She called to say that she had slept in after being up late because she was upset, and could she have a telephone appointment. I said that I thought that it would be difficult to pick up on the phone where we left off last week. I said that the prospect of continuing last week's discussion might have contributed to her sleeping in. She agreed, and said that was why she just had to talk to me, and please couldn't I give it a try?

I welcomed her continuing the discussion despite her resistance. Still it could wait until the next day. But the abruption image was in my mind, and I felt worried about the dangers of rigidity. I had been unexpectedly pleased with the effectiveness of some telephone supervision I had done recently and of a brief therapy for someone in a rural area with no access to a therapist, but I had not had a telephone session with an analytic patient. I had read an article that inspired to me to free myself from the guilt of deviating from the traditional when doing analysis on the telephone (Zalusky 1996). So I agreed to Esther's request. Looking back on it, I think that here Esther was changing the frame without discussion and agreement yet again, and I fell into the enactment.

"Well," Esther said portentously, and then launched into a report of her news, as if there was no problem between us. "The big news is, I got a studio apartment, first one I saw. And I love it. Art loved it too. Mom says she's fine with it, but she didn't meet us at her house after I had taken Art over to see it. She said she would be there, so she was clearly avoiding meeting him. Finally Art had to leave, but I waited for her. She got home at 11 P.M. and she seemed upset. Eventually, she just exploded at me. She went off. She's raving on about how Art will never be in her life, I'm not to marry him, she can't sleep since I started seeing him, because he's a nobody, and she thinks I deserve someone rich and important like Dad. She just went on and on: she's already had too much pain to bear in her life. She had to mourn the loss of two children, and this time she won't deal with it; she's having to take medication to help her sleep. She has even gone to a therapist! She thinks I have terribly low self-esteem to date a struggling artist and can't understand how could I think Art was anything like our family. And she never wants to meet Art's mother who has no education. On and on. I've never seen her so upset. She hates him. I said, 'Mom, you've never even talked to him.' She said, 'Esther, he's 50 years old and has nothing. Why doesn't he own a house? He has no goals except to get you—you're beautiful, educated, and rich. And you're going to spend your life poor and watching television while he messes with his paints.'

"I was proud of myself. I just listened. I didn't get sick. I never screamed back. I didn't even correct her about his age. I said, 'I hoped you'd be gracious, but if not you will not come to his art shows. He'll never come back to your home, but he will be in my home and at my parties.' She said, 'Then I won't come to see you any more.' I begged her to be reasonable, even if she had to pretend. She finally agreed to fake it and be nice even though she hates him. I was stunned. I had nothing to say. She says she's been thinking of death a lot lately, and she's glad that she no longer has to worry about me killing myself, but she says that this is a psychological death for me anyway. She said, 'You didn't fix the low self-esteem. Your analysis hasn't dealt with that. Dr. Scharff should have told you that. She shouldn't be letting you finish, while all this is going on. You think Art is so great, but he's not successful like your father and he isn't smart like the brothers you loved so much. You think you're trying to replace them, but trust me, you haven't come even close. You should look around some more, before you finish with Dr. Scharff.' I said, 'I'm happy with me, and it's too bad it's not good enough for you.'"

I felt sorry for Esther. She desperately wanted her mother to be proud of her choices and accomplishments. I was proud of how she stood up to her mother's barrage and remained calm and reasonable. On the other hand, I felt sorry for her mother. She must have been so disappointed that her daughter was not more like her. Perhaps she was speaking for her husband too in having to give up a failed fantasy that in finding a suitable husband by their standards Esther would bring back one of their lost sons. I agreed with her mother that the analysis was not fully complete. I would have liked to see Esther through another year of independent living, dating Art, reviewing the relationship, maybe considering other men as partners, maybe not. But I could see from her point of view that at some point she had to make and review her choices by herself. Was it better to insist on my criteria for termination being met or to accept her goals for herself?

"Mom went on and on about money and death and medication and said that I am killing her. If that's the way she feels, she is part of my past and not my future. I was good. I dealt well with this explosion, but I was shredded by it. I said to her, 'What about the man Rachel married, he's not upper class?' 'Well, but he is great in the business, and he is learning,' she says. 'He is reaching out to art and music, trying to learn. Art is your servant,' she says, 'and you think he's a prince.' Then she says, 'You're in love, Esther, and you can't hear a thing I say.' I said, 'Yes I am. I'm in love. And I'm listening, unlike you. You've never spoken to him. He's a really kind, gentle man. That's what's like my brothers. And yes he does things for me and I do things for him. I don't think he's a prince. He's just a decent guy who loves me.'"

I thought back to the times that Esther had reported similar rantings at her parents. Here was a role reversal. Perhaps it was her mother's way of holding on to the old Esther. Perhaps it was Esther's way of holding on to me, even though she felt ready to leave. Of course her mother had her reasons for being upset, but

I couldn't help but wonder if there was another role reversal going on in which Esther presented her mother as yelling at her with all the venom Esther would have liked to spit at me, while Esther did not betray her upset feelings like me. Now I could extricate myself from the enactment and release Esther's anger to me.

I said, "Your mother was having a tantrum like the ones you used to have before you got better, and that . . ."

Esther interrupted me to say, "You're right. That's a tactic I've used myself to separate."

"And that is a tactic you are using with me this last week," I continued.

"This is true," she acknowledged. "I want to keep talking about that, but I'll do it tomorrow when I see you. Meanwhile, I'm trying to get over this. I was already thinking about the things that she ranted and raved about. Mom is so disappointed in me."

"And in me, and so are you," I persisted.

"Oh you rat! Had to drag me in," she said. "Mom said 'Surely Dr. Scharff can help you do better than this. For years we thought you were going to kill yourself. Then you got over that in analysis. Now we see you're still going to die psychologically and you still hate everybody.' She's wrong. This is not who I am any more. I'll never be Miss Stupid Happy Face, but I'm happy for more than two hours at a time which is the most I ever managed before, and I'm happy about that. I have a job, an apartment, and a boyfriend who loves me, takes me out, and has sex with me.

"And as for you, you can't keep this analysis going just so you can see me graduate, get that new job, move up in my career, get engaged, get married to Art or the next guy, the bris of the first boy. Come on! Look Dr. Scharff, you've done fine by me. The only reason I'm unhappy with you is that I'm disappointed that you don't feel that I can do the rest alone. I'm happy with what I'm doing, where I'm going, and who I am. That's enough for me."

The next day Esther was late because of an accident that had not been her fault and which she had handled calmly and firmly. She told me that a car had swerved into her in the oncoming lane and the driver was found to have been drunk. Esther was preoccupied with the accident and could not continue the thread of our ongoing discussion over termination in the remaining time. In previous years when Esther had a car accident, she felt guilty and panicky about driving, even when someone else had been driving and she was merely the passenger. Back then, accidental damage recalling her brothers' fatal accident had stirred her longings for death.

At first I felt concerned that this accident had happened as a response to her talking about not being suicidal any more, or as a displacement of anger toward me and wishes to leave me. As if hanging on to old formulations, I wondered if a crash had to happen to reprise the loss of her two brothers for the termination. As it turned out, I became convinced that Esther had not contributed to this accident. I was relieved to note that she recovered her equilibrium in a few days and returned to the topic of termination. I realized that she had progressed to the point that a frightening life event did not result in regression toward deathly behavior, and I recovered my objectivity.

Esther reviewed her mother's criticisms of Art and his family thoughtfully. She acknowledged that she had not dated as much as she might have wished, and she worried that he might indeed be a replacement for her lost older brothers, but the men that her mother would choose for her were of no interest to her. She was profoundly grateful to have found a nice man like Art. She planned to get to know him over the next year and probably marry him, if all continued to go well. She said, "Maybe I am smarter than Art, but why be snooty about it? Mom gave examples of me not wanting to excel and being looked down on. She's right. I don't belong in the upper crust—or in the lower classes. I'm in the middle and so is Art. That's how it seems to me. We can be satisfied with that, and our kids will go to the local public school and hopefully they'll be happy and not suicidal at boarding school like I was."

Esther knew that I shared her mother's view that it would be better to continue for a while, but I acknowledged that her development was back on track at the young adult level, and that it was more important for her to decide for herself what made sense. In discussion over the next month, Esther decided that she would like to have a termination phase of four months. She would make do with a long July Fourth weekend vacation so as not to interrupt the process, and her termination date would be the last day of the last week of October. I agreed to the plan.

Readiness for Termination

Esther is living independently, she has a satisfactory social and sexual life, she has a committed, intimate relationship, and she manages difficult family relationships without regression. She can work and has found a career path. She can love and be loved. She can remember her dreams and analyze them herself. She can regulate her mood. She can engage in an angry debate with her therapist without self-destruction. She can assert her own point of view and back it up with logical reasons. She can feel devastated by an external event and recover within a day or two. Like other young adults who leave analysis short of their therapist's standard of completion, Esther is expressing her capacity for autonomy. The next chapter features a detailed account of the last eight sessions of the termination phase of Esther's analysis.

24

Termination

Termination is inevitable. It is intrinsic to the overall therapeutic plan. But as with birth and death, there is no single or predictable pattern. We think of termination from the beginning of every therapy. We experience its impact in advance by working on the loss of continuity of the therapeutic relationship experienced at the end of a session, or during planned vacations, and the unexpected absences of patient or therapist caused by life events.

The criteria for termination and the correct use of a termination phase of analysis and therapy have been considered at length (Becker 1993, Blum 1989, Firestein 1978, Nacht 1965, Ticho 1972). In practice, treatment is often not completed according to the ideal, and termination represents a compromise. We consider termination to be indicated when the patient's goals and our goals have been met. Of course these may differ. We measure the success of treatment according to the degree to which some or all of the following criteria have been met. These criteria interweave, and cannot usefully be ranked in importance, but when there is a sense that enough of them have been met, the patient is ready for a planned termination. See Table 24–1.

Criteria of Patient Readiness for Termination

When we consider patients' readiness for termination, we think of their growth in several areas, such as the ability to give and receive positive con-

TABLE 24–1. Termination Criteria

1. Accepting and providing holding in relationships
2. Improved capacity for relating
3. Reworking and owning of projective identifications
4. Enhanced capacity to bear loss, to tolerate developmental strain, and to mourn
5. Enhanced integration of self with better regulation of affect
6. Rehabilitation of inner objects, less splitting of good and bad
7. Ability to be separate while still in relationship
8. Continuing growth, perhaps partly by using self-analysis

textual holding in relation to their significant others. Patients whose treatment is completed are better able to relate than before, function with less anxiety, and have a greater capacity for resonating with others. This increase in mutuality comes by extricating themselves from distorted involvement with others. There has been a reworking of projective identifications so as to take responsibility for internal issues rather than unconsciously placing them in others and trying to work them out vicariously.

Patients whose therapy has been substantially successful also have an enhanced capacity to bear loss, tolerate developmental strain, and mourn. These gains reflect enhanced integration of the self, with smoother affect regulation, less vulnerability to disruptive situations, and less inclination to split the object. It is not possible to say which comes first—the integration of the self or the rehabilitation of the objects. They go together inextricably. The evidence for their integration is greater self-respect and an improved ability to appreciate others and balance individual needs with those of other members of the family and the social group—in other words, to be separate and autonomous within the context of caring relationships.

We can make a shorthand assessment of termination readiness from our overall sense of the patient's rehabilitation of inner objects. Parents formerly viewed unsympathetically by the patient as bad and harmful objects are often now viewed more charitably as people who suffered in their own right and did the best they could. Patients who have matured considerably have usually forgiven those at whose hands they have suffered, have a larger measure of compassion and understanding for others as a result of mourning their losses, deprivations, and trauma, and feel that they have an enlarged capacity to give to others.

Finally, we see a readiness to maintain the therapeutic process independently through continuing self-analysis in which the self and its parts are subject to review and processing. We are not expecting the deliberate adoption of the analytic method in slavish imitation of the therapist in the formal treatment process. We prefer to find a consistent capacity for digestion of painful material; reflection upon fears, fantasies, and behavior; and a more measured approach to life, love, work, and relationships.

The Evolution of Countertransference Leading to Termination

The therapist's countertransference is a significant marker for readiness for termination. Weigert (1952) and Searles (1959) noticed that therapists' feelings about patients change with the patients' growth. As patients near the end of their treatment, we feel differently about them, we are less constrained by countertransferential conflict and more able to work cooperatively at the level of the central self. For instance, we find that our dread of meeting certain aspects of a patient may evolve into a sense of understanding or fondness, or see our sadness about a patient's recurrent pattern of self-defeat maturing into pleasure at his gains and new abilities. Our sense of having to work carefully lest we injure the patient's self-esteem may metamorphose into working together freely with a shared acknowledgement of vulnerabilities which no longer seriously constrain the work.

The patient's termination process centers on mourning for the therapeutic opportunity and setting. Because each loss recalls previous losses, the loss of the therapeutic relationship at termination is a built-in opportunity for reviewing the losses that brought the patient to therapy and were the focus of work. Consequently, the anxiety concerning the loss of the therapy almost always brings a regression which, while superficially alarming and sometimes seeming to call into question the wisdom of the decision to terminate, actually offers an opportunity for review and reworking for a final time. While there are occasions when a reconsideration of the decision is called for, more often the decision holds, and the regression accompanying the termination process can be tolerated and used to advantage.

During termination, therapists also face the loss of their patients as objects and the trusted relationship that grew into a successful shared, cooperative venture. In an unsatisfactory or incomplete treatment, the therapist faces the loss of possibilities that were not realized. Most frequently, there is a mixture of positive gains and incomplete elements, which needs to be acknowledged by the therapist, and then mourned. The failure to mourn leaves the therapist depleted and reluctant to engage with new patients. Some patients leave us in a way that we agree is in their best interest. They fit our ideal of maturation and healing. But patients' circumstances and preferences do not necessarily fit with our therapeutic ideals.

The Range of Termination Experiences

To illustrate the variety of termination, we begin with a few vignettes of different ways that the treatments of patients described in this and previous books have ended. Then we give a detailed example from the completed analysis of Esther (Chapter 23) in order to fully illustrate the termination process.

The first four vignettes come from patients who planned their terminations in collaboration and agreement with the therapist. Even so, the pictures vary enormously.

> Rose Holt was 67 years old when she and her husband successfully terminated sex and marital therapy with me (DES) (described in D. Scharff and J. Scharff 1987). Over the years after that, she has come back herself to work on recurrent anger, depression, jealousy of her older sister, and the residue of her feeling that she had not got enough from her father and from me. I have seen her for about twenty sessions over the past fifteen years. Now over 80, Rose most recently came back for dizziness and fainting for which repeated medical workups found no organic cause. The fainting and the anxiety behind it improved—but was not completely gone—after six sessions of brief therapy.
>
> In her termination session, she reviewed this time of working together, the years we have known each other, and the way she is dealing with life in old age. She hates being old. It makes her mad—but she prefers it to not being alive. She has enjoyed her husband more in the last fifteen years than at any previous time in their marriage. Pleasurable intercourse, achieved for the first time after sex therapy fifteen years ago, is no longer available to them, as her husband's erectile potential, even with injection therapy, has failed in the last five years, and he is unwilling to use a penile prosthesis. Still, they are loving companions who enjoy other forms of sexual encounter and a great deal else about life and their family. She leaves therapy now, believing it is perhaps for the last time, still with disappoint-

ment that she cannot ever get rid of all her regrets, but with more satisfaction in her life than she ever would have expected.

Frieda (described in J. Scharff and D. Scharff 1994) spent fifteen years in therapy recovering from years of childhood sexual abuse from her father and extreme neglect from her mother. She ultimately found a fair amount of relief from her chronically relapsing depression and her fear of intercourse with her husband, whom she loved and trusted. She asked to terminate slowly, moving first to once a week for over a year, then to every other week, once a month, and once every couple of months. But Frieda failed to keep her final appointment—something she had never done before—and delayed paying the balance on her account for two years. By not showing up for her last appointment, not rescheduling, and not clearing her debt, she both held on to the relationship and "stuck it to" the therapist. So in this final phase of the relationship, she did something that traumatized patients almost always do in termination: she passed part of her early trauma back to the therapist.

Albert, aged 35 (Chapter 9 and J. Scharff and D. Scharff 1994), had come to analysis after seeing me (DES) intermittently since the age of 15. After three years of analysis, we agreed the work was stalemated, and he switched to twice-weekly therapy. Working in that way for another two years, he was able to understand a great deal about the reasons for the analytic stalemate, and finally to say, "I realize that what I want is for you to cure my parents." Following this realization, he decided that after these five years of therapy (plus three earlier therapies of about a year each), he was getting along as well as could be expected and should try life without therapy. His goals were not really met: he was not involved in a significant emotional relationship, and he was not working in a professionally satisfying career. It was not clear to him or to me that therapy was continuing to improve his life, although he did seem much less depressed and less in danger of chronic self-destruction. Accordingly, we agreed to meet for another three months, after which he stopped. He contacted me a year later to say that things were about the same, and so he would like to come back in a month or so, but he did not follow through. I hope to see him again at another point in his life, but I cannot say when that might be.

Angela (Chapter 12) whose analysis was punctuated by periodic episodes of wanting to quit, had a successful eight-year treatment which resulted in significant reduction of her depression, and improvement in her marriage. She planned a termination date in concert with her analyst, and, as reported earlier, experienced a termination regression which allowed her to rework the earlier fears that led to her recurrent wish to quit prematurely. This gave her an opportunity for review of the issues that brought her into analysis, an assessment of her gains, and a reworking of early losses and disappointments. Angela's experience bears a considerable similarity to the termination sequence described in detail later in this chapter.

The second group of examples illustrates patients who did not plan their terminations. In two cases geographic moves played a role, in one case the termination was triggered by the withdrawal of funding by a managed care company, and in the other case the therapist unsuccessfully confronted a characterologic pattern.

Ivan, whose distance from his therapist was described in Chapter 11, maintained the distance from treatment despite his gains. After two years of treatment, in which he had been absent freely, as though it had no emotional meaning, I (DES) decided to confront him, feeling that no further progress was likely unless Ivan could face the effect of his attitude on me, and by analogy, the effect that his avoidant and dismissive style had on other relationships. It was not a sucessful confrontation. Ivan accepted the validity of my contention that his coming and going at will without regard for its effect on the therapy represented his way of controlling me, minimizing my importance, and keeping me from owning and controlling him, a fate that he feared both in therapy and in other relationships. But the confrontation also frightened him. Although Ivan and I both acknowledged his fright and were working on it, Ivan suspended treatment, using the excuse of a work reassignment. He called me several months later to say he would be resuming, but he did not follow through.

I was disappointed, felt a mixture of guilt and relief, and wondered if I had acted out against Ivan. I asked myself whether it would have been more useful to tolerate his absences longer while solidifying the alliance and slowly working through the schizoid problem. But I had acknowledged to myself at the time of the confrontation that there was a substantial risk that Ivan would quit. I had decided that the work had been stalled for so long that it no longer seemed useful under the circumstances. I had taken a position and had to live with the consequences.

Bill Noonan is a 55-year-old man whose family I (DES) have seen through the years (D. Scharff 1982, D. Scharff and J. Scharff 1987). While I was seeing his wife Peggy many years ago, I referred Bill for analysis because he was unable to love her or continue a sexual relationship with her, although he thought she was wonderful, and because he was so anxious at work that he could barely keep his job. His analysis was completely successful: he could love Peggy fully, their sex life was good, and he became able to work effectively. Bill and Peggy subsequently had three children whom he adored, and he achieved a fair degree of professional success.

Ten years after finishing his analysis, and after I had helped the couple with developmental issues concerning their young son, he sought help from his analyst for midlife anxiety, but, because he was terminally ill, the analyst could not see Bill. Bill turned to me, saying he once again found himself anxious at work because his better judgment indicated that he should change jobs, and because he could not settle questions of his religious identity enough to help his children establish a spiritual life for themselves. Bill had to deal with the return of his anxiety, its exacerbation by the pain of his analyst dying, and its aggravation now that he was on his own without the analyst to help him. He worked with me twice a week for a year on the couch. The symptoms gradually abated and Bill's job anxiety settled down. He decided to stay in his job for the time being and he became more successful there. Bill and Peggy bought a bigger, more expensive house to accommodate their growing family. Then we moved on to his spiritual dilemma, which opened out to the more general questions of midlife identity that had produced his symptomatology.

Bill felt that this was an important area to explore, but in the middle of this phase, his managed care company denied further benefits, because I could no longer say he was occupationally at risk. Although the reviewer agreed that Bill could profit from more therapy, he denied the appeal for insurance coverage. Bill felt that he could not afford to pay for the therapy entirely out of pocket because of his increased mortgage payments. He decided that—however much he valued the work—he was no longer dealing with make-or-break issues. With his obligations to his children who were now nearing college age, and the expense of the new house, he would have to stop. Reality constraints played into his ambivalence and compounded the effect of the loss of his analyst, for whom I was a poor substitute. He discontinued therapy after a few more sessions. I have heard from his family periodically since. He is doing well in the same job but also continues to find it difficult to relate to his children's development and to Peggy's concerns about aging.

Peggy called me two years later to work on her relationship to her oldest child. She wanted to work on this problem alone because Bill was still preoccupied at work, they had no more insurance reimbursement, and he was reluctant to return to therapy. After a few sessions of brief therapy with Peggy, the problem with her son improved.

Marianne (Chapters 12 and 21) stayed in analysis for eighteen months, during which the work moved to deeper levels and enabled her eventually to leave a hopelessly destructive, sexless marriage. From the first year on, she had expressed an ambivalence about making a commitment to staying in Washington for the longer analysis that I (DES) thought she needed. She kept feeling victimized and shortchanged in her marriage and work situations, as she had in every relationship for the last fifteen years. From the beginning of the analysis, her mother had been in decline. As the analysis moved on, Marianne decided to leave her husband and take the chance of being on her own. She separated and she took a temporary job in another city, ending regular analytic sessions without an agreed-on plan to do so. But she kept in touch with me, and saw me during her irregular visits home. Then her mother died. Freed from the threat of her mother's impinging on her life, Marianne took a job in Paris—the first really good offer she had—and planned to move back there as a single woman. Now she came back to Washington for a final month of analytic sessions in which she reviewed the constraints she had put on her own analysis, the fears that I would impinge on her as her mother had, and the freeing effect that her mother's death had on her, even though she also felt sadness and regret. She experienced the loss of me and was grateful that I had stuck by her despite her shabby treatment of me, and she resumed treatment in Paris with an analyst whom she had seen as an adolescent. From my point of view, this was an aborted treatment of a person who could work well in analysis. From Marianne's point of view, analysis was a liberating experience that freed her to see her need for treatment and return to her own country for further growth.

Catherine (Chapter 11), who had been recently reassigned to Washington, DC by her Los Angeles–based company, had come for help with an acute work crisis which had quickly resolved. This had led to her investigating how the pain and rejection of her two divorces had caused her to seal herself off against emotional and sexual relationships. She began therapy twice a week on the couch, agreed reluctantly to take antidepressant medication, and worked on the parallel problems of the way she set herself up for trouble with exploitative people at work and in the new relationships that she was now willing to try. In romantic involvements, she came to understand a self-destructive pattern. Catherine could not extricate herself from relationships with men who were interested in her sexually but unwilling to commit to her emotionally. Several times she allowed men to exploit her. After fifteen months of treatment, she was able to end a relationship that threatened to repeat this pattern.

Then Catherine suffered a re-creation of the original work crisis. Although she was able to resolve this crisis more successfully, she decided that a large part of the fault lay in allowing herself to stay in an office that periodically exposed its workers to this kind of situation, and she decided to accept transfer back to Los Angeles where she knew she would have the support and understanding of a boss she could trust. She could see the parallel between the work crisis and the romantic difficulty she had been having. At the same time she met up with an old friend in another city with whom she now began a long-distance romantic relationship in which she was treated well. Catherine left therapy because of the move, but she was able to continue the new relationship on weekends. She wrote two months after moving to thank me and to tell me that she regretted that we could not continue such fruitful work. She had taken my referral to a colleague in Los Angeles and had begun therapy there. The relationship with her friend continued to be loving and might well result in marriage.

These vignettes present a few of the endless varieties of termination. We now turn to an illustration that presents the process in the full detail and depth that a leisurely termination affords.

Termination: Eight-Session Countdown

This example covers the last eight sessions of the analysis of which the pre-termination phase was presented in Chapter 23. Most of the criteria for successful treatment had been fulfilled, and the termination offered the patient an opportunity for review of her gains and vulnerabilities. We pick up the termination material as the patient proceeds through the last two weeks of treatment.

Esther had been in analysis with me (JSS) for eight years, three more than she had been led to expect by her father's best friend, a senior British analyst who had persuaded her father to make the referral to me. This family friend, who had been one of my supervisors before I left Britain years earlier, thought that she needed a woman analyst who had experience with adolescents. Not that Esther was adolescent at the time of the referral, but he correctly surmised, from talking with her father and visiting the family on yearly trips to the United States, that she had many adolescent issues in addition to profound depression that she had suffered when her family suddenly lost two older boys when she was young. It was sad for me that the referring analyst died of a sudden illness in the third year of treatment when Esther was only a little better, and so he did not get to see the good results.

In the course of her analysis, Esther had progressed from being totally debilitated by depression and hating school to living independently, working two jobs, studying part-time for a masters degree in business, and enjoying a loving, sexually satisfying relationship with a kind, devoted man ten years her senior. She could now communicate her experience in words rather than in bodily symptoms of stomach and bowel pain. She still had some anxiety about embracing the professional career in business for which she would soon qualify. She thought that she had fully mourned the loss of her two older brothers, but she was worried that her choice of partner had been determined by her wish to replace the one to whom she was closest, since her boyfriend resembled him in looks and was the age he would have been had he lived. She was upset that her parents did not accept her boyfriend because he was too old for her, was not Jewish, and, being an artist and not a businessman, he was not financially competitive like her father. Esther knew that her sister liked Art, but she was not sure what her father thought. Her mother was outspoken in her active dislike of Art. She took Esther's choice of boyfriend as a sign that Esther was not ready to terminate and begged her not to leave analysis.

Ideally, I would have preferred to continue the analysis through the period when Esther began more complex professional work and had time to review her choice of partner more thoroughly, but I respected Esther's point of view that she was ready to try things on her own. As Esther put it, she could not "hang around in analysis through every future life event."

As described in Chapter 23, Esther signalled her readiness to approach termination with a dream, entered a transference struggle over leaving on her own terms and being let go, and then independently chose an earlier date for termination than Dr. Jill Scharff would have preferred, but negotiated an agreeable format for ending. Esther approached the last two weeks of the termination phase as a countdown to freedom from sessions eight to one, like a rocket in blast-off.

Session 8

"This is the 8th day and I'm terrified!" she began.

> *I associated to the six days it took to make the world, and the seventh day of rest. The odd thought occurred to me, "What happened on the eighth day?" I must have been feeling that this termination was momentous.*

"I'm aware that this is a terrible time to finish," she said. "I could screw up, skip school, never get a permanent job, go back to live with my parents. But it doesn't change my mind. I'm feeling ready to finish. And I'm not giving up Art to please them. I won't finish with him unless I stop loving him. I admit that a part of me would like you to totally change your technique and tell me what to do with my parents to make them approve of me. And believe it or not, I had an orgasm with Art. So there's hope for me.

"I was very weepy last night. I saw a movie on television where various marriages turned into disasters. I had a rush of self-doubt. But Art listened and made me feel better. And I felt happy and calm before I went to sleep. I was worried that I won't be able to do everything about my car, an apartment for us, my parents' reservations, my career, my money, my work, my broken air-conditioner, my stopped-up drain. And I worried, if I was moving too fast with him, what would be the consequences. I don't have as much time to see anyone, so there's a loosening of the bond I had with my parents and my sister and brother-in-law. I am more on my own, but there's no reason to think I would screw up. If I study, I'll pass the exam. If I go to financial advisers, they'll help me manage my budget. Art doesn't have to move in. I can keep the job I have until I find something permanent I like or feel comfortable switching. There's no reason to worry. Nothing's going wrong, except Mom. There are no signs. It's just the potential."

"It's the forecast of doom that points you in the worry direction," I said, thinking of the impact of her mother's worry on her.

"Yes," she agreed. "But it's a much smaller part of me than before and only gets me when I'm down. My sister's husband told me that he really likes Art. My evaluations are good. Someone wrote something very nice about me being helpful and accommodating. Anyway, last night I was feeling pretty down but I feel much better today."

Esther's state of mind is reasonably independent of her mother's opinion, now that she uses feedback from a wider range of external objects to secure her self esteem. She is also reporting on the resilience of her internal object. She does not, however, deny her mother's reservations. She thinks about them, even worries over the reality of her mother's concerns, and decides after process and review that her choice is the best one for her at this time. Now she turns to examine her use of Dr. Scharff as an object, interwoven with her thoughts about her family.

"I wonder what you've been thinking in the last eight days?" she said inquiringly. "What would my brothers think of me in the last eight days? I can't pretend they'd be thrilled, because they would have wanted me to marry into a wealthy Jewish business family too, but they'd recognize more of my accomplishments than Mom and Dad and be more optimistic and positive. They'd let me talk to them and they'd listen. As for you, I can't imagine what you would want me to be like right now so I'm not even trying. There's a wish to fulfill your expectations, but they'd have to be in line with mine, 'cause I like mine too much! I'm not going to change them.

"It seems ridiculous when you think of how close we've been, but I may lose my mother altogether. But that's a long way off. Art told me of a dream he had where he and my parents were talking amicably. He is hopeful that my Dad will help her to come around. I can't think of anything more I would want to tell you.

"I've been using you as mother and father. I want you to tell me I'm fine, and that you approve of my choices, of which you can do neither, really. There's no reason why I wouldn't do well. If I put my mind to it," she finished.

Esther faces the potential loss of her mother with regret but without being manipulated by it. She recognizes that she has been using Dr. Scharff as a substitute object, but she does not try to keep her in that role. She has used her to form an intimate couple with, and now she has transferred that to building a couple relationship in her life. She maintains hope for her autonomy. Most of all she shows that she has a durable concept of the future despite attacks on her confidence.

Session 7

"I don't want to tell you anything," she began. "I don't want you to know what's in my mind and what I'm working on. Plus I'm in a bad mood. You would say it's because of leaving this. But I think it's because I can't get everything done before the end of my summer job. The person I'm substituting for in the summer school office wanted me to do a lot of cataloging, but I think she'd want me to do the other jobs first, so I do them and don't have time for the cataloging."

I said, "You can't get everything done here either, and because it was important to you to decide for yourself what needs doing, I agreed to the early date for termination that you proposed. Yet you long for me to tell you what to do."

"I don't know," she said. "I wish you'd give me an exit guide. There are seven days left, and I'm already done."

Earlier in her life when she was suicidal, and in previous therapies when she felt bored, Esther made for the nearest exit. So asking for help with this was different for her. I obliged with an exit guide of sorts. I said, "How about using them for doing the leaving?"

"What does that mean?" she demanded. "I don't have any stuff to put away, no desk to clean off. I don't need a reference letter. There aren't a lot of miserable things I wanted to say and never told you."

Immediately, I wondered if her protest was covering a degree of annoyance with me.

Referring to her earlier view of me as an irritating, crafty little rodent, I asked, "How am I doing in the rat department?"

"Very well," she replied, laughing. "I've nothing to criticize you for—well nothing that would do any good now since I'm leaving. I can't believe it, it's so exciting. I think I'm gonna be fine. I wonder if you're excited, or depressed, or let down, or hopeful. I don't know how the other half feels. But I'm happy I finally had the guts to stick to it, leaving I mean. I'm looking forward to sleeping a little later. Have you any advice on how long to wait before I get married? Ha ha!" she said, teasingly, as if daring me to fall out of my analytic role.

I felt taunted, and then bored, as she went off into the there-and-now and rattled on in a slightly manic style imagining details of her wedding. "It's the sort of thing she could be discussing with her mother," I thought. But her mother, who would have loved to plan for her daughter to marry a more suitable man, was not available to share in planning for a wedding to Art. I also felt irritated that the wedding was of such interest to Art. Maybe Esther's mother was right, and he really was unsuitable. I felt worried that the wool was being pulled over my eyes. I thought that here I was being given to identify with Esther's persecutory maternal object while she held on to confidence in her self and survived the threat of disapproval. Then I found myself shifting again to identify with her secure sense of self, her confidence in her choice, and her hope for the future. My identifications were switching between self and object quite rapidly, following the thread of her ambivalence and her individuation process. As she said her next words, I was drifting along, preoccupied with these thoughts.

"I figure next fall is the earliest," she said, "But Art keeps talking about wedding dresses and that means a real wedding and family involved. So I'll wait till the dress thing goes away. I don't want it their way. I want it my way. They may not want to be there anyway. Art thinks I'd be pretty in the dress. He likes the ritual and wants it formalized. It's a long way off. That's something I'd find it difficult to spend money on. Yet if I have a wedding I don't want nasty food and a cheap place. But I don't know if I want to spend my money that way. So I'll see if this dress thing runs its course and disappears. Oh well . . . This session is kind of a waste."

So she was bored with it too! Now she gets to the point.

"I think I'm staying another week just to please you. I wouldn't mind at all if we finished this week. Well, how long have I got?"

I gave no answer.

"Unless you're asleep, or dead!" she prompted.

"328 minutes," I said, feeling provoked to make a wisecrack about the time left in the remaining six sessions.

"Oh for heaven's sake, I mean today," she said.

"Twelve minutes," I conceded, and pointed out, "You want to do for yourself but you want me to track the time for you."

"Twelve is a nice short map," she said, not wanting to think of the fullness of time left in which to notice her separation from me. "I don't wear a watch. This is the only place I need a watch. Even in the store where I work. If I get a more serious job, I'll get a watch. Besides if I had a watch here, I'd be looking at it all the time."

Esther switches almost imperceptibly to talk about finishing up at her extra summer job. It sounds as if she is talking about leaving analysis.

"I'm gonna be tough today and get a lot done before I leave," she declared. "But if I don't, I don't care, 'cause I'm not there permanently. So either I do it, or I forget it. It hasn't been very pleasant; hasn't made me love the job. But it's been good experience working in school administration, and I liked having the money from the summer job as well."

Consciously returning to the analysis, she said, "I'll tell you what I won't miss here and that's your other patients. They end up parking in the one place you told them not to park. I'd love it if someone would back into one of those cars. I always imagined I'd get into an accident leaving a session so I'm holding my breath about that."

"You're wondering if you'll be able to leave here without injury," I noted.

"That's the kind of kooky thing that happens to me," she said. "I've only got seven days to get through. Six more illegal right turns and seven more backing out of the driveway. Then I don't have to be a patient, or see patients who have been here before me, or get up early unless I want to, and I don't have to tell you every stupid thing that goes through my brain."

"Are you scared to speak of how afraid you are in case it would seem that you aren't happy or ready?" I asked.

"Yes, I don't need self-doubt right now," she admitted. "Thinking about being worried makes me worry worse. If you just do it, you've minimized it. A melodramatic 'Am I going to survive this?' sounds just awful. I don't want that."

Esther wants to finish up in such a way as to never go back, and not sustain damage at the last moment. She is inhibiting herself in the last couple of weeks out of fear of having feelings that might prevent her leaving.

Session 6

Esther had nothing to say for ten minutes. At last, she spoke about her temporary second job that was about to end now that summer was almost over. "One thing I'll miss in that office is the opportunity to try finding things," she said.

"You are focusing on ending your search activity in that job rather than in your analysis because it exposes you to less self-doubt than looking at the ending of this," I said.

"I can't think of much I'll miss about here," she shot back. "I won't have to live my life around this anymore."

"You won't miss the structure that this provides?" I asked.

"I won't miss that I never got a vacation except one to coincide with yours," she replied. "I never liked that. But I don't want to complain. I'm happy and relieved to stop, but it's rude to dwell on it. And I don't want to dwell on what will go wrong. I can't predict what Mom will do, what she'll like or not like. I'm sure she'll see me moving into Art's apartment in the District as a direct result of stopping this. She'll think I'm under his influence, and in a sense I am! I resent her implication that her life experience would enable her to make a better decision about my life than me. Most people don't wait this long to be serious about someone. And I've already given up one person 'cause I was too young. I could have been stuck with him, someone who was too overweight. He was smart and funny but so competitive you could never be right. But he wasn't nasty. Funny guy, very talented. How can Mom think she knows better? Her life has been so different from mine. Stopping this, dating Art, and doing great isn't even going to convince her. She doesn't focus on what I do well. I have a weakness for feeling low, not liking other people, not being optimistic. I'm not Miss Happy Face and I don't love the world, but these things are not hurting me now. I'm not crawling back to her or hiding in the corner of the couch. When I have a child I'm not going to cast up things from the past. If you can't feel young with your parents, who can you feel young with? Who knows whether staying seeing you would make the big difference? I can't take that chance because it would be doing what she wants."

It would be tragic if Esther had to shortchange herself in analysis to prove that her actual mother had not been reinstalled as the guardian of her choices and her future. She might even get forced into remaining with Art, even if he began to seem unsuitable, just to maintain her autonomy. But at least she is aware of it. And now she counterbalances the weight of her mother's opinion with an account of her father's support.

"Dad thinks I really have come a long way. He appreciated how angry I was about his being so withdrawn all those years. He thinks dating, going to school, working, and being in analysis were good things for me. He even appreciated it when I got mad and told him off, but Mom thought the things I said were terrible, pointless, and mean. I don't know. I haven't the faintest idea. He's not saying much about Art. Hasn't been home to meet him. Mom is the one with all the feelings, about this as in everything else.

"Mom wants me to explore other boyfriends, but I feel like being monogamous. It's important to me that I keep having sex and enjoying it.

Otherwise, I'd either get no sex, or sex with a stranger. It's not worth it. My parents want me to date without sex, but that's not possible for me. If I'm not comfortable to have sex, I don't want to date either. It's safe with one person and it's comfortable. Are those terrible reasons? I can't play my own version of what my mom was like at 21, dating and choosing a husband from the select set presented to her. It's not like Dad was so select. I mean he'd been married before and he was older. He had two kids, but I suppose his financial success took care of that little problem. I didn't want to spend the last six days talking about my mother," she concluded ruefully.

I wished for a nice clean termination without this extremely painful complication of her mother's distress. Talking about her mother was inevitable, and it was always disquieting. I did not join her plea that Esther continue analysis, but what if her mother knew best? I myself would have preferred a longer termination, as they both knew. But I continued to feel that the choice of termination date had to be Esther's decision. I had to trust in her ability to continue growing after analysis.

Session 5

"Last Friday night I had a scary dream about a big spider, this big," Esther began, showing me with her hands a length of about two feet. She did not explain why it had taken her a week to tell this dream. "I was in bed and it's facing me. I do my thing. I leap up and get out of bed. Scared Art to death. Art couldn't find a spider so I went back to bed. Yesterday A.M. I had another spider dream and again I went back to bed. This dream was about me being in my parents' house. My mom was there I think, but I'm not sure. There were these big spiders in each new situation and that's what the dream became about—avoiding them, tricking them, killing them. I wonder if talking about my mom yesterday has triggered this spider dream."

Esther made the association between spider and entrapment by her mother. I settled back to see how she would interpret this dream for herself.

"In this spider dream, they could grow from teacup size to larger than a dinner plate. You could step on them if they were small, but if they were big, you couldn't. You never knew when they were going to enlarge themselves. It was frightening. Other people were concerned but didn't think it was as big a deal as I did. I said 'I'll put my clothes in a dresser to keep them away from the spiders.' They said, 'Any clothes you put on will have spiders. No matter what.'"

"Here you are analyzing for yourself the connection between your fear of spiders and your mother's power over you wherever you are," I noted with satisfaction, because Esther was showing her capacity for internal analytic process.

"No doubt about that," she agreed. "And it's not a bug dream, which I also have. Just spiders in these spider dreams. And they are not scaring me in a no-brain, crawly way. The spiders are big and terrifying. They affect me more as if they are a human presence. They are a real problem. They are big, they are not afraid of me, and they won't go away. I saw Mom at my sister's house when she was baby-sitting Saul right before the dream. There's nothing that she said that triggered this dream. It was a meaningless interaction. I could handle that just fine."

I noted that Esther was looking for a day residue that the dream had picked up, but she did not find one in her actual interaction with her mother. So the dream could be expressing split-off fears, or more likely old fears that reasserted themselves in dream life during the termination. I then thought it possible that her dream was revealing a temptation to have back the old fears and dependency gratifications that her illness used to bring her.

"Then did the visit leave you with a longing for your Mom to get bigger in your mind?" I asked.

"Well I don't like the way she is playing such a small part in my life because I'm with Art. Yesterday, when I drove away from the house, I could see her in my rear-view mirror holding Saul's hand, and getting smaller and smaller. Saul looks like me, with a soup-bowl haircut like Mom would have given me and wearing overalls like I wore. That's what my mom wants. She wants the little child that I'm leaving behind. She wants to go back and do the mother-thing all over again.

"I saw my old friend Celia and her baby. The baby is happy, healthy, and dainty. Art likes them dainty, but I don't. I'm used to chubby babies. This baby was happy, never cried. Celia's always been my role model as a career woman. But after she gets her PhD, she thinks she'll maybe work part-time as a tutor *at home*! That whole ambitious person has been replaced by this mother who'll fit her career around her family! Unlike my sister, who's back to work as soon as she can get up! It made me feel 'Celia can do it, I can do it.' It'll be okay for me to work part-time. She might go back to school for computer training and work at home. Or she might open a shop! Ugh! Totally different from the Celia I used to know.

"So I had a mother who devoted herself entirely to the kids, and is still devoting one half of her life to her two grandchildren, when my sister doesn't devote anything to the kids. Interesting. I'm working two jobs today again, for the last paid day. I got most of the cataloging done. It was tiring but I managed as long as I kept myself fed and watered. It's sneaky, because now I could say of the things I can't do, 'Wait till Monday and the real office manager will be back.' People are on vacation, that's nice, it's calmer with fewer students coming to sign up.

"The mom thing is bugging me in the back of my mind. But in the front of my mind everything is more calm."

I felt that Esther was highly ambivalent about her mother's continuing role as a mothering person, and about her own role as a woman who might choose to work and mother. I considered the dream in terms of object and self. Perhaps it also expressed fears in the transference, I thought. I did not feel like a spider woman, but I decided to check it out anyway.

"Does the spider dream connect to feelings about here?" I asked quite directly. "I remember you used to see spiders near the sliding doors here and kill them."

"No, I was just thinking I haven't seen a spider here for months and months," she corrected me. "You don't have a spider problem. It's been so long."

I felt amused by this reply and I took it to mean that Esther does not feel entrapped here in analysis, and that where she used to have a problem with me being a spiderlike edition of her mother, the transference has now resolved. To the extent that her mother actually does want to weave her into her web of desires for her child, the external object problem still exists, but I felt sure that the internal object had been transformed.

"Yesterday when I was with Mom, I saw an enormous beetle, on its back. I thought it was dead. I poked it and its legs started waving and I poked it till I turned it over. So I don't get it. Some bugs I help, some bugs I kill."

I thought that the bug that she righted stood for her dead self that she had turned over and revived in analysis.

"I'm trying to work through feelings about my mother trying to control and trap me, even though she doesn't actually call me up or visit me and tell me what to do," she said. "She's made it clear that she doesn't approve of what I'm doing, but she hasn't taken back the queen-size bed that she lent me."

Now she moves out of displacement and into the transference, where she shows some concern and appreciation for me.

"For some reason I'm real calm today. I'm really anxious to know what you think, but I'm not going to get to find out. This is vain of me, but I wonder what it will be like for you without me here? Of course, I'm not the only patient. I don't know. Usually I don't care. Other times I've left therapy have been after a short time. I know you think I'm not done, but I don't think you think of it negatively like Mom does.

"It's strange to think of your old supervisor checking up on how you did with me if he was still alive, but I think you feel you did a good job and so it's not a problem. Are you relieved he's dead? That sounds terrible. He's not around, so at least if he thought you didn't do a good job, you wouldn't hear about it, and it wouldn't change your references. Perhaps that's me thinking about myself. I was fond of him because he cared about my dad and us children, but we only saw him once a year when he visited, except for the year that the boys were killed. He came over for the funeral and he stayed to help us cope. I wish he was alive if he thought I was successful, but I'd rather have him dead if he was going to be disappointed in me."

This was painful to hear. Her need for parental approval was murderous. I had been fond of this man. He was like a parent to me, and I hated to think of his right to life depending on his view of her or of me as her therapist. If he had been so good to the family, where was her concern for him? And she had him coupled in her mind with me, which raised the question of what was on her mind about me. Perhaps, she felt like killing me off too, if I did not approve. I felt that her setting the termination date earlier than I would have was a test of whether I appreciated that she was acting independently to leave with integrity as a final step toward health.

"I'm left with a positive feeling about him," she said. "He was warm, stable, and he got me you, the first therapist that was any good. But he's not my father. The most important thing is that my father loves me and everything else is secondary."

"I think you're also wondering what you mean to me," I suggested.

"Yes," she allowed, then denied her curiosity. She thought she knew what I meant to her. "I'm a job, and whether or not you've done a good job is what I mean to you. It's businesslike. Like taking the car in to be fixed and it's a bigger job than they said. Then they do it right or just do a rush job. I have to be a client who is satisfied with the work done or services rendered. And you will evaluate whether you provided the service or not. And that's how you'll think of me. It's strange when you leave a job they give you a party. It's strange to think that here it's one more day, then that's it. The longest job I've ever had. Maybe the longest job you've ever had! Maybe that's the spot I've had, the longest living patient."

"I thought that was a spot you didn't want," I said, remembering how she had wished to finish in three years, and feeling that she was denying the value of her time with me.

"No I didn't, but it makes me a bit memorable," she said.

She was memorable anyway, memorable for the depth of her depression, her tenacity, and her spectacular improvement, and I did not want her belittling herself. I didn't see that she was also aggrandizing herself by making a claim of being special to me. She was reminding me that she was alive—a huge achievement in itself, and so why was I was arguing about the basis for her claim to feeling special? Of course I would miss her because I had known her for so long and especially now that it was such a pleasure to see how well she could work.

I said, "As far as the 'job' aspect is concerned, we both think your engine is running pretty well. I hope that if it goes out of kilter, you'll come back for a tuneup without feeling your mother was right in thinking that your engine was lousy. But all this talk of jobs done and services rendered obliterates our relationship. It takes away from the personal value of the relationship we have had for seven and a half years."

"Well it's work to have a relationship," she said, stubbornly holding to her point of view.

I felt hurt and obliterated. My thinking process stopped until the next session.

Esther may be backtracking from having told Dr. Scharff that she has been good for her. After recognizing this, Esther may have given a reply to diminish its importance, because she is hurt that Dr. Scharff does not recognize her longing to be special for being in treatment so long. Dr. Scharff fails to see that that in itself was a greater achievement than Esther had managed in previous therapies. Esther cannot accept that her length of time in analysis is the defining variable, and Dr. Scharff misses the point that her analytic longevity also represents her survival.

Session 4 (*After the Weekend*)

"Well I've been sick for days," she complained. "Killer headaches, four days now." She remained silent, looking ill.

She had been sick away from me, and I felt that she wanted to be sick with me, like it used to be. So many times, she had lain groaning on the couch or doubled over. I thought that she might be afraid and angry, but I didn't try to relieve her pain as I used to do by finding the words for her body language. I thought that perhaps she was sacrificing herself to illness to save me from caving in, but four days to termination, I wasn't going to interpret the symptoms for her.

"That's an old way of dealing with separation. How about trying the new way, and putting into words what you feel?" I asked.

"Okay," she replied quickly, and went on. "I will miss this place. That was some parting shot! 'Obliterated our relationship.' You're my psychoanalyst, not my friend. It's your job to have a relationship. In that case, I can understand why there is a finishing point and why you don't go back. I felt very needy with Art last night. Tomorrow is my first day of school, so I have other things to be edgy about than leaving here. But you don't get a going-away party here! And I'm going to be damned by my mother for leaving here, and I don't know how to handle that. But I was planning to see her tonight. I feel wary around her. I feel her tugging at me, trying to give me what she gave me before, but I don't need that anymore."

I thought that my decision to hold back was validated.

Esther reverts to the here-and-then of the transference, but becomes able to return to the here-and-now of the transference and the there-and-now of her family life.

"I want to do it all myself," she reiterated.

"On the other hand, I'm very conflicted," Esther continued. "I'd like to be tired with her and have my headaches with her. Now it's term time, I won't have Art because he'll be teaching his course at night at the art school again. I'm worried I'll miss him, that my feelings will be hurt, or I'll become dependent on Mom. I'm too much the sick one in the relationship with Mom. I know I need Art, but I don't need to be sick to get him to care for me. I'm scared of Art dying, because he is older, and his mother died in her fifties. So far I think it's worth it, being with him. We agree on a lot, especially on children things.

"I've gotten completely away from the subject of being here or not being here," she confronted herself. "There were times when it was nice to get up early and enjoy the way things smell, no traffic, the light. It won't be long before I'm getting up early again, for a job, for a kid, but it won't be for this." She fell silent, then she resumed briefly, "I was imagining what my job might be like in a few years. Well I guess I've shut down."

"You think of what you'll have instead of this, rather than confront the emptiness of the morning when you are not coming here," I said.

"Yes," she acknowledged. "Hmm. There will be a few mornings where I wake up early and I don't have to. And some when I'll worry because I don't have a professional to talk to. I'll worry that my relationship with my mother is disintegrating because I don't come here. I feel I've done with you for now, for my self. I could work with you on things for my mother's sake, but I don't want to enter into that right now.

"I told Art I was very hopeful about the fall. I have all sorts of plans. Somehow I'll have to work my mother into those plans. Some will have to include baby-sitting my sister's children so I get to see Mom. Maybe after school's begun.

"I wonder if I'll know if you get sick and die, like Dad's friend. My staying here didn't keep you well, so my leaving won't kill you. It might make *me* a little sick, but I'm ready to face that, too."

Esther is referring to my five-week absence for surgery last year. She used to think that leaving home would kill her mother, and had assumed for years that her leaving therapy would kill me.

Here Esther shows that she has gone beyond a grandiose fantasy about controlling her object, and can face loss and uncertainty.

"I wonder how interested you are in us?" she mused.

I found myself thinking, "Who's us?" Did she mean the parts of herself, her and her mother, Art and her, her whole family, or me and her? I mulled

this over, and thought that she meant herself and Art and was wondering if,
unlike her mother, I could accept her as a member of this couple that did not
include me.

Esther began to give a catalogue of her improvements, going from her
body self to her self in action on the job. "I certainly like my body, at least,"
she said with satisfaction. "I have improvements to make but I'm pleased
with the basic product. That's a big change. I dropped off my time sheet at
my summer job. I'll miss that now. I no longer feel like an inadequate replacement. I no longer felt bad if I couldn't find the statistic the teacher
wanted. I did the best I could and learned to ask them to wait until I could
get help if they needed more than I could do."

She fell silent, and I guessed that it was partly because I was fairly silent.

"I just wanna keep my thoughts to myself," she continued after a few
minutes. "I have learned to trust my self more. You have to do that when
your therapist doesn't say anything for long periods of time. I would tell my
friends that you don't speak to me, and they'd think I was wacko to stick
with you. But there's a reason for that. They'd want opinions, like me. They'd
want directed therapy. Sounds great, but there you haven't figured it out for
yourself and the other person's solution may be totally off the wall.

"I'm glad we did what we did. And I don't know if there is a right time
to stop, and if so, if this is the right time to stop, but I don't know when the
right time is, and I don't want it to be for Mom. I won't know if it is right,
until I do it. I just want to give it a try, and it seems like the right time,
because I'm not in the middle of a change. I'm in a good coasting period,
and yes I also have things to do. I'm apprehensive but not afraid, because
being afraid stops you, and I don't feel anything stopping me."

Esther succeeds in putting her organ language into words and dealing with
the separation of termination. She recognizes her need for a relationship and
reviews her vulnerability to sink into dependency. She feels good about herself and wants to function both as an autonomous person and as a member of
a generative couple. She feels ready to terminate because her fears of change
are not overwhelming. Dr. Scharff feels ready, too.

Session 3

"Three days left!

"I went to see my mom, and everyone was there. So I spent most of my
time with my nephew Saul because no one was paying any attention to him,

because it's easier to take care of his baby sister. Mom had nothing to say to me. She didn't ask about anything, not school, work, the apartment, or anything. It's interesting to be with someone who goes from being intrusive to not interested at all. It eases any guilt I feel in not having time to spend with her, because she doesn't want to know anything about the path I'm on. They caught me up on all that's going on with the business."

Esther gave a lot of financial and administrative information that demonstrated her knowledge of business, and her interest in her father's work—for the first time, even though she was in business school. Then she zeroed in on her own financial condition.

"I got my own Visa card," she said, triumphantly, knowing that I would understand that this meant that she would now pay for all her own expenses, rent, car repairs, and gas, out of earnings.

"Tonight's my first class. I have the book," she said rather purposefully.

"So what will you be studying tonight?" I asked, staying at that level.

"Accounting! It'd be nice to work in an office where precision is valued more. Knowing I'll be leaving my summer job in a few days, I've been pressing ahead to complete my projects of updating the catalogue of school courses. The amount of disarray is still dismaying. I don't know why the school system isn't interested in fixing the place up. They are so damned slow. Oh, I wish I could make more decisions there."

"I know you're a bit anxious about it, but mainly your career choice is something you want to work on by yourself, and you don't want me involved," I said.

"Well I bought lots of books," she said, confirming her identity as a serious student. "I'm planning to read one chapter a night." Shifting back to thoughts about terminating, she went on, "Tomorrow I come here at 8:20, then 9:10 on Thursday. That's it. Don't you feel it's strange?"

I felt a lot of things: pleasure in her accomplishment, sadness for the continuing strain between her and her mother, worry that her mother's disapproval and avoidance would push her into a dependence on her boyfriend, and mourning that this young woman that I had seen improve and grow through much of the young adult life stage would no longer be a patient of mine. I would have liked just a little more time for consolidation, but I felt quite tolerant of her disagreement with that. I even felt some pleasure in working together on our different preferences and arriving at the compromise. I did not feel it was strange to think of her finishing.

"I'm noticing how close the end is too, but it's only strange if I still were to think of you as the person you were when you first came here," I replied.

"When I came here I was very scared," she said. "It was a last-ditch effort. You seemed very sharp. Sharp Scharff! But I certainly didn't think it would be eight years. My father hasn't said anything about disagreeing with me finishing now, but I've no idea what he really thinks because he's not allowed to differ with Mom. I think he's pleased I've made the decision myself. I don't think I've done that often in my life. All the way through, there's been an undercurrent of trying to get away from Mom and get approval from him for being my own person. So his opinion matters more, because she was always jealous of you and of me working in therapy. I think she was jealous on two counts—that I got the therapy, and that you got *me*.

"It's weird to hear that now Mom doesn't want me to finish. I thought she would have been thinking, 'Ha ha to you Dr. Scharff. Now she'll leave you, too.' But that's what I'm supposed to do. I mean most people would agree. You're supposed to grow up and detach. I've done a lot of it in the last year. The only thing my parents pay for now is this month's analytic bill and my last tuition payment. In December when I get my MBA, that'll be over, and there won't be anything left, except in their basement, a couple of boxes from college I can go get. I'm glad I'm on my own and doing well. I'm not glad Mom's having trouble with it. I'm not glad she's not approving of me and Art. By being so against it so early on and unwilling to have a dialogue, she's got me feeling that I don't want to speak to her about him now. Why put myself in a position to be hurt by her? So I just keep in touch, show up every so often, and talk about the rest of the family. She and I don't really exist. It's too bad. I have a lot of good things going. I would have liked your old supervisor to know that. He was an old sweetie. He wouldn't have been hard to convince that, with or without Art, I'll be fine."

I thought she was right about that. He was an optimistic person, with a lot of faith in human nature.

"Is it sad for you that he's not here to see this?" I asked.

"Yes! If I'd just finished before he died, he might have got on Dad's case to talk Mom out of her opinion," she said regretfully. "But I wasn't ready then."

As I read this now that I am well, I get the idea that one reason she had to choose to finish on her own time schedule was to get out before I died too. It was too soon after my illness for me to think that then, and so it was not addressed.

"And I have a couple days to relax before the fall begins," she said, changing the subject to matters of everyday life. "That's my mini-vacation. I'm going to have my air-conditioner fixed. I'm going to put pictures on the walls. And I'm going to plan how I'm going to study. I'm going to write a schedule for exercising. I'm going to get my car engine tuned. I'm going to write my résumé and send it to all the accounting firms in Maryland. Then I'll look into the Maryland school administration system, or maybe Pennsylvania. If that doesn't work there are other things I can do. My job now is okay, a little boring, but not stressful. Sometimes I end up caring too much, and no one else does, so that's foolish.

"Well there I let you in a little bit!" she taunted me.

"Yes, you must have felt sure enough of yourself that you could afford to let me into your plans," I agreed.

This session is remarkable for its absence of pathology. Esther has completely recovered from her regression to psychosomatic forms of relating through her own analytic activity. She sounds like a healthy young adult, talking about her job, her degree, her parents, and her future.

Session 2

"One day left!" she began.

"Class was pretty good last night. I think I'll like it. One thing I noticed was the men. There were about twenty of them, and all of them had to give a brief summary of their business goals. Most of them are pretty average. I felt like I was trying to fulfill one of Mom's requests that I date around by looking at these men to see if any were attractive. There were a couple of cute ones who might've been interesting, but no one made me regret being with Art. He stacked up pretty well against that bunch in terms of looks and success. We went around the room talking of our career plans and I said my spiel too, but I really wanted to say 'I'm going to get married in the next couple of years, have a baby, and have fun!'

"Then I went to the summer school office and the woman I was substituting for showed me some of the pictures of her vacation and asked me to do a computer search in another room, while this headmaster I'd tried to help with some figures last week, and had such a hard time understanding what he wanted, asked her to do the same search all over again, the rat. I was pleased to hear him give her the same problem to deal with he'd given me last week. She had the same struggle as I had with him. It wasn't just me! The only difference was Mrs. Lowe was talking all the time about each item she pulled up and pushing him to make decisions, but I was silent and just waited for him to decide. I wanted him to make the decisions, like you do. But he doesn't want to learn.

"Mrs. Lowe thanked me for covering for her and said everything looked great, and she sympathized with me for how hard the teachers could be. Then she told me about how I messed up on the phone. It's just the way she is, I wasn't very offended. I just smiled and nodded. 'Give a reward and then criticize.' I read that in Psychology 101. The way I respond, is to ignore the pat on the head because it's superficial. But that's the way she operates and I don't have to work with her anymore, except to turn in my pay sheet and look at her vacation pictures. That'll be it, then.

"I saw a child here yesterday and I was curious how you'd act differently with child patients. I wonder if you sit there or play with them instead of just watch them. Mrs. Lowe said the teachers had said nice things about me. I don't know whether it's true or not, but it was nice of her to say it." Esther was quiet and lay very still for a few minutes.

I was thinking. I heard that Esther had reviewed alternative choices to please her mother, and had felt confirmed in her own opinion. She was able to enjoy positive feedback without overvaluing it and take negative feedback without much distress from the woman she was working for, but she was glad not to have to deal with her any more. I heard some remaining negative transference in Esther's description of Mrs. Lowe's more talkative way of working and in her thinking about whether I might be more engaged with a child in therapy. My attention was drawn mainly to her comments about getting feedback from the manager, and her silence led me to think that she was having thoughts about getting feedback from me.

Esther stirred on the couch. "I don't know what to say. I'm a little sleepy."

"You might want to know what I'd say about you," I guessed. "By this time you could have a good sense of it."

"I always want to know that," she agreed this time. "You want me to speculate. I can't imagine what it's like to be a therapist and have someone leave. I never thought of this as fun. You wouldn't say it's fun. You'd say it was interesting, but I don't know if I've been particularly interesting. I've been a frustrating patient, but I do seem to have made progress.

"You said last month if I ever had a problem I could come back. That makes me think you don't think I'll be 100 percent perfect from now on. I suppose that's realistic. It leaves the door open and all those good things, but it also says you might blow it. I don't think that way. I can't do this again. I can't start over with you or anybody else. And thinking about a fixer-upper set of sessions makes me feel, well 'she thinks I'll need them.' Certainly Mom does. She thinks I shouldn't stop at all. But I'm not like you two in that respect.

"It might happen that I'll not be as successful as I hope, but I don't tie it to coming back. I think if I disappoint myself, I'll have to live with it. I'll do it myself. I've used up my quota. I don't have endless resources of being receptive to treatment. For now I'm shutting down the whole treatment side. I don't want it and I won't squeeze anything out of it anymore. Saying yes I'll come back is just to make other people happy and I have a hard time actually visualizing that. I see myself as resolving the problems that crop up. But we'll see. Right now I'm anti-therapy, no doubt about it. But I recognized eight years ago that I needed help. I don't think that ability is gone. If I need help I'll be able to see it. And it was an edge I have over my family. No one has been in this intensive therapy. I was the one who was working on it, my older brothers' deaths, my parents' depression, and now I won't have to be the one."

In contrast to her therapy-rejecting words, she said quite tenderly, "Comfy couch! I don't know. Something else will have to get me up in the mornings. Job, baby, husband, studying for school. I will miss this long picture above the couch." She added quite abruptly and peevishly, "And I will miss my cat picture even though I haven't seen it in so long 'cause you've got so much in front of it."

Esther was making a brief mention of a sore spot we had been over before. The cat picture stands for her, covered over and forgotten. She always loved that cat picture and was upset that new child-patients' paintings now cover the old ones, just as someone will replace her on the couch. But she did not dwell on it. She was reinforcing her decision to end therapy and resisting the appeal of the comfort of having me to talk to. She had covered so much ground since the early days when she first responded to the cat picture, and she moved on now too.

She continued, "I have a hard time imagining what you're thinking now."

I was feeling that Esther seemed to be talking in such a way that I felt unnecessary to her and somewhat outside her experience. I wondered if she was shutting me out, or if I was letting go. Mainly I felt sorry that she was on the

*way out, because she was a gratifying patient now. But I did not answer, be-
cause I wanted to know what she could sense of my feelings. I was disappointed
when she proceeded to change the subject to make a cartoon of her loss of therapy.*

"I feel bad I'm dribbling off at the end," she apologized. "I fantasized
I'd come in and tell you my car had been stolen. I could just have the money
and go buy something that isn't what I have. I just wanted to have one more
dramatic incident with you."

"One big loss to represent the loss of this," I said, bringing her back to
the termination theme. "And a way to have the money to get on with your
life."

"I want to get on with it," she said. "I know I've been impatient. I want
it to be a few years from now, so it will be time to trade in the car, which I
should not do right now. Everything I want to do, I want to have done
yesterday, to have already begun. I'm into the not-wanting-to-let-you-in-
part.

"I will miss having a definite setup where I bring whatever's happening for discussion and dissection, especially when I have something big to
handle. But I just don't want a setup thing. I want to carry my life around
with me and work on it as I go along, any old time of day."

Here Esther confirmed that she was shutting me out to feel autonomous.

"Maybe there is a parallel between the summer school office and here.
I'm not as good as the professional, but on my own I can survive. People
like me and deal with me. I didn't crump there and I won't crump here. I
won't be devastated by doing it myself. Quite the opposite."

"You are sure that doing it yourself won't kill me and it won't kill you,"
I confirmed.

"Hmm, but it might kill my mother—according to her. I can't help that.
It's too bad she doesn't support me this time, but there's no rule that says
she has to, and no rule that I have to visit her once a week. There is a rule
in me that if I marry then my husband is number one, not my mother, or
my father, and they can either go along with it, or be out of the picture. To
be part of my family that I create, you will have to accept my mate. (There's
a rhyme!) But that's skipping way ahead."

"I was thinking back to a time when it looked as though you'd never be
able to take in what analysis could offer," I said. "A time when you were
so mad you would rather take pleasure in defeating me than in getting
better. Those times seem very far away."

"Yes they do. If I can ignore Mom's opinions, things look pretty good."

"Even though you chose to finish before a time when your mom's anxieties were assuaged, and before a time for completion determined by finishing school and reviewing your relationship with Art over time as I suggested, which is to some extent sad for me, I get satisfaction from hearing that you chart your own course," I said, telling her my main feeling.

"And I get to have satisfaction with life," she said. "There was a time when nothing was fun and people seemed awful. There are still jerks out there but that doesn't give me a sense of being cursed. I can have a life and enjoy it."

In general I feel satisfied. My mourning the loss of this patient has been going on unobtrusively. I share her optimism and feel confident that she will take care of herself now.

Session 1

Bounding in gleefully, Esther began immediately, "I never have to push the button any more. I never have to see what parking space is open. I don't have to get up early any more unless someone is paying me. Speaking of which, do you have my bill?"

I handed it to her and she held it without comment.

"I wish I had grand and important things to say but I don't. My summer school job is done so now I just have the store and school. Well, have you got anything to add?" she said in a challenging, somewhat manic way. When she received no response, she looked at her bill envelope.

"Well I'll open this," she decided. Reading the final date on her statement, she exclaimed, "Thirty-one! My age on terminating."

Getting a kick out of her pleasure, but wondering if there were other feelings, I said, "You seem to be most in touch with feelings of glee rather than sadness about finishing."

"Yes! I got my air-conditioner fixed yesterday," she said. "So now we'll work on the sink that doesn't drain properly."

"You take care of these things as you do your own self," I acknowledged.

I got the point that she could provide a good environment for herself, but I was wondering if she was using daily things to substitute for a more serious and direct exploration of sadness. I waited to see where her associations would take her.

"Drains and air-conditioners don't seem to belong to the grand good-bye," she acknowledged. Looking through the glass doors, she was distracted by a workman on a neighboring house and said, "And that person on the roof over there doesn't belong either. Now if he fell off the roof that'd be worth remembering as a grand goodbye. That house is never finished."

"I remember when you wanted to jump off the roof. That was when I had to call your parents," I said.

"It's one sure way to kill yourself. I am a bit dramatic but I'm not sorry I did it. I'm not sorry I frightened my parents, and I'm glad you called them. I've come out of it well. My parents haven't. They are still anxious about me." Oddly, the workman on the neighbor's roof was now joined by another, creating the image of a couple in danger. "Now there are two people on the roof. I wonder if they have special insurance?" she wondered. Returning to her conscious ideas about her parents, she went on, "Anyhow. I wish they would have come here for a family meeting so I could show you what they're like and how I felt about them, and to stick it to them, and make them do some hard work. I was resentful that I was always the only one working at anything emotional."

This odd coincidence of the people on the roof provided the opportunity for Esther to review the most difficult stage of her treatment, where she put me to a severe test. It also enabled her to state again her resentment at her parents in ordinary words without threats.

"I really don't know what I should be saying except that I'm glad I'm not coming back," she said gleefully.

Based on my sense that she was defending against deeper feelings, I said, "Yes, I realize that relief and pleasure at getting off on your own are your predominant feelings. Are there others being kept back, feelings that may have come out in your dreams perhaps?"

"I didn't have any dreams last night, because I woke up so many times last night to check the time," she said. "I was so scared I'd be late. So there is anxiety there." Suddenly she focused on my impending absence. "Oh you get to have your vacation now, that's nice! I almost forgot about that. I definitely was apprehensive a while ago, but not now. I'm really not that worried. The only thing clouding this is my mom. I really don't know what to do about her. If a good idea comes to me, I'll act on it. I guess I'm really trying to keep that external and not let it come inside. I have had a lot of diarrhea. I suppose I could attribute that to leaving, but it hasn't stopped me. The headaches have stopped, and the stomach will settle down. Probably had a lot to do with the weather."

"Your diarrhea seems to be an old bodily way of saying you have some worry about letting go here when things aren't solid with you and Mom," I said.

"Maybe, but it's not accompanied with pain, like it used to be and it hasn't interfered," she replied. "So I'm not letting it mess me up."

Esther was experiencing an empty symptom. It had the same form as her original symptom, but without pain or gain. She did not deny her areas of weakness, but she was not dominated by them any more.

"Neither my mom or anybody is going to stop me," she said. "It would be easier if I hated her guts, but I love her very much and that's not changing. I still have all those feelings of wanting to help her or keep her company, but there's no place for them. And since she won't be paying for things anymore after this last analytic bill, there'll be no reason to go to her for payment. I'll only go over if we are to visit.

"I'm glad you're getting a vacation, 'cause I know I won't have to suffer for it. I'm just very optimistic these days."

I said, "Yes. You have positive moods and you think in terms of your future. I remember the time when you were amazed that you had a good mood that lasted two hours."

Laughingly, she said, "Oh, better a glimpse than no glimpse at all. Now I'm on a soap box, telling the world, 'I have a right to be happy.' And I can do it without you. Boy, doesn't that sound cold. But I can! And I can do it without Mom—specially now."

"Now what?" I asked, looking for clarification.

"Now that she has nothing to offer me," she replied. "So there's no longing to be back with her. I know what she wants me to do and it's the opposite of what I want. She wants me to lead a different life and be a different person, and I just feel too good to do what she wants. She may be right that this is not a good time to stop, but I'm going to do it anyway, and we'll see what happens.

"I feel a little too comfortable here, you know," she confided.

"I don't know. What do you mean?" I asked.

"I could do this the rest of my life," she admitted. "Bring in what I feel, have you say things—every million years, always have this place to bring my self. It's riskier, stopping. It's safe to keep coming. It's safe to live at home with Mom and Dad. But I can't do that either. Safe in that I didn't have to face things. I'm not saying it was healthier. I had to be strong enough to feel that I could leave them and feel I'll have problems and solve them, figure out dreams myself, resolve conflicts, experience sadness without it becoming a depression. The next leaving will be leaving my present job and moving on in my career after I get my MBA.

"I feel like I should find some deep, dark, scary feelings for you to chew on, but I just don't feel them. I'm just in too good a mood."

Now I felt that I could not get a word in edgeways. I noted that I felt quite bleak compared to her terrifically good mood, even though I was also enjoying her pleasure in terminating.

"So what could I be anxious about?" she asked herself. "I guess I am worried about whether I'll find a job in my career field. I'm nervous that Art will have a heart attack and die. That's about it. That's all I can come up with. Hmm . . . I would like to say something that would make you happy."

Feeling that perhaps she had noticed a change in my expression, I asked, "Are you feeling I'm not?"

"No, I'm just feeling generous," she answered.

"What makes me happy is to feel you got what you came for," I began to say.

"No magic pill though," she interrupted. "I came for another chance. And I've gotten it. Now it just remains to be seen what I'll do with it."

I continued, "The stage you're at, when you now have confidence and hope for the future, means that I won't be seeing you anymore. I think you don't want to think about any sad feeling your mom might have to see you becoming independent or that I might have about losing you after all these years and the kind of work that you now do here, in case your awareness of my feelings might prevent you leaving."

"It's hard to imagine your missing me," she said. "No other relationship is this weird. There's no one else who doesn't tell me what's going on with them. There's no one else I don't face when I'm speaking. So I don't know what you'll feel. But the main thing is how I feel. I feel great. Mainly I won't miss it, because I don't need it. I guess it's time to go. Goodbye, and thank you."

It hurt a bit to be viewed as the therapy rather than the therapist, but I probably provoked this by harping on the underlying sadness. I got the point that Esther was thinking of her treatment rather than of me as "both mother and father" to whom she had turned. As she left, I continued to feel sad that she was leaving before all doubts about her choice of partner could be resolved, resigned to her decision to terminate before making the transition to a more demanding career, deeply gratified at the spectacular progress she had made through our work together, and pleased that she had grasped her future.

Dr. Scharff's task is to accept Esther's need to diminish her relevance as a person, so that she can leave her and find her autonomy. Like the parent who is being left when a child goes off to school, the analyst has to contain feelings of loss that the young adult who has to leave is normally defended against. Esther is ready to terminate because the analytic function is in place. She can interpret her dreams and her remaining bodily symptoms. She can study and work effectively. She can love a man who loves her and treats her with respect and devotion. She can bear the tremendous pain of losing the attention of her mother and the approval of her parents. She can set priorities, and she looks forward to a future for herself as a professional, wife, and mother. Lastly, she can make decisions independently of the analyst.

25

Narrative of a
Complete Analysis

Sylvia Kerr's Life Story

Sylvia Kerr, a petite, blonde, 39-year-old married woman, was worried that something would happen to kill her precious 5-year-old daughter Winnie. Mrs. Kerr had lost her mother when she was 12, and she was afraid that her child would be taken from her, too. Winnie was an anxious child with infuriating sleeping difficulties and irrational fears. Mrs. Kerr became enraged at the child, but saw no connection between her anger and her fears of Winnie coming to harm.

Sylvia Kerr had grown up on the West Coast, the only child of older parents both of whom had previously been unhappily married. As a child Sylvia felt that she should never express what she really felt so as to avoid any upset. She thought it her responsibility to keep her parents happy by being perfectly good. Her own daughter was more of a challenge.

Sylvia remembered her mother as an athletic woman who was not physically affectionate, but who was patient and devoted. They loved being together. Her mother never yelled or got angry at her, perhaps because Sylvia always went along with her wishes and modeled her own interests on her mother's, quite unlike the situation with her own difficult child. Sylvia and her mother had lots of enjoyable time together, much of it spent playing tennis at the club, or grooming, exercising, and training the champion Labradors that her mother bred. Her father, a Navy captain who was regularly at sea for months at a time, was a less constant figure, but, when he was there, he was more physically affectionate than her mother, and Sylvia adored him. He regretted that because she spent so much time playing with her mother and her dogs that she did not have enough friends her own age, and he tried to break up the closeness of the mother–daughter pair without success. During his leave and when he was on shore duty, she was allowed to lie in bed with her parents, and she remembered finding it exciting.

When she was 12, her father succeeded in sending her off to an eight-week tennis camp where she thrived on her newfound autonomy. When she returned, she was more rejecting of her mother's wishes for closeness and also upset to find that her mother did not seem to feel like doing much for her. It was a shock and a big letdown from the devoted care that she had come to expect. Irritated at the inconvenience, Sylvia complained angrily and became unpleasant around the house in protest. She failed to notice that the cause of the change was that her mother was ill. One day in late summer, her mother lost consciousness while changing out of her swimsuit. Sylvia's last image of her mother was of her naked body in collapse being lifted onto a stretcher and whisked off in an ambulance. She was not permitted to go to the hospital. Her mother was operated upon immediately. She remained in a coma for a week, and then died. Sylvia never saw her mother again. She behaved as if she were not upset, but she managed to twist her ankle while running with one of the dogs, and the limp gave her an acceptable way of asking for sympathy.

Sylvia's father, who wanted to retain his offshore command, sent her off to a coeducational boarding school, which she hated. Sylvia did not know that he had begun to date. Suddenly, before the end of the term, he remarried. So when she returned from school there was some other woman in her mother's place in the family house. But her new stepmother worked outside the home, could not spend all day with her, and could not relate to her stepchild. Even so, Sylvia only wanted to be home, and this her father would not permit.

A therapist tried to help with her misery at school, but Sylvia did not dare tell her that she felt abandoned, rejected, isolated, and out of her social class. She missed her wonderful mother, she felt awful about being a spoiled brat when her mother was dying, and she thought her behavior had killed her. She hated not being there to say goodbye, and she hated what she was left with. Her previously adored father was now consumed with his new wife, by whom she felt replaced, and whom she could not get to love her. The only thing to be glad about was that there were no children of the new marriage for her to envy. Eventually her father also found the relationship to his new wife difficult and the marriage ended, but not until Sylvia herself was married.

In college, Sylvia did well academically, but socially she was called a prude. She disapproved of her classmates' sexual involvements, and felt uncomfortably excited by them. She kept herself obese by bingeing, and then she starved herself to the point of dehydration, and thereby found a symptom to ensure that her father and stepmother had to take her in at home. But when they sent her back to complete college, she did well. After graduation she worked as a civilian administrator working for the Navy in San Diego, following her father's suggestion, rather than following her preference to be a dog trainer. She did not enjoy office work, but she liked living independently and began to have a social life. When she finally became sexually active, she found that she was surprisingly responsive. She developed a longterm relationship with a man that she cared for greatly, but he proved to be unreliable. She tried therapy again, but found the therapist to be too cold.

Sylvia left the man, left the therapist, quit her job in San Diego, and moved to Santa Barbara to pursue her dream of working with dogs. She worked as an assisant and lived with the family that owned the kennels. When they took her in and treated her like family, she blossomed. She met her husband, a generous and patient man, whom she describes as a "rock," and all seemed well until his career necessitated moving to Omaha. She lost the location of her dreams, the job that she had chosen independently of her father, and the everyday support of the loving second family for whom she worked. Now for the second time, her life was upended because of coming second to the ambitions of a man. But, at least this time, this man wanted to be with her.

Now married, Mrs. Kerr diverted herself from these losses by focusing on making a comfortable home, developing a new social network in the city, and working in a veterinary clinic until she could start a family. She longed for a baby girl, and when Winnie was born, she was overwhelmed by her feelings of love and responsibility. She loved being a mother and caring for such a sweet and adorable girl who was everything that she had wanted. When Winnie was 3, Mrs. Kerr's second pregnancy began to show. She seemed big for her dates, and was thrilled to learn that she was expecting two more girls. At the same time, her mother-in-law had a second stroke, and her condition fluctuated unpredictably. Mrs. Kerr had to go to the West Coast to supervise her care every few weeks, and she found it easier to travel if she left Winnie at home with her trusted housekeeper and her husband. Her mother-in-law's eventual placement in a nursing home brought back the pain of losing her own mother. Shortly after the birth of twin girls, her mother-in-law died. Winnie got upset by her mother's absences during the pregnancy, her mother's sadness at losing her mother-in-law, and her preoccupation with caring for her twin infants. Winnie became unremittingly oppositional, anxious, and hateful—a painful reminder of what a spoiled brat Mrs. Kerr had been as a preteen when her mother was ill. Mrs. Kerr felt that she had lost both her mother-in-law and her delightful daughter. On top of that, the family had to move again because of her husband's work, this time to Washington, DC.

The Symptoms

Under the additional stress, Mrs. Kerr's symptoms were aggravated and old fears from childhood re-emerged. As well as worrying that forces beyond her control would hurt Winnie, Mrs. Kerr was now afraid that she herself might hurt her. Anxiety that something bad would happen had troubled her since childhood even before she lost her mother. She woke up at night with her heart pounding. She was afraid that fire would break out, and so she had acquired a habit of secretly checking for gas leaks or electrical hazards. She obsessively made superstitious deals with God which she was deeply ashamed of, because this habit ran counter to her religious beliefs. She had bursts of rage, bouts of uncontrollable weeping, and binges of cookie-munching, interspersed with episodic dieting to keep herself slim and petite. She could not get along with her aging father, enjoy club tennis, or take pleasure in her family's love. She took pleasure in remembering stories about her mother, but it troubled her deeply that she was unable to remember her mother's voice. She had tried therapy twice with no relief. She constantly felt fatigued, and her self-esteem was rock bottom. Few people would guess this, because she functioned exceptionally well—as a reliable, devoted wife and mother, a good friend, and a selfless volunteer. She cared for others from morning to night.

From Consultation to Analysis

As she talked with me (JSS), Mrs. Kerr realized that she must have been depressed for twenty-five years, and that depression must be why everything she managed so well—excellent grades in college, a successful marriage, three children, "A" team at her tennis club, and skill as a dog trainer—cost her so much emotionally and left her so exhausted. She was grateful to me for providing the space in which she could arrive at this insight about the length and breadth of her distress. It led her to conclude that analysis was her last chance to get relief from years of suffering, and that I had to be her analyst. She called it a do-or-die opportunity.

Previous therapies had not been enough, probably because they did not offer the sufficiently intense, long-term therapeutic relationship that I thought would be needed to allow her to confront the loss of her mother. The history, the symptoms, the failure of previous attempts at therapy, and the use that she made of my linking comments pointed to a recommendation for analysis. Mrs. Kerr was a good candidate for analytic treatment, and she could afford to make the financial investment. She was bright, articulate, psychologically minded, emotionally expressive, energetic, and capable of commitment to her goals and principles of service. As the analyst offering to treat her, I felt privileged to be trusted by such a sensitive and dedicated person, but I sensed from her history of early loss, failed therapies, her obsessional symptoms, the depth of her rage, and her do-or-die approach to analysis that her treatment was likely to be a grueling experience because this time it would have to be thoroughgoing. I felt humbled at the prospect of the work ahead.

Anger at the Object, Badness in the Self, and the Threat of Death

Mrs. Kerr began analysis with trepidation. She was afraid of finding out bad things about herself. She was afraid of being angry and of making me angry. Every time she admitted to being angry, she worried that something awful would happen to Winnie or the twins, or she refused to eat and made herself feel ill. I talked to her about how she got rid of anger to keep a feeling of safety. She projected anger outside into forces beyond her control to avoid feeling full of badness herself, but then she felt frightened of bad things happening to her family. She also projected anger inside herself into her body (which was outside the imaginary space of her mind) and then felt like a bad person anyway.

When she projected anger in these ways in analysis, I said that she was trying not to realize that she was angry at me, just as she had avoided being angry at her mother and hated herself for being angry with Winnie. She responded, "I dare not be mad at you, because I'm afraid of being such a shit that anyone in her right mind would leave me. Both my parents did." Helping her to feel her anger and express it directly would be a major task.

The anniversary of her mother-in-law's death that first winter brought to the surface an explosion of grief. It was quite a relief to both of us. At the same time I caught a cold. Mrs. Kerr complained that I could not listen to her because of my coughing. I tried to suppress the cough, which only made it worse. She had no empathy for me, and was thoroughly annoyed that my sickness impinged on her as her mother's had done. When I took a day off to recover, Mrs. Kerr was unnerved, as she had been when her strong and healthy mother suddenly died. She could not contain her upset. Instead of preparing to express to me directly the rage that stemmed from her fear of losing me to illness, she displaced it from me to her children and yelled at them instead. She then spent a sleepless night worrying about whether they would die. She felt that she had caused my illness by a failure of her love for me. This was the first hint of her omnipotent wishes to control her mother and me, and most of all, to matter to me.

From discussing the idealized goodness of the relationship with her late mother, Mrs. Kerr moved on to the badness of the relationship with her difficult 5-year-old daughter, who seemed to have all Mrs. Kerr's anxiety and none of her father's steadiness. When she felt overwhelmed by the power of her hateful thoughts, Mrs. Kerr went about the house checking locks, sniffing for gas, and making deals with God to protect her family from her anger. She kept these rituals hidden even from her family. I thought that her telling me about them in detail showed that she could trust in the holding environment that I was providing. I said that she was trusting me enough to admit the destructive force of her anger. She wanted to challenge these entrenched rituals, but she was afraid of exploring their meanings, in case doing so would leave her unprotected from the constantly hovering threat of death.

The Exciting Object Relationship

One day during the early phase of her analysis Mrs. Kerr said bleakly, "Nobody cares for me as much as I need, nor can I. What I've learned so far in this analysis is that I want the love and caring a parent gives you. It's so strong a longing in me, and I can't have it because it doesn't exist. I don't want it in other forms, such as my husband and children. They don't make up to me for what I want. I feel furious because there's no escape. I have to have it. I just feel that I'm a mass of deprived cells. That's why I don't eat. I can't give myself a treat, not one cookie. I'll eat the whole bag, and then I'll wake up at night with my heart pounding. So I don't eat much of anything. I'm trying to starve those awful deprived cells to make them go away. I don't want to look like a ravenous monster that can't stop."

Mrs. Kerr could now express her anger at feeling so deprived, but she still rejected her feelings of neediness and longing. She was sad that she had to have such a grip on herself, because it inhibited her enjoyment of her life and family. I was worried by the outward signs of her internal struggle: she had become noticeably too thin, and anorexia had been a problem in her adolescence. Was she recreating her adolescent conflict now? Would I be able to understand her adult anorexia before it became dangerous?

Here we see the power of the internal exciting object relationship characterized by feelings of deprivation and craving, viciously repressed by the rejecting internal object relationship. The dynamic between these repressed internal object relationships worked in opposition to the functioning of her central self and its ideal object. Mrs. Kerr had reconstructed an ideal object in her satisfying relationship to a good husband and had refound her central self in relation to him and in satisfactory daily interactions in the community—but these brought little joy, because they paled in comparison to the onslaught from the repressed object relationships. We also see the projection of aggression and fear of death into her body. Mrs. Kerr re-created her connection to her mother at the scene of her death, through flirting with death by semistarvation.

Splitting and Projective Identification

In the early phase, I was often present in Mrs. Kerr's dreams as a good person, kindly inviting her into my house. At the same time, her good friend, a social worker at the agency where she volunteered, appeared as bad. I said to Mrs. Kerr that I thought that she had split off bad aspects of me and projected them onto this friend. After this interpretation, her dreams continued to express longing for a warm relationship with me, but she began to experience me as "full of unmitigated coldness," both in the office when I made comments, and outside the office when I drove by in my car without seeing her.

In the countertransference, I appreciated her commitment to being such a good patient, her gratitude, and her positive feelings for me. On the other hand, I felt controlled by her looking for me on the roads and expecting me to wave. I felt pressured both by her anxiety about my passing colds and by my anxiety about her weight loss. I felt somewhat oppressed by how incredibly often our driving

Object Relations Individual Therapy

paths crossed. In short, I became aware of her intense focus upon me—positive and negative—and of her constant attempts to get me to focus on her intently. The transference to me was one in which she wished to have me understand her perfectly, to care for her like her devoted mother, and to be eager to find her everywhere. Despite some anxiety and irritation on my part, I accepted her need for proximity to me. I said that she wished "to live in my pocket," and she felt that this image aptly expressed her desire to be accepted and to matter to me.

Splitting Good and Bad to Preserve the Disappearing Object

Mrs. Kerr found an old family photograph in which her mother was looking away, withdrawn from the young Sylvia. Her mother seemed troubled, remote, and depressed. I was supposed to be drawn in, to correct for that depressed, undemonstrative mother, to be concerned for her, and worried about her need to starve herself. But I was not there to provide a corrective emotional experience. I was worried, but I was thinking about the situation. I thought that she was starving herself so that her appearance would resemble her young self at an age before she had lost her mother.

At home, Mrs. Kerr was in despair about being unable to help Winnie, who was self-centered, stubborn, and tormenting. At least now she could be angry at her without worrying that the child would die. I said that she was taking out on Winnie anger that pertained to me. Mrs. Kerr did not take this interpretation well. She took it as a sign of lack of sympathy and of the awfulness of my unmitigated coldness. It proved that she must be a terrible person, and she could not bear to live with that. She was sobbing and feeling furious with me. She threw the box of tissues so that it fell apart against the wall, she threatened to put a chair through the window, and she almost drove her car into a tree to get rid of this terrible person she was that I could not love.

By now, Mrs. Kerr could express her need and longing for me and my care. She found it increasingly difficult to separate from me at the end of the session. She said, "I want to stay and scream and refuse to leave. Every session feels like a little death. Thoughts of analysis and you fill my life. You matter so much to me, I am sure I am going to lose you, like I lost my mother. Is it possible I think I'm responsible for my mother dying? Did I kill her off? Did I lose my father because I deserved to? I'll deserve to lose you too, so I'll kill you off before I do. I have to get fixed before I kill off anybody else." Mrs. Kerr convinced me that the strength of her destructiveness was awesome.

Oedipal Transference, Primal Scene, and Recovery of the Good Object

I often felt concerned for Mrs. Kerr's safety, but that is not how she saw me. She began to see me not only as uncaring, but as actively needling her. She complained that I poked her with everything I said. She was a greedy infant, a wild child who wanted to be a baby but could not get anything from me. I was a cold, nasty, provocative, hurtful mother who loved the man I met with before her. Thoughts of this man led Mrs. Kerr to recall longings for her father. She now thought that she had been sent away to boarding school because of wanting him too much—perhaps in a wicked sexual way. She put together for herself the idea that she may have felt "frustrated, angry, and upset by Mother and so turned to Father." Now she remembered how much she had loved her father when she was a little girl. The recovery of these wonderful feelings led to a slow but steady rehabilitation of her relationship with him. Then it led to more memories about her mother.

Mrs. Kerr felt more and more in touch with her longing for her mother. One day, for the first time, Mrs. Kerr vividly recalled being carried on her mother's hip and hearing her voice tone. She described hearing her mother's voice as "enormously comforting, an arrow of peace." It was a wonderful moment for her and for me. The next day she felt so awful that she was worried about damaging Winnie again.

I said, "You had to destroy something good because of your fury at not having it before."

She said, "She never said goodbye, and it's never finished. She never told me she loved me. I keep waiting to hear her say it." Then she insisted, "Since she's not around, you have to!" But she did not press the point yet. She told me that she was mad at not being carried by me, but still she thought what I was doing was right. I was impressed at her ability to respect the therapeutic relationship even while compelled to rail against it.

Mrs. Kerr reworked the experience of seeing her mother lifted unconscious on to the stretcher. Her naked, gray body with sagging breasts looked so vulnerable and so unlike the athletic mother who had been her caring companion. Thinking next of her own scrawny hip as looking like her mother's did that day, Mrs. Kerr led me to see that her weight loss was more than an attempt to get back to her prepubescent reality. It was a desperate effort to get others to see in her the body of the woman she missed.

I said, "You can starve yourself in the false hope of finding your mother in your own body until you have depleted yourself so thoroughly that you are unable to get to your analysis and then you will lose me as well. Gone will be the chance to understand your self-starvation and depression." My confrontation hit home. Mrs. Kerr began to imagine allowing herself to have a strong, well-nourished body like her champion Labrador, a fantasy that allowed her to separate from the dying mother of adolescence and identify with the healthy mother of childhood. On the other hand, she asserted that she still preferred to be weak and to explode in hysteria and madness so that I would have to take care of her. Nonetheless, she said, the thin person had to go.

Primal Scene

Mrs. Kerr had a dream of a male friend exposing himself and urinating on Winnie's food. Throughout the middle phase of the analysis there were many similar dreams. She kept thinking that there must have been some abusive experience in childhood that left her wild with anger. Each dream, each memory seemed to take us closer to a revelation of a traumatic incident. None was ever recovered. Then, late in the analysis, Mrs. Kerr had an intense reaction to hearing a couple fight loudly in an adjoining office. Even though she could not hear what they were saying, they were so loud that she felt included in an immense argument. Her breathing rate increased and her heart quickened until it was pounding. She was terrified by how much she felt pulled into their orgasmic release of rage. Mrs. Kerr associated to feeling overwhelmed with the excitement of her parents' intercourse which she remembered overhearing more than once when she had sought refuge from her childhood fears by crawling into their bed. Following this powerful re-creation of the anxiety of the primal scene, Mrs. Kerr revised her understanding of her fears of being overtaken by forces beyond her control. She now saw her fears of something bad happening to Winnie as an unconscious fantasy displaced from her anxiety of exposure to the primal scene. Her thoughts of sexual abuse faded away, and so did her nighttime heart pounding.

The sadomasochistic quality that Mrs. Kerr experienced in the therapeutic relationship can be viewed as a re-creation of the primal scene viewed through the eyes of an uncomprehending, overstimulated, and jealous child. The child projects the resulting aggression into the primal scene and thinks that the parental couple in intercourse are hurting each other, and feels frightened, wakeful, panicky, and guilty (J. Scharff 1992). The couple's excitement generates physiological arousal without sexual release in the child. By creating this arousal, exposure to the primal scene invades the boundary of the skin and threatens the autonomy of the self.

Envy of the Breast and Recovery from Self-Starvation

Three years into the analysis, at the time of the anniversary of her mother's death, two dreams, over a weekend separation, ushered in the next phase of the transference.

> In the dream, I was with you in a room like this office, with glass doors and bookshelves, but in the dream there were tennis cups as well as books on the shelves. I had lots of time staring at you, drinking in your face, as we looked together at your tennis trophies on the shelves, sharing that interest, and it gave me a good feeling that lasted all day. The tennis cups reminded me of your pin that I admired the other day. After this dream I cried for my mother all day.

I learned from her associations that my room stood for my body. The tennis trophies connected me to her mother, with whom she shared that interest. The pin I had worn was a Celtic shield, round with a single stone. The cups and the pin together reminded her of the breast. After listening to her associations, I said that the first dream was an image of closeness and satisfaction at the breast. She felt deeply understood. The next day she reported the second dream:

> I was in the breakfast room and the window was in shards. It was terrifying. Then I was in your room looking out the full-plate glass sliding doors. I wished I had glass doors like that in my breakfast room.

In the second dream, after drinking me in in the first dream and taking in my satisfying interpretation, she became envious of what I had. What she had taken in from me was destroyed. Invaded by envy, the internal space of her body was shattered. I said that she had taken in my interpretation of her first dream as a good, full feed, but then had to destroy it in anger in the second dream, because she had become envious of the full breast. Also, in giving an interpretation as clear as glass, I had rejected her wishes for closeness. She said that she wanted to be in the room with me with full-plate glass doors like in the dream. She thought that this meant that she wanted to be able to take her experience with her and keep it whole.

Later that week, Mrs. Kerr horrified herself by dreaming of sucking her nephew's "sweet little penis." I thought of this fantasy as a sexualization of the re-created nursing experience now transferred to a male figure. She associated to her father's friend drunkenly coming on to her. This led to the idea that she had seen her father enjoy her mother's breast, while she felt excluded, excited, and enraged. Immediately, she got furious at me. The feeling from the dream came straight into the transference. The good feeling from seeing my face in the earlier dream got lost in a torrent of rage in the session. She was angry that, for me, analysis was just a cool rational process of interpretation, and that analysis itself ends.

Mrs. Kerr got angry at me for the oral-level interpretation about the breast, for stimulating her to recast it in oedipal terms, and for causing her the pain of re-experiencing involvement in, and exclusion from, the primal scene. After this explosion of rage at oedipal and preoedipal levels, Mrs. Kerr began to eat normally, that weekend, and often enough after that so that her periods returned. This piece of analysis dramatically enabled her to get over anorexia, but the depression underlying that symptom required much more work.

The Negative Oedipal Transference

The transference was now moving into the negative oedipal domain, with the emergence of infantile sexual feelings for her mother. Mrs. Kerr told another dream:

> I was lying in the pitch black with my friend. Not only did I have a penis, I had it inside my friend, but in a neutral way.

Her social worker friend had used the word "neutral" to explain the analytic attitude the week before. So Mrs. Kerr's mention of the friend and the use of the word made me think of the analysis. I said that her idea was that if she had a penis she could relate to me and feel loved by me. She responded by remembering more dreams in which erect penises were everywhere and I was there comforting her. The dreams started to come in threes, a number traditionally associated with the male genitals and which for her was a superstitious number. She felt guilty about the strength of her wishes for me. She looked for me and found me everywhere—in her dreams, on the road, on the children's playground. Suddenly she had as much of me as she wanted, but her love for me was mixed with awful, guilty feelings. She felt that I was torturing her by evoking these feelings. Her sexual feelings made her anxious and hypervigilant. She went sniffing in the basement of her house for a gas leak that could cause a fire. She traced this to her childhood fears of fires. Then she remembered that she used to think that if she masturbated a fire might happen.

Mrs. Kerr is dealing with the basement of her body and its connection to the ruptured internal couple.

Birth into the Analysis

After talking of masturbation guilt—all this sexual nastiness as she called it—Mrs. Kerr had an unusual experience on the couch. Her head felt stuck and her arms and legs felt as if they were all over the place. At first I thought that this experience might be a re-creation of intercourse as witnessed by a child, but her associations led me to think otherwise. She thought of the umbilicus, a baby wrapped with the cord round its neck, and her own breech birth.

I said, "This body memory might represent a moment of birth into the analysis."

Mrs. Kerr replied, "The words 'I'm out' come to mind."

In relief, I took it to mean that she was out from having to dwell inside my pocket, but she disabused me of my interpretation: she meant that she was cruelly pushed out.

"I hate the 'out' place," she said. "You would have to be dead before you could understand how awful it was."

I said, "To some extent you already feel dead and so you have to be a part-person, always needing someone to complete you."

She sobbed, "It is scary to think of getting better. Right now I would rather stay a part-person than have to work on this. But I have no choice. I'm 'out' now and things will never be the same."

I said, "The 'out' place is scary and you don't want to be there, because of how 'in' you were with your mother."

She relaxed and said, "I took her in to me. When she was withdrawn, I'd be still so as not to lose her. I never wanted to be 'out' with her."

I got the impression of Mrs. Kerr as the young Sylvia—acutely sensitive to maintaining harmony with her mother. Now I understood her attempts to get a rise out of me as attempts to cure me of my silence, experienced as depression, rather than to get me out of my analytic role. Now that she was "out," Mrs. Kerr began to change. She no longer lived analysis twenty-four hours a day. She could wait and put her thoughts and feelings about me on hold until the next session when she returned to the re-creation of her memories.

Early Intensification of the Transference

The occasional negative transferences I have described so far now coalesced into an intense negative transference. Mrs. Kerr experienced me as torturing her with my silence or with my comments, picking at her skin, probing relentlessly, and provoking her wrath and envy by displaying what I had. Her envy focused on some landscaping work being done to screen the office parking area. A keen gardener, she was interested in the project, but furious at me for having too many plants. Over the next few weeks she realized that the profusion of plants in the gardener's truck made her think I had too many babies inside me. She wanted to join them there, freeze them to kill them off, and worst of all to steal them for herself. By envious comparison to my project, she felt that anything she was doing for her house was pathetic. I spoke to her about her worry that her admiration for her mother and her longing to have her was associated with losing her. Having expressed herself to me with great feeling, her envy of me lessened. She recovered a sense of her own value, and continued her own house renovation and landscaping with a new sense of accomplishment. But in the analysis she began to feel wordless and helpless.

At times I felt as wordless and helpless as she did, a complementary identification with her object that was based on her experience of the remote part of her mother. At other times I felt furious as she smashed my attempts at understanding (a concordant identification with a part of herself that was in protest against her objects). Sometimes the atmosphere was so fraught with anxiety that I thought it might be unsafe to speak at all. Mrs. Kerr's tension, the force of her fantasies of symbiotic union with me, and her demand for empathy evoked a tense, overinvolved feeling of concern; at other times when her regression turned out to be so painful for her and threatening to her family life I felt guilty and insecure about my decision to offer analysis. I had fantasies about being censured by a peer-review committee for not insisting on medication. Here I was substituting a there-and-now societal concern in place of a here-and-now countertransference because of my discomfort with thinking of myself as cruel.

I could hardly bear to be thought of as so cold and sadistic. Sometimes I felt as though I could not stand her berating me. It seemed that she would be too much for me. I wanted to get out of my commitment to her—but thankfully that feeling always passed.

"Not Love as Such; Love Such as It Is"

After months of telling me about her rage at me and destroying my helpfulness, Mrs. Kerr reported a hopeful dream that reflected a growing capacity for mourning and acceptance:

> You gave me all your notes and thoughts about me, and read me an explanatory message, "It is not love as such, but love such as it is."

She interpreted this dream to mean that I cared for her not in the way she wanted, but in a professional way that she could accept. For the first time, she did not wreck the good feeling of the dream, but enjoyed the ensuing fruitful discussion in which she began to think that her relationship to me could be different from the nasty, exciting, and rejecting way she had seen it. I said that she had realized that the relationship could be one of collaboration. At first, she hated that word of mine. She protested that collaboration was a poor second to love, but she got to like the idea. She enjoyed the feeling that she got from working on the dream with me, from actually collaborating. She reported that the dream got its color from the work she did on it. "I carry it around," she said, "like a lucky stone in my pocket."

This image of the dream being carried in her pocket recalls earlier references to a pocket. In the early phase, she had agreed with the interpretation that she wanted to live in Dr. Scharff's pocket. Later she had the dream in which she was "out" of the analyst's pocket. Now she has taken a dream and carries it in her pocket. She uses it as a transitional object. She is no longer in the analyst's pocket. Now she has something from the analysis in her pocket—not her analyst, but a product of hers that became a collaborative effort and led to a resolution of this phase of the transference.

Mrs. Kerr felt a renewed determination to work in analysis, but she was afraid I would misconstrue her good feeling as readiness to go. She need not have worried. I knew that she was not ready. "Love such as it is" fit my sense of the countertransference, and for now it was enough for her.

A second love dream followed:

> You had been feeding children. You stood up and said, "I will think of you, I do care about you, I do love you," and you kissed me on the cheek. I was flooded with happiness. This dream was a three-star event. After I woke up I clearly heard my mother's voice.

I was listening silently, appreciating how happy she felt to hear my words in the dream. I was contemplating the wonder of the moment of hearing her mother's voice as she had longed to do for so long. But she was expecting me to say, "Oh, what a nice dream." When I remained quiet, she felt that I had wrecked her experience.

Regressed and angry, she cried: "I can't bear to go away with nothing. I'm all alone. I have to have your comfort and there isn't any."

I said, "What you need is not for me to make up the love you lost but for me to help you through the loss."

"Oh," she groaned, "that means going through it."

Now that Mrs. Kerr has experienced "love such as it is" and has been satisfied with that, she feels safe to regress from central self functioning. The repressed exciting and rejecting internal object relationships begin to reassert themselves and push for reintegration into her personality.

Regression: Transference Longings and Fears of Annihilation

Mrs. Kerr reverted to her demands for "love as such." When I did not declare my love for her, she perceived me as cold and uncaring. I felt as though we were back at square one. In fact, things were getting worse. If she had a success, she had to spoil it. If she made good connections between her thoughts and her feelings, she had to break them. If she thought of something good about her relationship with me, she promptly forgot it. She felt crazy. She said that she was losing her internal picture of me and losing her memory of my words. She experienced in the transference the impact of the loss of her mother on her internal object relations. She developed an intense need for my face, and searched it anxiously before she lay down on the couch and as she left the office. Crying and sobbing, she begged me to let her look at me from the couch. I finally agreed that she should sit up for a while so that she could see me, but she did not need to. She said it helped to know that she could see my face if she wanted to, and she linked her need to see me to the anxious searching of a baby for the face of an alive, intact mother. She thought that her mother had been more depressed than she realized. As a young child, Sylvia must have been highly sensitive to her mother's moods and anxious about where she was emotionally. And then she had died. Now she felt that life was a living death, and so was analysis.

In the countertransference, I could feel what she meant. My understanding was often killed off. My view of myself as a kindly, concerned therapist confronting problems with useful ideas was buried in hatred. I was entombed as cruelly interpretive, all the love and hope wrung out of me. I felt hyperalert and worried that I might say something harmful. I felt like a sadist and a masochist. It was torture. I could hardly bear to have the sadistic, masochistic, and schizoid aspects of my personality brought to life and scrutinized so often. I felt too in tune with her affect, as she had felt with her mother. Sometimes I felt that we would not get through this, because the gains seemed so short-lived. But I had set "going through it" as our goal, and my conviction and her commitment helped us to endure the course.

The here-and-then of her relationship with her mother is recreated in the here-and-now of the transference.

Intensification of the Transference

Mrs. Kerr came to sessions tense and angry week after week. She wept uncontrollably. She despised her life and hated me. She demanded drugs because she was desperate, even though she did not want to take them. Her state terrified her friends and her family, who now begged her to take medication. She communicated her despair to her social worker friend, who reportedly suggested that "the problem might be preoedipal and preverbal and, therefore, unanalyzable." Mrs. Kerr was distraught. In saying this, her friend had been filled with Mrs. Kerr's hopelessness and her disappointment in me in the transference and was returning that projective identification in words that Mrs. Kerr then used to attack the analysis. I knew that the problem was preoedipal and preverbal, but I did not agree that this made it unanalyzable.

I thought that I had heard Mrs. Kerr's anger, but she was now directly, intensely furious. She screamed so loudly and intensely that people two rooms away could hear her. She yelled that she might have to kill herself, and only if I yelled back, ranted, and raved at her would she feel cared about and not despised. I said that she was creating a torturous, envious, and destructive relationship to me because she found the more collaborative, independent way of functioning so unfamiliar. After some weeks of this violent communication, her intense rage had been fully expressed.

The Post–Regression Relationship

After we had come through this period of analytic regression, Mrs. Kerr became able to collaborate with me. That was a great pleasure and a tremendous relief to both of us. She succeeded in getting a paying job as an office manager at a busy veterinarian's practice. Her office colleagues were delighted with her telephone manner, her patience with the animals, and her organizational skills. She adjusted easily to her new work life and felt very good about herself and her earnings. Her husband said how much he loved her and appreciated all her efforts to be cheerful and to take care of her work and her family. Life improved, and analysis became mostly free of intense anger and depression. Mrs. Kerr was pleased, except that she resented the fact that everyone took her ability for granted: no one knew her as the sick person she really was. She was not yet used to being healthy.

This was so delightful. I began to relax. I was no longer on the alert. I no longer felt mean and cruel. I could see why her husband loved her so much. I felt warmly toward her and admiring of how much she had accomplished.

Then, Mrs. Kerr told another dream:

You were simply holding my hand. I felt close to you and I knew that you were interested in me.

She said that the dream had assured her that I did care, and it was enough for her. After this dream, she made a remarkable shift in her capacity to find the good object in analysis. She told me that "love such as it is" had become "love as such."

Leaving the Neurosis Behind

Mrs. Kerr continued to progress. She began to mourn the loss of her neurosis. She thought of herself sitting in a rowboat, rowing with her back toward me, keeping a familiar yellow house in sight as her fixed point as she rowed to where I was waiting beyond a bend in the river. As she rowed closer to me, the house (looking like my office and standing for her neurosis) grew smaller and smaller, and she felt sad to see it go but she knew that it would always be there. Later in the analysis the same image returned, but now I was no longer ahead beckoning. I was now the yellow house that she had to row away from by herself. She began to feel that she would be able to finish analysis successfully, and intended to set a date for terminating in about a year's time.

After this insight about the imminence of separation from me, she immediately regressed again at the thought of finishing with me. I heard no more about a date for termination. She said, "I am terrified. If I think of leaving you, maybe you will get sick and die. Death took my mother, and my mother-in-law, and if it can happen to them, I'm afraid that it could as easily happen to you. I had to be a child so that my mother could be a mother, and I never had the chance to see whether we could both go on as women when I grew up. What I want is to separate without either one of us dying. Well, I'll be getting a taste of separation when my vacation comes, and I am not looking forward to it."

After the vacation, she confided that she had managed to enjoy herself away from me and yet to keep me in mind. For the first time she felt sure that I would be there after her return. This was a major improvement in her internalization of the good object. She still slipped back into agonizing over how to get me to love her, but these regressions were now short-lived. Over time, she consistently progressed beyond them to collaborate with me, mourn her losses, and embrace her life.

Preliminary Thoughts of Termination

In January of the fifth year of her analysis, Mrs. Kerr returned to the topic of termination and proposed finishing in the summer, eighteen months later. I said that she was expanding the length of time needed for termination because she was afraid of feeling the loss and was resisting being in the unfamiliar situation of functioning as an autonomous, self-sufficient adult. She was furious at me for using the word "autonomy."

"Is autonomy all that analysis gives?" she demanded. "I don't want autonomy. I want love. If I have that, then I'll leave."

On the other hand, she no longer felt that I loved the man with the appointment the hour before hers more than her. She realized that this must mean that she already had my love. Why else would she no longer hate the man? So she re-examined the nature of her love for me and mine for her, now and in the future. All possibilities fully explored, she concluded that I felt "love such as it is" for her, and that it did not have to be "love as such." I knew that she was ready to terminate. I waited for her to propose a closer date.

Readiness for Termination

After five years of analysis, Mrs. Kerr had become more secure. She experienced the change in her self-functioning as an internal drive for growth and autonomy pushing her on despite her periods of backsliding. She realized that I had been there after all throughout the analysis, that she now felt visible and connected to me, and that she had something to give. She said that she felt that the deprived part of her had been expressed and truly cared for in the analysis. She was relieved that she had not had to throw it away. Instead, having dealt with deprivation, she could now be fond of her emptied-out and shrunken "deprived cells." She knew she was at the beginning of the end of analysis.

What remained to be revisited was the issue of feeling loved and being loved by me. Mrs. Kerr decided to aim at feeling loved not in an all-encompassing, infantile way, but in a limited yet realistic way. She gave up the certainty of her view of me as uncaring, in favor of assuming that she was loved by me, but then she was driven crazy by the thought that she might be inventing my love. She begged me to be real. But what was the real relationship? She arrived at an appreciation of my understanding and commitment as a form of love that was real and that she had had in full from me.

Three major insights brought her relief and a feeling of space and energy. She listed them:

"1. I really did love my mother. I didn't just demand, and therefore I offered her something and didn't kill her. And I won't kill you.

"2. I can't make you or anyone else love me.

"3. Loving my parents as a perfect child and so canceling myself out was not bad; it just was not real because it canceled out the mixture of love and hate."

As Mrs. Kerr took on these new ways of thinking about these three issues, she shed the dreadful burden of the old ones. She said that she now felt somewhat loved as a whole person, with good and bad, love and hate not stringently kept apart. Her experience of feeling integrated continued to grow.

Regression at Termination

Mrs. Kerr called the summer vacation that year "the last break," and she hoped that she could get through it well. However, she did regress before the vacation and again felt desperate, convinced that I did not love her. At the moment of separating, she lost her tie to me that gave her the ability to love herself.

On her return, I learned that her regression had been massive—but not total. She had felt dead—not sad or angry—just dead. She felt devastatingly cut off from every human, including herself, but she never doubted that I would be there on her return. I said that she had been letting herself feel what she was afraid of feeling after termination. She confirmed that I was right, and then became stuck, tearful, and hopeless again. I said that she wanted me to think that I would be condemning her to an awful life if I finished with her. She defended herself from the pain by chit-chatting as if nothing was bothering her, but her tears allowed me to see that she was angry at me for making her do without me. When I said this, she responded by grunting and shaking furiously. She was so mad, she said, she could throw the sofa through the window.

For a moment I believed it possible. She seemed so angry and physically energized that I could imagine her lifting the sofa by herself. After all, she had actually smashed a tissue box against the wall. I imagined the sofa being hurled through the glass doors, and shards of glass flying. This image reminded me of the early dream of the shattering of good feeling due to envy after drinking in my face and my understanding. Then I realized that her intense experience was just a recapitulation of earlier themes, a regression that held on to the analysis that was about to be given up. This was not the time to delve back into the destructive effects of her rage and envy. It was time to progress and separate. My countertransference experience helped me to find the words for her experience that moved her forward.

I said that her feeling black and awful was her fantasy of what it would be like after finishing, now that analysis felt like a good place to be. It obliterated her feelings of hope and competence and prevented her from setting a termination date. Mrs. Kerr found this interpretation helpful because a fantasy, unlike a death sentence, can be accepted and worked on. The next day she had recovered from this major regression.

Under the stress of approaching termination, the remnants of the transference reappear. Exciting and rejecting object systems return from repression and are then detoxified. Her regression has been intense and her recovery swift, a common phenomenon in those who are near termination.

The Pretermination Dream of Readiness to Terminate

Mrs. Kerr began to think that whether or not I loved her was not the issue.
Perhaps the real issue was whether or not she could love herself, because if
she could not, she would not be able to feel anyone else's love for her. Still
she hoped that she was right that my feelings for her were love as such,
but what if she was fooling herself?

> *I examined my feelings for her. Did I love her too, and was the problem caused
> by my not acknowledging this? I did love her in a way, but I did not feel "love
> as such." My feelings were not those I have for a friend, a mother, or a daugh-
> ter. Her other expression, "love such as it is," decribed my feelings more accu-
> rately. My countertransference reflected my response to her love such as it was
> for me. But once the pressure of the transference no longer dictated the unpleasant
> form of her "love such as it is," my feelings for her approximated "love as such."
> "Love as such" and "love such as it is" no longer seemed to be distinct, and the
> one state of mind dissolved into the other. I did most of this work silently, so as
> not to prejudice her developing her own conclusion. Apart from the inciden-
> tally useful effect of refining my views on projective and introjective identifi-
> cation and the nature of transference and countertransference (J. Scharff 1992),
> I think that my analysis of the nature of my love in the countertransference
> cleared the way for Mrs. Kerr's continuing work on how I felt about her.*

Mrs. Kerr went round and round on the knotty issue of how she was loved,
until she felt that she was in a snare like one of the tangles in her daughter's
hair. Then she had a dream that clearly signalled the termination:

> The dream took place at the stables where my daughter takes her riding
> lessons. I was in a ring with another woman and a glossy, dark-brown horse.
> The woman and the horse fell down in a tangle but were okay. Then they
> fell again. They were all tangled up, and I was afraid the woman would be
> killed. But the horse remained still until the woman got up. I put my arms
> round the horse's neck. I filled up my arms and I leaned against her. It was
> the essence of being filled by something alive. Then she wanted to run away.

I rubbed on her withers like I've seen Winnie do, hoping she would stand still, but I knew she was going to back away.

Mrs. Kerr said that she had never wanted a horse, but in the dream she felt as close to that horse as to her dog. She added that the horse was the color of her mother's chocolate Labradors. She thought that the dream was of her mother dying and also of her own wish to love. She said she felt that if she had loved her mother she would not have died, her father would not have sent her away, and I would not either. To me, the dream was also about analysis. The first fall represented the tangle of the transference, which was resolved when she was able to give up the clinging, envious way of relating to me. The second tangle was a death tangle, about her struggle with me over her feeling dead without me.

She said, "So the horse becomes me leading you, me saddled up and ready to go."

I said, "Yes, and you were also holding that living part of you."

She replied, "We're all woven into it. I'm hugging the tangle goodbye. I love you, but I'm setting you free. And I'm the horse you're hugging goodbye." She continued, "Right now there is a possibility of a good goodbye. Earlier I might have said, 'I'm not the horse. I'm not leaving.' But right now I feel myself, the horse, slowly backing away and wanting to be free. I just wanted her to stay awhile, so I rubbed her withers."

The word "withers" made her think of withering, dying, and shriveling. She thought of the umbilical cord withering. I said that she had wanted the crying, dead part of her rubbed the previous week because being in that kind of relationship to me was familiar and soothing, and it delayed her parting. She realized that expressing herself through being terribly upset was a fantasy about making her mother come alive and be there when needed. She then returned to her dream.

"Now separation isn't a blank screen," she said. "The woman—and the horse, who is also a woman—feels tremendous love and, feeling complete, knows the horse is leaving and loves the beauty of the free horse. But there's still a connection."

Setting the Date

Mrs. Kerr now talked of being finished earlier than she had thought, perhaps by spring of the next year, rather than summer. She had now reduced the time needed for terminating to six months. There were some regressions from her autonomous position, with brief exacerbations of symptomatology, but she continued to function independently, assertively, competitively, and yet compassionately, in relation to me. She struggled intently on the final question of being loved by me, and settled for feeling loved by my understanding, my commitment to seeing her through the worst times, and my seeing her as a whole person. Mrs. Kerr concluded that what I had felt for her was indeed a kind of love, not love as such, but love in the context of having done the work and being in the new relationship with her. That being settled, she no longer needed six months to finish. She decided quite easily on a date that gave her eight weeks to go.

In the last year of the analysis, before agreeing on a date, Mrs. Kerr was terminating in fantasy, working down from eighteen months, one year, six months, to eight weeks. By the time she sets the date, nine months after first introducing the possibility of finishing, the hard part of the termination work has been done. She has recapitulated the major themes. She has had intense regressions that were, however, brief. She has revisited the transference and resolved it.

Feeling Loved and Loving Herself

The last eight weeks moved along without trouble. The major regressions had already come and gone. It was a pleasant time of continuing growth, consolidation, and self-affirmation. Mrs. Kerr now took the question about my love the next step, away from me and back to herself.

"Whether or not I am loved by you," she said, "I've earned the right to respect and love, and I AM, even as I feel those things for you."

Picking up on her emphasis on "I AM," I said, "Now that you give yourself the right to feel respected and loved, you say, 'I AM,' meaning 'I AM loved,' but I think you also mean 'I AM who I want to be.'"

"Well, I AM!" she said. She was able to feel loved and lovable. She was able to love and respect herself. She talked at length about her new energy. She enjoyed a feeling of space inside her mind. She felt competent at work, had plenty of love to give, confidence, and a welcome lightness of being. She told me with pride that her husband was offered a prestigious job in Asia, and she was thrilled to be able to encourage him wholeheartedly, no longer envious of him or afraid of leaving me.

Self-Analysis, Integration, and Consolidation of Gains

Two dreams of driving through different landscapes showed her progression in analysis and her shifting in termination between paranoid-schizoid and depressive position levels of functioning. Mrs. Kerr described the two dreams and analyzed them for herself:

> The first dream was just a barren landscape with a gun pointed at bald eagles. It was a still photograph in black and white. The second dream, a moving picture in full color, was of fertile, rolling countryside with farm animals and puppies.

She said that the first dream showed how frightened, sad, and remote she felt before, when she was still preoccupied with the loss of the endangered mother who had been her life. The second dream depicted her new way of living fully in her life. She loved her full-color brilliance. For instance, she had decided to compete for her boss's job as senior office manager. She only regretted her occasional backsliding to a more constricted way of relating. As she said, "The nice thing about recovery is it's unconscious, like a bowling pin that rights itself."

One day when she lost her temper at her stubborn daughter, she returned to her despair about her hasty way of dealing with Winnie's anxiety. She promptly called herself on this as a remnant of the transference. She said that it was a way of sidetracking her progress, a way of saying to me, "How can you let me go when you see what a mess I'm making?" Her feelings analyzed, Mrs. Kerr felt more patient with Winnie again. Unlike the time when she was upset at my having a cold, my absence now for one day because of illness did not trouble her. A rowdy patient in the waiting room was something to laugh about and compare to earlier times, when she would have been so angry about competition. She said that she did not feel bad that someone else would have her time, because she had what she needed and felt grateful.

Mrs. Kerr is able to enjoy her remaining time in analysis without denying her weaknesses. She has the terrible times and the good times balanced clearly in her mind. She is able to take pleasure in her family life, and be more assertive. She can retrieve past experience, mend it, and fuse past and present into something real and solid that will serve for the future. Her capacity for self-analysis, for integration, and for recovery from setbacks is consistently in evidence. She can make reparation for how upsetting she has been, and she can feel and express gratitude. She inhabits her life and loves herself and her family, now and with a good sense of the future.

In the last minutes of our final session, Mrs. Kerr returned to the subject of gardening, which had been the metaphor for her envy and competition with me, and was now an area of separate interest and pleasure to her. With a gardening image to capture her experience of analysis, Mrs. Kerr concluded, "This has meant everything to me. Like the bulbs I've just had planted, what we've done together is *in*. It's real. I don't have to see it to know it's there. It's not just mine, it's yours too—but the flowers will be mine."

26

Five Dreams:
Fractal of an Analysis

The analysis of a young adult man gives an unusual opportunity to experience in summary the process of a whole analysis through the progression of the material of five dreams, the only ones reported in this relatively short, three-year analysis with Dr. Jill Scharff. The same dream of a triangular situation recurs three times in variations. Of the two other dreams, one features a dead couple and the other a single individual, himself. We view the series of five dreams as a fractal of Mr. Hendry's endopsychic situation, each dream reflecting changes in the transference and in his object relations as he progresses over the course of the analysis.

   As a 4-year-old boy, Mr. Hendry had been there when his infant brother died of meningitis. He knew that this event was a family trauma, but since he had not had much to do with the baby, his death had not meant much to him. He knew that it was a terrible loss for his parents, but they put their grief behind them and did not talk about it. He did not know until late in his analysis that he had experienced other traumatic incidents, and that his parents had suffered other trauma, earlier and more extensive than any he had been exposed to.

   Mr. Hendry was referred to me (JSS) for analysis because his compulsive lifestyle was causing life-threatening damage to his body and because he was failing in law school. He had to change his personality to avoid losing his colon and ultimately to save his life. Severe colitis meant that he was losing blood and having to take steroid medication. He felt compelled to fake a socially charming self when in reality he felt remote, overly intellectual, and dismissive of attachments. His social grace made him seem well-related, although really he was not. He was a thin, blonde, good-looking man whose gentle manner exuded charm rather than sex appeal. He was well aware of his charm, as was I. He warned me that it was a feature of what he called "the unreality of his public persona." I took his phrase to mean that he had a competent false self that covered for his true self.

Mr. Hendry had been engaged to a pleasant, nice-looking, intelligent young woman who wanted to marry him, but he ended their long-term relationship because he thought of it as nothing but a performance. He could perform sexually with her, but he could not love her as she loved him. Free of obligation to her, he turned his attention to studying ferociously many hours a day and tried to stay fit by bicycling, both solitary activities. Instead of relaxing by being on top of his work and having time for leisurely exercise and friends, he put himself under extra stress. He worked and exercised so compulsively that he defeated his capacity to think and restore his body. When he developed severe colitis, he realized that he was destroying himself mentally and physically, or as he put it rather grandly, he was engaged in self-mortification.

He tried to master his weakened body, but he could not control the occasionally bloody diarrhea that was undermining his strength. Similarly, he tried to master what he called "the body of knowledge" presented to him in law school, but he could not, because he could not concentrate. He got lost in all the details, and the big picture slipped further away from him the harder he tried. In class, he was deadly serious and had little time for social breaks.

Mr. Hendry had no sexual relationship and little social life. He got along well with his male roommates because they were as busy as he was and needed little from him. He did go dancing once a week, but he did it assiduously to keep up his advanced level of skill as a ballroom dancer, not in a casual way to meet friends. His dance partners often asked him out, but he did not have the time or the inclination to date any of them. In contrast to his social charm, he had an extremely detached attitude toward intimacy. In analysis, he dealt with me politely, but used an intellectualized way of thinking about himself to ensure that I kept my distance and did not become too important to him.

During the assessment, he told me of a recurrent dream he had since the age of four:

The dream takes place in the black void. I take the form of a beam of energy seeking to connect thousands of miles away with another beam that represents a loved one. A third beam is intercepting the second beam and it represents destruction. I have to speed to intercept it and that means my destruction but I awake before that.

This struck me as the most inhuman dream I had ever heard. I found it hard to bear the pain of the 4-year-old boy whose dream life was full of terror and empty of humanity and love. I felt sad to think how incredibly remote his true self was, hidden by the false self "persona" of adulthood.

What was the source of Mr. Hendry's terror? He told me that his parents lost their infant son, who died of meningitis, when Mr Hendry was about that age, and so it seemed that his dream might be showing a fear of death and a wish to rejoin him. His parents had explained what happened to the infant, and then quickly tried to erase the signs of his existence, by giving away his clothes and redecorating his room. Mr. Hendry felt that his mother carried a huge burden of sorrow because of this great loss, and he felt a bit guilty that he had not felt similarly upset.

Mr. Hendry did not give any other history of trauma, but over the course of the analysis he discovered that he had been abused at three levels of development. He unpeeled the layers of the onion of repression in the following order.

As a young adult, he lost his place on the college ballroom dance team because he rejected a much-loved male coach who betrayed his friendship by trying to spank him in a sexually excited way. Mr. Hendry felt humiliated and upset by his sudden awareness of the homosexual dynamics that he had been fostering unwittingly. After he recovered the memory of the homosexual threat with his coach, his colitis cleared up.

Then an earlier memory of threatening abuse surfaced. As a very young child, he had been about to be sexually abused by a teenage babysitter, who hurt him as he wrenched free. Now it became clear that an unconscious fear of being found attractive by men had led him to choose solo bicycling so that he could avoid social exercise situations. After recovering this memory, he became able to enjoy investing in personal fitness at the gym.

Finally the deepest layer of repression gave way. He remembered that as a preteen he had been beaten repeatedly by his father. That memory was the most deeply repressed, because he was the most dependent on his father to care for him. His father's violence may have been a result of his

a. In addition to the trauma of losing their child, which Mr. Hendry did know about, both his parents had suffered in the Second World War, but he did not know how, because it was a topic not to be discussed. Mr. Hendry was indirectly affected by trauma transmitted from his parents.

Mr. Hendry felt far too close to his mother. He was caught up in helping her to feel cheerful without having any idea of the cause of her suffering beyond knowing that she had lost a child. He was furious at his father for being so absent that he had to function in his place as his mother's spouse. This led to his living in what he called "the fantasy"—a state of anxious concern and overinvolvement in his mother's states of mind.

This fantasy state was re-enacted in the interplay of transference and countertransference. I felt preoccupied and acutely attentive. I struggled to make sense of his intellectual descriptions and find their emotional meaning. He evoked in me a state of attunement to his unexpressed feelings and a preoccupied feeling of puzzlement over what he was talking about when his meaning was always buried in his highly abstruse, confusing language.

Mr. Hendry said that he realized that he had been talking in a very intellectual way to protect me from the full force of his feelings. I told him that I thought that this happened with me so as to keep alive his tie to his mother. I said that he wanted to stay at this early level of fusion with me to keep out of awareness any other emotional responses or sexual fantasies that he might have about me or his mother, about which he might feel guilty. When he had worked more on not wanting to recognize and feel guilty about feelings that he or I might have, he became able to recognize that I mattered to him. Having accomplished that, he wanted to deal with both parents as a couple, and began to imagine their sexual union. At this point he told me his second dream:

All there was in this dream was two dead bodies. I have no idea who they were. Just two dead bodies lying there piled together.

Working on this dream, his associations were to sexual and aggressive images. He wondered if he had killed the bodies, but he did not think so. He had the impression that they had been dead for a long time. I said that this dream was showing him his view of his parents as a dead couple, destroyed by their own suffering, and by his envy and rage at them for being so close with each other and keeping their secrets so closed off from him.

Mr. Hendry has a dead internal couple in his internal object relations and it leaves him unable to couple with a woman in an intimate and sexual relationship or engage emotionally with his female analyst.

Mr. Hendry began to feel more separate from his parents and less worried about their feelings. He thought of confronting them about their ways of relating to him and their unexplained suffering. The original dream then recurred.

> This time I took the form of a beam of energy streaking toward the other beam, now identified as my mother. As I approach her to rescue her from the intercepting beam, I recognize it is my father and I veer off. I was not anxious and did not need to wake up. I was relieved that there was an ending to it.

The most striking thing about this dream is that the objects are recognized as people. Mr. Hendry himself, however, still takes the form of a beam of energy.

In association to this dream, Mr. Hendry thought of a plan to visit his parents and get at the truth. I said that he intended to confront his parents in person and ask them to reveal their feelings, because he wanted to avoid his own feelings about them in the analysis. Instead of going to confront them, he proceeded to confront his own difficulty in thinking about both parents together. He was filled with fears for their safety. When he thought about both parents together, he became confused, confusing, and mysterious. He said that he was preoccupied with his perceptions of reality which he could not trust and with his need to use the false-self behaviors of the "public persona."

After working on his view of his parents and his self, Mr. Hendry turned to address his difficulty in achieving good results in law school commensurate with the effort he put into studying. With the same intense energy that he put into his schoolwork, he now focused singlemindedly on the problem of performing academically, to the exclusion of any further review of dreams, parental sexuality, or aggressive feelings. In session after session of trying to understand the school difficulty in analysis, he found that he could not concentrate, just as he could not concentrate on his studies at school, even though he spent hours in the library. He said that it felt like a black hole to climb out of.

In my countertransference, I had been feeling as though I might as well not have been there. I felt as though I did not mean anything to him. My value had been emptied out. I was the black hole.

Bearing in mind his dream in the void, and my countertransference feeling, I said that he was emptying out his feelings about his closeness to his mother and his rage at his father so that he didn't have to puzzle over their meaning any more. To avoid feeling empty, he displaced the feelings of rage, closeness, and fusion into his schoolwork, where he felt lost in all the details, and into his analysis where he felt stuck. He climbed out of the hole by talking at length about his mother and father separately and as a couple.

Having done the internal work on the parental couple, Mr. Hendry began to change. He got feedback from his family, roommates, and classmates that he was a more interesting, lively, and confident person than they had thought. He no longer needed his persona. He was still charming, but it was no longer a cover for emptiness. He was still polite, but he was no longer soft and sweet. As he regained weight and muscular development, he became more masculine and assertive. Feeling that he had the right to information, now that he had prepared himself thoroughly for what he might have to process, he went to ask his parents for details about their past. He chose to do this on Memorial Day weekend, because he was off school and because I would be away, and so he would not miss a session due to travel.

His parents complied with his request and tearfully told him about horrible wartime family losses. They had seen friends tortured and killed. Two family members had been reported missing and no final answer had been given to the family. At a certain point his parents had had enough, but Mr. Hendry had to know just one more thing. Abruptly his father told Mr. Hendry to stop upsetting his mother and punched him so that he was silenced and knocked down.

After this, Mr. Hendry gave me a dose of the abandonment and rage that he had felt from his father, by threatening to quit and by not showing up for a few sessions.

In the countertransference, I felt hit by his sudden announcement and dismissive behavior. I had put a lot into his analysis and I was about to lose my investment. I felt beaten and knocked over.

I told him that it was outrageous to talk of quitting as if it mattered nothing to me. I said that I felt hit and beaten by him as he had felt by his father. I thought that he was giving me a taste of what had happened to him so that he could stop feeling how painful it was. He said that he felt rage at me when I could be absent like his father and then waltz back in thinking wrongly that my presence was of importance to him. Having the transference addressed, he was now able to recall and tell me about the many other beatings from his father in adolescence. Until this moment, he had withheld this information from me, as he expected me to feel too much and be overwhelmed if he told me, just as he always protected his mother from the pain of feeling too much. For instance, he had not told his parents of his abuse at the hands of the babysitter when he was very young, because he did not want his mother to worry.

After working through his rage in the transference, Mr. Hendry became able to study the details and fit them into the big picture. There was no longer a black hole of confusion, emptiness, and despair. His internal space no longer had to be emptied out. He could contain his aggressive and sexual feelings and his image of the internal couple, so that feelings and images did not spill over into the work space. He got excellent grades at last, and he became able to date a classmate for whom he had both affectionate and sexual feelings. They had a good relationship, but he was not yet able to love, and the relationship ended by mutual agreement six months later.

Then his recurrent dream appeared in its final form:

> This time the dream is in human form. I am traveling through space as a child, and through time as well, maturing until the dream ends in the present. Instead of sacrificing myself, this time I actively destroy the deadly object and watch it explode. My mother and father are traveling toward each other and this time could continue on, undisturbed by the deadly object while I went on my way at a tangent. I saw you and then you turned to go on your way and both of us were satisfied with the outcome.

In this dream, he felt relieved by his father's presence, and so felt free to go on. As he himself noted, this time the dream is in human form, he grows from child to adult, saves himself from destruction, and explodes the deadly object. He then said that the last piece of unreality in his way of relating had now dropped out.

This dream reviews Mr. Hendry's analytic journey and his life, detonates the deadly encapsulation (his own and his parents' trauma fused with his oedipal complex), illustrates a satisfactory oedipal outcome in the transference, preserves the autonomy of the self, and heralds the termination.

Mr. Hendry noted how much he had progressed in working with his dance teacher so that now he anticipated all her corrections. He realized that he was outgrowing her as a teacher, but he liked dancing with her as a partner. One day he noticed to his surprise that she was an attractive young woman. He decided to ask her out, their relationship blossomed, and he fell in love for the first time. He reported a dream, strikingly unlike the recurrent dream of beams in a triangle, or the dream of the dead couple. Instead of being caught in a perverse triangle, he is functioning on his own in this last dream before terminating:

> I am all by myself on the dance floor practicing all the steps of a complicated dance something like the tango.

Mr. Hendry quickly agreed with my comment that in his dream, as in life, he felt no teacher was necessary. He took it as a compliment, rather than a comment on his defensive self-sufficiency. He added that he now felt that no analyst was necessary. He said that until now his pattern had been to facilitate someone else falling in love with him whom he then rejected, and in analysis to talk about what had happened to him rather than about what he felt and wished to do. He was determined that he would not be passive any more, and would go out into the world and feel, love, and think about life for himself. He was ready to finish and so he planned to stop analysis next week.

I felt stunned by his announcement, and it reminded me of how I had felt hit the time he threatened to quit when his father had punched him after giving him what he needed. I felt like protesting: surely he did not intend to leave analysis this time either; he had only just fallen in love. What about the need for process and review of the still fairly new relationship and its transference implications?

I reviewed the history of his wish to quit and pointed out that he wanted to avoid working through the termination in a leisurely way. Mr. Hendry was adamant that he must finish. He did, however, agree to continue coming for another month to work on termination. He repeated his reasons for terminating and summed up the phases of his analysis. He said, "I am leaving because now I have a sense of self and now I need to make love and to feel. At first, analysis was a space where I could think what I wouldn't otherwise think. Then it became the space where things occurred and I began to feel things. Now it feels as if I am having to think up things to keep the space there. Until now, there's been a sense of timelessness and openendedness to it, but yesterday I knew I should prepare myself for this to stop. I can't and I won't devote more time to this. I have got what I needed from you. Analysis is now a way of being. It won't end when I leave here."

In the dream, Mr. Hendry is doing a couple-dance solo, and is not demonstrating the mature level of interdependency that ballroom dancing and intimate relationships call for. No doubt there is an acting out of the transference in his turning a professional relationship with a teacher into a personal one. Some might say that his termination is a resistance against exploring this displacement of the transference. Through his abrupt manner of terminating with only one month for completion, he deals Dr. Scharff a swift blow. Here we see an element of identification with the aggressive object in Mr. Hendry's actions. Others might say that Mr. Hendry has failed to get in touch with his dream-life. We find, however, that paucity of dreaming is a not uncommon finding in the survivor of abuse and in the children of abuse survivors (Bollas 1989, J. Scharff and D. Scharff 1994).

On the other hand Mr. Hendry's spare dream series can be viewed as an economical communication of his state of mind. The five dreams function as fractals of his endopsychic situation at the time of each dream. As a series, they function as a fractal of the whole analysis. Mr. Hendry gives Dr. Scharff an experience of the impact of his various traumas, which he has previously avoided. We recognize the positive aspects of his feeling secure enough to convey this level of unconscious communication. Incidentally, we find that this mode of departure from treatment is typical of the survivor of trauma who finally feels safe and who is stimulated to traumatize the analyst by reversing the pain of losing that important object of safety (J. Scharff and D. Scharff 1994). Despite some reservations about the completeness of his analysis, it has to be admitted that Mr. Hendry's choice of partner is appropriate to his age, his interests, and his circumstances.

Applying the concepts from chaos theory that we presented in Chapter 8, we are studying the series of dreams as one of the folds representative of the whole topography of the analysis (Galatzer-Levy 1995). We find that each dream functions as a fractal of Mr. Hendry's endopsychic situation and of its representation in the here-and-now of the transference. In addition, the series of three versions of the repetitive dream reveals the parents' traumatic experience as encapsulated in the son's personality. So the son's dream functions as a fractal of the parents' experience. The dream is a fractal of his personality and his personality is a fractal of the parents' personalities. Dr.

Scharff's countertransference attitude to Mr. Hendry's confused and confusing descriptions of his mother may be said to act as a "strange attractor" (see Chapter 8) that draws the transference into a recognizable pattern and moves it toward change.

Of most importance, the final dream of the analysis features Mr. Hendry in an entirely human form. It presents an image of his achievement of autonomy and his practicing for an adult passionate relationship. Like many young adults, such as Esther in Chapters 23 and 24, Mr. Hendry leaves analysis to complete the work autonomously. He has reclaimed his vitality, his masculine self, his loved object, his work, and his capacity for genuine relatedness. Admittedly, he does not stay in analysis long enough for a perfect termination. He does not wait to have the final dream of himself with a loving partner. But he does not have to, because now his dream is alive.

Epilogue

Freud, Fairbairn, Klein, Winnicott, Bion, and many others since them have grappled with the complexity inherent in human behavior, thought, feeling, and relating, but each formulation, however sophisticated, inevitably did some injustice to the richness of that complexity. Any one explanation had to ignore some phenomena in order to explain others. Any one theory, any one clinical intervention, is only part of a whole that endlessly awaits full comprehension. Learning from clinical experience means living with confused and confusing areas of human relationship, accepting and expanding what can be known while tolerating the unknown.

To be useful, each small piece of theory has to provide an answer to some clinical problem that we do not understand until the right idea is supplied at the right moment. Then the penny drops; a bit of theory fits in place to give new understanding that is blended with what is already known. Like memories of actual experience with good objects, much theory is eventually lost to consciousness and permeates the unconscious as clinical intuition, the theoretical elements remaining difficult to remember discretely, perhaps until it comes time to teach a student or meet the challenge of a difficult patient. Sometimes students or patients repeat back to us something we thought we knew, and we find fresh learning in their way of putting things.

Research offers another way of understanding human growth and interaction, but it, too, has to overlook the full complexity of human psychology in order to clarify the aspects under study. Focusing on a few variables, measuring them, and seeking insight about the relationship among them, research methodology isolates them from the inherent disorder of their context. Researchers must inevitably simplify or omit some elements to narrow the field of study. This limitation of focus empowers their observations to generate useful models of segments of human behavior. For instance, attachment researchers' focus on observable separation and reunion behaviors has led to a schematic model for parent–infant behavior that is useful for sorting, quantifying, and testing otherwise intangible data in terms of attachment categories and applying them to the study of development, the transmission of personal qualities from parent to child, and related aspects of transference.

Our research laboratory is clinical practice. There the data are messy, uncontrolled, and free-form. Models, theories, and maps of transference act as guides to uncharted areas of thinking, feeling, and relating, but much still remains to be discovered, especially in the area of the growth and development of the self. The edges of self and object experience have fold upon fold of infinite potential for meaning. The predominating pattern embedded in life's chaos reveals itself through the organizing principle of the therapeutic relationship.

Chaos theory—developed by theoreticians working at the outer edges of mathematics, computer science, and physics in the last third of the twentieth century—describes the discovery of hidden patterns in the seeming disorder of the physical and biological universe. As clinicians, we find that the concepts of chaos theory help us think about our experience of working with the known and the unknown. *Limit-cycle attractors* define known and describable aspects of behavior, while *strange attractors* help us find pattern in the disorder of obscure areas. Some psychoanalytic theories appear to be formulated as limit-cycle attractors. For instance, Freud's ideas on the neurological correlates of the organization of the conscious and unconscious mind and on psychosexual development define boundaries of biological potential which he held to be universal. Other Freudian theories, such as the repetition compulsion or transference, function more like strange attractors, appearing to organize experience at the same time that they are actually created by it.

Interpersonal and intrapsychic interactions express infinite patterned variablity that nevertheless occurs within describable limits. The concept of the strange attractor helps us understand the way self and object interaction leads to behaviors that are repeated over and over, yet never exactly in the same way. At macrocosmic and microcosmic scales these patterns show *fractal scaling*: patterns seen in society at large echo individual and family behavior;

patterns of internal object relations built from many previous external interactions influence the quality of present interaction.

Psychoanalytic theory resembles physical and biological sciences both in successfully developing hypotheses about how the present has evolved from the past of our patients and in less successfully predicting the future. Chaos theory promises no more: how the future develops from strands of experience may be understood in retrospect but cannot be reliably predicted because of random fluctuations in current experience and the later effects of sensitivity to initial conditions. But chaos theory does take account of the predictably unpredictable forces of order and disorder, using new techniques to calculate phenomena that were previously unmeasurable. Therapy is a field of random patterns and infinite possibility, where the major factors are beyond both our control and our understanding for stretches of time. Chaos theory gives therapists a model for addressing the edges of our knowledge of theory and practice.

When we work to understand human experience by learning from the unending cycle of projective and introjective identification, and of transference and countertransference, we offer our own experience in the therapeutic relationship as a strange attractor for the patient's object relations. We give back to our patients the understanding we have gained in consultation with them so that they can modify their lives through insight. Even though our formulations are arrived at after careful consideration, they are not conclusive: they remain open to reinterpretation and modification as the therapeutic relationship develops. Repeating patterns in the transference that are at first similar to past expressions evolve until they are sufficiently different that patient and therapist, as they construct new internal objects, may experience their selves in fundamentally new ways. The therapeutic interaction repeats itself variously, now in a limited way, then in a cascade of diverging forms, and finally comes together as a shared view of what has been and what is.

In therapy and analysis we surrender to the chaos and, at the same time, strive to contribute to its organization.

References

Abelin, E. (1971). The role of the father in the separation-individuation process. In *Separation-Individuation*, ed. J. B. McDevitt and C. F. Settlage, pp. 229–252. New York: International Universities Press.

———— (1975). Some further observations and comments on the earliest role of the father. *International Journal of Psycho-Analysis* 56:293–302.

Ainsworth, M. D. S., Blehar, M. C., Waters, E., and Wall, S. (1978). *Patterns of Attachment: A Psychological Study of the Strange Situation*. Hillsdale, NJ: Lawrence Erlbaum.

Alexander, F., and French, T. M. (1946). The principle of corrective emotional experience. In *Psychoanalytic Theory: Principles and Application*, pp. 66–70. New York: Ronald Briggs.

Atwood G., and Stolorow, R. (1984). *Structures of Subjectivity: Explorations in Psychoanalytic Phenomenology*. Hillsdale, NJ: Analytic Press.

Bacal, H. (1987). British object relations theories and self-psychology: some critical reflections. *International Journal of Psycho-Analysis* 68:81–98.

Balint, M. (1952). *Primary Love and Psychoanalytic Technique*. London: Tavistock, 1965.

———— (1957). *The Doctor, His Patient, and the Illness*. London: Tavistock.

———— (1968). *The Basic Fault: Therapeutic Aspects of Regression*. London: Tavistock.

Balint, M., Ornstein, P. H., and Balint, E. (1972). *Focal Psychotherapy*. London: Tavistock.

Bartholomew, K. (1990). Avoidance of intimacy: an attachment perspective. *Journal of Social and Personal Relationships* 7:147–178.

Bartholomew, K., and Horowitz, L. M. (1991). Attachment styles among young adults: a test of a four-category model. *Journal of Personality and Social Psychology* 61:226–244.

Becker, T. C. (1993). The difference between termination in psychotherapy and psychoanalysis: panel report. *Journal of the American Psychoanalytic Association* 41(3):765–773.

Beebe, B., Jaffe, J., and Lachmann, F. (1993). A dyadic systems model of mother–infant mutual regulation: implications for the origins of representations and therapeutic action. *Newsletter of the Division of Psycho-Analysis, American Psychological Association* Winter xiv(1): 27–33.

Beebe, B., and Lachmann, F. M. (1988). The contribution of mother–infant mutual influence to the origins of self- and object-representations. *Psychoanalytic Psychology* 5:305–337.

Beebe, B., Lachmann, F. M., and Jaffe, J. (1997). Mother–infant interaction structures and presymbolic self and object representations. *Psychoanalytic Dialogues* 7:133–182.

Bell, M. B., Billington, R., Cicchetti, D., and Gibbons, J. (1988). Do object relations deficits distinguish BPD from other diagnostic groups? *Journal of Clinical Psychology* 44:511–516.

Belsky, J., and Cassidy, J. (1994). Attachment theory and evidence. In *Development Through Life*, ed. M. Rutter and D. Hay, pp. 373–402. Oxford: Blackwell.

Belsky, J., and Nezworski, T. (1987). *Clinical Implications of Attachment Theory.* Hillsdale, NJ: Lawrence Erlbaum.

Benjamin, L. S. (1979). Structural analysis of social behavior. *Psychological Review* 81:394–425.

——— (1985). Use of structural analysis of social behavior (SASB) to guide intervention in psychotherapy. In *Handbook of Interpersonal Psychotherapy*, ed. J. C. Anchin and D. J. Keissler, pp. 190–214. New York: Pergamon.

——— (1996). *Interpersonal Diagnosis and Treatment of Personality Disorders.* New York: Guilford.

Benjamin, L. S., Foster, S. W., Roberto, L. G., and Estroff, S. E. (1986). Breaking the family code: analysis of videotapes of family interactions by structural analysis of social behavior (SASB). In *The Psychotherapeutic Process: A Research Handbook*, ed. L. S. Greenberg and W. M. Pinsoff, pp. 391–438. New York: Guilford.

Benjamin, L. S., and Friedrich, F. J. (1991). Contributions of structural analysis of social behavior (SASB) to the bridge between cognitive science and a science of object relations. In *Person Schemas and Maladaptive Interpersonal Patterns*, ed. M. J. Horowitz, pp. 379–412. Chicago: University of Chicago Press.

Bertalanffy, L. von. (1950). The theory of open systems in physics and biology. *Science* 111:23–29.

Bettelheim, B. (1982). Reflections: Freud and the soul. *The New Yorker*, March 1, pp. 59–93.

Bibring, E. (1954). Psychoanalysis and the dynamic therapies. *Journal of the American Psychoanalytic Association* 2:745–770.

Bick, E. (1964). Notes on infant observation in psychoanalytic training. *International Journal of Psycho-Analysis* 45:558–566.

Bion, W. (1956). Development of schizophrenic thought. *International Journal of Psycho-Analysis* 37:344–356. Reprinted in *Second Thoughts* (1967), pp. 36–42. London: Heinemann.

——— (1959). *Experiences in Groups*. New York: Basic Books, 1961.

——— (1962). *Learning from Experience*. New York: Basic Books.

——— (1967). *Second Thoughts*. London: Heinemann.

——— (1970). *Attention and Interpretation*. London: Tavistock.

Birtchnell, J. (1993). The interpersonal octagon. In *How Humans Relate: A New Interpersonal Theory*, pp. 215–229. Westport, CT: Praeger.

Birtles, E. F. (1996). The philosophical origins of Fairbairn's theory of object relations. Presented at The Fairbairn Conference of the International Institute of Object Relations Therapy, New York, October. In *Fairbairn Then and Now*, ed. N. Skolnick and D. Scharff. Hillsdale, NJ: Analytic Press, 1998.

Birtles, E. F., and Scharff, D. E., eds. (1994). *From Instinct to Self: Selected Papers of W. R. D. Fairbairn, vol. 2*. Northvale, NJ: Jason Aronson.

Blatt, S. J., and Blass, R. B. (1992). Relatedness and self-definition: Two primary dimensions in personality development, psychopathology, and psychotherapy. In *Interface of Psychoanalysis and Psychology*, pp. 399–428. Washington, DC: American Psychological Association.

Blatt, S. J., Brenneis, L. B., Schimek, J., and Glick, M. (1976). Normal development and the psychopathological impairment of the concept of the object on the Rorschach. *Journal of Abnormal Psychology* 85:364–373.

Bloom, B. L. (1981). Focused single session therapy: initial development and evaluation. In *Forms of Brief Therapy*, ed. S. Budman, pp. 167–216. New York: Guilford.

Blum, H. P. (1989). The concept of termination and the evolution of psychoanalytic thought. *Journal of the American Psychoanalytic Association* 37(2):2275–2295.

Bockneck, G., and Perna, F. (1994). Studies in self-representation beyond childhood. In *Empirical Perspectives on Object Relations*, ed. J. M. Masling and R. F. Bornstein, pp. 29–58. Washington, DC: American Psychological Association.

Bollas, C. (1987). *The Shadow of the Object*. New York: Columbia University Press.

——— (1989). *Forces of Destiny: Psychoanalysis and Human Idiom*. London: Free Association Books.

——— (1992). *Being a Character: Psychoanalysis and Self Experience*. New York: Hill and Wang.

——— (1995). *Cracking Up*. New York: Hill and Wang.

Bornstein R. F., and Masling, J. M. (1994). Introduction. From the consulting room to the laboratory: clinical evidence, empirical evidence, and the heuristic value of object relations theory. In *Empirical Perspectives on Object Relations*, ed. J. M. Masling and R. F. Bornstein, pp. xv–xxvi. Washington, DC: American Psychological Association.

Bowlby, J. (1958). The nature of the child's tie to his mother. *International Journal of Psycho-Analysis* 39:1–24.

——— (1969). *Attachment and Loss, Volume I*. New York: Basic Books.

——— (1973). *Attachment and Loss, Volume II. Separation: Anxiety and Anger*. New York: Basic Books.

——— (1977). The making and breaking of affectional bonds. *British Journal of Psychiatry* 130:201–210, 421–431. Reprinted in *The Making and Breaking of Affectional Bonds*, pp. 126–160. London: Tavistock, 1979.

——— (1980). *Attachment and Loss, Volume III. Loss: Sadness and Depression*. New York: Basic Books.

Bråten, S. (1992). The newborn's virtual other: a model for human communication. *Yearbook of Sociology* 8:101–118.

——— (1993). Infant attachment and self-organization in light of this thesis: born with the other in mind. In *Making Links: How Children Learn*, ed. I. L. Gomnaes and E. Osborne, pp. 25–38. Oslo: Yrkeslitteratur.

Brazelton, T. B., Koslowski, B., and Main, M. (1974). The origins of reciprocity: the early mother–infant interaction. In *The Effect of the Infant on Its Caregiver*, ed. M. Lewis and L. Rosenblum, pp. 49–77. New York: Wiley.

Bretherton, I. (1985). Atachment theory: retrospect and prospect. In *Growing Points of Attachment Theory and Research*, ed. I. Bretherton and E. Waters.

Monographs of the Society for Research in Child Development, vol. 50, nos. 1–2, pp. 3–35.

Breuer, J., and Freud, S. (1895). Studies on hysteria. *Standard Edition* 2:3–305.

Briggs, J. (1992). *Fractals: The Patterns of Chaos*. New York: Touchstone.

Briggs, J., and Peat, F. D. (1989). *Turbulent Mirror*. San Francisco: Harper and Row.

Budman, S. H., and Gurman, A. S. (1988). *Theory and Practice of Brief Therapy*. New York: Guilford.

Burke, W. F., Summers, F., Selinger, D., and Polonus, B. S. (1986). The comprehensive object relations profile: a preliminary report. *Psychoanalytic Psychology* 3:173–185.

Burston, D. (1991). *The Legacy of Erich Fromm*. Cambridge, MA: Harvard University Press.

Byrne, G. D., and Suomi, S. J. (1995). Development of activity patterns, social interactions, and exploratory behavior in tufted capuchins (Cebus apella). *American Journal of Primatology* 35:255–270.

Carlson, J., and Kjos, D. (1997). Object relations individual therapy. *Psychotherapy with the Experts Videotape Series*. New York: Allyn & Bacon.

Casement, P. J. (1991). *Learning from the Patient*. New York: Guilford.

Cassidy, J. (1994). Emotion regulation: influences of attachment relationships. In *Biological and Behavioral Foundations of Emotion Regulation*, ed. N. Fox. *Monographs of the Society for Research in Child Development* 59:228–250.

Cassidy, J., and Berlin, L. J. (1994). The insecure/ambivalent pattern of attachment: theory and research. *Child Development* 65:971–992.

Cassidy, J., and Kobak, R. (1988). Avoidance and its relation to other defensive processes. In *Clinical Implications of Attachment*, ed. J. Belsky and T. Nezworski, pp. 300–326. Hillsdale, NJ: Lawrence Erlbaum.

Chused, J. (1991). The evocative power of enactments. *Journal of the American Psychoanalytic Association* 39:615–639.

——— (1996). The therapeutic action of psychoanalysis: abstinence and informative experiences. *Journal of the American Psychoanalytic Association* 44(4):1047–1071.

Coates, S. (1997). Is it time to jettison the concept of developmental lines? Commentary on de Marnesse's paper "Bodies and Words." *Gender and Psychoanalysis* 2:35–53.

Collins, N. L., and Read, S. J. (1990). Adult attachment, working models, and relationship quality in dating couples. *Journal of Personality and Social Psychology* 58: 644–663.

Consumer Reports (Nov. 1995). Does therapy help? pp. 734–739.

Cortina, M., and Maccoby, M., eds. (1996a). *A Prophetic Analyst: Erich Fromm's Contributions to Psychoanalysis*. Northvale, NJ: Jason Aronson.

———— (1996b). Introduction: Erich Fromm's contributions to psychoanalysis. In *A Prophetic Analyst: Erich Fromm's Contributions to Psychoanalysis*, ed. M. Cortina and M. Maccoby. Northvale, NJ: Jason Aronson.

Davanloo, H. (1980). *Short-Term Dynamic Psychotherapy*. New York: Jason Aronson.

———— (1991). *Unlocking the Unconscious*. New York: Wiley.

Diagnostic and Statistical Manual of Mental Disorders, Fourth Edition. (1996). Washington, DC: American Psychiatric Association.

Dicks, H. V. (1967). *Marital Tensions: Clinical Studies Towards a Psychoanalytic Theory of Interaction*. London: Routledge & Kegan Paul.

Dozier, M. (1990). Attachment organization and treatment use for adults with serious psychopathological disorders. *Development and Psychopathology* 2:47–60.

Dozier, M., Cue, K., and Barnett, L. (1994). Clinicians as caregivers: role of attachment organization in treatment. *Journal of Consulting and Clinical Psychology* 62:793–800.

Dozier, M., and Kobak, R. R. (1992). Psychophysiology in attachment interviews: converging evidence for deactivating strategies. *Child Development* 63: 1473–1480.

Dozier, M., Lomax, L., and Tyrrell, C. (1996). *Psychotherapy's challenge for adults using deactivating attachment strategies*. Unpublished manuscript, University of Delaware.

Duncan, D. (1981). A thought on the nature of psychoanalytic theory. *International Journal of Psycho-Analysis* 62:339–349.

———— (1990). The feel of the session. *Psychoanalysis and Contemporary Thought* 13:3–22.

———— (1992). The meaning of psychoanalysis. Lecture at the Washington School of Psychiatry summer institute at the Tavistock Clinic, London, July.

Eissler, K. (1953). The effect of the structure of the ego on psychoanalytic technique. *Journal of the American Psychoanalytic Association* 1:104–143.

Emde, R. N. (1988a). Development terminable and interminable: I. Innate and motivational factors from infancy. *International Journal of Psycho-Analysis* 69:23–42.

———— (1988b). Development terminable and interminable: II. Recent psychoanalytic theory and therapeutic considerations. *International Journal of Psycho-Analysis* 69:283–296.

Erikson, E. H. (1950). *Childhood and Society*. New York: Norton, 1963.

———— (1959). *Identity and the Life Cycle*. (Psychological Issues 1:1–171.) New York: International Universities Press.

Ezriel, H. (1950). A psycho-analytic approach to group treatment. In *British Journal of Medical Psychology* 23:59–74.

———— (1952). Notes on psycho-analytic group therapy ii: Interpretation and process. *Psychiatry* 15:119–126.

Fairbairn, W. R. D. (1940). Schizoid factors in the personality. In *Psychoanalytic Studies of the Personality*, pp. 3–27. London: Routledge, 1952.

———— (1941). A revised psychopathology of the psychoses and the neuroses. In *Psychoanalytic Studies of the Personality*, pp. 28–58. London: Routledge.

———— (1943a). Phantasy and inner reality. In *From Instinct to Self: Selected Papers of W. R. D. Fairbairn, vol 2*, ed. E. F. Birtles and D. E. Scharff, pp. 293–295. Northvale, NJ: Jason Aronson, 1994.

———— (1943b). The repression and return of bad objects (with special reference to the 'war neuroses.') In *Psychoanalytic Studies of the Personality*, pp. 59–81. London: Routledge.

———— (1944). Endopsychic structure considered in terms of object-relationships. In *Psychoanalytic Studies of the Personality*, pp. 82–136. London: Routledge, 1952. Reprinted as *An Object Relations Theory of the Personality*, pp. 82–136. New York: Basic Books, 1954.

———— (1951). A synopsis of the development of the author's views regarding the structure of the personality. In *Psychoanalytic Studies of the Personality*, pp. 162–179. London: Routledge & Kegan Paul.

———— (1952). *Psychoanalytic Studies of the Personality*. London: Routledge & Kegan Paul.

———— (1954). The nature of hysterical states. In *From Instinct to Self: Selected Papers of W. R. D. Fairbairn, vol 1*, ed. D. E. Scharff and E. F. Birtles, pp. 13–40. Northvale, NJ: Jason Aronson, 1994.

———— (1956). Reevaluating some basic concepts. In *From Instinct to Self: Selected Papers of W. R. D. Fairbairn, vol. 1*, ed. D. E. Scharff and E. F. Birtles, pp. 129–138. Northvale, NJ: Jason Aronson, 1994.

———— (1958). On the nature and aims of psychoanalytic treatment. *International Journal of Psycho-Analysis* 39:374–385. Reprinted in *From Instinct to Self: Selected Papers of W. R. D. Fairbairn, vol. 1*, ed. D. E. Scharff and E. F. Birtles, pp. 74–92. Northvale, NJ: Jason Aronson.

———— (1963). Synopsis of an object-relations theory of the personality. *International Journal of Psycho-Analysis* 44:224–226. Reprinted in *From Instinct to Self: Selected Papers of W. R. D. Fairbairn, vol. 1*, ed. D. E. Scharff and E. F. Birtles, pp. 155–156. Northvale, NJ: Jason Aronson.

Ferenczi, S. (1933). Confusion of tongues between the adult and the child. In *Final Contributions to the Problems and Methods of Psychoanalysis*, pp. 156–167. London: Hogarth, 1955.

Field, M., and Golubitsky, M. (1992). *Symmetry in Chaos: A Search for Pattern in Mathematics, Art and Nature*. New York: Oxford University Press.

Firestein, S. (1978). *Termination in Psychoanalysis*. New York: International Universities Press.

Fisher, J., and Crandell, L. (1997). Complex attachment: patterns of relating in the couple. *Sexual and Marital Therapy* 12(3):211–223.

Fonagy, P. (1996). The Vulnerable Child: Research from the Anna Freud Centre. Discussion Group, American Psychoanalytic Association Fall Meeting, New York, December.

Fonagy, P., Moran, G. S., Steele, H., and Higgitt, A. C. (1991). The capacity for understanding mental states: the reflective self in parent and child and its significance for security of attachment. *Infant Mental Health Journal* 13:200–216.

Fonagy, P., Steele, M., and Steele, H. (1991). Maternal representations of attachment during pregnancy predict the organization of infant–mother attachment at one year. *Child Development* 62:880–893.

Fonagy, P., Steele, M., Steele, H., et al. (1995). Attachment, the reflective self, and borderline states: the predictive specificity of the Adult Attachment Interview and pathological emotional development. In *Attachment Theory: Social, Developmental and Clinical Perspectives,* ed. S. Goldberg, R. Muir, and J. Kerr, pp. 233–279. Hillsdale, NJ: Analytic Press.

Freud, A. (1936). *The Ego and The Mechanisms of Defence*. In *The Writings of Anna Freud, Vol. ll*. New York: International Universities Press, 1966.

———— (1964). *The Psychoanalytic Treatment of Children*. New York: Schocken.

———— (1965). *Normality and Pathology of Childhood*. New York: International Universities Press.

Freud, S. (1900). The interpretation of dreams. *Standard Edition* 4:1–338.

———— (1901). The psychopathology of everyday life. *Standard Edition* 6:53–105.

———— (1905a). Fragment of an analysis of a case of hysteria. *Standard Edition* 7: 7–122.

———— (1905b). Three essays on the theory of sexuality. *Standard Edition* 7:135–243.

———— (1910). Five lectures on psycho-analysis. *Standard Edition* 11:9–55.

———— (1911). Two principles of mental functioning. *Standard Edition* 12:218–226.

————— (1912). Recommendations to physicians practising psycho-analysis. *Standard Edition* 12:111–120.

————— (1915a). Instincts and their vicissitudes. *Standard Edition* 14:109–140.

————— (1915b). The unconscious. *Standard Edition* 14:166–204.

————— (1916–1917). Introductory lectures on psycho-analysis. *Standard Edition* 16:243–463.

————— (1917). Mourning and melancholia. *Standard Edition* 14:243–258.

————— (1920). Beyond the pleasure principle. *Standard Edition* 28:7–64.

————— (1921). Group psychology and the analysis of the ego. *Standard Edition* 18:69–143.

————— (1923). The ego and the id. *Standard Edition* 19:12–66.

————— (1930). Civilization and its discontents. *Standard Edition* 21:64–145.

Fromm, E. (1968). Puntos Centrales a Investigar en las Primeras Entravistas y en Entravistas de Recepcion del IMPAC. Mexico Biblioteca del IMPAC. Text in Spanish.

————— (1973). *The Anatomy of Human Destructiveness*. New York: Holt, Rinehart, Winston.

Fromm, E., and Maccoby, M. (1970). *Social Character in a Mexican Village*. Englewood, NJ: Prentice Hall.

Galatzer-Levy, R. (1995). Psychoanalysis and chaos theory. *Journal of the American Psychoanalytic Association* 43:1095–1113.

Gay, P. (1988). *Freud: A Life for Our Time*. New York: Norton.

Gill, M. (1984). Psychoanalysis and psychotherapy: a revision. *International Review of Psycho-Analysis* 11:161–169.

————— (1994). *Psychoanalysis in Transition*. Hillsdale, NJ: Analytic Press.

Gleick, J. (1987). *Chaos*. New York: Viking Penguin.

Gojman, S. (1996). The analyst as a person: Fromm's approach to psychoanalytic training and practice. In *A Prophetic Analyst: Erich Fromm's Contributions to Psychoanalysis*, ed. M. Cortina and M. Maccoby, pp. 235–258. Northvale, NJ: Jason Aronson.

Greenberg, J. R., and Mitchell, S. A. (1983). *Object Relations in Psychoanalytic Theory*. Cambridge, MA: Harvard University Press.

Grosskurth, P. (1986). *Melanie Klein: Her World and Her Work*. New York: Knopf.

————— (1991). *The Secret Ring*. Reading, MA: Addison-Wesley.

Grotstein, J. (1978). Innerspace: its dimensions and coordinates. *International Journal of Psycho-Analysis* 59:55–61.

————— (1981a). Wilfred R. Bion: the man, the psychoanalyst, the mystic: a perspective on his life and work. In *Do I Dare Disturb the Universe? A memorial to Wilfred R. Bion*, pp. 1–35. Beverly Hills, CA: Caesura.

——— (1981b). *Splitting and Projective Identification*. New York: Jason Aronson.

——— (1990). Nothingness, meaninglessness, chaos and the "black hole": II The "black hole." *Contemporary Psychoanalysis* 26(3):377–407.

——— (1994a). *The dual-track theorem: a newer paradigm for psychoanalytic theory and technique*. Unpublished paper.

——— (1994b). Notes on Fairbairn's metapsychology. In *Fairbairn and the Origins of Object Relations*, ed. J. Grotstein and D. Rinsley, pp. 112–148. London: Free Association Books.

——— (1994c). Foreword. In *Affect Regulation and the Origin of the Self: The Neurobiology of Emotional Development*, by A. N. Schore, pp. xxi–xxvii. Hillsdale, NJ: Lawrence Erlbaum.

Grotstein, J., and Rinsley, D., eds. (1994a). *Fairbairn and the Origins of Object Relations*. London: Free Association Books.

——— (1994b). Editors' introduction. In *Fairbairn and the Origins of Object Relations*, ed. J. Grotstein and D. Rinsley, pp. 3–16. London: Free Association Books.

Guntrip, H. S. (1961). *Personality and Human Interaction*. London: Hogarth.

——— (1969). *Schizoid Phenomena, Object Relations and the Self*. New York: International Universities Press.

——— (1975). My experience of analysis with Fairbairn and Winnicott. *International Review of Psycho-Analysis* 16:145–156.

Hamilton, N. G. (1988). *Self and Others: Object Relations Theory in Practice*. Northvale, NJ: Jason Aronson.

Hamilton, V. (1985). John Bowlby: an ethological basis for psychoanalysis. In *Beyond Freud: A Study of Modern Psychoanalytic Theorists*, ed. J. Reppen, pp. 1–28. Hillsdale, NJ: Analytic Press.

Harlow, H. F. (1958). The nature of love. *American Psychologist* 13:673–685.

Harlow, H. F., and Harlow, M. K. (1965). The affectional systems. In *Behavior of Non-Human Primates*, Vol. 2, ed. A. M. Schrier, H. F. Harlow, and F. Stollnitz, pp. 287–334. New York: Academia Press.

Harlow, H. F., and Suomi, S. J. (1970). The nature of love simplified. *American Psychologist* 25:161–168.

——— (1986). Parental behaviour in primates. In *Parental Behaviour*, ed. W. Slukin and M. Herbert, pp. 152–207. Oxford: Blackwell.

Harlow, H. F., and Zimmermann, R. R. (1959). Affectional responses in the infant monkey. *Science* 130:421–432.

Harrow, A. (1996). *The Scottish connection: Suttie, Fairbairn, Sutherland*. Paper presented at The Fairbairn Conference of the International Institute of Object Relations Therapy, New York, October. In *Fairbairn Then and Now*, ed. N. Skolnick and D. Scharff. Hillsdale, NJ: Analytic Press, 1998.

Harter, S. (1977). A cognitive-developmental approach to children's expression of conflicting feelings and a technique to facilitate such expression in play therapy. *Journal of Consulting and Clinical Psychology* 45:417–432.

———— (1986). Cognitive-developmental processes in the integration of concepts about emotions and the self. *Social Cognition* 4:119–151.

Hartmann, H. (1939). *Ego Psychology and the Problem of Adaptation*. New York: International Universities Press.

Hartmann, H., Kris, E., and Loewenstein, R. M. (1946). Comments on the formation of psychic structure. *Psychoanalytic Study of the Child* 2:11–38. New York: International Universities Press.

Hazan, C., and Shaver, P. R. (1987). Romantic love conceptualized as an attachment process. *Journal of Interpersonal and Social Psychology* 52:511–524.

———— (1994). Attachment as an organizational framework for research on close relationships. *Psychological Inquiry* 5:1–22.

Hazell, J., ed. (1994). *Personal Relations Therapy: The Collected Papers of H. J. S. Guntrip*. Northvale, NJ: Jason Aronson.

Hegel, G. W. F. (1807). *The Phenomenology of Spirit*, trans. A. V. Miller. London: Oxford University Press.

Heimann, P. (1950). On counter-transference. *International Journal of Psycho-Analysis* 31:81–84.

———— (1954). Problems of the training analysis. *International Journal of Psycho-Analysis* 35:163–168.

Henry, G. (1984). Reflections on infant observation and its applications. *Journal of Analytical Psychology* 29:155–169.

Hesse, E. (1996). Discourse, memory and the Adult Attachment Interview: a note with emphasis on the emerging Cannot Classify category. *Infant Mental Health Journal* 17:4–11.

Hinde, R. A., and Spencer-Booth, Y. (1967). The behaviour of socially living rhesus monkeys in their first two and a half years. *Animal Behavior* 15:169–196.

Hopper, E. (1985). The problem of context in group analytic psychotherapy: a clinical illustration and brief theoretical discussion. In *W. R. Bion and Group Psychotherapy: A Critical Reappraisal*, ed. M. Pines, pp. 330–353. London: Routledge & Kegan Paul.

———— (1991). Encapsulation as a defence against the fear of annihilation. *International Journal of Psycho-Analysis* 72(4):607–624.

———— (1995). *Wounded bird*. Unpublished paper.

———— (1996). The social unconscious in clinical work. *Group* 20(1):7–42.

Horowitz, M. J. (1991). Short-term dynamic therapy of stress response syndromes. In *Handbook of Short-Term Dynamic Psychotherapy*, ed. C. Crits-Christoph and J. P. Barber, pp. 166–198. New York: Basic Books.

Horowitz, M. J., Marmar, C., Krupnick, J., et al. (1984). *Personality Styles and Brief Psychotherapy*. New York: Basic Books.

Isaacs, S. (1948). The nature and function of phantasy. In *Developments in Psycho-Analysis*, ed. M. Klein, P. Heimann, S. Isaacs, and J. Riviere, pp. 67–121. London: Hogarth.

Jacobs, T. (1991). *The Use of the Self*. Madison, CT: International Universities Press.

Jacobson, E. (1954). The self and the object world. *Psychoanalytic Study of the Child* 9:75–127. New York: International Universities Press.

———— (1964). *The Self and the Object World*. New York: International Universities Press.

———— (1967). *Psychotic Conflict and Reality*. New York: International Universities Press.

Jones, E. (1955a). *The Life and Work of Sigmund Freud 1856–1900: The Formative Years and the Great Discoveries*. New York: Basic Books.

———— (1955b). *The Life and Work of Sigmund Freud 1901–1919: The Years of Maturity*. New York: Basic Books.

———— (1955c). *The Life and Work of Sigmund Freud 1919–1939: The Last Phase*. New York: Basic Books.

Joseph, B. (1975). The patient who is difficult to reach. In *Tactics and Techniques in Psychoanalytic Therapy*, vol. 2, *Countertransference*, ed. P. L. Giovacchini, pp. 205–216. New York: Jason Aronson.

———— (1985). Transference: the total situation. *International Journal of Psycho-Analysis* 66:447–454. and in *Psychic Equilibrium and Psychic Change: The Selected Papers of Betty Joseph*, ed. E. B. Spillius and M. Feldman, pp. 156–167. London: Routledge & Kegan Paul, 1989.

———— (1989). *Psychic Equilibrium and Psychic Change: The Selected Papers of Betty Joseph*, ed. E. B. Spillius and M. Feldman. London: Routledge & Kegan Paul.

Jung, C. G. (1953–1979). *The Collected Works* (Bollinger Series XX). 20 vols. Trans. R. F. C. Hull, ed. H. Read, M. Fordham, G. Adler, and W. McGuire. Princeton: Princeton University Press.

Kardiner, A. (1977). *My Analysis with Freud*. New York: Norton.

Karen, R. (1994). *Becoming Attached: Unfolding the Mystery of the Infant–Mother Bond and Its Impact on Later Life*. New York: Warner Books.

Kernberg, O. (1963). Discussion of paper by J. D. Sutherland (1963). Object relations theory and the conceptual model of psychoanalysis. *British Journal of Medical Psychology* 36:109–124. Reprinted in *The Autonomous Self: The Work of John D. Sutherland,* ed. J. S. Scharff, pp. 3–24. Northvale, NJ: Jason Aronson, 1994.

———— (1975). *Borderline Conditions and Pathological Narcissism*. New York: Jason Aronson.

———— (1976). *Object Relations Theory and Clinical Psychoanalysis*. New York: Jason Aronson.

———— (1979). An overview of Edith Jacobson's contributions. *Journal of the American Psychoanalytic Association* 30:793–819.

———— (1980). *Internal World and External Reality*. New York: Jason Aronson.

———— (1996). *The significance of Fairbairn's contribution*. Interview on videotape shown at The Fairbairn Conference of the International Institute of Object Relations Therapy, New York Academy of Medicine, New York, October. Transcribed in *Fairbairn Then and Now*, ed. N. Skolnick and D. Scharff. Hillsdale, NJ: Analytic Press, 1998.

Khan, M. (1974). *The Privacy of the Self*. London: Hogarth.

———— (1979). *Alienation in Perversions*. New York: International Universities Press.

Kihlstrom, J. F., and Cantor, N. (1984). Mental representations of the self. In *Advances in Experimental Social Psychology*, Vol. 17, ed. L. Berkowitz, pp. 1–47. Orlando, FL: Academic Press.

Kirkpatrick, L. A., and Davis, K. E. (1994). Attachment style, gender, and relationship stability: a longitudinal analysis. *Journal of Personality and Social Psychology* 66:502–512.

Klein, M. (1928). Early stages of the Oedipus conflict. In *Love, Guilt and Reparation and Other Works: 1921–1945,* pp. 186–198. London: Hogarth, 1975.

———— (1935). A contribution to the psychogenesis of manic-depressive states. In *Love, Guilt and Reparation and Other Works: 1921–1945*, pp. 262–289. London: Hogarth, 1975.

———— (1945). The Oedipus complex in the light of early anxieties. In *Love, Guilt and Reparation and Other Works: 1921–1945*, pp. 370–419. London: Hogarth, 1975.

———— (1946). Notes on some schizoid mechanisms. In *Envy and Gratitude and Other Works: 1946–1963*, pp. 1–24. London: Hogarth, 1975.

—— (1952). The origins of transference. *International Journal of Psycho-Analysis* 33:433–438.

—— (1955). *New Directions in Psycho-Analysis*. London: Tavistock.

Kohon, G., ed. (1986). *The British School of Psychoanalysis: The Independent Tradition*. London: Free Association Books.

—— (1996). Book review. *The Autonomous Self: The Work of John D. Sutherland*, ed. J. S. Scharff. In *Journal of the American Psychoanalytic Association* 44:1261–1262.

Kohut, H. (1971). *The Analysis of the Self: A Systematic Approach to the Psychoanalytic Treatment of Narcissistic Personality Disorder* (*Psychoanalytic Study of the Child*, Monogr. 4). New York: International Universities Press.

—— (1977). *The Restoration of the Self*. New York: International Universities Press.

—— (1984). *How Does Analysis Cure?*, ed. A. Goldberg. Chicago: University of Chicago Press.

Lacan, J. (1977). *Écrits: A Selection*, trans. A. Sheridan. New York: Norton.

—— (1988a). *The Seminar of Jacques Lacan Book 1: Freud's Papers on Technique, 1953–1954*, ed. J. A. Miller, trans. J. Forrester. New York: Norton.

—— (1988b). *The Seminar of Jacques Lacan Book 2: The Ego in Freud's Theory and in the Technique of Psychoanalysis, 1954–1955*, ed. J. A. Miller, trans. J. Forrester. New York: Norton.

Laing, R. (1960). *The Divided Self*. London: Tavistock.

Leigh, J., Westen, D., Barends, A., and Mendel, M. (1992). Assessing complexity of representations of people from TAT and interview data. *Journal of Personality* 60:809–837.

Lerner, H. D., and St. Peter, S. (1984). Patterns of object relations in neurotic, borderline, and schizophrenic patients. *Psychiatry* 47:77–92.

Lichtenberg, J. (1989). *Psychoanalysis and Motivation*. Hillsdale, NJ: Analytic Press.

Lichtenberg, J. D., Lachmann, F. M., and Fosshage, J. L. (1992). *Self and Motivational Systems: Toward a Theory of Psychoanalytic Technique*. Hillsdale, NJ: Analytic Press.

Lichtenstein, H. (1977). *The Dilemma of Human Identity*. New York: Jason Aronson.

Loewald, H. (1960). On the therapeutic action of psychoanalysis. *International Journal of Psycho-Analysis* 41:16–33.

—— (1980). *Papers on Psychoanalysis*. New Haven, CT: Yale University Press.

Lorenz, E. (1963). Deterministic non-periodic flow. *Journal of Atmospheric Science* 20:130–141.

Luborsky, L., and Crits-Christoph, P. (1989). A relationship pattern measure: The Core Conflictual Relationship Theme. *Psychiatry* 52:250–259.

———— (1998). *Understanding Transference: The Core Conflictual Relationship Theme Method*, 2nd edition. Washington, DC: American Psychological Association.

Mahler, M. (1968). *On Human Symbiosis and the Vicissitudes of Individuation, Vol. 1: Infantile Psychosis.* New York: International Universities Press.

———— (1974). Symbiosis and individuation: the psychological birth of the human infant. In *The Selected Papers of Margaret Mahler, Vol. 2*, pp. 149–165. New York: Jason Aronson.

———— (1980). Rapprochement sub-phase of the separation-individuation process. In *Rapprochement: The Critical Sub-phase of Separation-Individuation*, ed. R. Lax, S. Bach, and J. S. Burland, pp. 3–19. New York: Jason Aronson.

Mahler, M., Pine, F., and Bergman, A. (1974). *The Psychological Birth of the Human Infant.* New York: Basic Books.

Main, M. (1990). Cross-cultural studies of attachment organization: recent studies, changing methodologies, and the concept of conditional strategies. *Human Development* 33:48–61.

———— (1995). Attachment: overview, with implications for clinical work. In *Attachment Theory: Social, Developmental and Clinical Perspectives*, ed. S. Goldberg, R. Muir, and J. Kerr, pp. 407–475. Hillsdale, NJ: Analytic Press.

Main, M., and Goldwyn, R. (in press). Interview based adult attachment classification: related to infant–mother and infant–father attachment. *Developmental Psychology*.

Main, M., and Hesse, E. (1990). Lack of mourning in adulthood and its relationship to infant disorganization: some speculations regarding causal mechanisms. In *Attachment in Preschool Years: Theory, Research, and Intervention*, ed. M. Greenberg, D. Cichetti, and M. Cummings, pp. 161–182. Chicago: University of Chicago Press.

Main, M., and Solomon, J. (1986). Discovery of an insecure/disorganized/disoriented attachment pattern. In *Affective Development in Infancy*, ed. T. B. Brazelton and M. W. Yogman, pp. 95–124. Norwood, NJ: Ablex.

———— (1990). Procedures for identifying infants as disorganized/disoriented during the Ainsworth Strange Situation. In *Attachment in Preschool Years:*

Theory, Research, and Intervention, ed. M. Greenberg, D. Cichetti, and M. Cummings, pp. 121–159. Chicago: University of Chicago Press.

Malan, D. H. (1963). *A Study of Brief Psychotherapy*. London: Tavistock.

———— (1976). *The Frontier of Brief Psychotherapy*. New York: Plenum.

Mandelbrot, B. (1982). *The Fractal Geometry of Nature*. San Francisco: W. H. Freeman.

Mann, J. (1973). *Time-Limited Psychotherapy*. Cambridge, MA: Harvard University Press.

Marcia, J. E. (1994). Ego identity and object relations. In *Empirical Perspectives on Object Relations*, ed. J. M. Masling and R. F. Bornstein, pp. 59–103. Washington, DC: American Psychological Association.

Mayman, M. (1967). Object-representations and object relationships in Rorschach responses. *Journal of Projective Techniques and Personality Assessment* 31:17–24.

McDougall, J. (1978). *Plea for a Measure of Abnormality*. New York: International Universities Press.

———— (1985). *Theaters of the Mind*. New York: Basic Books.

———— (1989). *Theaters of the Body*. New York: Norton.

———— (1995). *The Many Faces of Eros*. New York: Norton.

McKenna, J., Thoman, E., Anders, T. F., et al. (1993). Infant–parent co-sleeping in an evolutionary perspective: implications for understanding infant sleep development and the sudden infant death syndrome. *Sleep* 16:263–282.

Millán, S. (1994). *The importance of initial interviews in psychoanalysis*. Paper presented at seminar "Fromm's Psychoanalytical Thinking and Clinical Practice." Therapeia Säätio Institute, Helsinki, Finland, September, 1995.

Miller, J. G. (1965). Living systems, basic concepts. *Behavioral Science* 10:337–379.

Miller, L., Rustin, M., Rustin, M., and Shuttleworth, J., eds. (1989). *Closely Observed Infants*. London: Duckworth.

Mitchell, S. (1988). *Relational Concepts in Psychoanalysis*. Cambridge, MA: Harvard University Press.

———— (1993). *Hope and Dread in Psychoanalysis*. New York: Basic Books.

Michell, S., and Black, M. (1995). *Freud and Beyond*. New York: Basic Books.

Modell, A. (1984). *Psychoanalysis in a New Context*. Madison, CT: International Universities Press.

Money-Kyrle, R. (1956). Normal counter-transference and some of its deviations. *International Journal of Psycho-Analysis* 37:360–366.

———— (1978). *The Collected Papers of Roger Money-Kyrle*, ed. D. Meltzer and E. O'Shaughnessy. Strath Tay, Scotland: Clunie.

Moore, M. S. (1990). Presentation. John Bowlby Memorial Attachment Conference. London.

———— (1992). *Early disturbed attachment: clinical implications for work with children with learning difficulties*. Paper presented at the 7th International Educational Therapy Conference, Oslo.

———— (1996). Attachment theory and brain research. Lecture at the International Institute of Object Relations Therapy, Chevy Chase MD, July.

Moran, M. (1991). Chaos and psychoanalysis: the fluidic nature of mind. *International Review of Psycho-Analysis* 18:211–221.

Morrison, T., Urquiza, Anthony J., and Goodlin-Jones, B. (1995). *Object relations theory and marital interaction: integrating theory with the known facts*. Unpublished manuscript. University of California, Davis.

———— (1997a). Attachment and the representation of intimate relationships in adulthood. *Journal of Psychology* 131:57–71.

———— (1997b). Attachment, perceptions of interaction, and relationship adjustment. *Journal of Social and Personal Relationships* 14:627–642.

Murray, J. M. (1955). *Keats*. New York: Noonday Press.

Murray, L. (1988). Effects of postnatal depression on infant development: direct studies of early mother–infant interactions. In *Motherhood and Mental Illness, Vol 2: Causes and Consequences*, ed. R. Kumar and I. F. Brockington. London: Wright.

———— (1991). Intersubjectivity, object relations theory and empirical evidence from mother–infant interactions. *Infant Mental Health Journal* 12:219–232.

Murray, L., and Trevarthen, C. (1985). Emotional regulation of interactions between two-month-olds and their mothers. In *Social Perceptions in Infants*, ed. T. Fields and N. Fox, pp. 137–154. Norwood, NJ: Ablex.

Nacht, S. (1965). Criteria and technique for the termination of analysis. *International Journal of Psycho-Analysis* 46:107–116.

Nelson, K., and Greundel, J. M. (1981). Generalized event representation: basic building blocks of cognitive development. In *Advances in Developmental Psychology, Vol. I*, ed. M. E. Lamb and A. L. Brown, pp. 131–158. Hillsdale, NJ: Lawrence Erlbaum.

Noller, P., and Ruzzene, M. (1991). Communication in marriage: the influence of affect and cognition. In *Cognition in Close Relationships*, ed.

G. J. O. Fletcher and F. D. Fincham, pp. 203–233. Hillsdale, NJ: Lawrence Erlbaum.

Ogden, T. (1982). *Projective Identification and Psychotherapeutic Technique.* New York: Jason Aronson.

————— (1986). *The Matrix of the Mind: Object Relations and the Psychoanalytic Dialogue.* Northvale, NJ: Jason Aronson.

————— (1989). *The Primitive Edge of Experience.* Northvale, NJ: Jason Aronson.

————— (1994). *Subjects of Analysis.* Northvale, NJ: Jason Aronson.

Osofsky, J. D. (1988). Perspectives on attachment and psychoanalysis. *Psychoanalytic Psychology* 12:347–363.

Padel, J. (1995). Book review. *The Autonomous Self: The Work of John D. Sutherland*, ed. J. S. Scharff. *International Journal of Psycho-Analysis* 76(1):177–179.

Parkes, C. M. (1973). Factors determining the persistence of phantom pain in the amputee. *Journal of Psychosomatic Research* 17:97–108.

Peitgen, H. O., Jurgens, H., and Saupe, D. (1992). *Chaos and Fractals: New Frontiers of Science.* New York: Springer-Verlag.

Peterfreund, E. (1978). Some critical comments on psychoanalytic conceptualization of infancy. *International Journal of Psychoanalysis* 50:427–441.

Piper, W. E., Azim, H. F. A., Joyce, A. S., and McCallum, M. (1991a). Transference interpretations, therapeutic alliance, and outcome in short-term individual psychotherapy. *Archives of General Psychiatry* 48:946–953.

Piper, W. E., Azim, H. F. A., Joyce, A. S., et al. (1991b). Quality of object relations versus interpersonal functioning as predictors of therapeutic alliance and psychotherapy outcome. *The Journal of Nervous and Mental Disease* 179:432–438.

Piper, W. E., Azim, H. F. A., McCallum, M., and Joyce, A. S. (1990). Patient suitability and outcome in short-term individual psychotherapy. *Journal of Consulting and Clinical Psychology* 58:475–481.

Porges, S. W. (1976). Peripheral and neurochemical parallels of psychopathology: a psychophysiological model relating autonomic imbalance to hyperactivity, psychopathy and autism. *Advances in Child Development and Behavior* 11:33–65.

Prigogine, I. (1976). Order through fluctuation: self-organization and social system. In *Evolution and Consciousness: Human Systems in Transition*, ed. C. H. Waddington and E. Jantsch, pp. 93–126, 130–133. Reading, MA: Addison-Wesley.

Prigogine, I., and Stengers, I. (1984). *Order Out of Chaos: Man's New Dialogue with Nature.* New York: Bantam.

Quinodoz, J-M. (1997). Transitions in psychic structures in the light of deterministic chaos theory. *International Journal of Psycho-Analysis* 78(4): 699–718.

Racker, H. (1957). The meanings and uses of countertransference. *Psychoanalytic Quarterly* 26:303–357, and in *Transference and Countertransference*, pp. 127–173. New York: International Universities Press, 1968.

————— (1968). *Transference and Countertransference*. New York: International Universities Press.

Rapaport, D. (1960). The structure of psychoanalytic theory. *Psychological Issues Vol. 2, No. 2, Monograph 6*. New York: International Universities Press.

Rayner, E. (1991). *The Independent Mind in British Psychoanalysis*. Northvale, NJ: Jason Aronson.

Rickman, J. (1951). Function and organization of a psychoanalytical institution. *International Journal of Psycho-Analysis* 32:218–237.

Robertson, J., and Robertson, J. (1972). Young children in brief separation: a fresh look. *Psychoanalytic Study of the Child* 26:264–315. New Haven, CT: Yale University Press.

Rustin, M. (1989). Encountering primitive anxieties. In *Closely Observed Infants*, ed. L. Miller, M. Rustin, M. Rustin, and J. Shuttleworth, pp. 7–21. London: Duckworth.

Sameroff, A., and Suomi, S. (1996). Primates and persons: a comparative developmental understanding of social organization. In *Developmental Science*, ed. R. B. Cairns, G. H. Elder, E. J. Costello, and A. McGuire, pp. 97–120. Cambridge, England and New York: Cambridge University Press.

Sandler, J. (1976). Actualization and object relationships. *Journal of the Philadelphia Association for Psychoanalysis* 3:59–70.

—————, ed. (1987). *Projection, Identification and Projective Identification*. Madison, CT: International Universities Press.

Schacht, T. E., Binder, J. L., and Strupp, H. H. (1984). The dynamic focus. In *Psychotherapy in a New Key: A Guide to Time-Limited Dynamic Psychotherapy,* ed. H. H. Strupp and J. L. Binder, pp. 65–109. New York: Basic Books.

Schacter, D. L. (1987). Implicit memory: history and current status. *Journal of Experimental Psychology: Learning, Memory, and Cognition* 13:501–518.

Schafer, R. (1976). *A New Action Language for Psychoanalysis*. New Haven, CT: Yale University Press.

———— (1992). *Retelling a Life*. New York: Basic Books.

Scharff, D. E. (1982). *The Sexual Relationship: An Object Relations View of Sex and the Family*. London: Routledge & Kegan Paul. Reprinted 1998, Northvale, NJ: Jason Aronson.

———— (1990). Book review. *Relational Concepts in Psychoanalysis* by S. A. Mitchell. *Psychoanalytic Psychology* 7(3):429–438.

———— (1992). *Refinding the Object and Reclaiming the Self*. Northvale, NJ: Jason Aronson.

———— (1994). Foreword. In *Empirical Perspectives on Object Relations Therapy*, ed. R. F. Bernstein and J. M. Masling, pp. xi–xiv. Washington, DC: American Psychological Association.

————, ed. (1996). *Object Relations Theory and Practice*. Northvale, NJ: Jason Aronson.

Scharff, D. E., and Birtles, E. F., eds. (1994). *From Instinct to Self: Selected Papers of W. R. D. Fairbairn, Vol. 1*. Northvale, NJ: Jason Aronson.

Scharff, D. E., and Scharff, J. S. (1987). *Object Relations Family Therapy*. Northvale, NJ: Jason Aronson.

———— (1991). *Object Relations Couple Therapy*. Northvale, NJ: Jason Aronson.

Scharff, J. S. (1992). *Projective and Introjective Identification and the Use of the Therapist's Self*. Northvale, NJ: Jason Aronson.

————, ed. (1994). *The Autonomous Self: The Work of John D. Sutherland*. Northvale, NJ: Jason Aronson.

———— (in press). *Object Relations Child Therapy*. Northvale, NJ: Jason Aronson.

Scharff, J. S., and Scharff, D. E. (1992). *A Primer of Object Relations Therapy* (formerly *Scharff Notes*). Northvale, NJ: Jason Aronson.

———— (1994). *Object Relations Therapy of Physical and Sexual Trauma*. Northvale, NJ: Jason Aronson.

Schore, A. (1994). *Affect Regulation and the Origin of the Self: The Neurobiology of Emotional Development*. Hillsdale, NJ: Lawrence Erlbaum.

Searles, H. F. (1959). Oedipal love in the countertransference. *International Journal of Psycho-Analysis* 40:180–190. And in *Collected Papers on Schizophrenia and Related Subjects*, pp. 284–303. New York: International Universities Press, 1965.

———— (1963). The place of neutral therapist responses in psychotherapy with the schizophrenic patient. In *Collected Papers on Schizophrenia and Related Subjects*, pp. 626–653. New York: International Universities Press.

———— (1965). *Collected Papers on Schizophrenia and Related Subjects*. New York: International Universities Press.

———— (1979). *Countertransference and Related Subjects: Selected Papers*. New York: International Universities Press.

———— (1986). *My Work with Borderline Patients*. Northvale, NJ: Jason Aronson.

Segal, H. (1964). *Introduction to The Work of Melanie Klein*. London: Heinemann.

———— (1979). *Klein*. Glasgow: Fontana.

———— (1981). *The Work of Hanna Segal: A Kleinian Approach to Clinical Practice*. New York: Jason Aronson.

———— (1991). *Dream, Phantasy and Art. The New Library of Psychoanalysis*, vol. 12., ed. E. B. Spillius. London: Tavistock/Routledge.

Shapiro, E., Zinner, J., Shapiro, R., and Berkowitz, D. (1975). The influence of family experience on borderline personality development. *International Review of Psycho-Analysis* 2(4):399–411 and in *Foundations of Object Relations Family Therapy*, ed. J. S. Scharff, pp. 127–154. Northvale, NJ: Jason Aronson, 1989.

Shapiro, R. (1978). Ego psychology: its relations to Sullivan, Erikson and the object relations theorists. In *American Psychoanalysis*, ed. J. Quen and E. Carlson, pp. 162–179. New York: Brunner/Mazel.

———— (1979). Family dynamics and object relations theory: an analytic, group interpretive approach to family therapy. In *Adolescent Psychiatry: Developmental and Clinical Studies*, ed. S. C. Feinstein and P. Giovacchini, 7:118–135. Chicago: University of Chicago Press.

Shaver, P. R., and Clark, M. (1994). The psychodynamics of adult attachment. In *Empirical Perspectives on Object Relations*, ed. J. M. Masling and R. F. Bornstein, pp. 105–147. Washington, DC: American Psychological Association.

Shuttleworth, J. (1989). Psychoanalytic theory and infant development. In *Closely Observed Infants*, ed. L. Miller, M. Rustin, M. Rustin, and J. Shuttleworth, pp. 22–51. London: Duckworth.

Sifneos, P. E. (1972). *Short-term Psychotherapy and Emotional Crisis*. Cambridge, MA: Harvard University Press.

———— (1987). *Short-term Dynamic Psychotherapy: Evaluation and Technique*, 2nd ed. New York: Plenum.

Simon, R. M., and Simon, R. H. (1995). Mid-atlantic salt-marsh shorelines: mathematical commonalities. *Estuaries* 18:199–206.

Singer, J., and Singer, J. (1994). Social-cognitive and narrative perspectives on transference. In *Empirical Perspectives on Object Relations*, ed. J. M. Masling and R. F. Bornstein, pp. 157–193. Washington, DC: American Psychological Association.

Slade, A. (1996). Attachment theory and research: implications for the theory and practice of individual psychotherapy. In preparation for *Handbook of Attachment Theory and Research*, ed. J. Cassidy and P. R. Shaver. New York: Guilford.

Spillius, E. B. (1994). Developments in Kleinian thought: overview and personal view. *Psychoanalytic Inquiry* 14(3):324–364.

――――, ed. (1987–1997). *The New Library of Psychoanalysis*. London: Tavistock/ Routledge.

Spruiell, V. (1993). Deterministic chaos and the sciences of complexity: psychoanalysis in the midst of a general scientific revolution. *Journal of the American Psychoanalytic Association* 41:3–41.

Sroufe, L. A., and Fleeson, J. (1986). Attachment and the construction of relationships. In *Relationships and Development*, pp. 51–71. Hillsdale, NJ: Lawrence Erlbaum.

Stadter, M. (1996). *Object Relations Brief Therapy: The Therapeutic Relationship in Short-Term Work*. Northvale, NJ: Jason Aronson.

Steiner, J. (1994). Patient-centered and analyst-centered interpretations: some implications of containment and countertransference. *Psychoanalytic Inquiry* 14(3):406–422.

Stern, D. N. (1985). *The Interpersonal World of the Infant: A View from Psychoanalysis and Developmental Psychology*. New York: Basic Books.

Stolorow, R., and Atwood, G. (1992). *Contexts of Being: The Intersubjective Foundations of Psychological Life*. Hillsdale, NJ: Analytic Press.

Stolorow, R., Brandchaft, B., and Atwood, G. (1987). *Psychoanalytic Treatment: An Intersubjective Approach*. Hillsdale, NJ: Analytic Press.

Strachey, J. (1934). The nature of therapeutic action of psycho-analysis. *International Journal of Psycho-Analysis* 15:127–159.

Strupp, H. H., and Binder, J. L., eds. (1984). *Psychotherapy in a New Key: A Guide to Time-Limited Dynamic Psychotherapy*. New York: Basic Books.

Sullivan, H. S. (1953). *The Interpersonal Theory of Psychiatry*. New York: Norton.

―――― (1962). *Schizophrenia as a Human Process*. New York: Norton.

―――― (1964). *The Fusion of Psychiatry and Social Process*. New York: Norton.

Suomi, S. J. (1984). The development of affect in rhesus monkeys. In *The Psychobiology of Affective Development*, ed. N. A. Fox and R. J. Davidson, pp. 119–160. Hillsdale, NJ: Lawrence Erlbaum.

―――― (1991). Early stress and adult emotional reactivity in rhesus monkeys. In *The Childhood Environment and Adult Disease*, ed. D. Barker, pp. 171–188. Chichester, England: Wiley.

―――― (1994). Social and biological pathways that contribute to variations in health status: evidence from primate studies. Proceedings of the 11th *Honda Foundation Discoveries Symposium on Prosperity, Health and Well-being*, pp. 105–112. Toronto: Canadian Institute for Advanced Research.

———— (1995). Influence of attachment theory on ethological studies of bio-behavioral development in nonhuman primates. In *Attachment Theory: Social, Developmental and Clinical Perspectives*, ed. S. Goldberg, R. Muir, and J. Kerr, pp. 185–200. Hillsdale, NJ: Analytic Press.

Sutherland, J. D. (1963). Object relations theory and the conceptual model of psychoanalysis. *British Journal of Medical Psychology* 36:109–124, reprinted in *The Autonomous Self: The Work of John D. Sutherland*, ed. J. S. Scharff, pp. 3–24. Northvale, NJ: Jason Aronson, 1994.

———— (1980). The British object relations theorists: Balint, Winnicott, Fairbairn, Guntrip. *Journal of the American Psychoanalytic Association* 28(4):829–860. Reprinted in *The Autonomous Self: The Work of John D. Sutherland*, ed. J. S. Scharff, pp. 25–44. Northvale, NJ: Jason Aronson.

———— (1989). *Fairbairn's Journey into the Interior*. London: Free Association Books.

———— (1990a). On becoming and being a person. In *The Autonomous Self: The Work of John D. Sutherland*, ed. J. S. Scharff, pp. 372–391. Northvale, NJ: Jason Aronson.

———— (1990b). Reminiscences. In *The Autonomous Self: The Work of John D. Sutherland*, ed. J. S. Scharff, pp. 392–423. Northvale, NJ: Jason Aronson.

———— (1994a). The autonomous self. In *The Autonomous Self: The Work of John D. Sutherland,* ed. J. S. Scharff, pp. 303–330. Northvale, NJ: Jason Aronson.

———— (1994b). Fairbairn and the self. In *The Autonomous Self: The Work of John D. Sutherland*, ed. J. S. Scharff, pp. 331–349. Northvale, NJ: Jason Aronson.

Suttie, I. (1935). *The Origins of Love and Hate*. New York: Matrix House, 1952, and London: Free Association Books, 1988.

Symington, N. (1983). The analyst's act of freedom as agent of therapeutic change. *International Review of Psycho-Analysis* 10:283–291.

Tangney, J. P. (1994). The mixed legacy of the superego: adaptive and maladaptive aspects of shame and guilt. In *Empirical Perspectives on Object Relations*, ed. J. M. Masling and R. F. Bornstein, pp. 1–28. Washington, DC: American Psychological Association.

Ticho, E. (1972). Termination of psychoanalysis: treatment goals, life goals. *Psychoanalytic Quarterly* 41:315–333.

Trevarthen, C. (1989). Development of early social interactions and the affective regulations of brain growth. In *The Neurobiology of Early Infant Behavior*, ed. C. von Euler and H. Forssberg. New York: MacMillan.

———— (1990). Growth and education of the hemispheres. In *Brain Circuits and Functions of the Mind*, pp. 334–363. Cambridge: Cambridge University Press.

———— (1992). Emotions of human infants and mothers and development of the brain. *Behavioral and Brain Sciences* 15(3):524–525.

Trevarthen, C., and Aitken, K. J. (1986). Brain development, infant communication, and empathy disorders: intrinsic factors in child mental health. *Development and Psychopathology* 6:597–633.

Tronick, E. Z. (1989). Emotions and emotional communication in infants. *American Psychologist* 44:112–119.

Urist, J. (1977). The Rorschach test and the assessment of object relations. *Journal of Personality Assessment* 41:3–9.

———— (1980). Object relations. In *Encyclopedia of Clinical Assessment*, Vol.2, ed. R. W. Woody, pp. 821–833. San Francisco: Jossey-Bass.

Van Eenwyck, J. R. (1977). *Archetypes and Strange Attractors: The Chaotic World of Symbols*. Toronto: Inner City Books.

Vygotsky, L. S. (1988). Thinking and speaking. In *The Collected Papers of L. S. Vygotsky, Vol 1*, ed. R. W. Rieber and A. S. Carton, pp. 39–288. New York: Plenum.

Wallerstein, R. S. (1988). One psychoanalysis or many? *International Journal of Psycho-Analysis* 69:5–21.

Weigert, E. (1952). Contribution to the problem of termination of psychoanalysis. *Psychoanalytic Quarterly* 21:465–480.

Welker, C., Becker, P., Hohman, H., and Schafer-Witt, C. (1987). Social relations in groups of the black-capped capuchin (Cebus apella) in captivity: interactions of group-born infants during their first 6 months of life. *Folia Primatologica* 49:33–47.

———— (1990). Social relations in groups of the black-capped capuchin (Cebus apella) in captivity: Interactions of group-born infants during their second half-year of life. *Folia Primatologica* 54:16–33.

Westen, D. W. (1990). Towards a revised theory of borderline object relations: contributions of empirical research. *International Journal of Psycho-Analysis* 71:661–693.

Westen, D. W., Barends, A., Leigh, J., et al. (1988). *Assessing object relations and social cognition from interview data*. Unpublished manuscript. Department of Psychology, University of Michigan.

Westen, D. W., Lohr, N., Silk, K., and Kerber, K. (1985). *Measuring object relations and social cognition using the TAT: scoring manual.* Unpublished manuscript, Department of Psychology, University of Michigan.

Westen, D. W., and Segal, H. (1988). *Assessing object relations and social cognition from Picture Arrangement Stories: scoring manual.* Unpublished manuscript. Department of Psychology, University of Michigan.

Wilder, T. (1973). *Theophilus North.* New York: Harper & Row.

Williams, G. (1984). Reflections on infant observation and its applications. *Journal of Analytical Psychology* 29:155–169.

Winnicott, D. W. (1945). Primitive emotional development. In *Through Paediatrics to Psycho-Analysis*, pp. 145–156. London: Hogarth, 1975.

——— (1947). Hate in the countertransference. In *Through Paediatrics to Psycho-Analysis*, pp. 194–203. London: Hogarth, 1975.

——— (1951). Transitional objects and transitional phenomena. In *Through Paediatrics to Psycho-Analysis*, pp. 229–242. London: Hogarth, 1975.

——— (1958). *Collected Papers: Through Paediatrics to Psycho-Analysis.* London: Tavistock, 1975.

——— (1960a). The theory of the parent–infant relationship. In *The Maturational Processes and the Facilitating Environment*, pp. 37–55. London: Hogarth, 1965.

——— (1960b). Ego distortion in terms of true and false self. In *The Maturational Processes and the Facilitating Environment: Studies in the Theory of Emotional Development*, pp. 140–152. London: Hogarth, 1965.

——— (1963a). Communicating and not communicating leading to a study of certain opposites. In *The Maturational Processes and the Facilitating Environment*, pp. 179–192. London: Hogarth, 1965.

——— (1963b). The development of the capacity for concern. In *The Maturational Processes and the Facilitating Environment*, pp. 73–81. London: Hogarth, 1965.

——— (1965). *The Maturational Processes and the Facilitating Environment.* London: Hogarth.

——— (1971a). *Playing and Reality.* London: Tavistock.

——— (1971b). *Therapeutic Consultations in Child Psychiatry.* London: Hogarth.

Wright, K. (1991). *Vision and Separation between Mother and Baby.* Northvale, NJ: Jason Aronson.

Yankelovich, D., and Barrett, W. (1970). *Ego and Instinct.* New York: Random House.

Yogman, M. (1982). Observations on the father–infant relationship. In *Fa-*

ther and Child: Developmental and Clinical Perspectives, ed. S. Cath, A. R. Gurwitt, and J. M. Ross, pp. 107–122. Boston: Little, Brown.

Zalusky, S. (1996). *Telephone analysis: out of sight, but not out of mind*. Paper presented at workshop "Telephone Analysis," American Psychoanalytic Association Annual Meeting, New York, December.

Zeanah, C. H., and Zeanah, P. D. (1989). Intergenerational transmission of maltreatment: insights from attachment theory and research. *Psychiatry* 52:177–196.

Zelnick, L., and Bucholz, E. S. (1990). The concept of mental health in the light of recent infant research. *Psychoanalytic Psychology* 7:29–58.

Zinner, J. (1976). The implications of projective identification for marital interaction. In *Foundations of Object Relations Family Therapy*, ed. J. S. Scharff, pp. 155–173. Northvale, NJ: Jason Aronson.

Zinner, J., and Shapiro, R. L. (1972). Projective identification as a mode of perception and behavior in the families of adolescents. *International Journal of Psycho-Analysis* 53:523–530.

Index

About the Authors

Jill Savege Scharff, M.D., is Co-Director of the International Institute of Object Relations Therapy and Clinical Professor of Psychiatry at Georgetown University. Educated in Scotland, she moved to England for further training at the Tavistock Clinic and received membership in the Royal College of Psychiatrists. Dr. Scharff is board certified in adult and child psychiatry and certified by the American Psychoanalytic Association in adult and child psychoanalysis.

David E. Scharff, M.D., is Co-Director of the International Institute of Object Relations Therapy and Clinical Professor of Psychiatry at Georgetown University and the Uniformed Services University of the Health Sciences. Dr. Scharff earned his M.D. from Harvard and is board certified in adult and child psychiatry and certified by the American Psychoanalytic Association in psychoanalysis. He is a former President of the American Association of Sex Educators, Counselors, and Therapists.

The Scharffs have a national and international reputation as authors, editors, teachers, and therapists. Among their books are *Object Relations Couple Therapy*, *Object Relations Family Therapy*, and *The Primer of Object Relations Therapy*. Both maintain private practices in individual, couple, and family object relations therapy and individual psychoanalysis with adults and children.